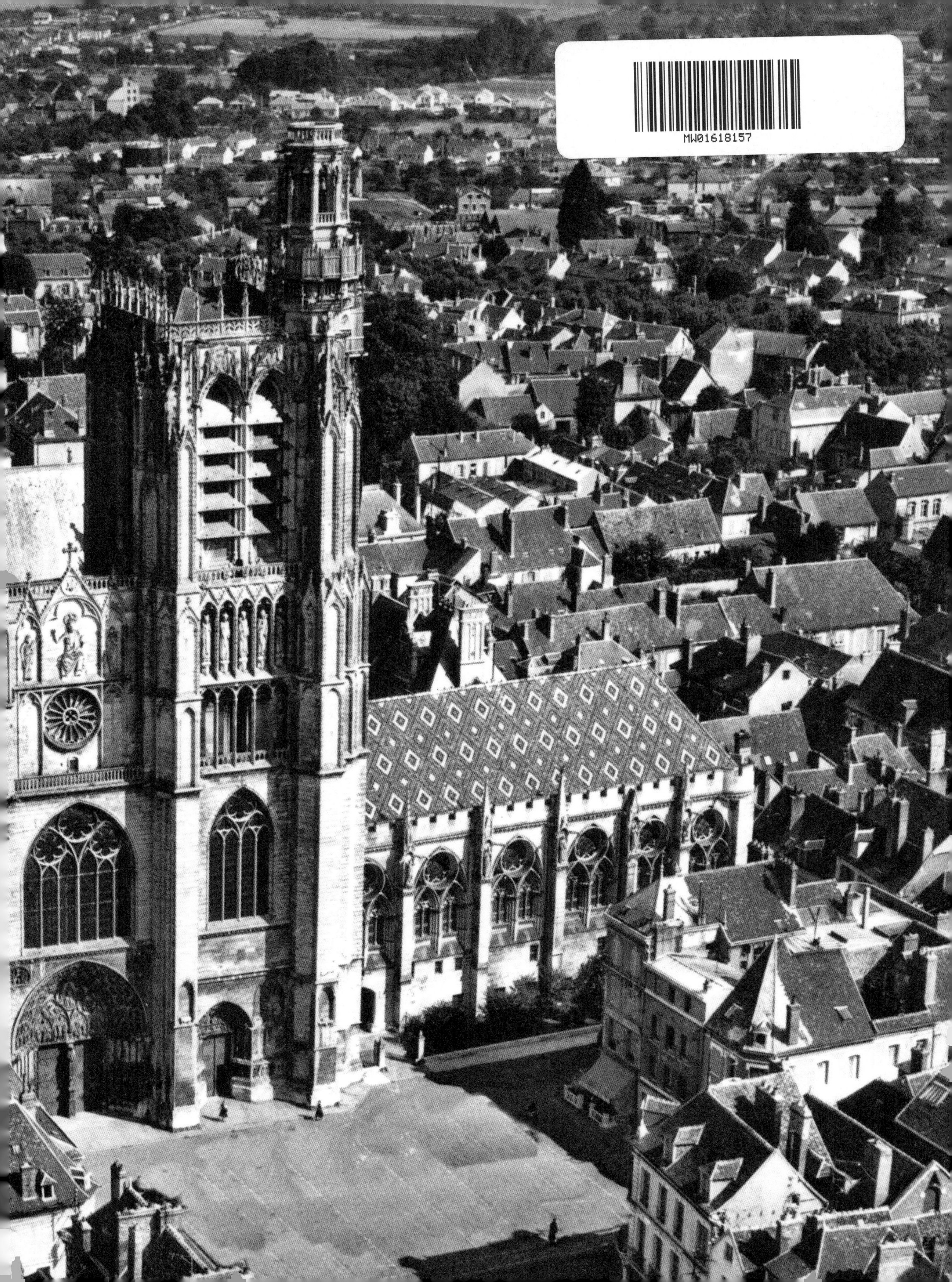
MW01618157

GOTHIC ART AND THOUGHT IN THE LATER MEDIEVAL PERIOD

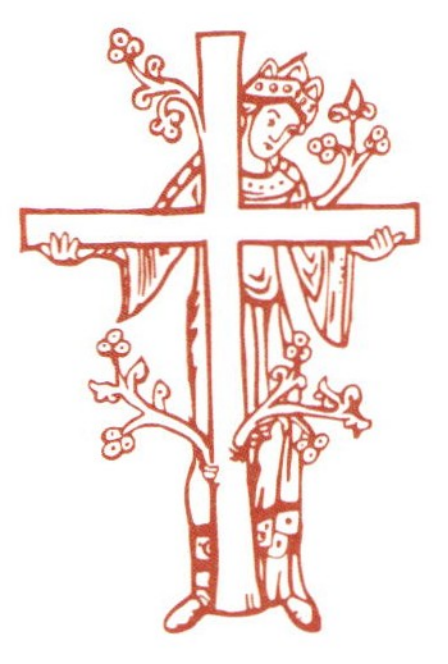

THE INDEX OF CHRISTIAN ART

Occasional Papers · XII

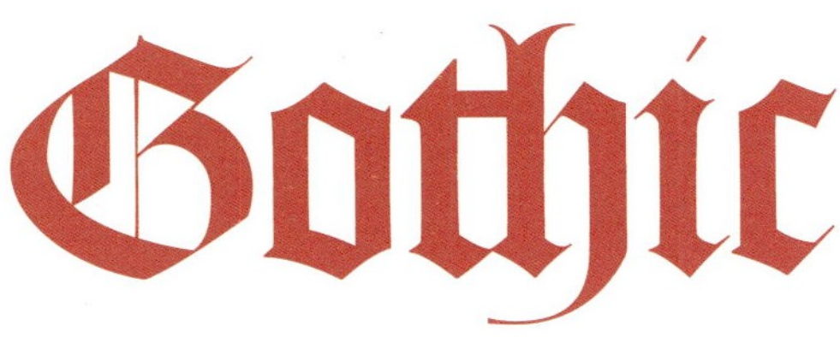

Gothic

ART & THOUGHT IN THE LATER MEDIEVAL PERIOD

Essays in Honor of Willibald Sauerländer

EDITED BY

COLUM HOURIHANE

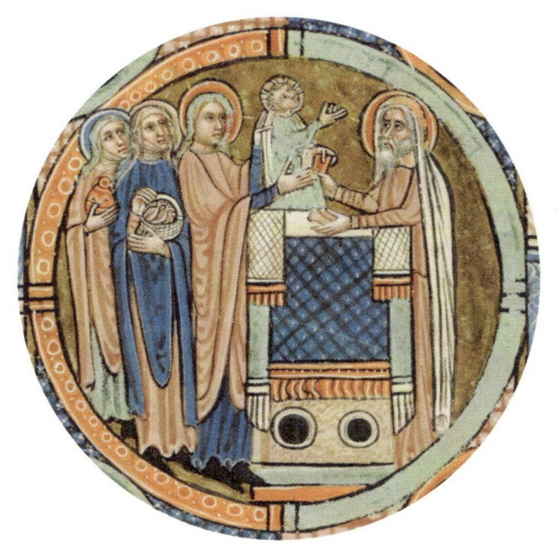

INDEX OF CHRISTIAN ART

DEPARTMENT OF ART & ARCHÆOLOGY

PRINCETON UNIVERSITY

in association with

PENN STATE UNIVERSITY PRESS

MM · XI

In the Nation's Service
and in the Service of all Nations

DISTRIBUTED BY
PENNSYLVANIA STATE UNIVERSITY PRESS
820 NORTH UNIVERSITY DRIVE, USB 1, SUITE C
UNIVERSITY PARK, PENNSYLVANIA 16802

❖

Library of Congress Cataloging-in-Publication Data

GOTHIC ART AND THOUGHT IN THE LATER MEDIEVAL PERIOD:
ESSAYS IN HONOR OF WILLIBALD SAUERLÄNDER / EDITED BY COLUM HOURIHANE.
P. CM. — (THE INDEX OF CHRISTIAN ART: OCCASIONAL PAPERS ; 12)
INCLUDES BIBLIOGRAPHICAL REFERENCES AND INDEX.
ISBN 978–0–9768202–9–1 (PBK. : ALK. PAPER)
1. ART, GOTHIC. 2. CIVILIZATION, MEDIEVAL.
I. SAUERLÄNDER, WILLIBALD, 1924– HONOUREE.
II. HOURIHANE, COLUM, 1955– EDITOR OF COMPILATION.
N6310.G56 2011 709.02'2–DC22 2010048094

TITLE PAGE IMAGE:

Presentation in the Temple (detail). Psalter, French, possibly by The Alexander Master Workshop, *circa* 1220–1230. New York, Morgan Library and Museum, Ms. M. 231, fol. 10v. Photo: John Blazejewski, © Morgan Library and Museum.

BOOKS PUBLISHED BY THE INDEX OF CHRISTIAN ART,
PRINCETON UNIVERSITY, ARE PRINTED ON ACID-FREE PAPER
AND MEET THE GUIDELINES FOR
PERMANENCE AND DURABILITY OF THE
COMMITTEE ON PRODUCTION
GUIDELINES FOR BOOK LONGEVITY OF THE
COUNCIL ON LIBRARY RESOURCES

CONTENTS

PREFACE

THE CONFERENCE on the Gothic that took place in Princeton in March 2009 was a follow-up to the successful event devoted to the Romanesque held two years earlier.[1] After looking at recent trends in the study of Romanesque art, it was a logical step for us to see what was happening in the later medieval period and to examine the Gothic. The results of that examination are published in this volume. The essays aim to look at what we have researched—and perhaps over emphasized at times—in the field of Gothic studies, but they also aim to see what has been neglected and to look at the reasons why. This volume strives to expand the fields for study in the period and to show the younger generation of scholars what still remains to be done. Its twin goals are historiographic and iconographic. The latter, of course, reflects the focus of the Index of Christian Art, which has now been in existence for over ninety years.

The general problem with the term Gothic is that it is too broad, attempting to cover too great a period of time as well as too expansive a geographic area. It is impossible to apply the same classificatory terms, for instance, to the art produced in western Ireland of the thirteenth century to that in eastern Europe of the same period; yet we continue to do so, albeit reluctantly in some cases. It is our need to classify and analyze which causes such problems, but many of the essays in this volume suggest alternatives, or at least make us aware of the problems in applying such limited terms.

It was impossible to cover every area or medium in the space of a two-day conference, but we made valiant efforts, and I hope you will understand and excuse us for lingering on such areas as French architectural sculpture or manuscripts. These essays demonstrate the value of having continued to work so conscientiously in the field of Gothic art. They are interdisciplinary and holistic in their approaches: some criticize while others applaud, but all make serious efforts to see where we are in terms of the Gothic period. All of the authors attempted to combine an overview of their respective field with new material, and I am grateful to

1. The conference on the Romanesque, which was organized by The Index of Christian Art (October 26th and 27th, 2006), was subsequently published as *Romanesque Art and Thought in the Twelfth Century, Essays in Honor of Walter Cahn*, Index of Christian Art, Occasional Papers, x, ed. Colum Hourihane (University Park and Princeton, 2008). See also *Representing History, 900–1300: Art, Music, History*, ed. Robert A. Maxwell (University Park, 2010). The conference on the Gothic, which shares the same title as this volume, was held on March 19th and 20th, 2009.

them for undertaking this task with charm and ease. With one or two exceptions, all of the speakers at the conference decided to include their essays in this volume and I thank them for working so assiduously and meeting my rigorous deadlines.

The volume is dedicated to Willibald Sauerländer whose work has inspired all of us for the last fifty years and will hopefully do so for many more years to come. Despite his wide interests in many art-historical fields, we all like to think of him as a medievalist and one whose feet are firmly placed in the Gothic. It was unfortunate that he could not be present at the event, but his lecture—which was delivered on his behalf by Jonathan Alexander, and which is also published in this volume—was inspirational and encapsulates his expansive knowledge and learning. It is published as it was delivered (and without footnotes) in an effort to capture the orality and spontaneity of his message. I remain grateful to him for all his help.

Many other people deserve to be thanked for making the conference and this publication possible. My thanks are extended to the moderators of the event—Peter Barnet, Michael Curschmann, and Alison Stones. The conference was generously supported by the Council of the Humanities in Princeton University and I wish to thank Alexander Nehamas and Carol Rigolot for their valuable help. My colleagues in the Index of Christian Art all contributed in many ways and my thanks go to them for their collegiality and willingness to help. Robin Dunham deserves to be singled out for dedicating so much of her energy and ability to the organization of a successful event; I am particularly grateful to her. My thanks also go to Mark Syp as well as Michelle Horgan from the Conference and Events Service in Princeton University for their help.

This is the fifth book that Mark Argetsinger has worked on for the Index and his imprint and skill as a master of design and detail is visible throughout the work. I am delighted to work with him and thank him for yet another fine addition to the Index library. Accomplishing the copy-editing, indexing, and design, he has coped with all my requests and made the volume that you now see before you what it is today—the work of a *magister super omnis*.

COLUM HOURIHANE
Director, Index of Christian Art

NOTES ON THE CONTRIBUTORS

MICHELLE P. BROWN is Professor of Medieval Manuscript Studies at the School of Advanced Study, University of London, and is Tutor to the M.A. Programme in the History of the Book. She was for many years the Curator of Medieval and Illuminated Manuscripts at the British Library, where she remains as a part-time project officer. She was also, until recently, a Lay Canon and member of Chapter at St. Paul's Cathedral, London. She has lectured, published, and broadcast widely on medieval manuscripts, history, and Christian culture. She has curated several major exhibitions, including "Painted Labyrinth: The World of the Lindisfarne Gospels" (British Library, 2003), and "In the Beginning: Bibles Before the Year 1000" (Smithsonian Institution, Washington, D.C., 2006–2007). She has an extensive list of publications, amongst which are *A Guide to Western Historical Scripts from Antiquity to 1600* (1990); J. Bately, M. P. Brown, and J. Roberts, eds., *A Palaeographer's View: Selected Writings of Julian Brown* (1991); *Anglo-Saxon Manuscripts* (1991); *Understanding Illuminated Manuscripts: A Glossary of Technical Terms* (1994); *The Book of Cerne: Prayer, Patronage and Power in Ninth-Century England* (1996); M. P. Brown and S. McKendrick, eds., *The Illuminated Book in the Later Middle Ages: Studies in Honour of Janet Backhouse* (1997); *The British Library Guide to Writing and Scripts: History and Techniques* (1998); *The Lindisfarne Gospels: Society, Spirituality and the Scribe* (2003); and *Painted Labyrinth: The World of the Lindisfarne Gospels* (2003).

CAROLINE BRUZELIUS is the Anne Murnick Cogan Professor in the Department of Art and Art History at Duke University. She graduated from Wellesley College with honors in 1971 and subsequently received her Ph.D. from Yale University in 1977. She taught at Dickinson College (1977–1979), before joining Duke University in 1981. She has taught at various colleges throughout her distinguished career, including Harvard University (1980–1981), The University of Rome "La Sapienza" (1998), and the Istituto Universitario di Architettura di Venezia (2003–), where she has been a Visiting and Adjunct Professor. She was Director of The American Academy in Rome between 1994–1998. She has received many awards and honors, and was a Paul Mellon Senior Fellow in the Center for Advanced Study in the Visual Arts (2004). Amongst her many publications are *The Stones of Naples: Church Building in the Angevin Kingdom, 1266–1343* (2004); *The Brummer Collection of Medieval Art*, with Jill Meredith (1991); *The Thirteenth-Century Church at Saint-Denis* (1985); and *Cistercian High Gothic: The Abbey Church of Longpont and the Architecture of the Cistercians in the Early Thirteenth Century*, Analecta Cisterciensia, XXV (1979). She is currently working on *Bodies, Buildings and the Medieval City: The Mendicant Orders, Lay Burial, and the Transformation of the Medieval City* (forthcoming).

MADELINE H. CAVINESS is the Mary Richardson Professor of Art History in Tufts University and Professeur Associé, Faculté des Lettres, Université Laval, Québec (honorary). She received her Ph.D. from Harvard University and is one of the foremost experts in the study of painted glass of the medieval period. She was President of the International Center of Medieval Art from 1984 to 1987 and President of the Medieval Academy of America from 1993 to 1994. Amongst her publications are *Sumptuous Arts at the Royal Abbeys in Reims and Braine: Ornatus elegantiae, varietate stupendes* (1990); *Visualizing Women in the Middle Ages: Sight, Spectacle, and Scopic Economy* (2001); *Medieval Art in the West and Its Audience: Viewers, Patrons, Interpreters* (2001); and "Unnatural Spectacles: Aristotelian Precepts and the

Construction of Gender around 1300," in *Tributes to Jonathan J. G. Alexander: Making and Meaning in the Middle Ages and Renaissance* (2006). A collection of essays in her honor has recently been published as *The Four Modes of Seeing: Approaches to Medieval imagery in Honor of Madeline Harrison Caviness* (2009).

LUCY FREEMAN SANDLER received her Ph.D. from the Institute of Fine Arts, New York University, in 1964. She joined the faculty of New York University the same year as assistant professor before becoming full professor in 1975. She became the Helen Gould Sheppard Professor of Art History Emerita in 2003. She has served on the boards and as an advisor to a number of learned organizations, amongst which are the Medieval Academy of North America, the International Center of Medieval Art, the Medieval Manuscripts Society, and the American Council of Learned Societies. She is a Fellow of the Society of Antiquaries of London and a Fellow of the Medieval Academy of America. Her many publications include *Gothic Manuscripts, 1285–1385*, A Survey of Manuscripts Illuminated in the British Isles, Vol. V, 2 vols. (1986); *The Lichtenthal Psalter and the Patronage of the Bohun Family* (2004); and *The Splendor of the Word: Medieval and Renaissance Illuminated Manuscripts at The New York Public Library* (co-edited with J. J. G. Alexander and James H. Marrow, 2005).

DANIELLE GABORIT-CHOPIN studied at the École Nationale des Chartes in Paris where she received her diploma in archival studies and palaeography in 1967. She then joined the Louvre Museum in 1967 as curator in the Department of Art Objects (département des Objets d'art), where she was based until her retirement in 2005. In that post she was responsible for the study and presentation of all medieval objects. Throughout her distinguished career she has researched many objects and is known for the scope and breath of her research, which has ranged from Romanesque to Crusader art, from the treasuries of Conques to St.-Denis, from manuscripts to objects of kingship. She is best known for her work on medieval enamels and ivories. She contributed to the publication of Volume II of the *Corpus of Medieval Enamels*, initiated by Marie-Madeline Gauthier (*Corpus des Emaux méridionaux*). As a curator she was involved in some of the major exhibitions of the last thirty years to be held in Paris, including "Les Fastes du Gothique, Paris. Le siècle de Charles V" (1981); "Trésors d'Irlande" (1982); "Les Vikings et l'Europe" (1992); and "Byzance" (1992). Her publications include *Ivoires du Moyen Âge* (1978); *Les ivoires médiévaux, Ve–XVe siècle. Catalogue. Musée du Louvre* (2003); and *L'art roman au Louvre* (edited by Jean-René Gaborit, Jannic Durand, and Danielle Gaborit-Chopin) (2005).

CHARLES T. LITTLE is curator in the Department of Medieval Art and the Cloisters, The Metropolitan Museum of Art, New York. He received his Ph.D. for a study on the Magdeburg Ivory Group in 1977. A former president of the International Center of Medieval Art (1996–1999), he is the author of over thirty articles and has curated some of the most important exhibitions on medieval art held in New York over the last twenty years. Amongst his many publications are *The Cloisters Cross: Its Art and Meaning* (co-authored with Elizabeth C. Parker) (1994); *Europe in the Middle Ages* (1987); *From Attila to Charlemagne: Arts of the Early Medieval Period in the Metropolitan Museum of Art*, with Katharine Reynolds Brown and Dafydd Kidd, (2000); and *Set in Stone: The Face in Medieval Sculpture* (2006).

RICHARD MARKS is Emeritus Professor of the History of Art in the University of York (appointed 2008) and Honorary Professor of the History of Art in the University of Cambridge (appointed 2008). He started his career as Assistant Keeper in the Department of Mediaeval & Later Antiquities in the British Museum (1973–1979), before moving to the Burrell Collection in Glasgow where he was Assistant (1979–1985). He was Director of The Royal Pavilion, Art Gallery & Museums in Brighton (1985–1992) before becoming Professor of Medieval Stained Glass in the Department of the History of Art in the University of York (1992–2008). He was Vice-President of The Society of Antiquaries of London (1991–1994) and the International President of the Corpus Vitrearum Medii Aevi (1995–2004). Amongst his many publications are *Stained Glass in England during the Middle Ages* (1993); *Image and Devotion in Late Medieval England* (2004); *Gothic: Art for England, 1400–1547*, with P. Williamson (2003–2004); and *Late*

Gothic England: Art and Display, ed. (2007). He is currently researching the function, reception, and audiences of devotional images in western Europe and the Orthodox world, and has two monographs in progress, one is on *The Rood in Medieval England & Wales* (a companion to *Image and Devotion in Late Medieval England*), the other is provisionally entitled *In a Perpetual State of Becoming: The Icon of the Mother of God of Vladimir*, which examines the history of a famous Byzantine icon from its creation in the twelfth century to the present day.

STEPHEN MURRAY is Professor of Art History and Archaeology at Columbia University. He was educated at Oxford and London Universities. Throughout his distinguished career he has held grants and fellowships from the Guggenheim Foundation, the Stanford Center for Advanced Studies in the Behavioral Sciences, the National Humanities Center, the National Endowment for the Humanities, and the Andrew Mellon Foundation. He was Founding Director of the Media Center for Art History at Columbia. In his research and publications he has explored the life of the great Gothic cathedrals of France (Notre-Dame de Paris, Amiens, Beauvais, and Troyes). His work has focused on all aspects of the cathedral, including design, construction, social context, and liturgical function. This inclusive agenda inspired his most recent book, *A Gothic Sermon* (2004). Under the auspices of a grant from the Andrew W. Mellon Foundation, he currently directs a project to create a database for French Gothic cathedrals.

AMY NEFF is Associate Professor in the School of Art and Art History at the University of Tennessee. She was an undergraduate at Barnard College in 1969 and received her Ph.D. in Art History from the University of Pennsylvania in 1977. She has received numerous awards and honors, including an NEH Fellowship for College Teachers in 2001–2002, a Gladys Krieble Delmas Foundation Fellowship, 1988, and the Rome Prize from the American Academy in Rome, 1974–1976. She received a Samuel H. Kress Foundation Fellowship in 1973–1974 and was Senior Fellow at Harvard University's Center for Italian Renaissance Studies at Villa I Tatti, in 1983–1984, as well as being a Senior Fellow at the Center for Advanced Study in the Visual Arts in the National Gallery of Art, Washington, D.C., 1982–1983. Her studies have focused on Italian as well as Byzantine art, and include "'This Unnatural Flow': Bleeding Demons in the *Supplicationes variae*, the Arena Chapel, and Notre-Dame des Fontaines, La Brigue," in *Anathemata Eortia: Studies in Honor of Thomas F. Mathews* (2009), as well as "Byzantine Icons and Franciscan Prayer: Images of Intercession and Ascent in the Upper Church of San Francesco, Assisi," in *Franciscan Prayer*, The Medieval Franciscans, 3 (2007); "An Aristocratic Copy of a Mendicant Text: James of Milan's Stimulus amoris in 1293," *Franciscan Studies* (2007); and "Lesser Brothers: Franciscan Mission and Identity at Assisi," *Art Bulletin* (2006).

BERND NICOLAI started his academic career in Mainz, Göttingen, and Berlin, before receiving his Ph.D. from The Free University of Berlin in 1990 for a study on Cistercian art and architecture around 1200. After teaching at the Technical University Berlin and Trier University, he moved to the University of Berne, where he has held the chair of Architectural History and Monument Preservation since 2005. His current research is a study on the cathedral of Santiago de Compostela as "Knowledge-Space," which is a collaborative project with the Brandenburg Technical University of Cottbus. His recent publications include *Moderne und Exil. Deutschsprachige Architekten in der Türkei 1925–1955* (1998); *Andreas Schlüter's Equestrian Monument in Berlin* (2002); *Architecture and Exile: Cultural Transfer and Architectural Emigration*, ed. (2003); "Orders in Stone: Social Reality and Artistic Approach. The Case of the Strasbourg South Portal," *Gesta* (2002/2); and *Gotik* (2007).

NINA ROWE received her Ph.D. from Northwestern University in 2002 and is Associate Professor in the Department of Art History and Music at Fordham University. Her essay "Synagoga Tumbles, a Rider Triumphs: Clerical Viewers and the Fürstenportal of Bamberg Cathedral," *Gesta* (2006), received the Van Courtlandt Elliott Prize for best first article in the field of Medieval Studies, from the Medieval Academy of America in 2008. She is the co-author of *Manuscript Illumination in the Modern Age: Recovery and Reconstruction*, with Sandra Hindman, Michael Camille, and Rowan Watson (2007), and she co-edited *Excavating the Medieval Image: Manuscripts, Artists, Audiences—Essays in Honor of Sandra Hindman*, with David Areford (2004). Her monograph *The Jew, the Cathedral, and the Medieval City: Synagoga and Ecclesia in the Thirteenth Century* (Cambridge) will be published in 2011, as will her article "Pocket Crucifixions: Jesus, Jews and Ownership in Fourteenth-Century Ivories," *Studies in Iconography*.

ROCÍO SÁNCHEZ AMEIJEIRAS received her Ph.D. in 1993 from the University of Santiago de Compostela for a study undertaken with Moralejo Alvarez entitled "Iconographic Researches on Thirteenth-century Castilian Funerary Sculpture." She is now Profesora Titular in the History of Art at the same university. Although an expert on funerary sculpture, she is best known for her many studies on thirteenth- and fourteenth-century Gothic sculpture in the kingdoms of León and Castile. Her particular focus has always been iconographical and she has attempted to look at the complex inter-relationships between Gothic and Islamic art in the Iberian Peninsula. Her publications include *El Tímpano Románico, Imágines, Estructura y Audienca*, with José Luís Senra Gabriel y Galán (2003), and *Iconographic Research on Funerary Sculpture of the Thirteenth Century in Castile and León* (1993). She is also the director of a project to compile a corpus of medieval Galician iconography (CIMGA) and is an advisor to the International Center of Medieval Art (ICMA).

DANY SANDRON received his Ph.D. in 1993 from the Université Paris Sorbonne-Paris IV for a study entitled "La cathédrale de Soissons. Etude architectural." He was a conservator in the Musée National du Moyen Âge, Thermes de Cluny, from 1989 to 1993, before becoming Research Director in the history of Western Art in the Centre André Chastel, Paris. He is currently Professor in the Université Paris Sorbonne-Paris IV where he has been based since 1998. His studies have focused mainly on French Gothic architecture and on sculpture in particular. He has several books to his credit, including *La Cathédrale de Soissons, architecture du pouvoir* (1998); *Picardie gothique. Autour de Laon et Soissons. L'architecture religieuse*, Collection Les Monuments de la France gothique (2001); *Amiens, la cathédrale* (2004); and *Les Monuments de la France gothique* (2006). A volume that he co-edited with Philippe Lorentz, *Atlas de Paris au Moyen Âge* (2006), was awarded Prix Le Senne de l'Académie des Inscriptions et belles-lettres in 2007. He is a member of the Scientific Council of the Institut National d'histoire de l'art (INHA) and is on the board of directors of the Centre International d'Etudes Romanes.

KATHERINE H. TACHAU is Professor of History at the University of Iowa, where she has been since 1985. She was an undergraduate at Oberlin College (B.A. in Spanish and Medieval Studies in 1972) and continued her studies at the University of Wisconsin, Madison. She was at the Institute for Medieval Greek and Latin Philology at Copenhagen University between 1979–1981, and subsequently held faculty positions at Montana State University and Pomona College. An interdisciplinary scholar, her studies have focused on the histories of medieval science, philosophy, and religious thought (with special emphasis on their development at the thirteenth- and fourteenth-century medieval universities), as well as the history of medieval art. Her many publications include *Vision and Certitude in the Age of Ockham: Optics, Epistemology, and the Foundations of Semantics, 1250–1345* (1988), which was awarded the Medieval Academy of America's John Nicholas Brown Prize (1992). She is currently writing a monograph, *Bible Lessons for Kings: Scholars and Friars in Thirteenth-Century Paris and the Creation of the Bibles Moralisées.*

GIUSEPPA ZANICHELLI received her Ph.D. in the History of Art in 1987 before becoming Associate Professor at Parma University in 1998. In 2007 she joined Salerno University as full professor. Throughout her career she has focused on the medieval arts of northern Italy and on manuscript production. While in Parma, she organized many exhibitions, including "Romanico Padano: strada, città, ecclesia" (1978), "Benedetto Antelami" (1990), "Wiligelmo e Matilde" (1991), "Il Medioevo delle cattedrali: Chiese e Impero: la lotta delle immagini, secoli XI e XII" (2006), and "La sapienza degli angeli" (2003). Another favored subject for her research has been the illustration of law manuscripts from the early medieval and Lombard periods with the particular aim of documenting the role of images in the transition from oral to written law. She has recently published a number of essays on the structure and function of the book for women in twelfth-century Italy. She has also published in the field of Renaissance studies with a particular focus on Mantua, Milan, and Parma in the fourteenth and fifteenth centuries, published as *Iconografia di Alessandro Araldi nel monastero di San Paolo* (1978); *Parma: le immagini del potere* (1994); and *I conti e il minio: codici miniati dei Rossi, 1325–1482* (1994). She is a member of the scientific committees of the journals *Rivista di Storia della Miniatura* (Pavia University), and *Civiltà mantovana*.

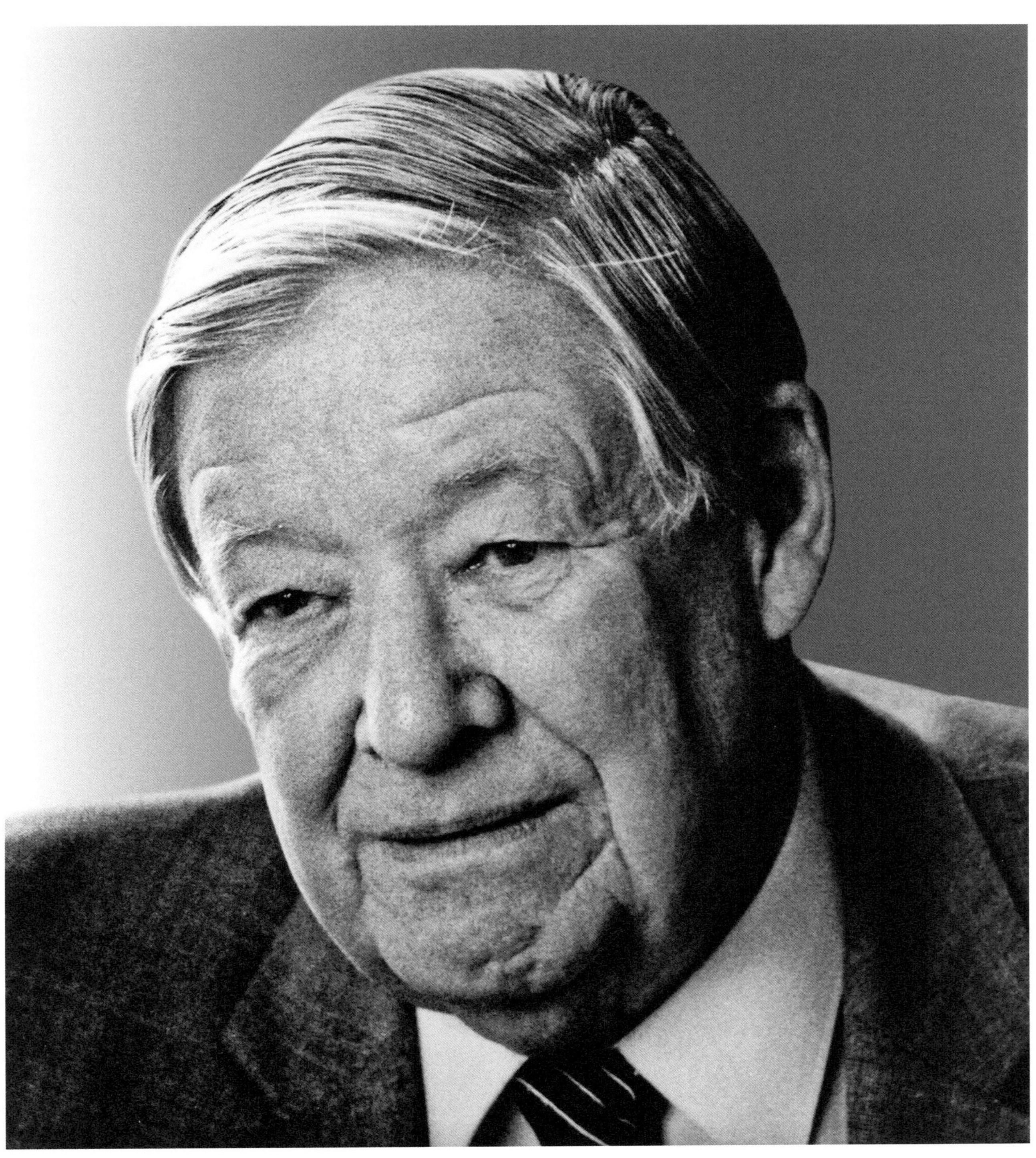

Willibald Sauerländer (photo © Regina Schmeken).

INTRODUCTION

THIS COLLECTION of essays on the Gothic follows the first in a series of review studies that looked at Romanesque art. In that volume we examined how the style developed, or failed to do so in certain areas.[1] The success of that study led us to propose a similar treatment for the other major medieval art styles, and these volumes are really designed to evaluate where we stand in relation to the various fields of study.[2] What has been studied, over emphasized, neglected, or ignored are all dealt with for the various media. Some of these essays certainly adopt a historiographic narrative, but in themselves they also analyze and propose future directions for research. In looking at the various styles it is clear that much remains to be done, and the value of these collections lies in making us aware of what remains. In these essays we are able to evaluate personal and communal methodologies and see what forces have been at play in the field.

Gothic studies have always been to the fore in medieval art history, and there is no shortage of eager new students willing to undertake research on the Pre-Reformation period. Even though the term Gothic is usually seen as an unproblematic classificatory term, it is in fact quite the opposite. As these essays show, we are all too casual in using the term, and whereas it may be the *lingua franca* for the period, we also need to look at local dialects. It is a style that has had much bad press over time, starting with Vasari in the mid-sixteenth century, and continuing to the present. The style has generally been criticized in relation to what preceded and followed it, and some countries, such as Italy and Ireland, even have difficulties in applying the term Gothic to various media outside of architecture. Willibald Sauerländer and others have pointed out that the style has an element of transubstantiality and etherealness, which attributes have also militated against it. Whether "rationalist and secular" or "mystical and literary," Gothic is above all else a classificatory term that is in need of re-evaluation.[3] Its nationalistic associations are every bit as strong as those of the Romanesque, and these developed mainly in the mid-nineteenth century. These essays address all of these issues and certainly make us aware of the inadequacies of the term, but it is generally agreed that it will remain with us. Accepting its permanency, they also suggest ways of working with it so that we are able to unravel the full meaning of the period and style.

One scholar who has moved with charm and enviable abilities between all the periods of art history, and not just the medieval time span, is the person to whom this collection is dedicated, Willibald Sauerländer. He has been an inspiration for all, as Charles Little demonstrates in his homage. Words cannot adequately describe the debt we all owe him for the life-long contributions he has made to our understanding of the medieval period. I do not think there is a single essay in this collection that does not reference one or more of his many studies. Of the many fields that he has researched, the Gothic is clearly the one for which he is best known, and it is more than fitting that this volume should be dedicated to him. It comes a few years after the occasion of his eighty-fifth birthday, but it is offered to him in celebration of that occasion and with a wish that he continue to share his profound thoughts for many more years to come.

The collection opens with an homage by Willibald's close friend and colleague, Charles T. Little. Their friendship developed over many years, and in this essay,

1. Published as *Romanesque Art and Thought in the Twelfth Century, Essays in Honor of Walter Cahn*, Index of Christian Art Occasional Papers, x, ed. Colum Hourihane (University Park and Princeton, 2008).

2. After the Gothic, the most recent style to be evaluated was Insular and Anglo-Saxon, which was the subject of a two-day conference in the Index of Christian Art series, "Insular and Anglo-Saxon Art and Thought in the Early Medieval Period," March 16th and 17th, 2010, the proceedings of which are forthcoming.

3. M. Camille, *Gothic Art, Glorious Visions* (New York, 1996), 10.

which is a finely written and succinct life narrative, we are also able to see the motivation and contextualization of Willibald's studies in the broader field of scholarship. Charles writes of the influences behind many of the studies and also gives us insight into the bountiful areas of research outside the medieval that have been examined by Willibald. He points out some of the common characteristics of Willibald's studies, such as the historical contextualization of the subject with which he is dealing, and his ability to reference sources from the contemporary to the early medieval—always with erudite knowledge. Willibald's base line, however, is that everything needs to be understood and explained to his readers as trenchantly as possible.

Many of the Index publications that have been dedicated to scholars over the last ten years have included an essay by the person being celebrated, and this one is no exception. Willibald's essay immediately follows Charles's homage and brings us straight away into one of the problems of the Gothic. It was with regret that Willibald could not attend the conference in Princeton, but his paper was delivered with charm and confidence by his colleague, Jonathan Alexander. I wanted to preserve the orality of that occasion, and the essay is published here as it was delivered—and remains unencumbered by footnotes or references. As one reads the words, it is possible to hear him *viva voce*. Although the essay nominally looks at the Gothic cathedral, its message is far more expansive. He looks at the perceptions and interpretations of the Gothic cathedral from Vasari to the twenty-first century and evaluates how it underwent change and responded to different concepts, from the idea of it representing a destructive style to it being an image of transcendental space. As in all of his studies, he attempts to understand how these buildings work—why they were built as they were, and what reasons lay behind them—portraying a holistic understanding of the structures in society. In typical form, he not only documents and analyzes, but he also suggests how future research might benefit from understanding some of the useful insights still extant from the Middle Ages concerning what went on in these structures. The essay shows how our concepts and images of the period in many ways influence our perception of what remains. The devil is in the details, and not necessarily in our lofty and erudite theories on functionality and structure. What we need to do is firstly understand what went on in these buildings as described in the asides that still survive. We need to look at the totality of these structures to see what they meant, and functionality and ritual serve as the keys.

The opening essay deals with the perception of the cathedral throughout time; the second is an erudite and scholarly analysis by Katherine Tachau that looks at an equally complex historiographical subject, the relationship of Gothic architecture and scholasticism—a topic close to the heart of one of the Index of Christian Art's biggest supporters, Erwin Panofsky. In an essay ranging from Aristotle to Hegel to von Simpson, Katherine surveys and analyzes Panofsky's five significant claims first made in his pivotal study, *Gothic Architecture and Scholasticism*, extending even further our knowledge of his work. It is a finely structured essay that interweaves the historical, the historiographical, and the art historical, over and above the architectural, into a benchmark essay that is certain to open further research.

We continue with architecture in the third essay. It moves us from the theoretical and historiographical into the actual, with an analysis of the often-overlooked, large-scale statuary found on the upper levels of cathedrals in northern France from the thirteenth to the sixteenth centuries. Dany Sandron in an insightful study whets our appetites and shows how such carvings elicited the responses of an audience on a local as well as regional level. Selecting three or four case studies, he analyzes the figures in terms of placement, iconography, sources, audience, and response. These carvings usually worked not as isolated images but were part of much larger ensembles, and we need to integrate them into general research to fully understand their purpose.

It is not surprising to find the fourth essay continue with the general theme of Gothic French architecture. One of the foremost experts in the field, Stephen Murray, provides us with an interesting and insightful study that has never before been attempted. He endeavors to narrate the story of Gothic architecture, not through formal stylistic analysis, but by plotting out and often uniting the careers and accounts of three witnesses to the development of the style. These three different individuals, who held three different roles in the building of cathedrals—Villard de Honnecourt, Gervase of Canterbury, and Abbot Suger of St.-Denis—are used to provide us with a unified and individual insight into the Gothic style and the whole process of construction. Structural analogies are used in support of the writings of these three individuals in a revelatory essay showing what can be accomplished with meager sources. It is one of the first attempts to really narrate the story of the style.

The Index of Christian Art has always attempted to be as inclusive as possible, and the conferences have dealt with as many media, styles, and geographies as is practical. The primacy of France in Gothic studies is understandable, but it is only within the last twenty or thirty years that regional and local manifestations have questioned the whole process by which it was transferred from its center in the Île de France to other countries. Studies by Richard Marks, Rocío Sánchez Ameijeiras, Caroline Bruzelius, Bernd Nicolai, and Giuseppa Zanichelli address this issue in a series of case studies or encyclopaedic analyses. They all point out the centrality of France in older scholarship, which in many ways has hindered the real appreciation of manifestations of the Gothic in other regions, in as much as they are seen as mirror images or reflections of the parent style. Whereas many of these studies still acknowledge that point of view, they also highlight the independence and indigenous qualities of the style, and indeed the variety of sub-styles within national borders.

The essay by Richard Marks questions the Englishness of English Gothic art. It is expertly done, using the relatively modern historiography of the style and providing us with an in-depth analysis as to why it was seen as a national style. It does not concentrate on the traditional analysis of forms and style, except where it underpins Richard's arguments, but instead provides us with a unique analysis of the people (beginning with Nicholas Pevsner), background, political and cultural *milieux*, and reasons why such a style as English Gothic developed. Richard, not content to simply provide us with an insightful study, then offers avenues for future research into the style itself.

Lucy Freeman Sandler, one of the foremost experts on English manuscript studies selects the Bohun family and their patronage of some one hundred and fifty manuscripts in the second half of fourteenth-century England as her case study into English Gothic manuscripts. It is an essay that could apply to any country, as she details the historiographic principles that have evolved in the study of these works from the late nineteenth century to the present. Looking at what could be called early or historical concepts, such as documentation (mapping, codicological analyses), the determination of ownership, style, influences, and iconography, Lucy shows how the study of these works has evolved since the 1930s into painting a broader picture—one that looks at ideas drawn from evidence outside of as well as within the works to see their full meaning. Anthropological, social, and literary theories have been used to analyze these works in order to understand more fully their meaning in society. We are clearly now in the age of minute analyses, and it promises to yield beneficial results.

A similar picture to that painted by Richard Marks emerges in Bernd Nicolai's examination of the Gothic in Germany of the Holy Roman Empire. His essay focuses equally on the centrality of the Île de France as well as the dynastic affiliations and strengths that lay behind the Gothic as found in his case study of Madgeburg Cathedral, the earliest example of the classic French-style cathedral in Germany. By any standard, the style of Madgeburg is unusual and reflects a local as well as international architectural and sculptural language, with influences from Lausanne and Basel. The style, however, was introduced, as Bernd explains, into a confident and secure empire and not, as we usually believe, into an area in need of outside influences.

In her essay on Spanish Gothic, Rocío Sánchez Ameijeiras looks at a much-neglected subject, and in particular at León Cathedral as a case study. Spanish Romanesque, as in most other countries, has superseded the Gothic in terms of research, popularity, and above all as a symbol of national identity, if such a concept exists. It is only in the last few years that such styles as Mudejar (both Romanesque and Gothic), Hispano-Moorish, Plateresque, Hispano-Flemish, and

Isabelline Gothic have been studied. We have to be constantly reminded that Spanish Gothic does exist in such fine buildings as the cathedrals in Ávila, Barcelona, Burgos, Girona, Oviedo, Seville, and Zaragoza, to name just a few, as well as in the many houses of the Mendicant orders found throughout the peninsula. Even though Rocío has previously examined some of these buildings in relation to French models, as she also does in this article, her focus here is on the inspiration for the iconography and its links to rhetorical education and texts.[4] In a revelatory work she convincingly traces the origins for many of the León motifs and provides us with a benchmark essay for future research in the whole field of Gothic iconography.

Although Michelle Brown claims, slightly apologetically, to be more comfortable studying the earlier rather than the later medieval manuscript, it is clear in her essay that she is also very much at home in book production of the Gothic period. Her encyclopaedic article covering three centuries resonates with many other studies in the volume and provides an overview that only someone such as Michelle could give. Her measured and engaging study starts with a historiographic perspective, but then very deftly looks at a range of factors, from the urban nature of production, to patronage, to technical aspects that characterize the Gothic book. Her article questions the validity of the word, and she views it in practical terms while at the same time not ignoring its problems. Like so many other contributors to this volume, she paves the way for future research and highlights the paths that should be taken, especially that of integrating manuscript study with that of other media and providing a broader understanding of the socio-historical context in which these works were made.

Italy's long and rich artistic tradition prior to and after the Gothic era has lead to the relative neglect of this style within the Italian art-historical tradition. Coming as it does between the Romanesque and Renaissance has led to difficulties in accepting the Gothic—especially since, as a number of essays in this volume indicate, it had national associations outside of the areas concerned and was seen as a foreign style to begin with. The two case studies on Italy in this collection, by Caroline Bruzelius and Giuseppa Zanichelli, differ from other national studies in that the Italians refused to recognize the style or to call it Gothic.

This is more than obvious in Giuseppa's rigorous and detailed historiographcial survey of Gothic manuscripts in Italy. In her finely paced analysis, she shows how the term is even more ambiguous as a means of classification than elsewhere, but practical needs justify its use. Even though it was in book illumination in Italy that the term Gothic acquired specific meaning, it is clearly still a term that rests uncomfortably, and in this respect it is not unique to Italy. The same situation, for example, is found in twenty-first-century Ireland where the term Gothic is applied to architecture and sculpture of the Norman period, but not to other media such as metalwork or book illumination.[5] Three different issues provide a background to Giuseppa's study. The first is the geographic regional fragmentation of thirteenth- and fourteenth-century Italy; the second the chronological breakup of the Gothic period in Italy, with Giotto as a watershed in the middle; and, third, the reluctance to accept the style both historigraphically and generally. Against all three factors, the essay presents a magisterial survey of the historiography of the term Gothic and its application to Italian medieval manuscripts. Like many other contributors to this volume, the author concludes with a wish for future scholarship to look at these manuscripts in a broader European context.

The second study to deal exclusively with Italy is by Caroline Bruzelius. She looks at what may seem to be three disparate subjects in the sculptural repertoire: Nicola Pisano, monumental free-standing pulpits, and the double-sided tomb or *arca* and its variants. Fully realizing what could be seen as a lack of cohesiveness in selecting these three topics, Caroline paints a detailed

4. As for example in her study of the south portal of Burgos Cathedral in "Church Reform and the Poetics of Gothic Sculpture in Burgos and Amiens," in *Spanish Medieval Art, Recent Studies*, ed. Colum Hourihane (Tempe, Ariz., 2007), 155–186.

5. See Colum Hourihane, *Gothic Art in Ireland, 1169–1550: Enduring Vitality* (New Haven, 2003).

and concise background—from historiography to political and cultural—before uniting all in a finely structured study. Noting the political power of sculpture when used as a public agent of gesture and statement (many examples of which are discussed), she proceeds to analyze these works as means of expression and rhetoric. It is an encyclopaedic study in which the political and social uses of monumental sculpture are discussed, and she seamlessly moves the reader from the north to the south, from Antiquity to the fifteenth century, and from the personal carving to the pubic monument.

No study on the Gothic would be complete without essays on ivories and stained or painted glass. The first of these is by Danielle Gaborit-Chopin, a scholar who has devoted much of her distinguished career to the study of medieval ivories. She follows in the tradition of Raymond Koechlin (1860–1931), whose three-volume publication on Gothic French ivories, *Les ivories gothiques Français* (1924), is the reference bible for the medium. In this essay and with the utmost of respect, Danielle examines Koechlin's work and what recent research can add to our understanding of the field. It is a subject far too expansive to be dealt with completely, but under a series of trenchant subheadings Danielle looks at how the field has changed: how we now know that schools of ivory working existed outside of France—in England and Germany, for example—and how previously understood views of polychromy, workshops, and the primacy of Paris need to be redefined. Like a number of other scholars in this volume, Danielle pleads for ivories to be researched in the future against other media, such as manuscript illumination and stone sculpture, so that we may see the larger picture.

It is with her customary modesty that Madeline Caviness describes herself in the introduction to her essay as a "former expert" in the field of stained glass. As her work here shows, she is still very much an expert in the field. In a finely paced historiographical essay, Madeline makes some very necessary and interesting challenges to our assumptions. The first of these is the actual terminology that we use, and she expresses her wish to see this medium referred to as painted (and not stained) glass. The secondary and neglected status of research in the field, along with the actual destruction of the fabric itself, is discussed in considerable detail against a historiography of the medium by a scholar who knows the material intimately. Her conclusion is a case study and detective story dealing with fragments of glass from Hereford Cathedral (with Hampton Court Palace also thrown in!) that vouchsafes and confirms Madeline's expertise as one of the foremost scholars in the field.

The primary interest of the Index of Christian Art and its major contribution to the field of medieval studies for nearly one hundred years is undoubtedly iconographic, and I am very grateful to all of the contributors for including aspects of this in their studies. The purpose of these volumes has been not only to evaluate what research has been undertaken in the field of Gothic art history, but also to stimulate new scholarship in the field. For the Index, this has meant the inclusion of dedicated and stimulating iconographical studies, and this volume includes two that are totally devoted to that end. Amy Neff and Nina Rowe conclude this collection with riveting essays on, respectively, the Wedding Feast at Cana and Ecclesia and Synagoga. Amy's study looks at two different images of the wedding feast, one at Assisi in the upper church of San Francesco and the other in the *Supplicationes variae*, both dating to the 1290s. It is an essay that looks at imagery of food and abstention from it, both of which link the Miracle at Cana fresco and the *Supplicationes* and can be viewed as carnal and sacred eating. Underlying both images, however, is a Franciscan connection, and it is this that is beautifully explored in a finely structured essay that looks at the different ways the same story can be told, and the need to address particular and encompassing audiences. This is a model as to what can be achieved by looking at the picture beyond the image itself. An equally fine model of iconographic research is found in Nina Rowe's study on Ecclesia and Synagoga. This is a topic to which Nina has dedicated much research, and here she focuses on those monumental carvings found on cathedral façades in the early to mid-thirteenth century (*c.* 1225–1240), on such buildings as the cathedrals at Reims, Bamberg, and Strasbourg, all of which are also linked to images of strong male rulership. Against a historiographical analysis of the subject from the antique to the medieval, Nina looks at issues of reception and perception and argues that this subject mediated between the real and ideal worlds. In conclusion, she has a finely painted case study of Strasbourg cathedral that convincingly weaves political, social, and religious factors into a convincing argument.

This collection of essays highlights our constant need to re-evaluate what we are doing, so that we may proceed with the advantage of an ever-greater perspective. I am grateful to all the authors for undertaking that task so admirably in this volume.

GOTHIC ART AND THOUGHT IN THE LATER MEDIEVAL PERIOD

CHARLES T. LITTLE

Willibald Sauerländer: Gothic Art and Beyond

ON March 28th, 2009, Willibald Sauerländer celebrated his eighty-fifth birthday in Munich with many friends, colleagues, and admirers joining him at the Zentralinstitut für Kunstgeschichte.[1] He was honored on the occasion with tributes from Martin Warnke, Pierre Rosenberg, Neil Stratford, and Thomas Gaehtgens, followed by a lecture presented by Carlo Ginsburg. Added to that celebratory occasion, Princeton is the ideal place to recognize Sauerländer's contribution to Gothic in America, for it was in 1961, at Erwin Panofsky's invitation, that he first came to the United States to the Institute for Advanced Study at Princeton. It was at Princeton that he developed his investigations on the cloister sculpture of Châlons-sur-Marne, among other topics, presenting the results that year at the 1961 International Congress of Art History in New York.[2] He was the first to recognize the significance of these astonishing discoveries of the cloister fragments, a project continued by Léon Pressouyre, and culminating in one of most beautiful new museums devoted to the archaeology, reconstruction, and significance of cloister sculptures. On different occasions, Sauerländer also taught in the United States, especially at the Institute of Fine Arts of New York University (1963–1965; 1969–1970; 1992–1993), but also at the University of California at Berkeley (1989), and at Harvard University (1984–1985). Although most of his doctoral students were in Germany, he advised several Americans as well. In 1973 at the Institute of Fine Arts, Sharon Jones prepared a thesis on French Gothic sculpture and its influence on north Italian sculpture in the first half of the thirteenth century. Then in 1978, Michael Ward prepared a dissertation on the Pórtico da Gloria at Santiago de Compostela.

One gets an overview of Sauerländer's life and work in his short 1999 autobiography prepared as part of an anthology of his writings, *Geschichte der Kunst–Gegenwart der Kritik*,[3] which highlighted his intellectual formation and included a comprehensive list of his published works. In addition, in 2000, his lasting mark on the field of study of cathedral and sculpture could be gauged by the selection of his writings published by Pindar Press.[4]

Sauerländer's early training was with Hans Jantzen—he clashed with Hans Sedlmayr (a member of the Nazi Party)—at the University of Munich immediately after World War II, but equally important was his early friendship with Louis Grodecki in Paris and Strasbourg, whom he saw—due to his wide-ranging interests, from ivory carving, to architecture, to stained glass—as a kind of oracle for the study of medieval art in France. Working in Paris in the early 1950s—and also under the spell of André Chastel, the "prince of French Art History"—he began his pioneering studies

1. See Thomas E. Gaehtgens, "Spielarten der Neugier—Kunsthistoriker und kritischer Essayist: Willibald Sauerländer wird 85," *Süddeutsche Zeitung*, 28 February – 1 March 2009, 14.

2. "Twelfth Century Sculpture at Châlons-sur-Marne," *Romanesque and Gothic Art: Studies in Western Art*, Acts of the Twentieth International Congress of the History of Art, I (Princeton, 1963), 119–128.

3. Willibald Sauerländer, *Geschichte der Kunst—Gegenwart der Kritik*, ed. Werner Busch, Wolfgang Kemp, Monika Steinhauer, and Martin Warnke (Cologne: Dumont, 1999), Bibliography, 343–359 (202 items). See now: Sasha Suda, "In Conversation: Willibald Sauerländer with Sasha Suda," *The Brooklyn Rail: Critical Perspectives on Arts, Politics and Culture*, February, 2010, and Willibald Sauerländer, "Afterthoughts to a Conversation with Sasha Suda," *The Brooklyn Rail*, April, 2010.

4. Willibald Sauerländer, *Cathedrals and Sculpture*, I (London, 1999), II (2000); "Publications of Willibald Sauerländer on Medieval Art," 921–934 (140 items).

of early Gothic sculpture on Senlis and Mantes cathedrals, followed shortly by his penetrating study of the façade sculpture of Notre-Dame de Paris that literally redefined how we approach Gothic sculpture.[5] He also looked to England for innovations in sculpture and recognized the importance of the figures from the Chapter House at St. Mary's at York.[6] His method allowed for a nuanced investigation of the interrelationships between monuments and the reality of the sculptors and masons working at many sites. While teaching at Freiburg University (1962–1970), he utilized the remarkable photo collection of Wilhelm Vöge, which included many photos of sculpture that recorded their state before the commencement of World War I. These became a critical starting point for his reassessment of Gothic sculpture. Thus his initial approach was much indebted to Vöge. The power of juxtaposing works took on a new significance in telling a progressive story.

Although sculpture became his forte, one must see his penetrating reviews of pivotal medieval exhibitions as reflections of his wider range of interests, many being published in the *Süddeutsche Zeitung*, where he became one of their principal critics after retiring as Director of the Zentralinstitut für Kunstgeschichte in 1989.[7] The culmination of his research on monumental sculpture in *Gotische Skulptur in Frankreich, 1140–1270* (1970) established his preëminence in the field. Coincidentally, that publishing event paralleled a project for the 1970 centenary of The Metropolitan Museum of Art. The ambitious "The Year 1200" Exhibition and Symposium, mostly the brainchild of the then Museum Director Thomas Hoving, was curated by a team lead by Florens Deuchler, Chairman of the Department of Medieval Art and The Cloisters. As Sauerländer was just about to launch his landmark volume *Gotische Skulptur in Frankreich* and was moving from Freiburg to Munich to take up the Directorship at the Zentralinstitut für Kunstgeschichte, the timing of the exhibition was fortuitous. A lecture course on monumental Gothic sculpture in the Spring of 1970 at the Institute of Fine Art was supplemented by an important seminar on "The Year 1200" Exhibition, one that I participated in as a graduate student. But as fate would have it, world events intervened with the Vietnam War and the invasion of Cambodia leading to the cancellation of classes—thus eclipsing our dreams of fully penetrating the glories of the Gothic world then being showcased at the museum. The students treasured the hours in the exhibition on Mondays, however, when the galleries were closed. In his element with the great objects assembled, Sauerländer was ever sensitive to the objects and the aesthetic spirit these works evoked. Having lively debates and reports in front of such celebrated works as Nicholas of Verdun's enamels from the Klosterneuburg ambo or his Tournai shrine is not something one easily forgets. But his *Gothic Sculpture in France*—as it was translated the next year—stands as the best testimony to his approach to sculpture, and as the subject of his lecture course, that clearly demonstrates the truth of what one reviewer enthused: "it is not too much to say that he has been responsible for largely rewriting its history."[8]

Since the 50s, Sauerländer had been pondering, and publishing extensively, on the transmission of style, especially regarding sculpture in France during the twelfth and thirteenth centuries. As a lead up to "The Year 1200" exhibition, his 1966 study "Von Sens bis Strasbourg" became something of a lightning rod for the debate concerning the role of style as an agent of change from the narrative and expressive tendencies of Romanesque to the naturalism of Gothic. Some felt the wisdom of Wilhelm Vöge and his imitable powers of observation of style distorted the actuality of the monuments and the historical situation. At the 1970 symposium to mark "The Year 1200" exhibition, one scholar (Jan van der Meulen) made an acerbic remark that was both whimsical and serious, maintaining that "the

5. Willibald Sauerländer, Die Marienkrönungsportale von Senlis und Mantes," *Wallraf-Richartz-Jahrbuch* 20 (1958), 115–162, and "Die kunsgeschichtliche Stellung der Westportale von Notre Dame in Paris. Ein Beitrag zur Genesis des hochgotischen Stiles in der französischen Skulptur," *Marburger Jahrbuch für Kunstwissenschaft* 17 (1959), 1–56.

6. Willibald Sauerländer, "'Sens and York': An Inquiry into the Sculptures from St. Mary's Abbey in the Yorkshire Museum," *The Journal of the British Archaeological Association* 22 (1958), 53–69.

7. A selection is found in Willibald Sauerländer, *Die Luft auf der Spitze des Pinsel—Kritische Spaziergänge durch Bildersäle* (Munich, 2002).

8. "Comparable Carving," *Times Literary Supplement*, 13 April 1973, 410.

result of style transmission was not so much leading from 'Von Sens bis Strasbourg' but from 'Von Sens bis non-Sense' "! For me, as a young graduate student, the power of this art, and especially the sculpture, never failed to impress me and continually forced questions of attribution, meaning, and context.

This is not the moment to comprehensively review the extraordinary contribution that his *Gothic Sculpture in France* has made to a generation of art historians since being published in 1970. Sauerländer utilizes an approach that one might call "strata-graphic Gothic," or "integrated Gothic," linking synchronic parallel developments of monuments both in their chronological relationships to other media and in the fabric of ideas generating them, rather than merely reviewing the linear history of sculpture at a particular monument. Although style is the key, iconography, and even political intention, is equally critical, as seen in his study of the typography and typology of the coronation cathedral of Reims.[9]

Sauerländer is a polymath in so many areas of artistic endeavor, from the Middle Ages to Jasper Johns and beyond. He proposes no unified theory of Gothic. Instead, he has often looked to "Gothic" Europe as a wellspring for capturing the past and antiquity and for foretelling trends of the future, especially in the nineteenth century, as seen in his provocative essay "La cathédrale et la révolution."[10] A look at his literary, art-historical, and critical essays over six decades reveals that Gothic is just a slice of an incredible range of interest; of more than four hundred published works, only a third covers the Middle Ages. Without abusing the old *topos* of Ovid concerning "the workmanship surpassing the material," his classic works strive to surpass with an élan, insight, and breadth of knowledge that one rarely finds in art-historical criticism. Most recently, his early interest in Nicolas Poussin, especially in the landscapes, has again blossomed into a series of discerning rhapsodies on these bucolic settings. These studies are unmatched in their grounding of the literary and poetic sources and are further exemplified in his incisive essay for the recent Metropolitan Museum exhibition devoted to Poussin's landscapes. Such an amazing understanding of antiquity and modernity surfaces again and again, seen, for example, in his study of the Hercules slaying the Hydra tapestry, now in the Munich Residenz.[11]

His 1991 Mellon lecture at the National Gallery, Washington, D.C., opened new possibilities of critical inquiry. Entitled "Changing Faces: Art and Physiognomy through the Ages," he brought science and art together to explore the nature of expression and how the face is mapped over time, whether it be the corbels of Reims Cathedral or the zoömorphism and caricatures of Franz Xaver Messerschmidt. For the Gothic aspects of physiognomy in the Washington lectures, Sauerländer intended them as a roadmap to the moralizing opposites between the beautiful and the ugly, and between the good and the bad. Fascinated by Michael Scotus' "Liber phisionomiae" and by Albertus Magnus' comment that "by the parts of the body one can recognize how a man is naturally disposed, but what habits he exercises and uses, one cannot recognize," Sauerländer explored the range of such possibilities in the Gothic age.[12] He uses physiognomy in innovative ways to explore the face as integral to the study of European art. Some of these ideas emerged in his study "The Fate of the Face in Medieval Art" for the 2006–2007 Metropolitan Museum exhibition entitled "Set in Stone: The Face in Medieval Sculpture."[13]

His contributions to Gothic art often start by looking through the lens of nineteenth-century commentators, regarding their insights and poetry of expression

9. Willibald Sauerländer, "Observations sur la typographie et l'iconologie de la cathédrale du sacre," *Académie des inscriptions et belles-lettres. Comptes-rendus des séances de l'année* (1992), 463–479. See also his "*Antiqui et Moderni* at Reims," *Gesta* XLII/I (2003), 19–37.

10. Willibald Sauerländer, "La cathédral et la révolution," in *Cathedral and Sculpture*, Vol. II, 830–864.

11. Willibald Sauerländer and Sabine Heym, *Herkules besiegt die lernäische Hydra: der Kerkules-Teppich im Vortragssaal der Bayerischen Akademie der Wissenschaften* (Munich, 2006).

12. See Willibald Sauerländer, "*Phisionomia est doctrina salutis.* Über Physiognomik und Porträt im Jahrhundert Ludwigs des Heilgen," in *Das Porträt vor der Erfindung des Porträts*, ed. Martin Büchsel and Peter Schmidt (Mainz am Rhein, 2003), 101–122, esp. 101.

13. Willibald Sauerländer, "The Fate of the Face in Medieval Art," in Charles T. Little, ed., *Set in Stone: The Face in Medieval Sculpture* (New York, 2006), 2–17.

as both revealing and as a critical point of departure. He usually launches a commentary on a topic of Gothic art or architecture with a quote from Marcel Proust, Gustave Flaubert, Victor Hugo, Goethe, Heinrich Heine, John Ruskin, or Mark Twain—the last of whom, after a visit to Paris in 1869, could only lament that Notre-Dame de Paris was a "brown old gothic pile." Since the nineteenth-century writers invariably captured the essence of the issues, their insights, wisdom, and elegance of expression often paralleled his aims and objectives. However, his view is more pan-European than looking at just local problems; but he does that too with incisive results, such as his revelations concerning the "tomb" of Henry the Lion and Mathilde in St. Blasius in Braunschweig.[14] Linking the architecture of Notre-Dame de Paris with León in Castile, or Uppsala Cathedral in Sweden, or Westminster Abbey reveals a more open playing field. At the same time, he recognizes the limitations of style: "We should also realize that the traditional concept of 'style' as being a sort of Platonic idea existing before creation and then producing a work of art, is worthless when studying works of Medieval art. The workshop seems here to depend very pragmatically and sometimes even accidentally on external condition, local demand, and models at hand."[15] To him, "the history of medieval art must be reintegrated with medieval history—not only with the history of ideas, but with political, economic, and social history. The dream of the Gothic cathedral as the visual and monumental symbol of a Christian past without conflict—the dream of all reactionaries and Romanticists from Chateaubriand to Sedlmayr—is, one hopes, finished for good."[16]

In the early days at Freiburg University he was a formidable intellect and teacher. His generosity was more characteristically showered on American students with whom he was both supportive and engaged. At the Institute of Fine Arts the students often enjoyed the way he turned German, French, Italian, or Latin phrases into English with amusing results, such as "the great apes (apse) of Cluny" or "here is the Qveen of Saba, mit de goose's fuss."

When studying, for example, the sculpture of the collection of Raymond Pitcairn, now the Glencairn Museum, he saw the collector, an incredible accumulator of Gothic sculpture and stained glass, as becoming the "true Connecticut Yankee in King Arthur's Court." A relief with the Adoration of the Magi in the collection caught his eye and, instantly seeing the relationship with the sculpture at the cathedral of Besançon, it became the subject of a charming study of Gothic in the Rhône valley.[17] Even Princeton Gothic architecture came under his spell. The octagonal structure erected in 1863, called the "Green library," looks directly to the so-called "rheinischen Übergangsstils—transition style" of the type of structure seen at St. Matthias in Kobern with its Hohenstaufen *Gralsbau* or grail structure. Even looking at the origins of The Cloisters, George Grey Barnard's original museum known as "America's First Gothic Museum," opening December 14th, 1914, was cause for repeated observations.[18] Whereas Barnard saw his Gothic museum as a kind of dream vehicle to transport one back to the Middle Ages, Sauerländer saw it as a specifically American phenomenon that evolved into an entirely new museum experience.

Willibald Sauerländer has pioneered so many pivotal studies on Gothic art that the field has truly been transformed because of his work. His present paper in this volume opens new probing matters of definition: he asks where the field is going next, and, most importantly, ponders what critical questions to ask.

14. Willibald Sauerländer, "Zur Stiftertumba für Heinrich den Löwen und Herzogin Mathilde in St. Blasius in Braumschweig," in *Der Welfenschatz und sein Umkreis*, ed. Joachim Ehlers and Dietrich Kötzsche (Mainz, 1998), 439–488.

15. Willibald Sauerländer, "Sculpture on Early Gothic Churches: The State of Research and Open Questions," *Gesta* IX/2 (1970), 32–48, esp. 41.

16. Willibald Sauerländer, "'Premier architecture gothique' or 'Renaissance of the twelfth century?' Changing Perspective in the Evaluation of Architectural History," *Sewanee Medieval Studies* (1985), 25–41, esp. 41.

17. Willibald Sauerländer, "Ein amerikanischer Nachtrag zur 'Gotischen Skulptur in Frankreich,'" *Wiener Jahrbuch für Kunsgeschichte*. Beiträge zur mittelalterlichen Kunst. Festschrift für Gerhard Schmidt, 46/47 (1993/1994), 621–627.

18. Willibald Sauerländer, "'Connecticut Yankee in King Arthur's Court'–Mittelalterliche Kunst in Amerika," in his collected essays, *Cathedrals and Sculpture* (London, 2000), 865–901.

WILLIBALD SAUERLÄNDER

Gothic: The Dream of an Un-classical Style

THREE YEARS AGO—at the last Index of Christian Art conference I attended—I spoke on "Romanesque Art: A Worn Out Notion?"[1] Speaking and writing about Gothic is a very different task. "Romanesque" is an art-historical notion coined by archaeologists in France during the dreary years after 1815; "Gothic" is not only a much older notion, but of all the classifications that art historians have accepted in order to baptize a style or a period, Gothic is the most charged with conflicting meanings and disputed values. Invented by the Italian humanists in order to denounce the interruption of the classical tradition and the deterioration of Latin script, it is a notion embattled between classical and romantic taste, between the Ancients and the Moderns, between civilization and barbarism, between religion and anticlerical liberalism. "Romanesque" is a more or less neutral notion for a medieval style. Gothic is a classification that has been embedded with all sorts of ideological ingredients, and until well into the twentieth century this ideological involvement has also affected scholarly discussion of Gothic architecture and art.

Even if it may sound redundant or trivial, I must begin with Giorgio Vasari's notorious condemnation of Gothic architecture in the introduction to his *Lives of the Most Excellent Painters, Sculptors and Architects*. This condemnation is, as has often been observed, the first stylistic characterization of the Gothic way of building. Vasari's defamation of Gothic architecture is read in the third chapter of his introduction to architecture, which bears the telling title "De cinque ordini d'architettura: rustico, dorico, ionico, corinto, composto, e del lavoro Tedesco." He deals with the different orders of classical architecture and opposes them: "Un altra specie di lavori che si chiamano tedeschi i quali sono di ornamenti e di proporzione molto differenti dagli antichi e da' moderni (The German works, which are very different in their ornaments and proportions from the ancients and the moderns)."

Nothing of this distinction is wrong, and one may even say that Vasari, one of the fathers of art history, has for the first time spoken of that fateful polarization between the classical order and the Gothic deviation from it. In point of fact, this became a basic topic of architectural theory and architectural history right into the twentieth century, as shown by such defining monographs as Wilhelm Worringer's famous book *Griechentum und Gotik*, which may be called a sort of Vasari reversed.

The list of errors for which Vasari blames the "lavori tedeschi" are the following: "Porte ornate di colonne sottili' e attórte, le quali non possono aver forza a reggere il peso di che leggerezza che sia (Portals with columns so subtle and twisted, that they do not have the strength to stand upright, and that they cannot support the lightest weight)." Vasari probably thought that he had recognized the fundamental difference between classical and Gothic proportion in this passage on Italian Romanesque portals, that is, the extreme elongation and slenderness of Gothic columns and responds. He also states that "Facevano una maledizione di tabernacolini l'un sopra l'altre, che non ch'elle possono stare, pare impossibile ch'elle si possino reggere (They made such a malediction of tabernacles, put one

1. Published as "Romanesque Art 2000: A Worn Out Notion?" in *Romanesque Art and Thought in the Twelfth Century, Essays in Honor of Walter Cahn*, ed. Colum Hourihane (University Park and Princeton, 2008), 40–56.

above the other, that they cannot stand, and it seems impossible, that they remain upright)." Again, Vasari insists on the absence of proportion and weight in the Gothic German manner of building. Again he touches on characteristic features of Gothic buildings, which architectural historians have later discussed *ad infinitum*. Furthermore, he says, "Spesso con mettere cosa sopra cosa andavamo in tanta altezza, che la fine d'una porta toccava loro il tetto (Often in putting one thing over the other, they went to such a height, that the top of a portal touched the roof)." Here Vasari derided a characteristic of Gothic buildings, which four hundred years later Hans Sedlmayr praised emphatically as the *überschnittene Geschosse* (the overlapping stories). Vasari also says of Gothic constructions, "Hanno piu il modo da parer fatte di carta che di pietre o di marmo (They seem made more of paper than of stone or marble)." Here he touches on another characteristic of Gothic architecture, its de-materialization. So, Vasari's condemnation of the German or Gothic work was a very succinct stylistic characterization *ex negativo*. The "lavori tedeschi" were presented as the bad alternative to classical order and proportion. This characterization had consequences that Vasari himself could not have foreseen. Once the relation between the Ancient and the Moderns had been reversed, or at least relativized, during the "querelle des Anciens et des Modernes" at the end of the seventeenth century, the condemned "lavori tedeschi" became accepted and even regarded as a fanciful liberation from the stern rigor of the classical order. Vasari paved the way for this astonishing reversal, although his own intentions had been quite different.

The reappraisal of Gothic architecture in the course of the eighteenth century proved to be fundamentally different from Vasari's characterization *ex negativo*. The problem of the classical orders, which had been so essential for Italian architectural theory of the Cinquecento, played no role in the Pre-Romantic astonishment over the emotional power of Gothic architecture. The sensitive encounter with the solemnity and the mystical gloom of Gothic buildings belonged to the dark sides of the Enlightenment, and gave birth to Romantic visions and dreams, which were to linger into twentieth-century art history. To demonstrate this, let me begin with a famous passage from Alexander Pope's introduction to his edition of Shakespeare in 1725: "I will conclude by saying that Shakespeare with all his faults, with all the irregularity, one may look upon his works, in comparison of those that are more finished and regular, as on an ancient majestic piece of Gothic architecture, compared with a modern building: The latter is more elegant and more glaring but the former is more strong and more solemn." Strong and solemn! With these adjectives emerges an evaluation of Gothic architecture that, while still admitting part of the blame assigned by Vasari, nonetheless supersedes that blame with new emotional and sublime qualities. Pope does not speak of the shudder of devotion, nor is he seduced by the vastness of Gothic space. For such an appraisal of Gothic ecclesiastical architecture one must look in the second half of the eighteenth century and the rapture of Teutonic pens. In 1787 we hear Wilhelm Heinse, a writer well known to art historians for his famous letters on paintings in the princely gallery at Düsseldorf and, above all, for his praise of Rubens: "A solemn Gothic cathedral with its free vast space strikes awe into the heart of the boldest unbeliever." Here we are very far from Vasari and his discussion of the Orders. The space in the interior of a Gothic cathedral now becomes the catalyst and spiritual vessel of a de-ritualized religious belief. The romantic dream of Gothic ecclesiastical architecture and its transcendental mysteriousness has started. Heinse was a Catholic. But even a man very close to the most radical sides of the French Revolution, and therefore certainly not devote, such as Johann Georg Forster, well known as an important companion of Captain Cook, could write in 1794: "When I visit Cologne, I always go into the magnificent temple—will say the cathedral—in order to feel the thrill of the sublime … There is in this bold upward soaring of piers and walls a ceaseless energy that the imagination so easily prolongs into the illimitable." So, by the end of the century, the dream of the interior of the Gothic church as a sublime space, as a space unlimited and infinite, had run full circle. It emerged first with Pre-Romanticism in England, with the discovery of the sublime as an aesthetic category in its own right, but it was not by chance that it gained its full transcendental power in Germany. It was a dream with a double face. It secularized the Gothic churches by doing away with all their ritual traditions and installations, but it made the interior of Gothic churches appear more sacred than ever before in hailing them as powerful transcendental spaces.

Needless to say, neither Pope, Heinse, nor Forster were professional art historians. During their lifetime, art history or architectural history as a scholarly discipline in its own right did not exist. But the interpretation of the interior of the Gothic church as a symbol of transcendental space, which they had prepared and introduced, loomed large in the discussion about the deeper meaning of Gothic architecture until the mid-twentieth century. Perhaps I should be more precise and cautious and say that it dominated a certain main stream of this discussion, which flowed mainly in Germany. Only in its very latest phase did it spill over with cultural emigration into the United States. In order to show this, let me begin with Franz Kugler, who was around 1850 the finest and most subtle mind in the rising discipline of art history in Germany. In his *Geschichte der Baukunst* (History of Architecture) he laid out a detailed and precise knowledge of the technical principles of Gothic construction. He even cited Viollet-le-Duc. But once having explained the rational side of Gothic architecture, he turned back to the romantic dream of the Gothic. He was ravished by "the effulgent sublimity of space" and says, "The builders very consciously aimed at the mystical effect," and finally he called the interior of the Gothic church "the revelation of a mystery." One might imagine, given the triumph of positivism in the later nineteenth century, that the momentous achievement of such a rationalist architect and scholar as Viollet-le-Duc would have put to rest this romantic dream about the mysterious space of the Gothic interior. But this was not the case. The dream re-emerged during the spiritual excitement in art at the beginning of modernity. In 1927, the German art historian Hans Jantzen started his much-debated lecture "Über den gotischen Kirchenraum" (On the Space of the Gothic Church) by citing Kugler's words about the "revelation of a mystery," and described the Gothic walls as "diaphanous," and finally called the Gothic interior "space as a symbol of the space-less." After the passage of 150 years, we are back to the Pre-Romantic dreams of the eighteenth century. The last and most seducing turn of this romantic dream of the transcendental and illuminated interior space of the Gothic church was Erwin Panofsky's proposal to connect this dream with the philosophy of Neoplatonism as it seemed to survive in St.-Denis with the writings of Dionysius the pseudo-Areopagite. Not in his famous edition of Suger's writings on St.-Denis from 1946, but in a shorter text of 1944, Panofsky even expressively cited Jantzen's lecture on the space of Gothic churches and their diaphanous walls. The diaphanous wall had become a Neoplatonic wall. The introduction of Neoplatonism in this discussion seems to give the romantic dream of the sublime and illuminated Gothic space a place in the history of ideas.

Looking back from 2009, these dreams of Gothic space and Gothic light look sadly faded. The idea of Neoplatonism as a catalystic force for the birth of Gothic in Suger's St.-Denis has been dismantled by Peter Kidson and Christoph Markschies, and must probably be put to rest. But it should not be forgotten that the dream of Gothic space as the revelation of a transcendental mystery had created a celestial aura around the Gothic churches, the loss of which one may mourn. After its disillusion we should ask if nowadays Gothic means anything more than a conventional stylistic classification for the daily business of instrumentalized art history. I shall return to this issue but, before that I must briefly turn to another facet of the dream of the Gothic as an essential and transcendental style.

Although there are countless Gothic castles, town halls, and houses all over Europe, Gothic was always mostly seen as a religious, or more specifically as an ecclesiastical, and in certain moments, even a Catholic style. When the fear of Jacobinism led in England in 1818 to the so-called Church Building Act, no less than 174 of the 214 newly erected churches were Gothic. Gothic churches were regarded as most convenient to raise religious feeling in the souls of the poor and to keep them devoted and quiet. So there was really a reactionary element in the preference for and the adoration of the Gothic style. One of the greatest representatives of the "Gothic Revival" in England, Augustus Welby Pugin, wrote: "I feel convinced that the Roman catholic church is the only true one and the only one in which the grand and sublime style of church architecture can ever be restored." And he meant Gothic. Nowhere did this reactionary preference for the Gothic becomes more sensible than in the beautiful pages that Chateaubriant wrote just after the end of the French Revolution in his "Genie du Christianisme." In his chapter on Gothic churches he states "On aura beau bâtir des temples grecs bien élégants, bien éclaires, pour rassembler le bon peuple de Saint Louis et lui faire adorer un Dieu métaphysique. Il regrettera toujours ces Notre-Dame de Reims et de Paris (One may well build elegant Greek temples, beautifully lighted, to assemble the good people of Saint Louis in order to adore a metaphysical God, this people will always regret Notre-Dame of Reims and of Paris)." The nineteenth century in France resounds with the aesthetic of, the sentimental attachment to, and the political nostalgia for the ancient Gothic cathedrals. One hears the voices of such great liberals such as Victor Hugo, who exclaimed: "I like the cathedral but not the middle ages," and who even said: "La cathédrale, cet édifice dogmatique, envahie par la bourgeoisie, par la commune, par la liberté (The cathedral, this dogmatic building, invaded by the bourgeoisie, by the commune, by the liberty)." One hears a laical rationalist such as Viollet-le-Duc confess pompously: "Les cathédrales du XIIe et XIIIe siècle sont ... le symbole de la nationalité française et la plus puissante tentative vers l'unité (The cathedrals of the twelfth and the thirteenth centuries are the symbols of French nationality and the most powerful effort towards unity)." The Gothic cathedrals were in the midst of the ideological battles that split post-revolutionary France in radically opposing camps. At the end of the nineteenth century—in the moment of separation of Church and State, but also of the "Renouveau Catholique"—we hear the noble voice of the erudite and pious Émile Mâle say, "Dans la cathédrale toute entière ont sent la certitude et la foi, nulle part le doute (In the cathedral one feels only certainty and belief, no doubt)." All these confessions, debates, and quarrels sound odd and far away today, but one can become envious in remembering what public and civic passions and enthusiasms the admiration for the Gothic cathedrals could once arouse. Today the dream of the cathedral is over, and there it is destined to remain.

But the story is not yet finished. It was in Weimar-Germany after 1918 that a new variation of the dream of the Gothic cathedral began to emerge. This was the nostalgic dream of the unity of all the arts in a sort of *Gesamtkunstwerk*, the great model being none other than the Gothic cathedral. Walter Gropius, the founder of the Bauhaus, postulated the rebirth of the spiritual unity that was once miraculously revealed in the Gothic cathedral. He addressed the artists of the new Weimar Republic: "Let us throw down the walls which were erected by pedestrian academic teaching between the different branches of the arts and let us become workers for the ultimate goal of all the arts: the cathedral of the future." The nostalgic dream of the Gothic cathedral, which had begun with the Romantics, and which aroused public passion in nineteenth-century France, is transformed into a program for the renewal of the arts in post-revolutionary Germany. In a text for an exhibition of the Bauhaus in 1923, the painter Oscar Schlemmer even proclaimed the construction of a "cathedral of socialism."

What have these drunken confessions of modern architects and painters over future cathedrals to do with the art-historical study of Gothic art and architecture? After 1950, after the end of the terrible ideological cataclysms of the twentieth century, the dream of the Gothic cathedral as the never-surpassed symbol of the spiritual unity of the Christian Middle Ages finally arrived among the art historians with the publication of two spectacular books. In 1951 Hans Sedlmayr published a volume of more than five hundred pages entitled *Die Entstehung der Kathedrale* (The birth of the cathedral), and five years later Otto von Simson presented a book with the ponderous title: *The Gothic Cathedral: Origins of Gothic Architecture and the Medieval Concept of Order*. Both books were rooted in the Germanic traditions of art history. Sedlmayr was Austrian, a Catholic, who mourned the decay of the ancient European order before 1918. Otto von Simson was a refugee from Berlin, a student of Wilhelm Pinder, a prominent figure in the very conservative *milieu* of the German emigration in Chicago. Both authors argued as professional art historians. Both were widely read in the specialized literature on Gothic architecture and sculpture, but also on medieval philosophy, religion, and poetry. Both had an admiration and nostalgia for the Gothic cathedral that transcended a mere scholarly interest and exuded a deep religious and even political sympathy for the lost spirituality and religious unity and order during the Christian Middle Ages.

The two books, however, were very different from one another. Sedlmayr's text resounds with pathetic empathy. It is a very unreliable bit of scholarship, because the author is always haunted by his surrealistic dream of the celestial beauty of the cathedral. Reading him, one must listen to his curious digressions on the responds of Notre-Dame as "air-roots" or on medieval poetry around the Holy "Gral," and sometimes one even gets lost in an eccentric text on Scheerbart or other expressionist architects. But Sedlmayr had an ingenious poetical vision of the Gothic cathedral as an image of the heavenly Jerusalem. It was the kind of idea that can never be exactly proved and yet has an inescapable illuminating radiance. Von Simson also understands Gothic architecture as the "representation of supernatural reality," and he writes, "to those who designed the cathedrals, as to their contemporaries, who worshipped in them the symbolic aspect or function of sacred architecture overshadowed all others. For us, it has become the least comprehensible. We have become curiously blind to the cathedral." That sounds like Chateaubriant redivivus.

Sedlmayr's and von Simson's books may be the answer of professional art history to the romantic dream of the cathedral. But the specialists of Gothic art and architecture didn't know what to do with these strange intruders into their bibliography. Their reviewers focused on the numerous factual errors, which can be easily found in both books, and they were dismissed.

But they left us with a problem. Over the last few decades an astonishing number of books, monographs, and studies on Gothic art and architecture have appeared. We certainly know a lot more than fifty years ago about Gothic stained glass, manuscripts, metalwork, and eventually even about Gothic architecture and sculpture. But I shall never forget my shock after having read a very flattering review of my book on Gothic sculpture in France nearly forty years ago in the *Times Literary Supplement*. The review was titled "Comparable Sculptures." I had to ask myself, if the only interest in these sculptures for the specialized art historian was to compare them with one another in order to classify so-called styles and to resolve uncertain dates, how could we ever arrive at an understanding of the substance and the message of these works? In 2009 the dream of the cathedral is over, or it has been transplanted into the Luna Park of the three million visitors that stream to Chartres every year to look at the cathedral as if it were another Disneyland. But what then does Gothic mean today for us—the representatives of specialized art-historical research? As much as we may dislike the boastful and reactionary books by Sedlmayr and von Simson, they have left us with a problem. Let me try to explain what I mean in the light of one single work. In the second quarter of the fifteenth century, an altar retable for the Chapel of St. Anthony in the church of Poligny in the Franche-Comté was painted by Rogier van der Weyden (Antwerp, Koninklijk Museum voor Schone Kunsten, inv. 393-394-395). It was commissioned by Bishop Jean Chevrot of Tournai, who was born in Poligny, and eventually was connected with a local brotherhood of the Holy Sacraments. Rogier's altar-painting mirrors the interior of a Gothic cathedral with the nave in its higher central part and the aisles and chapels in the lower lateral parts (Fig. 1). Certain details of the architecture may be Flemish—the round pillars in the nave—others, like the barrel-vaults of the chapels, recall the cathedral of Tournai, of bishop Chevrot's own church. But the shining interior on Rogier's altar is not an abstract space, nor the symbol or the image of a supernatural reality. It shows a well-organized liturgical topography. It represents the Holy Mass with the Eucharist before the main altar in the nave—and the six other sacraments in the chapels, beginning to the left with baptism and ending to the right with viaticum, the last anointing. Needless to say, Rogier's representation of these liturgical functions is fiction. And yet the sacraments were administered in the lateral chapels of any real cathedral, which in fact held the altars of private donors, and were a welcome source of income for the chapters. Rogier's painting shows us that in order to understand the meaning of the cathedral, we should less think of symbolism and turn to the careful study of function and ritual.

If something is urgently needed in our present studies of Gothic art and architecture—and not only of cathedrals but also monastic churches and great parish churches of the later Middle Ages—it is the reconstruction of the numerous customs, feasts, and ceremonies that once filled these gigantic buildings with a colorful life. It is true: there has been in the last decades a renewed interest in the study of liturgy, and this is very welcome. But the old customs in the cathedrals went much further than liturgy. They filled the vast space in the interior of the cathedral with all sorts of furniture—from shrines and reliquaries, to images, flags, watches, carriages, and other curiosities. Customs also differed from one place to the other. They explain the choice of the remaining images, which are still found nowadays in the cathedrals and churches. Statues at the entrances point to venerated images and relics in the interior. I have recently tried to show that the curious pillar of the angels in the transept of the cathedral at Strasbourg, which has troubled art historians, was connected with the tombs in the cathedral and with the local liturgy at Easter. An important recent study by Claudine Lautier has shown the relevance of relics for the program of stained glass at Chartres. Of the manifold functions that once filled—until the reformation or until the French revolution—Gothic churches with rites and ceremonies, theater, and even jokes, nothing has survived today. The romantic dream of the cathedral emerged from seeing the empty metaphysical space, after the iconoclasm of the Protestants and the Jacobins had done away with all paraphernalia. It was a dream without the noise of the pilgrims and without the laughter of Rabelais. It had neither room for the feast of the fools nor for the flowers, which were showered down in the nave of Amiens at certain great feasts. In order to reconstruct at least a part of this original life in the cathedrals, Dionysius the pseudo-Areopagite can only be dangerous reading. It is better to study the Ordinaries, the local descriptions from pre-revolutionary days in France, to see many of the traditions that were then still alive but which have now disappeared. These sources have not been sufficiently exploited. I have the impression that historians of music have made more productive use of these texts than have art historians.

One problem still remains and that centers on Otto von Simson's phrase concerning "the Gothic cathedral and the medieval concept of order," which provokes a final question and at the same time a grave contradiction. At the time when the great French cathedrals were being built, popular heresies emerged all over Europe. The bishop of Chartres, who oversaw the construction of the Cathedral with his chapter was present in the crusade against the Albigeois in 1208, where the papal legate is said to have cried at Béziers: "Kill them all. God will recognize those who are his." In the light of such possible sinister connections, the word "order" gains a quite different and less harmonious and lofty meaning. The great nobles who participated in the crusade against the Albigeois in 1216 appear in the windows of the choir at Chartres Cathedral. All are on horseback with their gonfalon. They ride as knights toward their lady Notre-Dame de Chartres in the central window: it is the iconography of a holy war. Seen in the light of such a program, the cathedrals with the images of the saints on their portals and in their windows appear not only as monuments of the Church triumphant, but of the Church in defense against such movements and upheavals that questioned its power and tradition. So, even if the dream of the cathedral is over, even if we mistrust ideas about the cathedral and medieval order, it remains our task to transform the dream of the cathedral into the concrete history of various cathedrals. By doing so—by enlarging our vista—we can make certain that the study of Gothic art and architecture remains a scholarly adventure worthwhile and of interest far beyond the limits of art history.

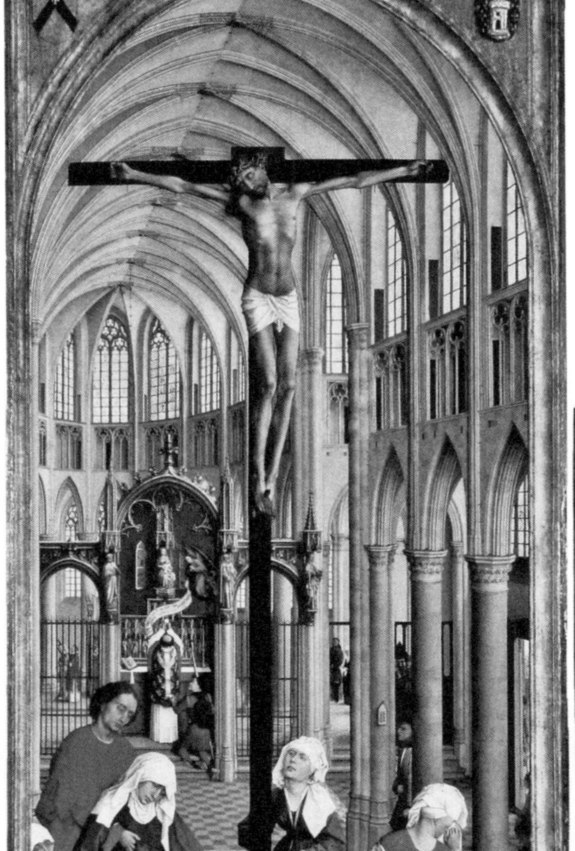

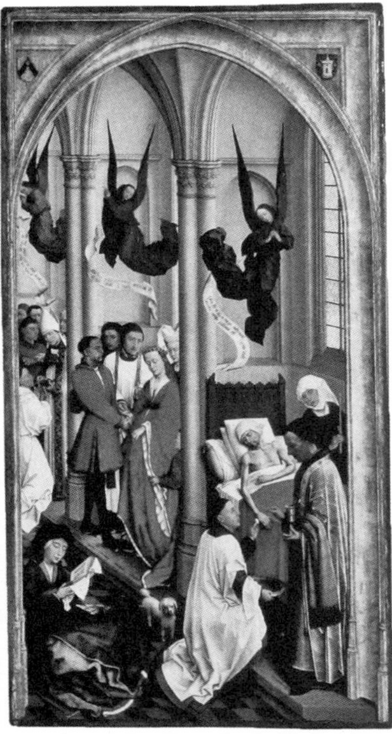

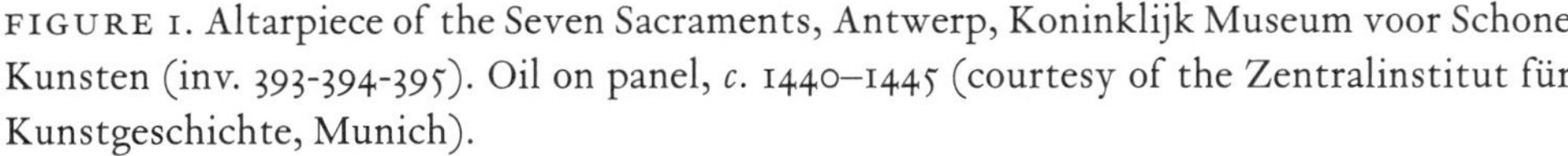

FIGURE 1. Altarpiece of the Seven Sacraments, Antwerp, Koninklijk Museum voor Schone Kunsten (inv. 393-394-395). Oil on panel, *c.* 1440–1445 (courtesy of the Zentralinstitut für Kunstgeschichte, Munich).

KATHERINE H. TACHAU

What Has Gothic to Do With Scholasticism?

THE TITLE of the present contribution alludes not only to Erwin Panofsky's *Gothic Architecture and Scholasticism*,[1] but also to the question, well-known to medievalists, posed rhetorically by Tertullian in the late second or early third century, "what has Athens to do with Jerusalem?" What Tertullian queried and thereby rejected was the pertinence of pagan Greek philosophy, sought in Athens, to Christian education and, hence, salvation, which began in the earthly Jerusalem and will, for the faithful elect, lead to the heavenly Jerusalem.[2] In denying that pagan learning—and specifically Stoicism and Platonism—had any utility for the Christian, Tertullian stood at one end of the continuum of attitudes on the matter. At the opposite terminus was Augustine, whose crystalization within his own teaching of Neoplatonic thought, with its significant Stoic and Aristotelian components, lent generations of theologians a telescope through which they would see ancient wisdom.[3]

The pairing of Athens and Jerusalem in Tertullian's question makes sense in its historic context, when early Christians were debating whether the usefulness of the classical education of the Roman elites outweighed its likelihood of perpetuating values and beliefs that Christians ought to reject. But why would anyone have sought in the first place to connect Gothic architecture and scholasticism, as did not only Panofsky, but also Max Dvořák, Hans Sedlmayr, Otto von Simson, and, to a degree, Paul Frankl? Paul Crossley and Albert Levi are surely correct in seeing Hegelian philosophy as the ultimate source of each of these great scholars' thinking, even when mediated by Ernst Cassirer or Alois Riegl.[4] The structuring of Panofsky's interpretation of works of art and architecture upon Hegelian tenets was reinforced for him by reading the history of medieval philosophy through the lens of Maurice De Wulf, the Hegelian-imbued historian and editor of medieval scholars' philosophical *oeuvres* from manuscript.[5]

1. Erwin Panofsky, *Gothic Architecture and Scholasticism* (Latrobe: 1951; I use the edition of Cleveland, Ohio: Meridian Books, 1957).

2. Tertullian, *De praescriptione haereticorum*, VII 9–13, VIII 1–2, in *Quinti Septimi Florentis Tertulliani Opera, pars I, Opera catholica adversus Marcionem*, ed. R. F. Refoulé, in *Corpus Christianorum, series Latina*, vol. 1, *pars* 1 (Turnhout: 1954), 187–224, at 192–93: "(9) Quid ergo Athenis et Hierosolymis? Quid academiae et ecclesiae? Quid haereticis et christianis? (10) Nostra institutio de portico Solomonis est qui et ipse tradiderat Dominum in simplicitate cordis esse quaerendum. (11) Viderint qui Stoicum et Platonicum et dialecticum christianismum protulerunt. (12) Nobis curiositate opus non est post Christum Iesum nec inquisitione post evangelium. (13) Cum credimus nihil desideramus ultra credere. Hoc enim prius credimus non esse quod ultra credere debeamus."

3. For discussion of this point, see D. C. Lindberg, "Science and the Early Church," in *idem* and R. L. Numbers, *God and Nature: Historical Essays on the Encounter between Christianity and Science* (Berkeley: University of California, 1986), 19–48.

4. P. Crossley, "Medieval Architecture and Meaning: The Limits of Iconography," *Burlington Magazine* 130 (1988), *Special Issue on English Gothic Art*, 116–121, at 118; A. W. Levi, "*Kunstgeschichte als Geistesgeschichte*: The Lesson of Panofsky," *Journal of Aesthetic Education*, 20.4 (Winter, 1986), 79–83, esp. 80–81; see also D. R. Topper, "On a Ghost of Historiography Past," *Leonardo*, 21.1 (1988), 76–78; D. P. Verene, "Kant, Hegel, and Cassirer: the Origins of the Philosophy of Symbolic Forms," *Journal of the History of Ideas* 30 (1969), 33–46; C. Rudolph, "Introduction: A Sense of Loss: An Overview of the Historiography of Romanesque and Gothic Art," in *idem*, ed., *A Companion to Medieval Art*, Blackwell Companions to Art History (Oxford, 2008), 1–43, esp. at 28–33. For Paul Frankl, see also his foreword to the first edition of his *Gothic Architecture*, for the Penguin History of Art, in the edition revised by P. Crossley (New Haven, 2000), 34, as well as Crossley's introduction.

5. In addition to M. Dvořak's "Idealismus und naturalismus in der gotischen Skulptur und Malerei" (1918); A. Dempf, *Die Hauptform mittelalterlicher Weltanschauung: eine geisteswissenschaftliche Stu-*

By describing these scholars' work as based in Hegelian philosophy,[6] I mean that these influential historians of art not only deployed Hegel's historical dialectic to explain or describe change from one period to another, but far more importantly, they were committed to the existence of *Zeitgeister*, as Hegelians defined these. For Hegelians, the *Zeitgeist* is the "spirit" or "mind of an age," and it is the unifying spirit that is manifested in the worldview and in the particular cultural practices, beliefs, art, and phenomena of an age.[7] It is intrinsic to the nature of a *Zeitgeist* that, like a phoenix, there can be only one in existence at a time.[8] Consequently, the hypothesis of *Zeitgeister* is problematic for those of us who believe that minorities or marginalized communities within a larger culture do not have the same *Weltanschauung* as that of the dominant population, for by definition, a *Zeitgeist* ... requires "that cultures [be] monolithic," indeed, "that each element of the culture must be independently monolithic, otherwise the *Zeitgeist* does not encompass the culture."[9]

If one thinks of western philosophy through the early nineteenth century as developing between the theories of Plato and Aristotle, Hegel would be located at Plato's end of the continuum.[10] Although Plato's epistemology

---

die über die Summa; and M. de Wulf's *History of Mediaeval Philosophy* (1938), as remarked by other scholars, Panofsky cites, in his *Gothic Architecture and Scholasticism*: M. Grabmann, *Die Geschichte der scholastischen Methode* (1909); R. Guelluy, *Philosophie et Théologie chez Guillaume d'Ockham* (1947); J. Weinberg, *Nicholas of Autrecourt, A Study in Fourteenth-Century Thought* (1948), as well as two then recent works by R. Arnheim, "Gestalt and Art," *Journal of Aesthetics and Art Criticism* (1943), and "Perceptual Abstraction and Art," *Psychological Review* (1947).

6. For an accessible overview of Hegel's thought, see H. B. Acton, "Georg Wilhelm Friedrich Hegel," in *The Encyclopedia of Philosophy*, vol. 3 (1967), 435–451; for his role as "the father of art history," in Gombrich's appelation, see S. Houlgate, "Hegel, Georg Wilhelm Friedrich, Survey of Thought," and M. Donougho, "Hegel on the Historicity of Art," in *Encyclopedia of Aesthetics*, vol. 2 (Oxford, 1998), 361–365, 365–368; and A. Speight, "Hegel and Aesthetics: The Practice and 'Pastness' of Art," in F. G. Beiser, ed., *The Cambridge Companion to Hegel and Nineteenth-Century Philosophy* (Cambridge, 2008), 378–393.

7. In lieu of Herder's term *Zeitgeist*, Hegel tended to describe rather than name it through his explication of a *Weltgeist* that is actualized over time, its different stages being embodied as the *Volksgeist* (or *Geist des Volkes*) of a specific people for a temporally delimited period. See for example G. W. F. Hegel, *Vorlesungen über die Philosophie der Geschichte*, in Hegel, *Werke*, eds. E. Molderhauer, K. M. Michel, H. Reinike, vol. 12 (Frankfurt-am-Main, 1970), 72–73: "Es ist diese geistige Gesamtheit, welche *ein* Wesen, der Geist *eines* Volkes ist. Ihm gehören die Individuen an; jeder Einzelne ist der Sohn seines Volkes und zugleich ... der Sohn seiner Zeit; keiner bleibt hinter derselven zurück, noch weniger überspringt er dieselbe. Diese geistige Wesen ist das seinige, er ist ein Repräsentant desselben; es ist das, woraus er hervorgeht und worin er steht. Bei den Athenern hatte Athen eine doppelte Bedeutung: zuerst bezeichnete sie die Gesamtheit der Einrichtungen, dann aber die Göttin, welche den Geist des Volkes, die Einheit darstellte. Dieser Geist eines Volkes ist ein *bestimmter* Geist und, wie soeben gesagt, auch nach der geschichtlichen Stufe seiner Entwicklung bestimmt.... Das andere und weitere ist, dass der bestimmte Volksgeist selbst nur *ein* Individuum ist im Gange der Weltgeschichte.... Die Gestaltungen dieser Stufen [des Weltgeistes] sind die welthistorischen Volksgeister, die Bestimmtheit ihres sittlichen Lebens, ihrer Verfassung, ihrer Kunst, Religion und Wissenschaft. Diese Stufen zu realisieren, ist der unendliche Trieb des Weltgeistes...." (emphases in original). Again, 96–97: "Der konkrete Geist eines Volkes ist es, den wir bestimmt zu erkennen haben, und weil er Geist ist, lässt er sich nur geistig, durch den Gedanken erfassen. Er allein ist es, der in allen Taten und Richtungen des Volkes sich hervortreibt, der sich zu seiner Verwirklichung, zum Selbstgenuss und Selbsterfassen bringt ... Dies muss und wird er auch vollbringen, aber diese Vollbringung ist zugleich sein Untergang und das Hervortreten eines anderen Geistes, eines anderen welthistorischen Volkes, einer anderen Epoche der Weltgeschichte.... Die Weltgeschichte, wissen wir, ist also überhaupt die Auslegung des Geistes in der *Zeit*, wie die Idee als Natur sich im Raume auslegt." This is the version of Hegel's lectures on world history translated in the nineteenth century as *The Philosophy of History* by J. Sibree (1896), repr. (Mineola, 1956, reissued 2004), 52–53; see also 63, 71–72.

The first of these passages is similarly reported in the lecture notes of other students, as edited in *Vorlesungen über die Philosophie der Weltgeschichte Berlin 1822/1823*, ed. K. H. Ilting, K. Brehmer, H. N. Seelmann, et al., in *Georg Wilhelm Friedrich Hegel Vorlesungen. Ausgewählte Nachschriften und Manuskripte*, vol. 12 (Hamburg, 1996), 37, 45; for the second, see 14–15. See also Hegel, *Vorlesungen über die Philosophie des Geistes, Berlin 1827/1828*, ed. F. Hespe, B. Tuschling, et al., in *Hegel Vorlesungen* vol. 13 (Hamburg, 1994), 7.

8. This is Hegel's simile, writing of the *Weltgeist* as it is born, grows, and dies in the series of *Volksgeister* that make up the world's history, in *Philosophie der Geschichte*, 98, quoted below, note 53; similarly, *Philosophie der Weltgeschichte*, 18.

9. Topper, "Ghost of Historiography," (as in note 4) at 76.

10. Hegel himself indicated that he saw his own idealism as a revision of Plato's; see J. Halfwassen, "Idee, Dialektik und Transzendenz. Zur Platondeutung Hegels und Schellings am Beispiel ihrer Deutung des *Timaios*," in T. Kobusch and B. Mojsisch, eds., *Platon*

is often labeled "realism," it can be—and has been—described just as accurately as (non-subjective) "idealism."[11] For Plato, Ideas, also called Forms, are the only truly real entities; they have existed and would continue to exist even if our minds were not there to recognize them. Not so the material particulars that seem real to us if we use our senses, rather than our intellects' mathematical reasoning: particulars are merely imperfect embodiments and copies of Ideas.[12] Similarly, Hegel insists upon the real existence of Spirit, or *Geist*, rather than matter, as the substance of the world. Thus, he elaborates,

> The nature of Spirit must be understood by a glance at its direct opposite—Matter. As the essence of Matter is gravity, so, on the other hand, we may affirm that the substance, the essence of Freedom.... [Spirit] may be defined as that which has its center in itself. [Unlike Matter, Spirit] has not a unity outside itself, but has already found it; it exists *in* and *with* itself.... Spirit is *self-contained existence*.[13]

Aristotle held roughly the reverse of Plato's ontology: that material particulars being truly real, our senses are the starting point for informing us empirically about reality, on the basis of which our minds construct universal forms or ideas. These universals have no mind-independent reality.[14] Put in that way, many of us would find ourselves more Aristotelian than Platonic or Hegelian regarding historical periodization, seeing periods as labels (or names) and temporal boundaries that we find heuristically useful to impose upon the past, on the basis of what *we define* as characteristics of, say, "modernity," "romanticism," "romanesque," "gothic," or the like; and we then look for and find, or do not find, or overlook these characteristics in particular times and places. That is, the periods do not exist independently from our constructions; and if periods do not exist, then neither, concomitantly, do *Zeitgeister*.

Nevertheless, the Hegelian *Zeitgeist* is a notion at the core of the original *geistesgeschichte*, which we now term, with some impoverishment of meaning, "intellectual history."[15] Although what constitutes medieval intellectual history has diversified over the course of the

---

in der abendländischen Geistesgeschichte (Darmstadt: 1997), 193–209. Nevertheless, Hegel also explicitly adopted Aristotle's explanation of change or development as the actualization of innate potential, as at Hegel, *Philosophie der Geschichte*, 78: "Hier ist nur anzudeuten, dass der Geist von seiner unendlichen Möglichkeit, aber *nur* Möglichkeit anfängt, die seinen absoluten Gehalt als Ansich enthält, als den Zweck und das Ziel, das er nur erst in seinem Resultate erreicht, welches dann erst seine Wirklichkeit ist. So erscheint in der Existenz der Fortgang als ein Fortschreiten von dem Unvollkommenen zum Vollkommneren ... Ebenso weist wenigstens reflektierterweise die Möglichkeit auf ein solches hin, das wirklich werden soll, und näher ist die Aristotelische *dynamis* auch *potentia*, Kraft und Macht. Das Unvollkommene so als das Gegenteil seiner in ihm selbst ist der Widerspruch, der wohl existiert, aber ebensosehr aufgehoben und gelöst wird ..." (emphases in original).

11. Leibniz may have been the first to label Plato's ontology as "Idealist." For Plato's (non-subjective) idealism, see especially F. M. Cornford, *Plato's Theory of Knowledge (The Thaetetus and the Sophist of Plato)* (Indianapolis, 1957), esp. 2, 8–11, 228–232, 239–252; more generally, H. B. Acton, "Idealism," and J. O. Urmson, "Ideas," in *The Encyclopedia of Philosophy*, vol. 4 (1967), 110–121.

12. See for example Plato, *The Republic*, ch. 24 (vi.509d–511e), "Four stages of Cognition," ch. 25 (vii.514a–521b), "The Allegory of the Cave," and ch. 26 (vii.521c–531c), "Higher Education: Mathematics," in F. M. Cornford, *The Republic of Plato, Translated with Introduction and Notes* (Oxford, 1945, repr. 1964), 221–240; *Timaeus*, 51e–52d, 53c–55c, in Cornford, *Plato's Timaeus* (Indianapolis, 1959), 53–59. For Plato, our minds would exist so long as the "world of Ideas" does, for our intellects were part of it before being conjoined to our bodies, and will be part of it again.

13. The translation is Sibree's, *Philosophy of History*, 17 (his italics), of Hegel, *Philosophie der Geschichte*, 30: "Die Natur des Geistes lässt sich durch den vollkommenen Gegensatz desselben erkennen. Wie die Substanz der Materie die Schwere ist, so, müssen wir sagen, ist die Substanz, das Wesen des Geistes die Freiheit.... Die Materie ist insofern schwer, als sie nach einem Mittelpunkte treibt; sie ist wesentlich zusammengesetzt, sie besteht außereinander, sie sucht ihre Einheit und sucht also sich selbst aufzuheben, sucht ihr Gegenteil. Wenn sie dieses erreichte, so wäre sie keine Materie mehr, sondern sie wäre untergegangen; sie strebt nach Idealität, denn in der Einheit ist sie ideell. Der Geist im Gegenteil ist eben das, in sich den Mittelpunkt zu haben; er hat nicht die Einheit außer sich, sondern er hat sie gefunden; er ist in sich selbst und bei sich selbst. Die Materie hat ihre Substanz außer ihr; der Geist ist das *Bei-sich-selbst-Sein*" (emphases in original). Again, 31–32, "Es ist also als die Bestimmung der geistigen Welt und—indem diese die substantielle Welt ist und die physische ihr untergeordnet bleibt oder, im spekulativen Ausdruck, keine Wahrheit gegen die erste hat—als der *Endzweck der Welt* das Bewusstsein des Geistes von seiner Freiheit und ebendamit die Wirklichkeit seiner Freiheit überhaupt angegeben worden."

14. See G. E. R. Lloyd, *Aristotle: The Growth and Structure of his Thought* (Cambridge, 1968).

15. Hegel repeatedly provides a rationale for investigating the

last half century or so, for its early twentieth-century exponents, the worldview and, hence, the spirit of the times, was what an era's art revealed. To put this in the words of Max Dvořák, from his manifesto, *Kunstgeschichte als Geistesgeschichte*:

> Art depends not only on the solution and development of formal issues and problems, but is also, and before anything else, an expression of the leading ideas of mankind, and the history of art, no less than the history of religion, philosophy, or poetry, is part of the general history of the spirit.[16]

Panofsky described the *Zeitgeist* instead as "mental habits [that] are at work in all and every civilization,"[17] and Gombrich, recalling mutual conversations, regretted that Panofsky's *Gothic Architecture and Scholasticism* was "another attempt to justify the Hegelian tradition of governing spirits."[18] Von Simson too expressed his acceptance of a "spirit of the times" in similar terms in his *The Gothic Cathedral: Origins of Gothic Architecture and the Medieval Concept of Order*.[19]

Given the fact that many survey texts of western art, or of medieval art in particular (not to mention popularizing works), continue to disseminate the views of von Simson and especially Panofsky, even if with caveats,[20] let us survey what we, who edit and study the writings of medieval scholastics, have learned since Panofsky published his *Gothic Architecture and Scholasticism*. In that work, in addition to the better-known and disputed assertions, he makes at least five basic claims worth examining.

First, according to Panofsky, historical periods really exist and are not mere figments of the historians' imagination. An historical era is distinguishable by its particular unity of "such overtly disparate phenomena as the arts, literature, philosophy, social and political currents," and so on. In any real period, there will have been what Panofsky describes as "*intrinsic* analogies" among these manifestations of culture—that is to say, the analogies are or were real features of the period's culture, independent of any historian's search for or discovery of them.[21] Panofsky's second major claim is

---

"history of ideas" as a part of *Geistesgeschichte*, as, for instance, *Philosophie der Weltgeschichte*, 14: "Die Idee ist der Führer der Völker und der Welt. Der Geist führt die Welt, und seine Führung wollen wir kennenlernen." On the difference between "intellectual history" and "history of ideas," see: A. O. Lovejoy, "Reflections on the History of Ideas," *Journal of the History of Ideas*, 1 (1940), 3–23; W. E. Kleinbauer, "*Geistesgeschichte* and Art History," *Art Journal* 30.2 (Winter, 1970–1971), 148–153, is also germane.

16. M. Dvořák, "Über Kunstbetrachtung," 1920, part of a lecture printed in *Kunstgeschichte als Geistesgeschichte* (Munich, 1924), x., as quoted by Crossley, "Medieval Architecture and Meaning," p. 118 (compare to Hegel, *Philosophie der Geschichte*, 72–73, quoted above in note 7). Crossley stresses that "for Dvořak the relationships between art and other aspects of a civilisation were not causative but parallel," in as much as both *manifest* but do not cause the *Zeitgeist*. To confirm this point, Crossley adduces a statement from Dvořak's "Idealismus und Naturalismus in der gotischen Skulptur und Malerei" (as translated into English by R. J. Klawiter; *Idealism and Naturalism in Gothic Art* [South Bend, 1967], 12): "I do not suggest that one should attempt to relate artistic phenomena in any causative sense to the development of new economic social or religious conditions, or deduce the spiritual content of medieval works of art from the writings of the great contemporary theologians whose influence on art, if it had ever existed at all, could hardly be historically comprehended."

17. Panofsky, *Gothic Architecture and Scholasticism*, 21.

18. E. H. Gombrich, *The Sense of Order: A Study in the Psychology of Decorative Art* (London, 1979), 199, quoted by Topper, "Ghost of Historiography" (as in note 4), 77.

19. O. von Simson, *The Gothic Cathedral, Origins of Gothic Architecture and the Medieval Concept of Order*, 2nd ed. (Princeton, 1974), xvii–xviii, xx. See also Crossley, "Medieval Architecture and Meaning" (as in note 4), at 120.

20. This is not really surprising, given Hegel's role in creating art history as an area of study, and in providing the impetus for early survey texts; see M. Schwarzer, "Rethinking the Introductory Art History Survey," *Art Journal* 54. 3 (Autumn, 1995), 24–29. For the reliance on a hybrid Panofskian-von Simson explanation of the rise of Gothic architecture in recent survey texts, see F. S. Kleiner and C. J. Mamiya, eds., [*Helen*] *Gardner's Art Through the Ages*, 11th ed., vol. 1 (2000), 489, 496; M. Stokstad, *Medieval Art*, 2nd ed. (Boulder, 2004), 244, where she is careful to treat Panofsky as having "*suggested* that the pattern of thought typified by Abelard's rationalism, the balance of opposites, *Sic et Non*, permeated architectural thinking" (my emphasis). Other historians of art have long expressed skepticism; see, for instance, W. Sauerländer, "Romanesque Art 2000: A Worn out Notion?" in C. Hourihane, ed., *Romanesque Art and Thought in the Twelfth Century, Essays in Honor of Walter Cahn* (Princeton, 2008), 40–56, at 44–45.

21. Panofsky, *Gothic Architecture and Scholasticism*, 1, opening paragraph; see also 20. Although Panofsky refers to the historian as doing the dividing of history into periods, if the latter have unities that the historian can "verify ... instead of merely presupposing," then the period's unities must (have) exist(ed) *in re*, regardless of

that "Early Scholasticism was born at the same moment and in the same environment in which Early Gothic architecture was born in Suger's Saint-Denis."[22] That "same environment," Panofsky specifies elsewhere, is the "100-mile zone around Paris."[23] Third, the transition from "Early Gothic" to "High Gothic" coincided again with a transition from "Early" to "High Scholasticism" at "the turn of the twelfth" and thirteenth centuries; both occurred in the Île de France.[24] Fourth, "High Gothic" art and architecture, that is to say, the culminating stage of Gothic, coincided with the development of the age of *summae* that was the stage of "High Scholasticism."[25] As "High Gothic" architecture was the achievement of Jean de Loup, Jean d'Orbais, Robert de Luzarches, Jean de Chelles, Hugues Libergier, and Pierre de Montereau, "High Scholasticism" was reached in the great syntheses of faith and reason by "Alexander of Hales, Albert the Great, William of Auvergne, St. Bonaventure, and St. Thomas Aquinas"—to give Panofsky's ordering.[26] Fifth and finally, after reaching their height, both Gothic style and Scholastic thought experienced a declining end stage, marked by decomposition of an achieved unity.[27]

The first of these claims is Panofsky's description of how the *Zeitgeist* manifests itself, and alerts us that what follows will be a discussion of such objectively—not subjectively—existing analogies.[28] Let us turn to the second Panofskian claim, that the phenomena of "Early Scholasticism" and "Early Gothic" art emerged at the same time and "environment." The first "intrinsic analogy" unifying "Early Scholasticism" and "Early Gothic" sculpture to which Panofsky draws attention is a supposed "renewed interest in psychology"—albeit still an Augustinian psychology—that, Panofsky states, "had been dormant for several centuries," and "the gentle animation" of such human figures as the Early Gothic sculptures of Chartres' west façade (Fig. 1).[29] Setting aside the obvious question as to whether the feature thus described is subjectively personal, that is, whether the "animation" may not actually be an objectively real feature of the statues themselves, but only a (possibly arbitrary) creation of the viewer's mind, we should focus upon the choice of that word "animation," for it merits our notice. Panofsky's use of the word "animation" is not casual. Given his classical *Bildung*, we can be sure that he was aware that the Latin word *anima*, from which we derive "animation," which is what makes us living beings, but which we usually translate as "soul," rendered the Greek word *psyche*. Thus, the word "animation" is, for Panofsky, a technical term, one that clues us into understanding why Panofsky discerned any "intrinsic analogy" between psychology, or theories of the psyche, and the evolution of Gothic naturalism in the first instance.

We should expect, therefore, to find Panofsky correlating changes in scholarly theories of the mind to parallel developments in Gothic figuration, and that is indeed what he does. Thus, he claims, when intellectuals in the era of "High Scholasticism" turned from Augustinian to Aristotelian psychology, ultimately based, presumably, on the *De anima* (or Περὶ ψυχῆς) and *parva naturalia*, High Gothic artists managed a similar transformation from mere animation to the greater semblance of life, as at Reims (Fig. 2).[30]

Only in the Late Gothic phase did sculptors and other artists achieve complete naturalism and portraiture, according to Panofsky, and in the half century or so after the deaths of Louis IX, Thomas Aquinas, and Bonaventure, the "end phases" both of Late Gothic and Late Scholasticism coincided. Here the transition

---

whether any historian ever discovers that they did so or that there was such a period constituted by them.

22. Panofsky, *Gothic Architecture and Scholasticism*, 4.

23. *Ibid.*, 21. 24. *Ibid.*, 5. 25. *Ibid.*, 7–8.

26. *Ibid.*, 5, 7–8. 27. *Ibid.*, 8–10.

28. Earlier, Panofsky in his *Die Deutsche Plastik* had been explicit in his adoption of the Hegelian historical dialectic: "The Hegelian notion that the historical process unfolds in a sequence of thesis, antithesis, and synthesis appears equally valid for the development of art," as quoted in C. Wood, "Introduction," to his translation of Panofsky, *Perspective as Symbolic Form* (New York, 1991), 19. For an important discussion of the evolution of Panofsky's thought, see now B. Mitrovic, "Humanist Art History and Its Enemies: Erwin Panofsky on the Individualism-Collectivism Debate," *Konsthistorisk Tidskrift*, 78/2 (2009), 57–76.

29. Panofsky, *Gothic Architecture and Scholasticism*, 6. Panofsky provided no images to illustrate this description, so the choice of figures is mine.

30. Panofsky, *Gothic Architecture and Scholasticism*, 6. The choice of figures is mine.

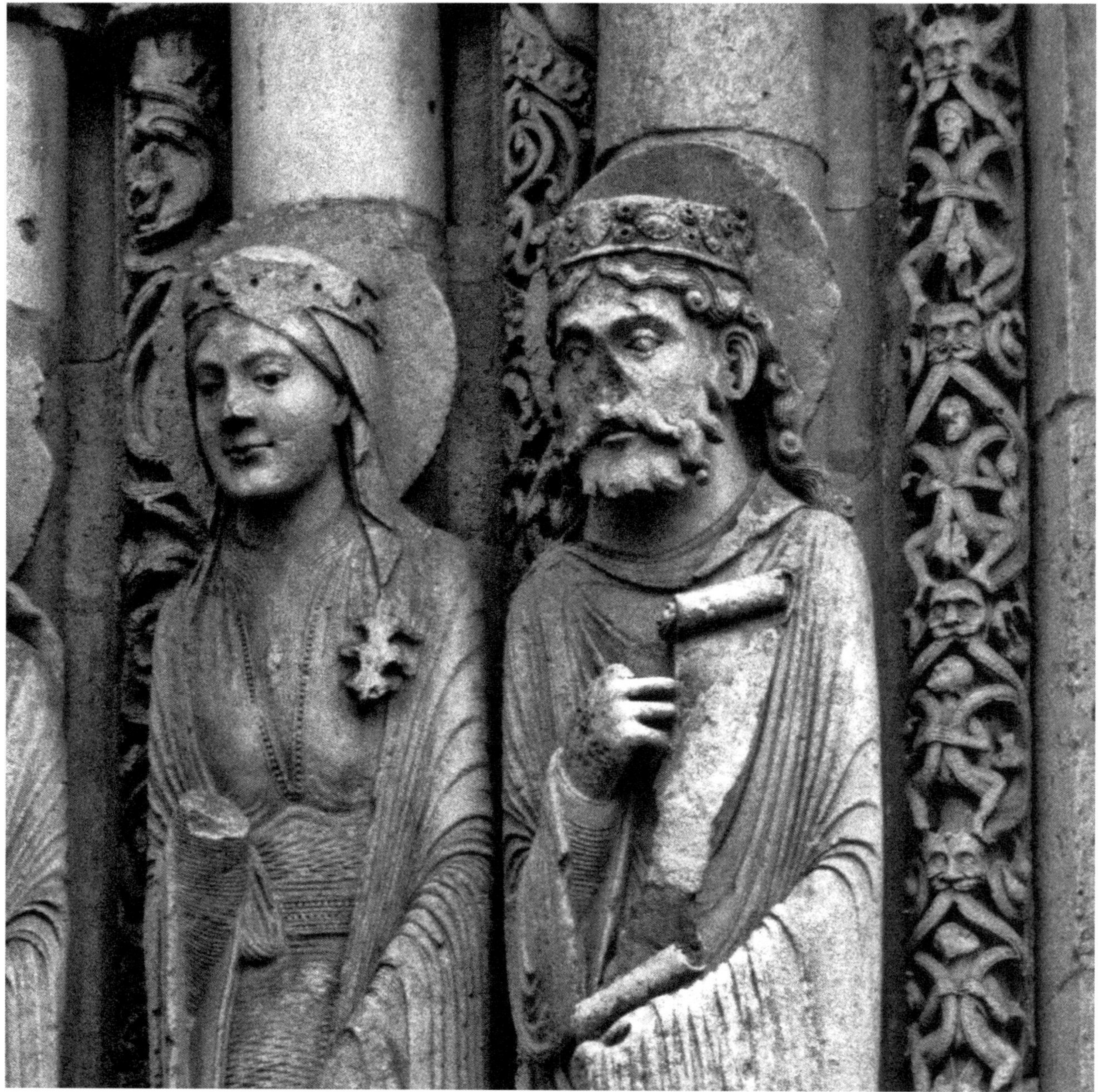

FIGURE 1. Chartres, Cathedral of Notre Dame, west façade, Portail Royal, mid-twelfth century. Detail of column statues, exemplifying what Panofsky described as "gentle animation" (photo: Vanni/Art Resource, N.Y.).

on the part of intellectuals, specifically with regard to philosophy of the mind, was marked by "a decrease in confidence in the supremely synthetic power of reason," purportedly based on a supplanting of Aristotelian psychology—as epitomized by Aquinas' *Summae*—with a revived Augustinian emphasis upon the will rather than reason.[31] In turn, somehow, this loss of confidence led to an "agnosticism," most importantly "in th[e] mighty movement, rightly called 'modern' by the later schoolmen," namely, "critical nominalism."[32]

31. Panofsky, *Gothic Architecture and Scholasticism*, 9, 28–29.

32. *Ibid.*, 11–12.

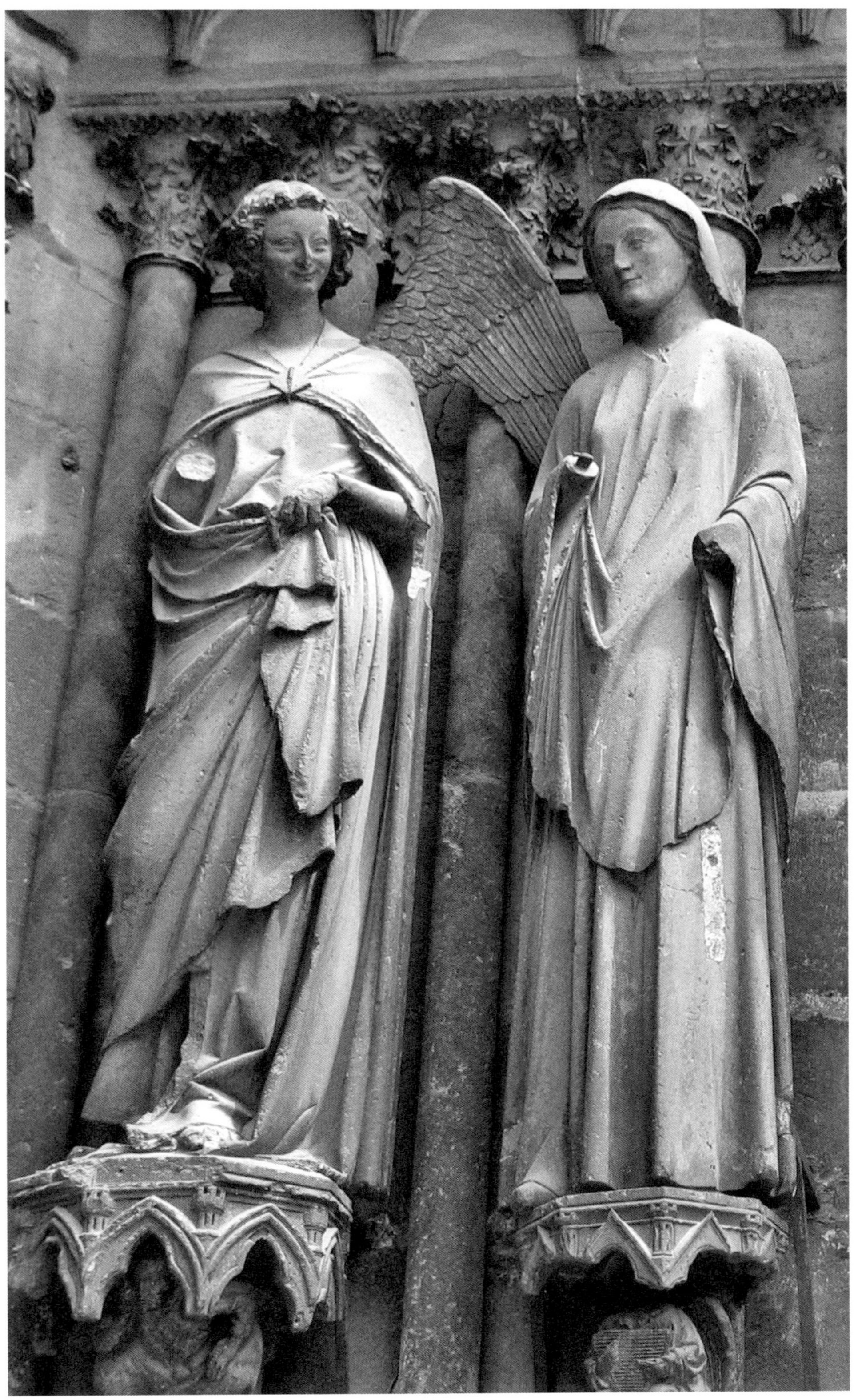

FIGURE 2. Reims, Cathedral of Notre Dame, west façade, central portal, right side, thirteenth century. Detail of column statues representing the Annunciation, which, for Panofsky, showed the "greater semblance of life" that Gothic sculptors achieved during the thirteenth-century (photo: Scala/Art Resource, N.Y.).

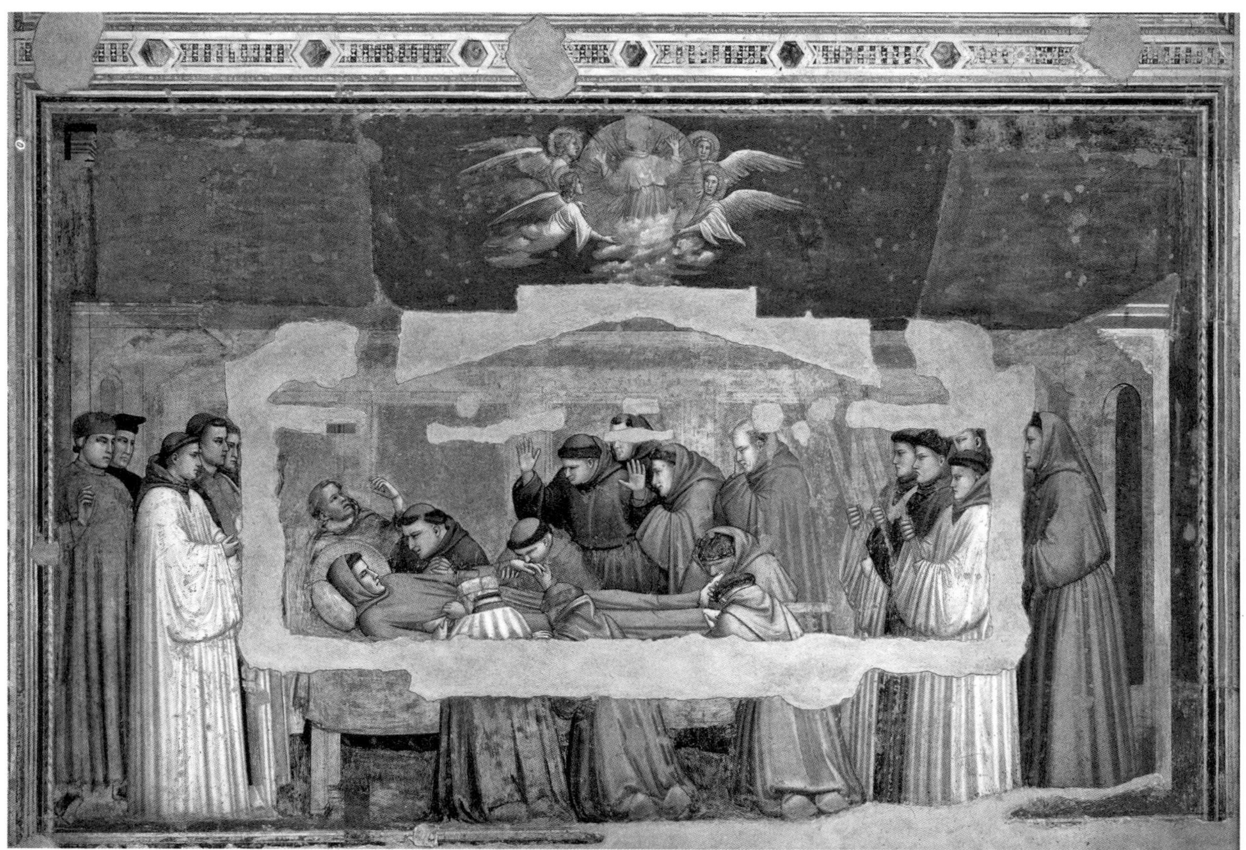

FIGURE 3. Giotto di Bondone (1266–1336), Detail of the Death of Saint Francis, Cappella Bardi, Basilica of Santa Croce, Florence, *c.* 1318, an example of what Panofsky considered Giotto's attainment of the "subjectivism ... of the visual sphere," through the "perspectiv[al] interpretation of space" (photo: Alinari/Art Resource, N.Y.).

Panofsky attributed to "critical nominalists" a theory of knowledge that treated particular psychological states, acts, or processes as entirely subjective experiences rather than objective realities.[33] Moreover, the epistemological subjectivism of the so-called "critical nominalists" did not admit of universals, finding only particulars: "particular things and particular psychological processes"[34] in Panofsky's words.

Late scholastics' subjectivism is, for Panofsky, a manifestation of a fourteenth-century *Zeitgeist* that reveals itself also in the "aesthetic subjectivism of the poet and humanist, the religious subjectivism ... of the mystic,"[35] and in a corresponding "subjectivism ... of the visual sphere," the "most characteristic expression" of which is "the emergence of a perspectiv[al] interpretation of space" by Giotto and Duccio (Fig. 3).[36] Moreover, Panofsky asserts, the "new way of seeing—or rather, of designing with reference to the very process of sight" was soon applied in Late Gothic sculpture and architecture as well.[37]

With respect to the Gothic side of Panofsky's equation, the work of other scholars contributing to this volume has expanded our knowledge considerably beyond what was available to him when he composed his

33. Panofsky, *Gothic Architecture and Scholasticism*, 13.

34. *Ibid.*, 15. 35. *Ibid.*, 13–14.

36. Panofsky, *Gothic Architecture and Scholasticism*, 16. The choice of figure is mine. To understand how a "perspective interpretation of space" produces subjectivism in the other arts and architecture, as Panofsky states, 17–18, one must also take into account his *Perspective as Symbolic Form.*

37. Panofsky, *Gothic Architecture and Scholasticism*, 17–18.

Gothic Architecture and Scholasticism; the history of medieval philosophical, scientific, and theological development has similarly advanced beyond the pioneering surveys upon which Panofsky relied for his general conceptualization of medieval thought. This essay will not address his formal analysis of scholastic writings, which although comprising much of the book, can and has been critiqued on other grounds;[38] nor is it feasible here to do much more than point out some of the ways that our understanding of medieval logic, psychology, and theories of knowledge has changed. Meanwhile, it is worth keeping in mind that if our ontology does not include *Zeitgeister*—that is, if we do not posit their existence as objects in the real world that would exist even if there were no historians to find them—the analogies that Panofsky has elaborated are not intrinsic to the world.

Since Panofsky wrote, greater familiarity with the *oeuvre* of a far more extensive range of authors has been encouraged by the production of facsimile editions, easier access to medieval manuscripts containing unpublished works, and consequent progress on critical editions. The latter have demonstrated how unreliable were the incunabula and sixteenth-century printings of medieval scholastic works, the chief primary sources available to most historians.[39] Not surprisingly, therefore, if one had only Panofsky's footnotes in *Gothic Architecture and Scholasticism* to go by, one would infer that, of all the twelfth- through fourteenth-century scholastic authors whom he cited, he knew only Aquinas through published primary sources,[40] depending otherwise upon the surveys of the great philosophical editors of medieval texts, Martin Grabmann and Maurice De Wulf. We have already encountered De Wulf as an "Hegelian imbued" source for Panofsky. More important for Panofsky's understanding of medieval philosophy than De Wulf's Hegelianism, however, was De Wulf's Neo-Thomism. De Wulf was among the first generation of Neo-Scholastics in late nineteenth-century Belgium who, in accord with the recent papal encyclical *Aeterni Patris* (1879), were intent upon recuperating the thought of Aquinas as a basis for modern thought. This was an agenda that De Wulf was able to advance significantly through his professorship, then directorship of the Institut Supérieur de Philosophie in Leuven, an Institute that remains among the major centers of medieval scholarship today.[41] Panofsky may have found De Wulf's thinking congenial in part be-

38. Among the most significant problems with respect to Panofsky's claims about formal structures of the lectures, disputations, and *Summae* of scholastic authors is that there was no uniformity of the sort he presupposes. Instead, for those of us who study and edit such sources, it is clear that their structures varied considerably from one discipline or university to another, and according to a work's origin in an extemporized oral exercise or instead as a written creation, as well as to the stage in a scholastic's academic career at which such works were produced. See, for example, A. Kenny and J. Pinborg, "Medieval Philosophical Literature," in N. Kretzmann, A. Kenny, and J. Pinborg, eds., *The Cambridge History of Later Medieval Philosophy* (Cambridge, 1982), 11–42.

39. Although B. Geyer had published Abelard's *Logica 'Ingredientibus'* in 1919–27, the first reliable critical editions of his remaining logical and theological *oeuvre* appeared in print in 1956 (and those of his contemporaries and teachers since 1959); the first volume of the ongoing critical edition of John Duns Scotus was published in 1950; the philosophical and theological *Opera omnia* of William Ockham appeared in 1965–85, and his ecclesiopolitical writings are still being edited—to name three of the most significant medieval scholars whose views were described by Panofsky. For an introduction to the immense volume of new critical editions completed or in progress, see A. Cacciotti, B. Faes de Mottoni, eds., *Editori di Quaracchi 100 Anni Dopo: Bilancio e Prospettive* (Rome, 1997); W. J. Courtenay, "Late Medieval Nominalism Revisited: 1972–1982," *Journal of the History of Ideas* 44 (1983), 159–164.

40. I am grateful to Dr. Gerda Panofsky for confirming, in conversation after this paper was read at the symposium in Princeton, March 2009, that this inference would be mistaken. Reading Panofsky's treatise in light of the sources available to a scholar at the time of its writing, an historian of medieval scholasticism would have to be impressed by the number of medieval authors whom he named, and whose ideas he endeavored to convey.

41. According to J. L. Perrier, *The Revival of Scholastic Philosophy in the Nineteenth Century* (New York, 1909), ch. 13, at http://maritain.nd.edu/jmc/etext/perrierd.html (accessed March 2009), "In his *Histoire de la Philosophie Médievale* [1900], Mr. de Wulf departs from the common view which identifies Scholasticism with Mediaeval philosophy, and discovers in the Middle Ages two antithetical currents: Scholasticism proper, represented by Thomas Aquinas, Duns Scotus, Albert the Great, etc.; and anti-Scholasticism, of which Scotus Erigena is the father, and which is continued by the Catharists, the Albigenses and the Pantheistic schools. Mr. de Wulf's view on this point has not met with a ready acceptance.... Mr. De Wulf, however, still holds the same opinion, and has defended it again in his *Introduction à la Philosophie Néo-scolastique*" of 1904.

cause the Belgian scholar had already endeavored to draw connections between the aesthetics of art and the philosophy of its era.[42] Be that as it may, Panofsky adopted the Neo-Thomistic view of scholasticism as having prepared in an early phase, then climbed to its apogee with Aquinas (and his contemporaries), before losing appreciation for the heights and abandoning them to descend into incoherence and unwarranted skepticism.

For Panofsky, the preparation stage, or "Early Scholasticism" was born in the work of "Gilbert de la Porrée (d. 1154) and Abelard (d. 1142)," listed in that order, and adduced as belonging to the same cultural environment as Abbot Suger of St.-Denis.[43] Historians of medieval philosophy would now find it hard to agree. For these three scholars, although roughly the same age, belonged to two different scholarly generations, and the distinguishing views of Gilbert and Abelard bore little resemblance.[44] Nor was either of them a "nominalist" as generalists have used that term, namely, for a philosopher who maintains that universals do not have any existence extramentally in reality. Indeed, in the last forty years or so it has become clear that the twelfth-century terms for the propounders of two logical positions, "*nominales*" and "*reales*," described answers to a different question than that regarding the existence of universals.[45] Moreover, "*nominales*" and "*reales*," were labels from the second half of the twelfth century, and so did not refer precisely to the stance of Abelard from several decades earlier. More surprising still, we have discovered that these were labels for only two of *several* schools of thought, or "*sectae*," which also included *vocales*, *Porretani* (followers of Gilbert de la Porrée), *Parvipontani* or *Adamitae* (followers of Adam of Petit Pont), *Albricani* (followers of Alberic of Paris), and *Meludinenses* (followers of Robert of Melun), *Montani*, and several others.[46]

The arguments of these competing schools began

42. See F. van Steenbergen's article on De Wulf in H. Damico et al., *Mediaeval Scholarship, Biographical Studies on the Formation of A Discipline*, vol. 3, *Philosophy and the Arts* (1995), 43–54, at 46.

43. Panofsky, *Gothic Architecture and Scholasticism*, 4. Thus, Suger (*c.* 1081–1151), whose years of schooling were 1091–1106, was a few years younger than Pierre Abelard (1079–1142), who had arrived for the first time in Paris while in his teens, probably 1092–1096, and by 1101 had set up his own schools, first in Melun, then Corbeil, before returning to Paris in 1108, where he taught through 1118. Youngest of the three was Gilbert de la Porrée, also known as Gilbert of Poitiers, Gilbert Porreta, Gilbertus Porretanus or Pictaviensis (1085/90–1154), regarding whom see especially L. O. Nielsen, *Theology and Philosophy in the Twelfth Century : A Study of Gilbert Porreta's Thinking and the Theological Expositions of the Doctrine of the Incarnation During the Period 1130–1180*, (Leiden, 1982); T. Gross-Diaz, *The Psalms Commentary of Gilbert of Poitiers : From Lectio Divina to the Lecture Room* (Leiden, 1996).

44. See also: L. Grodecki, "Abélard et Suger," in *Pierre Abélard, Pierre le Vénérable: les courants philosophiques, littéraires et artistiques en Occident au milieu du XIIe siècle: [actes et mémoires du colloque international], Abbaye de Cluny, 2 au 9 juillet 1972* (Paris, 1975), 279–286.

45. The major turning point in the historiography of purported nominalism in the twelfth to fourteenth centuries was the publication of the first volume of L. M. de Rijk's, *Logica Modernorum: A Contribution to the History of Early Terminist Logic*, 2 vols. (Assen, 1962), which provided new texts from manuscripts of numerous twelfth-century logical treatises and offered a new conceptual framework for reading Abelard in context, as achieved in J. Jolivet, *Arts du langage et théologie chez Abailard*, Etudes de philosophie médiévale 58 (Paris, 1975); *idem*, "Comparaison des théories du langage chez Abélard et chez les nominalistes du XIVe siècle," in E. M. Buytaert, ed., *Peter Abelard*, Mediaevalia Lovaniensia I/2 (Louvain, 1974), 163–178; G. Nuchelmans, *Theory of the Proposition: Ancient and Medieval Conceptions of the Bearers of Truth and Falsity* (Amsterdam, 1973).

46. See Y. Iwakuma, "Twelfth-Century *Nominales*: The Posthumous School of Peter Abelard," *Vivarium* 30:1 (1992), 97–109; S. Ebbesen, "What Must One Have an Opinion About," *Vivarium* 30:1 (1992), 62–79; Iwakuma and Ebbesen, "Logico-Theological Schools from the Second Half of the 12th Century: A List of Sources," *Vivarium* 30 (1992), 173–210; C. J. Martin, "The Logic of the 'Nominales,' or the Rise and Fall of Impossible 'Positio,'" *Vivarium* 30 (1992), 111–126; M. Lenz, "Are Thoughts and Sentences Compositional? A Controversy between Abelard and a Pupil of Alberic on the Reconciliation of Ancient Theses on Mind and Language," *Vivarium* 45 (2007), 169–188. For other approaches, see C. Mews, "Philosophy, Communities of Learning, and Theological Dissent in the Twelfth Century," forthcoming in G. d'Onofrio, ed., Acts of *Il Paradigma Medievale* (Rome, 2005); W. J. Courtenay, "*Nominales* and Nominalism in the Twelfth Century," in J. Jolivet, Z. Kaluza, A. de Libera, *Lectionum Varietates* (Paris, 1991), 11–48, reprinted in Courtenay, *Ockham and Ockhamism: Studies in the Dissemination and Impact of His Thought* (Leiden, 2008), 39–80; Courtenay, "*Nominales* and Rules of Inference," K. Jacobi, ed., *Argumentationstheorie: Scholastische Forschungen zu den logischen und semantischen Regeln korrekten Folgerns* (Leiden, 1993), 153–160, reprinted in Courtenay, *Ockham and Ockhamism*, 81–87; I. Rosier-Catach, "Priscian on Divine Ideas and Mental Conceptions: The Discussions in the Glosulae in

before the *logica nova*—that is, those logical works by Aristotle that had not been translated into Latin by the sixth century—became available again in the academic generation *after* Abelard to scholars approaching Aristotle through Latin; and the arguments of the various *sectae* had been abandoned long enough before the early thirteenth century that Parisian authors writing then could misdescribe, obfuscate, or simply forget the tenets of the *nominales*, *reales*, and their competitors. Probably the disappearance of these "sects" (*sectae*) or "schools of thought" was an effect of the coalescence of a scholarly guild of Masters of Arts in the 1170s or 1180s, which meant that individual masters no longer had to compete for students, whose tuition ceased in turn to be the masters' *direct* source of income. In the words of Sten Ebbesen, "[i]n the competition for pupils, a list of the school's paradoxical opinions may have had an advertising function similar to that of a restaurant menu displayed in a window."[47] Absent competition, distinctive positions attributable to a master and his school became otiose.

We still do not fully comprehend which question(s) were at the root of the disparate tenets that each school of thought defended—theorems such as, "from an affirmative [proposition] a negative does not follow;" "there is no time except the present;" and, "what was once true is always true"[48]—but we do know that the thirteenth-century authors upon whom De Wulf, Grabmann, and many other historians had relied for their understanding, were simply wrong.[49] After decades of research into early twelfth-century logic, Christopher J. Martin has recently presented in lectures, but has not yet published, the most persuasive, comprehensive historical and philosophical explanation to date. Martin locates the origin of the logical debates, with their resultant school tenets, in the recognition among teachers of Boethius' *Topics* at Paris around 1100, of flaws in his treatment of hypothetical syllogisms, and Abelard's response: the development of a theory of entailment.[50] At present, then, as a general rule it would be wise not to speak of "nominalists" or "realists" in the twelfth century—much less to impute any views to them.

What about the fourteenth century, and such authors as Pierre Auriol, William of Ockham, and Nicolas of Autrecourt, whom Panofsky described as the "critical nominalists" of Late Scholasticism, and whose alleged subjectivism he rooted in their epistemologies of intuitive and abstractive cognition?[51] Here, too, we have learned a great deal since World War II, when the publications of Paul Vignaux, Philotheus Boehner, and E. A. Moody finally sparked the reassessment of these so-called "nominalists" from a *non*-Neo-Thomist point of view, that is, without the assumption that Thomas Aquinas was the best that the Middle Ages had to offer the modern world.[52] Absent also the biological model of youth, maturity, and senescence, the historian of medieval thought need not search for decline, disinte-

---

Priscianum, the Notae Dunelmenses, William of Champeaux and Abelard," *Vivarium* 45 (2007), 219–237.

47. Ebbesen, "What Must One Have," 63. On the stages of the introduction of Aristotle's *oeuvre*, see B. G. Dod, "Aristoteles latinus," in N. Kretzmann et al., eds., *Cambridge Later Medieval Philosophy*, 45–79; on Abelard's formation in and concern with those works of Aristotelian and Stoic/Neoplatonic logic known as the *logica vetus*, see in the same volume, M. Tweedale, "Abelard and the Culmination of the Old Logic," 143–157.

48. Iwakuma, "Twelfth-Century *Nominales*," 104: "*ex affirmativa non sequitur negativa*;" "*nullum tempus est nisi praesens*," "*quicquid semel verum, semper verum*;" but cf. Ebbesen, "What Must One Have," 67.

49. Iwakuma, "Twelfth-Century *Nominales*," 105–109.

50. C. J. Martin, four lectures on "Inconvenient Consequences: Peter Abaelard's Revolution in Logic and its Failure," presented at Paris, École pratique des hautes études, Section des Sciences Religieuses, 12 May–2 June 2009; forthcoming in the series *Conférences Pierre Abélard* (Paris).

51. Panofsky, *Scholasticism and Gothic Architecture*, 13; see also 8–12.

52. P. Vignaux actually began to publish his re-evaluation in the 1930s, thus roughly contemporaneously with E. Hochstetter's *Studien zur Metaphysik und Erkenntnislehre Wilhelms von Ockham* (Berlin, 1927). See the rich historiographic essays of W. J. Courtenay, "In Search of Nominalism: Two Centuries of Historical Debate," in A. Maierù, ed., *Gli studi di filosofia medievale fra Otto e Novecento, contributo a un bilancio storiografico: atti del convegno internazionale Roma 21–23 settembre 1989* (Rome, 1991), 233–251, reprinted in Courtenay, *Ockham and Ockhamism*, 1–19; M. L. Colish, *Remapping Scholasticism*, The Étienne Gilson Series 21 (Toronto, 2000), esp. at 10–15.

gration, or loss of vigor after the era of Bonaventure, Aquinas, and their contemporary patron of the arts, Louis IX.[53]

Thus, in the last fifty years, we have learned to appreciate that, far from opening the door to skepticism and subjectivism, the dichotomy of intuitive and abstractive cognition was introduced as the mechanism by which we attain certitude about reality, and achieve standardized—that is, non-arbitrary—universal concepts by the innate powers with which God has endowed the human mind. Moreover, Auriol, Ockham, and Autrecourt had quite dissimilar theories of how intuitive and abstractive cognition worked; the acceptance of this dichotomy did not commit its holder to either nominalism or realism, but was compatible with both.[54]

While Ockham was claimed in the late fifteenth century as a nominalist by Parisian scholars who so labeled themselves, Auriol never was named as a nominalist by any medieval author, so far as I have been able to discover.[55] It is not actually obvious in any case that the fifteenth-century self-styled nominalists, who were on other matters patently unreliable historians, were correct to see Ockham as their forerunner or as one of themselves.[56] But if *we* deploy the label "nominalist" as it has generally been used for the last hundred years or

53. Hegel had argued for such a biological model in his *Philosophie der Geschichte*, 98–100: "Die nächste Bestimmung aber, welche sich an die Veränderung anknüpft, ist, dass die Veränderung, welche Untergang ist, zugleich Hervorgehen eines neuen Lebens ist, dass aus dem Leben Tod, aber aus dem Tod Leben hervorgeht.... In der Vorstellung von der Seelenwanderung ist er in Beziehung auf das Individuelle enthalten; allgemeiner bekannt ist aber das Bild des *Phönix*, von dem Naturleben, das ewig sich selbst seinen Scheiterhaufen bereitet und sich darauf verzehrt, so dass aus seiner Asche ewig das neue, verjüngte, frische Leben hervorgeht. Dies Bild ist aber nur asiatisch, morgenländisch, nicht abendländisch. Der Geist, die Hülle seiner Existenz verzehrend, wandert nicht bloß in eine andere Hülle über, noch steht er nur verjüngt aus der Asche seiner Gestaltung auf, sondern er geht erhoben, verklärt, ein reinerer Geist aus derselben hervor.... Der Geist *handelt* wesentlich, er macht sich zu dem, was er an sich ist, zu seiner Tat, zu seinem Werk; so wird er sich Gegenstand, so hat er sich als ein Dasein vor sich. So der Geist eines Volkes: er ist ein bestimmter Geist, der sich zu einer vorhandenen Welt erbaut, die jetzt steht und besteht, in seiner Religion, in seinem Kultus, in seinen Gebräuchen, seiner Verfassung und seinen politischen Gesetzen, im ganzen Umfang seiner Einrichtungen, in seinen Begebenheiten und Taten. Das ist sein Werk—das *ist* dies Volk. Was ihre Taten sind, das sind die Völker.... Das Volk lebt so, wie das vom Manne zum Greisenalter übergehende Individuum, im Genusse seiner selbst, das gerade zu sein, was es wollte und erreichen konnte.... Diese Gewohnheit (die Uhr ist aufgezogen und geht von selbst fort) ist, was den natürlichen Tod herbeiführt.... So sterben Individuen, so sterben Völker eines natürlichen Todes;" similarly, *Philosophie der Weltgeschichte*, 45–47. See too his 1820 *Vorlesungen über die Geschichte der Philosophie*, as quoted in A. De Laurentiis, "Metaphysical Foundations of the History of Philosophy: Hegel's 1820 Introduction to the 'Lectures on the History of Philosophy,'" *The Review of Metaphysics* 59 (2005), 3–31, at 13, n. 25.

54. Tachau, *Vision and Certitude in the Age of Ockham: Optics, Epistemology, and the Foundations of Semantics, 1250–1345*, in the series *Studien und Texte zur Geistesgeschichte des Mittelalters* (Leiden, 1988). The argument of this book is now widely accepted among historians of fourteenth-century thought. See, for example, Colish, *Remapping Scholasticism*, 15. While Panofsky relied for his appreciation of Autrecourt on Julius Weinberg's *Nicolaus of Autrecourt: A Study in 14th Century Thought* (Princeton, 1948), which was the first sympathetic modern philosophical reading of Autrecourt, all studies of the latter's thought before my *Vision and Certitude* were—as I established in that work—based on misleading, inaccurate editions of Autrecourt's *Exigit ordo*, letters, and even the Papal condemnation of theses he had defended. See now: L. M. de Rijk, *Nicholas of Autrecourt, His Correspondence with Master Giles and Bernard of Arezzo, A Critical Edition and English Translation* (Leiden, 1994); Z. Kaluza, *Nicolas d'Autrécourt. Ami de la Vérité*, Histoire Littéraire de la France, 42–1 (Paris, 1995); C. Grellard, *Croire et savoir: Les principes de la connaissance selon Nicolas d'Autrécourt*, Etudes de philosophie médiévale 88 (Paris, 2005).

55. I base this claim on research in the manuscripts of medieval readers of Pierre Auriol's work. On Auriol (Aureol) and the re-evaluation of his thought, see my *Vision and Certitude* and "The Preparation of a Critical Edition of Pierre Auriol's *Sentences* Lectures," in Cacciotti, Faes de Mottoni, eds., *Editori di Quaracchi*, 205–216; O. Grassi, "Probabilismo teologico e certezza filosofica: Pietro Aureoli e il dibattito sulla conoscenza nel '300," in G. d'Onofrio, ed., *Storia della teologia nel Medioevo III: La teologia delle scuole* (Casale Monferrato, 1996), 515–40; C. D. Schabel, *Theology at Paris 1316–1345: Peter Auriol and the Problem of Divine Foreknowledge and Future Contingents* (Ashgate, 2000).

56. The 1474 petition of the *Nominalistae* at Paris to King Louis XI is discussed in Tachau and William J. Courtenay, "Ockham, Ockhamists, and the English-German Nation at Paris, 1339–1341," *History of Universities* 2 (1982), 53–96, at 75–79. According to the *Nominalistae* of 1474, it was not any opinion regarding the extramental reality of universals that had led to controversy over

more,[57] Aristotle arguably should be deemed the first nominalist. After all, as mentioned above, Aristotle can and has been read as denying that universals have any fully mind-independent existence. Thus, it is very odd, to say the least, that historians have lauded the use to which Aquinas put Aristotle in harmonizing faith or revelation with reason, taken as a synonym for "Aristotle's theories," while castigating nominalists for accepting particulars as the only extramental realities. For the fourteenth as for the twelfth century, we should be wary of resorting to the labels "nominalist" or "realist" as adequate or even useful descriptors of any scholastic's views.[58]

This leads me to the third and most important "ism" where the evolution of scholarship on the part of historians of medieval thought has a bearing on our appreciation of Gothic art and architecture, namely "Neoplatonism." With regard to the impact of Neoplatonism upon intellectual culture, I would side in part with Panofsky, Sedelmayr, and von Simson—but only in part. They were right, I think, in seeing Neoplatonism as important in theologically educated ecclesiastics' explanations of and justifications for the aesthetic decisions that they had approved as patrons. But this does not mean that Abbot Suger had access to or read the writings of Dionysius the pseudo-Areopagite, nor that Suger thought deeply about the latter's distinctive teachings about the workings of light as opposed, say, to the views of Augustine,[59] whose works, as have already been mentioned, were also important vehicles for conveying the substance of late antique Neoplatonism to later generations.[60]

Those of us who study the history of medieval and early modern theories of light and vision, which, it turns out, were inseverable from astrology and alchemy, do not see in the sources the thesis-antithesis struggle between Neoplatonism and Aristotelianism that was the structure upon which such early twentieth-century historians as De Wulf, Martin Grabmann, or Étienne Gilson constructed their surveys of medieval thought.[61] I believe we can make much more sense of the centuries from Abelard to Newton if we think of

---

Ockham's thought, but rather his stance in the political battles between Pope John XXII and the Franciscans: "Among the nominalists the first to be condemned is said to have been William Ockham, whom John XXII persecuted, first because the said William Ockham took opposite sides from the pope on the heresy [on the part of the pope] of the souls of the blessed, which the same pope said would not see God face to face before the day of final judgment.... and [second] ... because Ockham, in his *Dialogue*, defended the royal authority [against John XXII] by holy scripture and the pronouncements of popes, general councils, and doctors of the church ... For these reasons, John XXII bestowed many privileges upon the University of Paris that it might condemn Ockham's doctrines; yet the said university was unwilling to condemn it. But the Faculty of Arts, overcome by importunity, made a statute in which it enjoined that the said doctrine should not be taught because it was not yet examined and approved." See also Z. Kaluza, "La Crise des années 1474–1482: L'Interdiction du nominalisme par Louis XI," in Hoenen et al., eds., *Philosophy and Learning*, 293–327.

57. See Courtenay, "In Search of Nominalism," and above, note 45.

58. Indeed, Carl Prantl had already insisted on the inaccuracy of describing Ockham's views as "nominalist" in volume three of his *Geschichte der Logik in Abendlande* (Leipzig, 1867); see also Tachau and Courtenay, "Ockham, Ockhamists."

59. See P. Kidson, "Panofsky, Suger and St Denis," *Journal of the Warburg and Courtauld Institutes* 50 (1987), 1–17, at 4–6, esp. his argument (p. 5) that "[i]n the absence of explicit references, how could the presence of the Pseudo-Dionysius be detected? The only satisfactory answer would be through characteristic doctrines in Suger which were otherwise peculiar to the Pseudo-Dionysius, or which could have reached Suger only by way of the Pseudo-Dionysius.... Panofsky makes a great fuss about light metaphysics in his essay, but there is not much to go on in Suger, and what there is lacks sharpness and precision."

60. Maurice de Sully, who had studied *theologia* before succeeding Peter Lombard as bishop of Paris and launching the rebuilding of the Cathedral of Notre-Dame (the building that we know today), is more likely to have been familiar with and thoughtful about Augustinian Neoplatonism, but we cannot be sure. For an introduction to more recent studies of Neoplatonism, see the essays in L. G. Benakis, *Néoplatonisme et philosophie médiévale. Actes du colloque international de Corfou 6–8 octobre 1995 organisé par la Société Internationale pour l'Étude de la Philosophie Médiévale* (Turnhout, 1997); also articles in Kobusch and Mojsisch, eds., *Platon in der abendländischen.*

61. In addition to Tachau, *Vision and Certitude*, see also Tachau, "'*Et maxime visus, cuius species venit ad stellas et ad quem species stellarum veniunt*': *Perspectiva* and *Astrologia* in Late Medieval Thought," *Micrologus* 5: *La Visione e lo sguardo nel Medio Evo* (1998), 201–224; Tachau and D. C. Lindberg, "*Perspectiva*: La scienza della luce, del colore e della visione," *La scienze medievale*, vol. 4 of *Storia della scienza* (Rome: *Enciclopedia Italiana*, 2002), 397a–406b; and Lindberg, *Theories of Vision from Al-Kindi to Kepler* (Chicago, 1976).

Neoplatonism as a rainbow that, like all rainbows, contains more than one hue, and in which each of the colors transitions subtly into the next so that there is no clear distinction visible to the eye of the historian. Because Neoplatonism had expressly incorporated Stoic and Aristotelian thought within itself; and because throughout the period we are discussing today, Aristotelian theories were refracted through the Neoplatonic lens of Porphyry's *Introduction* to Aristotle's *Categories*, the arrival of the rest of the Aristotelian *corpus* during the 1140s–1260s added intensity to the rainbow's hues, but did not alter or reposition it beyond recognition. Moreover, the diffusion of Euclidean, Ptolemaic, and Galenic thought—also available, albeit in shadowy form, in the Neoplatonism of Augustine—added further hues to the rainbow of *prisca sapientia*, or "pristine wisdom,"[62] as medieval scholastics referred to the entire spectrum that we call "Neoplatonisms."

There were, to be sure, twelfth- and thirteenth-century "Tertullians," so to speak, who inveighed against any philosophy beyond that conveyed by Jerome and Augustine; but these contemporaries could not "unweave the rainbow" that fellow scholars were entwining.[63] That is a nineteenth- and twentieth-century project, not a medieval one. Nevertheless, because the Greek and Arabic works were translated and absorbed over 120 years or so, and because academic institutions changed, the content and emphases of the ongoing conversation of scholarly generations did change over time, such that the preoccupations of one were not inevitably those of another. Hence, we must pay close attention to the differences among generations if we are to discover the particular intellectual context that provides us with the key to unlock iconography that we "see through a glass obscurely" but that was not so enigmatic at the time of its production.

For the twelfth century, the most significant shifts would include, among others, the rise to predominance of the intellectuals associated with St.-Victor, other monasteries, and the cathedral of Paris—these are the institutions from which the logical *sectae* emerged—and away from the scholastics associated with Chartres. After roughly a half-century of treating the creation accounts of the *Timaeus* and *Genesis* as compatible, that Chartrain project had been roundly rejected by the middle of the twelfth century. By then, Peter Lombard, in his *Sentences*, encapsulated the arguments against the Chartrain theories soon to be echoed by his younger colleague (and former student) Peter Comestor, in the *Historia scholastica*, and, a generation later, by Peter the Chanter.[64]

For all three of these authors, the account of creation presented by Plato in the *Timaeus* was not the only erroneous cosmogony from Antiquity that they confronted, for they also took aim at Aristotle, "the Epicureans," and most important of all, the Manichaeans.[65] For these mid-century authors—who wrote before the influx of Aristotle's non-logical writings, and

62. See G. Molland, "Addressing Ancient Authority: Thomas Bradwardine and *Prisca Sapientia*," *Annals of Science* 53 (1996), 213–33.

63. The phrase "unweaving the rainbow," is from Keats' poem *Lamia*, and is well-known to historians of science as a veiled criticism of Newton who, by studying prisms, provided the modern analysis of the visible spectrum of light. In Keats' words, "Do not all charms fly | At the mere touch of cold philosophy? | There was an awful rainbow once in heaven: | We know her woof, her texture; she is given | In the dull catalogue of common things. | Philosophy will clip an Angel's wings, | Conquer all mysteries by rule and line, | Empty the haunted air, and gnomed mine— | Unweave a rainbow ..."

64. Peter Lombard (*c.* 1100–1160 in Paris), about whose views see below at notes 80–83; Petrus Cantor, taught theology at Paris from 1170s, d. 1197; Petrus Comestor became Chancellor at Notre-Dame de Paris in 1160, and died 1178. The best points of departure for studying these authors remain: J. W. Baldwin, *Masters, Princes, and Merchants: The Social Views of Peter the Chanter and His Circle*, 2 vols. (Princeton, 1970); M. L. Colish, *Peter Lombard*, 2 vols. (Leiden, 1994); J. Morey, "Peter Comestor, Biblical Paraphrase, and the Medieval Popular Bible," *Speculum* 68 (1993), 6–35; M. J. Clark, "Peter Comestor and Peter Lombard: Brothers in Deed," *Traditio* 60 (2005), 85–142, esp. 89–90, 120–21. To put the work of the three Peters in context and appreciate the first generation of Victorine scholars, see B. Smalley, *Study of the Bible in the Middle Ages* (Oxford, 1952; 3rd ed. 1983); also, R. W. Southern, "The Schools of Paris and the School of Chartres," in R. L. Benson and G. Constable, eds., *Renaissance and Renewal in the Twelfth Century* (Cambridge, Mass., 1982), 113–137.

65. In what follows, I condense materials discussed in greater detail in "At the Beginning: The Meaning of Creation," Chapter 3 of my forthcoming *Bible Lessons for Kings: Scholars and Friars in Thirteenth-Century Paris and the Creation of the "Bibles Moralisées."*

who knew Epicurean thought only through Augustine's rebuttals—what these four cosmogonies had in common was that all shared the erroneous assumption that God the Creator was not the only eternally existent, and therefore uncreated, entity. If Peters the Lombard, Comestor, and the Chanter did not know contemporary proponents of the Aristotelian or Epicurean opinions that they opposed, they did know of Cathars, whom they considered to be the Manichaeans of old resurgent in their time. To defeat them, the Lombard and his followers wielded Augustinian—not Chartrain—Neoplatonism. In other words, we cannot safely infer from a given scholar's embrace (or rejection) of a specific Neoplatonic tenet what his attitude toward other Platonic tenets would be.[66]

After the middle of the twelfth century, we may discern another generational transition when Peter the Chanter began to teach, and the continuity of his worldview through the teaching and ecclesiastical authority wielded for a second generation by his students and such other scholars as Philip the Chancellor—known to historians of music as a composer of no small moment.[67] Then, beginning in the last decade of the twelfth century and continuing into the first two decades of the thirteenth, the works of Greco-Arabic scholarship began to reach Latin readers in Paris, provoking reaction and counter-reaction, a dynamic that began to change with the arrival of the first Franciscan and Dominican friars. Two further intellectual shifts appear to me to be apparent. The first had as its terminus the late 1250s, when most of the works coming from the Arabic-speaking world had arrived and been fit into a curriculum.[68] From that point on, the masters and preoccupations of the Franciscan Order predominated until roughly a decade after the death of John Duns Scotus. In this, to be clear, I am rejecting the textbook picture of this as the era of Aquinas; but his impact largely came later.[69]

One could continue, but this much may suffice to suggest how greatly a current survey of Parisian thought would diverge from those available when Panofsky wrote—and we have not even broached the periodization of Bolognese or Oxonian scholasticism.[70] We could also reverse the relation of the Gothic and scholasticism under discussion. That is, we might think about how the architectural spaces influenced the masters and students singing, praying, working, and living in them; we could consider, for instance, Peter the Chanter's condemnation of the expense and ambition of bishop Sully's project for building the Notre-Dame that exists

66. M.-D. Chenu, in *La théologie au douzième siècle* (Paris, 1976), 108–141, in a chapter titled "Les platonismes du XIIe siècle." For recent discussions, see A. de Libera, *La philosophie médiévale* (Paris, 1993), 307–354, esp. 314–317; Benakis, ed., *Néoplatonisme et philosophie médiévale*; and J. Marenbon, "Platonismus im zwölften Jahrhundert: alte und neue Zugangsweisen," in Kobusch and Mojsisch, eds., *Platon in der abendländischen*, 101–119, an especially helpful historiographic introduction.

67. T. B. Payne, "Poetry, Politics, and Polyphony: Philip the Chancellor's Contribution to the Music of the Notre Dame School," Ph.D. Diss., University of Chicago, 1991; C. Wright, *Music and Ceremony at Notre Dame de Paris, 500–1550* (Cambridge, 1989), 294–300. For his theologico-philosophical *oeuvre*, see: H. Meylan, "Les 'Questions' de Philippe le Chancelier," *Ecole Nationale des Chartes: Positions des thèses soutenues par les élèves de la promotion de 1927* (Paris, 1927), 89-94; *Corpus philosophorum medii aevi, opera philosophica mediae aetatis selecta*, 2 (Bern, 1985), *pars prior*, Introduction, 11*–28*; N. Wicki, ed., *Philippus Cancellarius Parisiensis*, "*Summa de Bono*" 2 vols. (Bern, 1985).

68. In addition to Dodd, "Aristoteles Latinus" (as in note 47, above), convenient starting points for tracing the arrival of Greco-Arabic learning remain M.-T. d'Alverny, "Translations and Translators," in Benson and Constable, eds., *Renaissance and Renewal*, 421–62; D. C. Lindberg, "The Transmission of Greek and Arabic Learning to the West," in *idem*, *Science in the Middle Ages* (Chicago, 1978), 52–90; C. Lafleur, "Les 'guides de l'étudiant' de la Faculté des arts de l'Université de Paris au XIIIe siècle," in M. J. F. M. Hoenen, J. H. J. Schneider, and G. Wieland, eds., *Philosophy and Learning, Universities in the Middle Ages* (Leiden, 1995), 137–199.

69. Moreover, it is important to recognize that Aquinas was far from the last to compose *summae*; fourteenth-century authors did so, too, to take Ockham's *Summa totius logicae* or Thomas Bradwardine's *Summa de causa Dei* as two prominent examples; nor, despite Panofsky, did the title *Summa* ever connote the "totality"—something that theologians would have condemned as audacious—but rather something closer to "a summary" or a "summing up."

70. Ockham, for instance, was never a resident of the Paris Franciscan convent, much less a student or teacher at the *studium* there; given the slowness with which his theological and logical work became accessible and gained readers at Paris (for which see Tachau, *Vision and Certitude*), Ockham's thought was, in my opinion, never truly germane to Panofsky's argument.

today.[71] I would like, instead, to illustrate the difference that this "periodization" makes for our interpretation of the context for specific iconography. And my example concerns the kind of project in which it can be demonstrated that scholars actually worked with and directed the work of artisans, namely the earliest *Bible moralisée*. This is not to claim that artisans *always* produced their work under such close supervision; nor is it to claim that the scholars involved were particularly fine scholars. Rather, I am only stating that in this particular instance, there is evidence that scholars actually planned the work of artisans at a level of detail that allows us to arrive at the probable intended "meaning" of the resultant images. Moreover, it is useful to call the illuminators "artisans" because that was their status in Paris in the first decades of the thirteenth century, and that is how they are depicted in the *Bible moralisées* themselves; no matter how skilled and exceptional, illuminators were *tradesmen* in the eyes of the clergy and anyone who hired them, and so would not have had the autonomy that willy-nilly the word "artist" conjures up for us.

My example is an image about which I have written a decade ago, but to which I have lately returned, in part to explain why the makers of the subsequent *Bible moralisées* changed it, and what the changes mean, and in part to answer a critique (Fig. 4). Over the last century, this illumination has increasingly become a visual cliché, vaguely appropriated from its original manuscript context and disseminated in both scholarly and less academic venues to illustrate medieval thought, art, or worldview.[72] It is fair to say that for at least a century, this image has emerged from the manuscript that contains it, to function within the domain of historians of art as though it were a freestanding work. Isolated from the folios that this miniature actually introduces, their evidence has been lost to those scholars determined to decode its iconographical significance.

Erwin Panofsky and Fritz Saxl initiated one strand of interpretation in the 1920s. Only in passing, but influentially, did Panofsky and Saxl refer to medieval depictions of "God the Father with Compass in hand as architect of the world" as exemplifying an intermediate conceptual step from the symbolism of divine to human creative genius. For their purposes, the frontispieces of the *Bible moralisées* were interchangeable, as they quoted the words above the Old French creation scene and illustrated the genre with the first folio of the Vienna Latin manuscript.[73] Otto von Simson drew a second strand into the interpretive weave. In his explication of emergent Gothic architecture, von Simson proposed that the Platonism of scholars at Chartres and at Paris in the twelfth century informed "the dramatiz[ation] of the image of the architect ... by depicting God as a master builder," and discerned sources for this valorization in Augustine and in the Neoplatonic writings of Boethius. Von Simson discerned in a passage of Boethius' *De musica* the choice "precisely [of] the compass to represent an art [i.e., architecture] that truly 'comprehends the whole,'" as the reason for placing a compass in God's hand to represent him "as the Creator who composed the universe according to geometrical laws."[74]

Taken together, the views of Panofsky and Saxl on

71. Cf. Sir Winston Churchill's remark: "We shape our buildings; thereafter they shape us." Petrus Cantor (Peter the Chanter), *Verbum abbreviatum*, Biblioteca apostolica Vaticana, MS. Reg. Lat. 106, fol. 113[vb], 115[ra]: "Sicut in vestium et cibariorum superfluitate et curiositate labor nature in culpa vertitur et res in vitium cadit, sic in superfluitate et curiositate et sumptuositate edificiorum.... (115[ra]) Incastellantur multotiens turrite ecclesie et loca deo sacrata. Et multa mala ex hac edificatione superflua proveniunt: iusticia spiritualis minus exercetur, religio minus observatur, et fere omnia pervertiuntur. Peccatur etiam in ecclesiis construendis, cum enim capita earum humiliora deberent esse corporibus ipsarum pro misterio, quia capud nostrum Christus scilicet humilior est ecclesia sua altiora nunc eriguntur. Et nota quod hic morbus etiam a senibus et litteratis et religiosis non potest eradicari, quod mirum est. Si homines tacent, lapides clamant." See also: Baldwin, *Masters*, vol. 1, 66–69; vol. 2, 47–48. Peter the Chanter held that office among the canons of the Cathedral while Maurice de Sully was its bishop.

72. Here I expand upon portions of my article, "God's Compass and *Vana Curiositas*: Scientific Study in the Old French *Bible moralisée*," *Art Bulletin* 80 (1998), 7–33.

73. E. Panofsky and F. Saxl, *Dürers 'Melencolia I': Eine Quellen- und typengeschichtliche Untersuchung*, Studien der Bibliothek Warburg 2 (Leipzig-Berlin, 1923), esp. 1, 62, and 67, note 3; plate 17, figure 29. The figure is mistakenly labelled the Bodleian *Bible moralisée* "of around 1250," an error the authors corrected in later works.

74. Otto von Simson, *The Gothic Cathedral*, 32–37, esp. 35, where von Simson cites Boethius' *De musica 5.1*. See also: J. M. Heinlen,

the one hand, and von Simson on the other, have proven mutually reinforcing and come to dominate art-historical interpretation; in survey textbooks, they have launched flights of fancy from which sight of the ground has long receded. Among historians of medieval science, the illumination is widely interpreted as depicting God as the world's Architect, thus translating the "*Artifex*" or "Demiurge" of Plato's *Timaeus*.[75] The suggestion is that the *titulus* above the image—which reads, "here God creates the heavens and the earth, the sun and the moon, and all the elements"—purportedly combines the opening words of Genesis with the gist of the Demiurge's work in the *Timaeus*. Many of the early twelfth-century platonizing authors whom von Simson adduced in support of his view continue to be cited as pertinent to the meaning of an illumination from the first decades of the thirteenth century. Recently, for instance, Conrad Rudolph has on this basis rejected departure from this now traditional reading.[76]

Yet, by 1200, the Lombard's *Sentences* and Comestor's *Historia scholastica* were well established as essential works of reference for the scholarly study of the Bible at Paris, even at the most introductory level. What the Lombard and Comestor had to say, therefore, are likely to have informed any intellectuals involved in determining the content of the *Bible moralisées*, and, as we have already noted, they explicitly repudiated the Platonist cosmogony of the very same Chartrain authors of the previous generation whom twentieth-century scholars would eventually invoke in their interpretations of the Old French and Vienna Latin frontispieces.[77] In fact, the Old French *titulus* accords well with the title of the first chapter of Comestor's *Historia scholastica* in numerous manuscripts already available to students of the Bible at Paris when the Old French *Bible moralisée* was planned. His title, "Concerning the creation of the empyrean heaven and of the four elements,"[78] introduces the following explanation:

> "In the beginning"... God created the empyrean and sensible worlds and the sublunary regions, from nothing (*ex nihilo*).... The legislator [Moses] says: "In the beginning God created the heavens and the earth" ... the earth, namely, the matter of all bodies, that is the four elements, and so the sensible world constituted

"The Ideology of Reform," ch. 1, "God as Architect of the Cosmos," esp. 12–26; J. Zahlten, *Creatio mundi: Darstellungen der sechs Schöpfungstage und naturwissenschaftliches Weltbilt im Mittelalter* (= *Stuttgarter Beiträge zur Geschichte und Politik*, 13) (1979), 154–56 and *passim*; R. W. Hanning, "'Ut enim faber ... sic Creator:' Divine Creation as Context for Human Creativity in the Twelfth Century," in *Word, Picture and Spectacle*, Early Drama, Art, and Music Monograph Series 5 (Kalamazoo, 1984), 95–149, a volume that uses the Old French frontispiece for its own. Zahlten cites von Simson (156n); Hanning acknowledges his intellectual debt to both Panofsky and von Simson, among others.

75. J. Murdoch, *Album of Science: Antiquity and the Middle Ages* (New York, 1984), his figure 273, pp. 330–331, states: "*In principio creavit Deus celum et terram.* This opening verse of the first chapter of the Book of Genesis was often interpreted as God's creation 'in the beginning,' not simply of the heavens and the earth, but of the four elements.... [T]his interpretation naturally related the Genesis account of creation to natural philosophy.... A compass appeared frequently in medieval creation miniatures such as this one. The theme behind this motif most likely was that of the Creator as designer or architect of the universe; its ultimate source probably was Plato's *Timaeus*, in which the notion of a craftsman god who impressed forms on a preexistent unformed matter or chaos was central to the world's creation. Indeed, in this miniature, one might imagine that the amorphous mass flanked by the sun and the moon at the center of the universe, of which God is taking measure with his compass, in some way reflects this Platonic idea of unformed matter, even though there is no textual basis for such a suggestion." See other citations in my *God's Compass*.

76. C. Rudolph, "In the Beginning: Theories and Images of Creation in Northern Europe in the Twelfth Century," *Art History* 22 (1999), 3–55.

77. For the literature on and discussion of the Lombard's opposition to the positions of Chartrain authors in his treatment of Genesis, see Colish, *Lombard*, vol. 1, 303, 305, 323–24, 336–341. Especially notable among his direct sources is Abelard, and among his targets are: Bernard of Chartres, who stated in his commentary on Chalcidius' translation of Plato's *Timaeus* that the principles of creation are God, *hyle*, and *ydeas* (see Colish, *Lombard*, 1, 305 and Comestor, below, at note 79); Bernard Silvestris (Colish, *Lombard*, 1, 306–07); Thierry of Chartres (Colish, *Lombard*, 1, 310); Clarenbald of Arras (Colish, *Lombard*, 1, 316–17). Bernard Silvestris and especially Thierry of Chartres were, for von Simson, *Gothic Cathedral*, 26–30, the major creators of the Chartrain "system" of theology and cosmology underlying their emphasis upon God as (p. 27) "the divine artist of creation;" he also accords weight to Clarembald, William of Conches, and (inaccurately) Abelard.

78. Peter Comestor, *Hist. scholastica*, in *Petri Comestoris Scolastica historia, Liber Genesis*, A. Sylwan, ed., Corpus Christianorum Continuatio Mediaevalis, 191 (Turnhout, 2005), 6; in the apparatus to

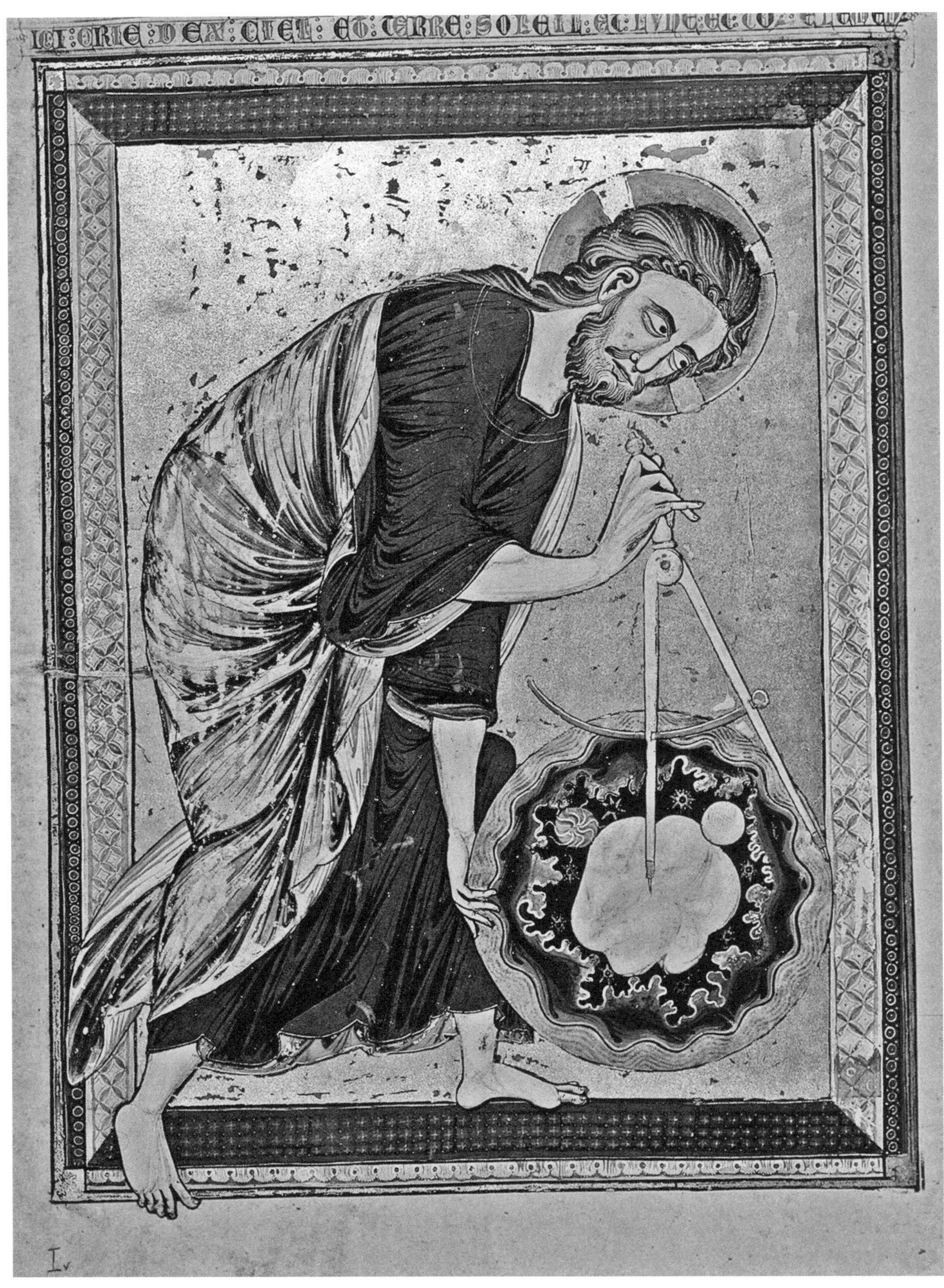

FIGURE 4. God Using a Compass While Creating the Universe, *Old French Bible moralisée*, produced in Paris *c.* 1210, Vienna (Österreichische Nationalbibliothek, Cod. 2554), fol. I[v].

from them.... When Moses says [God] "created," he avoids three errors: those of Plato, Aristotle, and Epicurus....[79]

Comestor is actually just condensing Peter Lombard's more theologically detailed discussion. The Lombard embarks upon the second book of his *Sentences* by paraphrasing Bede and Strabo from the *Glossa ordinaria* to explain just what was the error of Plato, Aristotle, and Epicurus, that Moses had avoided:

> God is the creator, the beginning of time and of all created things, visible and invisible ... Moses, inspired by the Spirit of God, relates that the world was created in one beginning (*principium*) by God the creator, [thus] avoiding the error of some authors who claimed that there were many principles (*principia*) that were themselves without beginning.

When it comes to Plato, Lombard continues:

> Plato thought that there were three beginning [entities], namely God, the exemplar, and matter; that matter was uncreated (without a beginning), and that God was like an artisan (*artifex*), not a creator.[80]

But this, Lombard says, is mistaken, for God is not an *artisan*, a designation that would include architects. This is because, unlike artisans—who use material to make objects—the Creator made the very material itself. As Lombard states:

> He who makes *ex nihilo* is a Creator, for strictly speaking 'to create' is 'to make *ex nihilo*,' while 'to make,' [refers] not just to working from nothing, but also from matter. Hence a man or an angel is said strictly speaking to make, but not to create, and he is called a 'maker' or an 'artisan' (*artifex*), but not a 'creator.' For the latter name strictly speaking applies only to God.[81]

---

lin. 1, Sylwan indicates that four entire manuscript families—her ς, β, γ, δ—substitute "de creatione empyrei celi et quatuor elementorum" for the *incipit* she prefers, "de prima creatione celi et terre." I have ascertained through examination of the codices that various late twelfth- and early thirteenth-century Parisian manuscripts (made and still preserved in Paris) do indeed have the *incipit* that Sylwan relegates to the variant readings.

79. Peter Comestor, *Hist. scholastica*, *Liber Genesis*, ed. Sylwan, p. 6, lin. 3 – p. 7, lin. 34: "*In principio erat verbum, et verbum erat principium*, in quo et per quod pater creavit mundum. Mundum quatuor modis dicitur. Quandoque empyreum celum 'mundus' dicitur propter sui mundiciam. Quandoque sensilis 'mundus' ... Quandoque sola regio sublunaris 'mundus' dicitur ... Quandoque homo 'mundus' dicitur, quia in se totius mundus ymaginem representat. Unde a Domino omnis creatura dictus est, et Grecus ipsum 'microcosmum,' id est 'minorem mundum,' vocat. Empyreum autem et sensilem mundum et sublunarem regionem creavit Deus, id est de nichilo fecit; hominem vero creavit, id est *plasmavit*. De creatione ergo illorum trium inquit legislator: *In principio creavit Deus celum et terram*: celum id est continens et contentum, id est celum empyreum *et angelicam naturam*; terram materiam omnium corporum, id est quattuor elementa, id est mundum sensilem ex his constantem. Quidam celum superiores partes mundi sensilis intelligunt, terram inferiores et palpabiles.... Cum vero dixit Moysis 'Creavit,' trium errores elidit: Platonis, Aristotelis, Epicuri. Plato dixit tria fuisse ab eterno: deum, ydeas, *ylem* et in principio temporis de *yle* mundum factum. Aristotelis duo: mundum et opificem qui de duobus principiis, scilicet materia et forma, operatus est sine principio et operatur sine fine. Epicurus duo: inane et athomos, et in principio Natura quosdam athomos solidavit in terram, alios in aquam, alios in aera, alios in ignem. Moyses vero solum Deum eternum prophetavit et sine preiacenti materia mundum creatum. Creatus est autem in principio sic: *In principio fecit Deus celum et terram*, 'in principio,' id est in filio, et iterandum est 'in principio,' temporis scilicet, coeva enim sunt mundus et tempus. Sicut autem solus Deus eternus, sic mundus sempiternus, id est semper eternus, id est temporaliter eternus" (punctuation and translation mine).

With few verbal discrepancies, the Comestor's wording is taken over by Peter the Chanter (Petrus Cantor), *In Genesim*, Paris, Bibl. Mazarine MS. 44, fol. 2^{rb-va}.

80. Peter Lombard, *Sententiae*, bk. 2, d. 1, c. 1, in *Magistri Petri Lombardi Parisiensis episcopi Sententiae in IV libris distinctae*, Collegium S. Bonaventurae ad Claras Aquas, eds. (Grottaferrata, 1971–1981) [hereafter: ed. Quaracchi], vol. 1, p. 329, lin. 9 – p. 330, lin. 6: "1. Unum esse rerum principium ostendit, non plura, ut quidam putaverunt.—Beda. Creationem rerum insinuans Scriptura, Deum esse creatorem initiumque temporis atque omnium, visibilium vel invisibilium creaturarum, in primordio sui ostendit dicens: *In principio creavit Deus caelum et terram*. His etenim verbis Moyses, Spiritu Dei afflatus, in uno principio a Deo creatore mundum factum refert, elidens errorem quorundam plura sine principio fuisse principia opinantium. 2. Strabus: Plato tria dixit principia. Plato namque tria initia existimavit, Deum scilicet, et exemplar, et materiam; et ipsa increata, sine principio, et Deum quasi artificem, non creatorem." This passage and that in the next note, 81, were crucially important for shaping the debate over one of the major sticking points for the acceptance of Aristotelian physics during the thirteenth century, and are discussed in the valuable R. C. Dales, *Medieval Discussions of the Eternity of the World* (Leiden, 1990), 37–38.

81. Lombard, *Sententiae*, bk. 2, d. 1, c. 2, ed. Quaracchi, vol. 1, p. 330, lin. 8–14: "(Cap. 2). Ex qua ratione proprie dicitur creator, et quid sit creare, quid facere. Creator enim est, qui de nihilo ali-

There is more that one could say about Lombard's reasoning, and why he thinks it crucial to understand that God is no artisan, but the point is that the explicit rejection, in sources closer in time and place to their production, of the Christian God as Plato's "Maker" is crucial evidence against the assumption that the Christ of the Old French frontispiece was to be read by that particular Platonic light, as either an architect or geometer. But there was also an alternative way of imagining God the Creator, namely as *Conditor*, or Founder of the universe, for the planning and laying out of which a compass might come in handy.[82]

The understanding of God as *Conditor mundi* could hardly have been more familiar to Parisian clergy, for what more omnipresent shapers of the their imagination were there than the liturgical evocations of the universe's first week? Peter Lombard himself quoted the Gregorian hymn *Magne Deus potentie* sung at Vespers on Thursdays when he expounded in the *Sentences* upon God's production of seabirds and other sea creatures on the fifth day of creation.[83] Like him, monks and canons throughout Paris and its environs would have been reminded through the liturgy of God's identity as Founder (*Conditor*) of the world while, year in and year out, they sang the Gregorian hymns of the divine offices that so addressed God. Awakened at night on the first day of each week for Sunday Matins, monks were reminded of the unity of the creation and end of the world by the hymn *Primo dierum omnium*:

> On the first day of all,
> On which the world was founded,
> On which the founder, having risen again,
> Vanquished death and freed us from it.[84]

At Vespers on Monday, the second day of each week, they recalled the second day of creation while singing to the "immense founder of the heavens" (*Immense caeli conditor*).[85] Similarly, at Tuesday's Vespers they praised the creator who separated the waters from the land on the universe's third day through the hymn, *Telluris ingens conditor*.[86] During Advent, the beginning of the liturgical year, Vespers included the anonymous

---

qua facit, et 'creare' proprie <loquendo> est de nihilo aliquid facere; 'facere' vero, non modo de nihilo aliquid operari, sed etiam de materia. Unde et homo vel angelus dicitur aliquid facere, sed non creare; vocaturque 'factor' sive 'artifex,' sed non 'creator.' Hoc enim nomen soli Deo proprie congruit, qui et de nihilo quaedam, et de aliquo aliqua facit. Ipse est ergo creator et opifex et factor. Sed creationis nomen sibi proprie retinuit, alia vero etiam creaturis communicavit. In Scriptura tamen saepe 'creator' accipitur tanquam 'factor' et 'creare' sicut 'facere,' sine distinctione significationis" (my punctuation and translation). See also: Hugh of St. Victor, *De Sacramentis*, bk. 1, c. 1 (Migne PL: 176), col. 187.

82. Consider the use of the verb *condo* from which *conditor* derives in the title of Livy's history of Rome, *Ab urbe condita*; by the early thirteenth century, French kings were founding cities, so the notion that one had to devise a putative urban "layout" was available to the intended recipients of the *Bibles moralisées*.

83. Lombard's allusion to the hymn was noted by the editors of his *Sententiae*; see the critical apparatus at Bk. 2, d. 15, c. 1, ed. Quaracchi, vol. 1, p. 400, lin. 21, their note 5. The hymn was used in former Carolingian domains from Charlemagne's time for Thursday Vespers. It appears in this position, for instance, in the Carolingian manuscripts Trier, Stadtbibliothek Mss. 1404 and 1418, according to F. J. Mone, *Hymni latini medii aevi e codd. mss.*, 3 vols. (Freiburg-im-Breisgau, 1853), vol. 1, 372; it was also part of the office practiced at Molesme retained among the earliest Cistercians, then rejected as foreign to the Ambrosian hymnal that Benedict had employed, and, in the last quarter of the twelfth century, restored in a revised Cistercian liturgy that reintegrated the hymns once rejected, but that were of long-standing use by all clergy and monastics, in the words of Abelard, in his contemporaneous criticism of the early twelfth-century Cistercians. Abelard thus confirms indirectly that the Office hymns we know from other Parisian sources would have been in general use in the Île de France, including among Cistercians, by 1200. See C. Waddell, *The Twelfth-Century Cistercian Hymnal*, 2 vols, Cistercian Liturgy Series (Kalamazoo, 1984), vol. 1, bk. 1, 14, 64–67; vol. 2, 6.

84. The first stanza in Mone, *Hymni latini*, vol. 1, 370, 372: "Primo dierum omnium | quo mundus exstat conditus | vel quo resurgens conditor | nos morte victa liberat...." In Trier, Stadtbib. MS. 1418, this is instead to be sung during Sunday Nocturns; see also Waddell, *Twelfth-Century Cistercian Hymnal*, vol. 1, bk. 1, p. 13, for its presence in the Molesme liturgy. At Paris, *Primo dierum omnium* was the hymn for Septuagesima Matins (i.e., the first portion of Nocturns) according to the Proper of Time for Notre-Dame, in Wright, *Music and Ceremony*, Appendix B, "Parisian Hymnal." On the time of celebration of Matins at the cathedral of Notre-Dame at Paris, see Wright's 103, 110.

85. "Immense caeli conditor | qui, mixta ne confunderent | aque fluenta dividens | celum dedisti limitem | firmans locum celestibus | simulque terre rivulis...." Listed in Mone, *Hymni latini*, vol. 1, 372, as a hymn for Monday Vespers in Trier, Stadtbib. Mss. 1404, 1418; for Molesme, see Waddell, *Twelfth-Century Cistercian Hymnal*, vol. 1, bk. 1, p. 13.

86. "Telluris *ingens* Conditor | mundi solum qui separans | pul-

seventh-century hymn *Conditor alme siderum*.[87] Between Epiphany and Lent, religious in Paris would have called God "founder" yet again in chanting the hymn *Eterne rerum conditor* at Lauds.[88] Finally, during Lent their hymn, *Audi, benigne conditor*, would have been added to the liturgy of Terce.[89]

I hope to have shown by dissecting this example how, by looking at sources that come from precisely the time and place in which a work of medieval art or architecture was produced, we improve the likelihood that the iconological meanings we read are those that the planners and creators of the work expected viewers to comprehend. The rich troves of documents and treatises that are now available to scholars, with an ease of access that historians of art active in the 1950s could never have imagined, can help us to do so. Such examinations, to my mind, are far more precise than searching out a *Zeitgeist* in formal elements or structures, as a means to understanding past eras.

---

sis aque molestiis | terram dedisti immobilem | ut germen aptum proferens | fulvis decora floribus | fecunda fructu sisteret | pastumque gratum redderet...." Listed in Mone, *Hymni latini*, vol. 1, 372, for Tuesday Vespers in Trier, Stadtbib. MSS. 1404, 1418; also Waddell, *Twelfth-Century Cistercian Hymnal*, vol. 1, bk. 1, p. 13. Since the reforms under Urban VIII, this hymn has been altered.

87. "Conditor alme siderum | eterna lux credentium | Christe redemptor omnium | exaudi preces supplicum ..." When the Cistercians reformed their liturgy late in the twelfth century, they reworded the hymn to fit a more Pauline reading of the bible, so the actual text of the hymn sung by other religious in Paris would not have been precisely identical; Waddell, *Twelfth-Century Cistercian Hymnal*, vol. 1, bk. 1, 98; also vol. 1, bk. 1, 13, 96; vol. 2, 65, 67 (labeling the hymn as to be sung at Terce). See Wright, *Music and Ceremony*, Appendix B, "Parisian Hymnal," where this is the first hymn of the Proper of Time for Notre-Dame. By combining the services of the eight canonical hours into three, cathedral practice differed from that of monastic houses, so the clergy at Notre-Dame may not have sung every hymn included in the offices of nearby monastaries.

88. See Wright, *Music and Ceremony*, Appendix B, "Parisian Hymnal," where this hymn is accorded to Septuagesima Lauds; also listed in Mone, *Hymni latini*, vol. 1, 372 among the hymns for Sunday Lauds in Trier, Stadtbib. MS. 1418. This hymn was specifically named by Stephen Harding as the one to be sung every night of the year. Abelard confirms that they were doing so in the early twelfth century, and states that this was contrary to the practice of the rest of the Church, who varied the hymn by time of year and according to the proper of saints, Waddell, *Twelfth-Century Cistercian Hymnal*, vol. 2, p. 6, for Abelard's remarks; also, vol. 1, bk. 1, 7; vol. 2, 9, 14–15.

89. See Waddell, *Twelfth-Century Cistercian Hymnal*, vol. 1, bk. 1, 14, bk. 2, 102; vol. 2, 115, 117. There had been theologians at Paris who identified God the Creator as *conditor mundi* since the early twelfth century; see e.g. Hugh of St. Victor, *De Sacramentis*, prolog., c. 2 (Migne PL: 176), col. 183: "Materia divinarum Scripturarum omnium sunt opera restaurationis humanae. Duo enim sunt opera ... Primum est opus conditionis.... Ergo opus conditionis est creatio mundi cum omnibus elementis suis."

DANY SANDRON

The Cathedral Façade: Monumental Sculpture in Context from the Twelfth to the Sixteenth Centuries[1]

IN THIS ESSAY the works of art at which I will be looking are large-scale carvings that, although located in high places, can be seen from considerable distances. Large isolated figures or series of statues, or even combinations of both, were used to address and engage the public. The examples chosen for this study are found in the northern part of France, and are dated from the twelfth to the sixteenth centuries. Large buildings, such as Gothic cathedrals, are typical locations in which this monumental sculpture is found. Interestingly, this kind of sculpture, especially when it is of a declamatory nature, has been less studied than the portals in such buildings, which, of course, are more accessible and easier to view. One exception to this lack of research are the many galleries of the kings, which really are the perfect example of sculpted monumentalization in the Gothic period, but whose meaning still remains problematic.[2] The fact that there is a focus on sculptural iconography in the upper elevations of these buildings, which are more densely placed compared to the particularly spacious portals in the lower parts, is a unifying factor in all these monuments.

Patron Saints

It is not surprising that the patron of the church is placed in a prominent position on the outside of many buildings. In Notre-Dame de Paris, for example (Fig. 1), the Virgin, between two angels, surmounts the gallery of the kings in front of the western rose window.[3] At Chartres (Fig. 2), the mother of God is found on three gables (nave and transept arms).[4] At Strasbourg, the statue of the Virgin was planned to top the cathedral's spire.[5] The statue of St. Firmin, first bishop and martyr, was placed on top of the north tower of the façade of Amiens Cathedral at the beginning of the fifteenth century (Fig. 3).[6]

As another example, histories, both local and legendary, are frequently evoked in the sculpture of many such buildings. The eight large oxen on top of Laon

1. I am grateful to Panayota Volti for the translation of the text into English.

2. J. G. von Katzenellenbogen, *Die Königsgalerie der französischen Kathedrale, Herkunft, Bedeutung, Nachfolge* (Munich, 1965); D. Sandron, "Galerie des Rois," in *Dictionnaire d'Histoire de l'Art du Moyen Âge occidental*, P. Charron and J.-M. Guillouët, eds. (Paris, 2009), 384–385.

3. A. Erlande-Brandenburg, *Notre-Dame de Paris, Histoire, architecture, sculpture* (Paris, 1990); D. Sandron, "La galerie des rois de Notre-Dame de Paris," in *Commission du Vieux Paris, Procès-verbaux*, 2 mai 2002, no. 5, 10–15.

4. A. Prache, *La cathédrale de Chartres, image de la Jérusalem Céleste* (Paris, 1993); P. Kurmann, B. Kurmann-Schwarz, *Chartres: la cathédrale* (Saint-Léger-Vauban, 2001).

5. D. Sandron, "'L'art n'a jamais rien produit de plus élevé': l'octogone et la fleche," in *Strasbourg 1400. Un foyer d'art dans l'Europe gothique*, Ph. Lorentz, ed. (Strasbourg, 2008), 100–117, with bibliography.

6. G. Durand, *Monographie de l'église Notre-Dame, cathédrale d'Amiens*, 3 vols. (Paris, 1901–1903); D. Sandron, *Amiens, la cathédrale* (Paris, 2004).

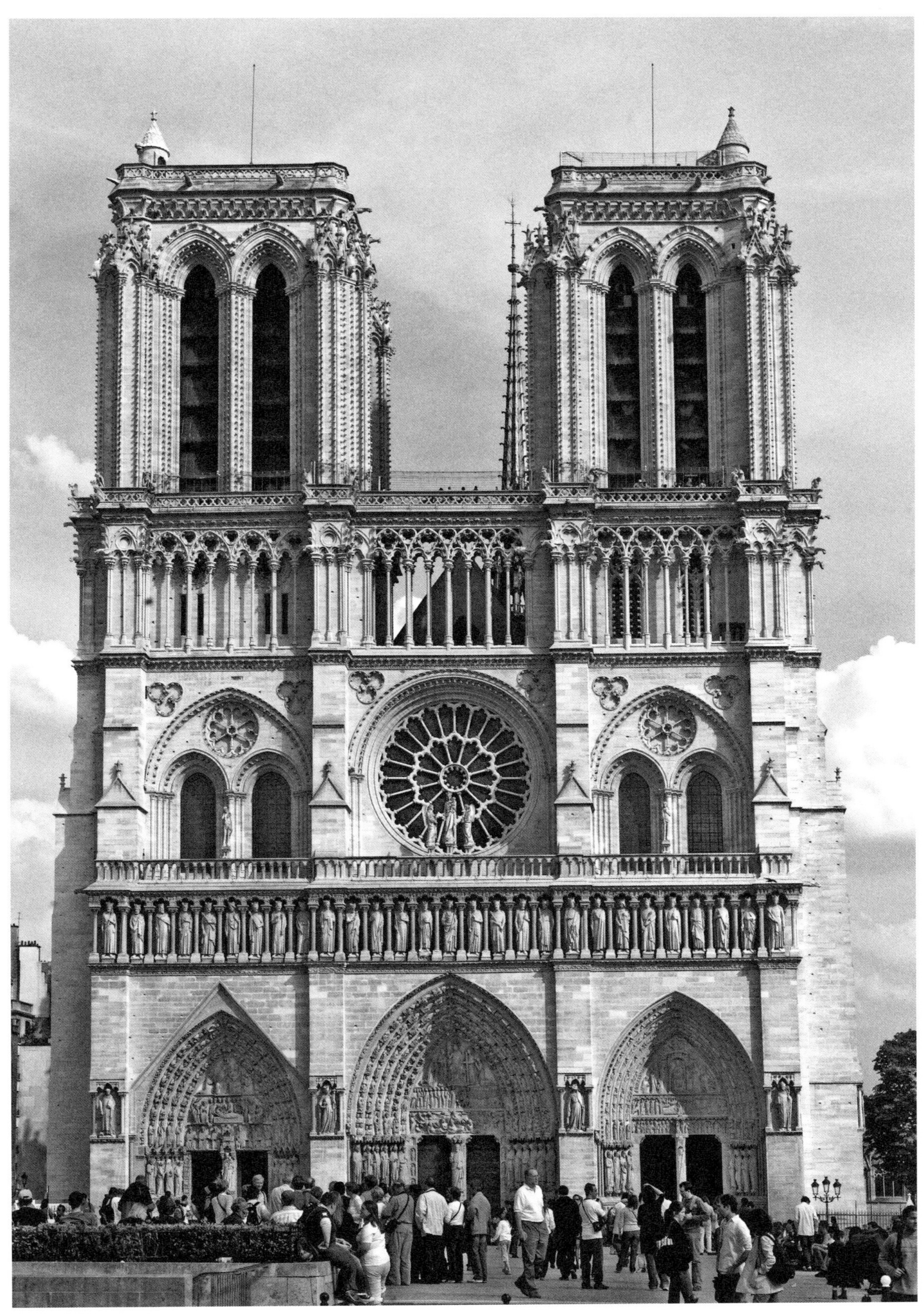

FIGURE 1. Paris, Notre-Dame Cathedral, west façade (photo: Centre Chastel, Christian Lemzaouda).

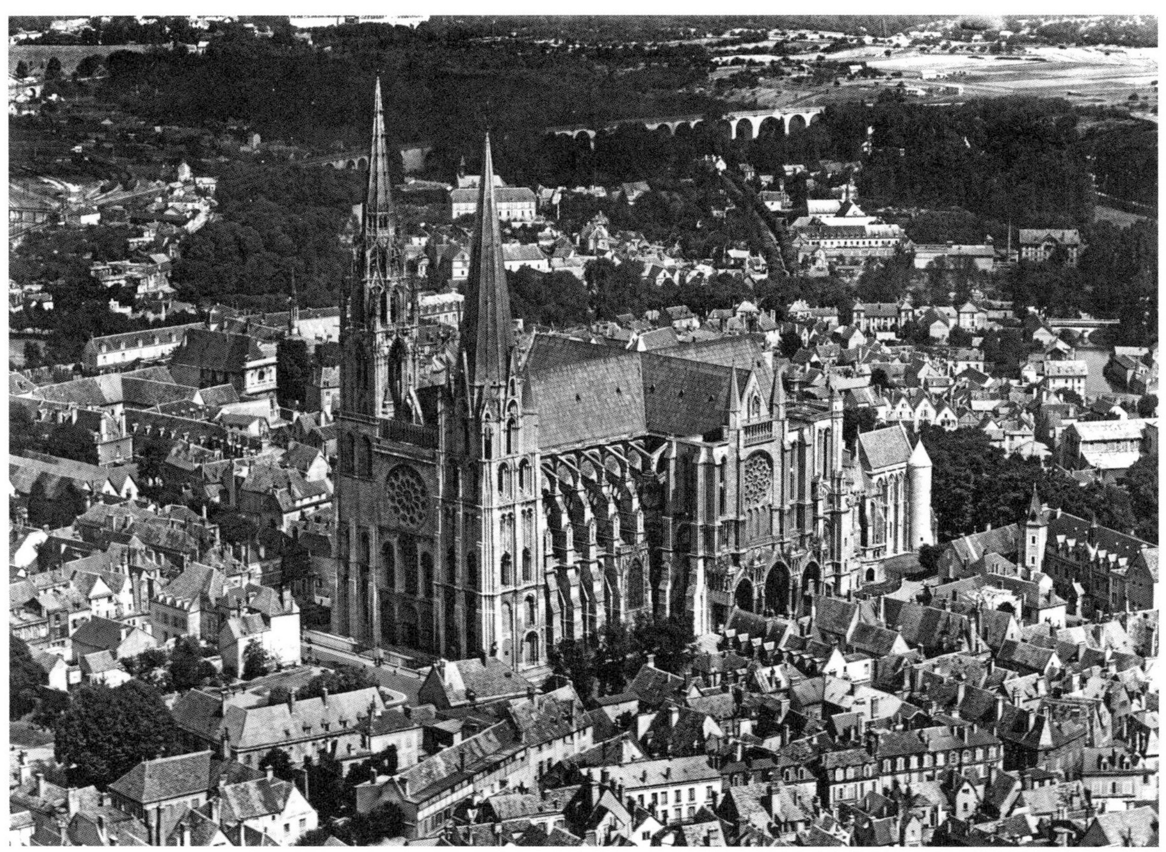

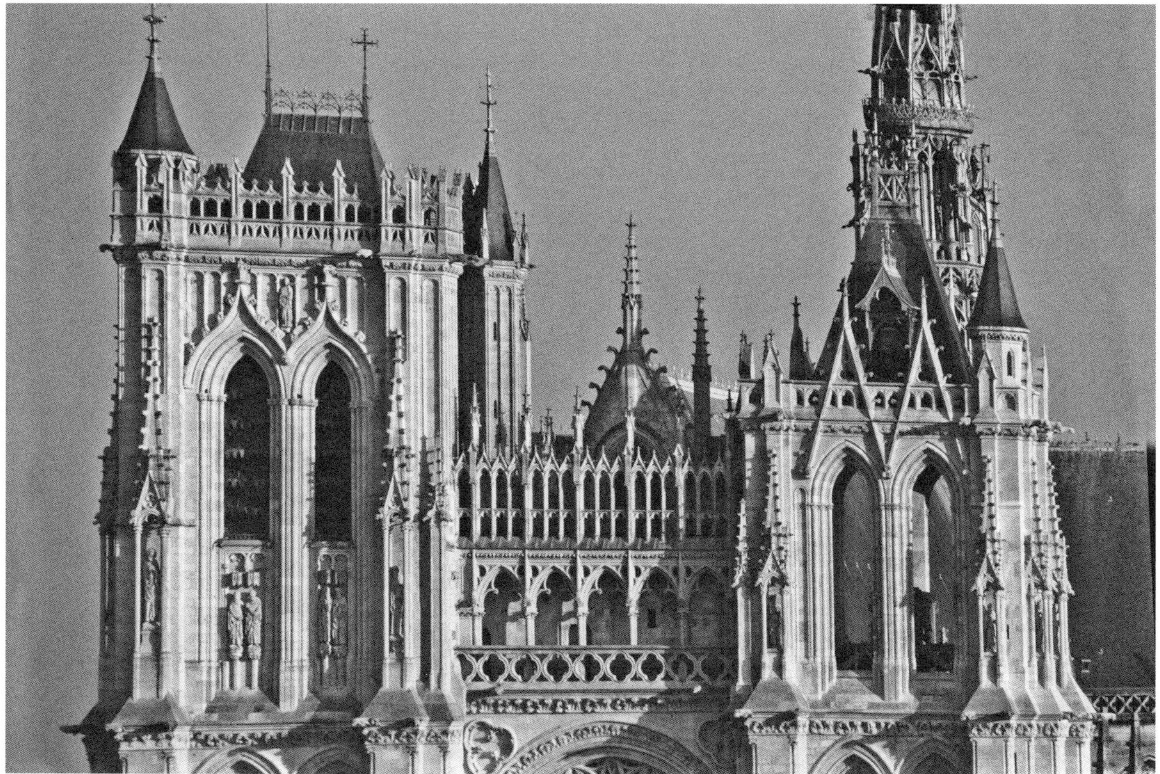

FIGURE 2. Chartres Cathedral, aerial view from the southwest (photo: Centre Chastel).

FIGURE 3. Amiens Cathedral, upper elevation of the west towers (photo: Centre Chastel, Christian Lemzaouda).

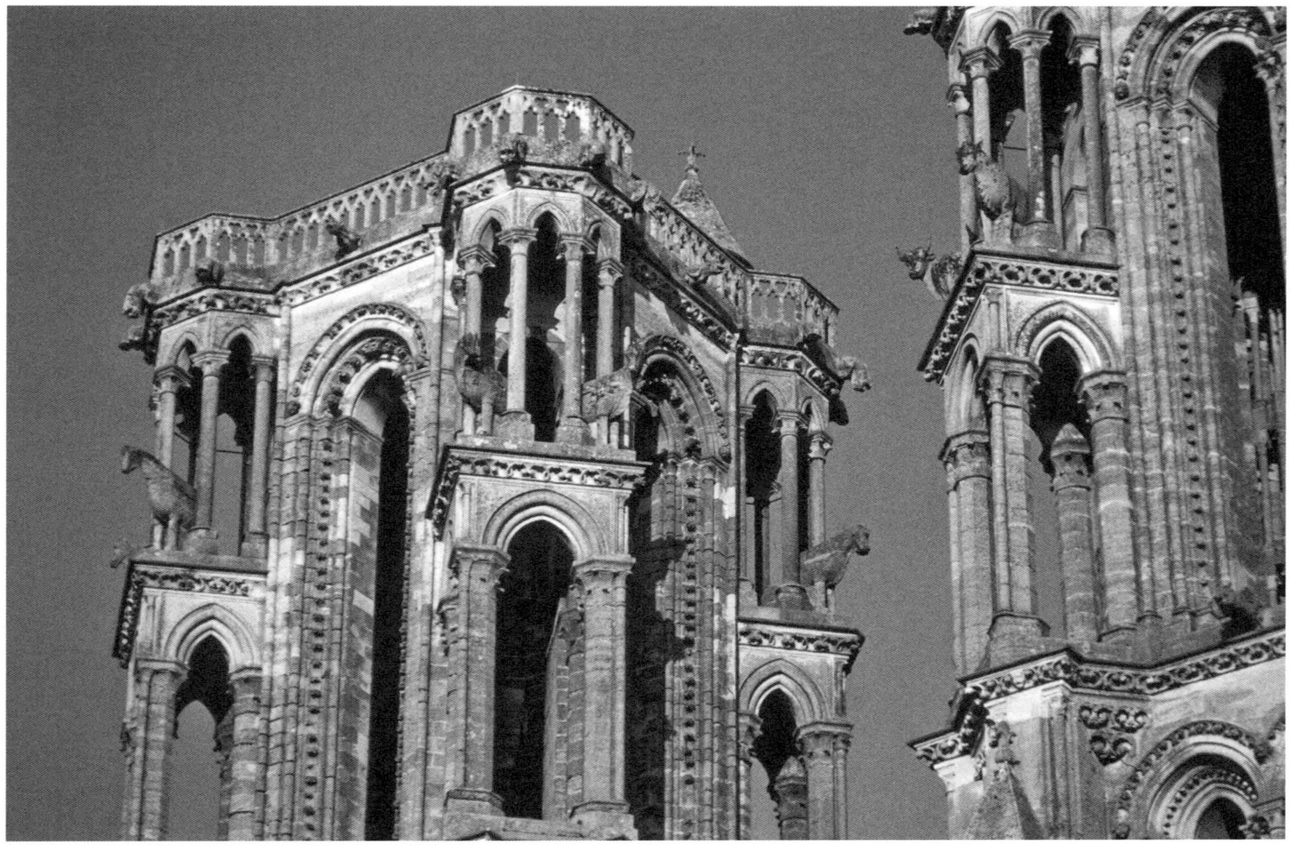

FIGURE 4. Laon Cathedral, upper elevation of the west towers (photo: Centre Chastel).

Cathedral's towers are associated with a miracle mentioned by Guibert de Nogent in the first half of the twelfth century (Fig. 4).[7] This relates to an event that happened as the site was being built, before the actual construction of the church began. After a fire in 1112, an ox miraculously appeared to help with the work and was replaced by another one when the first was tired. These oxen helped carry the stones and there was, thus, no interruption to the work. After almost a century, these oxen high up on the cathedral's façade still commemorate that miraculous event in Laon's ecclesiastical history. Other local saints are frequently evoked and commemorated in the form of statues on top of the gables in such buildings. St. Marcel stands on top of the gable of the southern transept of the cathedral of Notre-Dame de Paris,[8] and St. Denis is on the western gable of the nave in the royal abbey-church near Paris.[9]

Dating to around 1300, the kings who are shown rid-

7. Guibert de Nogent, *Autobiographie*, ed. E.-R. Labande (Paris, 1981), Book III, Chap. 13: 392–393: ... *un clerc fort estimable, qui avait été chargé d'assurer les transports de matériaux pour la réparation des toits de l'église, m'a raconté comment un jour, en gravissant la montagne, un des boeufs, épuisé, s'effondra. Le clerc alors s'affaire fort, mais il ne trouvait pas de boeuf à placer sous le joug de celui qui était défaillant. Et voici que, tout à coup, un boeuf accourut là s'offrir, comme si de propos délibéré, il était venu se mettre à son service. Ce nouvel auxiliaire tira gaillardement avec les autres le chariot jusqu'à l'église, mais ensuite le clerc était très anxieux de savoir à qui il devait restituer ce boeuf inconnu. Or celui-ci, à peine détaché, sans attendre guide ni conducteur, s'en retourne encore plus vite dans la direction même d'où il était venu.*

8. D. Kimpel, *Die Querhausarme von Notre-Dame zu Paris und ihre Skulpturen* (Bonn, 1971).

9. Louvre, inv. RF 436, F. Baron, *Sculpture française I Moyen Age. Musée du Louvre. Département des sculptures du Moyen Âge, de la Renaissance et des temps modernes* (Paris, 1996), 94, High: 1, 925 m. On the Rayonnant church of St.-Denis, see C. Bruzelius, *The Thirteenth-Century Church at St. Denis* (New Haven, London, 1985).

ing on the façade of Strasbourg Cathedral represent the royal protection of Clovis, Dagobert, and Rudolph of Habsbourg at the end of the thirteenth century (Fig. 5).[10] Louis XIV added his own effigy in 1681 after the incorporation of the city into the French kingdom.

Functions

These carvings found in the upper levels of the buildings also have definite purposes. The western façade of Reims Cathedral (Fig. 6) offers an eloquent example with its gallery of kings who are focused on Clovis' baptism. This must be an allusion to the coronation of the French kings that took place below in the cathedral itself. The scenes of Solomon and David in the arches and spandrels of the western rose window in the same building are also easily explained in relation to the many biblical references of the contemporary French coronation ceremony.[11]

The monumental sculpture of the coronation of the Virgin at the top of the façade in the southern transept of Rouen Cathedral (Fig. 7) is another example of the same scene that is found in the gable of the central portal of the Cathedral at Reims. Markus Schlicht has recently discussed the significance of the ducal title given by the first Valois king, Philippe VI, in honor of his elder son, Jean, the future Jean le Bon.[12] In much the same way, the coronation of the Virgin, patroness of the cathedral, could also be an allusion to the ancestral quality of Rouen Cathedral, which had been the church in which the dukes of Normandy were crowned. This could explain why the scene was borrowed from the coronation church and was given such a formal treatment, found as it is under a baldachin, which is shaped by the spreading out of innumerable canopies.

Relics & Shrines

We have already seen the statue of St. Marcel above the façade of the southern transept in the Cathedral of Notre-Dame de Paris (Fig. 8). Its presence there raises the question as to whether this representation of the saintly bishop of Paris is closely related to the nearby sanctuary. The body of St. Marcel was kept in an impressively large reliquary directly above the cathedral's sanctuary. This expensive shrine was made around 1260 in an architectural form, consisting of a large structure flanked by long side aisles of six bays and crowned in the middle by a spire. The transept, which was modified by architects Jean de Chelles and Pierre de Montreuil, would have offered a reflection of what lay below.[13] In this case, the architecture and sculpture (that of the portals, as well as that of the upper levels) resonated with the main treasure of the cathedral's sanctuary, the shrine.

Similarly, the façade of Auxerre Cathedral was designed to inspire (Fig. 9). The number of recesses is astonishing; seventy-four were built, and there were some 111 in all, if the symmetrical façade with two towers is included. It is clear that it was a building meant to hold many statues.[14] Here, prophets, apostles, or saints, scenes related to their lives, and even episodes from Christ's life were found. Sadly, only the statue of St. Christopher has been preserved. Although, if we compare it to the nearby St. Peter's church (to the north of the cathedral), it is very likely that the cathedral's

10. The oldest mention of the kings dates from 1521; R. Will, "Les statues équestres d'empereurs et de rois—un décor de façade insolite à la cathédrale de Strasbourg," in *Bulletin de la cathédrale de Strasbourg* 21 (1994), 21–26; P. Kurmann, "Deutsche Kaiser und Könige. Zum spätstaufischen Herrscherzyklus und zur Reiterfigur Rudolfs von Habsburg am Strassburger Münster," in *Kunst im Reich Kaiser Friedrichs II. von Hohenstaufen*, vol. 2, A. Knaak ed. (Munich, Berlin, 1997), 154–169.

11. W. Sauerländer, "Observations sur la topographie et l'iconologie de la cathédrale du sacre," in *Comptes rendus de l'Académie des inscriptions et belles-lettres*, 1992 (1994), 463–479.

12. M. Schlicht, "La cathédrale de Rouen vers 1300. Portail des Libraires, portail de la Calende, chapelle de la Vierge," in *Mémoires de la Société des Antiquaires de Normandie*, XLI (2005), 357–359.

13. D. Sandron, "Une savante mise en scène des reliques: l'architecture et le décor monumental de Notre-Dame de Paris dans la seconde moitié du XIIIe siècle," *Revue d'Histoire Ecclésiastique* (forthcoming).

14. H. Titus, "The Architectural History of Auxerre Cathedral," Ph.D. Diss., Princeton (1984); D. Sandron, "Auxerre, la façade," in *Une cathédrale en chantier: Saint-Etienne d'Auxerre*, C. Sapin, ed., colloquium Auxerre (forthcoming).

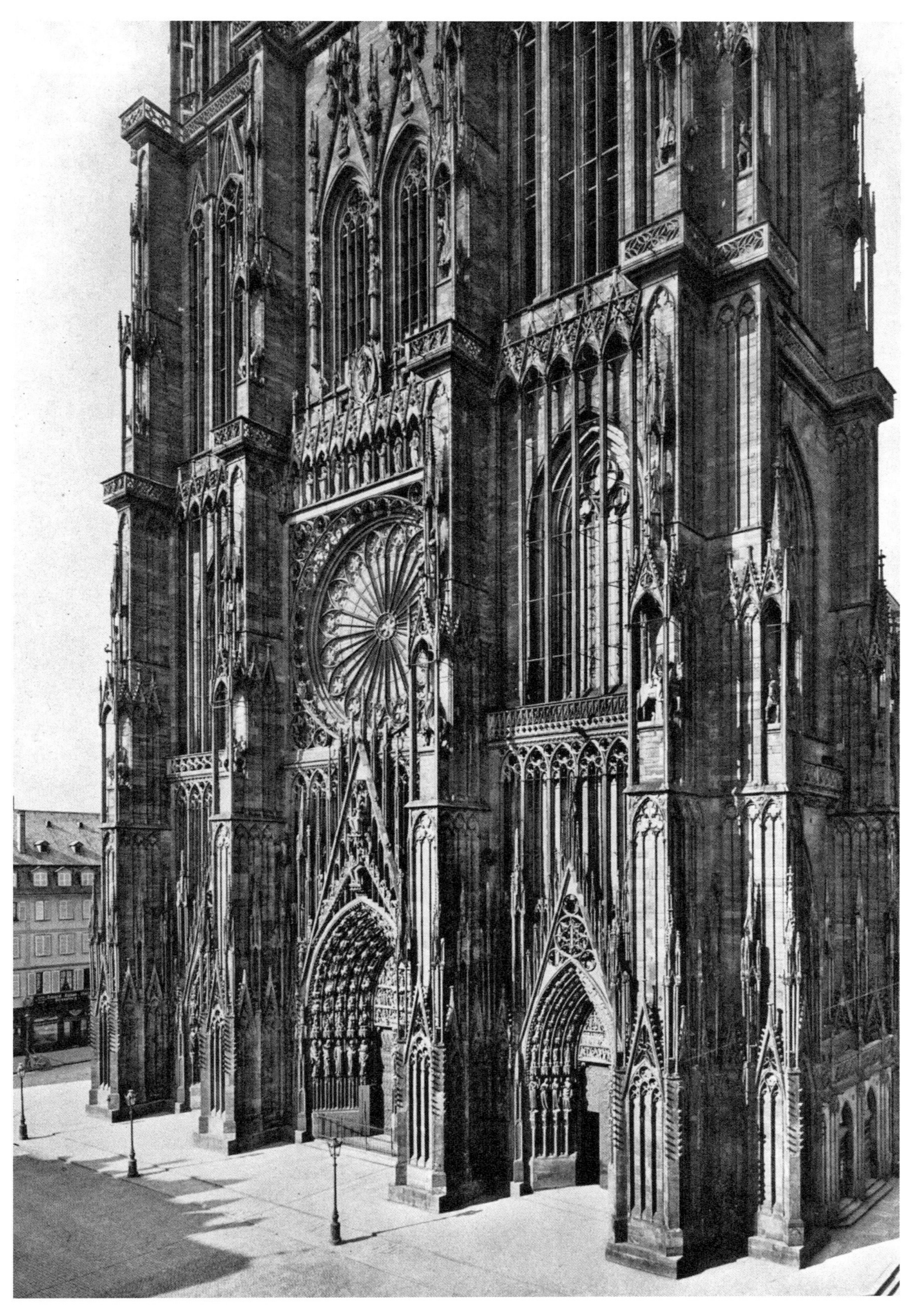

FIGURE 5. Strasbourg Cathedral, west façade (photo: Centre Chastel).

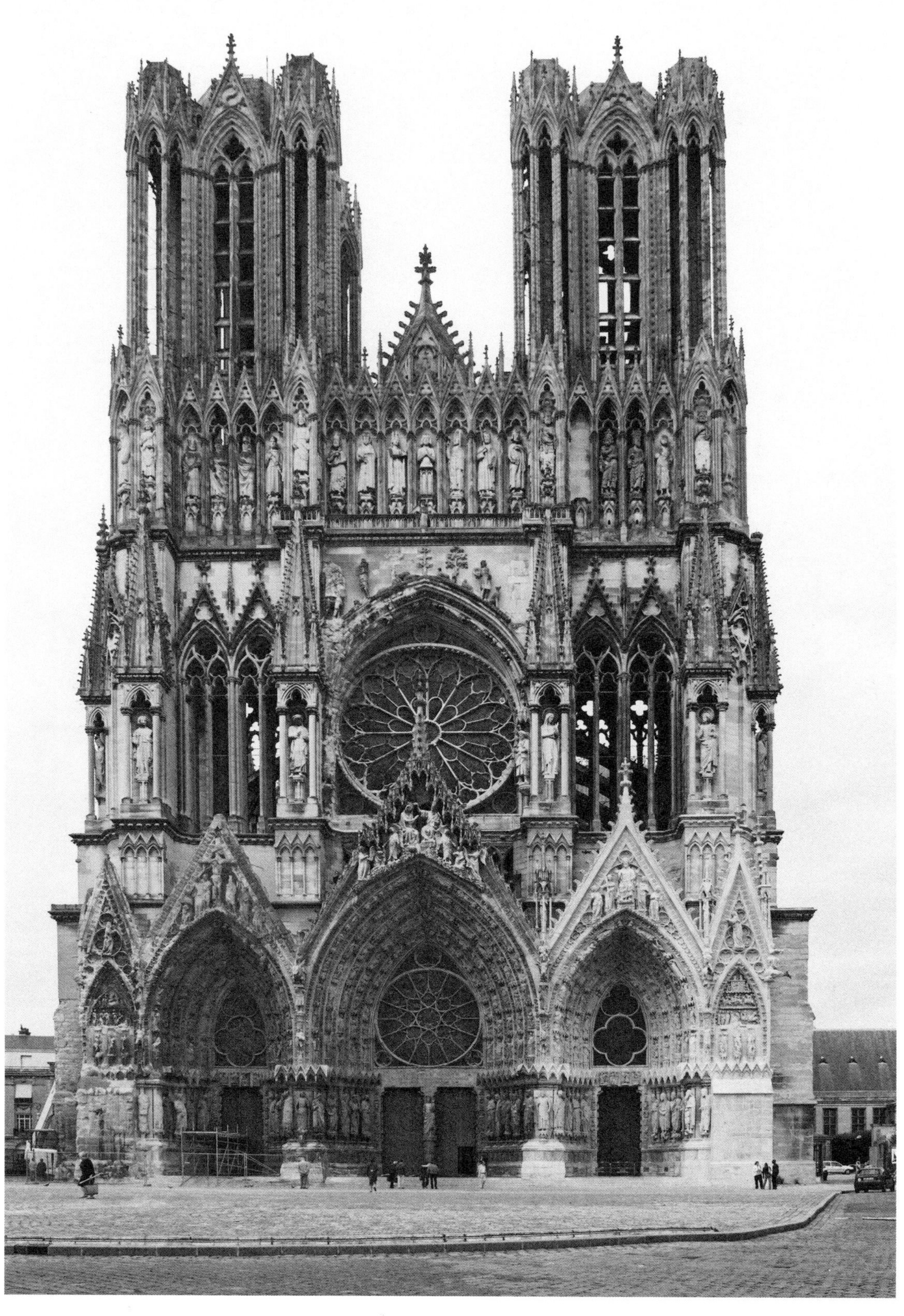

FIGURE 6. Reims Cathedral, west façade (photo: Centre Chastel, Christian Lemzaouda).

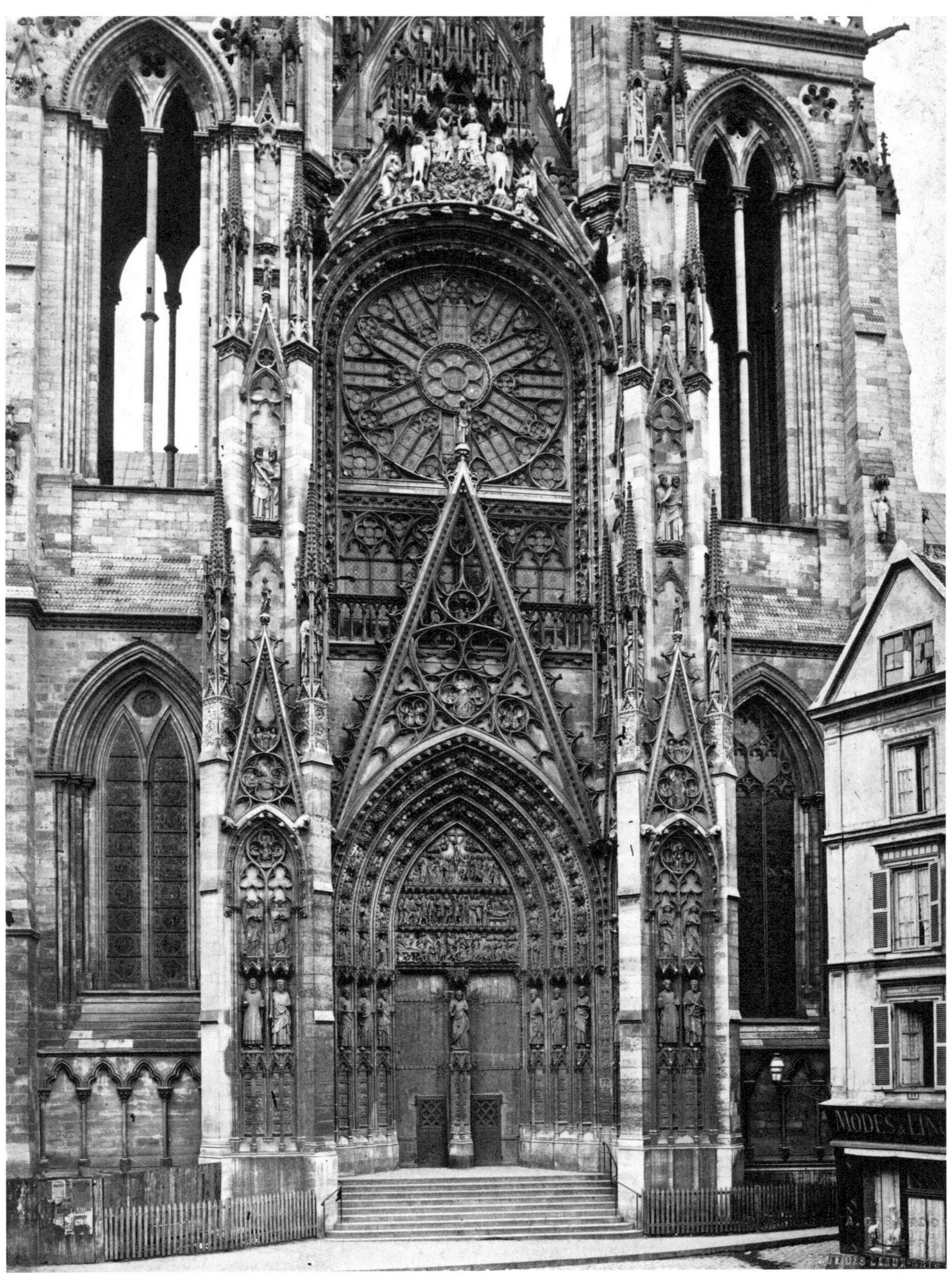

FIGURE 7. Rouen Cathedral, Portal in the south transept façade (photo: Centre Chastel).

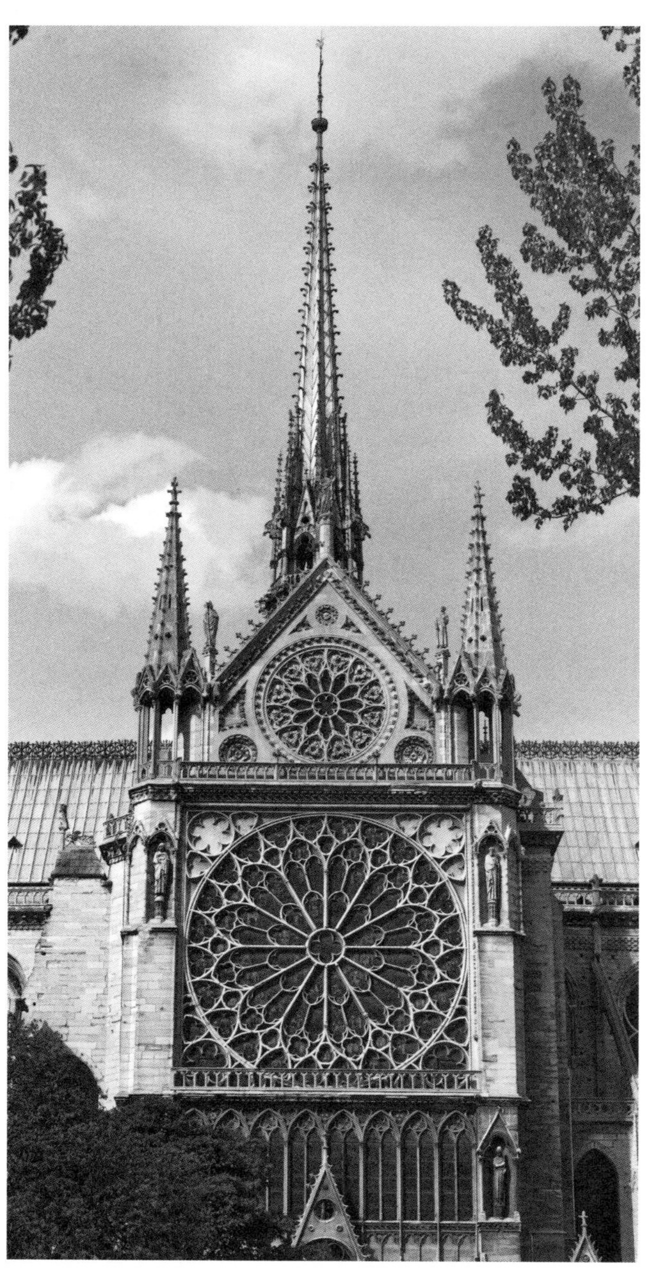

FIGURE 8. Paris, Notre-Dame Cathedral, south transept (photo: Centre Chastel, Christian Lemzaouda).

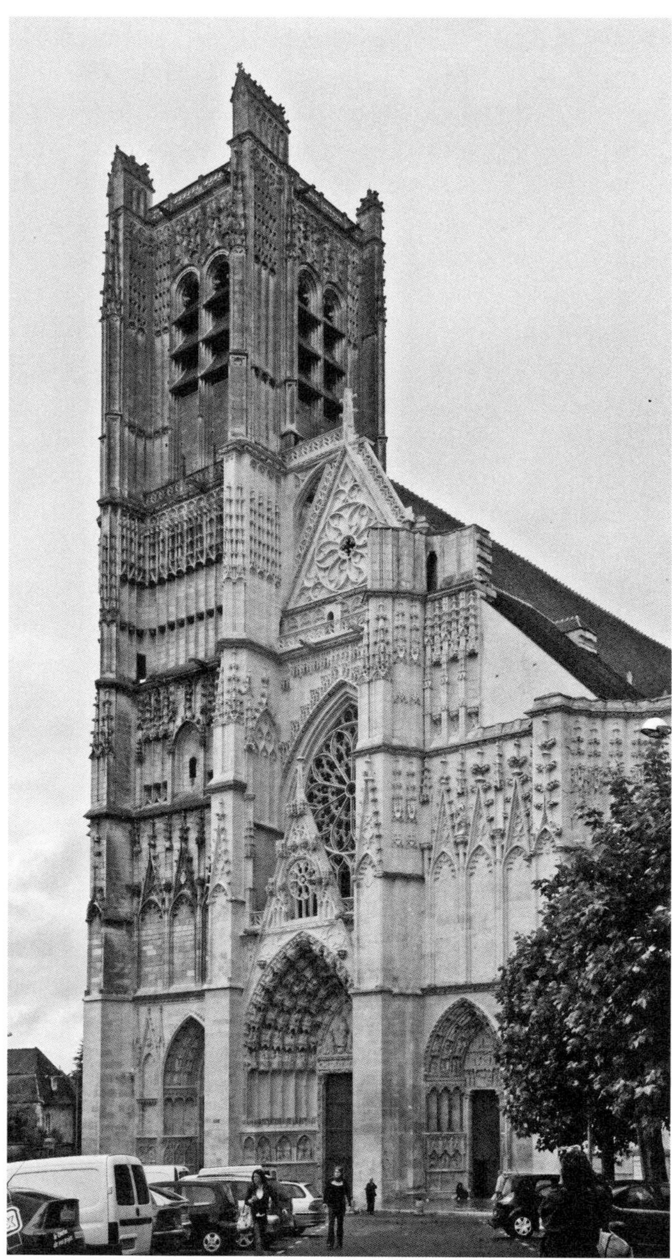

FIGURE 9. Auxerre Cathedral, west façade (photo: Centre Chastel, Céline Gumiel).

façade also had statues of local bishops. A bishops' cycle would not have been out of place in this church, where bishops were honored and celebrated since the early Middle Ages.[15] A series of stained glass windows showing their lineage is found in the cathedral. When the tower in the façade was finished, sometime before 1543, the bishop François II de Dinteville took care to commemorate his predecessors with a series of paintings he commissioned on St. Peter's life and miracles and then installed in the Chapel of St.-Germain.[16] He also installed other paintings that decorated the walls of the Chapel of St.-Sébastien depicting the "bishops of Auxerre for whom we celebrate the office or who are considered blessed."[17] The fact that the tower of Auxerre's Cathedral was decorated at its summit with statues of bishops and other saints could then explain the unusual treatment of the buttresses' ridge that stands higher than the roof of the bell-tower (Fig. 10). Unusually shaped, the saddle-roof is marked in the middle with a pinnacle (only the lower bit remains), which recalls the gold-plated shrines in the sanctuary. Here, the bodies and earthly remains of saints, such as St. Amâtre, who preceded the famous St. Germain, were kept. Nothing less than magnificent reliquaries could be used to indicate the sacred character of the place and the building itself, which was prominently displayed in the city as well as the countryside for miles around.

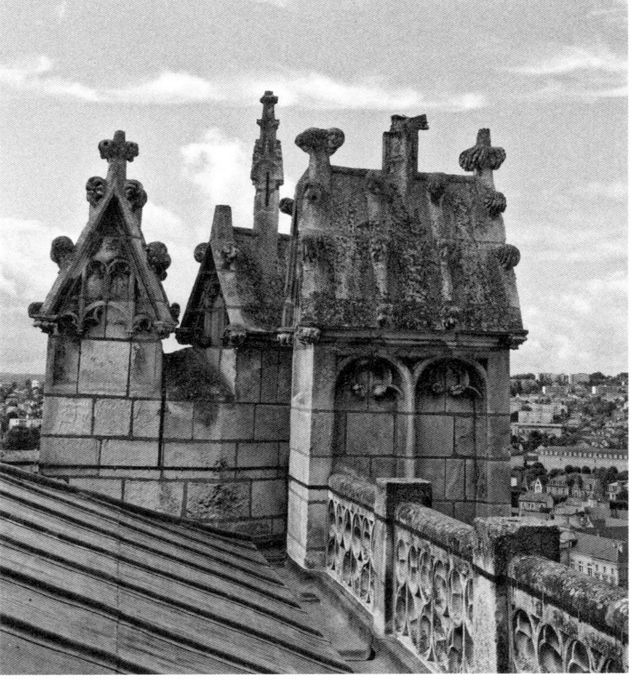

FIGURE 10. Auxerre Cathedral, top of the buttresses (photo: Centre Chastel, Céline Gumiel).

Monumental sculpture can also be used in a more general way to highlight special subjects not found elsewhere in such buildings. The oxen on top of Laon's towers, setting aside the anecdotal legend of the miracle, repeat the theme found below in the archivolts of the windows beside the rose window on the façade (Fig. 11). Iliana Kasarska has recently shown how the subject of exalting man's work (liberal arts, medicine, architecture on the north side), parallels that of God (Creation on the south side).[18] An echo of this is also found in the oxen on top of the building that shows divine intervention in miraculously replacing the failing animal. Villard de Honnecourt's sketch of one of Laon's towers adds a significant detail showing the hand of God (Fig. 12).[19]

At Strasbourg, the representation of the Last Judgment on the belfry, which was added between the towers of the façade in the last third of the fourteenth century (Fig. 13),[20] also repeats the theme found inside the building close to the Angels' pillar, erected in the

15. C. Sapin, ed., *Auxerre*, Centre national d'Archéologie urbaine (Tours, 1998), 34.

16. J. Lebeuf, *Mémoire concernant l'histoire ecclésiastique et civile d'Auxerre...*, vol. 2 (Paris, 1743), 127.

17. *Ibid.*

18. I. Kasarska, *La sculpture de la façade de la cathédrale de Laon. Eschatologie et humanisme* (Paris, 2008).

19. Paris, Bibliothèque nationale de France, MS. fr. 19093, fol. 10r; cf. H. Hahnloser, *Villard de Honnecourt, Kritische Gesamtausgabe*, 2nd ed. (Graz, 1972), 49–55, and D. Sandron, "La cathédrale et l'architecte: à propos de la façade occidentale de Laon," in *Pierre, lumière, couleurs. Études d'histoire de l'art du Moyen Âge offertes à Anne Prache*, F. Joubert and D. Sandron, eds. (Paris, 1999), 133–150.

20. D. Borlée, "Le beffroi de la cathédrale de Strasbourg: un singulier aménagement de la fin du XIVe siècle," in *Strasbourg 1400. Un foyer d'art dans l'Europe gothique*, P. Lorentz, ed. (Strasbourg, 2008), 80–93; D. Borlée and D. Sandron, "La place du beffroi dans l'espace urbain," in *Strasbourg 1400. Un foyer d'art dans l'Europe gothique*, Ph. Lorentz, ed. (Strasbourg, 2008), 94–99.

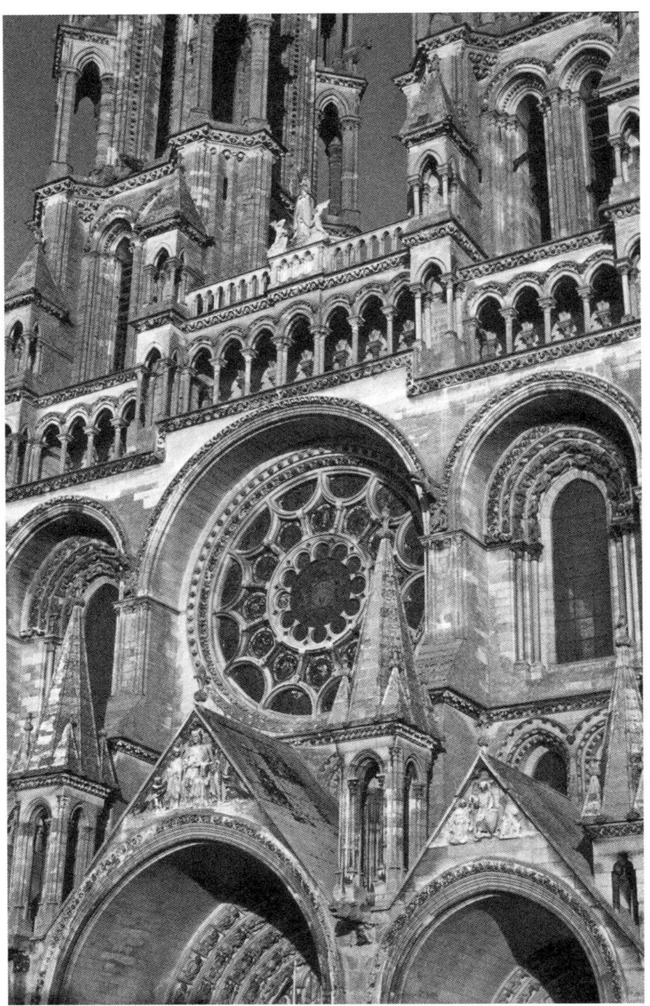

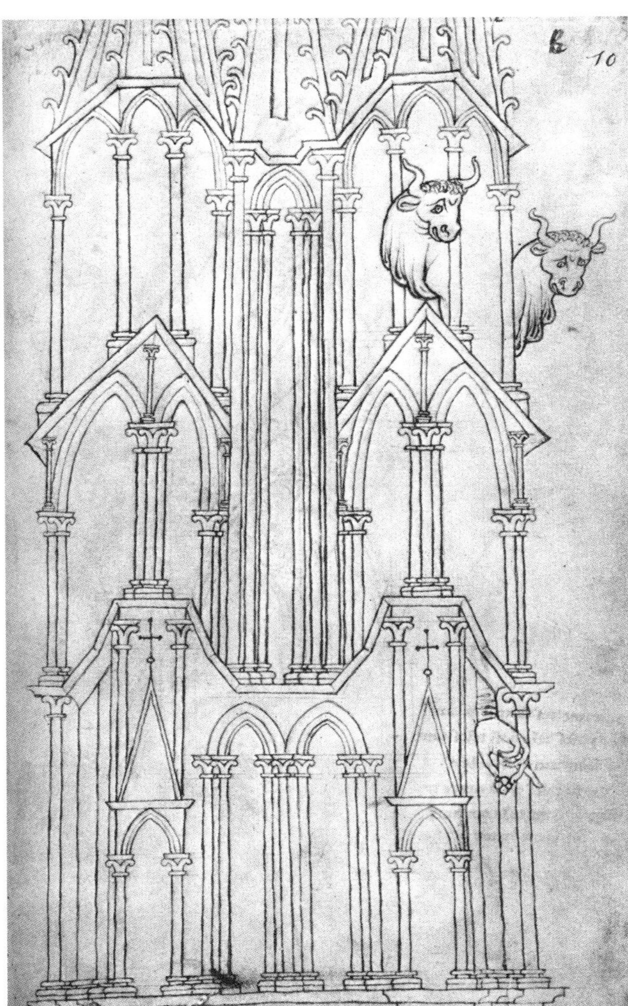

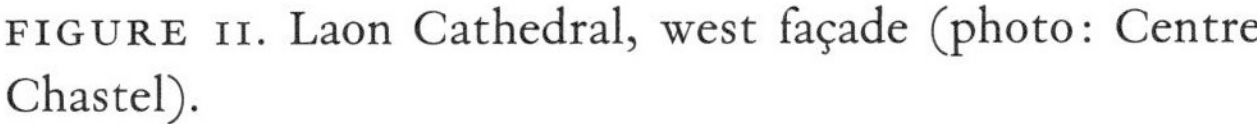

FIGURE 11. Laon Cathedral, west façade (photo: Centre Chastel).

FIGURE 12. Villard de Honnecourt, drawing of a tower in Laon Cathedral, Paris, Bibliothèque nationale de France, MS. fr. 19093, fol. 10r (photo: Bibliothèque nationale de France).

1220s.[21] This was certainly not accidental, as it is possible to see the municipality's wish to commemorate itself through the church. This was done on the one hand by adding the very intrusive belfry, and on the other by repeating the same iconographical themes, and even by replacing the clergy's time keeping by its own means and with its own bells.

Similarly, in Strasbourg, the spire of Jean Hültz (Fig. 14), which was finished in 1439, was surmounted by a statue of the Virgin and child. With its characteristic silhouette, it was unique and echoed the theme of the central portal which was the Virgin/Solomon's throne, and on the degrees occupied by lions (Fig. 15).[22]

This leads us to question the integration (or lack thereof) within the urban landscape for monumental sculpture located in high places. The churches at Laon

21. W. Sauerländer, "Strasbourg, cathédrale. Le bras sud du transept: architecture et sculpture," in *Congrès Archéologique de France. Strasbourg et Basse-Alsace*, 2004 (Paris, 2006), 171–184.

22. D. Sandron, "'L'art n'a jamais rien produit de plus élevé': l'octogone et la flèche," in *Strasbourg 1400. Un foyer d'art dans l'Europe gothique*, Ph. Lorentz, ed. (Strasbourg, 2008), 100–117. On the Central Portal, see B. Van Den Bossche, *La cathédrale de Strasbourg. Sculpture des portails occidentaux* (Paris, 2006), and B. Boerner,

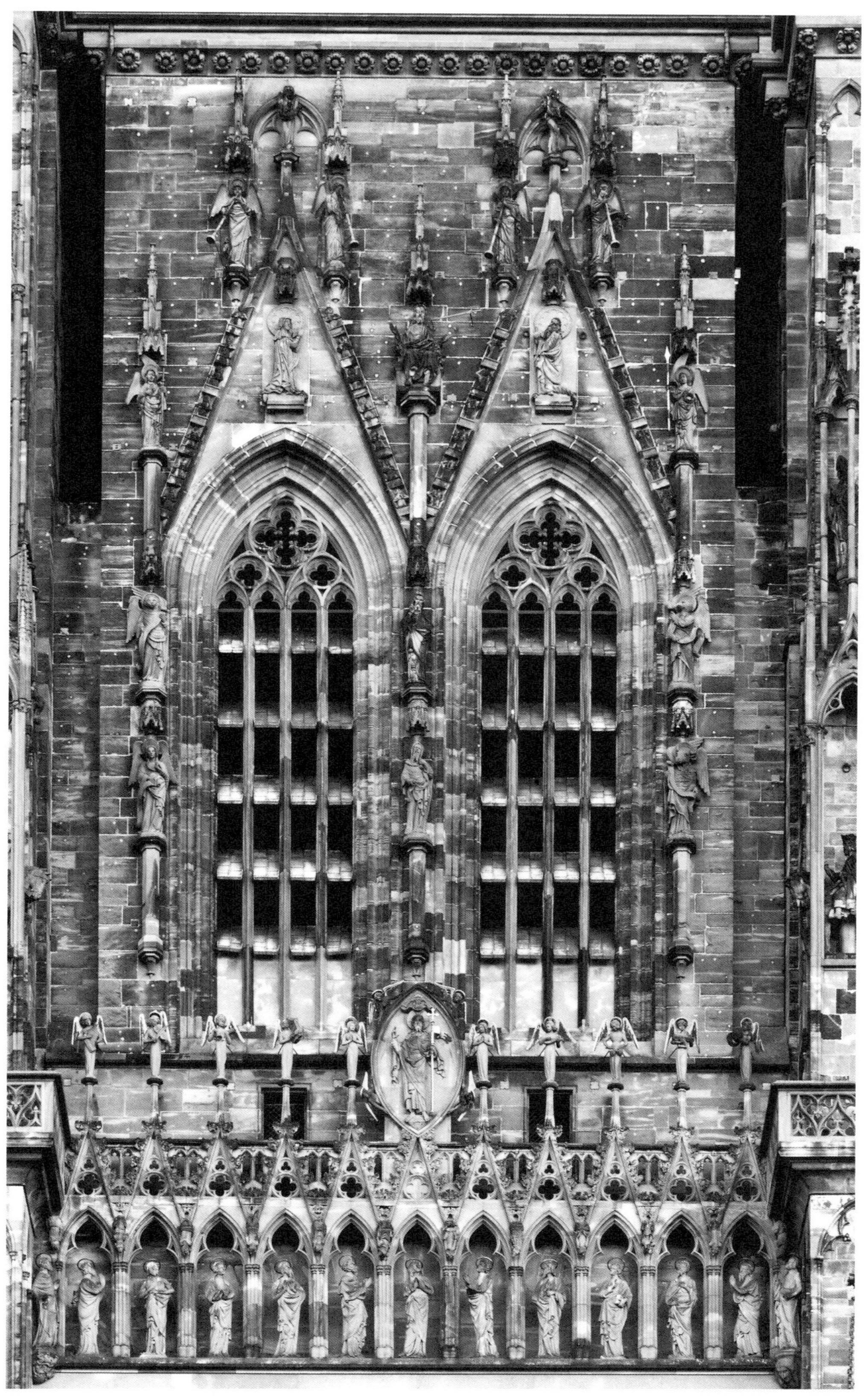

FIGURE 13. Strasbourg Cathedral, detail of belfry (photo: musées de Strasbourg, Mathieu Bertola).

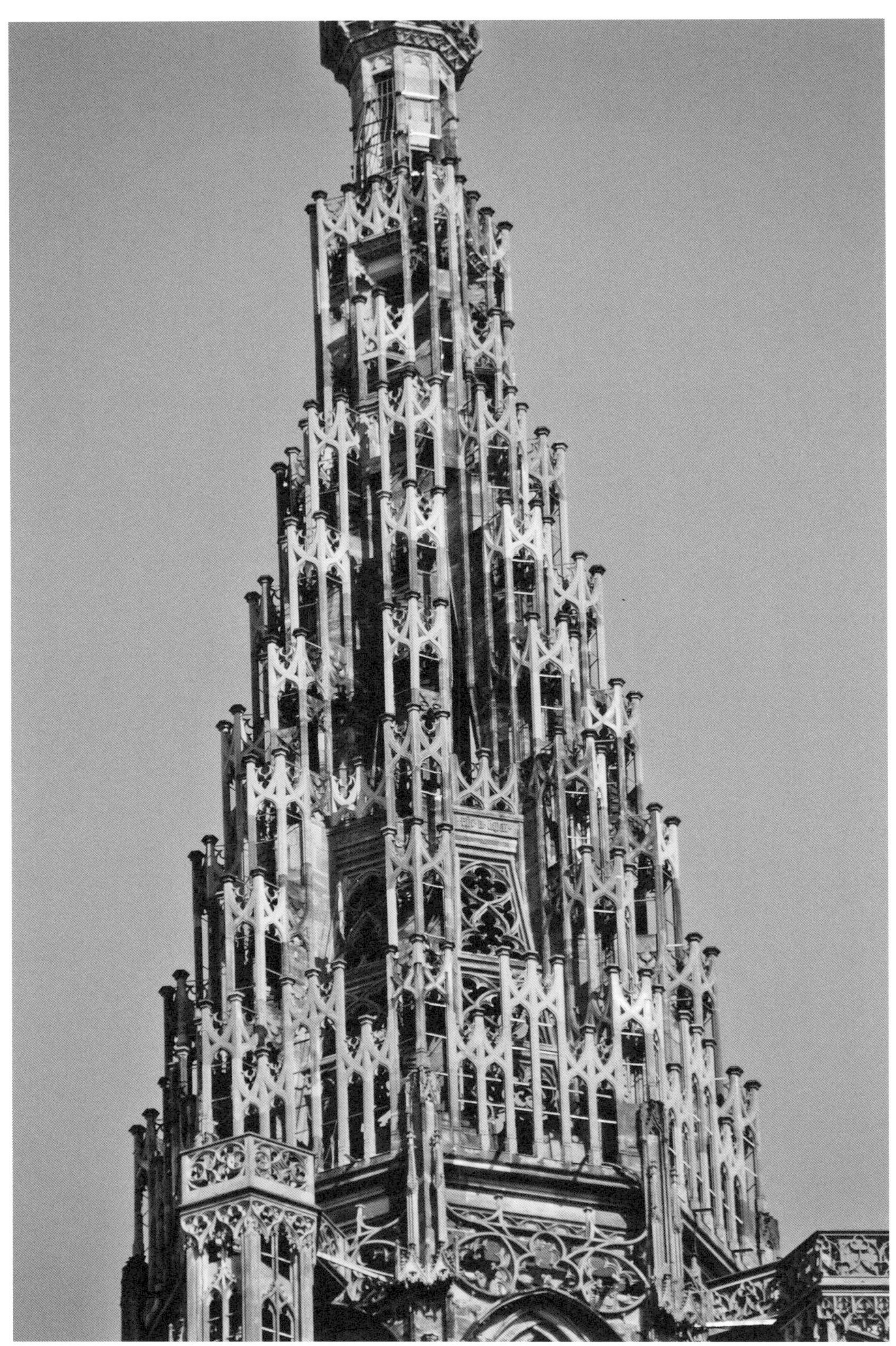

FIGURE 14. Strasbourg Cathedral, detail of spire (photo: author).

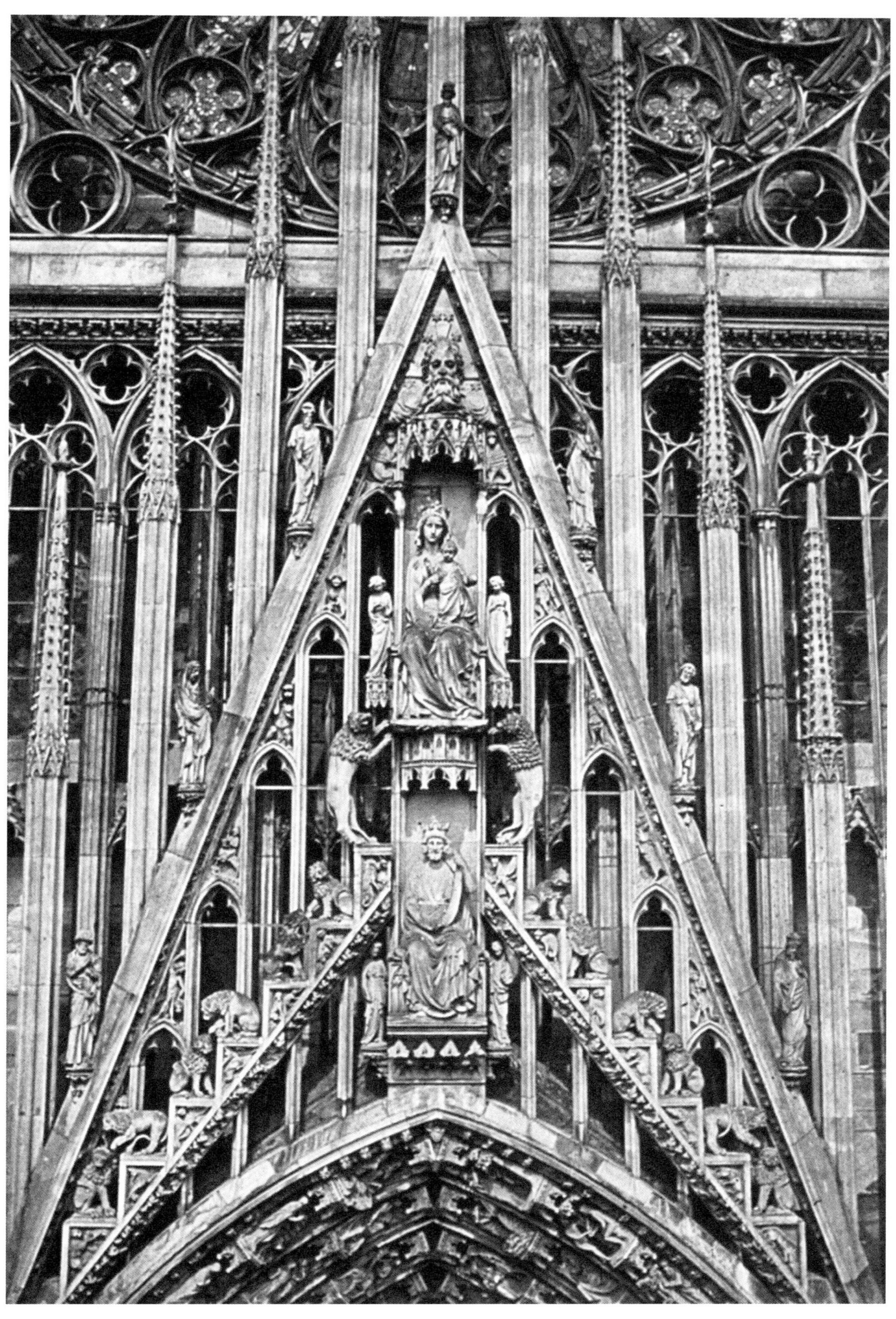

FIGURE 15. Strasbourg Cathedral, detail of central portal of the west façade (photo: musées de Strasbourg, Mathieu Bertola).

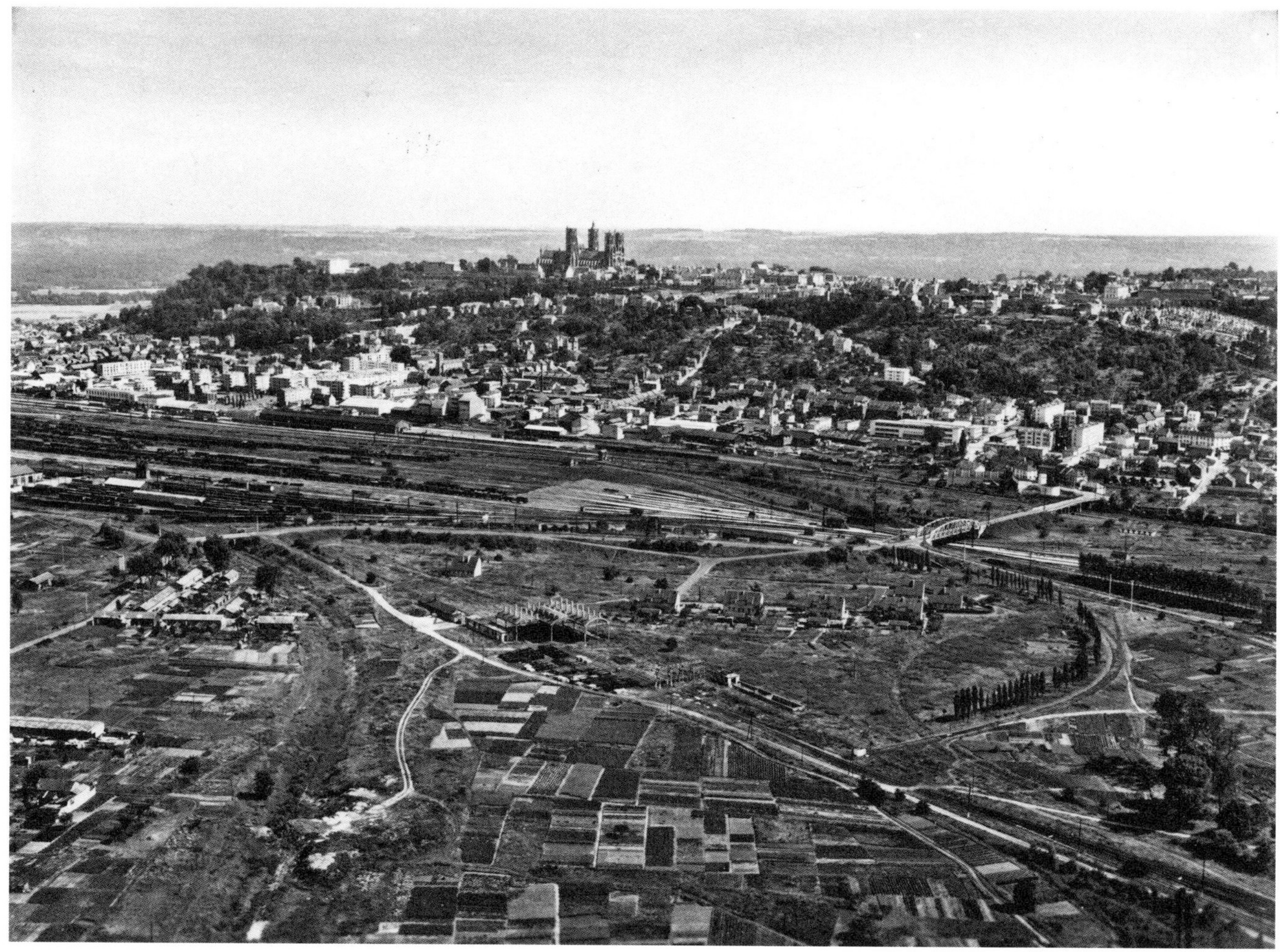

FIGURE 16. Laon, view of the town from the north-west (photo: Centre Chastel).

(Fig. 16) and Strasbourg can be readily seen from considerable distances. At Rouen Cathedral, the Coronation of the Virgin under the gable over the rose window in the south transept can be seen best in the town and especially from the river Seine (Fig. 17).

In the Cathedral of Notre-Dame de Paris, the gallery of the kings on the façade could not be seen in the Middle Ages, except from the parvis, which was considerably smaller than the present square. Only the central part could be seen from further away—perhaps only from the corner of the Rue Neuve Notre-Dame. The Virgin flanked by two angels clearly indicated the submission of the kings to the patron of the church, and this iconography is also found on the tympanum of the Ste.-Anne Portal, which dates to the middle of the twelfth century.[23] Even though the façade of the south transept was only partially visible from the narrow courtyard of the medieval bishop's palace, its upper parts could definitely be seen from the south bank. Here, the statue of St. Marcel was definitely visible, as

"Strasbourg, cathédrale. L'iconographie des portails de la façade," in *Congrès archéologique de France, 2004. Monuments de Strasbourg et du Bas-Rhin* (Paris, 2006), 201–209.

23. J. Thirion, "Les plus anciennes sculptures de Notre-Dame de Paris," in *Comptes-rendus de l'Académie des inscriptions et belles-lettres* (1970), 85–112; D. Sandron, "Notre-Dame de Paris: observations sur la structure et la sculpture des portails de la façade," *Monumental* (2000), 10–19.

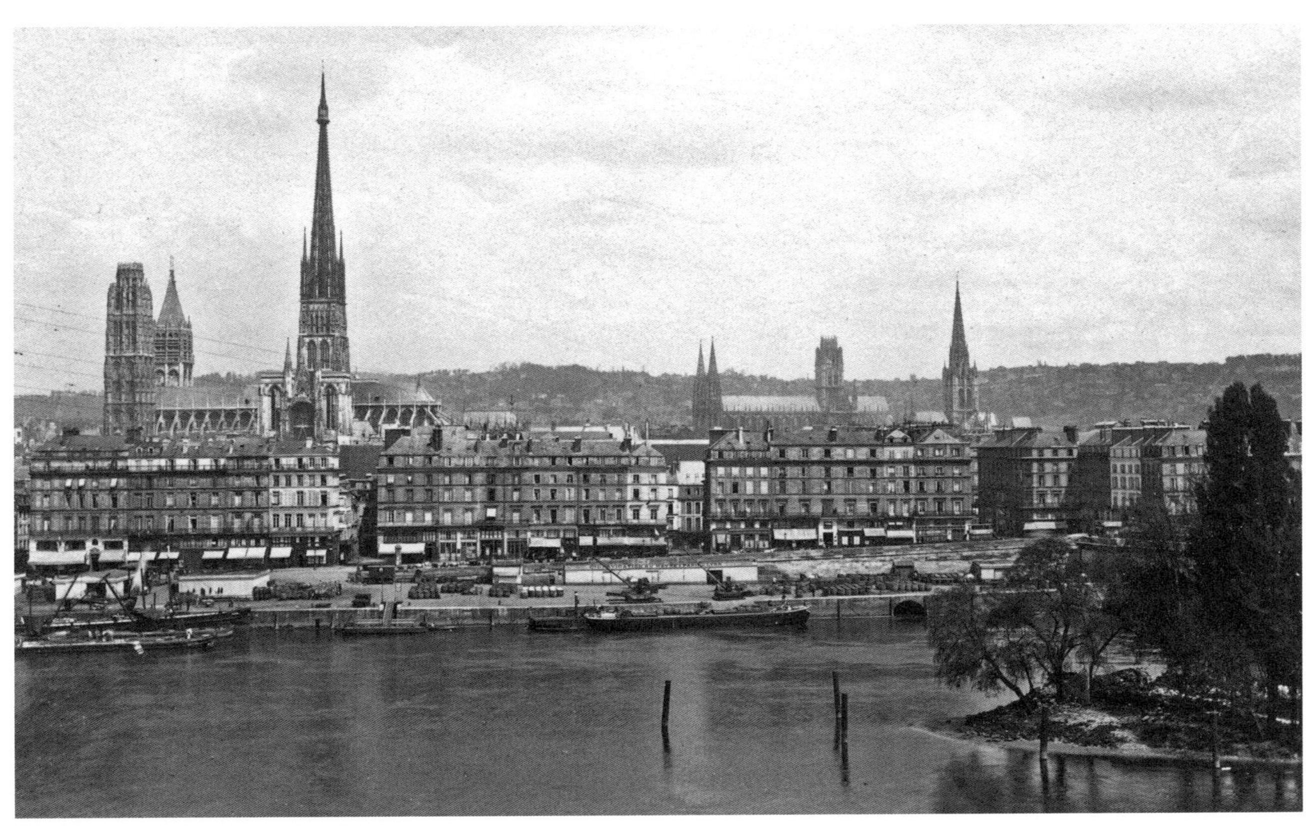

FIGURE 17. Rouen, General view of the town and Cathedral from the Seine (photo: Centre Chastel).

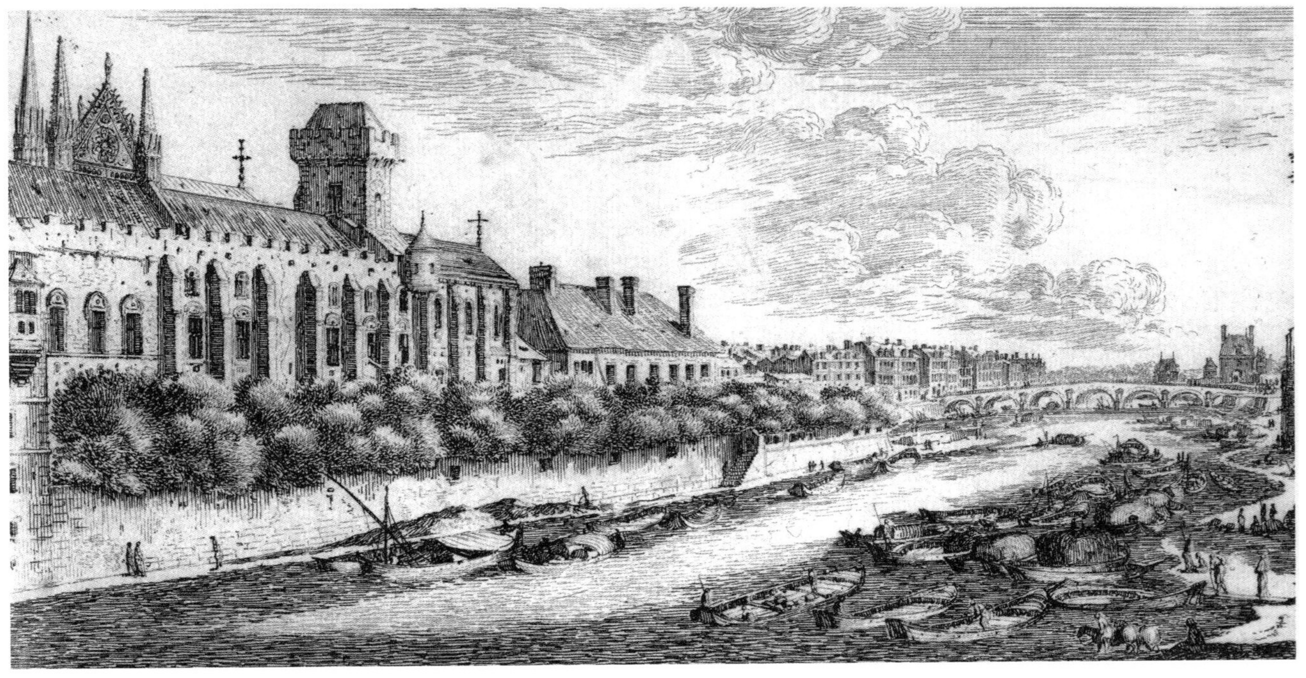

FIGURE 18. Israël Sylvestre, *Vue de l'archevêché de Paris et du pont de la Tournelle*, 17th c. (Paris, Musée Carnavalet, 13264, photothèque Musées de la Ville de Paris).

it was higher than the roof of the palace's big hall (end of the twelfth century). This view is also confirmed in an engraving by Israël Silvestre that dates to the start of the seventeenth century (Fig. 18).[24]

At Reims Cathedral, the gallery of the kings in the western façade was also very high up in terms of the surrounding structures (Fig. 6). It loomed over the roofs of the town, over the statues of angels or kings in the tabernacles along the choir, the transept, or nave. The relative height of the gallery of the kings allowed it to be seen from even outside the town. It is still possible to recreate the strong impression that it must have had as the royal procession approached the coronation city from the west on the eve of the ceremonies. The last coronation, that of Charles X in 1824, was organized according to the standard tradition of passing through the gate of Vesle, which was dominated in the distance by the mass of the cathedral.[25]

The external angle (northwest) of the north tower on the façade of Auxerre Cathedral is noticeably emphasized by a chamfered design (Fig. 19). This emphasis on the angle is extremely rare, and it has many niches culminating in an exceptional combination of stone shrines that form the top of the buttresses. It faces the direction of one of the principal city gates, the gate of Paris, located precisely to the northwest. The ornament of the chamfered northwest buttress and the shrines that surmount it could be clearly seen from the Paris gate, which was one of the principal points of access to the city from the northwest. It was prominently displayed to all who approached the city and as such has to be seen as a program exalting the relics of the cathedral. Without any doubt, this spectacular setting also confirmed the presence of the saint relics facing the nearby abbey of St.-Germain. The abbey prided itself on being the principal necropolis of the city and of having relics that were at the center of an important pilgrimage route.[26]

The cathedrals of Laon, Paris, Chartres, Amiens, Reims, Auxerre, Rouen, and Strasbourg have allowed us to see in a small way the importance of monumental sculpture mounted high up on these structures. These buildings integrated the carvings into an urban fabric—they focused on or related to some particular element or elements of the churches they surmounted, such as patronage, relics, or functionality, and as such were far more powerful than has hitherto been suggested.

In his distinguished career, Willibald Sauerländer has expressed an interest in these ensembles, especially that at Reims Cathedral. He has also studied the miscellaneous fragments that remain of the upper parts of Sens Cathedral (Fig. 20), which he examined in a pioneering study in 1966.[27] These carvings, together with the *Majestas Domini* from the gable, were one of the sources of inspiration for the upper parts of the façade at Vézelay that was remodeled in the thirteenth century (Fig. 21).[28] The subject is rich, and many other buildings such as those at Rouen (western façade), Meaux, Troyes, Soissons, and so forth, remain to be examined. Their monumental figurative carvings need to be discussed in relation to the rest of the sculptural, painting, or stained glass programs so that we can understand the totality of these works of art (*Gesamtkunstwerke*). These cathedrals are the places where phenomena of redundancy and resonance so familiar in the Middle Ages will be seen to have played a major role.

24. P. Lorentz and D. Sandron, *Atlas de Paris au Moyen Âge* (Paris, 2006), 123.

25. Laurent et Adam, *Vue de la porte de Vesle le 28 mai 1825*, lithograph, Reims, musée Saint-Remi, reproduced in *Mythes et réalités de la cathédrale de Reims de 1825 à 1975*, Exhib. Cat. (Reims, 2001), 39. The "Porte de Vesle" or "Porte Vesloise" was first called "Porte de Soissons"; P. Desportes, *Reims et les Rémois aux XIII*[e] *et XIV*[e] *siècles* (Paris, 1979), 68, 232.

26. C. Sapin, ed., *Archéologie et architecture d'un site monastique, V*[e]*–XX*[e] *siècles. 10 ans de recherche à l'abbaye Saint-Germain d'Auxerre* (Auxerre, Paris, 2000).

27. W. Sauerländer, *Von Sens bis Strasbourg. Ein Beitrag zur kunstgeschichtliche Stellung der Strassburger Querhausskulpturen* (Berlin, 1966), 29.

28. I. Plein, *Die Frühgotische Skulptur an der Westfassade der Kathedrale von Sens*, Beiträge zur Kunstgeschichte des Mittelalters und der Renaissance (Münster, 2005), 201. The original fragments of the sculpture of Vézelay have been studied by L. Saulnier and N. Stratford, *La sculpture oubliée de Vézelay. Catalogue du musée lapidaire*, Bibliothèque de la Société française d'archéologie (Paris, 1984), 41–42, 50–62, 175–176.

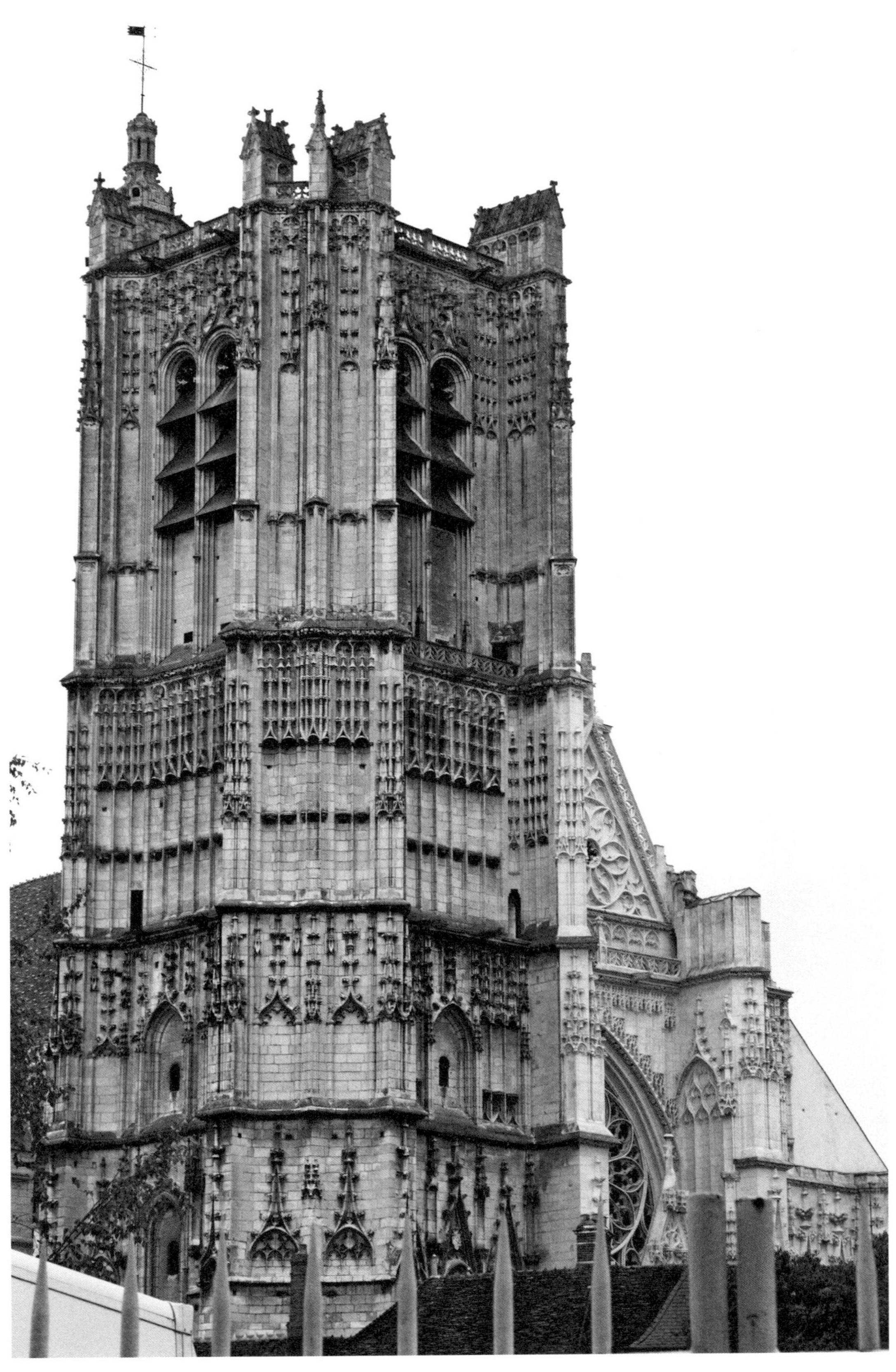

FIGURE 19. Auxerre Cathedral, north tower from the northwest (photo: Centre Chastel, Céline Gumiel).

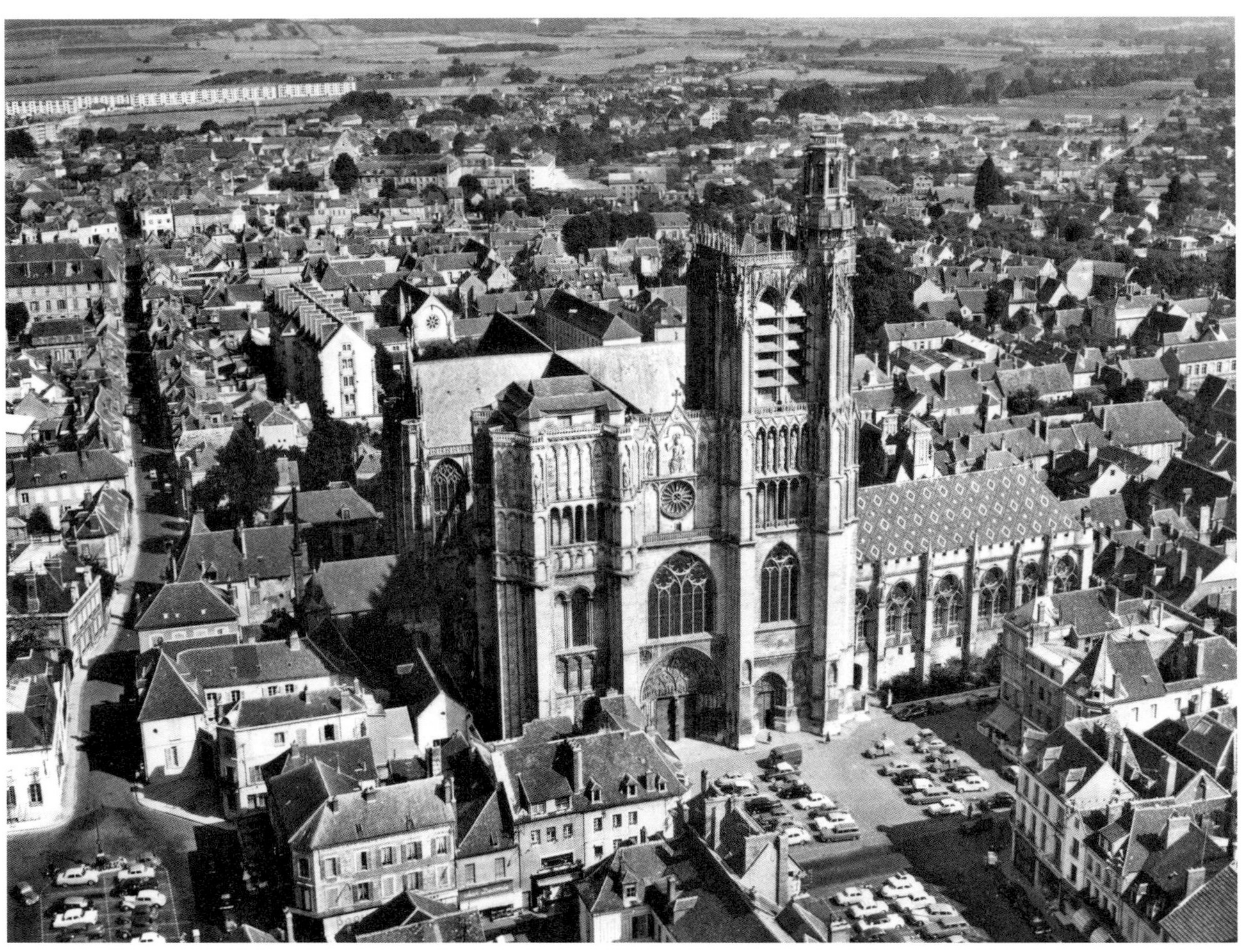

FIGURE 20. Sens Cathedral, aerial view of the cathedral and west façade from the northwest (photo: Centre Chastel).

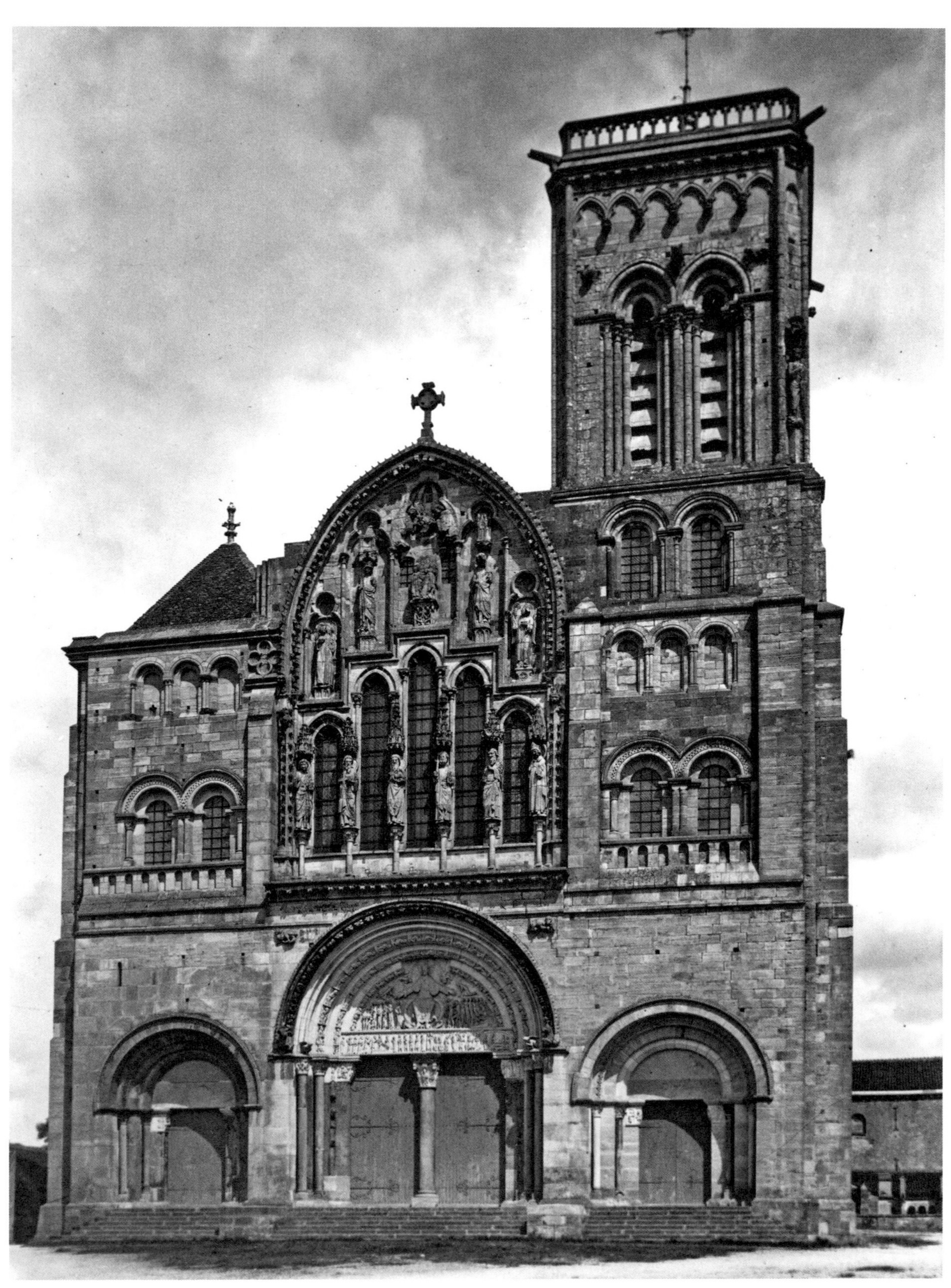

FIGURE 21. Vézelay Abbey, west façade (photo: Centre Chastel).

STEPHEN MURRAY

Narrating Gothic: The Cathedral Plot

THE PHENOMENON known as "Gothic" has been created as much *with words* as with images and with architectural forms and spaces. Yet, while much effort has been devoted to establishing the formal patterns of sameness and difference in Gothic buildings and artifacts that we categorize as "style," little attention has been paid to the rhetorical commonplaces—the *topoi*—that result from the art historian's mission to translate the forms and spaces of Gothic architecture into words—whether in the chapters of a book, or in the classroom or on-site lecture.

Jean Bony, in *French Gothic Architecture of the Twelfth and Thirteenth Centuries*, used the forms of Soissons Cathedral to represent the "essential" features of Gothic: pointed arches, rib vaults, enhanced height and spaciousness.[1] Looking to Romanesque antecedents and beyond, he then tracked how each feature "developed." His story is one of "influences," "urges," and architectural elements that somehow "travel" from one place to the next. Thus, for example, we are told that rib vaults "entered" the Île de France from Normandy "along two roads."[2] The storytelling strategy where the ending is already known at the beginning creates a self-fulfilling *entelechy*—as old as Creation in *Genesis* or Plato's account of the creative action of the Divine Craftsman (*Demiurge*) in the *Timaeus*.

In recent decades, however, the deterministic style-based narrative of Gothic has fallen entirely out of fashion: Willibald Sauerländer certainly played a key role in challenging the old means of representation.[3] Little consensus now exists among interlocutors on how the big story might best be told.

There is clearly a need to move beyond the attempt to construct a unified, teleological, style-based master narrative, toward spatial, *synchronic*, modes of thought that will allow us to recognize, control, and correlate characteristic patterns in multiple stories over an extended period of time, from the period of construction to the present. How can this be achieved?[4]

This essay proposes to build upon the recognition—already established in Antiquity and well known in the Middle Ages—of structural analogies between rhetoric and architectural space. Thus, Quintilian (V : 10, 20) defined *topoi*, or "commonplaces" as a "storehouses for trains of thought."[5] Such spatial thinking may best be pursued in relation to the stories of Gothic by invoking the multiple meanings of the word "plot." Roget's *Thesaurus* recognizes three principal meanings of the noun "plot." First, and most ancient, a controlled lot or parcel of land (a building plot, for example); second, a covert plan, pursued by multiple agents, to achieve a desired end; and third, a series of events and relationships

1. J. Bony, *French Gothic Architecture of the 12th and 13th Centuries* (Berkeley, 1983), 5.

2. Bony, *French Gothic Architecture* (as in note 1), 26.

3. W. Sauerländer, "Mod Gothic," *New York Times Review of Books*, 31 (Nov. 1984), 43–44; H. Belting, *Das Ende der Kunstgeschichte?* (Munich, 1983); M. Davis, "Sic et Non: Recent Trends in the Study of Gothic Ecclesiastical Architecture, *J.S.A.H.* 58 (1999), 414–423; P. Crossley, "Introduction," in P. Frankl, *Gothic Architecture*, revised by P. Crossley (New Haven, 2000), 7–34.

4. "Mapping Gothic France," a collaborative project currently under way at Columbia University and Vassar College with support from the Andrew Mellon Foundation, aims to develop just such a synchronic, spatial context, providing access to hundreds of Gothic churches embedded in a modified Google map of France, www.mappinggothicfrance.org. H. Lefebvre, *La production de l'espace* (Paris, 1974), provides a theoretical framework for spatial thinking.

5. E. R. Curtius, *European Literature and the Latin Middle Ages*, transl. W. R. Trask (Princeton, 1973), 70.

forming the dynamic basis of a rhetorical composition or story.[6] As a verb, "to plot" may convey the meaning of *showing graphically* the location or direction of something; or, alternatively, working out a secret plan to achieve a desired end.

In order to explore the notion of "plotting," as applied to Gothic, I have examined the rhetoric, narrative structures, and *topoi* employed by three witnesses close to the construction of twelfth- and thirteenth-century Gothic edifices.[7] The writing of each individual is well known, yet no attempt has been made to *correlate* their testimonies and rhetorical strategies. The correlation proposed here is embedded within the spatial context of a plot.

The name of the first witness, Villard de Honnecourt, certainly one of the most illustrious in the story of Gothic, was entered in an introductory annotation in a little book containing multiple images of Gothic edifices and devices, sculpture, furniture, as well as natural forms, that now resides in the *Grande reserve* of the Bibliothèque Nationale.[8] The little book has inspired the passionate engagement of a continuing procession of interpreters, who, reading between the lines, have generated their own apocryphal stories around the central questions of who was Villard de Honnecourt and what was the intended purpose of his book? In fact, such are the ambiguities in the relationships between the images and their prototypes; between annotations that have been added around the images that they "explain" and the images themselves; and between the original intention behind the gathering of images and the didactic application applied by several subsequent contributors, that it is best to remain skeptical of any final "explanation" of Villard's mission. For the purposes of this short essay, I shall limit my conclusions to the following direct observations. First, the little book is the work of an *imagier*—one whose eyes have encountered a range of visual phenomena which were collected somewhat randomly, as *objects of desire*, and entered, as "virtual reality" images, upon multiple unbound pages. Although mocked by modern art historians for multiple inaccuracies, the *imagier* was interested in creating in the mind of the viewer slippage and ambiguity in the relationship between image and prototype.[9] He wanted illusion; the reality effect: *verisimilitude*.[10] Rather than reading between the lines, it is best to focus upon the images themselves, considered as virtual reality *surrogates* for the real thing, inviting members of his audience with the repeated word, *vesci*..., to just *come and look*.[11] It is this performative function

6. On the plot as story line, see P. Brooks, *Reading for the Plot: Design and Intention in Narrative* (New York, 1984).

7. The present paper forms part of a larger book project, *Narrating Gothic*.

8. For many years the best means of access to Villard de Honnecourt was the facsimile edition by H. Hahnloser, *Villard de Honnecourt: Kritische Gesamtausgabe des Bauhüttenbuches, ms. fr. 19093 der Pariser Nationalbibliotek* (Vienna, 1935, reprint Graz, 1972). More recently, see R. Bechmann, *Villard de Honnecourt: la pensée technique au XIIIe. siècle et sa communication* (Paris, 1991); C. Barnes, *Villard de Honnecourt: The Artist and His Drawings* (Boston, 1982). I am grateful to C. Barnes and J. Smedley for allowing me access to the new edition, *The Portfolio of Villard de Honnecourt (Paris, Bibliothèque nationale de France, MS Fr 19093): A New Critical Edition and Color Facsimile* (Ashgate, 2008). As we await the appearance of the new edition, the pages of Villard's little book are most readily accessible in the Bibliothèque nationale edition online: http://classes.bnf.fr/villard/. The editors of this web edition have applied consecutive numbers to the folios rather than the traditional recto and verso: despite my own preference for the traditional system, my references to specific pages in Villard will, for convenience, follow the online edition (referred to here as *bnf*). The introductory annotation was added to a page of images of the Apostles, see *bnf*, 02.

9. See, for example, the renderings (interior and exterior) of a chapel and the elevation of Reims Cathedral (*bnf*, 60, 61 and 62). Rather than excoriating Villard for his inaccuracies (the tripled rib springer in *bnf*, 60 or the mistaken proportions in *bnf*, 62) we might rather remark on the skill with which the artist captured the essential features of Reims Cathedral.

10. This verisimilitude is apparent in the simple "perspective" construction that conveys the spaciousness of the Reims chapel (*bnf*, 60 and 61); in the deep shadowing that allows the colonnettes and the passages of the same chapel to stand out in relief, and in the corrugated effect gained by the use of the hook-fold technique (*Muldenfaltenstil*) to render drapery (*bnf*, 32, for example). On Villard's representation of "Gothic" as a system of colonnettes, see M. F. Hearn, "Villard de Honnecourt's Perception of Gothic Architecture," *Medieval Architecture and Its Intellectual Context: Studies in Honor of Peter Kidson* (London, 1990), 127–136. On the reality effect, see F. R. Ankersmit, *The Reality Effect in the Writing of History: The Dynamics of Historiographical Topography* (Amsterdam, 1989), and R. Barthes, *The Rustle of Language*, transl. R. Howard (Berkeley, 1989).

11. Thus, for example, the image of the housing of a clock tower

that enables Villard to be characterized not just as an *imagier*, but also as an *interlocutor*—one who wanted to insert himself between viewer and object with his "virtual reality" surrogates and his verbal explanations.[12]

Imagier, *interlocutor* ... and one who, through a strategy of half revealing and half concealing, wanted to create ambiguity and doubt in the mind of his audience.[13] And, finally, the images penned by Villard and the subsequent contributors to the book provide valuable insights into "plotting" understood as spatial *control*, extending also to the logistics of construction.[14]

In his *Tractatus de Combustione*, the second witness, Gervase of Canterbury, with the help of dramatic narrative and graphic circumstantial detail, weaves together time and space to tell a story that rolls along with all the inevitability of the opening chapters of *Genesis*.[15] In six days God created the earth, and it was seen to be good; after six years of work the monks entered the new choir and the new work was good. The construction of a great new building has been witnessed by many, but who would be able to piece together a year-by-year narrative some twenty years after the event?[16] Others have already suggested that Gervase, in his role as sacristan, was the "ingenious and industrious monk" who directed the work of construction after the first master mason, William of Sens, tumbled from the scaffold.[17] However, it has never been proposed that Gervase, in order to reconstruct the complex building history of the Gothic choir of his cathedral more than twenty years after the event, had recourse to "artificial memory"—written administrative sources (building accounts).[18] Gervase certainly demonstrated considerable knowledge about the business of architectural *production:* the procurement of stone, hiring of the master mason, design of templates, and the day-to-day business of construction.

As with Villard, apocryphal stories have developed around this extraordinary witness of Gothic: the most dramatic being Peter Kidson's suggestion that Gervase's artful narrative was actually a cover-up to mask the disarray of the community after the martyrdom of Thomas Becket.[19]

In his book, *De consecratione*, the third and final witness, Abbot Suger of St.-Denis, left a rhetorical struc-

---

(*bnf*, 12): *Ki veult faire la maison d'une ierloge vesent ci une que io vu une fois*; "Who[ever] wants to make the housing of a clock, see, here is one that I saw once ..."

12. On the role of the interlocutor and the performance of the work of art, see R. Brilliant, *Visual Narratives: Storytelling in Etruscan and Roman Art* (Ithaca, 1984); also, "The Bayeux Tapestry: A Stripped Narrative for their Ears and Eyes," *Word and Image* 7 (1991), 98–126. "*Voici*" in Villard is the equivalent of "*ubi*" and "*hoc*" in the Bayeux Tapestry.

13. This strategy of half-revealing and half-concealing is demonstrated most strikingly in pages like the one with the enigmatic male nude in front of a draped altar with an image of a king (*bnf*, 22) and the "Tomb of a Saracen" (*bnf*, 11). On Villard's deceptiveness, see R. Bechmann, "The Saracen's Sepulcher: An Interpretation of Folio 6r in the Portfolio of Villard de Honnecourt," in *Villard's Legacy: Studies in Medieval Technology, Science and Art in Memory of Jean Gimpel*, ed. M.-T. Zenner, AVISTA studies II (Ashgate, 2004), 121–134.

14. Plotting as spatial control was achieved in the Middle Ages by means of ropes stretched out on the ground: we catch a glimpse of such spatial control in Villard's plan for a cloister and in the Cistercian Church, *bnf*, 28 and 39. Control over the logistics of construction was achieved through the rigorous use of templates; Villard provides a glimpse of the templates designed for use at Reims in *bnf*, 63.

15. The old source for Gervase was W. Stubbs, *Rerum Britannicarum Medii Aevi Scriptores, or, Chronicles and Memorials of Great Britain and Ireland during the Middle Ages, the Historical Works of Gervase of Canterbury*, 2 vols. (London, 1879–89). More recently, see B. Tammen, "Gervasius von Canterbury und sein *Tractatus de Combustione et Reparatione Cantuariensis Ecclesiae*," in *Mittelalterliche Kunsterleben nach Quellen des 11. bis 13. Jahrhunderts*, ed. G. Binding and A. Speer (Stuttgart, 1994), 264–309; J. Schröder, *Gervasius von Canterbury, Richard von Saint-Victor und die Methodik der Bauverfassung im 12. Jahrhundert* (Cologne, 2000); C. D. Cragoe, "Reading and Rereading Gervase of Canterbury," *Journal of the British Archaeological Association* 154 (2001), 40–53. The comparison between the six days of Creation and the six years of construction was observed by B. Tammen, "Gervasius," 292.

16. Cragoe puts the writing well into the 1190s, see C. D. Cragoe, "Reading and Rereading," as in note 15, 49.

17. A. Gransden, *Historical Writing in England, c. 550–c. 1307* (Ithaca, 1974), 39.

18. On the early development of accounting systems at Canterbury, see R. A. L. Smith, "The Central Finance System of Christ Church, Canterbury, 1186–1512," *English Historical Review* 55 (1940), 353–69; also, *Canterbury Cathedral Priory: A Study in Monastic Administration* (Cambridge, 1943).

19. P. Kidson, "Gervase, Becket, and William of Sens," *Speculum* 68 (1993), 969–991.

ture that is entirely different from that of Gervase of Canterbury's *Tractatus*.[20] Whereas Gervase combined precise information about logistics and the sequence of construction in the grand sweep of his creation narrative, and Villard artfully (and deceitfully) projected his "reality effect," Suger provides only whispy glimpses of "reality" within a carefully-constructed structure based upon a series of rhetorical units each bearing the appearance of a syllogism. The prologue is, indeed, a true syllogistic reconciliation of thesis of Divine Harmony with the antithesis of the trials of the flesh through the mediation of the Holy Spirit. What follows, however, is a series of manipulated tripartite rhetorical constructions, in which *pressing circumstances* demand immediate *intervention*, which intervention is then justified through some manifestation of approval—either a miracle or a flashy liturgical event. Gabrielle Spiegel, in her study of Suger's *Life of Louis the Fat*, characterized these tripartite structures as "event units."[21] In the case of the book on the Consecration, three such event units end with three crescendos: the spectacular foundation-laying of the new chevet, the rapid completion of that chevet, and the final consecration. The *first problem* is that Dagobert's basilica, founded on the tomb of the saints, is not big enough; its entrance, narrow and ruinous, is overwhelmed by crowds. *Intervention:* fulfilling youthful hopes, we laid foundations for twin towers and extension of the nave. *Justification:* funding, at first in short supply, becomes abundant; a quarry for the columns is miraculously discovered; a column is miraculously retrieved. The *second problem* is that the new frontispiece must be joined to a nave threatened with "gaping cracks" and damaged capitals and bases; difficulty in finding appropriate beams. *Intervention:* preparations are made to repair walls and rebuild roof; renewed search for beams. *Justification:* miraculous discovery of wooden timbers of appropriate size to serve as tie beams; signs of divine approval in the spectacular dedication of the western frontispiece and its chapels. The *third problem* is the crush of people around the relic chamber in the crypt. *Intervention:* postpone completion of upper towers; enlargement of church. *Justification:* monastic assent as the construction and form of the new chevet is *anticipated*.

CRESCENDO 1: the spectacular foundation-laying of the chevet with royal participation; the due provision of funds.

CRESCENDO 2: rapid completion of the chevet; creation of the *châsses* and special altar for the use of dignitaries. The gold and gems, presented by pontiffs and the king, were procured with the aid of the martyrs themselves; miracles of the escape from damage from the windstorm and provision of the mutton.

CRESCENDO 3 (*climax*): the consecration of the chevet with controlled liturgical spectacle contrasted to the uncontrolled milling of the mob; translation of the relics; *châsses* opened and bodies inspected; spontaneous self-insertion on the part of the king; spectacular consecration of all the altars.

Brother William, Suger's biographer, has provided a clue to the circumstances under which this unique composition was realized: "Indeed, he [Suger] would tell stories—because he was a most agreeable man—sometimes about his own deeds, sometimes about [the deeds of] other great men he had seen or heard told of—sometimes into the middle of the night."[22] Suger's "book" on the consecration clearly resulted from the telling of such stories, honed through repetition to meet the needs of his audiences—stories that were then recorded in pen and ink for posterity, for example, in the context of readings from the *pulpitum* in the mo-

20. E. Panfosky, *Abbot Suger on the Abbey Church of St.-Denis and Its Art Treasures* (Princeton, 1946); F. Gasparri, ed., *Abbé Suger: Oeuvres. Ecrit sur la consecration de Saint-Denis; l'oeuvre administrative; histoire de Louis VI* (Paris, 1996); A Speer, A. G. Binding, et al., *Abt Suger von Saint-Denis: Ausgewählte Schriften* (Darmstadt, 2000).

21. G. Spiegel, "History as Enlightenment: Suger and the *Mos Anagogicus*," in *Abbot Suger and Saint-Denis: A Symposium*, ed. P. Gerson (New York, 1986), 151–158; also in *The Past As Text: The Theory and Practice of Medieval Historiography* (Baltimore, 1997), 163–177.

22. Speer, Binding, et al., *Abt Suger von Saint-Denis* (as in note 20), 390–391, "Lectio quidem erat de libris Patrum autenticis; aliquando de ecclesiasticis aliquid legebatur historiis. Narrabat vero, ut erat jocundissimus, nunc sua, nunc aliorum, quae vel vidisset vel didicisset gesta virorum fortium, aliquotiens usque ad noctis medium...." See also Panofsky, *Abbot Suger* (as in note 20), 13; H. Glaser, "Wilhelm von Saint-Denis: Ein Humanist aus der Umgebung des Abtes Suger und die Krise seiner Abtei von 1151–1153," *Historisches Jahrbuch* 85 (1965), 257–322.

nastic refectory.[23] The manipulated syllogism was just the device needed to propel the community to the construction of a new church, which probably surpassed the needs and aspirations of many of the brothers.

At the end of his life, and with the construction of the great church far from complete, the abbot became aware of the pressing need to connect signifier with signified; Alpha with Omega; a good start with a good ending though a safe middle.[24] Suger faced death in the realization that he would not live to see the completion of the "middle,"—the nave. This desire to *connect* went beyond the need to link the new frontispiece with the new chevet—it included, most importantly, the need to link signifier with signified, text with image, and the material with the immaterial in the famous "anagogical" upward-lifting movement.[25]

Thus, in each of the three case studies, the witnesses have hastened to add words to images in order to control; to fix meaning.

Having introduced the three witnesses, I now propose to develop a spatial means to correlate their testimonies. In order to accomplish this end, two senses of "plot" will be invoked. The first is "to show graphically" the location of something, and secondly, as a means of controlling space. Thus, I will show graphically or *visualize* a building plot—every medieval building project would begin with the stretching of ropes extended on the ground intersecting at right angles in order to define and control space.[26] A similar spatial mechanism may be applied to organize and correlate multiple stories told about Gothic.

The beginning involves the laying out of a plot that will allow the visualization of a space in which stories of Gothic may be told. The plot's first two essential boundaries are those that locate, constrain, and animate an interlocutor—one who talks or writes about one or

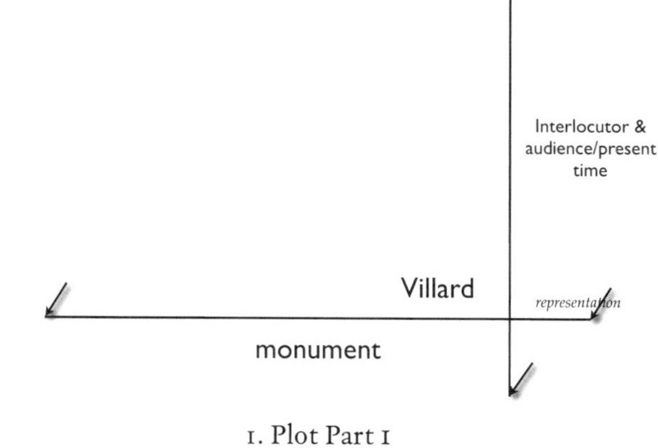

1. Plot Part 1

more work(s) of architecture (Fig. 1). In this plot, the monument, represented by the bottom edge, is understood *diachronically*—stretching in time from the period of its initial construction to its completion, through all the subsequent interventions that may have modified it, down to the present, when it intersects with our own time. That intersection point is marked (to the right) by a second bound, representing today's reception of the monument, and responses in words, oral as well as written (the role of the interlocutor). The activity undertaken at the point of intersection between monument and interlocutor is essentially the work of *representation*—amongst the three witnesses it is Villard de Honnecourt who most completely fulfills this task: *Come and look....*

As the interlocutor begins to speak about the monument, he will find that it is quite impossible to locate his story entirely within the time and space of the edifice. The interlocutor will tell members of the audience what they can see as well as *what they cannot see*. The very language that is used to designate the various parts of the building is largely figurative: defining what a thing *is* by invoking what *it looks like*. Thus, the body of the

23. E. P. Schmitz, "Les lectures de table à l'abbaye de Saint-Denis vers la fin du moyen-âge," *Revue Benedictine* 42 (1930), 163–167.

24. Glaser, "Wilhelm von Saint-Denis" (as in note 22), 305; L. Grant, *Abbot Suger of Saint-Denis: Church and State in Early Twelfth-Century France* (London, 1998), 206–7; 288.

25. Panofsky, *Abbot Suger* (as in note 20), 44–5. The vision of the new chevet was the moment prayed for by Suger with his monks, who had "implored Divine mercy that He Who is the One, *the beginning and the ending, Alpha and Omega*, might join a good end to a good beginning by a safe middle..." On Suger's understanding of "anagogical," see D. Poirel, "*Symbolice et anagoge*: l'école de Saint-Victor et la naissance du style gothique," in *L'abbé Suger, le manifeste gothique de Saint-Denis et la pensée victorine, Actes du Colloque organisé à la Fondation Singer-Polignac* (Turnhout, 2001), 141–170.

26. Control of the land through stretched ropes (plotting) went back to the Roman *agrimensores* and beyond, see O. A. Dilke, *The Roman Land Surveyors: An Introduction to the agrimensores* (New York, 1971).

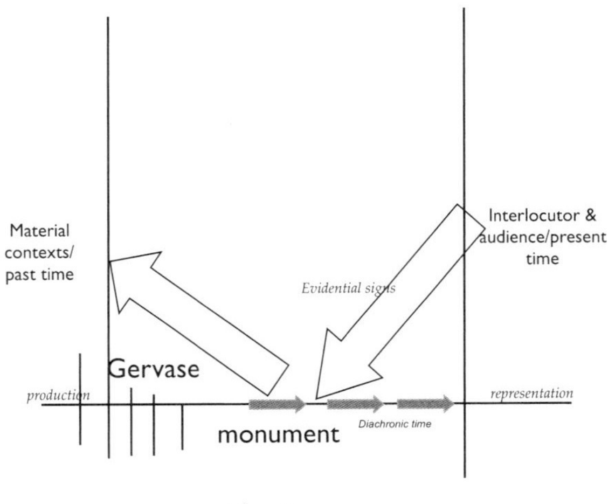

2. Plot Part II

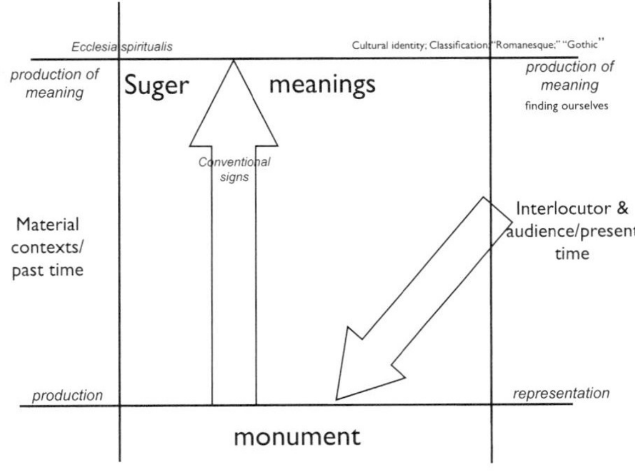

3. Plot Part III

cathedral looks like a boat—hence, nave, *navis*, *Schiff*. At the sides of the cathedral are wings (*aisles*). The choir is the head (*chevet*). The application of such figurative language often brings levels of signification—thus the boat of the nave might signify Noah's Ark, a vehicle of salvation.[27] Similarly, the interlocutor's announcement that "this is a *Gothic* cathedral," is only intelligible in relation to the audience's awareness of the thousands of other look-alike buildings—beyond their range of vision—that constitute "Gothic."[28] In explaining the forms of the building, moreover, the interlocutor may invite his audience to leave the present time and to consider the past and the circumstances of construction with its promises and challenges.

These considerations present the other two sides of the plot. When the forms of the building are interpreted as *evidential signs* leading to an understanding of the circumstances and sequence of construction, the interlocutor assumes the role of a detective (Fig. 2).[29] He may announce that he is merely allowing the stones to "speak for themselves," yet without his intervention most visitors or students will be unable to envisage the building process. This aspect of the past, then, is represented in the left side of our plot, and the monument's intersection with that past is understood in terms of material *production*. Amongst our three witnesses, Gervase of Canterbury tells us most about the hiring of the master mason, the procuring of stone and other materials, and the yearly sequence of operations. He is appointed as the logistics man.[30] These three boundaries of our plot are thus linked by the "life" of the monument over time, tying together past with present: what, then, is the fourth side? This has already been alluded to: the interlocutor's use of figurative language that conveys meaning: thus, the top line of the plot may be understood in terms of the production of meaning, or *semiosis* (Fig. 3).[31] It concerns the immaterial: the aesthetic, spiritual, and practical values assigned to the building. Amongst the three witnesses it is the Abbot Suger who most completely invokes the power

27. William Durand, Bishop of Mende, tells us about how the church can nudge the viewer to an understanding of levels of meaning through what it looks like (a human body, for example, the Body of Christ) and through analogy: see *The Rationale Divinorum Officiorum of William Durand of Mende*, ed. Timothy M. Thibodeau, Records of Western Civilization (New York, 2007).

28. We are dealing with the problem of universals: see D. M. Armstrong, *Universals, An Opinionated Introduction* (Boulder, 1989).

29. On the art historian as detective, see C. Ginzburg, *Clues, Myths and the Historical Method*, transl. John and Anne Tedeschi (Baltimore, 1992).

30. Villard and his followers, with their drawings of templates and stone-cutting strategies, also reveal important information on production.

31. On ways in which buildings may convey meanings, see J. Onians, *Bearers of Meaning: The Classical Orders in Antiquity, the Middle Ages and the Renaissance* (Princeton, 1988); G. Bandman, *Mittelalterliche Architektur als Bedeutungsträger* (Berlin, 1951); O. von Simson, The Gothic Cathedral: Origins of Gothic Architecture and the Medieval Concept of Order (London, 1956); H. Sedlmeyr, *Die Entstehung der Kathedrale* (Zurich, 1950).

of the material church as *medium*—as a means of transporting the user from one place to another; from the material to the immaterial. Meaning is produced not only through the agendas and choices of the builders but also through the responses of later audiences who read the building as a kind of language in terms of *conventional signs*, the interpretation of these signs being, of course, variable over time and location.

This fourth dimension of the Gothic cathedral—meaning—has been largely neglected by Anglo-Saxon positivists and French archaeologists, and the German scholarship that has focused upon the cathedral as an image of the Celestial City or as resulting from Neoplatonic light theory remained under continuing attack for decades. By representing the production of meaning at two points of intersection (construction and response) it is hoped that our visualization will stimulate new understanding of the slipperiness of signification.

A *common place* with clearly defined edges that constrain the limits of not one, but multiple stories of Gothic has been visualized. Such stories must, perforce, result from the storyteller's response to the monument(s) and his desire to inform his stories with knowledge of the conditions that attended initial construction of the edifice and the ways that the edifice might generate meaning for multiple audiences through an extended period of time. But our task remains unfinished, since our *post festum* scheme responds to the monument only as a *fait accompli* and does not accommodate the dynamic mechanisms understood in "plot" as a verb—to collude or conspire to work out a plan to achieve a desired outcome. Jean Bony never entirely met his own challenge: "the only productive line of approach for the historian is to try to uncover the urges which at each stage dictated the new orientations that were taken by the Gothic movement..."[32] How can we reach an understanding of the dynamics of production of the as-yet-unbuilt cathedral by plotting the sociological scenario of construction? Here we need to represent the human agents who work or conspire together to fix a desired outcome of some kind—in our case this outcome will be the Gothic cathedral or great church.

The three witnesses can be of enormous help in the visualization of the dynamic plot, since their testimony can be applied to represent the agency of the three kinds of person engaged in cathedral construction: churchman, master mason, and budget/logistics provider/organizer (Fig. 4).[33] Thus, Suger was the churchman *par excellence;* Gervase, the sacristan, was the organizer of construction work on the Canterbury choir; and Villard de Honnecourt, while not himself a practicing master mason, brings us close to the world of the artisan. For each of these agents, the great church, the object of desire, was not just an end in itself—it was also a means of accomplishing a personal, soteriological, or ideological agenda of some kind.[34] In other words,

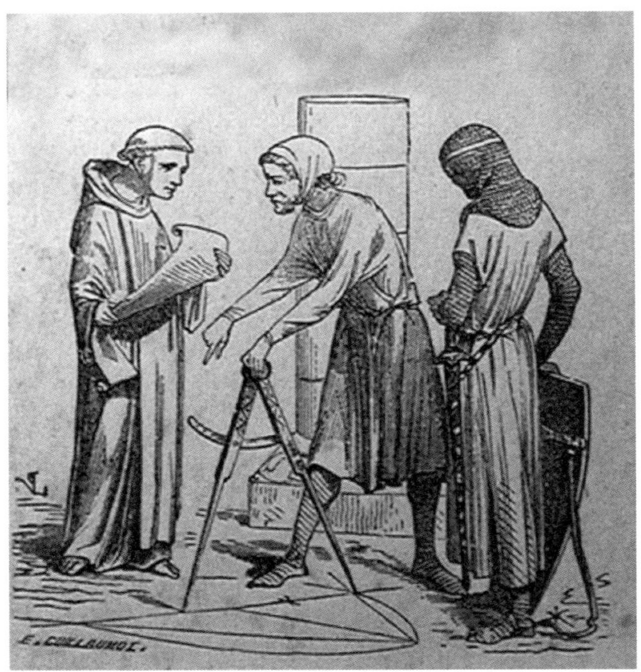

4. The Three Builders

32. Bony, *French Gothic Architecture* (as in note 1), 1.

33. E. E. Viollet-le-Duc, *Dictionnaire raisonné de l'architecture française, du XIe. au XVIe. siécle* (Paris, 1856), 1, frontispiece. The author's prejudices about the social framing of Gothic are, of course, built into this image, which glorifies the role of the mason and marginalizes the knightly patron. In a Gothic cathedral, however, there was frequently no such patron at all, and the third "builder" should be understood as the logistics person, sacristan, or *proviseur*. I have proposed that Gervase of Canterbury played just such a role.

34. This notion is inherent in Krautheimer's "iconography of

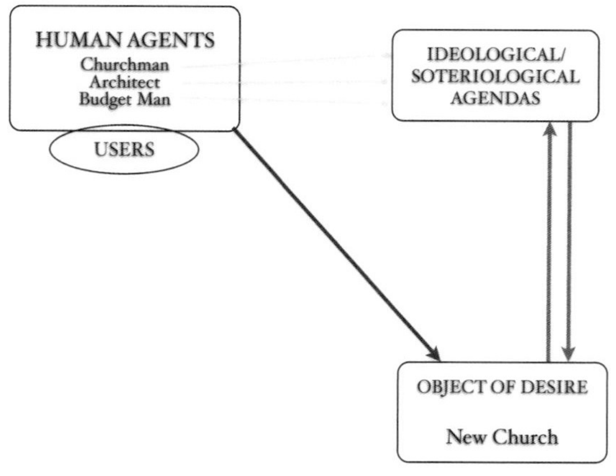

5. Sociology Part I

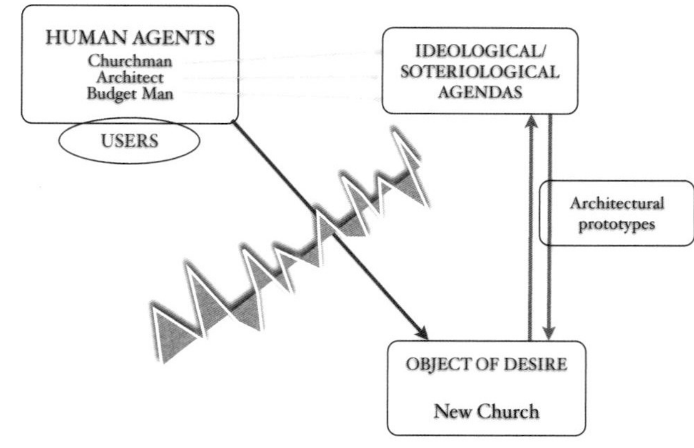

6. Sociology Part II

desire is triangulated (Fig. 5). Thus, Abbot Suger wanted not just a new church, but also to cement the special relationship between the monastery of St.-Denis and the Capetian kings of France and to secure his own salvation. It has been alleged by Peter Kidson that Gervase of Canterbury wanted to use the construction of the Gothic cathedral as a means to transcend the divisions that followed the martyrdom of Thomas Becket and profit from the ensuing pilgrimage.[35]

Between the agency of the builders and the realization of their object of desire, however, lies a gap—representing the enormity of the task of demolishing the beloved old building that had occupied the site, reaching consensus on how to start, and undertaking the rigorous daily tasks of a construction project that none of the initial builders would live to see finally accomplished (Fig. 6).[36] Transcending that gap is only possible through a process of *compression and expansion*, as mnemonic images of the unbuilt cathedral are formed in relation to myriad memories of known structures, as these images are processed and represented graphically and rehearsed rhetorically (Fig. 7).[37] *Expansion* involves the translation of these images into material architectural forms as the means of production are secured and the space of the future cathedral controlled by means of stretching ropes on the ground. Both compression and expansion may, of course, be understood in terms of *plotting*.

This essay has provided visualizations of two kinds of plot. While the first goes back to ancient writings on rhetoric (Quintilian) that envisage a common place as a storehouse for thought, the second plot resembles a dynamic scenario for a filmscript. It allows us to fulfill Bony's challenge to think of the past in forward motion, projecting us beyond the old story of "style" and "influences." The imaging of the as-yet-unbuilt cathedral

architecture." Thus, builders might want the new edifice to refer to an ancient prototype not just because it is beautiful, but because of the levels of meaning that it might convey through association, see R. Krautheimer, "Introduction to an 'Iconography of Medieval Architecture,'" *JWCI* 5 (1942); also, "The Carolingian Revival of Early Christian Architecture," originally *Art Bulletin* 24 (1942); reprinted in *Studies in Early Christian, Medieval and Renaissance Art*, (New York, 1969), 203–25.

35. P. Kidson, "Gervase, Becket, and William of Sens," as in note 19.

36. The decision to rebuild was sometimes not as clear cut as modern students might assume: thus, the older building might be demolished progressively and parts might be incorporated in the new work.

37. On such mnemonic images, see M. Carruthers, *The Book of Memory: A Study of Memory in Medieval Culture* (Cambridge, 1992); also, *The Craft of Thought: Meditation, Rhetoric and the Making of Images, 400–1200* (Cambridge, 1998); and, "The Poet as Master Builder: Composition and Locational Memory in the Middle Ages," *New Literary History* (1993), 24, 881–904. On compression and expansion, see S. Murray, "Slippage of Form and Meaning," in *The Artful Mind: Cognitive Science and the Riddle of Human Creativity*, ed. M. Turner (Oxford, 2006), 189–207.

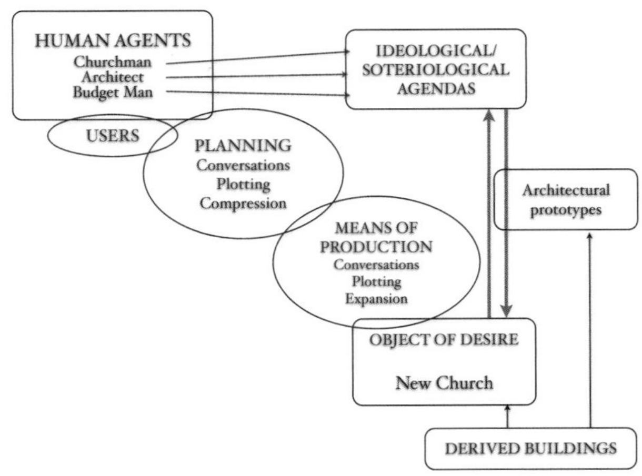

7. Sociology Part III

is achieved in reference to models of various kinds (the builders of Amiens Cathedral, for example, may have first envisaged their cathedral with reference to Soissons and Laon). Similarly, the builders of future cathedrals might themselves make reference to Amiens as well as to the same cathedrals referenced by the builders of Amiens. Transmission of ideas and "change" must, finally, be represented in terms of the desires and agendas of makers and users and not as some disembodied force "out there." It is only through such means of representation that it is possible to finally escape from old animistic notions of the "development" of "style" through "influences" and rewrite the stories of Gothic in terms of human desires, challenges, and patterns of production.

There is another dimension to the cathedral plot that can only be briefly alluded to here. In recent decades, scholars have returned to the theme that "Gothic," understood as a set of look-alike features achieved when one building "quotes" another, is embodied in hundreds of buildings that occupy the space and time of the "birth of France."[38] When relative chronology is considered, it is clear that the architectural phenomenon came before, or *anticipated* the political and institution manifestation: creating in the mind of the traveler encountering look-alike buildings embedded in the landscape of nascent France the illusion of *manifest destiny*. And was this not the builders' *plot*?

38. D. Kimpel and R. Suckale, *Die gotische Architektur in Frankreich, 1130–1270* (Munich, 1985), 67, "Wir gehen in unserem Buch von der These aus, dass das Entstehungs-und Verbreitungsgebiet der Gotik bis 1200 identish is mit dem französischen Kronland."

RICHARD MARKS

The Englishness of English Gothic Art?

THIS PAPER does not seek to identify (or re-discover) traits by which English Gothic art and architecture may be defined. Rather, it is concerned with historiography: the role played by concepts of national mode and identity in narratives of the buildings and visual arts of England between the late twelfth and early sixteenth centuries. Behind the title, which is structured as an interrogative, lies a wider question: is it possible, even desirable, to write meaningfully about a "national" art?

The issue of an English "national" art is a field that has been well-tilled in a number of recent studies, notably in the papers of two conferences: *The Geographies of English: Landscape and the National Past, 1880–1940*, published in 2002; and *Reassessing Nikolaus Pevsner*, which appeared two years later.[1] As their titles suggest, both collections range further than the Middle Ages (indeed, the former makes only passing reference to this period), but both contain much of relevance to medievalists.

The *locus classicus* of the identification of art as a "national" style and linked with the "spirit of an age" is of course Pevsner's *The Englishness of English Art* (Fig. 1).[2] He was not breaking new ground. There had been a renewed interest in "Englishness" and English medieval art from the nineteenth century (especially in the context of the Gothic Revival) and further stimulated by a

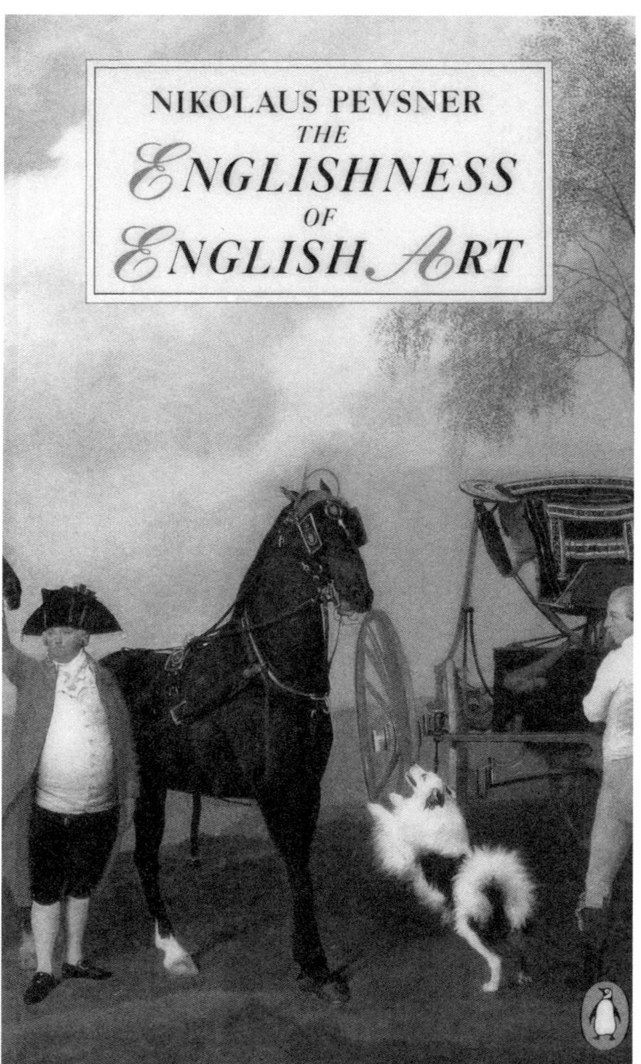

FIGURE 1. Cover of N. Pevsner, *The Englishness of English Art* (Penguin edition, 1993).

1. D. Peters Corbett, Y. Holt, and F. Russell, eds., *The Geographies of Englishness: Landscape and the National Past, 1880–1940*, Studies in British Art 10 (New Haven and London, 2002); P. Draper, ed., *Reassessing Nikolaus Pevsner* (Aldershot, 2004). For a recent wide-ranging survey of the historiography of medieval art, see Conrad Rudolph, "Introduction: A Sense of Loss: An Overview of the Historiography of Romanesque and Gothic Art," in C. Rudolph, ed., *A Companion to Medieval Art: Romanesque and Gothic in Northern Europe* (Oxford, 2006), 1–43.

2. N. Pevsner, *The Englishness of English Art* (London, 1956). This has been re-published by Penguin Books in several editions; the page references in this article are taken from the Penguin edition of 1993.

series of exhibitions of "English primitives" at regular intervals from 1890, as Alexandrina Buchanan and Andrew Causey have discussed.[3] Nationalism arising from the First World War added to this, as did the concept of "national character" rooted in a pastoral England, which emerged in the 1930s and found proponents in the likes of the historian Sir Arthur Bryant.[4] This vision notably found expression in a series of books published between the 1930s and 1950s by Batsford under the heading of *The Face of Britain*, enfolded in seductively evocative dust-jackets designed by Brian Cook (Fig. 2). This veneration of the "traditional" values of English landscape and rural crafts, then perceived to be under threat of extinction through urbanization and industrialization, has been studied by historical geographers, especially David Matless, who has applied Foucaultian notions of contestation and instability to claims to authority over rural spaces and activities.[5] Less attention has been paid to the related (and sometimes overlapping) series of monographs published by Batsford between the First World War and the 1970s under such headings as *British Art and Buildings*, which brought medieval architecture and ancillary arts to both the general public and the scholarly world. Although the word "British" recurs in the titles of the various Batsford series, the overwhelming majority of the books themselves are Anglocentric. The writings of John Harvey (of whom more anon) and other Batsford authors like the prolific J. C. Cox (parish churches and fittings), Aymer Vallance (on screens), and F. H. Crossley and Katharine Esdaile (funerary monuments) meshed with the publishing house's extolling of ancient craft skills, such as stonemasonry and carpentry.[6] To

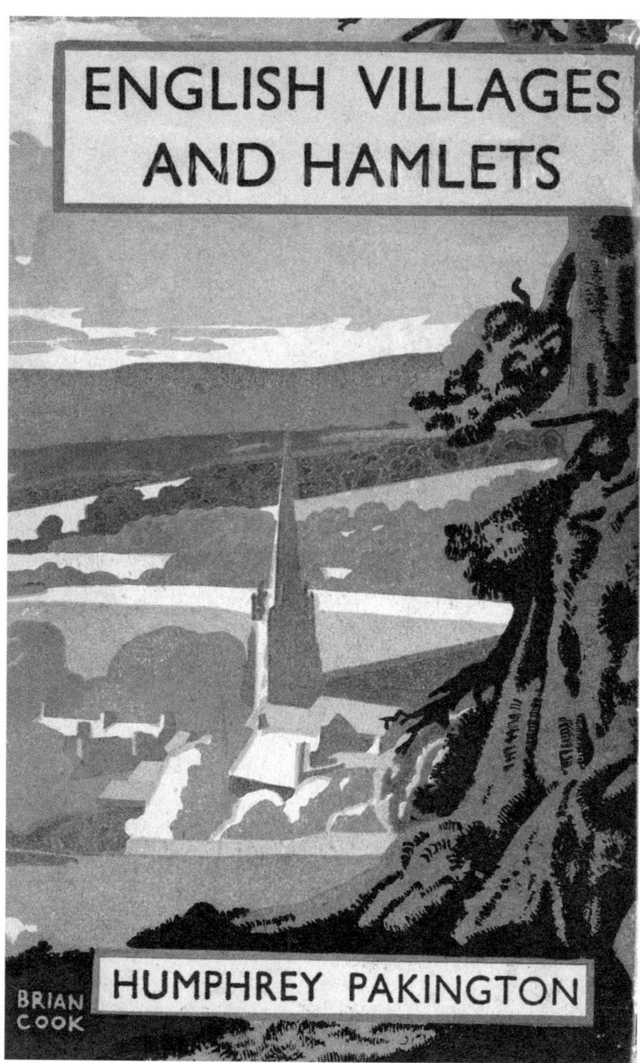

FIGURE 2. Dust-jacket designed by Brian Cook for H. Pakington, *English Villages & Hamlets* (Batsford, 4th revised ed., 1945).

3. A. Buchanan, "Perspectives of the Past: Perceptions of Late Gothic Art in England," in R. Marks and P. Williamson, eds., *Gothic: Art for England, 1400–1547*, Exhib. Cat. (Victoria & Albert Museum, London, 2003), 128–139; *idem*, "Show and Tell: Late Medieval Art and the Cultures of Display," in R. Marks, ed., *Late Gothic England: Art and Display* (Donington, 2007), 124–137; *idem*, "Perceptions of British Medieval Art," in T. Ayers, ed., *The History of British Art 600–1600* (Tate Britain, Yale Center for British Art, London, 2008), 247–259; A. Causey, "English Art and 'The National Character,' 1933–34," in Peters Corbett, Holt, and Russell, *Geographies of Englishness* (as in note 1), 275–302.

4. The idealization of English rural life dates back to the middle of the nineteenth century; for a summary of recent scholarship on the subject, see P. Crossley, "Between Spectacle and History: Art History and the Medieval Exhibitions," in Marks, *Late Gothic England* (as in note 3), 144; this article (pp. 138–153) is a very valuable contribution to the historiography of English medieval art. For Bryant, see Causey, "English Art" (as in note 3), esp. 278–280.

5. D. Matless, *Landscape and Englishness* (London, 1998).

6. J. C. Cox, *The English Parish Church* (London, 1914); *idem*, *The Parish Churches of England*, edited with additional material by C. B. Ford (London, 1935, 1950); *idem*, *English Church Fittings* (London, 1923); A. Vallance, *English Church Screens* (London, 1936); *idem*, *Greater English Church Screens* (London, New York & Toronto, 1947); F. H. Crossley, *English Church Monuments AD 1150–1550* (London,

inject a personal note, my own adolescent interests in medieval art and architecture were nurtured by Batsford's cheap paperback editions of Cox and Ford on English parish churches and Crossley on English abbeys. If the books emit a gentlemanly tweedy or clerical flavor this is not to undervalue the scholarship and contribution to knowledge of their authors. They were rooted in the antiquarian tradition, because at this time there was no other academic structure available for their ilk.

Pevsner's grounding was very different. No only did he bring to English art the perspectives of a non-Englishman, but also the vast knowledge of European art and architecture as well as intellectual grounding in the discipline of art history (as propounded by his doctoral supervisor Wilhelm Pinder). This formation was of course one he shared with other refugees from Nazism that have so enriched medieval art history in England (Saxl, Pächt, and Zarnecki are names that immediately spring to mind). For these reasons—plus the fact that, as far as I am aware, Pevsner's book still remains the only authoritative monograph on English artistic identity over the *longue durée*—it provides a convenient starting-point.[7]

The Englishness of English Art originated in the Reith Lectures broadcast on the wireless in 1955, and first appeared in the following year under this title (Fig. 1). However, the concept was already germinating in Pevsner's mind over a decade earlier, in 1941–2, while he was giving lectures on English art at Birkbeck College in the University of London.[8] The lectures more or less coincided with the publication by the Viennese art historian Dagobert Frey of his *Englisches Wesen in der Bildenden Kunst* (*English Character in the Visual Arts*), which made the same link between art and national *psyche*.[9] Whereas Frey took a chronological approach, Pevsner used a series of diachronic case-studies as a means of categorization. The philosophical underpinnings of *The Englishness of English Art* are spelt out succinctly: "There is the spirit of an age, and there is national character. The existence of neither can be denied ..." Soon after, a caveat is applied: "National character does not at all moments and in all situations appear equally distinct. The spirit of a moment may reinforce national character or repel it."[10] Determinants of the national character, amongst which meteorology features, are articulated: "A decent home, a temperate climate, and a moderate nation," which finds expression in conservatism.[11] This notion of a distinctive "geography of art" (*Kunstgeographie*), the title of the first chapter in the book, was conceived by neither Pevsner nor Frey, but was inherited from Pinder, as Ute Engel has pointed out.[12] Perpendicular architecture is the subject of the one chapter dedicated to the medieval period, but sprinkled throughout the book are observations about English medieval art in ways that demonstrate Pevsner's enormous breadth of knowledge. For example, he sees Hogarth's powers of observation and flair for portraying quotidian life as a characteristic of English art from Romanesque times

---

1921); K. A. Esdaile, *English Church Monuments 1510–1840* (London, 1946). This list is exemplary, not exhaustive. For Batsford and its eponymous proprietor, see Matless, *Landscape* (as in note 5), 64, 68, 75, 129–133, 180; also P. Crossley, "Anglia Perdita. English Medieval Architecture and Neo-Romanticism," in S. L'Engle and G. B. Guest, eds., *Tributes to Jonathan J. G. Alexander: The Making and Meaning of Illuminated Medieval & Renaissance Manuscripts, Art & Architecture* (London/Turnhout, 2007), 471–481, esp. 472–473.

7. Another seminal study by Paul Crossley is his "Introduction" to Draper, *Reassessing Nikolaus Pevsner*, 1–25 (as in note 1).

8. Pevsner, *Englishness* (as in note 2), 9–10. I am indebted to Paul Crossley for clarifying the role played by the 1941–2 lecture series.

9. D. Frey, *Englisches Wesen in der Bildenden Kunst* (Stuttgart & Berlin, 1942). For an analysis of this and Pevsner's *Englishness of English Art*, see W. Vaughan, "Behind Pevsner: Englishness as an Art Historical Category," in Corbett, Holt, and Russell, *Geographies of Englishness*, 347–368. Also A. Causey, "Pevsner and Englishness," in Draper, *Reassessing Pevsner*, 161–174 (as in note 1).

10. Pevsner, *Englishness* (as in note 2), 21, 23.

11. Pevsner, *Englishness* (as in note 2), 80.

12. U. Engel, "The formation of Pevsner's Art History: Nikolaus Pevsner in Germany 1902–1935," in Draper, *Reassessing Pevsner*, 29–55, esp. 33–4 (as in note 1); *idem*, "British Art and the Continent," in Ayers, *History of British Art* (as in note 3), 53–80, esp. 54–55. On the concept of *Kunstgeographie*, see also T. Da Costa Kaufmann, *Toward a Geography of Art* (Chicago and London, 2004), and B. Kurmann-Schwarz, "Zur Geschichte der Begriffe 'Kunstlandschaft' und 'Oberrrhein' in der Kunstgeschichte," in P. Kurmann and T. Zotz, eds., *Historische Landschaft—Kunstlandschaft? Der Oberrhein im späten Mittelalter*, Vorträge und Forschungen LXVIII. Herausgegeben vom Konstanzer Arbeitskreis für mittelalterliche Geschichte (Ostfildern, 2008), 65–90.

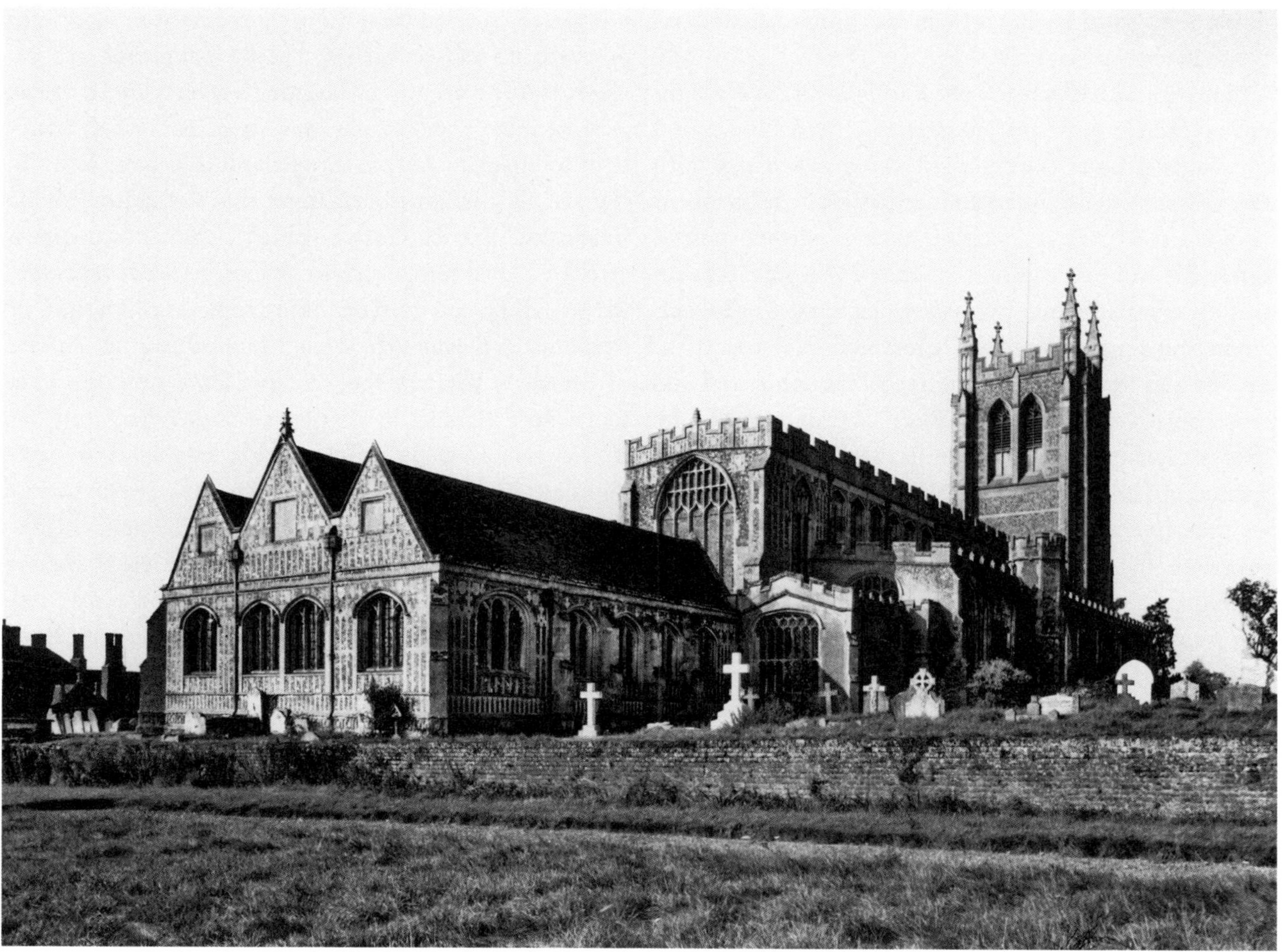

FIGURE 3. Long Melford church (Suffolk) (photo: National Monuments Record).

via the marginalia and *bas-de-page* vignettes of Gothic illumination: "No continental country has anything like these riches of observed life in medieval art"[13] (Fig. 8).

The opening sentence of the chapter on Perpendicular firmly associates it with national identity: "There is little that is in every respect so completely and so profoundly English as are the big parish churches of the Late Middle Ages ..." (Fig. 3). As the chapter unfolds Pevsner links the "matter-of-factness of Perpendicular space and tracery" with phonetics ("the clipped sound of the English monosyllable").[14] Recently the relationship between language and architecture in medieval England has been revisited by Peter Draper.[15] Pevsner also cites illogicality as an English quality: "The distaste of the English for carrying a thought or a system of thought to its logical extreme is too familiar to need comment." Subsequently he appears to contradict this by citing rationalism/reasonableness as a feature of much English Gothic architecture and ventures into social causality, associating the architecture of this

13. Pevsner, *Englishness* (as in note 2), 45.

14. Pevsner, *Englishness* (as in note 2), 90, 95.

15. P. Draper, "English with a French Accent: Architectural *Franglais* in Late-Twelfth-Century England?" in G. Clarke and P. Crossley, eds., *Architecture and Language: Constructing Identity in European Architecture c. 1000–c. 1650* (Cambridge, 2000), 21–35; *idem*, *The Formation of English Gothic: Architecture and Identity* (New Haven and London, 2006), 53.

period with the growing influence of a mercantile class in late medieval England.[16]

Linearity as a distinctively English trait is the subject of the chapter appropriately entitled "Blake and the Flaming Line." Pevsner has some difficulties with this signifier of English ethnic identity, as he is forced to cite Irish manuscript illumination and even hesitantly the Iron Age Celts in tracing its origins. Indeed, for Pevsner as for many Batsford authors, *English* was synonymous with *British*.[17] Decorated and Perpendicular, Pevsner argues, are two sides of the same coin and hence both are reconcilably English traits, unified by "line"—as we shall see, a familiar *topos*: "Decorated is the flowing line, Perpendicular is the straight line, but both are line and not body." This he justifies through asserting that "The history of styles ... can only be successful ... if it is conducted in terms of polarities, that is in pairs of apparently contradictory qualities."[18]

If one strand linked Pevsner with Frey and the Viennese school, a second found an echo in the theoretical standpoint of a number of contemporary scholars whose first language was English. Pevsner was editor of the *Pelican History of Art* series, and the fact that it was to a very considerable extent structured around current national boundaries was determined by the concept of a geography of art. A number of volumes (arguably disproportionately large) were devoted to British art and architecture, and it is instructive to look at the observations made by the authors of the three covering the Middle Ages.[19] Geoffrey Webb's *Architecture in Britain: The Middle Ages* (Harmondsworth, 1956; 2nd ed., 1965) eschewed any attempt to invoke a "national style," but this is not the case with both Margaret Rickert and Lawrence Stone in their highly important monographs on painting and sculpture that first appeared respectively in 1954 and 1955. Margaret Rickert, an American art historian, invoked national character as a determinant of insular traits in English Gothic painting: "In the end, it was not the Channel that saved English art [from the "French Gothic flame"], but the sturdiness of the English temperament, which refused to surrender to fads but insisted on taking time to weigh the new elements and consider what, if anything, it wanted of them."[20] Rickert was far from alone amongst contemporary scholars in evoking national character, but those who followed this line were by no means in agreement as to what peculiarly English qualities shaped its Gothic art. For Joan Evans, author of the period 1307–1461 in the *Oxford History of English Art* series, they were ethereal: "The most shining beauties of its architecture depend, as English beauties should, on fortuitous changes of light and shadow." We are in Constable or Turner country here. Evans again: "English art has the qualities of the art of a small country—it is more often decorative and pretty than monumental or noble." Rickert attempted to identify consistent features of English medieval art: "love of nature, of the whimsical, and of rich decorative pattern."[21] This characterization was not new; over twenty-five years previously, Eric Millar had identified lavish and robust ornament as a distinctive feature of English fourteenth-century illumination.[22] In her concluding remarks, Rickert like Pevsner invoked line as a distinguishing trait: "On the technique of outline drawing ... rests the continuity of English painting in the Middle Ages, and this is true not only of figural compositions but of the decorative

16. Pevsner, *Englishness* (as in note 2), 101, 122–123. Paul Crossley believes that Pevsner's emphasis on the significance of a burgeoning mercantile class was taken from Wilhelm Pinder's *Die Kunst der ersten Bürgerzeit bis zur Mitte des 15. Jahrhunderts* (Leipzig, 1937) (personal communication).

17. Pevsner, *Englishness* (as in note 2), 136–137; see also, Causey, "Pevsner and Englishness" (as in note 9), 165.

18. Pevsner, *Englishness* (as in note 2), 24; also 132.

19. I owe this observation to Paul Crossley. In the 1955 series plan, no fewer than seven volumes out of the total of about 50 were devoted to the British Isles. See S. Slive, "Nikolaus Pevsner's contribution as editor of *The Pelican History of Art* Series," in Draper, *Reassessing Pevsner* (as in note 1), 73–86.

20. M. Rickert, *Painting in Britain: The Middle Ages* (Harmondsworth, 1954), 7. A second edition was published in 1965.

21. J. Evans, *English Art, 1307–1461* (Oxford, 1949), 223, 224; Rickert, *Painting* (as in note 20), 8.

22. E. G. Millar, *English Illuminated Manuscripts of the XIVth and XVth Centuries* (Paris, 1928), ix. This passage was noted in Lucy Freeman Sandler, "Illuminated in the British Isles: French Influence and/or the Englishness of English Art 1285–1345," *Gesta* 45/2 (2006), 177–188 (177).

work as well."[23] Significantly, Francis Wormald, in his *English Drawings of the Tenth and Eleventh Centuries* (1952), conspicuously omitted any attempt to identify consistent "English" traits in a medium that by its nature would appear to be prime evidence for "line."[24]

Stone, primarily a renowned socio-economic historian, considered that English medieval sculpture was permeated by "a strong sense of dynamism and of movement." Another passage is very reminiscent of Rickert: "the tendency to linear abstraction and rhythmic pattern, which again and again triumphed over more naturalistic styles imported from the Continent." Stone concluded his Introduction with eloquent advocacy of the qualities of the insular carver: "His was an art circumscribed by somewhat narrow limits; but within these limits his resource and genius, inventiveness and power were certainly equal to those of his fellow-craftsmen in other countries. Though hemmed in by steep banks, the stream ran deep and fast."[25] There is more than an echo here of observations made by Arthur Gardner, the pre-eminent scholar of English medieval sculpture of a previous generation, which had appeared in print only four years earlier; Gardner cited a certain conservatism and "a loving attention to craftsmanship of detail" as distinctive traits of English sculpture.[26] Pevsner was somewhat less impressed by the qualities of carving in England: "The English are not a sculptural nation."[27] He was, however, ignoring the sculptural treatment of surfaces in early English and Decorated architecture and also overlooking the vast scale of losses. Stone estimated that more than ninety percent of English medieval religious sculpture has been lost; I would put the scale of destruction even higher and almost total in the case of wood carving: the Annunciation group at Wells Cathedral is an all-too-rare survivor (Fig. 4).[28] Unlike Rickert and Evans, absent from Stone is any attempt to link medieval sculpture with national character.

As with Pevsner, the focus in both Stone and Rickert is on English art, but with less excuse as the word "Britain," not "England" is used in their titles. Works of art originating in Celtic cultures (and in some instances still located in Scotland and Ireland) are discussed solely in their respective chapters on the pre-Viking period, and neither book addresses the question of what is "British" and what is "English."

English ethnicity looms large in the ideology of John Hooper Harvey (1911–1997), much of whose work appeared under the Batsford imprint, including his pioneering study of English late medieval architecture and its creators, the architects/masons. In common with Pevsner, Harvey (an architect by training) was the progeny of Hegelian *Zeitgeist*, and, also in common with Pevsner, he considered Perpendicular architecture to be a (or the) quintessential national style; indeed, he used this label as a chapter title in both *Gothic England* (1947) and in *The Perpendicular Style*, published three decades later (Fig. 5).[29] Harvey pushed more explicitly the idea of Perpendicular as a manifestation of national character, for which his terms of reference were both vague and diverse. In *Gothic England* he speaks of "a fundamental mysticism which lies beneath the surface rawness of the English temperament; ideas hardly to be spoken in words or drawn in clear outline, but which reflect an inner world ..."[30] *The Perpendicular Style* invokes the more quotidian virtues of practical commonsense and an aptitude for organization and improvisation. To these ingredients Harvey added that of the ruler's personality and character (and particularly Edward III) as both arbiter and imparter of taste. Some quotations from *The Perpendicular Style* give the flavor: "The reaction away from Curvilinear and the

23. Rickert, *Painting* (as in note 20), 218.

24. F. Wormald, *English Drawings of the Tenth and Eleventh Centuries* (London, 1952).

25. L. Stone, *Sculpture in Britain: The Middle Ages* (Harmondsworth, 1955), 5–6. A second edition appeared in 1972.

26. A. Gardner, *English Medieval Sculpture* (Cambridge, revised and enlarged ed. 1951), 1.

27. Pevsner, *Englishness* (as in note 2), 137.

28. Stone, *Sculpture* (as in note 25), 2.

29. J. Harvey, *Gothic England: A Survey of National Culture, 1300–1550* (London, 1947); *idem*, *The Perpendicular Style, 1330–1485* (London, 1978).

30. Harvey, *Gothic England* (as in note 29), 8.

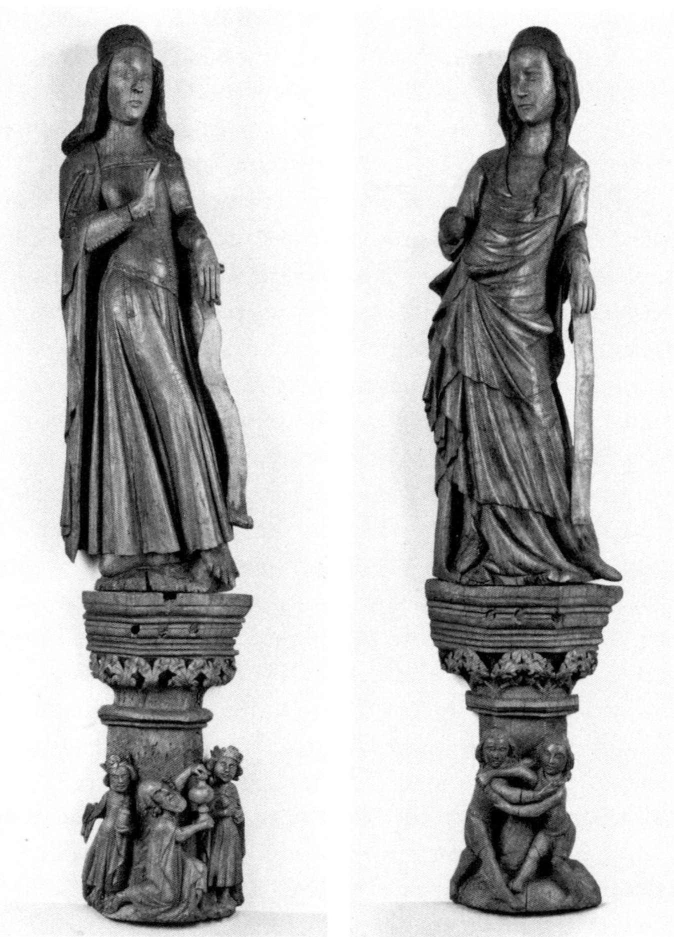

FIGURE 4. Wells Cathedral: Annunciation group (photo: Victoria & Albert Museum).

artistic licence which was its logical outcome lay in fundamental traits of English character, full of practical commonsense. Our deeply imbedded love of the line, especially the clear outline, was offended by convolutions ... England was ready to turn away in dislike, and for once found itself behind the personal taste of a great sovereign. Edward III was no ascetic ... he was a soldier ... [who] assured the creation of an English national style of architecture."

Again: "Perpendicular was the artistic style of the later Plantagenets and reflected their personalities and their manner of exercising a national sovereignty... The style ... was an aesthetic as well as a structural and technical reflection of the political purpose which in the same period engaged in fighting the Hundred Years War."[31] In other passages Harvey equates the emergence of Perpendicular with the development of English as a literary language (an analogy shared with Pevsner) and of music as practised by composers like John Dunstable. In Harvey's writings a celebration of distinctive English qualities is seasoned with a hint of superiority over the island's Continental neighbors: "The greater part of England was, by the opening of Edward III's reign, a highly civilised country. Embroidered hangings, clothes and accoutrements ... illuminated books, were produced to a standard of exquisite quality hardly ever equalled, and in western Europe, never excelled."[32] And more in the same vein.

31. Harvey, *Perpendicular* (as in note 29), 159, 234.

32. Harvey, *Perpendicular* (as in note 29), 42.

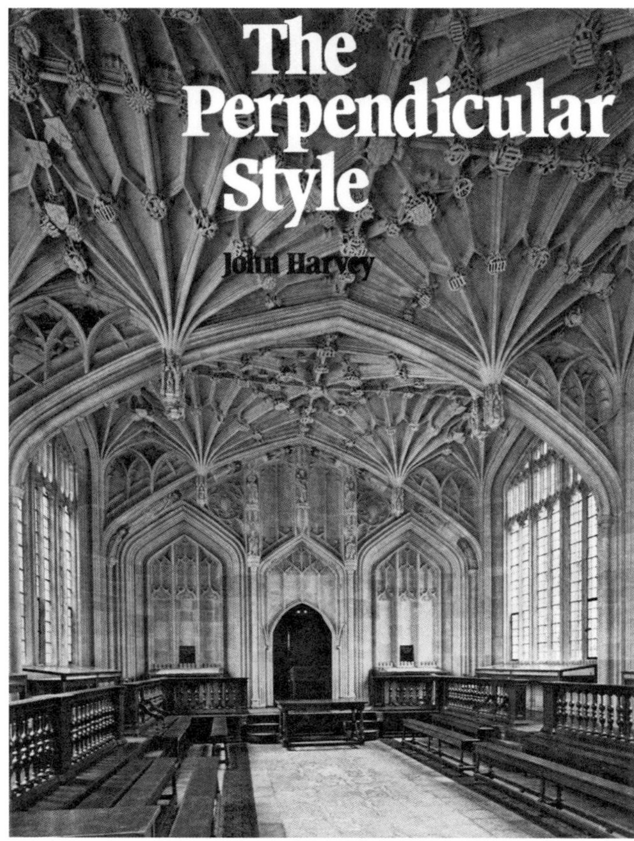

FIGURE 5. Dust-jacket of J. Harvey, *The Perpendicular Style 1330–1485* (Batsford, 1978).

It is not the least ironic of situations that similar theories of *Zeitgeist* and a synergy between art and national character art were propounded on the one hand by a German-speaking art historian (Pevsner) opposed to the racial theories of fascism (Frey's book however was part of a Nazi research program) and on the other by an English right-wing authoritarian, whose own fascist leanings have recently been exposed by Graham Macklin.[33] Despite an occasional whiff from Harvey—more pronounced in his historical writings than in his architectural studies—the issue of art as a signifier of national identity this side of the Channel never developed the toxicity that it did in Germany, firstly under Bismarck and then the Nazis.[34] Nonetheless, it was perhaps sufficiently in evidence to account for the absence of any reference to Harvey's writings by Pevsner in *The Englishness of English Art.* It is also worth observing that some of Harvey's pre-World War II contemporaries, who were advocates of traditional rural life, also admired aspects of Nazi Germany, notably Arthur Bryant.[35]

From the outset, the association of style with transmitted national genetics did not go unchallenged. Jonathan Alexander has pointed out that as long ago as 1936 Meyer Schapiro attacked the premise that art was an expression of national character. Not surprisingly, it was the first aspect of these headings to disappear.[36] Even before the publication of *The Englishness of English Art*, Tom Boase had rejected the nexus in his *English Art 1100–1216*: "It is ... seldom true to talk of the arts in terms of nationalism." The concept is also absent from Peter Brieger's volume on the period 1216–1307 in the same *Oxford History of English Art* series, published in 1957, where the traces of "spirit of the age," which infiltrate into the Conclusion, look strangely alien to the tenor of the book as a whole.[37] Like Lawrence Stone, my own tutor, George Zarnecki, in the two seminal monographs on English Romanesque sculpture he published in the early 1950s, remained mute on the subject—unsurprisingly considering his personal experiences of virulent nationalism.[38] Curiously, absent from both the proponents and opponents of the concept of

33. G. Macklin, "The Two Lives of John Hooper Harvey," *Patterns of Prejudice* 42, no. 2 (2008), 167–190.

34. Crossley, "Between Spectacle and History" (as in note 4), 143-4; for the appropriation of German medieval art to fit the ideology of National Socialism, see M. H. Caviness, "The Politics of Taste: An Historiography of 'Romanesque' Art in the Twentieth Century," in C. Hourihane, ed., *Romanesque Art and Thought in the Twelfth Century, Essays in Honor of Walter Cahn* (Princeton, 2008), 57–81, esp. 75–6.

35. Matless, *Landscape* (as in note 5), 199–123; Macklin, "Harvey" (as in note 33), 185.

36. J. J. G. Alexander, "Medieval Art and Modern Nationalism," in G. R. Owen-Crocker and T. Graham, eds., *Medieval Art: Recent Perspectives, A Memorial Tribute to C. R. Dodwell* (Manchester and New York, 1998), 218.

37. T. S. R. Boase, *English Art, 1100–1216* (Oxford, 1953), 297; P. Brieger, *English Art, 1216–1307* (Oxford, 1957), 271–4.

38. G. Zarnecki, *English Romanesque Sculpture, 1066–1140* (London, 1951); *idem, Later English Romanesque Sculpture, 1140–1210* (London, 1953). See also Peter Kidson's obituary of George Zarnecki in *The Burlington Magazine* 150 (2008), 830–1.

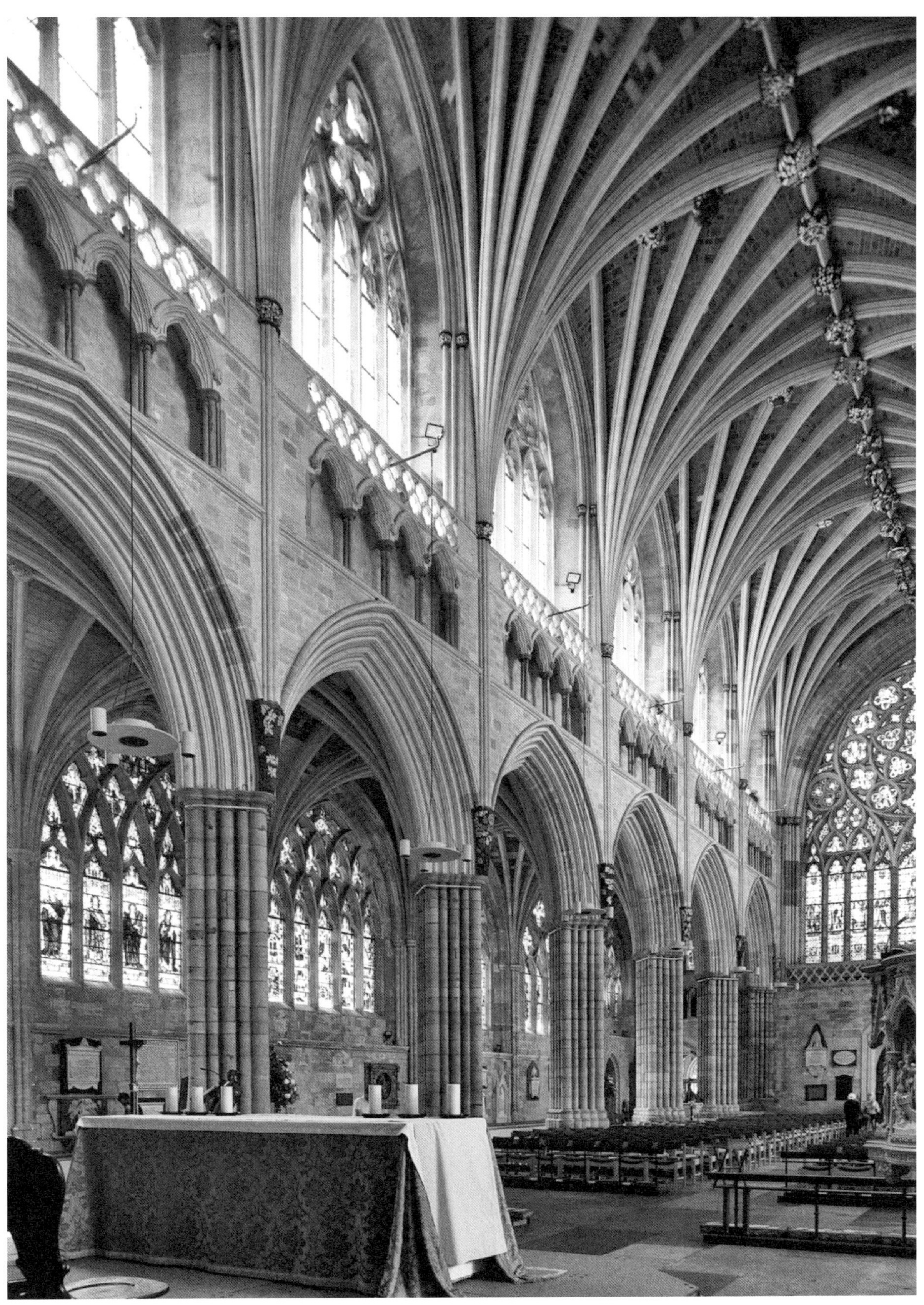

FIGURE 6. Exeter Cathedral, nave (photo: Christopher Wilson).

a national style in the Middle Ages was any appeal to contemporary sources. Had they done so, the critics of the construct would have rejoiced in the fact that there is little sign that medieval Englishmen and women had any perception of a "national" architecture, as Jane Geddes has recently observed.[39]

The Age of "The Age of Chivalry"

In his foreword to the Penguin edition of *The Englishness of English Art*, Pevsner writes: "It has been gratifying to see that no changes worth mentioning had to be made between 1955 and 1963."[40] The second edition of Rickert's *Painting in Britain: The Middle Ages*, published in 1965, also retained the passages about national character and consistent identifiable traits. But by the late 60s and 70s issues of "national style" as well as *Zeitgeist* had disappeared from the scholarly radar screen. Despite the occasional late echo from historians rather than art historians, it would be a brave scholar who would argue today that English art and architecture between the late twelfth and early sixteenth centuries exhibits recognizable stylistic continuity, let alone seek to identify ethnic characteristics underpinning it.[41] Only the most blinkered, I suspect, would maintain that the naves of Exeter Cathedral and St. George's Chapel, Windsor (Figs. 6, 7) are both manifestations of one and the same national character, or that a consistent interest in linearity unites the Packham Clifford Hours and the Bedford Hours and Psalter (Figs. 8, 9).

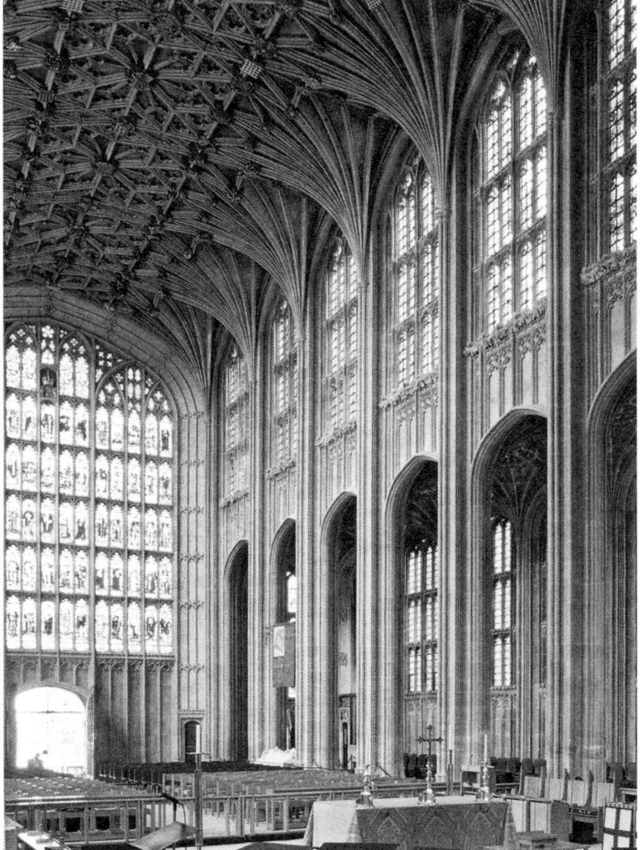

FIGURE 7. Windsor Castle, St. George's Chapel, nave (photo: Christopher Wilson).

From the 1960s, in the place of "grand narrative," three distinct trends have emerged, trends that coincided with, and were fueled by the spread of art history as an academic discipline in British and American universities. The first was the systematic and scholarly cataloguing of medieval manuscript and glass painting through *A Survey of Manuscripts Illuminated in the British Isles* (Fig. 10), published by Harvey Miller under the general editorship of Jonathan Alexander, and the English volumes in the international *Corpus Vitrearum Medii Aevi* project (Fig. 11); the first publications of both appeared in the 1970s. The two series differ in that whereas the *Illuminated Manuscripts* are selective, the *Corpus Vitrearum* leaves no stone (or more accurately, no sliver of glass) unturned. All three of the *Illuminated Manuscripts* series for the Gothic period eschew the concept of continuity, although to varying extents each argues for consistent stylistic traits in their respective periods. All of them have made available far more material than had hitherto been the case, dressed with the necessary bibliographical paraphernalia and copious illustrations, etc.

Secondly, there have been more detailed and better-informed explorations of individual and groups of buildings and artifacts. An important vehicle here is

39. J. Geddes, "Ideas and Images of Britain, 600–1600," in Ayers, *History of British Art*, 19–52 (as in note 3), 38.

40. Pevsner, *Englishness* (as in note 2), 11.

41. Notably C. Richmond, "The Visual Culture of Fifteenth-Century England," in A. J. Pollard, ed., *The Wars of the Roses* (Basingstoke, 1995), 186–209.

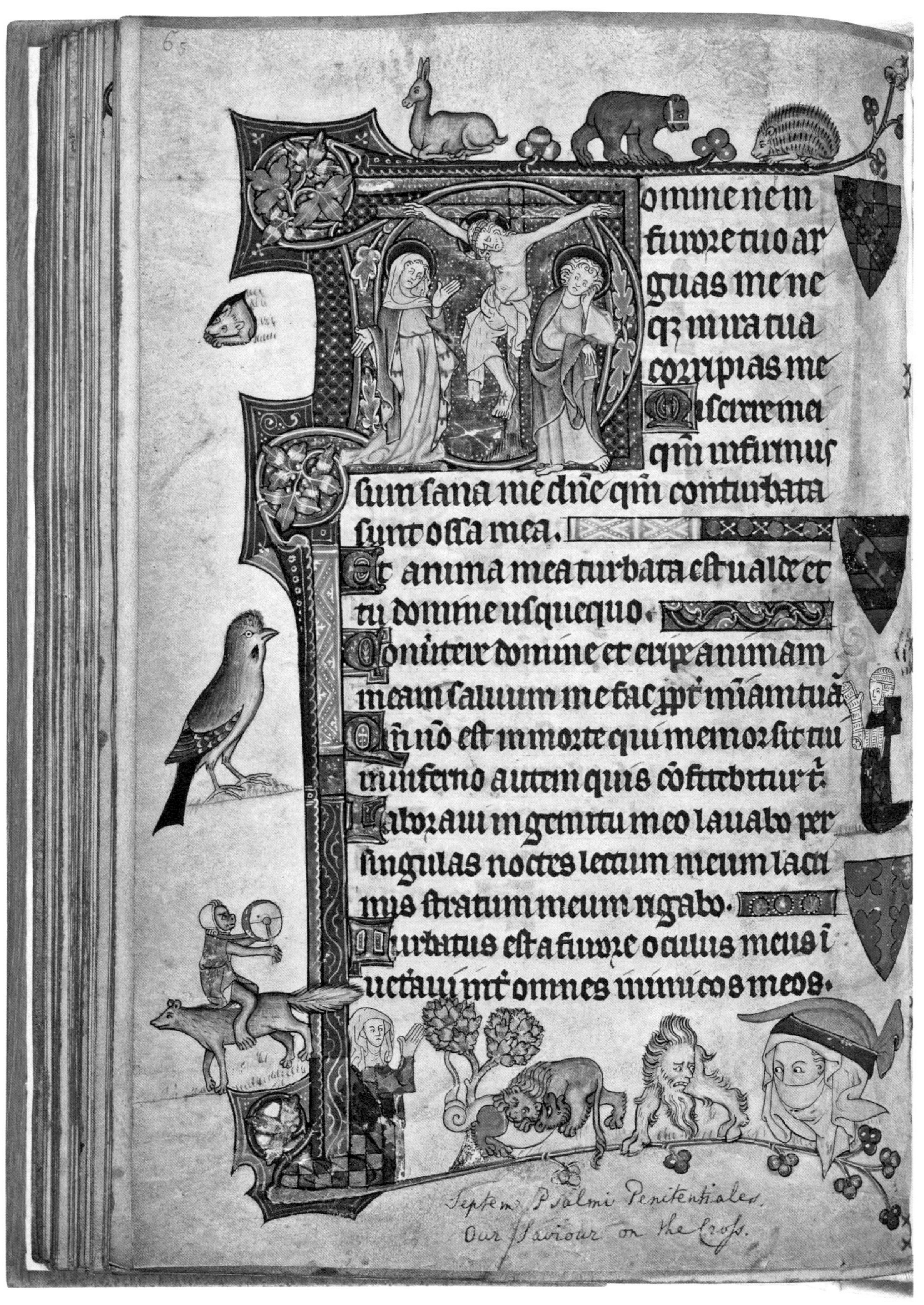

FIGURE 8. *Packham Clifford Hours* (Cambridge, Fitzwilliam Museum MS. 242, fol. 55^{v}) (photo: Fitzwilliam Museum).

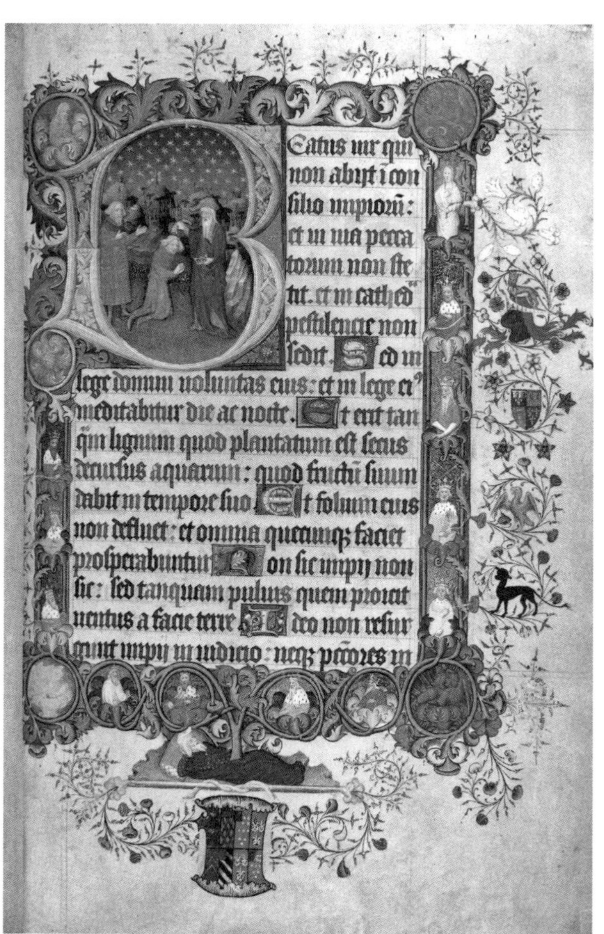

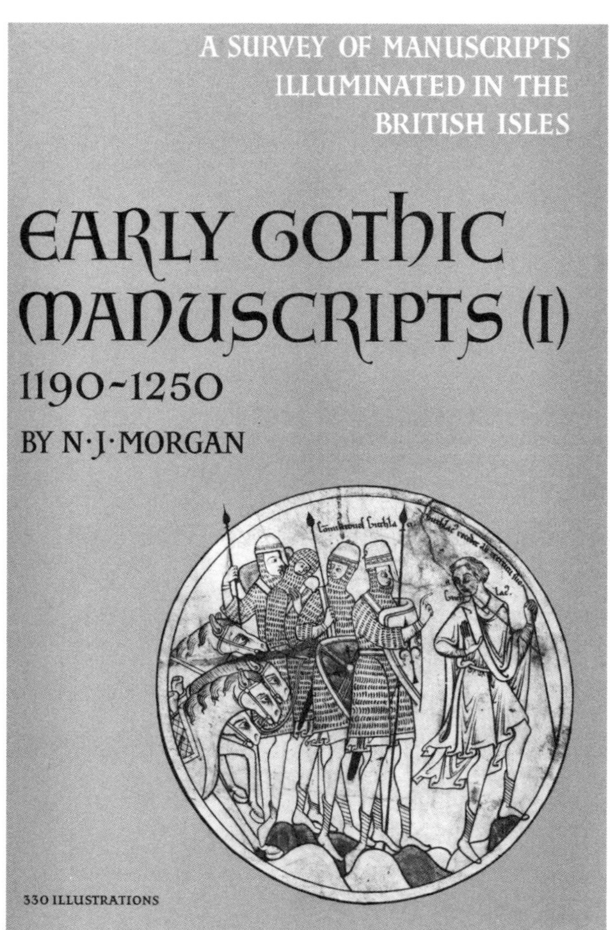

FIGURE 9. *Bedford Hours and Psalter* (London, British Library MS. Add. 42131, fol. 73ʳ) (photo: British Library Board).

FIGURE 10. Dust-jacket of N. J. Morgan, *Early Gothic Manuscripts (I) 1190–1250* (London, 1982).

FIGURE 11. Dust-jacket of P. Hebgin-Barnes, *The Medieval Stained Glass of the County of Lincolnshire* (Oxford, 1996).

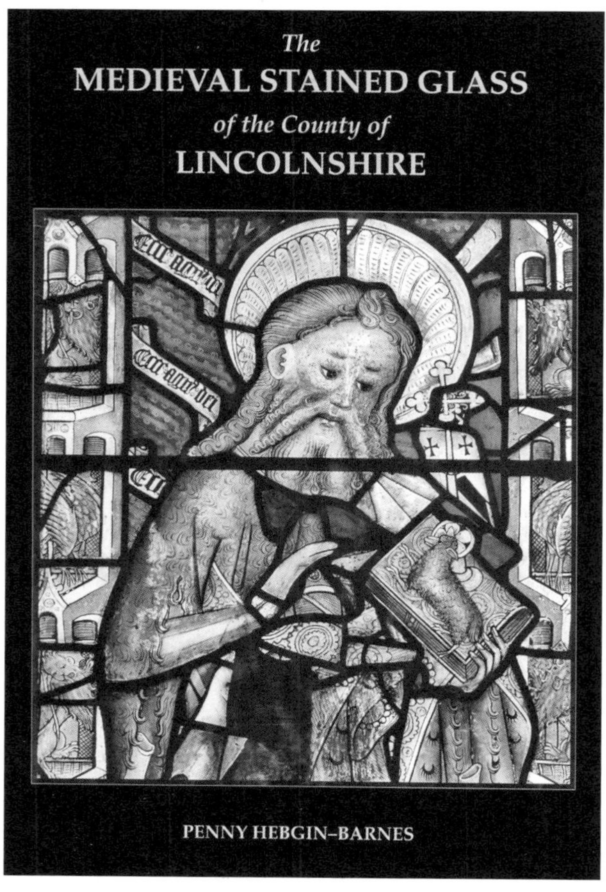

the annual British Archaeological Association Conference, the proceedings of which first appeared in 1978. These have tended to be focused around cathedrals and great churches and thus have supplemented a series of scholarly monographs on English cathedrals that began with York Minster (1977).[42]

Through all these and many other studies, England's medieval art has become better known and interpreted. While the underlying assumption remains that there was an *English* Gothic, its diversity has been made more apparent: there is more than one English Gothic. At the same time, a more nuanced and refined exploration of its relationship with the Continent has emerged. Doctrinally, England was part of Western (Catholic) Christendom and the religious orders established there were important agents for the movement of art and architecture. Christopher Wilson has highlighted the role of the Cistercians in introducing Gothic architecture into northern England.[43] Tom Boase and later Walter Cahn demonstrated the inseparability of manuscript illumination in southern England and northern France during the late twelfth century, coining the label "Channel Style."[44] Madeline Caviness extended the "Channel Style" concept to embrace stained glass by showing that the glazing of the eastern parts of Canterbury Cathedral in the same period not only shared the same design features as northern French schemes but that some of the glaziers moved between the principal programs.[45] As long ago as 1949 Jean Bony placed Canterbury Cathedral within a group of northeastern French buildings that he saw as "resistant to the Chartres model," a concept revisited and glossed recently by Christopher Wilson.[46] All of this, to varying degrees, problematizes the notion of a "national" English Gothic. In some instances, recognizably foreign influences were assimilated into English visual idioms. The French "band window" formula was applied within the context of English Decorated window design (Fig. 12). Christopher Wilson has put into perspective the notion of Perpendicular as the "national style" by identifying much of its origins in French Rayonnant architecture ("There is a very real sense in which Perpendicular is Rayonnant taken to its ultimate conclusion").[47] Lucy Sandler and others have drawn attention to the reception (and re-working) of Italianate modeling and spatial settings in English fourteenth-century painting in various media, largely but not exclusively filtered through Parisian art of the 1320s and 30s (Fig. 13).[48] The focus has not been entirely on either style or dependency on foreign models. George Henderson, followed by Peter Klein, Nigel Morgan, and Suzanne Lewis, has underlined the indigenous predilection for high-status illuminated Apocalypse manuscripts in the thirteenth century.[49]

42. G. E. Aylmer and R. Cant, eds., *A History of York Minster* (Oxford, 1977).

43. C. Wilson, "The Cistercians as 'Missionaries of Gothic' in Northern England," in C. Norton and D. Park, eds., *Cistercian Art and Architecture in the British Isles* (Cambridge, 1986), 86–116.

44. Boase, *English Art, 1100-1216* (as in note 37), 181–184; W. Cahn, "St Albans and the Channel Style in England," in *The Year 1200: A Symposium* (Metropolitan Museum of Art, New York, 1975), 187–230.

45. M. H. Caviness, *The Early Stained Glass of Canterbury Cathedral, c. 1175–1220* (Princeton, 1977), esp. 49–58, 77–100; *idem*, *The Windows of Christ Church Cathedral Canterbury*, Corpus Vitrearum Medii Aevi Great Britain, vol. II (London, 1981), *passim*.

46. J. Bony, "The Resistance to Chartres in Early Thirteenth-Century Architecture," *Journal of the British Archaeological Association*, 3rd series, 20/21 (1957–8), 35-52; C. Wilson, "Lausanne and Canterbury: A 'Special Relationship' Re-considered," in P. Kurmann and Martin Rohde, eds., *Die Kathedrale von Lausanne und ihr Marienportal im Kontext der europäischen Gotik*, *Scrinium Friburgense*, 13 (Berlin and New York, 2004), 89–124.

47. C. Wilson, "The English Response to French Gothic Architecture, c. 1200–1350," in J. Alexander and P. Binski, eds., *Age of Chivalry: Art in Plantagenet England, 1200–1400*, Exhib. Cat., Royal Academy of Arts (London, 1987), 82; *idem*, "'Excellent, New and Uniforme': Perpendicular Architecture c. 1400–1547," in Marks and Williamson, *Gothic: Art for England* (as in note 3), 99, 103.

48. L. F. Sandler, "A Follower of Jean Pucelle in England," *Art Bulletin* 52 (1970), 363–372; *idem*, *The Psalter of Robert de Lisle in the British Library* (London, 1999); see also her discussion of French and English illumination of the same period in "Illuminated in the British Isles" (as in note 22); P. Binski and D. Park, "A Ducciesque Episode at Ely: The Mural Decorations of Prior Crauden's Chapel," in M. Ormrod, ed., *England in the Fourteenth Century: Proceedings of the 1985 Harlaxton Symposium* (Woodbridge, 1986), 28–41; C. Norton, "Klosterneuburg and York: Artistic Cross-Currents at an English Cathedral, c. 1330," *Wiener Jahrbuch für Kunstgeschichte*, 46/47(1993/94), 519–532.

49. See the bibliographies and discussion of individual manuscripts in N. J. Morgan, *Early Gothic Manuscripts (II) 1250–1285*, A Survey of Manuscripts Illuminated in the British Isles, Vol. IV

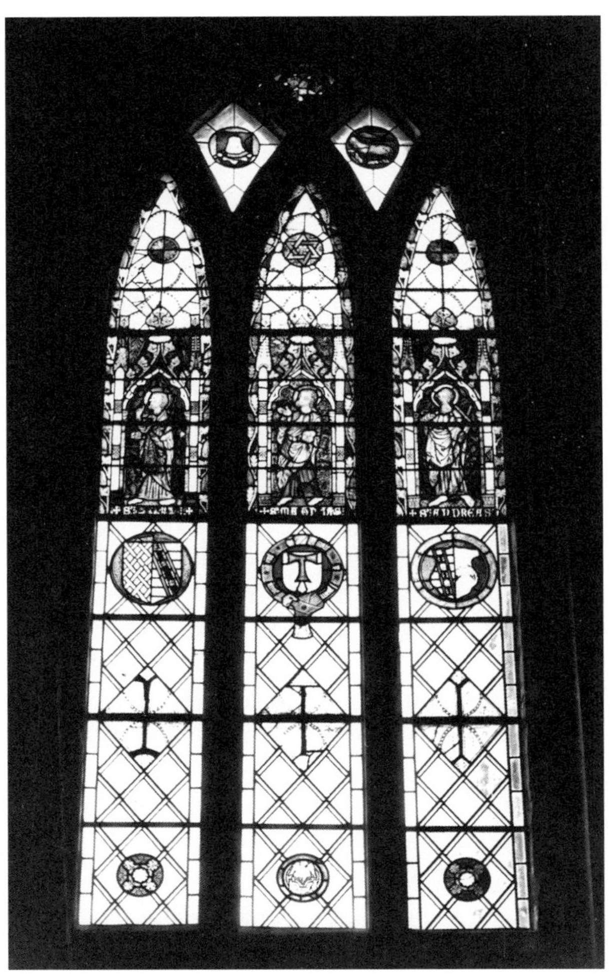

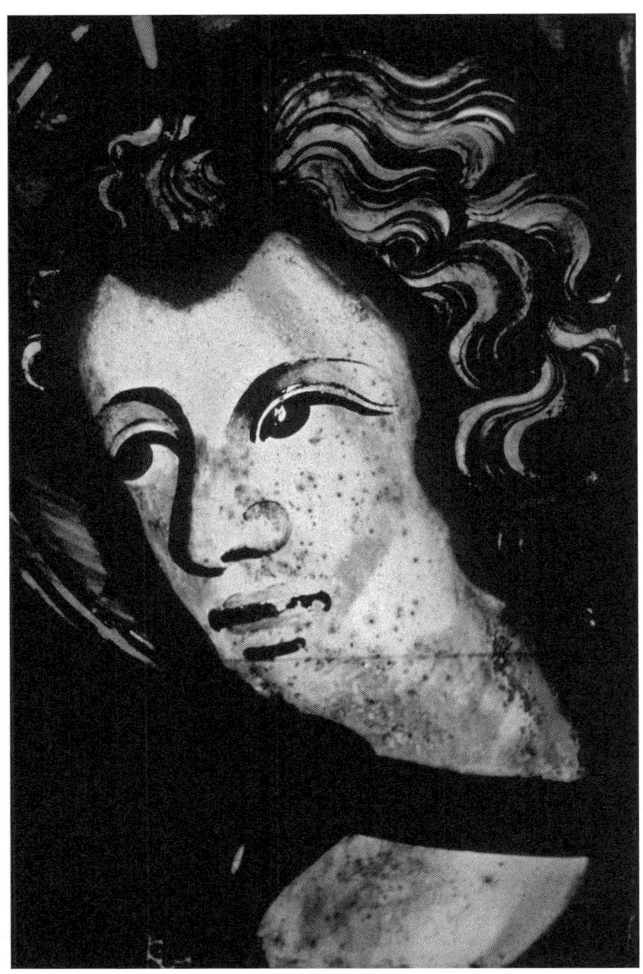

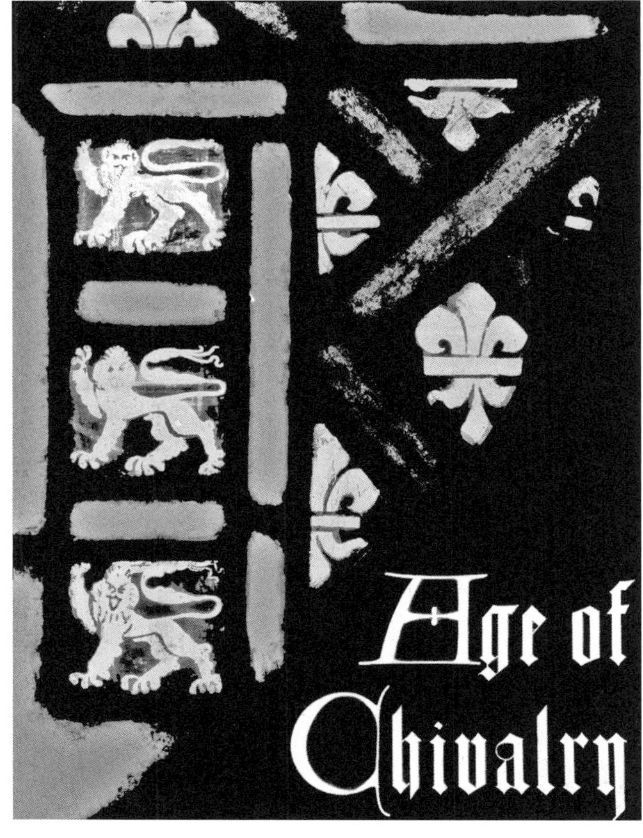

FIGURE 12. Stanford on Avon church (Northamptonshire), chancel window (photo: author).

FIGURE 13. York Minster nave west window: head of St. John the Evangelist (photo: author).

FIGURE 14. Cover of *Age of Chivalry: Art in Plantagenet England 1200–1400* catalogue (London, Royal Academy of Arts, 1987).

These two strands, which might loosely be categorized as discovery and recovery, were rooted in the discourse of empiricism. The third began to make its impact in the 1980s with the adoption by some medievalists of what was then the "New Art History" with its social readings of art (or "visual culture"—a label abhorred by traditionalists), which challenged the discipline's historic monolithic focus on style, aesthetic value-judgements, and attribution, in favor of alternative narratives embracing deconstruction, *Rezeptiontheorie*, function, audience, and meaning, the challenging of the notion of the great artist/work of art, and introducing feminism, and, latterly, gender. Michael Camille and others contested the use of images in the likes of the Luttrell Psalter as mirrors of life as it was lived in the fourteenth century, arguing that on the contrary they were active as opposed to reflective agents in the construction of history and self-identity; he also applied Bakhtinian theories of carnival as controlled subversion to marginalia and misericords, etc. (Fig. 8).[50] In this environment the writing of "national" meta-narratives did not sit comfortably.

In the midst of this intellectual transformation of the discipline of Art History occurred the *Age of Chivalry: Art in Plantagenet England, 1200–1400* exhibition, held at the Royal Academy in 1987 (Fig. 14). Curated by Jonathan Alexander, the exhibition and its catalogue, co-edited with Jonathan by Paul Binski, was a seminal event in the historiography of English Gothic art: a *Summa* in which the varying fruits of past and recent research were harvested and where the New Art History rubbed shoulders with the old.[51] On reflection—and indeed I think at the time—the inclusion of such a wide spectrum of intellectual inquiry came across as complementary rather than adversarial.

Unsurprisingly, the exhibition made no attempt to define an overarching national Gothic style. It did however chime with a reaction against the notions of a hegemonic culture—in the case of the thirteenth and fourteenth centuries, that of Paris and the Île de France. As Jonathan Alexander wrote in the catalogue: "It is no longer the case that scholars see English Gothic art as some sort of provincial offshoot under the shadow of French Gothic art..."[52] Hegemony depends of course on where you are and who is exercising it. From the Irish nationalist perspective, as Colum Hourihane reminds us, the Gothic style was perceived not in terms of a dominant French cultural form but as a manifestation of an alien (English) occupying power.[53] Only one essay in the *Age of Chivalry* catalogue (by Christopher Wilson) explicitly explored the relationship between France and England and that in respect of architecture. As he observed, the major English early thirteenth-century cathedrals were the equals of their French contemporaries in "aesthetic sophistication" and were more costly—unsurprisingly perhaps as at the time a dozen of Catholic Europe's richest forty sees were in England.[54] Significantly too the concept of a "Court Style" rooted in the Paris of Louis IX and his successors, already under attack by Paul Binski amongst others, only attracted fleeting mention (Fig. 15).[55]

Gothic: Art for England

The *Age of Chivalry* took 1400 as its *terminus ante quem*. It is a curious paradox that while Harvey and Pevsner predicated much of their case for the "Englishness of English art" on Perpendicular architecture, they were far more reticent about the pictorial arts of the fifteenth and early sixteenth centuries. Indeed, in the welter of publications on English Gothic art that have

---

(London, 1988), 16–19, and catalogue entries. Also S. Lewis, *Reading Images: Narrative Discourse and Reception in the Thirteenth-Century Illuminated Apocalypse* (Cambridge, 1995).

50. M. Camille, "Labouring for the Lord: The Ploughman and the Social Order in the Luttrell Psalter," *Art History* 10 (1987), 423–454; subsequently incorporated into *Mirror in Parchment: The Luttrell Psalter and the Making of England* (London, 1998); *idem*, *Image on the Edge: The Margins of Medieval Art* (London, 1992).

51. Alexander and Binski, *Age of Chivalry* (as in note 47), 82. See also the perceptive observations on the exhibition in Crossley, "Between Spectacle and History"(as in note 4), esp. 144–147.

52. Alexander and Binski, *Age of Chivalry* (as in note 47), 13.

53. C. Hourihane, *Gothic Art in Ireland, 1169–1550: Enduring Vitality* (New Haven, 2003), 19–34.

54. Wilson, "The English Response to French Gothic Architecture" (as in note 47), 74.

55. P. Binski, *The Painted Chamber at Westminster*, Society of Antiquaries of London Occasional Paper 9 (London, 1986); *idem*,

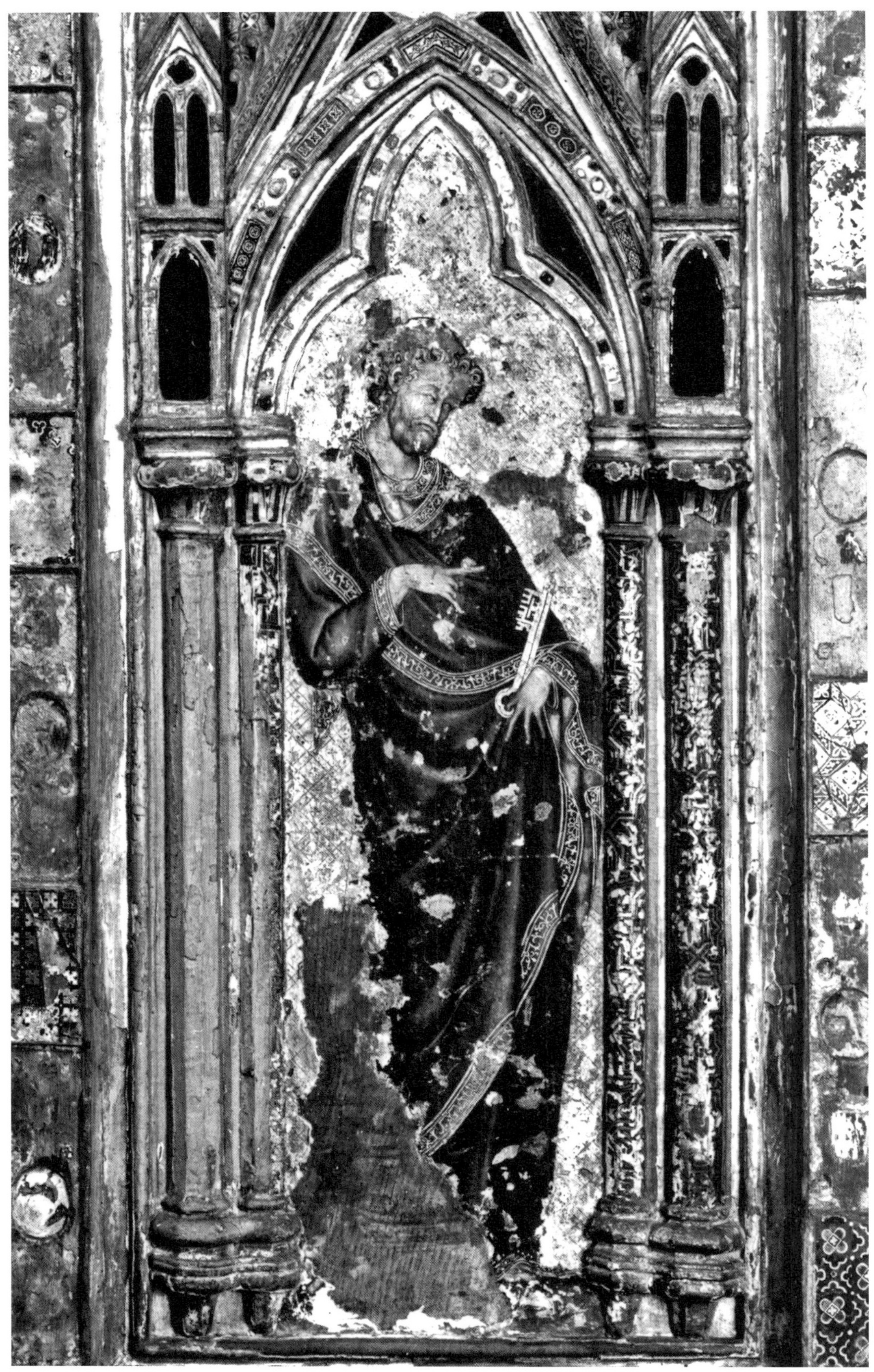

FIGURE 15. Westminster Abbey: Westminster Retable, detail (photo: Conway Library, Courtauld Institute of Art).

appeared since Pevsner's time, the emphasis very decidedly has been on the late twelfth to the fourteenth centuries. This bias is epitomized by the joint acquisition in 1929 of the Luttrell Psalter and Bedford Hours and Psalter by the British Museum. Whereas the former was published in a lavish part-facsimile by Eric Millar only three years later, it was not until 1962 that even a brief article was dedicated to the latter (by Derek Turner)(Fig. 9).[56] Even leaving aside the obvious appeal of the Luttrell Psalter, this is a remarkable *longeur*. The same picture emerges on the larger canvas of the general surveys of English Gothic art. Rickert only devoted one chapter (out of eight) and twenty-two pages (out of 226 text pages) to English painting from *c*. 1425. Stone was slightly more generous: two chapters for the period *c*. 1410–1540 and thirty-nine pages (from 233).[57] With regard to wall-painting, Tristram's monumental volumes on the twelfth and thirteenth centuries were followed solely by a more modest monograph on the fourteenth century.[58] Quantitative analysis of course is not the only measure that can be applied, and the balance has begun to be redressed in recent decades, especially in one particular field, as we will see shortly.

A factor in this relative neglect of the fifteenth and early sixteenth centuries has been an underlying assumption that the history of art and architecture at this time was determined by, and hence mirrored, political history: i.e., just as England descended into internecine strife and chaos from which it was rescued only by the Tudor monarchy, so in the visual arts it was very much downhill all the way from the glories of the thirteenth and fourteenth centuries until the Renaissance crossed the Channel in the sixteenth century. As a result, there has been a perception that the Late Gothic period at best was an "Age of Transition" sandwiched between peaks of creativity.[59] I suspect that another barrier is that, with the exception of Perpendicular architecture, whose salient technical and design features had been established before 1400, the diversity exhibited by English art after this date does not lend itself to being molded into a neat linear formalist narrative. The picture is not merely one of stylistic heterogeneity, but also of much greater (or more apparent) regional variation than hitherto. For the first time too the scale of imported works of art and of numbers of immigrant craftsmen became significant. Uncertainty over the parameters of Late Gothic art in England extends into chronology: when does "Gothic" England come to an end? This depends on which of the alternative determinants (style, patronage, religion, etc.) is adopted. Thus the *terminus ante quem* in the *Pelican History of Art* and *Oxford History of Art* has varied between 1461 (Evans) and 1540 (Stone).[60] The *Corpus Vitrearum* county survey volumes have opted for the 1550s, and in placing its endpoint as late as 1600, the recent medieval volume in the *History of British Art* series has emphasized continuities in the secular sphere.[61]

The study of this period therefore raises once again the defining of a "national" art—or rather, a period-specific "national art": What should be included and what excluded under the label of English Late Gothic art? Is it "art *of* England," limited either to what was made by indigenous craftsmen, or also encompassing the output of foreign-born artists resident in England? Is it "art *for* England," i.e., taking into consideration works of art created abroad—primarily in France (especially Paris) and increasingly the southern Netherlands—which were commissioned or purchased by English patrons (Figs. 16, 19)?

The response depends on the kind of Art History that is being written. Seen from the perspectives of patronage, consumption, function, and reception, to con-

---

Westminster Abbey and the Plantagenets: Kingship and the Representation of Power 1200–1400 (New Haven and London, 1995), 8–9, 44–46, 112, 175.

56. E. G. Millar, *The Luttrell Psalter* (London, 1932); D. H. Turner, "The Bedford Hours and Psalter," *Apollo* 76 (1962), 265–270.

57. Rickert, *Painting* (as in note 20); Stone, *Sculpture* (as in note 25).

58. E. W. Tristram, *English Medieval Wall Painting: The Twelfth Century* (London, 1944); *idem*, *English Medieval Wall Painting: The Thirteenth Century* (London, 1950); *idem*, *English Medieval Wall Painting: The Fourteenth Century* (London, 1954).

59. As in D. Gaimster and P. Stamper, eds., *The Age of Transition: The Archaeology of English Culture, 1400–1600* (Oxford, 1997).

60. Evans, *English Art, 1307–1461* (as in note 21); Stone, *Sculpture* (as in note 25).

61. Ayers, *History of British Art* (as in note 3).

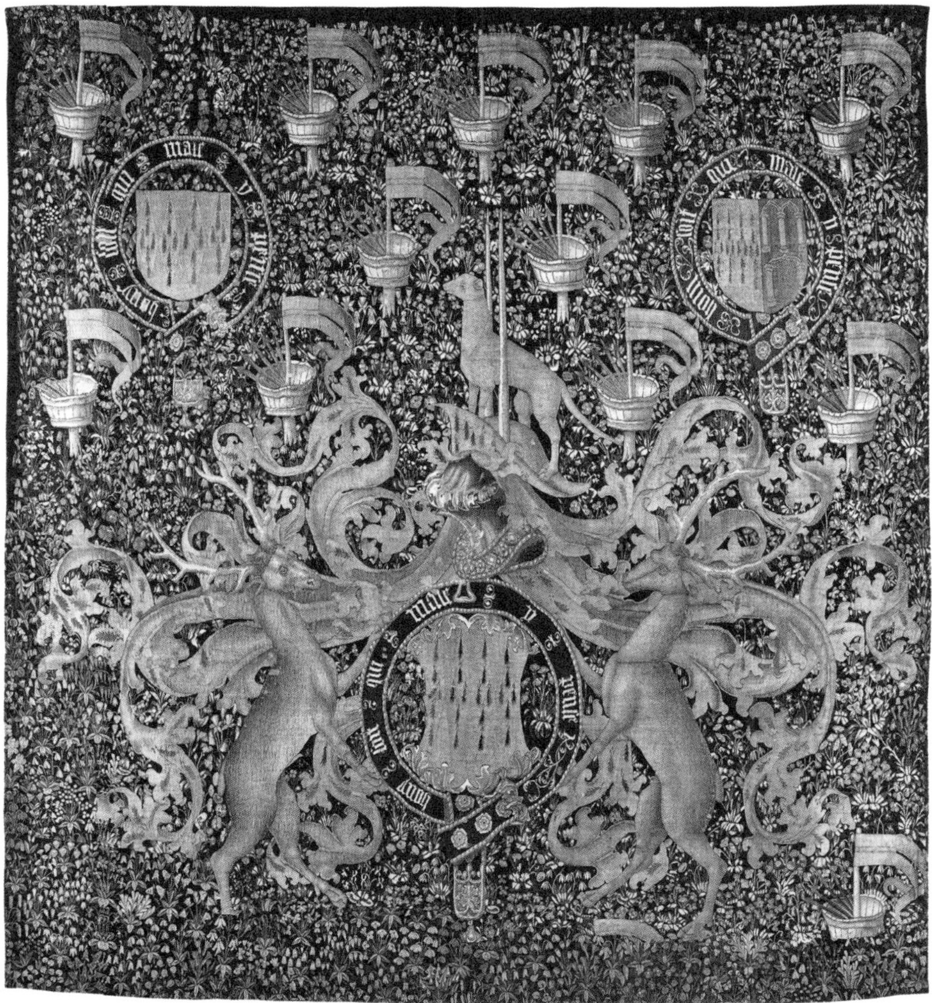

FIGURE 16. Tapestry of John Lord Dynham (New York, The Metropolitan Museum of Art, The Cloisters Collection, 1960 [60.127.1]) (photo: The Metropolitan Museum of Art).

fine the history of art in England to what is deemed to be the work of indigenous craftsmen would be to present a very confused and distorted picture, especially at the highest levels. It is often difficult, sometimes even pointless, to characterize a work as "English" or "foreign." Judgement is still out as to the nationalities of the painter of the Wilton Diptych, owing to lack of any comparable extant works, and also of the carvers of the ranks of saints in Henry VII's Chapel, Westminster Abbey (Figs. 17, 18).[62] The Donne Triptych is self-evidently the work of Hans Memling and was executed in Bruges (Fig. 19), but what label should be applied to the tomb of Richard Beauchamp, Earl of Warwick (d. 1439) a collaborative exercise involving several craftsmen, including the "Dutchman" Bartholomew Lambespringe, who chased and gilded the earl's bronze effigy (Fig. 20)? It is unhelpful to distinguish between the Donne Triptych and the glazing of Fairford (Fig. 22), on the basis that one was painted in Flanders and the other was made by immigrant craftsmen from the same region.

62. For a summary of conflicting opinions on the nationalities of the carvers of the Henry VII Chapel stone figures, see P. Lindley, "'The singuler mediacions and praiers of al the holie companie of Heven': Sculptural Functions and Forms in Henry VII's Chapel," in T. Tatton-Brown and R. Mortimer, eds., *Westminster Abbey The Lady Chapel of Henry VII* (Woodbridge, 2004), 275–293, esp. 287–293.

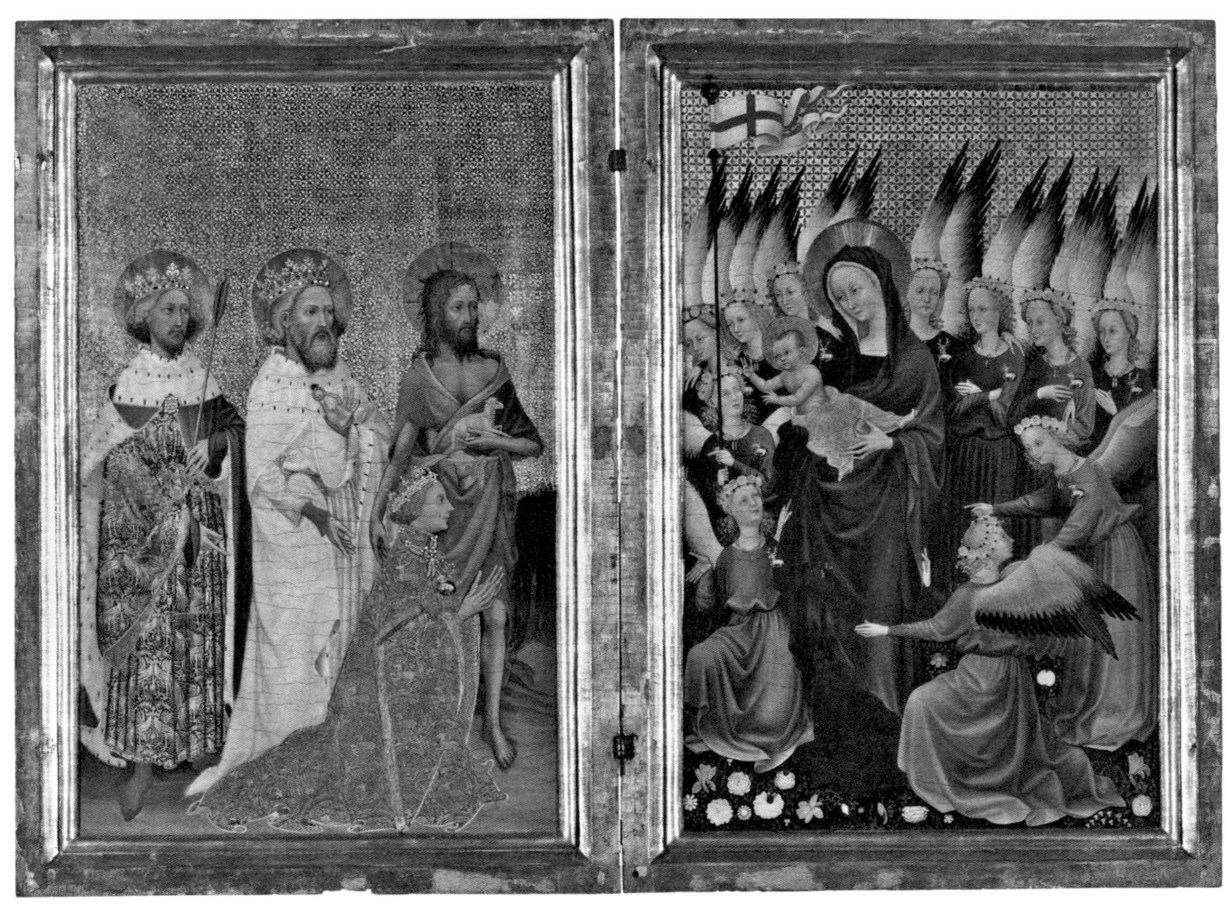

FIGURE 17. *Wilton Diptych* (London, National Gallery) (photo: National Gallery).

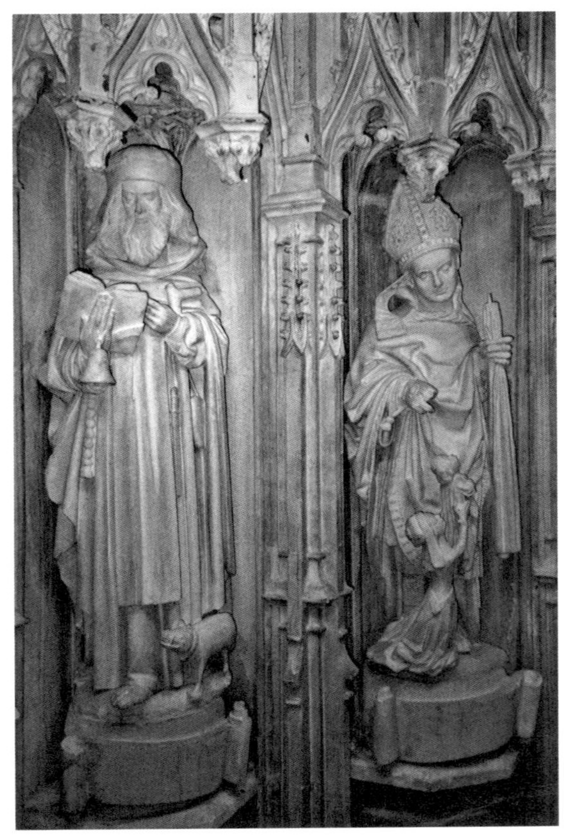

FIGURE 18. Westminster Abbey, Henry VII's Chapel, interior sculpture (photo: author).

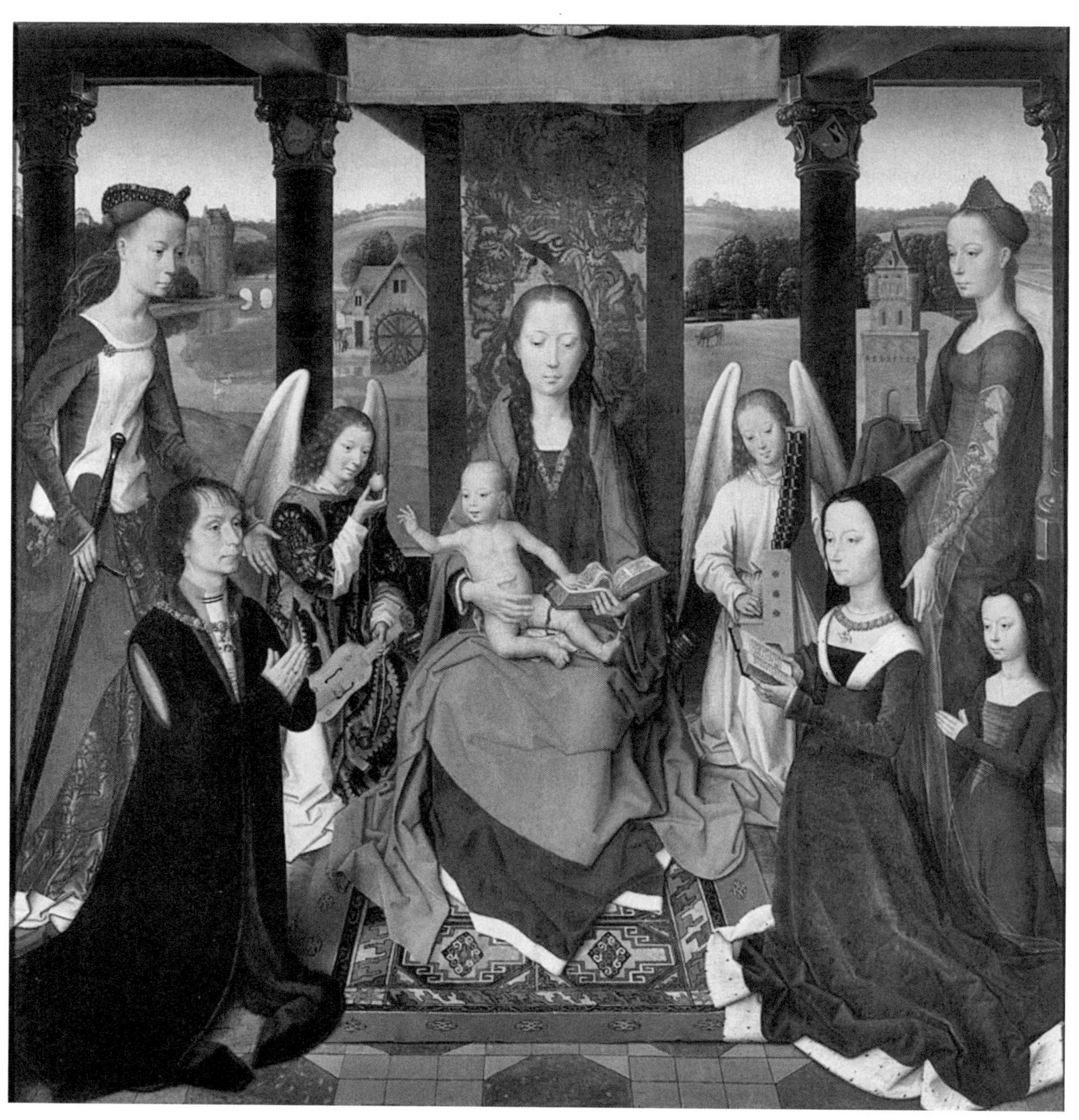

FIGURE 19. Hans Memling: *Donne Triptych*, center panel (London, National Gallery) (photo: National Gallery).

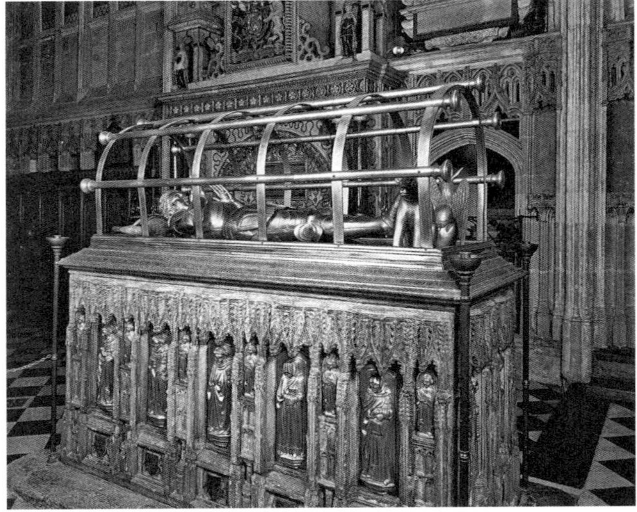

FIGURE 20. Warwick, Beauchamp Chapel, tomb of Richard Beauchamp, Earl of Warwick (d. 1439) (photo: author).

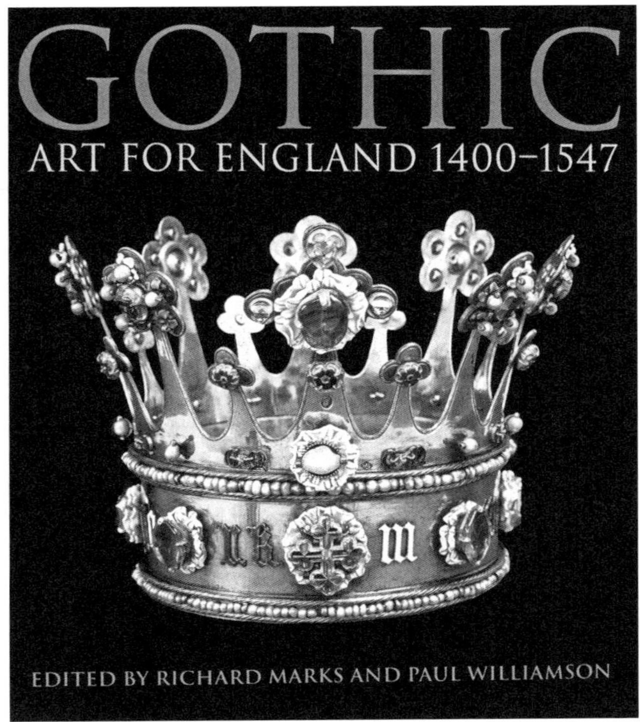

FIGURE 21. Dust-jacket of *Gothic: Art for England 1400–1547* catalogue.

The Donne Triptych and a Fairford window were displayed alongside indigenous artifacts in the *Gothic: Art for England, 1400–1547* exhibition held at the Victoria and Albert Museum in 2003/4, because, more unequivocally than the *Age of Chivalry* exhibition, its guiding principle was the desire to embed the art of the period within wider cultural contexts (Fig. 21).[63] As a consequence the *Gothic: Art for England* exhibition was more interdisciplinary than its predecessor, a methodology that did not meet with universal approval amongst art historians, some of whom (including Willibald Sauerländer) lamented what they perceived to be its subordination of style and attribution to historical criteria.[64] Prominent too in *Gothic: Art for England* was a new focus that has blossomed since the 1980s, one in which the fifteenth and early sixteenth centuries have figured prominently. Intention, meaning, and function have retained their place in the cultural agenda, but reception theory has morphed into religion. Instigated by the work of Hans Belting, David Freedberg, Henk van Os, and others, and *inter alia* drawing on the anthropological models (especially ritual theory) of the likes of Clifford Geertz, the Turners, and William Christian Jr., the emphasis has been on imagery and buildings as part of the frame of religious practices, both collective (i.e., liturgical) and personal—and hence whose purposes first and foremost were devotional (although the role of aesthetics *in* devotion remains problematic). This in turn has led to a broadening of the canon beyond what is predicated on aesthetic "quality" to encompass parish churches and their fittings and furnishings as well as imagery in manuscripts hitherto considered unworthy of attention. In this process, what is socially, visually, and iconographically distinctive about English late medieval religious imagery, and what is normative in respect of western Catholicism, is emerging. For example, the *Pietà*, an image known in Italy by the middle of the fourteenth century, had reached northern Europe, including England, by the late 1380s. There were a number of variations on the theme and

63. Marks and Williamson, *Gothic: Art for England* (as in note 3).

64. W. Sauerländer, review of *Gothic: Art for England* in *Apollo* 159 (2004), 59–60. The review by N. Coldstream took much the same line in *Burlington Magazine* 145 (2003), 869–871; see also Crossley, "Between Spectacle and History" (as in note 4), 147–153.

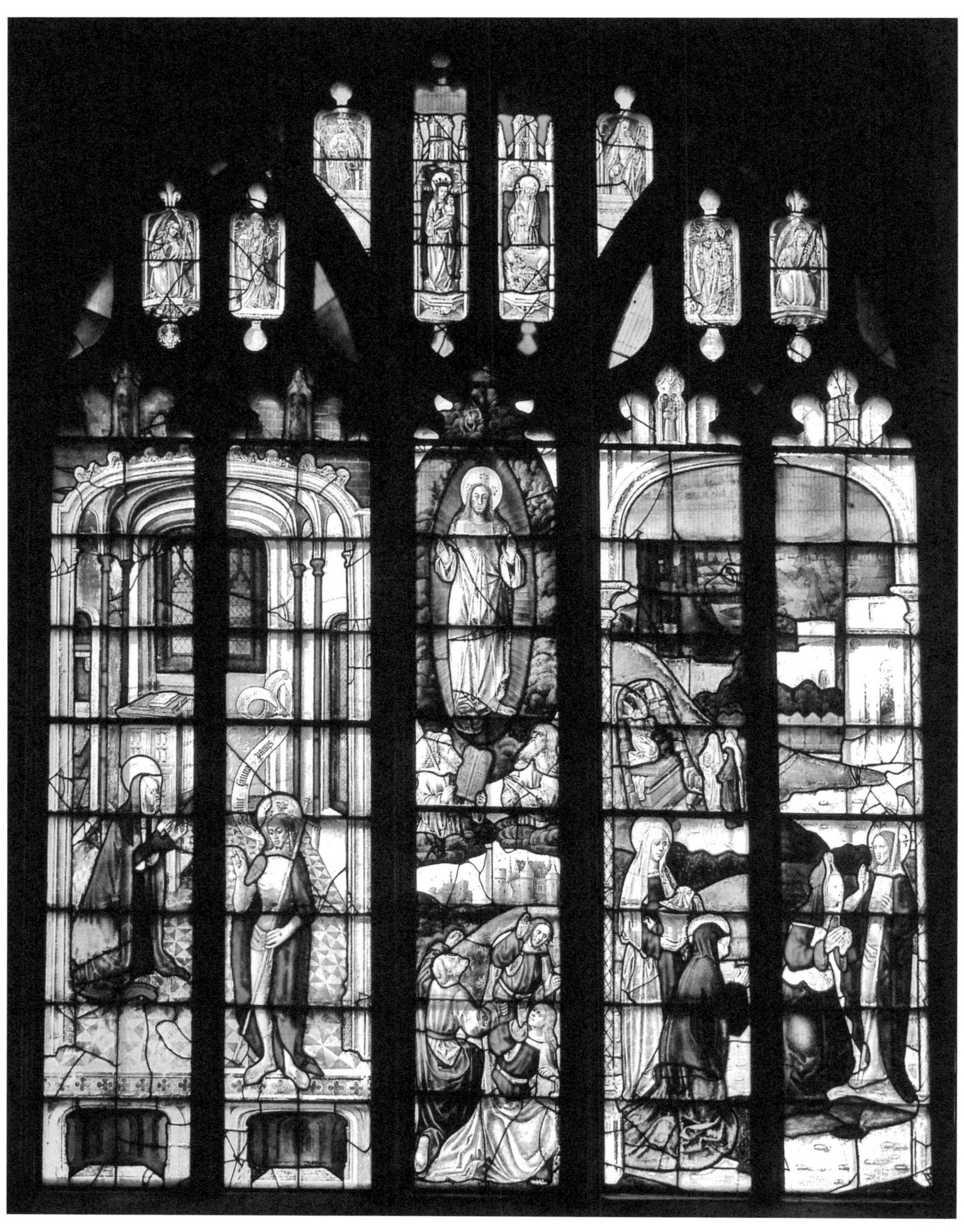

FIGURE 22. Fairford church (Gloucestershire), east window of chancel south chapel (photo : Keith Barley).

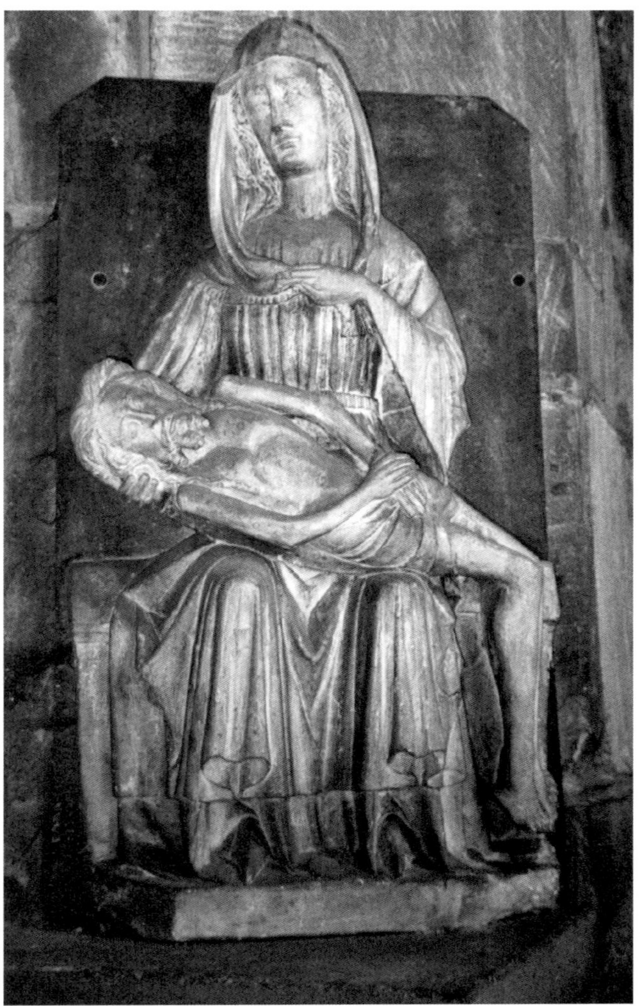

FIGURE 23. Breadsall church (Derbyshire), alabaster *Pietà* (photo: author).

surviving representations suggest that one in which the Virgin touches her veil was much favored in England (Fig. 23).[65] This aspect of scholarship is one where the increasing cross-fertilization of disciplines is well to the fore, *inter alia* fostered by the growth of interdisciplinary centers of medieval studies in universities and the popularity of the annual Kalamazoo, Harlaxton, and Leeds conferences. As regards England, in the van of revisionist scholarship on late medieval religion and its imagery have been historians, above all Margaret Aston and Eamon Duffy, and such literary specialists as Gail McMurray Gibson and Kathleen Kamerick, all of whom have roamed freely over territory previously the preserve of art historians.[66] Amongst the latter, Paul Binski has added a new dimension to the understanding of English thirteenth- and fourteenth-century architecture and art by embedding it within contemporary political, intellectual, and spiritual developments and pastoral concerns.[67] In a real sense, it is cultural history rather than art history that is making the intellectual running today.

Whither Now?

The titles in the *Oxford History of Art* series and Phaidon's *Art and Ideas* volumes suggest that the current flow is against monographs on "national" art, at least within the western hemisphere. As art historians we are creatures of our own time. England is a different country from that of Pevsner's era—less ethnically homogenous and more culturally diverse, factors that, consciously or otherwise, have impacted on the discipline of Art History: difference, not uniformity, is today's mantra. No longer too is it acceptable to relegate wider cultural perspectives to a chapter or section labeled "Historical Background" or towards crude equating of artistic developments with political events: art history does not dance to the same tune as history in its various manifestations, but has its own autonomy.[68]

I have no intention of assuming the powers of clairvoyancy in predicting future directions of research on

65. R. Marks, *Image and Devotion in Late Medieval England* (Stroud, 2004), 123–143.

66. Notably M. Aston, *England's Iconoclasts. Volume 1, Laws Against Images* (Oxford, 1988); and E. Duffy, *The Stripping of the Altars: Traditional Religion in England c. 1400–c. 1580* (New Haven and London, 1992); G. M. Gibson, *The Theater of Devotion: East Anglian Drama and Society in the Late Middle Ages* (Chicago and London, 1989); K. Kamerick, *Popular Piety and Art in the Late Middle Ages: Image Worship and Idolatry in England, 1350–1500* (New York, 2002).

67. Binski, *Westminster Abbey* (as in note 55); *idem*, *Becket's Crown: Art and Imagination in Gothic England, 1170–1300* (New Haven and London, 2004).

68. As pointed out by Willibald Sauerländer, "From Stilus to Style: Reflections on the Fate of a Nation," *Art History* 6 (1983), 253–270; *idem*, review of the *Age of Chivalry* in *The Burlington Magazine* 130 (1988), 149–151. See also Crossley, "Between Spectacle and History" (as in note 4), 150–151.

English medieval art, but will close by highlighting one potentially rewarding approach, which might be termed geocultural. Just as there is more than one history of English Gothic art, so there are several Gothic Englands, whose physical, artistic, social, and devotional boundaries could be elucidated by applying the kinds of overlaying and overlapping human and natural considerations (and complexities) identified in a recent essay by the urban historian Derek Keene. These embrace geography, topography, communications, demography, occupational and familial networks, prosperity (or its absence), trade, manufacture, markets, ecclesiastical institutions and jurisdictions and local administrative structures and patronage.[69]

There is the England that culturally forms part of the Continent (especially northern Europe) and with which it is linked rather than separated by the Channel and North Sea. Here a key issue is that of geographical parameters: are they defined by the borders of the modern national state or by those of medieval realms? The former of course do not equate with the latter, which in addition fluctuated during the course of the Middle Ages. Does it make sense, for example, to ignore those parts of present-day France that formed part of the Angevin Empire in the twelfth century when considering English Romanesque art?

And then there is the England composed of regions. In respect of architecture, a pioneering study was T. D. Atkinson's *Local Style in English Architecture*, a Batsford publication of 1947; subsequently Pevsner's magisterial *Buildings of England* series has been an indispensable research tool; both amongst other studies have underlined the diversity of design in parish churches throughout the country, especially in the fifteenth and early sixteenth centuries (Figs. 3, 24).[70] Here too, wider cultural considerations have enormous potential.

69. D. Keene, "National and Regional Identities" in Marks and Williamson, *Gothic: Art for England* (as in note 3), 46–55.

70. T. D. Atkinson, *Local Style in English Architecture: An Enquiry into its Origin and Development* (London, New York, and Toronto, 1947); For the *Buildings of England*, see P. Crossley, "Introduction" in Draper, *Reassessing Pevsner* (as in note 1), 19–21.

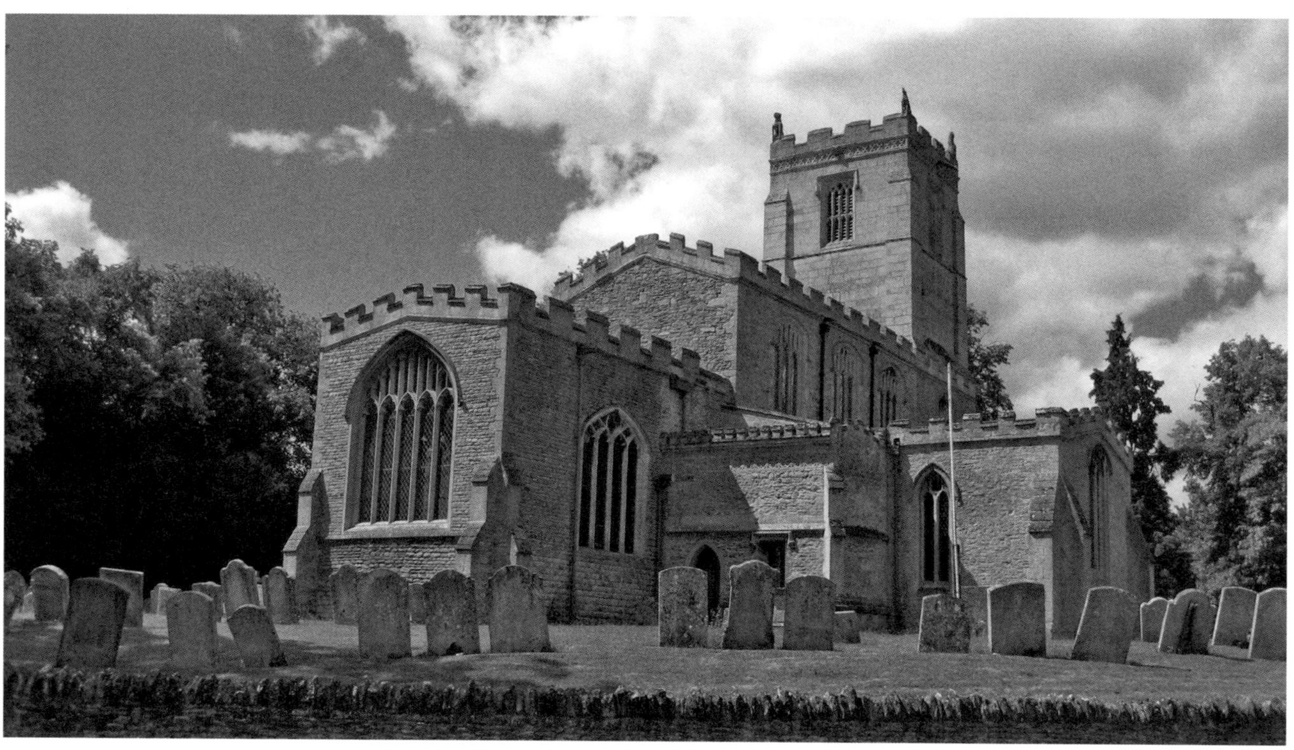

FIGURE 24. Glatton (Cambridgeshire), St. Nicholas's church (photo: author).

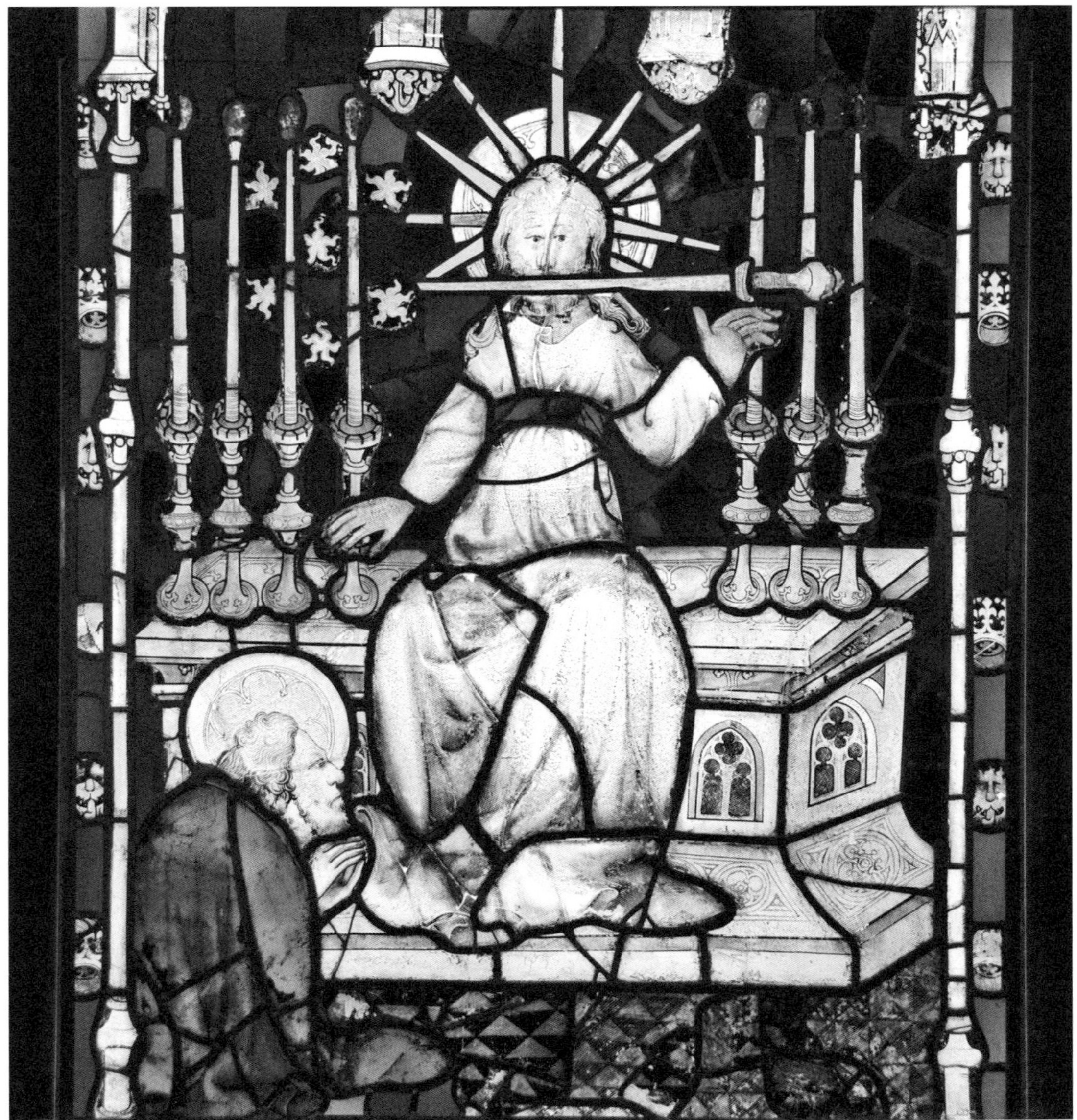

FIGURE 25. John Thornton: panel from York Minster east window (photo: Dean and Chapter of York Minster).

In respect of certain media, for example, stained glass, London may well emerge as of less significance in the fifteenth century than Coventry and York, where John Thornton, evidently a leading practitioner of the craft, was employed (Fig. 25). The historiographical concentration on East Anglia (which itself comprised more than one region) needs redressing, as it can give the impression that nowhere else was of any artistic importance, especially in the later Middle Ages. To comprehend why architecture, screens, and stained glass are so different in eastern England from, say, the West Country, it is necessary to consider the respective landholding patterns and social structures as well as devotional concerns: the early sixteenth-century windows of the parish church of St. Neot in Cornwall are instructive in this respect (Figs. 26, 27).[71] Nevertheless, it remains

71. See J. Mattingly, "Stories in the Glass—Reconstructing the St Neot Pre-Reformation Glazing Scheme," *Journal of the Royal Institution of Cornwall*, new series 2, vol. 3 (2000), 9–55.

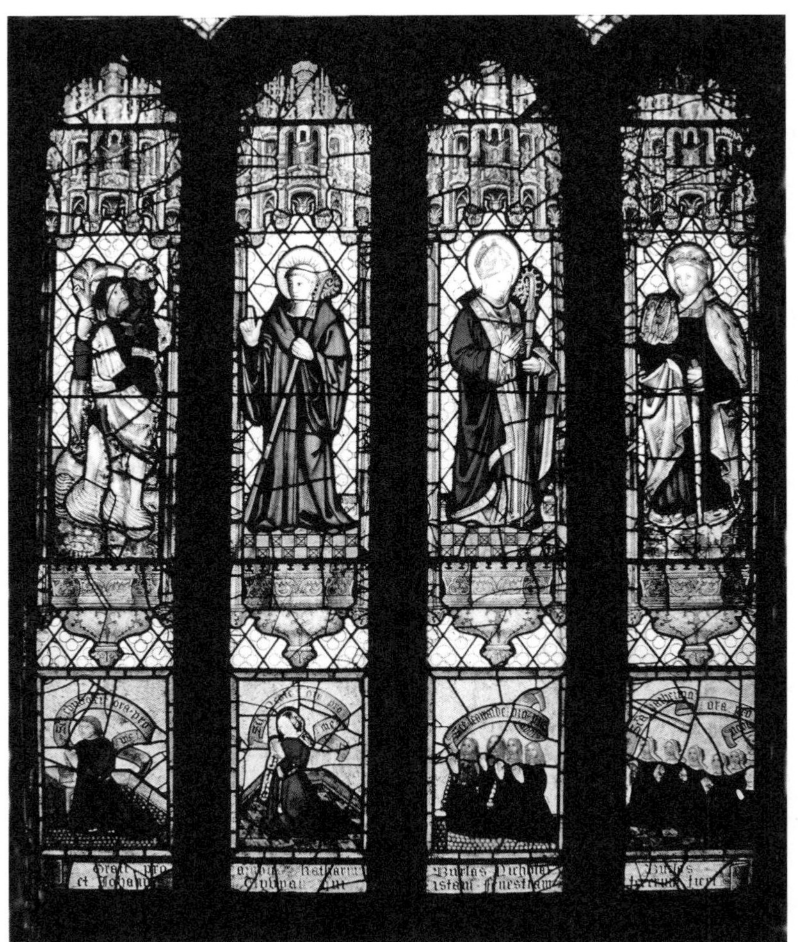

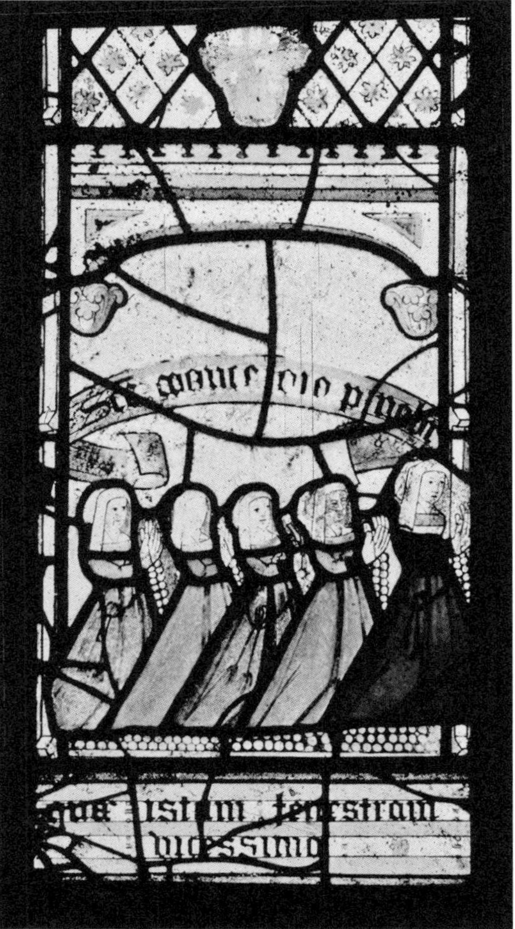

FIGURE 26. St. Neot church (Cornwall), north aisle (Borlase) window (photo: author).

FIGURE 27. St. Neot church (Cornwall), north aisle window (detail) (photo: author).

a *sine qua non* to date, locate stylistically, and even attribute works of art like the St. Neot's windows—also to distinguish between what is original and what is restored (particularly an issue with stained glass and textiles). To do so means the application of the subject-specific skills of the art historian. I hope that Willibald Sauerländer would approve of this affirmation of "traditional" values.

ACKNOWLEDGEMENTS

I am indebted to Colum Hourihane for the invitation to participate in this conference, which turned out to be so stimulating. Also to Paul Crossley for reading this paper; it has been improved immeasurably by his comments, suggestions, and references. A fortuitous meeting with Timothy Auger at a school reunion dinner shed invaluable light on the history of Batsford and its founders as well as on the personality of John Harvey. The following illustrations are reproduced by permission of: (9) British Library Board, (15) Conway Library, Courtauld Institute of Art, (8) Fitzwilliam Museum, Cambridge, (16) The Metropolitan Museum of Art, New York, (17, 19) National Gallery, London, (3) National Monuments Record, (4) Victoria and Albert Museum, London, (6, 7) Professor Christopher Wilson, (22) Keith Barley, (25) York Minster, Dean and Chapter.

ROCÍO SÁNCHEZ AMEIJEIRAS

The Faces of the Words: Aesthetic Notions and Artistic Practice in the Thirteenth Century[1]

Whether short or long, let the discourse always be colored inwards and outwards; but choose among colors with discretion. First examine the soul of the word and then its face, whose outward appearance alone you should not trust. Unless the inner color conforms to the outer form, the relationship between the two is worthless. Painting only the face of an expression results in a vile picture, a falsified thing, a fake form, a whitewashed wall, a verbal hypocrite which pretends to be something when it is nothing. Its form covers up its deformity; it vaunts itself outwardly but has no inner substance. This is the kind of picture which pleases at a distance, but displeases close up.[2]

DRAWING comparisons with the visual arts in order to explain rhetorical styles, as Geoffrey of Vinsauf does in his *Poetria Nova* (*c.* 1210), quoted above, was a common practice in medieval treatises on Rhetoric, a practice inherited from their Roman ancestors, Horace, Cicero, and Quintilian.[3] The Horatian *topos* of picture and poetry was well known in the Middle Ages. The theory of the *colores rhetorici*, in particular, acquired an extraordinary development in thirteenth-century treatises,[4] both in the Arts of Poetry (*Artes poeticae*) and the Arts of Preaching (*Artes praedicandi*).[5] Of the many examples comparing speech with images that can be found in the period, I shall only quote another significant one, which lies hidden in King Alfonso

1. I should like to express my gratitude to Colum Hourihane for inviting me to participate in this *Festschrift* to Willibald Sauerländer, whose writings have stimulated several generations of medieval art historians. I should also like to thank Francisco Prado-Vilar for his effort in the final edition of the text and for his enlightening conversations while writing it; and to the staff of the Library of the Sacro Convento at Assisi for the facilities they have offered in consulting an unedited manuscript by Fray Juan Gil de Zamora.

2. E. Gallo, *The Poetria Nova and its Sources in Early Rhetorical Doctrine* (The Hague, Paris, 1971), 53. Geoffrey of Vinsauf's *Poetria Nova* was one of the most influential books in the Middle Ages. The *Documentum de modo et arte dictandi et versificandi*, which has been attributed to him, includes another essay on the similarities and differences between a literary essay and a painting, see *Documentum*, II, 3, 1, in E. Faral, *Les Arts Poétiques du XIIe et du XIIIe siècle* (Paris, 1971; 1st ed. Paris, 1924), 284. On the problems of attribution of the *Documentum* and the *Tria sunt* to this author, see M. Camargo "Tria sunt: The Long and the Short of Geoffrey of Vinsauf's 'Documentum de modo et arte dictandi et versificandi,'" *Speculum* 74 (1999), 935–955.

3. G. A. Kennedy, *Classical Rhetoric and its Christian and Secular Tradition: From Ancient to Modern Times* (London, 1999). As is well known, the classical corpus became reduced in the thirteenth century to Horace's *Ars Poetica*, Cicero's *De inventione* and the pseudo Ciceronian *Rhetorica ad Herennium*, a compendium that preserved important extracts of Quintilian's *Insitutiones Oratoria.* See J. O. Ward, "Quintilian and the Rhetorical revolution of the Middle Ages," *Rhetorica* XIII (Summer, 1995), 231–283; *idem*, "From Antiquity to the Renaissance: Glosses and Commentaries on Cicero's Rhetorica," in *Medieval Eloquence: Studies in the Theory and Practice of Medieval Rhetoric*, J. J. Murphy ed. (Berkeley and Los Angeles, 1978), 25–67; and *The Rhetoric of Cicero in its Medieval and Early Renaissance Commentary Tradition*, V. Cox and John O. Ward, eds. (Leyden, 2006).

4. A basic introduction to the *colores rhetorici* is in L. Arbusow, *Colores Rhetorici. Eine Auswahl rhetorischer Figuren und Gemeinpläze als Hilfsmittel für Übungen an mittelalterlichen Texten*, Gottingen, 1963. For further and more comprehensive discussions related to Medieval Rhetoric, see notes 5, 9, and 10.

5. For Rhetorical theory in the Middle Ages, see J. J. Murphy,

the Wise's *General Estoria* and is said to have been copied from a still unidentified *Summa de Rhetorica*: "Grammar sets the foundations, Dialectics builds up the walls, and then Rhetoric paints all the building and decorates the ceiling with stars."[6] Rhetoric is here compared with the polychrome decoration of the building, including the monumental portals, which were originally animated with colors.[7]

The comparison between words and painted faces was inserted by Geoffrey of Vinsauf in his discourse on topical styles (*qualitates materiae*), within the theoretical context of the classical notion of *decorum* as it was applied to the theory of Rhetoric. The notion of *decorum*, as formulated by Cicero and Quintilian, is an aesthetic principle that regulated the harmonious coordination between discourses, and the poetics used to fashion them, paying attention to the suitability to their intended audiences. The homiletic tradition preserved this notion, which had been introduced into the Christian discourse on Rhetoric by Augustine and Gregory the Great. Nevertheless, it underwent an unexpected development by the end of the twelfth and into the thirteenth centuries, when the old tree of the Rhetorical treatises became more diversified in the branches of the Arts of Poetry and Prose, the Arts of Preaching, and the Arts of Letter-writing (*Artes dictaminis*), where the notions related to this principle were expanded in several ways.[8] In the *Poetriae*, the classical distinction of *genera dicendi*—the high, middle, and low styles—was transformed into *qualitates materiae* (topical styles or styles of subject matter), which articulated the relationship between subject matter and social class, but also invaded the field of style, in the opposition between "difficulty" and "facility," formulated for the first time by Geoffrey of Vinsauf. Accordingly, the ornate *difficilis* or *gravis* called for tropes, the ornate *facilis* or *levis* used the figures of thought and diction, and this classification became the formal complement of the system of *qualitates materiae*.[9]

The notion of suitability was also developed in the Arts of Preaching.[10] Hence, in his *Ars de modo predicandi* written *c.* 1220, Alexander of Ashby not only echoed the classical notions of *decorum* applied to the theory of Rhetoric, filtered through the lens of the writings

---

La Retórica en la Edad Media: Historia de la teoría de la retórica desde San Agustín hasta el Renacimiento (Mexico, 1986; 1st ed. Berkeley, 1974); *idem*, *Medieval Rhetoric: A select Bibliography* (Toronto, 1971); *Medieval Eloquence* (as in note 3); R. H. Rouse and Mary A. Rouse, "'*Statim invenire*': Schools, Preachers, and the New Attitudes to the Page," in *Renaissance and Renewal in the Twelfth Century*, R. L. Benson, G. Constable, and C. D. Lanham, eds., (Oxford, 1982), 201–225; *Rhetoric and Renewal in the Latin West, 1100–1540. Essays in Honor of John O. Ward* (Turnhout, 2003).

6. See *General estoria*, II 57a.21–b.16; quoted by Ch. Faulhaber, *Latin Rhetorical Theory in Thirteenth and Fourteenth Century Castile* (Berkeley, Los Angeles, London, 1972), 89.

7. *La couleur de la Pierre. Polychromie des portails gothiques. Actes du colloque d'Amiens, 12–14 octobre 2000* (Paris, 2002).

8. As is well known, the idea of *decorum* permeated visual aesthetic statements, and opened an inflamed debate in the monastic realm of the mid-twelfth century, see C. Rudolph, *The Things of Greater Importance: Bernanrd of Clairvaux's* Apologia *and the Medieval Attitutude toward Art* (Philadelphia, 1990); and L. Donkin, "*Ornata decenter*: Perceptions of 'fitting decoration' Amongst Augustinian Canons of Sant'Orso in Aosta in the Mid-Twelfth Century," *Journal of the Warburg and Courtauld Institutes*, LXXI (2008), 75–93. Somewhat earlier, the idea of fitting decorations was related to the fitting of the fabric or material rather than with imagery, and when it is related to it in the monastic world, it is usually understood in analogical terms. This is also the case with the statements related to images by Lucas, Bishop of Tuy, at the end of his life, after being canon of the monastery of Saint Isidoro in León. On this text, see S. Moralejo Álvarez, "D. Lucas de Tuy y la 'actitud estética' en el arte medieval," *Euphrosyne. Revista de Filología Clásica*, 22 (1994), 241–346, reprinted in *Patrimonio Artístico de Galicia y otros estudios.Homenaje al Prof. Serafín Moralejo* (Santiago de Compostela, 2004), II, 299–302.

9. D. Kelly, *The Arts of Poetry and Prose* (Turnhout, 1991), 71, continues to be the best introduction to the genre. See also J. Murphy, *Retórica* (as in note 5), 135–193; W. Purcell, "Ars Poetriae": Rhetorical and *Grammatical Invention at the Margins of Literacy* (Columbia, 1996); A. Leupin, *Fiction and Incarnation: Rhetoric, Theology, and Literature in the Middle Ages* (University of Minnesota Press, 2002). An essential book that deals with different styles of rhetoric is by E. Auerbach, *Mimesis, Dargestellte Wirklich Keit in der abendländischen literature* (Bern, 1946).

10. On the Arts of Preaching, see T. M. Charland, *Artes praedicandi: Contribution a l'histoire de la rhétorique au Moyen Âge* (Ottawa, 1936); H. Caplan and H. King, "Latin Tractates on Preaching: A Book-List," *Harvard Theological Review*, 42 (1949), 185–206; Murphy, *Rhetoric* (as in note 5), 275–361; M.-G. Briscoe and B .H. Jaye, *Artes Praedicandi. Artes Orandi* (Turnhout, 1992); a revision of the editions of these authors in A. Alberte, *Retórica medieval: Historia de las artes predicatorias* (Madrid, 2003). For other titles related to medieval preaching, see note 12.

of Pope Gregory the Great, but he also expanded the doctrine of suitability to the formal verbal expression—the *elocutio*—explaining that the style of the sermon must be modest, sweet, simple, and appropriate to the subject matter. Furthermore, quoting the Horatian *topos*, he advised that not only the style (*elocutio*), but also the delivery and gestures (*actio*) must accord to the tone and the message, providing his discourse on the *decorum* of preaching with a visual dimension. The same ideas were repeated later by Humbert de Romans, or Thomas of Chobham;[11] and this principle acquired a systematic enunciation when scholastic norms permeated the Arts of Preaching. The concept of the thematic sermon was fashioned by William of Auvergne, the pseudo-Bonaventure, or John of Wales, to the point that they articulated technical considerations to the audience, and began to consider preaching in vernacular or macaronic combinations of two or more languages.[12] Therefore, the *Artes praedicandi* take into consideration a wider range of possibilities regarding form, content, and audience than the Arts of Poetry and Prose or the *Artes dictaminis*. The treatises on preaching encompassed a variety of media, a variety of modes of expression according to the *thema* and the audience.

In this paper, I shall argue that the aesthetic principles that permeated Rhetorical treatises, which were readily assumed as natural choices by the clerics in charge of the massive thirteenth-century sculptural portals, came to exert an important influence on the design of the portals themselves. As it has been said, the treatises on Rhetoric in fact facilitate the enunciation of a comparison between preaching and seeing, between voice and image.

A comparison of preaching and monumental sculpture is not, obviously, a new idea. A long tradition of discussion emerged from the interpretation of Pope Gregory's *topos* that images are visual sermons for the illiterate[13]—a tradition to which Willibald Sauerländer added his own contribution by defining the Last Judgement Portal at Conques "*als Bildpredigt*," as a sermon, for the portal inscriptions accompanying the images were intended to be performed "out loud."[14] Quite different attempts to associate Rhetoric and Gothic figurative programs have been made in the art-historical literature, the most recent being those by Wolfgang Kemp, Jacqueline Jung, and Stephen Murray. Kemp noted formal parallels between clusters of images framed by the decorative armatures of the Prodigal Son Window at Chartres and the divisions articulating a thirteenth-century sermon.[15] Jung called attention to what she qualifies as a new narrative visual trend appearing in the reliefs decorating Gothic choir screens, which is characterized by a formal idiom rich in detailed descriptions and humoris-

11. See the editions of Humbert de Romans, *De eruditione praedicatorum*, in Bibliotheca Veterum Patrum (Lyon, 1677), vol. XXV, 424–567; and Thomas of Chobhan, *Summa de arte praedicatoria*, F. Morenzoni ed. (Turnhout, 1988), CCCM, 82.

12. On the *Ars praedicandi* of William of Auvergne, see A. de Pooter, "Un manuel de Prédication medieval," *Révue neo-scolastique de Philosophie*, 25 (1923), 192–209; the Pseudo-Bonaventure in *Sancti Bonaventurae Opera Omnia* (Florence, 1903). On John of Wales' *Forma pedicandi*, see W. O. Ross, "Brief Forma predicandi," *Modern Philology* (1937/4), 337–344. Obviously, the theory conveyed in the treatises was but one propaedeutic tool to compose sermons. As Louis Jacques Bataillon has demonstrated, the *dilatatio* or amplification let the preachers put in practice several strategies, as the use of images, see "Les images dans les sermons du XIIIe siècle," *Freiburger Zeitschrift für Philosophie und Theologie* 37/3 (1990), 327–395, reprinted in *La predication au XIIIe siècle en France et en Italie* (Aldershot, 1993), 327–395. On Medieval preaching, see J. Longère, *La prédiaction médiévale* (Paris, 1983); N. Bériou, *L'avènement des maîtres de la parole: La prédication à Paris au XIIIe siècle* (Paris, 1998); D. L. d'Avray, *The Preaching of the Friars: Sermons Diffused from Paris before 1300* (New York, 1985); M. Zink, *La predication en langue romane avant 1300* (Paris, 1976); J. Hamese et al, *Medieval Sermons and Society: Cloister, City, University* (Louvain, 1998).

13. The most recent discussion is in H. Kessler, "Gregory the Great and Image Theory in Northern Europe During the Twelfth and Thirteenth Centuries," in *A Companion to Medieval Art: Romanesque and Gothic in Northern Europe*, C. Rudolph, ed. (Oxford, 2006), 151–172, with subsequent bibliography.

14. W. Sauerländer, "*Omnes perversi sic sunt in tartara mersi*. Skulpture als Bildpredigt. Das Weltgerichts tympanon von Sainte-Foy in Conques," *Jahrbuch der Akademie der Wissenshaften in Göttingen* (1979), 34–47.

15. W. Kemp, *The Narratives of Gothic Stained Glass*, (Cambridge, 1997, 1st ed. Munich, 1987). The work of L. E. Saurma-Jeltsh, "Das Zackenstil als *ornatus difficilis*," *Aachener Kunstblätter* 6 (1994), *Festshrift für Hermann Fillitz*, 257–266, appears to have had less of an impact.

tic anecdotes—a trend that she has called "vernacular imagery," due to the fact that it seems to present features also found in contemporary vernacular sermons.[16] And last, but not least, to reconstruct the medieval perception of Amiens western portal, Stephen Murray used a sermon written and preached in the diocese of Amiens that was used to raise funds to finish the building of the cathedral.[17]

Here I shall propose a different approach to the issue of the relationship between preaching and imagery.[18] The changes that occurred in the theory of Rhetoric from the late twelfth century to 1300 could help define one of the major differences between what art historians have traditionally called "Romanesque imagery" and "Gothic imagery." Concepts found in the theory of Rhetoric also seem to have been used in the field of medieval imagery. The sculptural programs found in a Gothic cathedral should not be compared to a sermon, but instead to a set of thematic sermons, which were determined by the same rules and dictates that determined the composition of verbal sermons. The portals of a Gothic façade, and especially a western Gothic façade, may have different thematic sermons that were fashioned according to different "topical styles," and these were then expressed in different formal idioms—or elocutionary styles. Each was based upon a particular visual poetic, chosen from a formal repertoire that was especially suited to its intended audience. As the scholastic practice abandoned the aesthetic notion of *brevitas*, and transformed the concept of preaching, creating the idea of the thematic sermon which was expanded according to *partitiones* and *amplificationes*, so also did the figurative programs of the Gothic portals expand in response in an effort to cover a lot of issues by means of amplification.

Inverting the Code: Periphery as a Means to Understand the Center

The western portals of León Cathedral will be the point of departure for my study (Figs. 1a and 1b).[19] León has been chosen not only because of the extraordinary quality of its sculpture, but also because Castilian Gothic monumental sculpture has been largely neglected in general surveys of medieval art. Even if Sauerländer has flirted with Spanish Virgins,[20] or scholars such as Peter Kurmann, Regine Abbeg, or Fabienne Joubert have recently focused their attention on a few specific monuments,[21] Castilian Gothic is seldom given any serious

16. J. E. Jung, "Beyond the Barrier: The Unifying Role of the Choir Screen in Gothic Churches," *Art Bulletin* LXXXII/4 (2000), 622–657.

17. S. Murray, *A Gothic Sermon: Making a Contract with the Mother of God, Saint Mary of Amiens* (Berkeley, 2004).

18. This approach could be related to E. Perry's *The Aesthetics of Emulation in the Visual Arts of Ancient Rome* (Cambridge, 2005), esp. 28–29 (for the notion of *decorum*); and Eric R. Varner, "Reading Replications: Roman Rhetoric and Greek Quotations," *Art History* 29/2 (2006), 280–303. Quite different insights on the relationship of Rhetorical theory and artistic practice is in C. van Eck, *Classical Rhetoric and the Visual Arts in Early Modern Europe* (Cambridge, 2007).

19. I have already discussed the southern and western portals of León cathedral and its suitability to its topography and function in R. Sánchez Ameijeiras, "Poéticas y discursos en la escultura leonesa del siglo XIII," in *Actas del Congreso La catedral de León en la Edad Media*, G. Boto Varela, M. V. Herráez Ortega, and J. Yarza Luaces, eds. (León, 2005), 203–239. My purpose here is to expand the argument to other examples related to Leonese western portals in the frame of the aesthetic notions as conveyed in Rhetorical treatises. Traditional Spanish scholarship focusing on the León western portal was engaged, instead, in categorizing styles and looking for their possible sources, or for the iconographic sources of each subject represented there. See M. Gómez Moreno, *Catálogo Monumental de España: Provincia de León* (Madrid, 1925), I, 231–240; J. Ainaud and A. Durán Sempere, *Escultura Gótica* (Madrid, 1954), 41–60; J. Yarza Luaces, *La Edad Media* (Madrid, 1978) 235–237; J. Azcárate Ristori, *El arte gótico en España* (Madrid, 1990), 162–169; J. Ara Gil, "Escultura Gótica," in *Historia del Arte de Castilla y León* (Valladolid, 1994), 219–329, esp. 240–249; P. Williamson, *Gothic Sculpture, 1140–1300* (London, 1995), 343–345; A. Franco Mata, *Escultura gótica en León y su provincia (1230–1530)* (León, 1998), 102–298 (on iconography) and 321–358 (on styles).

20. W. Sauerländer, "Von der Glykophilousa to 'Amie gracieuse.' Überlungen und Fragen zur 'Virgen Blanca' in der Kathedrale von Toledo," *De la création a la restauration. Travaux d'histoire de l'art offerts à Marcel Durliat pour son 79e anniversaire* (Toulouse, 1992), 449–461; *idem*, "La escultura de la sede leonesa a la luz de los grandes talleres europeos," *La catedral de León* (León, 2005) (as in note 19), 177–202.

21. P. Kurmann, "Französischer als in Frankreich: Zur Architektur und Skulptur der Kathedrale von León,"in *Gotishe Architektur in Spanien: La arquitectura gótica en España. Akten des Kolloquiums der Carl-Justi Vereinigung und des Kunstgeschichtlichen Seminars der Universität Göttingen.Göttingen, 4.–6. Februar* 1994, Ch. Freigang ed. (Frankfurt,

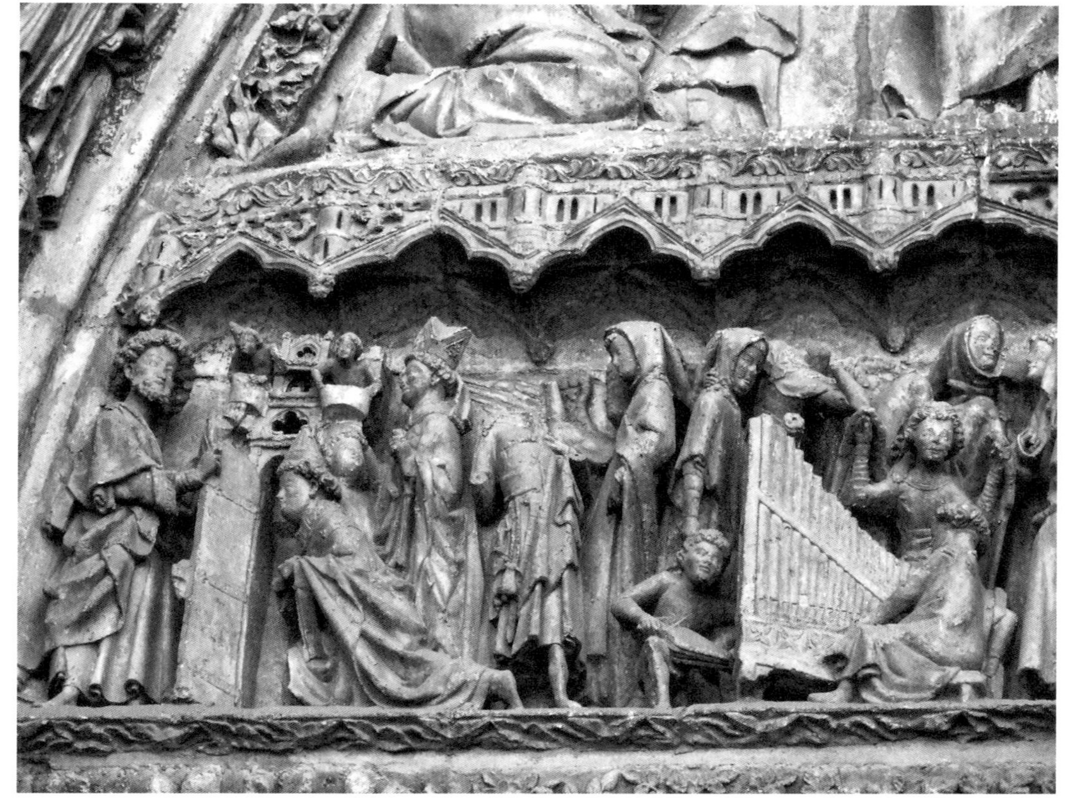

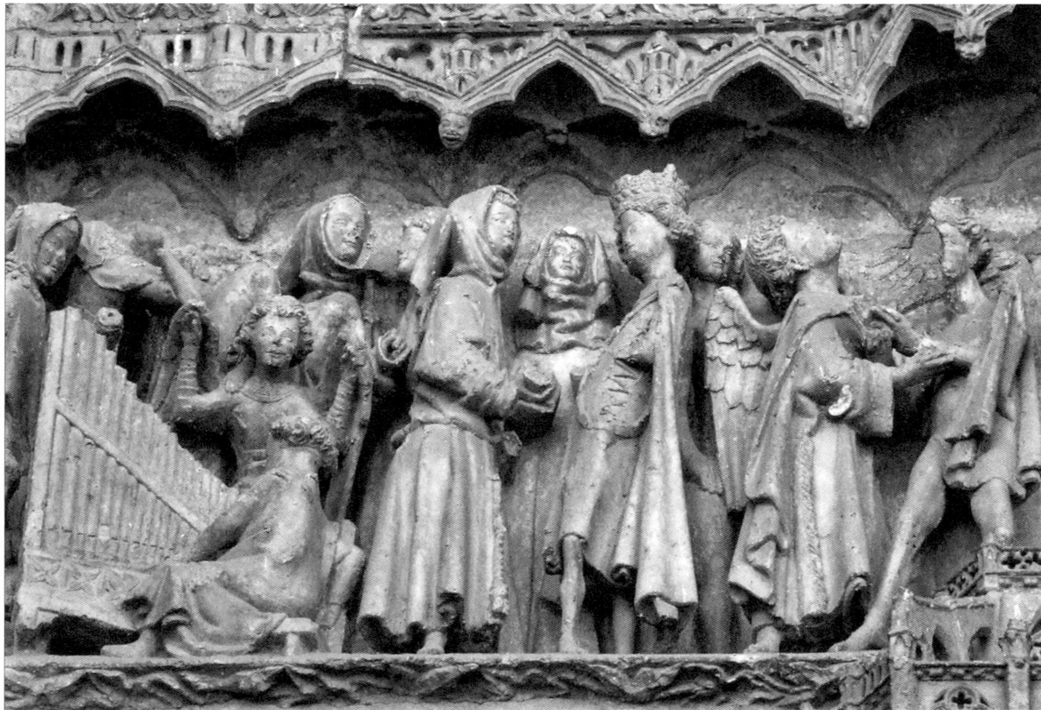

FIGURE 1a. León Cathedral, western façade, Last Judgement Portal. General view of the lintel showing the elect in the Hall of Paradise (1255–1275) (photo: author).

FIGURE 1b. León Cathedral, western façade, Last Judgement Portal. Detail of the lintel showing the elect in the Hall of Paradise (1255–1275) (photo: author).

consideration in international scholarship.[22] It seems that Castilian sculpture has lost the glamor it enjoyed in the 1920s and 30s, when Émile Bertaux, Georg Weise, August L. Mayer, Hanshubert Mann, and Frederick Deknatel, praised the Leonese Last Judgement Portal as one of the most remarkable sculptural ensembles to be found in the thirteenth century.[23] Using Wölfflin's categories, these scholars agreed in qualifying this sculpture as pictorial, rather than plastic, and in appreciating the exaggerated proportions and slenderness of the figures in terms of mannerism and primitivism.[24] One cannot help but compare the laughing devil who in León throws the lusty woman into the cauldron of Hell with the diabolic characterization of the knight in Emil Nolde's *Enthusiast*, and the shameless naked prostitute who inspired the title of the picture with the naked Leonese sinner. Or, one can find a kind of familiarity between the slenderness of Kirchner's *Women in the Street* and the mannered attitudes of the elect in the Hall of the Leonese paradise. Even if some German scholars felt pressured to accept the National Socialist ideology, they remained supporters of what Nazis called "degenerate art." So was Deknatel, whose loves were, significantly, Castilian sculpture and Edvard Munch.[25]

There is another important reason to choose León. Many Gothic façades, such as at Paris, Sens, and Auxerre, cannot be seen as unified structures or as worked out in response to an original or single masterplan. Portals were frequently carved in different periods; however, the western façade portals in León were conceived as an original ensemble by those responsible for the work.[26] Chief among them was, with all probability, Bishop Martín Fernández, chancellor to King Alfonso the Wise, who ruled the see from 1250 to 1289.[27] A prominent member of his entourage was the prolific Franciscan writer Fray Juan Gil of Zamora—Johannes Aegidii Zamorensis—an advanced disciple of Bonaventure.[28] The friendship between these two

Madrid, 1999), 105–117; R. Abegg, *Könings–und Bischofsmonumente. Die Skulpturen des 13. Jahrhunderts im Kreuzgang der Kathedrale von Burgos* (Zürich, 1999); F. Joubert, *La sculpture gothique en France. XIIe–XIIIe siècles* (Paris, 2008), 190–191 (on León); and *idem*, "De Bourges à León: réflexions sur l'elaboration de la sculpture au XIIIe siècle," *Actes du colloque international de Tolède, 15-18 mai 2004*, Y. Christe and C. Hediger, eds. (forthcoming).

22. This absence can be explained by ideologies relying on historical constructions. As Madeline Caviness concluded when analyzing German medieval art, "period's styles are ideological," see M. H. Caviness, "The Politics of Taste: An Historiography of 'Romanesque' Art in the Twentieth Century," in *Romanesque Art and Thought in the Twelfth Century, Essays in Honor of Walter Cahn*, C. Hourihane, ed., (Princeton, 2008), 57–80, esp. 76.

23. É. Bertaux, "La sculpture chrétienne en Espagne, des origines au XIVe siècle," *Histoire de l'Art*, A. Michel, ed., (Paris, 1906), vol. 2/1, 214–295, esp. 284–292; A. L. Mayer, *Gotische Portal-Skulpturen in Spanien* (Leipzig, 1922), figs. 6 and 8; G. Weise, *Spanische Plastik aus sieben Jahrhunderts*, vol. 1 (Reutlingen, 1925), 18–34; A. L. Mayer, *Gotik in Spanien* (Leipzig, 1928), 50–55; H. Mann, *Kathedral Plastik in Spanien* (Leipzig, 1935), 39–43; F. B. Deknatel, "TheThirteenth Century Gothic Sculpture of the Cathedrals of Burgos and León," *The Art Bulletin* 17 (1935), 234–389, esp. 326–346 (on iconography) and 357–383 (on styles).

24. On German scholarship under the Nazis, see N. Hille, "Kunstgeschichte in Tübingen, 1933–1945," in *Kunst und Politik. Jahrbuch der Guernica-Gesellschaft* 5 (2003). *Kunstgeschichte und den Universitäten im Nazionalsozialismus*, 93–122; *idem*, "Eine Kontroverse des Jahres 1932 und ihre Folgen für das Tübinger Institut für Kunstgeschichte," in *Kunstgeschichte im Nationalsozialismus: Beiträge zur Geschichte einer Wissenschaft zwischen 1930 und 1950*, N. Doll et al., eds. (Weimar, 2005), 99–115. The case of Bertaux is different, he was more interested in fifteenth-century painting than in thirteenth-century sculpture and he worked on the Spanish art for the *Histoire de L'art*, edited by André Michel between 1905 and 1913, see V. Papa Malatesta, *Émile Bertaux: Tra storia dell'Arte e Meridionalismo* (Rome, 2007), 24–27.

25. On Deknatel, see S. Freedberg, "Tribute to Frederick Deknatel," *Art Journal* 33/3 (Spring 1974), 283; and G. Bazin, *Histoire de l'histoire de l'art: de Vasari à nos jours* (Paris, 1986), 276–277.

26. The tympana and archivolts of León's western façade can be dated to between 1255 and 1280. The statues of the embrasures and those decorating the piers of the porch were carved later. It must be said that during the restorations carried out in the nineteenth century, the portals were dismantled and mounted again. One can see that some of the *voussoirs* were relocated in the wrong place, and others were newly carved. On the restorations of the architecture of León Cathedral, see I. González-Varas Ibáñez, *Las catedrales de León: Historia y restauración, 1859–1901* (León, 1989); and J. Rivera Blanco, *Historia de las restauraciones de la catedral de León* (Valladolid, 1993). Nevertheless, it lacks a comprehensive study on the restorations of the portals sculpture.

27. P. Linehan, "La iglesia de León a mediados del siglo XIII," *León y su historia*, vol. 3 (León, 1975), 1–30, reprinted in *Spanish Church and Society 1150–1300* (London, 1983), 12–76; *idem*, *The Spanish Church and the Papacy in the Thirteenth Century* (Cambridge, 1971), 268–275.

28. The best study on this figure continues to be M. Castro y Castro, *Fray Juan Gil de Zamora, O.F.M. De Preconiis Hispaniae*,

clerics is shown in Juan Gil of Zamora's sermons, as well as in a treatise on virtues and vices that he dedicated to Bishop Martín Fernandez.[29] In turn, don Martín, aware of the spiritual revolution that was developing thanks to the new monastic orders, promoted their pastoral activity in his see, and this is recorded in his synodal constitution dictated in 1267.[30] The friars had license to preach and administer confession in the cathedral, and we know that the ministry of the word was not only delivered in the pulpit but also in the squares or in the parvis of the churches. The western façade of León served, therefore, as a stage set before which the friars could preach. Using such a backdrop also enabled them to identify themselves, at a spiritual and personal level, with those attending the divine concert in the realms of paradise shown on the lintel (Fig. 1b).

Owing to Don Martín's friendship with Fray Juan Gil, the principles guiding the Rhetorical treatises were incorporated by the patrons of León Cathedral into its sculptural programs. In contrast to the rest of Europe, the Castilian world did not see this discipline flourish in the thirteenth century, but there were exceptions, such as the *Ars Epistolaris ornatus* which Geoffrey of Eversley dedicated to King Alfonso the Wise, the Art of Letter-writing by John of Zamora, and his collection of sermons, which, however meager, still show evidence in the León area of the thematic sermon as developed in Franciscan scholastic treatises.[31] Thus, inverting the terms of the common hermeneutical pattern, an ostensibly "peripheric" example could illuminate the understanding of the more celebrated centers of Gothic sculpture.

Water Pouring from the Stone: A Forgotten Tradition of Baptismal Visual Sermons

Like so many other Gothic cathedrals, the western façade of León Cathedral has three portals: a central Last Judgement Portal, flanked by a Coronation of the Virgin portal, to the right, and one dedicated to Christ's infancy, to the left, a combination which is characteristic of the so called "high Gothic." Laon inaugurated the pattern, and if Martin Büchsel is right, the southern façade of Chartres Cathedral was originally planned following the same model. Also at Notre-Dame de Paris, the old portal of Ste.-Anne which included a cycle of Christ's infancy was reused to accompany the Last Judgement and the Coronation of the Virgin portals.[32] But the subjects were not chosen at random. An aspect recently emphasized in the interpretation of the imagery of Gothic cathedrals, but brought to attention years ago by Willibald Sauerländer, was its relation to the specific liturgy celebrated in each part of the building.[33] Thus, cathedral western portals were conceived,

Estudio preliminar y edición crítica (Madrid, 1955), even if it needs an urgent revision. See also M. C. Díaz y Díaz, "Tres compiladores latinos en el ambiente de Sancho IV," *La Literatura en la época de Sancho IV. Actas del Congreso Internacional "La literatura en la época de Sancho IV," Alcalá de Henares, 21–24 de febrero de 1994* (Alcalá de Henares, 1994), 35–52, esp. 46–52. His scientific work has been relatively recently published: *Johannes Aegidii Zamorensis, Historia Naturalis*, A. Domínguez García and L. García Ballester, eds. (Salamanca, 1994).

29. The manuscript, preserved in the Library of the Sacro Convento at Assisi was catalogued with the number 699 in C. Censi, O.F.M., *Bibliotheca manuscripta ad Sacrum Conventum asssisiensem* (Assisi, 1981). In the first column of folio 217 one can read: "Reverendo ... M(artini Fernandi) diuina prouidentia legionem. antistiti, fr. iohannes egidij sue mangnificentie humilis apocrifarius aliquorum sermonum breviloquium vobis mitti."

30. See Linehan, *Papacy* (as in note 27), 319.

31. For Geoffrey of Eversley and Fray Juan Gil of Zamora's rhetorical works, see Faulhaber, *Rhetorical Theory in Castile* (as in note 6), 98–103 and 103–121. Among the many works of Fray Juan Gil it must be remember in this context, an unedited collection of sermons. See F. Lillo Redonet, "El sermonario inédito de Juan Gil de Zamora a la luz de las *Artes Praedicandi*," in *Actas del I Congreso Nacional de Latín Medieval* (León, 1995), 285–292. On the idea of *decorum* in Fray Juan Gil's Art of Letter-writing: "Quia ergo, Karissime, nos pulcris (*sic*) verbis indegemus et congruis, non solum in literis faciendis, verum eciam in sermonibus et collacionisbus componendis ..., see Juan Gil de Zamora, *Dictaminis Epithalamium* ed., Ch. Faulhaber (Pisa, 1978), 41.

32. On Laon, see I. Kasarska, *La sculpture de la façade occidentale de la cathédrale de Laon. Escathologie et humanisme* (Paris, 2008); on Chartres, see M. Büchsel, *Die Skulptur der Querhauses der Kathedrale von Chartres* (Berlin, 1995); and B. Kurmann-Scharzw and P. Kurmann, *Chartres. Die Kathedrale* (Regensburg, 2001). On Paris, A. Erlande-Brandenburg, *Notre-Dame de Paris* (Paris, 1997).

33. W. Sauerländer, "Observations sur la topographie et l'iconographie de la cathédrale du sacré," *Académie des Inscriptions et Belles-Lettres, Comptes-Rendus* (1992), 463–79, reprinted in *Cathedrals and Sculpture* (London, 1999), vol. 2, 254–272. The author also develops the idea in "Integrated Fragments and the Unintegrated Whole: Scattered Examples from Reims, Strasbourg, Chartres, and Naum-

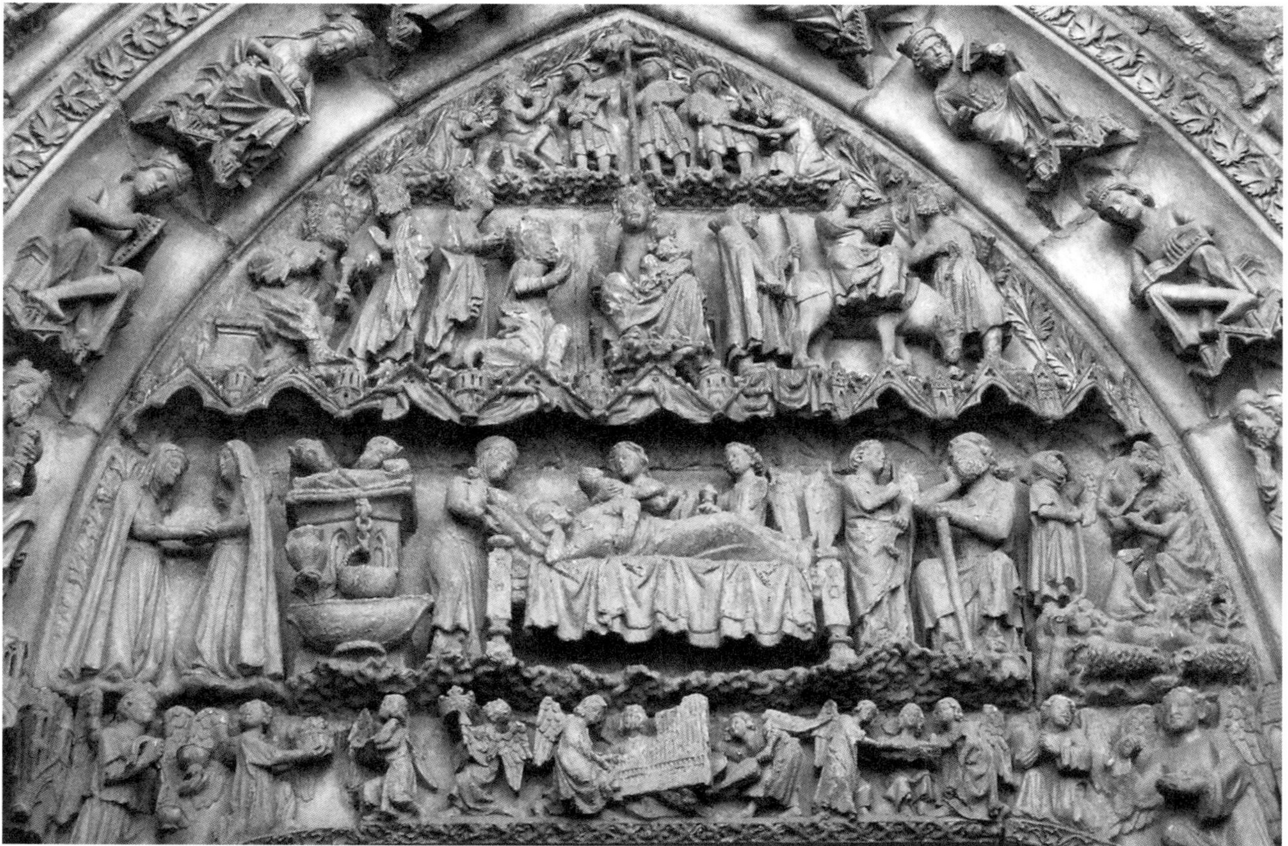

FIGURE 2. León Cathedral, western façade, Portal of St. John the Baptist (1255–1275) (photo: author).

not as a frame for the cannon's offices but mainly for compelling the laity to participate in the sacraments of the Church.

In León Cathedral, this pastoral function must be assigned to the left portal of the western façade (Fig. 2). Even if it is usually referred to as a Christ's Infancy Portal and traditionally known as St. John's Portal, it differs notably from its alleged French models, such as the portals of Laon and Chartres. The sermon in stone in León is an expanded one, whose implications are much more ambitious than those of earlier ones. Indeed, the design of the visual narratives at Laon and Paris cathedrals is still linked to the notion of *brevitas*, praised by authors such as Alain de Lille in his *Summa de arte praedicatoria* (*c.* 1200).[34] In contrast, the main rhetorical device used by the promoters of the León portal in the creation of their sermons was amplification, both by devising a chain of typological sub-themes and by taking pleasure in detailed descriptions. In following these compositional rules, the Leonese portal did not differ from the major trends found in contemporary rhetorical manuals. For instance, the *Ars dilatandi sermones* of Richard of Thetford (*fl.* 1245), which was widely circulated, discussed eight ways of amplification: concordances, metaphors, four exegetical senses of scripture, contrast, or description.[35]

burg," *Artistic Integration in the Gothic Buildings*, V. Chieffo Raguin, K. Brush and P. Draper, eds. (Toronto, Buffalo, London, 1995), 153–166, esp. 157–158; and his publication quoted in note 70; and Kasarska (as in note 32), 93–97.

34. On *brevitas* as a main aesthetic value in rhetorical treatises around 1200, see Alberte, *Artes predicatorias* (as in note 10), 63.

35. Murphy, *Retórica* (as in note 5), 333–334. Also Guillaume of Auvergne in his *De Arte Praedicandi* (*fl.* 1250) dedicated half of the

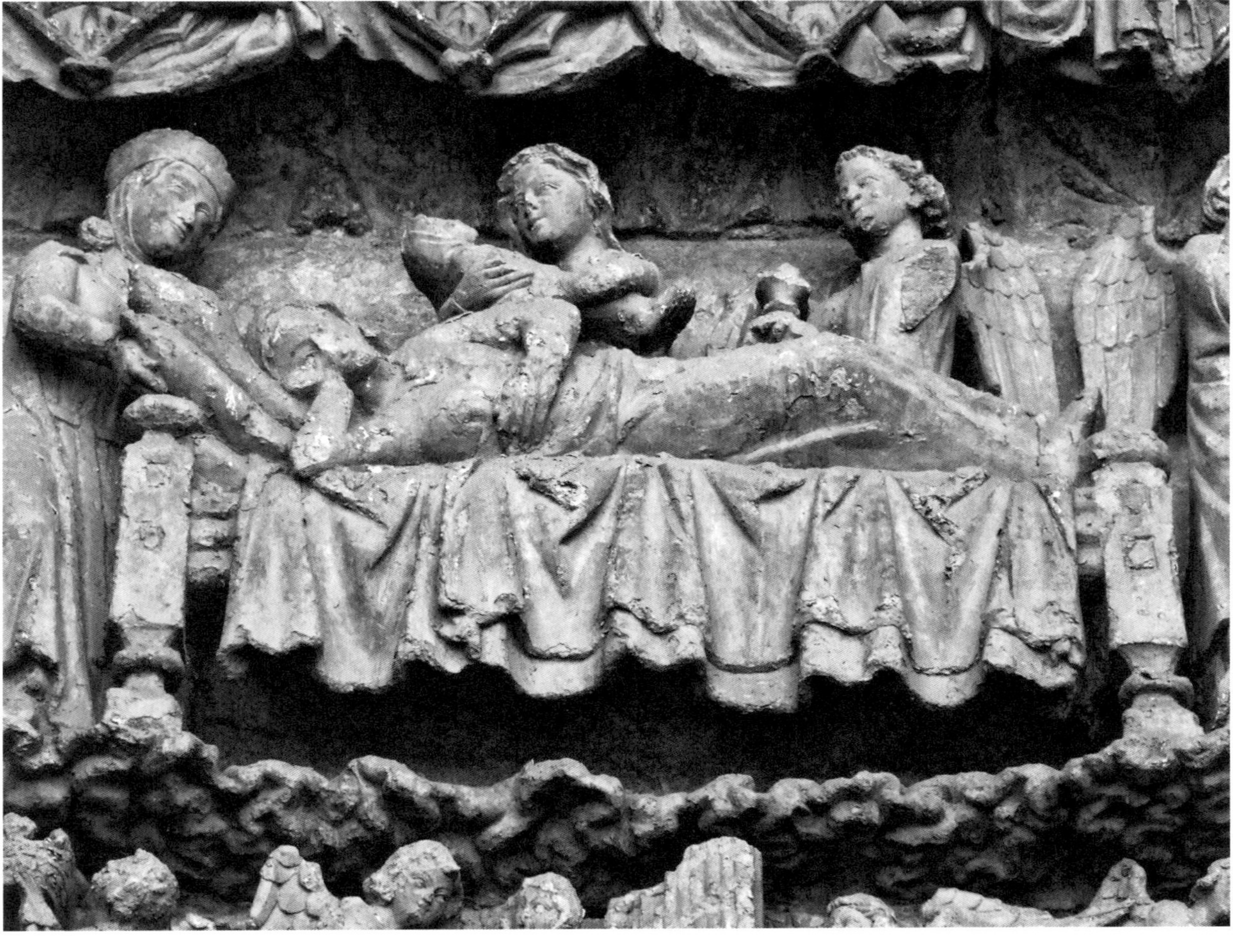

FIGURE 3a. León Cathedral, western façade, Portal of St. John the Baptist, tympanum. Christ's First Bath (1255–1275) (photo: author).

At first sight, another fundamental difference with respect to its French ancestors is that the main theme of the Leonese portal is not, as it might appear, Christ's Infancy, but instead, Baptism. Indeed, the first bath of Christ, an apocryphal episode, dominates the central register, although we cannot see the naked holy baby in the water, due to a sort of narrative ellipsis. One of the midwives who assisted Mary in her labor holds the baby in her arms while Mary rests exhausted in bed (Fig. 3a). To the left, we can see a kind of domestic still-life composed by a huge boat-shaped incense basin, a cauldron hanging from a chain, and a jug hooked onto the manger-altar, where the newborn baby we have already seen lies, now tidy, wrapped in the blanket, and being warmed up by the ox and the mule's humid breath (Fig. 2).[36] The theological discourse on Baptism is am-

treatise to different ways of amplification, see Murphy, *Retórica* (as in note 5), 337–338. See also Briscoe, *Artes Praedicandi* (as in note 10), 55–56.

36. Christ's First Bath was not a usual subject in French Gothic portals. See V. Juhel, "Le bain de l'enfant-Jésus: des origines à la fin de douzième siècle," *Cahiers archéologiques* 39 (1991), 111–132. On Hispanic theological sources of the Baptismal typology associated to the scene, see P. A. Patton, "*Et partu fontis exceptum*: The Typology of Birth and Baptism in an Unusual Spanish Image of Jesus Baptized in a Font," *Gesta* 33.2 (1994), 79–92, esp. 85–88. A wider treatment of the theme is in H. Sonne de Torrens, "*De fontibus salvatoris*: A Survey of Twelfth-Century Baptismal Fonts Ornamented with Events from the Childhood of Christ," in *Objects, Images, and the Word: Art in the Service of the Liturgy*, C. Hourihane, ed. (Princeton, 2003), 105–137, esp. 127–128.

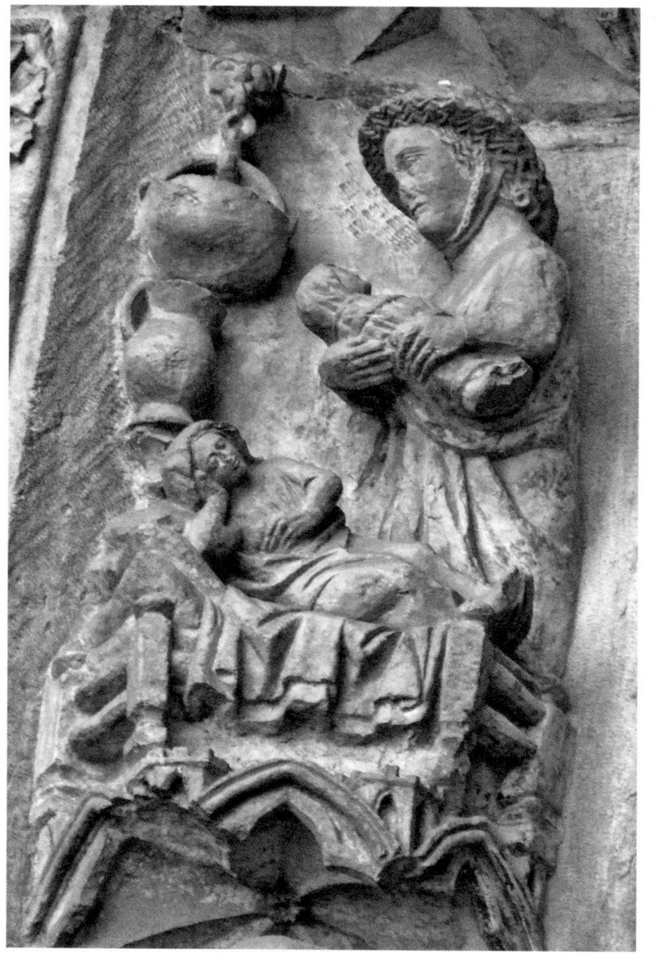

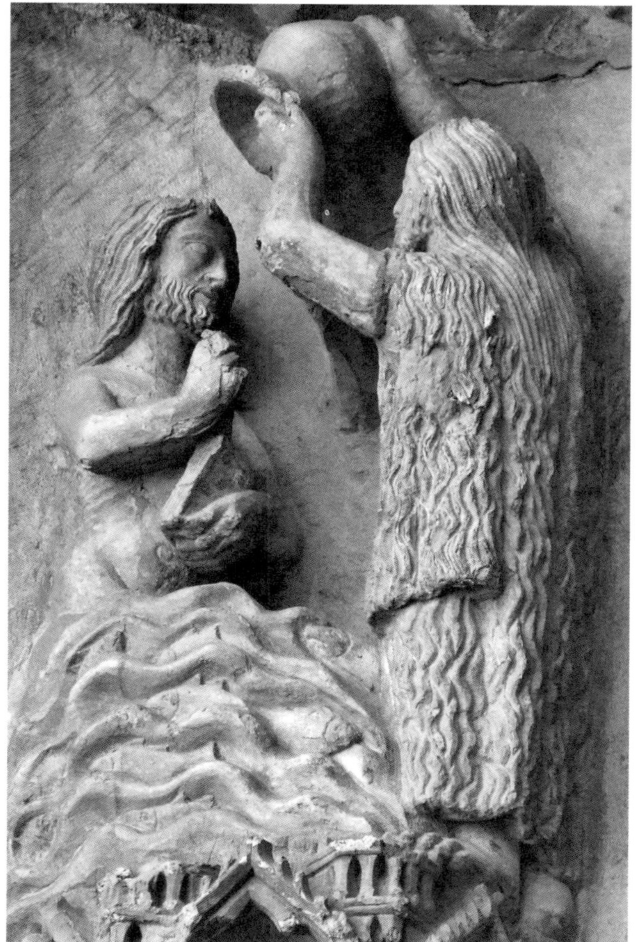

FIGURE 3b. León Cathedral, western façade, Portal of St. John the Baptist, archivolt. St. John's First Bath (*top left*) (1255–1275) (photo: author)

FIGURES 4a & b. León Cathedral, western façade, Portal of St. John the Baptist. Baptism of Christ (*top right*) and St. John's circumcision (*bottom right*) (1255–1275) (photo: author).

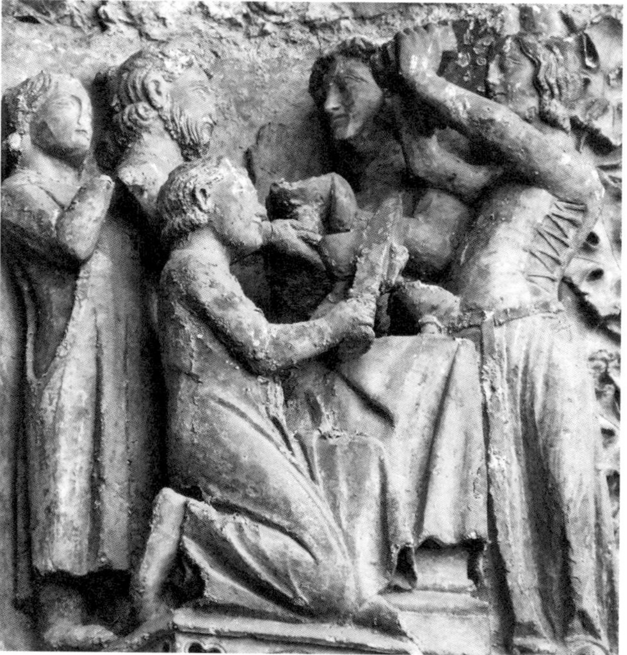

plified by echoing typological parallels in the archivolts, where the stories of St. John's life and afterlife and those of St. Paul are carved. Hence, water is alluded to in the first bath of the St. John (Fig. 3b); and flows abundantly through the sculpture in the Baptism of Christ (Fig. 4a), and in the Baptism of St. Paul.

And not only does water flow, but also infant's blood, which runs forth in the crude scene of St. John's circumcision, thus establishing a contrast between the "filthiness" of the Jewish initiation rite and the cleanliness of the Christian one (Figs. 4a, 4b).[37] It runs also in the scene of the Massacre of Innocents, another example of Jewish extreme cruelty, with its physical and symbolic climax in the image of the baby pierced by the lance of a Roman soldier, who shows him as a triumph, which occupies the center of the composition (Fig. 2). The Massacre of the Innocents is here alluded to as a veritable Baptism of Blood, to use St. Paul's description of martyrdom, although the Innocents were Jewish nonbaptized children.[38]

But the figurative sermon on Baptism in the Leonese portal is even more complex. Both the liturgical order and a long exegetical tradition justified the association of the Baptism of Christ with the Epiphany, which is carved on the upper register of the tympanum (Fig. 2). The Roman Church celebrated both Feasts on January 6th, and late twelfth- and thirteenth-century theological treatises and sermons consistently equated the baptismal font with Mary's womb and the sacrament with the Incarnation. As Harriet Sonne de Torrens has recently noted, that is the reason why cycles of Christ's Infancy and especially the Adoration of the Magi came to decorate thirteenth-century baptismal fonts.[39] A relatively rough baptismal font from León, dated by Sonne de Torrens to around the middle of the thirteenth century demonstrates the success of this evangelic imagery in the context of baptismal liturgy. Baptismal repertoires were used, then, both in fonts and in the portals, where this flooding of Baptismal imagery announced to the faithful, at the very threshold of the physical Church, the sacrament by which they could have access to the Spiritual Church.

As I have demonstrated elsewhere, the choice of a Baptismal sermon in stone for the Leonese portal was determined by its topography, which responded to a wish to adhere to the theory of *decorum*. If the matter of the sermon had to be suited to a specific audience, similarly the matter—the *thema*, to use the specific rhetorical term—of portal imagery should be adapted to the specific audience determined by its topography. The left portal of the western façade at León provided entry to St. John's Chapel, located on the ground floor of the

37. This scene was traditionally misunderstood. Displaced from its original location during the restorations carried on in the nineteenth century, and set between two scenes related to the martyrdom of St. John, it was identified as St. John's decollation, see Franco Mata, *Escultura Gótica* (as in note 19), 129 and 135. New digital photography confirms this new identification. If further evidence were needed, it is also found in Sens Cathedral's northwestern portal, see I. Plein, *Die Frühgotische Skulptur an der West fassade der Kathedrale von Sens* (Münster, 2005), 109–110 and fig. 64. Other examples once existed at Amiens or Auxerre. See *infra*. On circumcision, see E. Frojmovic, "Gendered Representations of the Circumcision Between Family and Community," in *Framing the Family: Representation and Narrative in the Medieval and Early Modern Period*, R. Voaden and D. Wolfthal, eds. (Temple, 2005), 221–243. Medieval blood has been studied by a number of scholars recently, see *Le Sang au Moyen Âge: Actes du quatrième colloque international de Montpellier Université Paul-Valery 27–29 novembre 1997*, M. Faure, ed. (Montpellier, 1999); *Blood: Art, Power, Politics and Pathology*, J. M. Bradburne, ed. (Munich, 2001); and B. Bildhauer, *Medieval Blood* (Cardiff, 2006).

38. A kind of persuasive visual rhetoric directed towards the Jews is clearly concealed in this portal, where the allegory of Synagogue appears in the outer porch. The cruelty with which the Jews are treated in scenes on the upper part of the portal accords with the extreme negativity used to represent Synagoga, showing her eyes and ears being devoured by a pair of dragons, see Sauerländer, "La escultura"(as in note 20), 199–200, fig. 35. For an analysis of the representation of Jews and the issue of conversion in the contemporary *Cantigas de Santa María*, see F. Prado-Vilar, "*Iudeus sacer:* Life, Law, and Identity in the 'State of Exception' called 'Marian Miracle,'" in *Judaism and Christian Art*, ed., H. L. Kessler and D. Nirenberg (Philadelphia: University of Pennsylvania Press, forthcoming).

39. Many years ago M. W. Bedard, in a chapter entitled "The Font as Mother or as Womb of the Church," in *The Symbolism of the Baptismal Font in Early Christian Thought* (Washington, D.C., 1951), focused his attention on these topics. H. Sonne de Torrens, in "*De fontibus salvatoris*" (as in note 36), *passim*, explained the popularity of images of Christ's Infancy in western baptismal fonts dating from the second half of the twelfth century to the late thirteenth with the success of these metaphors in contemporary pastoral and exegetical literature. She stresses Nordstrom's reflection on the coincidence between the celebration of the Baptism of Christ and the Epiphany in the Roman liturgy. See F. Nordstrom, *Medieval Baptismal Fonts: An Iconographical Study* (Umea University, 1984), 110. The legal texts related to King Alfonso the Learned (Partida I, Titulo IV, Ley VII) witness the current circulation of these metaphors in the contemporary Castilian realm, see *Las Siete Partidas del Rey Don Alfonso el Sabio*, (Madrid, 1972), 66. Among the Castilian examples must be quoted the baptismal fonts from Renedo de Valadavia (Palencia) and Valcobero (Museo Diocesano de Palencia), see G. Bilbao López, *Iconografía de las pilas bautismales del románico castellano. Burgos y Palencia* (Burgos, 1996).

northern tower, and this chapel functioned as a Baptistery and main place for celebrating parochial liturgy.[40] The portal was, then, the frame for the door through which the citizens of León entered for the first time into the physical and spiritual body of the Church. Furthermore, the portal served as a backdrop to the beginning of the ceremony. The ritual of Baptism began at the door of the Church, where the Priest asked the parents or the godfathers what prompted them to become Christians.[41] Echoing this liturgical setting, water and blood, parents and children are the main protagonists of the visual discourse of St. John's Portal at León. The families of the Leonese neophytes could identify themselves with their Biblical archetypes rejoicing or suffering in domestic interiors quite similar to their own.

Other Gothic portals with the story of St. John displayed on their tympana and archivolts confirm its Baptismal character. For instance, St. John the Baptist is featured on the north portal of the west façade of the cathedral of Sens (Fig. 5), on the northwest portal of Rouen, and on the southwest portal of Auxerre. At Sens, which is the seminal work in this tradition, the River Jordan floods the Baptism of Christ on the tympanum, while St. John is being bathed for the first time on a voussoir of the archivolt (Fig. 6a). These scenes were included in a long narrative with the turbulent story of St. John's relics, a story that stresses the resurrectional character of the sacrament. St. John's body, once burnt and reduced to ashes, recovered its original appearance and had the power to resurrect the devoted petitioners.[42] Irene Plein has recently tried to justify the choice of this program as a way of celebrating the translation of the relics of the Saint to the church in 1192, nevertheless, the idea could have been conceived earlier.[43] This portal's door was axially aligned with the chapel of St. John the Baptist, which was the north chapel of the chevet, and this had already been built before 1156.[44] Perhaps because the model was sanctioned by the arch-episcopal character of the see, it was imitated at Rouen. Here an original portal of St. John, carved at the end of the twelfth century, was severely damaged by fire in 1200, but was also restored when the western façade was rebuilt, thereby evoking the older one in a new tympanum, carved around 1240.[45] The relationship between Rouen and Sens is even closer, as one cathedral's plan imitated the other, and the cycle of St. John served to announce (at the threshold of the church) the dedication of the northern chapel to the Saint and its Baptismal character.

As was seen at Sens and Rouen, the discourses on Baptism and its regenerative power could be qualified as homiletic. Following the long tradition of preaching in the twelfth century, it is possible to find a long narrative at Auxerre that was carved around 1260, as well as an expanded sermon in León.[46] Both portals encompass Christ's Infancy and St. John's life, although in the Burgundian program St. John is found in the tympanum, while Christ is relegated to the archivolts. Both portals multiply the water imagery with the scenes of Christ's and John's First Bath, and the Baptism of Christ. However, at Auxerre, the rhetorical strategy used to amplify the theme was contrast. Here a moral contrast is shown between the holy fluids alluded to and the lusty waters of Bethseba's bath in the reliefs of the socle (Fig. 6b). At Auxerre the question of the relationship between topography and imagery remains

40. Sánchez Ameijeiras, "Poéticas y discursos" (as in note 19), 216–217.

41. The ritual is attested to in Castile, as it is described in *Las Siete Partidas* (as in note 39), 66.

42. Plein, *Sens* (as in note 37), 96–127, figs. 49–80. For another interpretation of the story of the relics of St. John at Sens, see N. Kenaan-Kedar, "Aspects des relations entre 'centre' et 'périphérie': les catedrales Saint-Etiènne de Sens et Saint-Jean de Sebaste," *Pèlerinages et Croisades. Actes du 118e Congrès Nacional Annuel des Sociétés historiques et scientifiques* (Paris, 1993), 315–319.

43. Plein, *Sens* (as in note 37), 288–290. I have already pointed to the Baptismal character of this iconography in Sánchez Ameijeiras, "Poéticas y discursos" (as in note 19), 218–221. A. Martin is also engaged in demonstrating the sacramental tone of the portal, see A. Martin, "Nouvelles observations sur le portail Saint-Jean de la cathedrale de saint-Étienne de Sens," *Bulletin Monumental* 163 (2005), 315–327.

44. The dedication of the north chapel to St. John is discussed in literary sources, see J. Bony, *French Gothic Architecture of the 12th and 13th Centuries* (Berkeley, 1983), 58–59.

45. Y. Bottineau-Fuchs, *Haute-Normandie Gothique* (Paris, 2001), 287, 308–309; on the architecture, see L. Grant, *Architecture and Society in Normandy (1120–1270)*, (New Haven, London, 2005) 123–127.

46. On Auxerre, see U. Quednau, *Die Westportale der Kathedrale von Auxerre* (Weisbaden, 1979).

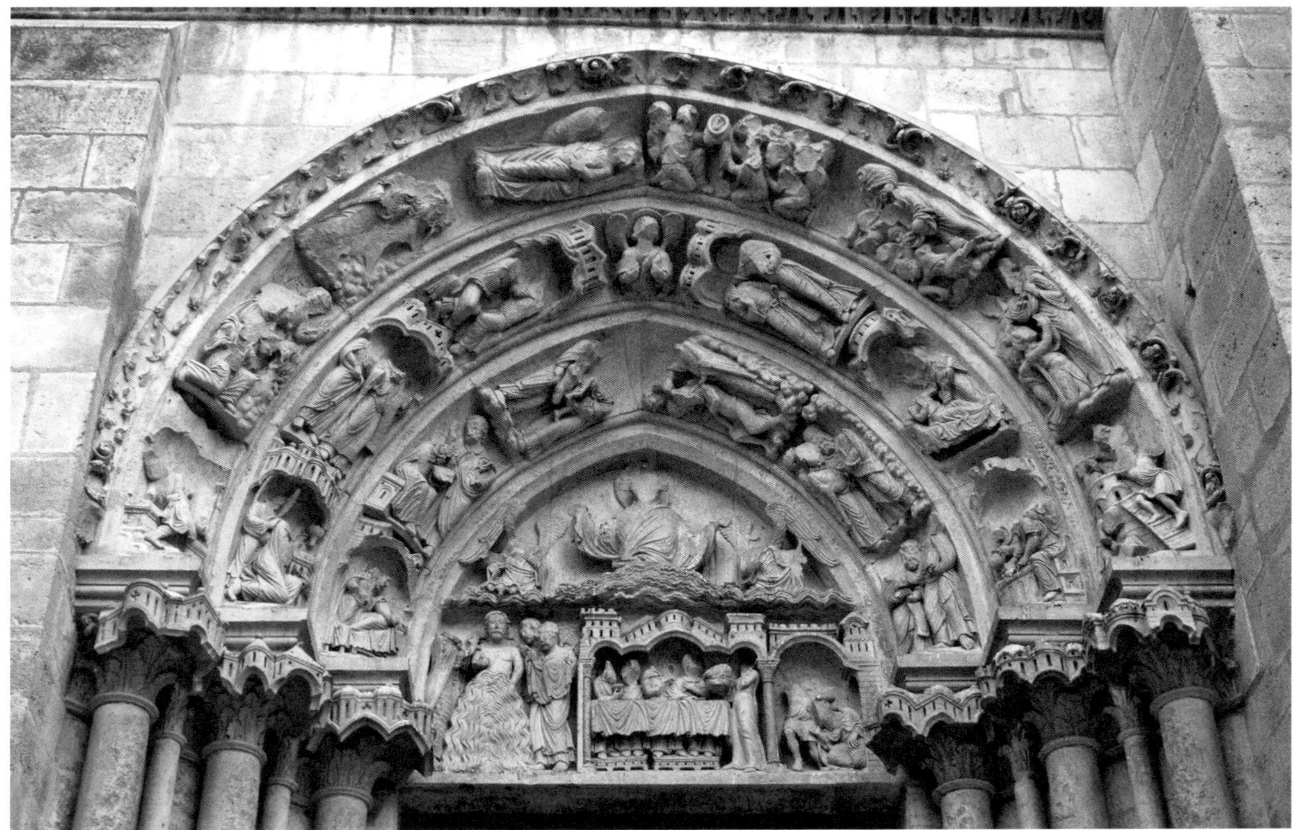

FIGURE 5. Sens Cathedral, western façade, north portal. St. John's Portal (1185–1195) (photo: Colum Hourihane).

elusive.[47] Nevertheless, other examples confirm the existence of a tradition of baptismal portals at least from the end of the twelfth century.[48] Visual narratives with the life of St. John the Baptist also decorate the socle of the southwestern portal of Amiens Cathedral and the lintel of the central portal of the Cathedral of St.-Jean, Bazas.[49] If instead of analyzing the portals' imagery using established categories rooted in Mâle's seminal work—hagiography, Christology, Mariology—a semiotic approach is used, and this is framed by the idea of "semantic field" offering a kind of kinship with the medieval rhetorical notion of *catena*. Other subjects come to convey the Baptismal discourse, and to fill the gaps in the already mentioned tradition. As has been pointed out, cycles of Christ's Infancy with the Epiphany could have been figuratively perceived as an allusion to Bap-

47. On the episodic construction of this Gothic cathedral, and the survival of the twelfth-century baptistery, see M. Dabas and H. B. Titus, Jr. "Non-destructive Sensing Projects Beneath Auxerre Cathedral," *Gesta* XL/2 (2001), 181–188, esp. 181, figs. 5 and 6.

48. Vincent Juhel has traced a Baptismal tradition in French, Catalan, and Italian late-Romanesque portals where Christ's First Bath is represented. He believes that this tradition is absent from early Gothic in northern France, the only exemption being the south portal of the collegiate church of Notre-Dame d'Étampes (1145–1155), see Juhel, "Le bain de l'enfant-Jésus" (as in note 36), *passim*. At Étampes, Christ's infancy is found on a capital frieze, and its immediate model is a "female" allusion to baptism on a capital frieze of the northwestern portal of Chartres, where an apocryphal cycle of the Virgin's infancy also included Mary's First Bath. On this last example, see L. Spitzer, "The Cult of the Virgin and Gothic Sculpture: Evaluating Opposition in the Chartres West Façade Frieze," *Gesta* 33 (1994), 132–50. Another early model is Christ's Infancy on the archivolts of the western portal of the Priory of St.-Loup-de-Naud.

49. On Amiens, see S. Murray, *Notre-Dame Cathedral of Amiens: The Power of Change in Gothic* (Cambridge, 1996), esp. 176. On Bazas, see J. Gardelles, "Les portails occidentaux de la cathédrale de

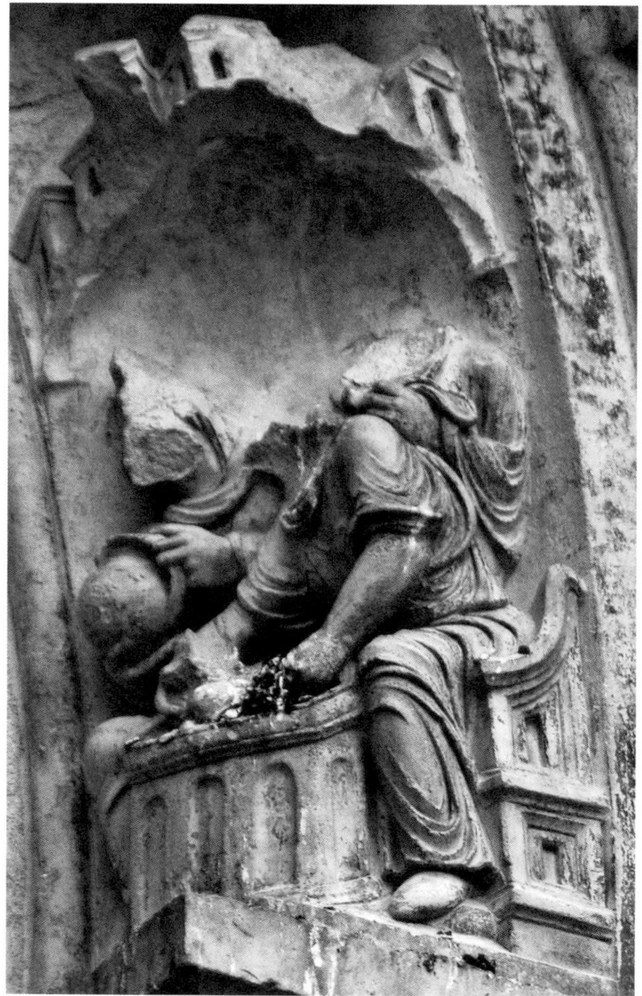

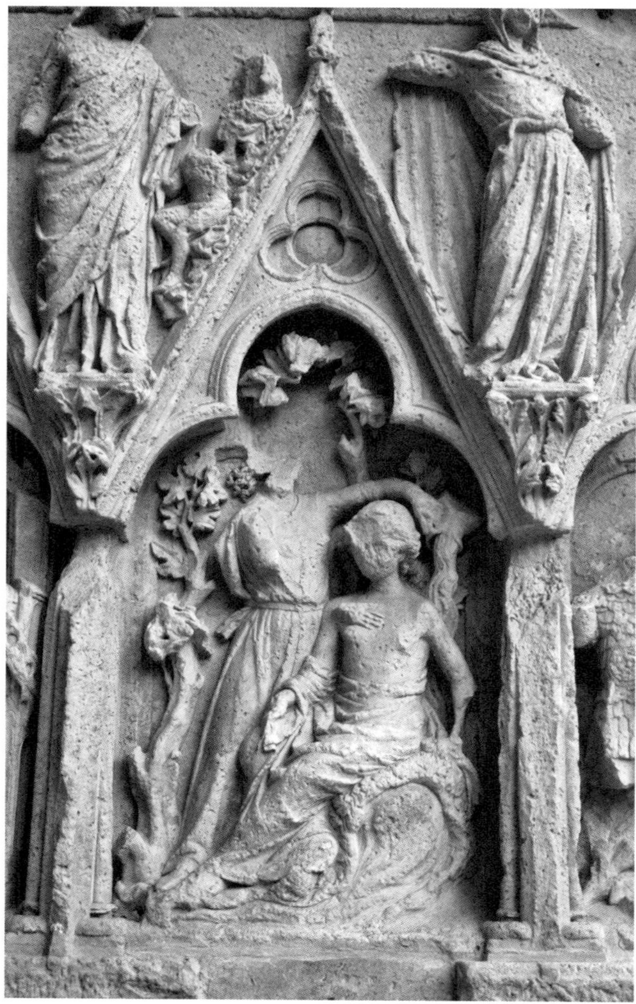

FIGURE 6a. Sens Cathedral, western façade, north portal. St. John's Portal, St. John's First Bath (1185–1195) (photo: author).

FIGURE 6b. Auxerre Cathedral, western façade, south portal. St. John's Portal, Bathsheba's Bath (*c.* 1260) (photo: author).

tism. Therefore the northwestern portal of Laon, the Ste.-Anne Portal of Paris, or the statues on the embrasures of the Virgin Portal at Amiens would join this Baptismal parade.

But other subjects were also likely to be incorporated in a visual sermon on the sacrament. When hagiographic narratives invaded the expanded portals, Baptism was not exclusively alluded to (figuratively) by its canonical or apocryphal Biblical types, which followed a clear homiletic rhetorical strategy. The saint/bishop was shown actually officiating at his cathedral's portal (Fig. 7). At Bourges, an expanded sermon on Baptism can be seen in the extreme southwestern portal. The life of St. Ursinus is narrated there, beginning

Bazas," *Bulletin Monumental* 133 (1975), 285–310; and Y. Criste, "Un cycle inédite de l'Apocalipse au portail du Jugement dernier de la cathédrale de Bazas," *De l'art comme mystagogie: Iconographie du Jugement dernier et des fins dernières à l'époque gothique. Actes du Colloque de la Fondation Hardt tenu à Génève des 13 au 16 février 1994* (Poitiers, 1996), 167–174.

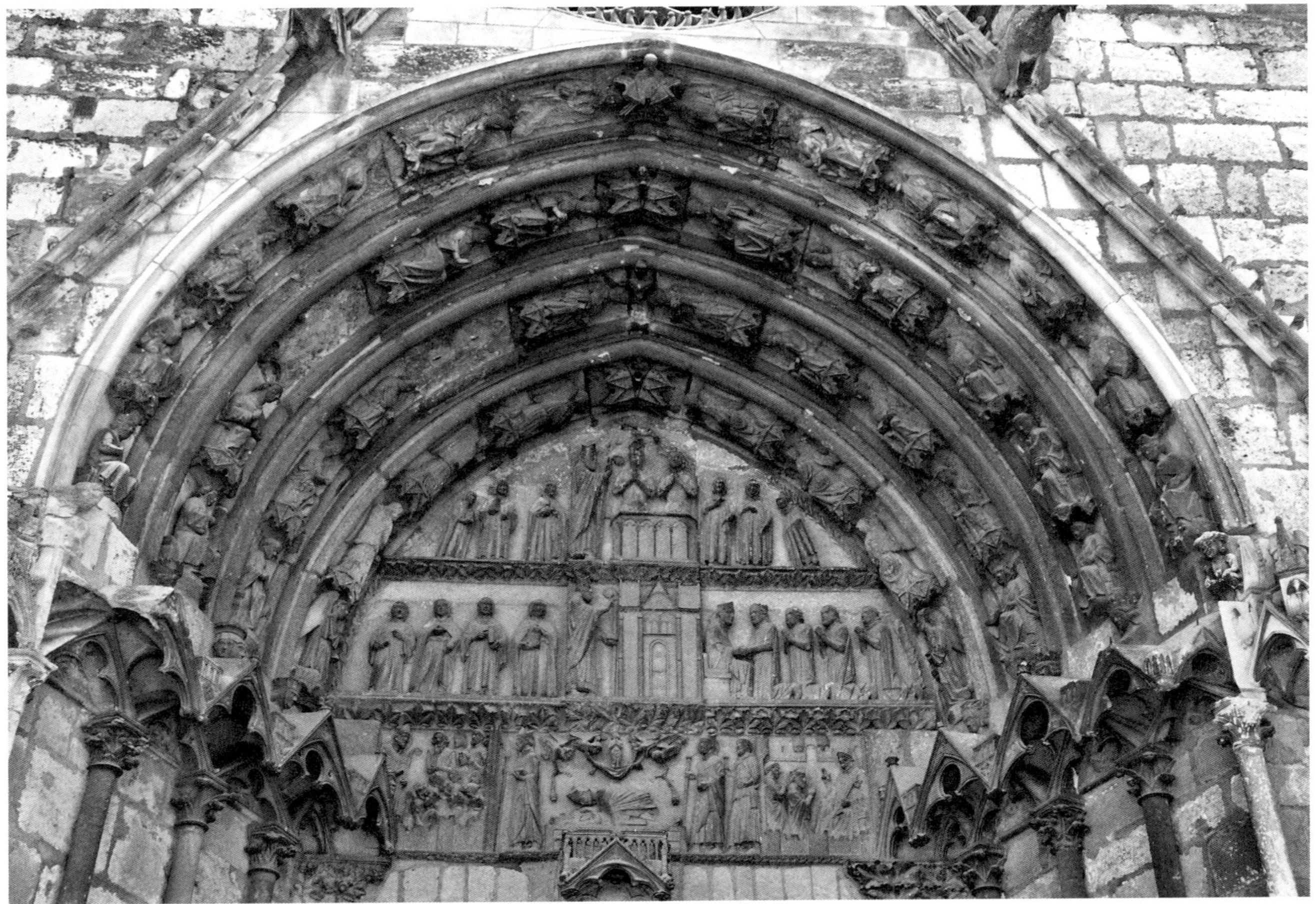

FIGURE 7. Bourges Cathedral, western façade, Portal of St. Ursinus (1230–1250) (photo: Colum Hourihane).

with his departure from Rome to undertake his apostolic mission in France, continuing with the building of Bourges Cathedral and the Baptism of the Roman governor of Aquitaine, Leocadius and his son Ludre, who crown the tympanum.[50] The still waters of the Gothic-shaped Baptismal basin, the troubled water of the Biblical Flood, and the story of Noah's ark are dramatically rendered on the sprandels of the socles, in such a way that the portal seems to be grounded in the troubles of the cosmic revolution (Fig. 12a).[51] At Bourges, as in León, Baptismal imagery changed the stone into water.

Sacraments & Transitional Imagery of Passage

Baptism was not the only sacrament announced at the western doors of the cathedral. The doors were usually intended for the citizens of the town. León Cathedral again confirms the importance of sacramental imagery on the main entrance to the Gothic cathedral. The central and right doors of the western portal offer two different sermons on the Resurrrection of the Body (Figs. 8, 10). This pairing of the Last Judgment with the Coronation of the Virgin was perhaps premiered in the

50. L. Brugger, "La cathedrale de Bourges au regard du tympan de Saint-Ursin," in *Mélanges J.-Y. Ribault. Cahiers d'Archeologie et d'Histoire du Berry* (November 1996), 67–72; *idem*, *La façade de Saint-Étienne de Bourges: Le Middrash comme fondement du message chrétien* (Poitiers, 2000), 55–58. The case of Reims Cathedral is more complex, as it was the consecration site of the Kings of France. Baptismal fonts are found in several parts of the building, but the main theme in this case is the image of the Baptism of Clovis.

51. Brugger, "Saint-Ursin," 67–72; *idem*, *Bourges* (as in note 50), 55–58.

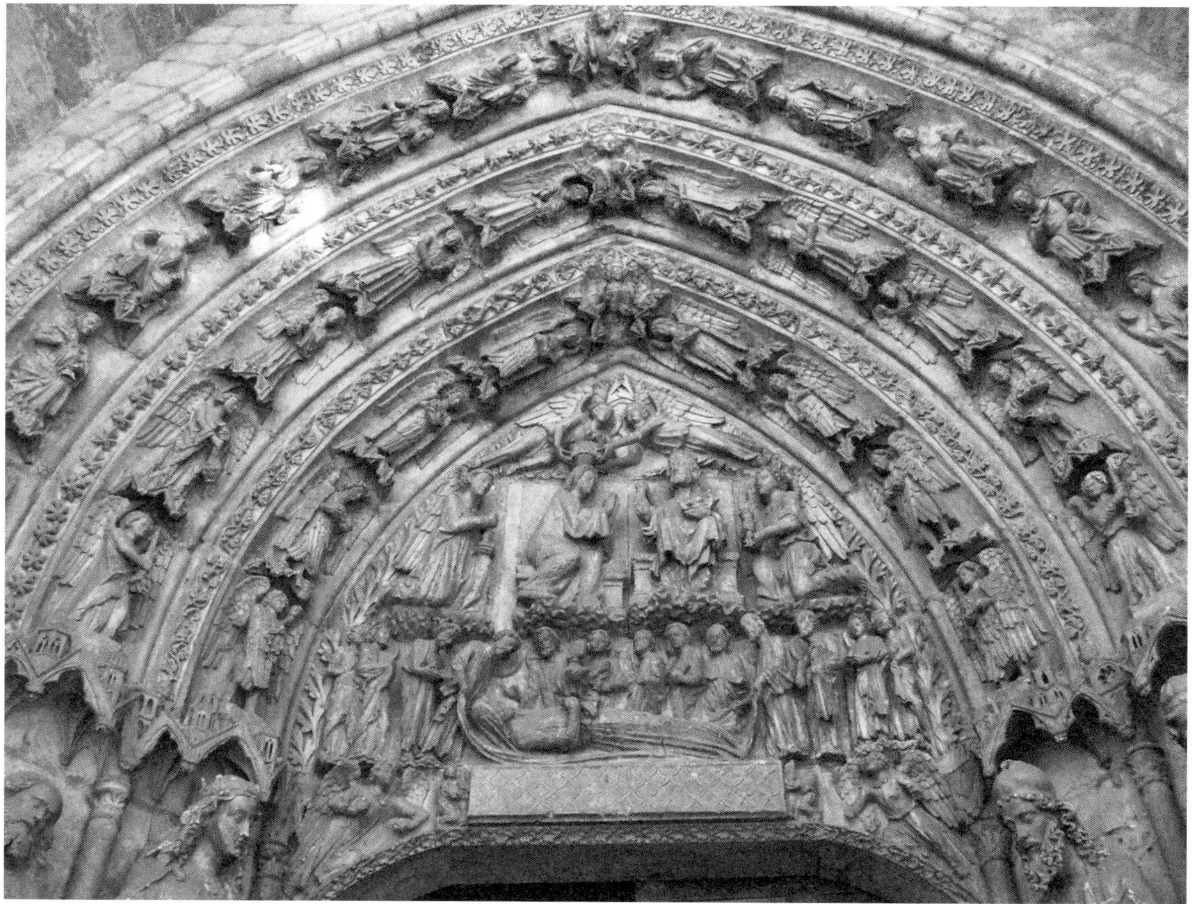

FIGURE 8. León Cathedral, western façade, Portal of the Coronation of the Virgin (1255–1275) (photo: author).

western portal of the abbey church of St.-Denis, and repeated later on the western façades of Laon, Paris, Amiens, Auxerre, and Bazas.[52] Aside from the complex ecclesiological meanings embedded in the Coronation of the Virgin Portals, as Marie-Louise Thérel has argued in relation to Senlis,[53] the combination of both programs could be understood in simpler terms as relating to the idea of death and regeneration of the flesh. The Last Judgement shows the glorious body of the resurrected Christ as well as the resurrection of the dead, while the so-called Coronation Portals offer proof of the real historical bodily resurrection of Mary and her Assumption. Furthermore, the discourse on the reunion of body and soul is also a common sub-theme in sermons dedicated to the Feast of the Assumption of Mary.[54]

52. P. Z. Blum, "The Lateral Portals of the West Façade of the Abbey Church of Saint-Denis," in *Abbot Suger and Saint Denis: A Symposium*, P. L. Gerson, ed. (New York, 1986), 199–227.

53. M.-L. Thérel, *Le triomphe de la Vierge-Église: Sources historiques, littéraires et iconographiques* (Paris, 1984). On the theme of the Coronation of the Virgin, see also Ph. Vedier, *Le courennement de la Vierge. Les origines et les premiers dévéloppements d'un theme iconographique* (Montréal, Paris, 1980); T. A. Heslop, "The English Origins of the Coronation of the Virgin," *Burlington Magazine* 147 (2005), 790–797; J. C. Schmitt, "L'Exception corporelle: à propos de l'Assomption de Marie," *The Mind's Eye: Art and Theological Argument in the Middle Ages*, J. Hamburger and A.-M. Bouché (Princeton, 2006), 151–185.

54. C. W. Bynum, *The Resurrection of the Body in Western Christianity 200–1336*, (New York, 1995), 249, n. 77; and *idem*, "Material Continuity, Personal Survival and the Resurrection of the Body: A Scholastic Discussion in its Medieval and Modern Contexts," in

If topography determined the location of some Baptismal portals, it also did so in this pairing of the Last Judgement and Coronation of the Virgin, which are clearly colored by eschatological connotations.[55] Much has been written about the funerary function of the parvis in Romanesque churches, but the possible survival of this function in the new and larger Gothic building has not been examined. New parvises located at the western end of the church were enclosed to serve as cemeteries.[56] It is known that the higher nobility and ecclesiastical hierarchy had the privilege of being buried in the interior of the Church, but common people continued to be buried in the sacred ground of the western parvis. An eighteenth-century engraving shows the western parvis of Notre-Dame de Paris, with the portals of the Last Judgement and the Coronation of the Virgin.[57] In the western portal of León Cathedral it is still possible to see the heraldic signs that must have served as marking the places for privileged burials near the southwestern entrance of the Church.[58]

There is no shortage of other examples showing this juxtaposition of themes on western portals. Such is the case, for instance, in the Portal of "la Majestad" in Toro (Zamora), where the Coronation of the Virgin occupies the tympanum and the Last Judgement is found on the outer archivolt on a portal that opens onto a privileged enclosed cemetery.[59] Even in cases when the western façade features only a Coronation of the Virgin Portal—as happens at Longpont or St.-Thibault-en-Auxois—an eschatological dimension is added by the presence of the Wise and Foolish Virgins, which serves as a reminder to the audience of the saying: "Watch therefore, for ye know neither the day nor the hour wherein the Son of man cometh."[60]

The Coronation Portal at León seems to emphasize the sub-theme of the resurrection of the flesh and this stresses the intricate ties that bind them. If the stone sermon on Baptism in the left portal can be qualified as an expanded discourse, the Coronation of the Virgin shows a kind of contraction that follows the aesthetic notion of *brevitas* even more so than the similar *brevitas* observed in French examples. Compared to the Parisian western portal, the tripartite structure of the tympanum has been reduced to a simpler binary pattern (Figs. 8, 9). The lower part shows the scenes of the death and entombment of the Virgin, which spreads to the lintel where a contemporaneous sarcophagus is depicted. The tympanum is reserved for the coronation. The sub-theme of the ancestors and prophets at Paris or Amiens linked the archivolts and the lintel, thereby glorifying Mary's earthly genealogy. This, however, has disappeared in León. The conflation of the death and entombment scenes stress the eschatological tone,[61] as similar sarcophagi would have been

---

Fragmentation and Redemption: Essays on Gender and the Human Body in Medieval Religión (New York, 1992), 257.

55. The placement of the Last Judgement in the western-most parts of Romanesque churches was analyzed by P. Klein, "L'emplacement du Jugement dernier et de la Seconde Parousie dans l'art monumental du Haut Moyen Âge," *Cahiers du Centre International de l'Art Mural* 2 (1988), 89–101; afterwards he expanded the idea to St.-Denis, and other Gothic examples, see P. Klein, "Programmes escathologiques, fonction et réception historique des portails du XIIe siècle: Moissac-Beaulieu-Saint-Denis," *Cahiers de Civilisation Médiévale* XXXIII/4 (1990), 317–349, esp. 342.

56. P. Ariès, *Images of Man and Death* (Cambridge, London, 1985), 13-23. See, for Castilan examples, I. G. Bango Torviso, "El espacio para enterramientos privilegiados en la arquitectura medieval española," *Anuario del Departamento de Historia y Teoría del Arte* (1992), 93–132.

57. The engraving was earlier published by A. Erlande Brandenburg, *La cathédrale* (Paris, 1989), pl. 118.

58. Franco, *Escultura Gótica* (as in note 19), 488, pl. 355.

59. On the Portal of Toro, see J. Navarro Talegón, *Portada de la Majestad: Colegiata de Toro* (Toro, 1996). The chronology of the portal is revisited by R. Sánchez Ameijeiras, "Algo más sobre Salomón y Sancho IV," *Homenaje a la Prof. Socorro Ortega* (Santiago de Compostela, 2002), 165–171.

60. The eschatological dimension is stressed at Longpont by the opposing good and dry trees of Matt. 7:15, see I. Kasarka, "Entre Notre-Dame de Paris et Chartres: Le portail de Longpont-sur-Orge (vers 1235)," *Bulletin Monumental* 160–IV (2002), 331–344. On St.-Thibaut-en Auxois, dated to 1260, see Ch. Freigang and P. Kurmann, "L'eglise de l'ancien prieuré de Saint-Thibault-en-Auxois: sa chronologie, ses restaurations, sa place dans l'architecture gothique," *Congrès Auxois-Châtillonais* (Paris, 1989), 271–290. Other cases of conflation, such as those combining Baptismal allusions in Christ's Infancy cycles (lintel) with the Coronation of the Virgin (tympanum), are found in the north portal of Villeneuve-l'Archevêque, or on the western portal of St. Stephen of Beauvais.

61. Schmitt, "L'Exception" (as in note 53), 172–173, offers some parallels for the Leonese solution that stress the physical sense of Mary's death and resurrection. Examples can be found in the Ingeborg Psalter (Chantilly, Musée Condé, MS. 9, fol. 34[r]), in the

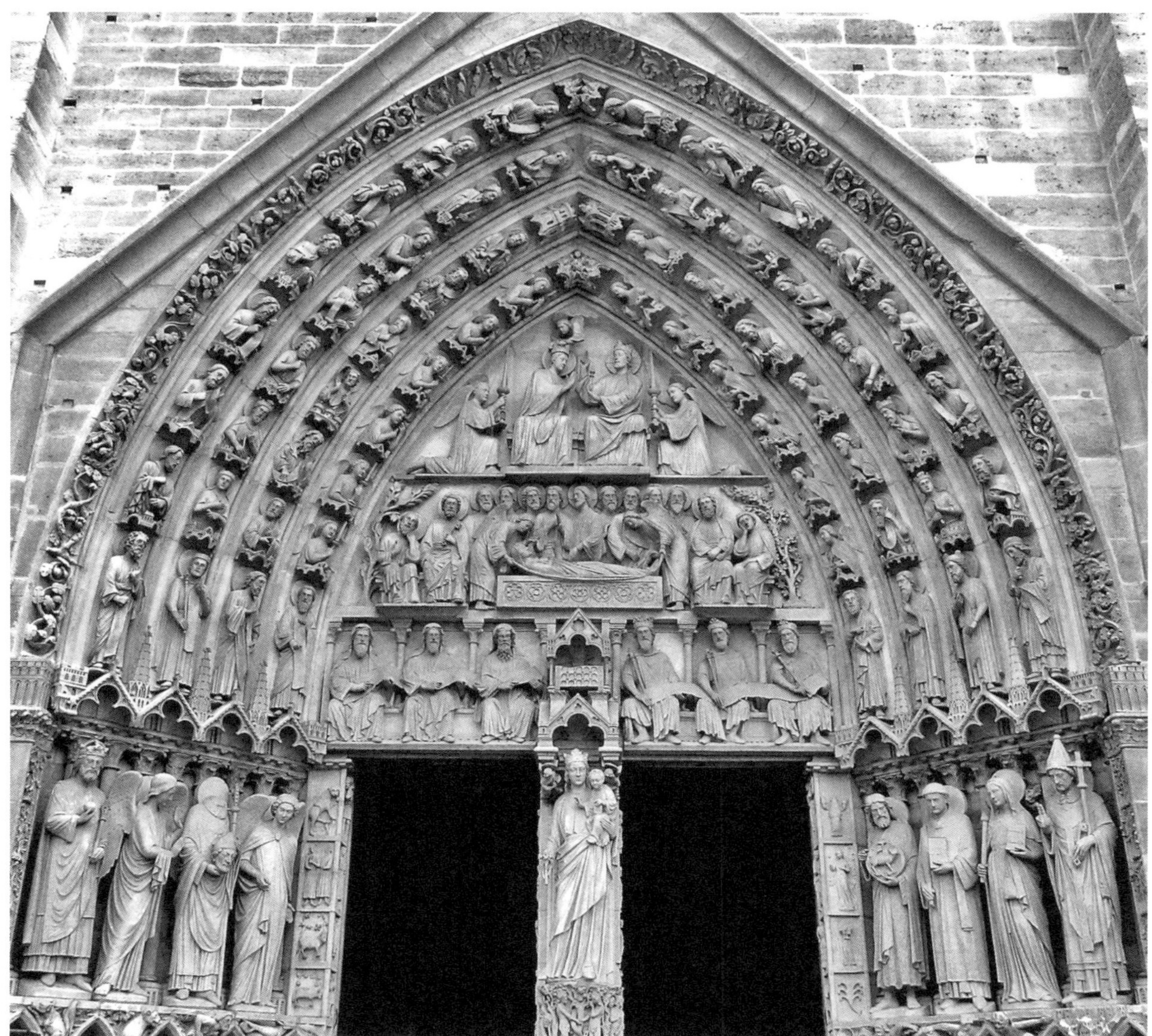

FIGURE 9. Paris, Cathedral de Notre-Dame, western façade, Portal of the Coronation of the Virgin (*c.* 1215–1225) (photo: Bildarchiv Photo Marburg).

found in the parvis, directly in front of the relief. The unified character and the eschatological tone spread to the archivolts, where the innermost ones present a kind of "office of the dead performed in Heaven"—as Erwin Panofsky would have said—with seraphim reading the prayers and angels censing and illuminating the ceremony,[62] while the outermost one is decorated with the Parable of the Wise and Foolish Virgins.

If the left portal borrowed its repertoire from baptismal fonts, the right one echoes contemporary funerary monuments, such as the Tombs of Bishops, where the absolution of the dead occupies the main register.[63] A

Psalter of Blanche of Castile (Paris, Bibliothéque de l'Arsenal, MS. 1186, fol. 29ᵛ).

62. E. Panofsky, *Tomb Sculpture: Its Changing Aspects from Ancient Egypt to Bernini* (London, 1964), 58–61.

63. R. Sánchez Ameijeiras, "*Monumenta* and *Memoria*: The XIIIth century episcopal pantheon of León cathedral," *Memory and the Medieval Tomb*, E. Valdez del Álamo with C. Pendergast, eds. (Cambridge, 2000), 269–300.

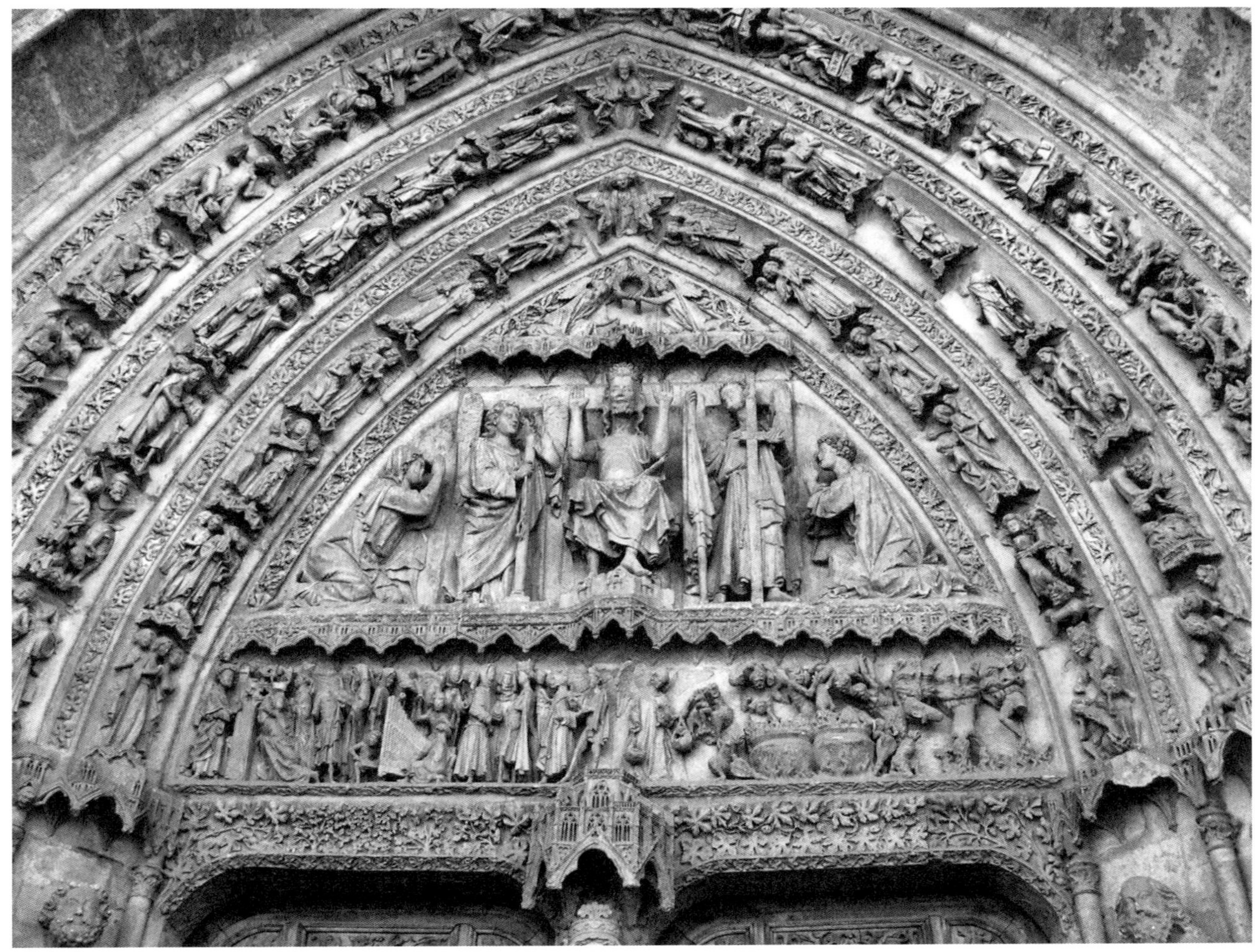

FIGURE 10. León Cathedral, western façade, the Last Judgement Portal (1220–1235) (photo: author).

clear symbolism of passage is stressed in both portals. Two rituals of passage—Baptism and the Absolution of the dead, the two sacraments that allow entrance into the earthly physical and spiritual Church, as well as the Heavenly Church—are alluded to on the portals flanking the central one, which features the Second Coming of Christ. Hence, a symbolism related to passage, entering, coming and leaving, dominates the whole composition.[64]

The discourse on the resurrection of the flesh that occupies the Last Judgement portal is again an expanded one, as was the case in Paris, Amiens, and Bourges (Figs. 10, 11). Nevertheless, the clerics designing the imagery at Paris and Amiens were interested in a didactical reflection on the fatal consequences of sin, as the figures of virtues and vices carved on their socles compelled the faithful to examine their consciences and remember their faults with the aid of the images, as well as being invited to repent and accept penance (Fig. 12b).[65] At Bourges, the allusion to sin is expressed in narra-

64. In "Beyond the Barrier," (as in note 16), 630–634, Jung drew on ethnographic and anthropological studies on the symbolism of passage by Arnold van Gnepp, Victor Turner, and Edmund Leach to understand the particular symbolism of the choir screen. In my opinion, the symbolism of passage achieved a quite wider transcendence in the figural decoration of other medieval architectural "sites of passage" or "structures of passage," a symbolism which acquires a deeper meaning when related to sacramental rites of passage.

65. B. Boerner, *Par caritas par meritum. Studien zur Theologie des gotischen Welgerichtsportals in Frankreich—am Beispiel des mittleren Westeingangs von Notre-Dame in Paris* (Fribourg, 1998).

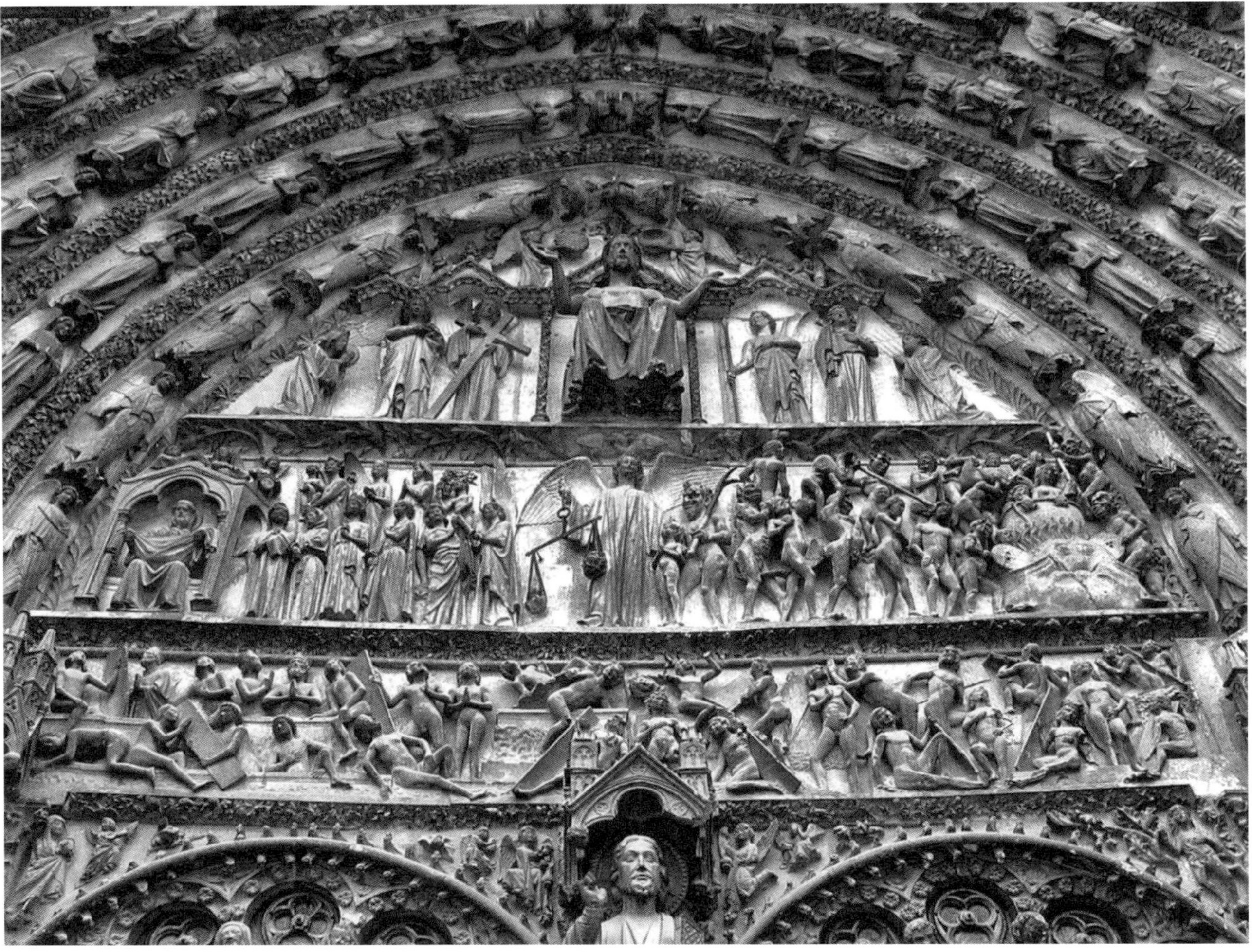

FIGURE 11. Bourges Cathedral, western façade, the Last Judgement (1230–1250) (photo: Colum Hourihane).

tive terms in the Genesis cycle on the spandrels, showing the female origin of sorrow and sin and confronting Eve's poisoned apple with the delicious fruits tasted by the elect in Paradise (Figs. 11, 12c).[66] Conversely, the León Last Judgement stresses the physical character of the resurrection of the body, and the power of the ecclesiastical hierarchy to forgive sins through the sacrament of Penance. While the Last Judgement, derived from Matthew 24–25, occupies the tympanum, the lintel, and the archivolts, the idea of resurrection is expanded to the intermediate archivolt, where the suffering bodies of Stephen, Peter, Lawrence, and others will be restored to their glorious appearance on the last day. (Fig. 12d).[67]

The discourse on the body and resurrection of the flesh reaches its climax in the persuasive rhetoric of contrast between the carnal suffering of the dammed devoured by a triple mouth of Hell (it must be noted that they preserve their sexual attributes) and the sensual, elegant, and joyful reunion of the elect in the realms of Paradise (Figs. 1a, 1b, 13). But there is another subtheme in this reunion because St. Peter is welcoming a hierarchically ordered elect, consisting of the pope, the bishop, and a cleric. The bishop puts his right hand on

66. Brugger, *Bourges* (as in note 50), 115–128.

67. The identification in A. Franco Mata, "Juicios Finales en la escultura monumental de las catedrales de Burgos y León," in *De L'art comme mystagogie: Iconographie du Jugement dernier et des fin dernières à l'epoque gothique. Actes du colloque de la Fondation Hadrt tenu à Genève du 13 au 16 février 1994* (Poitiers, 1996), 175–198.

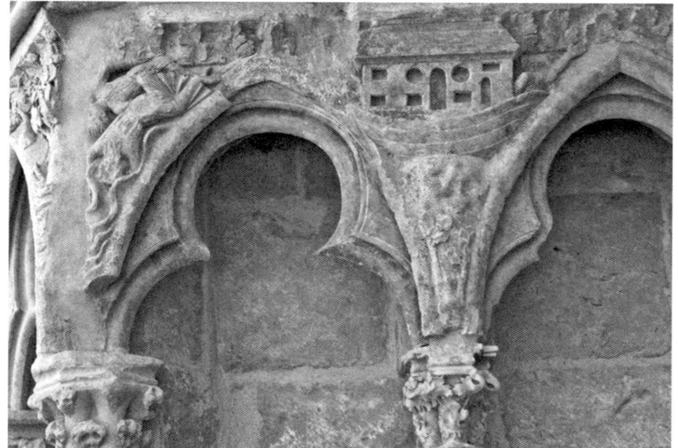

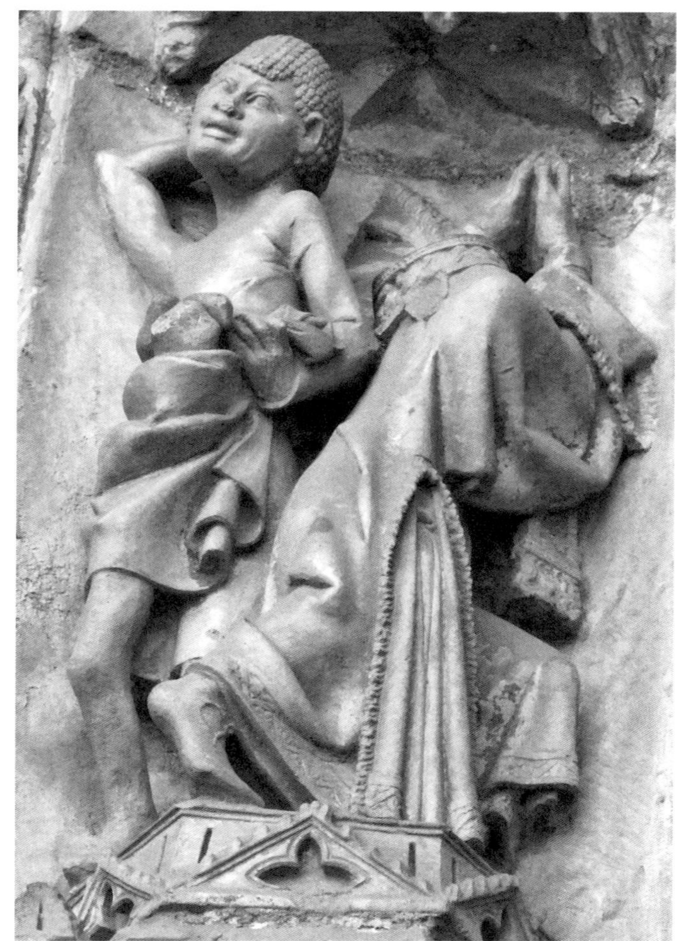

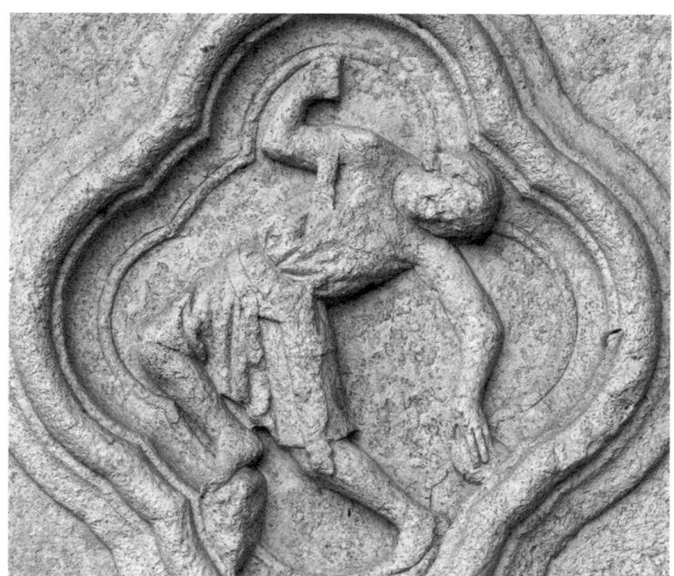

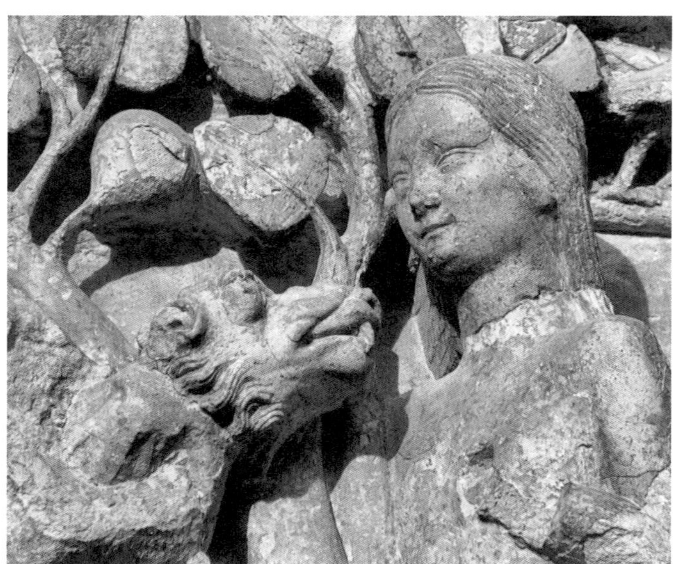

FIGURE 12a. Bourges Cathedral, western façade, St.-Ursinus Portal. Embrasures showing Noah's Ark (1230–1250) (photo: author).

FIGURE 12b. Amiens Cathedral, western façade, Last Judgement Portal. Bases of Portal embrasures and buttresses: Quatrefoil showing Despair from the Virtues and Vices (photo: Bildarchiv Photo Marburg).

FIGURE 12c. Bourges Cathedral, western façade, Last Judgement Portal. Spandrels of the socle showing The temptation of Adam and Eve (1230–1250) (photo: author).

FIGURE 12d. León Cathedral, western façade, Last Judgment Portal. *Voussoir* showing the Martyrdom of St. Stephen (1220–1235) (photo: author).

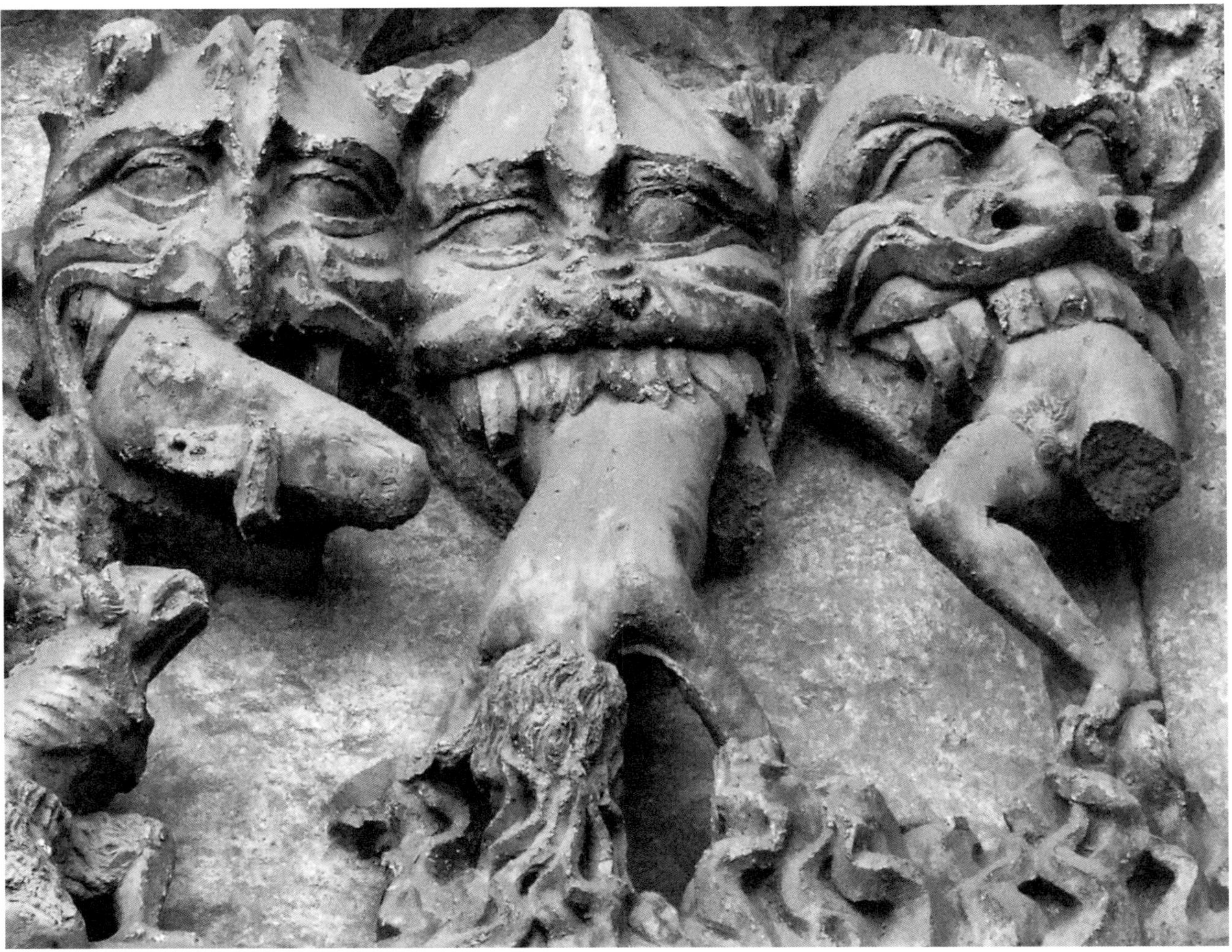

FIGURE 13. León Cathedral, western façade, Last Judgement Portal. Lintel showing the triple mouth of Hell (1255–1275) (photo: author).

the head of a boy, which is the standard gesture for absolution in the sacrament of Penance (Fig. 1a).[68] There is documentary evidence confirming that, at least from the early fifteenth century, the Last Judgement portal at León was known as the "Portal of the Pardon," thus confirming the penitential meaning of its imagery.[69]

With this reference to the sacrament of Penance, the symbolism of passage inherent in Baptism and the Absolution of the deceased is expanded. Penance has the power to allow or forbid entrance to the Christian to the spiritual benefits of the Church. Hence, the symbolism of passage is displayed on the western portal of Gothic cathedrals, a symbolism stressed not only by the visual allusion to the Christian rites of passage, but also amplified by the consistent repetition of iconographic motifs of passage. This visual strategy has been studied for St.-Firmin's Portal at Amiens as well as the doors of the cities of Thérouanne, Cambrai, Noyon, Beauvais, and Amiens, where the representation of a Bishop-Saint's journey echoes the actual processions celebrated in the cathedral.[70] But it is also found in Baptismal and Last Judgement penitential portals. St. Ursinus is shown

68. C. Vogel, *Le pecheur et la penitence au moyen âge* (Paris, 1969); *idem*, *En remission des péchés. Recherches sus les systèmes pénitentiels dans l'Eglise latine* (Aldershot, 1994).

69. R. Rodriguez, "Actas capitulares de la catedral de León," *Archivos Leoneses* (1957), 341–342.

70. W. Sauerländer, "Reliquien, Altäre und Portale," in *Kunst*

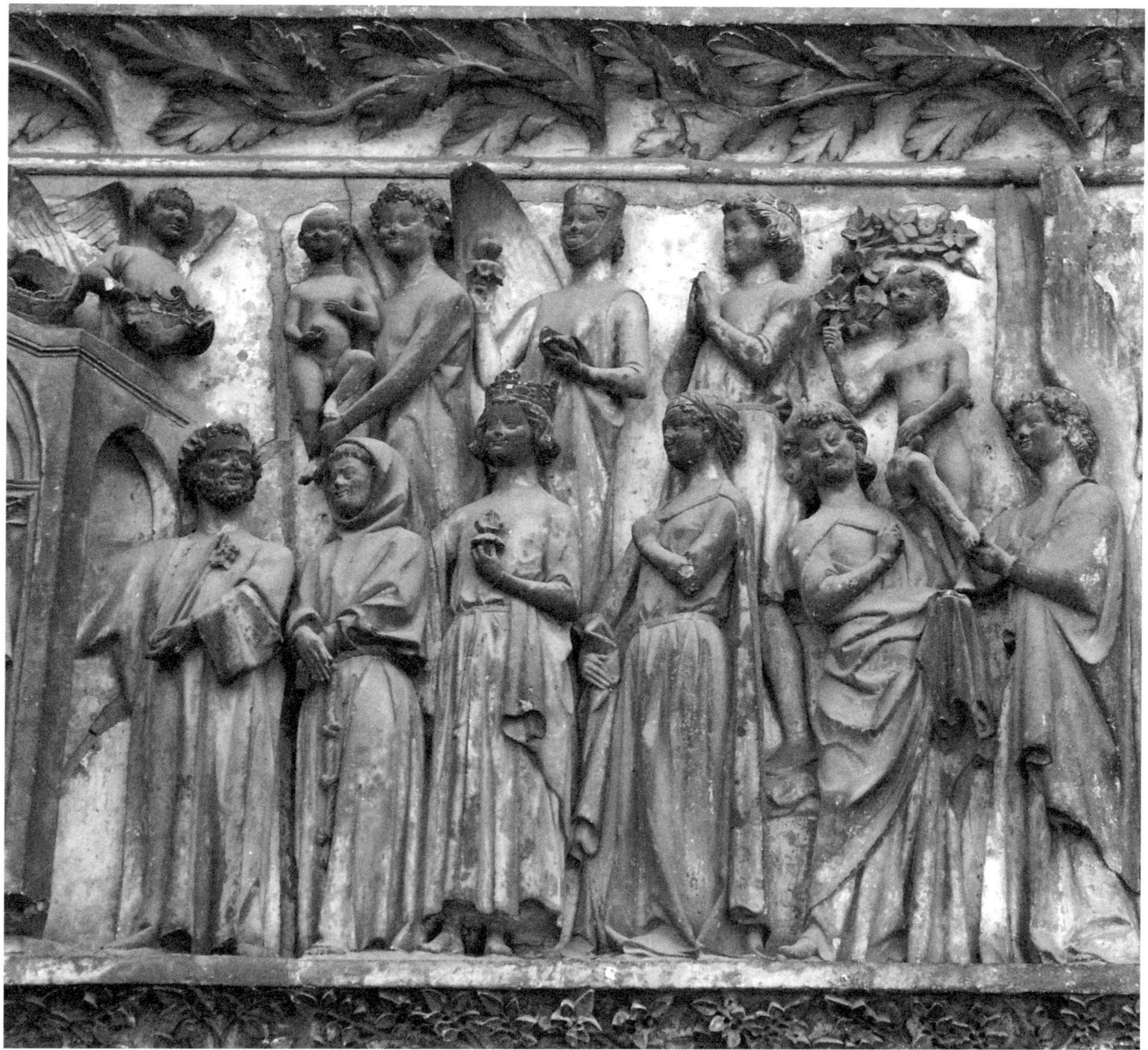

FIGURE 14. Bourges Cathedral, western façade, Last Judgement Portal. Lintel showing the Elect (1230–1250) (photo: Colum Hourihane).

passing through the doors of the cities of Rome and Bourges (first register of the Bourges tympanum), and consecrating the door of his own cathedral (Fig. 7).[71] In León the visual strategies of passage acquire a pronounced physicality. The door of Heaven on the lintel equates the physical earthly portal of the cathedral with the heavenly entrance. The blessed wait in front of the door of the realm of Paradise, which mirrored the

und Liturgie im Mittelalter. Akten des Internationales Kongresses der Bibliothe Herziana und des Nederlands Institut te Rome, Rome, 28–30 september 1997, N. Bock, S. de Blaauw, C. L. Frommel, and H. Kessler, eds. (Munich, 2000), 121–134; and C. M. Gaposchkin, "Portals, Pilgrimage, Processions and Piety: Saints Firmin and Honoré at Amiens," in *Art and Architecture of Late Medieval Pilgrimage in Northern Europe and the British Isles*, S. Blick and R. Tepikke, eds. (Leyden, 2004), 217–242.

71. Brugger, *Bourges* (as in note 50), 56–57.

Leonese citizens reunited under the porch or contemplating the portal imagery (Fig. 1a). Conversely, the devouring triple mouth of Hell endows the lintel with an illusion of a triple entrance to Hell, and this in turn mirrors the tripartite structure of the façade (Fig. 13). All of this imagery suits a place of passage, such as the entrance of the church.

If this is so, the guiding principle of *decorum* determined the choice of a reduced number of themes to decorate the western entrances to Gothic cathedrals, a principle that allows us to understand its obvious repetition. But these themes were likely to be expressed in different idioms and could be adapted to discourses and to intended audiences, as the Rhetorical manuals recommended. I shall now try to demonstrate that this aesthetic rule was followed in planning these vast monumental enterprises, which started in the second quarter of the thirteenth century.

The Variety of Poetics

Art historians who have written in the past on the Leonese western portals were mainly preoccupied with cataloguing each element and relating it to visual or iconographic sources; they sought to find formal prototypes for each figure on the tympanum or voussoir, and to place these in stylistic, iconographical, and chronological relationships with other portals with similar themes and styles. There has been a tendency in traditional scholarship to recognize three different artistic creators: "The Master of the Last Judgement Portal" would have carved most of the central portal, and the lintel of the one on the left side, which was erroneously assembled in this position in the nineteenth century (Figs. 1a, 1b, 10, 13). "The Master of the White Virgin" is credited with the Virgin of the *trumeau* on the central portal, and he was in charge of a second workshop responsible for the carvings on St. John's Portal (Fig. 2). Finally, there was the "Master of the jamb statues," whose followers were responsible for the sculpture of the Coronation of the Virgin Portal (Fig. 8). Previous scholarship was more interested in the series of statues than in the relief sculpture, and nobody realized that the stylistic differences between the portals in this Leonese façade result from each following a diverse formal idiom.

Since Peter Kurmann's study of the cathedral of Reims revolutionized our understanding of sculptural workshops in the high Gothic period, it is important to recognize that in the first half of the thirteenth century different forms and styles might appear in the same fabric at the same time. Kurmann showed how sculptors used little plaster models of heads, bodies, or members of the body, in such a way that figures with a Reims head on an Amiens body can be found.[72] I shall try to demonstrate that this practice continued in later generations of sculptors, and that specific sets of formal models were selected for their ability to convey a particular kind of discourse. What traditional historiography has understood as styles belonging to different chronological moments, must be seen instead as different idioms that were available at the same time. It was Cicero who said *tria sunt genera dicendi*, when proposing an ideal system of styles. It is easy to equate the Ciceronian division of oratory styles with the three visual idioms found at León. Nevertheless, the optional character of the formal idioms and the guiding principle of appropriateness is a practice related to medieval rhetorical propedeutics.[73]

The literary characterization of these styles as defined by the scholars who wrote on them allows us to find some formal continuities that remain despite changes in their taste or ideology. Every art historian agrees with the general belief that St. John's tympanum

72. P. Kurmann, *La façade de la cathédrale de Reims, Architecture et sculpture des portails. Etude archéologique et stylistique*, (Lausanne/Paris, 1987), *passim*; *idem*, "Un Colossse aux pieds d'argille. La chronologie de la sculpture française repose-t-elle sur des dates assurées?" in *Épigraphie et iconographie. Actes du colloque de Poitiers, 5–8 octobre 1995*, R. Favreau, ed., (Poitiers, 1996), 143–152; *idem*, "Mobilité des artistes ou mobilité des modèles? Á propos de l'atelier des sculpteurs rémois au XIIIe siècle," *Revue de l'Art* 120 (1998), 23–34; *idem*, "Jedem Meister seinen Stil? Zur Herstellungsproblematik französischer Monumentalskulptur in den grossen Bauhütten des 13. Jahrhunderts," *Stilfragen zur Kunst des Mittelalters: eine Einführung*, B. Klein, ed. (Berlin, 2006), 137–149.

73. This principle of the appropriateness of different visual idioms seems to have been already used in the western façade of Notre-Dame de Paris. There is no place here to expand the argument, but I hope to do so in the near future in the form of a book.

is "confused and overburdened with small figures," and they criticize its "excessive narrative character" and its "picturesque realism."[74] Nevertheless, the narrative character of this portal must have been deliberate. One of the persuasive strategies of the mendicants' sermons consisted in presenting the Evangelic episodes in terms of everyday life. This was a rhetorical strategy suited to the "low material style" presented in an "easy elocutionary way," or, as Madeline Caviness might say—they are suited to the "simple perception of (humble) matter."[75] And in terms of everyday life, Christ's Infancy is narrated in the Portal of St. John the Baptist. The detailed *descriptio* in the narratives was one of the means codified by the *Artes praedicandi* to amplify the sermon, and detailed description of the interior of common houses can be recognized in the scenes of Christ and St. John's first baths (Figs. 2, 3a, 3b). Furthermore, humoristic anecdotes were also recommended in the preaching manuals in order to attract the audience. The viewer cannot but smile upon seeing St. Joseph poking the lazy and obstinate mule with two sticks in the Flight into Egypt—a visual motif without known precedents, and lacking any biblical or Apocryphal justification (Fig. 2). The mule was obviously very much more comfortable resting in the manger. In fact, animals seem to play an important role in the humoristic repertoire of St. John's Portal. Another example can be seen in the Announcement to the Shepherds where ingenuous little goats climb on the rocks following their leader, while the already seated dog listens to the angelic concert.

When contemplating the humble and humoristic visual mode of the Leonese portal it is impossible to forget Jacqueline Jung's observations on the imagery of Choir screens. She has recently called attention to what she sees as a new narrative visual trend originating in this specific context, which is characterized by a formal idiom rich in detailed descriptions and humoristic anecdotes. Drawing heavily on arguments first proposed by James H. Stubblebine, she has qualified this narrative trend as "vernacular imagery," because it seems to present features that are also found in contemporary vernacular sermons, more geared towards the treatment of physical realities than the complex abstract metaphysical discourses of the Latin sermons that were clearly intended for a cultivated clerical audience.[76] According to Jung, the visual narrative of Christ's Infancy on the *jubé* of Chartres Cathedral (1230–1240) started this trend, which most befit this area of the church because it was the setting for preaching in the choir pulpit during the main liturgical feasts. Preaching was also performed in front of monumental portals, which served as stage sets, as is the case of the St. John Portal at León, whose program could have been inserted in this narrative tradition and linked to a lay audience. Although the León sculptors were probably trained in the workshops of Burgos, they developed a more narrative mode in León, a mode more suitable to the Baptismal discourse of the portal and its intended audience.

In reality, this narrative trend can be traced back even further than the Chartres *jubé*. The story of St. John at Sens, although severely damaged today, shows contemporary domestic interiors in the episodes of the birth of the Baptist, his first bath, and his naming by Zachariah—episodes where intimacy and tenderness come to the fore in the way the father holds the baby, in the sweet care with which the midwife bathes the child (Fig. 6a), and in Zachariah's delicate caress on Elizabeth's shoulder.[77] This particular narrative mode also permeates the portal of St. Ursinus at Bourges. In

74. Bertaux, "La sculpture chrétienne" (as in note 23), 281; Weise, *Spanishe* (as in note 23), 15; Gómez Moreno, *Catálogo* (as in note 19), 281; Mayer, *Gotik* (as in note 23), 52; Mahn, *Kathedraleplastik* (as in note 23), 34–35; Deknatel, "Thirteenth century" (as in note 23), 336; Ainaud and Durán, *Escultura gótica* (as in note 19), 56–59; Yarza, *Arte Hispánico* (as in note 19), 237; Azcárate, *Arte gótico* (as in note 19), 166–167; and Franco, *Escultura gótica* (as in note 19), 145–146 and 148.

75. M. H. Caviness, "The Simple Perception of Matter and the Representation of Narrative, ca. 1180–1280," *Gesta* 30 (1991), 48–64.

76. Jung, "Beyond the Barrier," (as in note 16), 648. The idea of a "vernacular imagery" has originally been proposed by James H. Stubblebine in relation to the frescoes of Assisi; and by Wolfgang Kemp when comparing the narratives of Chartres windows with vernacular poetry, see James H. Stubblebine, *Assisi and the Rise of Vernacular Art* (New York, 1985); and Kemp, *Narrative* (as in note 15). M. Camille, in "Visualizing the Vernacular: A New Cycle of Early Fourteenth-Century Bible Illustrations," *Burlington Magazine* 130 (Feb. 1988), 97–106, had already expressed his skepticism.

77. Plein, *Sens* (as in note 37), figs. 59–61.

the spandrels of the socle, which are decorated with the dramatic story of Noah's ark and in the tympanum, this anecdotal anachronism is not confined to the domestic interiors of the sacred narrative but also to its exterior stages (Figs. 12a, 7).[78] The backdrop to the preaching of St. Ursinus, which consists of small-scale representations of the contemporary cathedral, baptismal font, and city door, compel the mid-thirteenth century viewer to identify with the group of Bourges citizens who attentively listen to the bishop as if he were delivering his sermon in the space of the actual city. But was he preaching in the vernacular?

The contrast between vernacular and Latin preaching proposed by Jung to characterize the new narrative trend, which she sees as emerging only in choir screens, is perhaps rather simplistic. The Arts of Preaching contemplated a wide variety of idioms. Latin sermons were not always difficult, or *gravis*, and, conversely, vernacular ones were not always easy or *humilis*. The St. John Portal at León could, in fact, be characterized as vernacular and *humilis* (humble), not only on account of its narrative and anecdotal character, but also because the humble mode uses underlying meanings generated through typological linkage (Fig. 2).[79] Conversely, the portal of the Coronation of the Virgin could be labeled as vernacular, but, at the same time, *gravis*. In fact, scholars agree in praising the quality of its sculpture, the contained character and severity of the figures, but they criticize the monotonous repetition of facial types, and the lack of movement (Fig. 8).[80]

The genealogy of this idiom can be traced back, through the Coronation Portal at Amiens, to the Paris Coronation Portal (Fig. 9).[81] Stiffness, monotonous repetition of types, and subjection of the human figure to a geometrical ordering are some of the characteristics of this formal style, which was especially suited to the highly allegorical discourse found with complex tropes in the Coronation of the Virgin Portals.[82] In León the historical dimension of the imagery is stressed in the accentuated physical details of the mortal processes of the death and resurrection of Mary's body. Nevertheless the Coronation of the Virgin can also be understood as an ecclesiological metaphor, and, indeed, ecclesiological nuptial metaphors are expanded in the archivolts in the parable of the Wise and Foolish Virgins. This trend can be recognized also in Bourges—although the portal was highly restored in the sixteenth century—and in less ambitious programs such as those at Longpont or Toro. The case of Toro also seems to encapsulate the theory of styles in a single portal, because the sensual, lively, and expressive language in the Last Judgement of the outer archivolt contrasts with the geometrical stiffness of the Coronation of the Virgin on the tympanum.

But the sensual liveliness of the elect and dammed is not only found in Toro. A third and different formal mode in León dominates the Last Judgement Portal (Figs. 1a, 1b, 2, 10, 13). Scholars have traditionally attributed most of its sculpture to "The Master of the Last Judgement" whose formal idiom was labeled as "naturalistic expressionism," due to the elegance, imbalance, exaggerated disproportions, facial expressions and agitated movement of his figures. These features were seen as belonging to a "true Spanish genius," and have been considered to be a type of naturalism and expression of Aristotelian nominalism, or sometimes as an example of aesthetic mannerism present in "Court Styles."[83]

78. On the concepts of intimacy and extimacy as critical terms in analyzing Gothic visual discourses, see F. Prado-Vilar, "The Gothic Anamorphic Gaze: Regarding the Worth of Others," in *Under the Influence: Questioning the Comparative in Medieval Castile*, C. Robinson and L. Rouhi, eds. (Leiden, 2005), 67–100.

79. Auerbach, *Mimesis* (as in note 9), 34–39.

80. Bertaux, "La sculpture chrétienne" (as in note 23), 284; Weise, *Spanishe* (as in note 23), 18; Gómez Moreno, *Catálogo* (as in note 19), 281; Mayer, *Gotik* (as in note 23), 52; Mahn, *Kathedraleplastik* (as in note 23), 34–35; Deknatel, "Thirteenth Century" (as in note 23), 376; Ainaud and Durán, *Escultura gótica* (as in note 19), 59; Yarza, *Arte Hispánico* (as in note 19), 236; Azcárate, *arte gótico* (as in note 19), 168; Franco, *Escultura gótica* (as in note 19), 338–339.

81. On Amiens, see Murray, *Amiens* (as in note 17), 106–108.

82. The formal style also suited other programs, see R. Sánchez Ameijeiras, "Church Reform and the Poetics of Gothic Sculpture in Burgos and Amiens," in *Spanish Medieval Art: Recent Studies*, C. Hourihane, ed., (Princeton, 2007), 155–186.

83. Bertaux, "La sculpture chrétienne" (as in note 23), 281–282; Weise, *Spanische* (as in note 19) 18–34; Mayer, *Gotik* (as in note 23) 50–54; Gómez, *Catálogo* (as in note 19), 241–243; Mahn, *Kathedraleplastik* (as in note 23), 39–43; Deknatel, "Thirteenth Century" (as

In fact, the artistic genealogy of the León Last Judgement Portal goes back to the so-called Parisian "Court Style," with its immediate forerunners being the procession relief of the elect on the now-lost south portal of St.-Denis, as well as the Last Judgement Portal at Bourges (Figs. 11, 14).[84] It is my belief that this formal idiom must be understood in the context of its own modal tradition, and within the specific framework of mid-thirteenth-century Franciscan eschatological discourses.

Thirteenth-century Rhetorical treatises distinguished prophecy as a genre on its own, and one defined by its own features among the modes codified by the Arts of Preaching. Prophecy was a literary genre that had acquired its visual counterpart in the visionary portals as early as the Romanesque period. As Madeline Caviness has noted in a seminal article, the visionary mode was characterized by highly ordered and hierarchical compositions and a visual rhetoric of contrast. Whereas her case studies were the compositional similarities between the Last Judgement portals at Conques and Bourges, this is a type of composition that can also be recognized at León.[85] I am more interested in the differences between them, which do not only affect drapery and proportions, but also their discourses on the body.

When analyzing the expressive language of León's Last Judgement, it is possible to conclude that it was exclusively used in eschatological or prophetic contexts. I have already referred to St.-Denis and Bourges (Fig. 14). In Bourges, as in León (Fig. 1b), a Franciscan friar had been occasionally identified with the Saint of Assisi, and these portals inaugurate a new sensual, expressive, and bodily language in the representation of the Last Judgement. At Bourges, the blessed smile, as well as the fruits and flowers, evoke, through a synecdoche, the pleasant perfumes and delicious tastes of Paradise, while the singing angels echo harmonious heavenly melodies. The enlightened studies of Caroline Walker Bynum, Jerome Bashet, and Claudio Carozzi on theological disputes and eschatological questions that occupied theologians at the end of the twelfth and thirteenth centuries, allow us to recognize in these portals an increasing emphasis on the bodily and emotional character of the resurrected, which was defended by the Franciscans.[86]

But the ordered alignment of the elect in Bourges differs sharply from the imbalance and movement of the Leonese blessed, who flock to the door of Heaven (Figs. 1a, 1b, 10, 14). In order to understand León in a broader framework that goes beyond a unilinear genealogical pattern in monumental sculpture, it could be compared, using something like Deleuze and Guattari's epistemological idea of the *rhizome*,[87] to another visual eschatological discourse that developed in manuscript illumination. This is the one found in the Douce Apocalyse where, as Nigel Morgan has pointed out, we are presented with a "popular theology with pictures directed towards the laity."[88] This offers an interesting point of comparison to the Leonese ensemble. A kind of "rhizomatic" kinship can be established between the angel in the archivolt of

---

in note 23), 330–331; Ainaud and Durán, *Escultura* (as in note 19), 47–48; Yarza, *Arte Hispánico* (as in note 19), 235–235, insists in the "impression of deep unbalance"; Azcárate, *Arte gótico* (as in note 19), 163, qualifies the sculpture of "realism or expressionist naturalism"; Williamson, *Gothic Sculpture* (as in note 19), 344; Ara, "Escultura gótica" (as in note 19), 244–245; Franco, *Escultura gótica* (as in note 19), 331–332.

84. On the relationship between León and Bourges, see Joubert, "De Bourges a León" (as in note 21) (forthcoming).

85. Caviness, "The Simple Perception" (as in note 75), *passim*.

86. A detailed discussion on the new Franciscan sensual discourse and the sculpture of Bourges and León is found in "Poéticas y discursos"(as in note 19), 228–243. This new Franciscan bias in Last Judgement imagery seems to depart from Amiens, but, as I mentioned earlier, this aspect goes beyond the scope of this paper. On the eschatological disputes of the thirteenth century, see Bynum, *Resurrection* (as in note 54), and its review by J. Bashet in *Annales, H.S.S.* (1996), 135–139; Bynum, "Continuity" (as in note 54); J. Bashet, "Vision béatifique et représentations du paradis (XIe–XVe siècle)," *Micrologus* VI (1998), 73–93; *idem*, "Alma y cuerpo en el Occidente medieval: una dualidad dinámica, entre pluralidad y dualismo," in *Encuentros de almas y cuerpos entre Europa medieval y mundo americano* (Chiapas, 1999), 41–84; *idem*, "Le sein d'Abraham: un lieu de l'au-delà ambigu (théologie, liturgie, iconographie)," in *De l'art comme mystagogie* (as in note 67), 71–94; *idem*, *Le sein du père: Abraham et la paternité dans l'Occident médiéval* (Paris, 2000); and C. Carozzi, *Apocalypse et salut: dans le christianisme ancien et medieval* (Paris, 1999).

87. G. Deleuze and F. Guattari, *A Thousand Plateaus: Capitalism and Schizophrenia* (1987), introduction.

88. N. Morgan, *The Douce Apocalyse: Picturing the End of the World in the Middle Ages* (Oxford, 2007), 16.

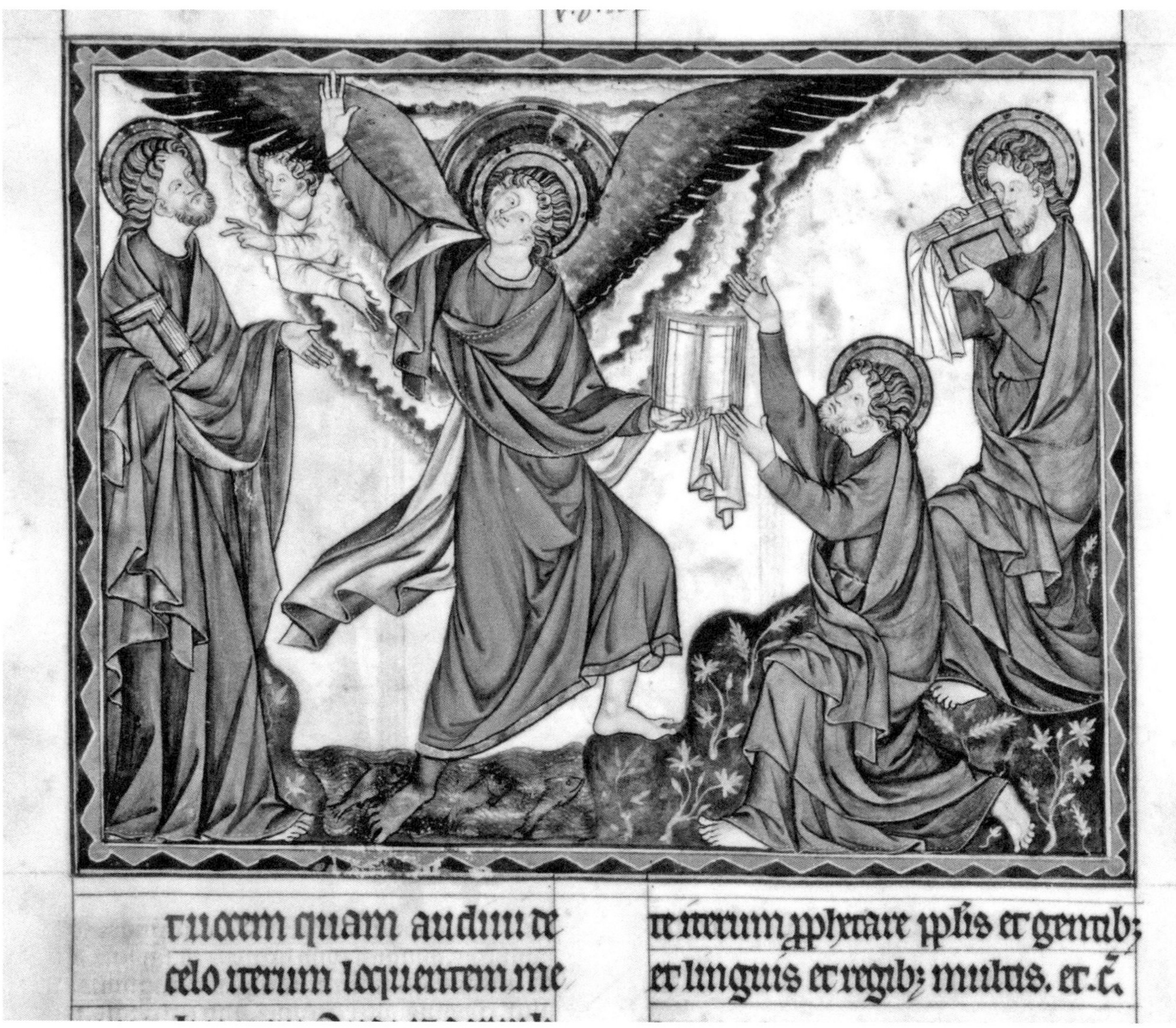

FIGURE 15a. Oxford, Bodleian Library, MS. Douce 180, p. 33. The angel gives John the book to eat (detail, *c.* 1270) (photo: Bodleian Library).

León and the smiling angel who offers St. John the book to eat in the English manuscript (Figs. 15a, 15b).[89] If the Leonese portal was considered as "more French than the French ones,"[90] the English manuscript was also related to the so-called Parisian "Court Style." The Franciscan bias permeating the Leonese eschatological discourse is clearly stated in the illustrations of the two witnesses in the Anglo-Saxon cycle.[91] As Paul Binski has observed, the Douce Apocalypse shows a "culture of spiritualized physical activity, its attendant contesting of

89. This kinship is not completely coincidental, for there are some historical connections between the two works. The manuscript was made for Prince Edward and Princess Eleanor of Castile, who bare shields with their arms and kneel before the Throne of Grace in the historiated initial of Fol. 1^{r}. Eleanor was the sister of king Alfonso the Wise, and don Martin, the Bishop of León, was the king's chancellor who officiated at the wedding celebrated at Burgos. See A. Ballesteros Beretta, *Alfonso X el Sabio* (Barcelona, 1984), 100–102.

90. Kurmann, "Französischer" (as in note 21).

91. Morgan, *Douce* (as in note 88) 18, on the manuscript's Franciscan bias; and 21–29, on its stylistic affiliation.

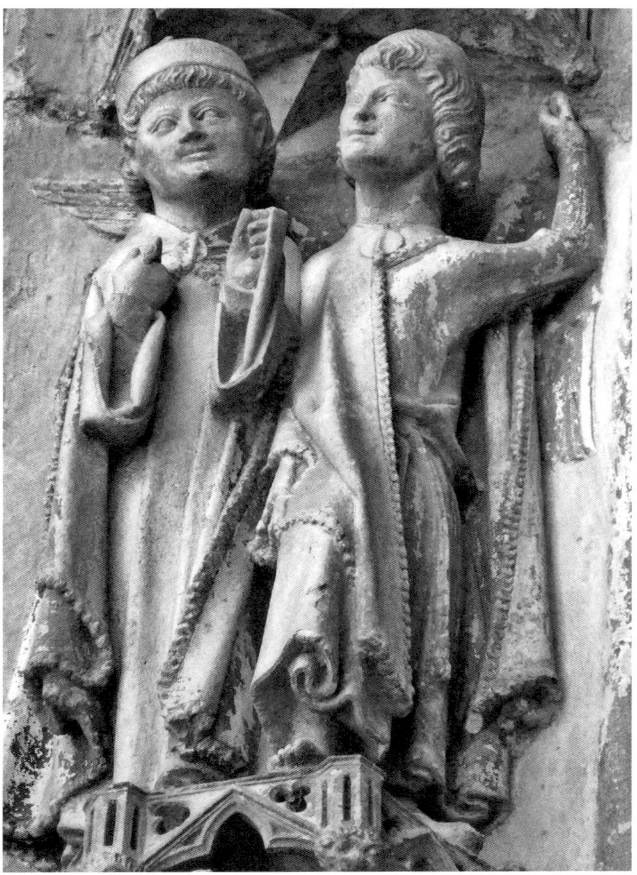

FIGURE 15b. León Cathedral, western façade, Last Judgment Portal. *Voussoir* possibly showing St. Dominic resurrected (1255–1275) (photo: author).

conventional norms of psychosomatic balance in service of religious transport."[92] The same words could be applied to León, because León and the Douce Apocalypse deal with prophetic imagery. The formal gifts of the angels in the English manuscript, and the elect as well as the angels in the Castilian Portal, translated into a visual idiom: the Bonaventurian discourse on the *dotes* (dowries) that were given to the angelic and the resurrected bodies, namely, *agilitas*, *subtilitas* and *claritas*.[93] *Agilitas* is the ability to move instantaneously everywhere; *subtilitas* is lightness; and *claritas*, a shining clearness. As John Gage and Paul Binski have demonstrated, the term *claritas* could be expressed in visual terms by means of a facial expression, the smile.[94] Thus, the smiles of the angels and the elect in both the manuscript and the Castilian Portal, their imbalance, the distorted proportions, and their agitated movement become an elocutionary style that from mid-thirteenth century on suited metaphysical bodies in prophetic visual discourses.

The idea of *decorum* preserved in the theory of Rhetoric was developed in the thirteenth century and must have played a role in the choice of subjects decorating Gothic portals, as well as in the choice of the visual idioms that suited them.

But the Rhetorical treatises not only defined the categories of difficult and easy, high, medium, and low, topical style, four genres of preaching, and so forth, they also codified a distinction between the arts of poetry and prose. Gothic portals could be seen as visual sermons in prose, but the thirteenth-century artists also developed the habit of rhyming images. While the León western portal was being carved, the illuminators of King Alfonso the Wise were composing the *Cantigas de Santa Maria*. The verses praising the Virgin were translated into rhyming images in this famous codex (Escorial MS. T.I.1),[95] and Gothic visual language can also be shown to have a wide sample of visual poetics as well.

92. P. Binski, "The Angel Choir at Lincoln and the Poetics of the Gothic Smile," *Art History* 20/3 (September 1997), 350–374, esp. 365–367.

93. Bynum, *Resurrection*, (as in note 54), 252–254.

94. J. Gage, *Color and Culture. y Cultura. La práctica y el significado del color de la Antigüedad a la abstracción* (Madrid, 1993), 69–79 and 277–280, esp. 77–78; Binski, "Angel Choir" (as in note 92), 367.

95. R. Sánchez Ameijeiras, "Rimando imágenes para Santa Maria. Teoría literaria y composiciones visuales de las *Cantigas de Santa Maria*," in *Cantigas de Santa Maria*. Ed. Facsímile Escorial I.1.1. Volúmen de estudios (forthcoming). On the relationship between the Theory of Rhetoric and the composition of the *Bible moralisées* where the habit of rhyming images cans also be found, see C. Hughes, "Typology and Its Uses in the Moralized Bible," in *The Mind's Eye: Art and Theological Argument in the Middle Ages*, Jeffrey F. Hamburger and Anne-Marie Bouché, eds. (Princeton, 2006), 133–150.

BERND NICOLAI

Transformation and Innovation of Rising Gothic in the Northern Holy Roman Empire: Transferring Gothic

ANY DISCUSSION on the Gothic moving outside the Île de France and the *Domaine Royale* faces the problem of having to deal with the gap between center and periphery. There has been much debate as to how this style was transferred to early thirteenth-century Germany, or more precisely, to the *Regnum Teutonicum* as part of the Holy Roman Empire under the Hohenstaufen. Willibald Sauerländer—who has worked on this topic and is celebrated with this volume for his life's work on Gothic art—speaks about the arts of the Hohenstaufen Empire as being in "an almost reacting position."[1]

More recently, Christopher Wilson in his study on *The Gothic Cathedral* claimed that: "German cathedral architecture during the first two thirds of the thirteenth century was conservative in style and modest in scope. Every major church built during this period incorporates French elements of some kind, but these vary greatly in their modernity and provenance."[2] What Wilson described *ex negativo* is the keystone for understanding the reception of the Gothic and the subsequent changes in the art and architecture of the northern Holy Roman Empire. It is important to realize, however, that these changes were undertaken by a self-assured, culturally and politically confident center.

Medievalists have proposed the idea of the Gothic culture radiating throughout Europe at different stages around the year 1200 from its original center in the Île de France. In mapping Gothic architecture outside of this core area we have to inquire as to what extent cultural models from the French kingdom were changed and at what stage this happened. Peter Cornelius Claussen's model of center, periphery, and "trans-periphery," exemplified by the figured portal of the Île de France, did not characterize the "trans-periphery" as distant geography, but was dependant on "the increasing orientation of different superior paradigms' respective traditions."[3] The concept of a trans-periphery follows it own rules, and this was the case in the northern Holy Roman Empire until 1250. This essay looks at the different processes in which the style changed, a style that ultimately ended when French models were completely taken over during the era of St. Louis by the Rayonnant style. For the Northern Empire it seems more likely that a paradigmatic change around 1200 can be seen less in architectural models than in fashion and troubadour epics.[4] Following these models, a second change

1. Willibald Sauerländer, "Intentio vera nostra est manifestare ea, que sunt, sicut sunt. Bildtradition und Wirklichkeitserfahrung im Spannungsfeld der staufischen Kunst" (1979), in *idem*, *Cathedrals and Sculpture*, Vol. 1 (London, 1999), 369–392; see also his "Style or Transition? The Fallacies of Classification Discussed in the Light of German Architecture 1190–1260," *Architectural History* 30 (1987), 1–29.

2. Christopher Wilson, *The Gothic Cathedral: The Architecture of the Great Church, 1130–1530* (London, 1990), 144.

3. Peter Cornelius Claussen, "Zentrum, Peripherie, Transperipherie. Überlegungen zum Erfolg des gotischen Figurenportals an den Beispielen Chartres, Sangüesa, Magdeburg, Bamberg und den Westportalen des Domes S. Lorenzo in Genua," in *Studien zur Geschichte der europäischen Skulptur im 12./13. Jahrhundert*, ed. by Herbert Beck and Kerstin Hengevoss-Dürkop, vol. 1 (Frankfurt a.M., 1994), 665–687, here 670.

4. See Nicola Zotz, *Intégration courtoise. Zur Rezeption okzitanischer und französischer Lyrik im klassischen deutschen Minnesang* (Heidelberg,

occurred around 1220 in illuminated manuscripts, paintings, and murals, as well as in sculpture.

Up to the 1240s, the model of the French cathedral was not transferred elsewhere. The first evidence of such a model being found outside of the center is in churches that were dynastically linked to the original. The Abbey Church of Westminster (1246 onwards) or the Cathedral of León (1240s onwards) are both coronation churches for the kings of England and Castile-León. Both dynasties were directly related to the Capetian kings of France.[5] In a later period, such Rayonnant buildings as Amiens and Beauvais were built using innovative building techniques, thanks to the prosperous economic conditions of Picardy's textile industry. These were based for the first time on exact plans, as was the Cologne Cathedral (1248 onwards), for example, where, the archbishop crowned the German king and emperor. The middle of the thirteenth century was the period when French architectural models really became international. At the same time the Hohenstaufen dynasty declined, giving way to an interregnum of two decades in the Holy Roman Empire with emperors, who up to 1300, could be described as weak.[6]

Why were the long-established architectural standards of the Holy Roman Empire changed around 1200? Why was an architectural model from what was essentially an entirely different cultural realm with strong links to the centralizing forces of the French crown as well as to the specific economic conditions of the northern French textile industry used? It represented what Jean Gimpel called the beginnings of the industrial revolution of the Middle Ages.[7] In contrast, the structurally organized Holy Roman Empire created an internal reference system that was based on older traditions as well as on the idea of the "imperial church." This was a church that had developed since the times of Charlemagne and Otto the Great and had a diocesan composition. This can best be described as Martin Warnke did some 30 years ago as "*repräsentativer Bauzwang*."[8] The dioceses, together with the mighty dukedoms and counties, formed the vigorous body politic of the Holy Roman Empire, a balance of *Sacerdotium* and *Regnum*.

Gothic Narratives

It is important to abandon national concepts of the Gothic, as Kimpel and Suckale did in their groundbreaking work on French Gothic architecture in 1985.[9] It is now possible to reconstruct new networks and to examine reasons beyond the aesthetic that lie behind the development and spread of Gothic art and architecture. German art history has concentrated on the French Gothic paradigm since Vöge's famous *Die Anfänge des monumentalen Stiles im Mittelalter* of 1894.[10] Here,

---

2005). Dynastic relations also have to be taken into consideration. For example, the influence of the Angevin court under Eleanor of Aquitaine for north Germany, esp. under the Guelphs, Cf. *Eleanor of Aquitain: Lord and Lady*, ed. Bonnie Wheeler and John Carmi Parsons (New York/Houndsmill, 2002); beyond the *Domaine Royale*, the English influence has been stressed by Robert Suckale, "Zur Bedeutung Englands für die welfische Skulptur um 1200," in *Heinrich der Löwe*, Exhib. Cat., ed. Jochen Luckardt and Franz Niehoff (Brunswick, 1995), vol. 2, 440–451.

5. Paul Binski, *Westminster Abbey and the Plantagenets: Kingship and the Representation of Power, 1200–1400* (London, 1995); Henrik Karge, "La arquitectura de la catedral de León en el contexto del gótico europeo," and Maria Victoria Herráez Ortega, "La construcción del templo gótico," both in *La catedral de León en la Edad Media*, Int. Congress Papers, ed. Joaquín Yarza Luaces, Ma Victoria Herráez Ortega, and Gerardo Boto Varela (León, 2004), 113–144, 145–176.

6. Cf. Reiner Haussherr, *Dombauten und Reichsepiskopat im Zeitalter der Staufer*, Akademie der Wissenschaften und Literatur, Abhandlungen der geistes- und sozialwissenschaftlichen Klasse, Nr. 5. (Mainz/Stuttgart, 1991). The shift in building industry was analyzed by Dieter Kimpel, "Le développement de la taille en série dans l'architecture médiévale et son rôle dans l'histoire économique," *Bulletin Monumental*, 135 (1977), 195–222. This aspect was also considered by Stephan Murray, in *Notre-Dame Cathedral of Amiens: The Power of Change in Gothic* (Cambridge, 1996); *idem*, *Beauvais Cathedral: Architecture of Transcendence* (Princeton, 1989).

7. Jean Gimpel, *The Medieval Machine: The Industrial Revolution of the Middle Ages* (New York, 1976).

8. Martin Warnke, *Bau und Überbau. Soziologie der mittelalterlichen Architektur nach den Schriftquellen* (Frankfurt a.M., 1976).

9. Dieter Kimpel and Robert Suckale, *Gotische Architektur in Frankreich, 1130–1270* (Munich, 1985), French edition, *L'Architecture gothique en France, 1130–1270* (Paris, 1990). The book, unfortunately, was never translated into English.

10. Wilhelm Vöge, *Die Anfänge des monumentalen Stiles im Mittelalter. Eine Untersuchung über die erste Blütezeit französischer Plastik* (Strasbourg, 1894, reprint Munich, 1988); see also *Wilhelm Vöge und Frankreich*, ed. Wilhelm Schlink, (Freiburg i. Br., 2003); Kathryn Brush, *The Shaping of Art History: Wilhelm Vöge, Adolph Goldschmidt, and the Study of Medieval Art* (Cambridge, Mass., 1996).

for the first time, two German traditions, the Classical and the Gothic, were transformed into one ideal—that of the "classical Gothic" and the "classical cathedral" (Jantzen) in a framework that had no national implications. This model was reshaped in the age of Imperialism and Totalitarism in the first half of the twentieth century. It aroused strong nationalistic tendencies and introduced the notion of *Deutsche Sondergotik*, which culminated in Wilhelm Pinder's *Sonderleistungen der deutschen Kunst*, a work that defined Hohenstaufen art and architecture as an exceptional creative force. In contrast, after World War I, French scholars such as Émile Mâle, and even architects such as Le Corbusier, pointed to the overall meagerness of German art and the poor reception in Germany of elegant French architecture.[11] Art history has been too concerned with this antagonism for far too long. It took the exiled German scholars Erwin Panofsky and Otto von Simson in the United States as well as Willibald Sauerländer in post-war West Germany to declare that the Gothic style was inherently modern, and even more importantly, that it was a prelude to Humanism.[12]

Recent approaches, including that of Sauerländer, are much more concerned with the concept of Gothic "as social practice"[13]—in terms of its quotidian function, liturgy, and perception, with a view toward reconstructing the complex cultural and historical impact of the style in different countries, regions, and periods. In this respect, the debate about stylistic transfer must be seen more in terms of a history of social norms, ritual, and ceremonial structures.[14] Contemporary art history faces a balancing act that combines hermeneutic with historic and social constructions.

As Brigitte Bedos-Rezak has stated, "Shaped by the encounter between life and a specific concept of visual structures, the Gothic cathedral articulates both life and concept through its form, which is itself a materialization, definition, and interpretation of a content."[15] Christian Freigang has recently highlighted the discrepancy between the rational approach of empirical architectural history, based on building archeology (*Bauforschung*), and the idea of an evolutionary development of style on the one hand and so-called theoretical constructions on the other. But this raises questions that can hardly be answered. What motivated clients? What experiences did architects have, or even more so the *magistri opera*? What constituted their formal vocabulary? And, last but not least, what constituted the reception of architecture in sociological terms? Can we conjure up notions of the different classes and their different levels of perception? Which references were important for kings and bishops? What moved the market-women or the canons when they entered huge porches in large-scale cathedral buildings?[16] But in posing such questions we must admit that medieval sources are all too rare and that contemporary interpretations might be highly speculative and driven by our own objectives. Descriptions of how architecture was perceived in the medieval world are not only quite rare but also lack uniformity. The two descriptions of the archiepiscopal cathedrals of Santiago de Compostela (around 1140) and Canterbury (around 1200) offer entirely different perspectives. One of these is so organized, it is possible to describe it as a "tourist's view" of Santiago, while the other claims to offer a liturgical continuity between old and new and really

11. Kurt Gerstenberg, *Deutsche Sondergotik* (Munich, 1913, reprint Darmstadt, 1968); Wilhelm Pinder, *Sonderleistungen deutscher Kunst* (Munich, 1944); Émile Mâle, *L'art allemand et l'art français du Moyen Âge* (Paris, 1922), and Le Corbusier-Saugnier, "Curiosité, non anomalie!" in *Esprit nouveau* 9 (June 1921), 1017.

12. Erwin Panofsky, *Abbot Suger on the Abbey Church of St. Denis and its Art Treasures* (Princeton, 1946); Otto von Simson, *The Gothic Cathedral: The Origins of Gothic Architecture and the Medieval Concept of Order* (London, 1956), and Willibald Sauerländer, for example, in his article "Die Kathedrale von Chartres" in *Meilensteine europäischer Kunst*, ed. Erich Steingräber (Munich, 1965), 131–170.

13. Brigitte Bedos-Rezak, "Towards a Cultural Biography of the Gothic Cathedral: Reflections on History and Art History" in *Artistic Integration in Gothic Buildings*, ed. Virginia Chieffo Raguin and Kathryn Brush (Toronto, 1995), 262–274, here 271.

14. Robert Suckale, "Stilgeschichte zu Beginn des 21. Jahrhunderts, Probleme und Möglichkeiten," in *Stilfragen zur Kunst des Mittelalter, eine Einführung*, ed. Bruno Klein and Bruno Boerner (Berlin, 2006) 271–281, 277.

15. Bedos-Rezak (as note 11), 271.

16. Christian Freigang, "Französische und deutsche Hochgotik. Interkulturalität und kulturelles Gedächtnis als Kriterien der mittelalterlichen Architekturgeschichte," in *Kulturelles Gedächtnis und interkulturelle Rezeption im europäischen Kontext*, ed. Eva Dewes and Sandra Duhem (Berlin, 2008), 397–413, here 398.

is a "liturgical view" of Canterbury (Rüffer). Although Gervase of Canterbury describes the new structure as William of Sens' architectural masterpiece, we have neither a modern notion of space nor a specific consciousness of style.[17]

Scholars such as Sauerländer discussed the *opus francigenum*—a term first used around 1260 in reference to the Wimpfen Capitulary Church—as an indication of aesthetic change. Nowadays, however, it is seen as referring to an entirely different concept. The *opus francigenum* offers no indication that it described a new style, but, according to Günter Binding, it was a technical term for French masonry.[18] Advanced building techniques rather than aesthetic decisions also might be one of the driving forces behind the reception of Gothic structural elements. They were firstly praised in inscriptions commemorating the architects of the twelfth and thirteenth centuries, as for example in the lintel inscription of the Cathedral of Santiago de Compostela, which was set in place in April 1188.[19] While emphasizing the rational and technical sides of Gothic architecture inherited from the nineteenth-century tradition, founded by Viollet-le-Duc, we are likely to miss the contextual dimensions of Gothic churches, which served as sites of liturgical and political performance.[20]

Architecture & Sculpture from Distant Fields

Nearly every cathedral built between 1200 and 1230 in the northern Holy Roman Empire followed the traditional ground plan of two choirs in the east and west, each flanked by two towers, a continuation of earlier Ottonian and Salian building traditions. Besides using such inherently older indigenous concepts, the Holy Roman Empire was also influenced by new concepts from areas other than France. Strong political connections existed with the dioceses of Northern Italy, which was also part of the Holy Empire. These were extended by dynastic relations with the powerful Angevin Empire and the Norman-Sicilian kingdom, both of which had well-developed court cultures. In the case of northern Italy, these influences can be seen in the huge cathedral churches, such as those in Vercelli, Parma, or Modena, or even more so in sculpture by the likes of Antelami. Dynastic relations brought more complex influences to bear as well. Just recently, Emperor Otto IV (r. 1198/1208–1218) was highlighted in an exhibition in Brunswick that showed the enormous impact on the Guelph court of courtly ceremony, poetry, and historiography from Aquitaine and England. Architectural relations with the Angevins were discussed by Ralf Dorn, as was the early Westphalian "Hallenkirchen" under the patronage of the counts of Lippe, close relations of the Guelphs between 1170 and 1230. Another transfer point was the court of Frederick II of Hohenstaufen who set up, as did his father Henry VI (r. 1189–1197), new cultural exchanges north of the Alps. His court culture was adopted at the palaces of Hagenau and Gelnhausen, and reached a climax with his triumphal entry into the countries of the *Regnum Teutonicum* in 1235. The riders of Bamberg and Magdeburg (*c.* 1230–1240) may be seen in this context.[21]

17. Jochen Schröder, *Gervasius von Canterbury, Richard von Saint-Victor und die Methodik der Bauerfassung im 12. Jahrhundert*, 2 vols. (Cologne, 2000); I should also draw attention to the contribution of Jens Rüffer to the ongoing project on the cathedral of Santiago de Compostela (with Bernd Nicolai, Berne, and Klaus Rheidt, Cottbus) that deals with medieval description formulae, as exemplified at Santiago and Canterbury: "'Ars sine scientia nihil est.' Überlegungen zur mittelalterlichen Gestaltungspraxis und zur Methodik ihrer Erschließung am Beispiel baugebundener Skulptur" (Habilitation thesis, Bern, 2010).

18. Günther Binding, "Opus Francigenum, ein Beitrag zur Begriffsbestimmung," in *Archiv für Kulturgeschichte* 71 (1989), 45–54, here 46.

19. Bernd Nicolai and Klaus Rheidt, "Nuevas investigaciones sobre la historia de la construcción de la catedral de Santiago de Compostela," in *Ad limina. Revista de investigacíon del Camino de Santiago y las peregrinaciones* 1 (2010), 53–80.

20. See Bedos-Rezak (as note 11), and Freigang (as note 16), 397–8.

21. Cf. Manfred Lucherhandt, *Die Kathedrale von Parma, Architektur und Skulptur im Zeitalter von Reichskirche und Kommunebildung* (Munich, 2009). The Angevin relations are discussed in *Otto IV., Traum vom welfischen Kaisertum*, Exhib. Cat., Braunschweigischen Landesmuseum, ed. Hans-Ulrich Hucker et al. (Petersberg, 2009); and Ralf Dorn, *Die Kirche des ehemaligen Damenstifts St. Marien und Pusinna in Herford, Architektur unter den Edelherren zur Lippe* (Petersberg, 2006); for the relation to the Norman kingdom of Sicily, see *Kaiser Friedrich II. (1194–1250), Welt und Kultur des Mittelmeerraums*, Exhib. Cat., Landesmuseum, Oldenburg, ed. Mamoun Fansa and Karen Ermete (Mainz, 2008); *Verwandlungen des Stauferreichs, Drei*

One particular work characterizes the different levels of reception that are found between sculpture and architecture. The carving of Queen Kunigunde on the Adam's Portal in Bamberg Cathedral, which is dated around 1230, shows her holding the model of a church, emphasizing her role as founder of the Bamberg diocese (Fig. 1). This model is of a cathedral choir with flying buttresses and towers flanking the transept, a structure that never existed in Bamberg, or in most of the cathedral buildings of that period anywhere in the Holy Roman Empire. Buildings such as those in Mainz, Trier, Strasbourg, or Naumburg are entirely different and must be seen as representing the different points of reference that sculpture took in comparison to architecture. The choir and transept of Strasbourg Cathedral are the best examples with which to bridge the gap between the two arts. Here, for the first time, the sculptural programs of the portals and the stained glass windows introduced new narratives that were related to new social practices, and represented a new sense of the visual and use new forms of *memoria*. The program of the south portal at Strasbourg Cathedral, for example, shows three levels of meaning, all connected with each other. It is possible to see a reflection of theological thought of the period when we examine the eschatological and mariological elements, all of which emphasize ecclesiastic authority. The program also reflects the *genius loci* and can be seen as a symbol of the court that was located inside and outside the transept. Finally, the program can be seen as a comment on the tendencies to include and exclude, which related in particular to the city of Strasbourg where a debate was going on at this time regarding the Jews and the various heretics. It has to be remembered that no comprehensive Gothic language was transferred to architecture until the second half of the 1220s.[22]

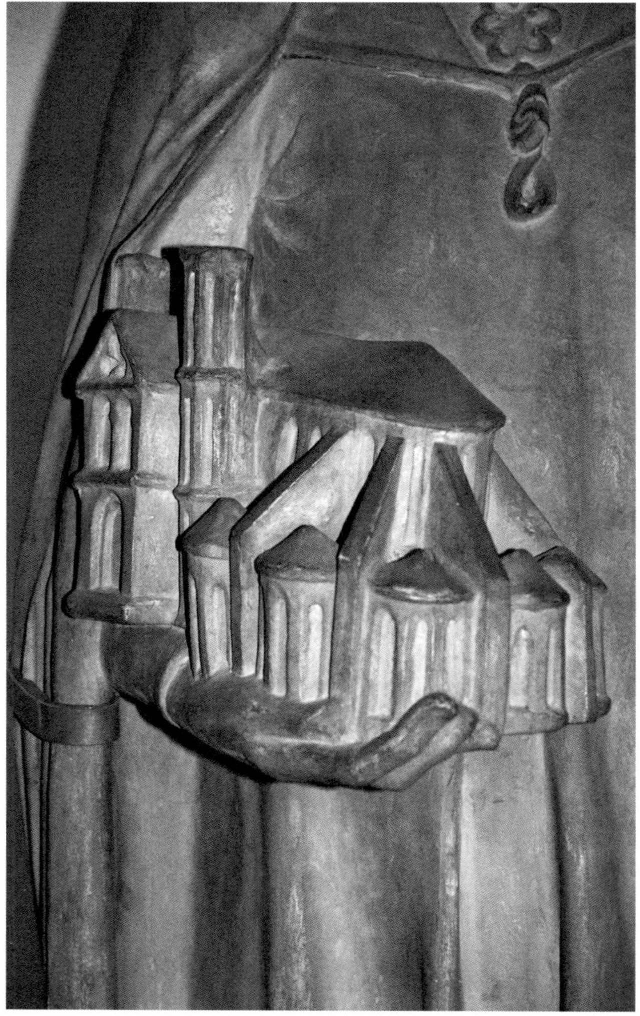

FIGURE 1. Replica of St. Kunigunde's model church, Bamberg Cathedral, Adam's Portal *c.* 1230. Plaster copy, Busch Hall, Harvard University (courtesy of Jeffrey Hamburger; photo: author).

This was also the case in the western part of the archdiocese of Trier with its suffragans Toul, Metz, and Verdun. Trier itself must be considered unique. Long-lasting links to the neighboring diocese of Reims opened a gate for the transfer of Champagnese models (Reims Cathedral itself and St.-Yved in Braine), including that of sculpture. A remarkable solution was

Innovationsregionen im mittelalterlichen Europa, ed. Bernd Schneidmüller, Stefan Weinfurter, and Alfried Wieczorek (Darmstadt, 2010); and Antje Middeldorf-Kosegarten, "Der Stauferkaiser Friedrich II. und die Pferde, Versuch über den Bamberger Reiter aus ikonographischer und hippologischer Sicht," *Zeitschrift für Kunstgeschichte* 71 (2008), 1–52.

22. Bernd Nicolai, "Orders in Stone, Social Reality and Artistic Approach: The Case of the Strasbourg South Portal," *Gesta* 41 (2002), 111–128, here 112; and also Willibald Sauerländer, "Strasbourg cathédrale, le bras sud du transept, architecture et sculpture," in Congrès archéologique de la France, vol. 162, session 2004 (Paris, 2006), 171–184.

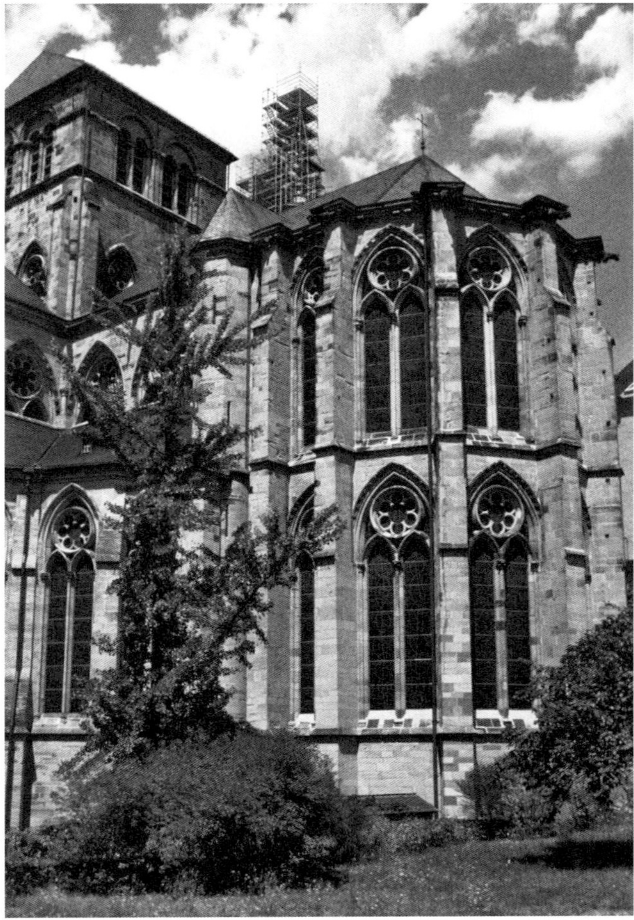

FIGURE 2. Trier, Liebfrauenkirche, 1228–1253, view from the east (photo: author).

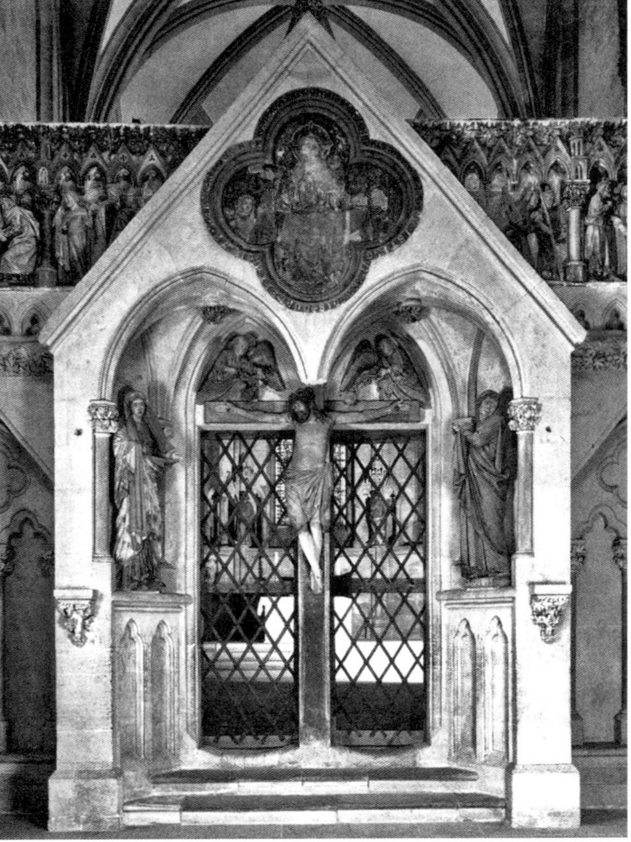

FIGURE 3. Naumburg Cathedral, rood screen portal at entrance to the west choir *c.* 1250 (photo: Bruno Klein, *Gotik*, Geschichte der bildenden Kunst in Deutschland, vol. 3 [Munich, 2007], p. 84).

created in the Liebfrauenkirche in Trier, a centralized building, later than the Roman *Maria Rotonda* type (Fig. 2). Maintaining tradition was a major factor here, in what was one of the oldest dioceses of the Empire. The façade of the Liebfrauenkirche shows a sensitive and sympathetic dialogue with the nearby and monumental eleventh-century west front of Trier Cathedral.[23] Issues such as the height and elevation of structures as well as the particulars of style can also be seen during the 1220s at Toul Cathedral and St.-Vincent in Metz. But these were also followed by innovations in the structure itself, such as a shaped double-storey interior elevation that in turn inspired such spectacular buildings as St. Elisabeth in Marburg.

The next stage, with a more complete adherence to Gothic formulae, is represented in Naumburg's west choir, begun in the 1240s. Here the choir screen not only unifies the western interior space but it also enhances its overall impression (Fig. 3). Its sculptural program marks a new shift as to how Gothic was perceived in "teaching through empathy and identification."[24] The new realism of the Naumburg benefactor figures repre-

23. See Andreas Waschbüsch, "Kunstlandschaft und Diözesanstil? Modelle zur Beschreibung des künstlerischen Austauschs am Beispiel lothringischer Portale des 12. und 13. Jahrhunderts," in *Neue Forschungen zur Bauskulptur in Frankreich und Spanien im Spannungsfeld des Portail Royal in Chartres und des Pórtico de la Gloria in Santiago de Compostela*, Congress Papers, ed. Claudia Rückert and Jochen Staebel (forthcoming, Munich, 2010).

24. Jacqueline E. Jung, "Beyond the Barrier: The Unifying Role of the Choir Screen in Gothic Churches," *The Art Bulletin* 82 (2000), 622–657, here 624.

sents an assembly of upper nobles in the manner of a literary "mirror of princes," while the narrative scenes on the rood screen showing Christ's passion address the senses and feelings of a wider audience in a dramatic manner.[25] This is also the case in French cathedral programs such as the north transept portals of Reims or the west front of Amiens, where for the first time a new realism in the form of scenes from everyday life was shown. Michael Camille and Wilhelm Schlink have pointed to the role of the Franciscan order in anchoring this new visual dimension to the style—what Roland Recht characterized as "*le croire et le voire*."[26]

In terms of the transition and transformation of early Gothic formulae, Magdeburg Cathedral does not have the typical ambulatory scheme found in most French cathedrals, but instead it has an ambulatory space with polygonal chapels, where both parts are characterized as separate spheres by entirely different vaulting systems. Magdeburg has been described as "Gothic in its plan, Romanesque in its elevation" (Fig. 4).[27] Because of this, it has been characterized as a "Transitional Style" (*Übergangsstil*), a not-too-useful descriptor that implies it lacks a coherent stylistic development. Here, the concept of style may have as broad a definition as that proposed by Robert Suckale, where the entirety of norms and habits is taken as background within chronological, regional, and social precincts.[28]

Besides all the problems of stylistic terminology, Magdeburg is a good example of a building that was altered throughout its history. Started by Archbishop Albrecht II in 1207–1209, it was built on an imperial Ottonian foundation—the mausoleum for Otto the Great and his first wife Editha—but the site was also the center of a cult that developed around St. Maurice (Fig. 5). Maurice was also incorporated into the imperial coronation ceremony. Apart from St. Peter and St. Catherine, he was the main saint of Magdeburg and the Holy Empire. From an iconological perspective, Magdeburg restated and redefined the "Imperial Cathedral" (*Reichskathedrale*) in the age of the last Hohenstaufen, and competed with the cathedrals of Basel, Bamberg, and Mainz.[29]

Because he was a henchman of the banned King Philip of Swabia and an opponent of the Hohenstaufen dynasty, it was with reservation that Albrecht II was accepted in 1206 as a new archbishop by Pope Innocent III. He was a cleric who was not only educated at the universities of Bologna and Paris, but was also experienced in law and scholastic theology. This wide perspective gained from Italy and the French *Domaine Royale* may have influenced his work in the building of Magdeburg Cathedral including the reception of Antiquity in the use of *spolia*, as well as the use of figured portals, the so-called "Goldschmidt portal," which must have come from Paris. Even though the portal was never completed, the carvings survive. In addition to this important and personal background to his life, there was also an official angle that was probably of equal importance. Albrecht became a mediator between *Imperium* and *Sacerdotium*, between emperor and pope. He had considerable influence in the imperial coronation of the Otto IV at Rome in 1209 as well as that of Frederick II of Hohenstaufen in 1220. In 1209 he insisted that the main relics of St. Maurice—parts of the cranium of the martyr which were in the Abbey of St.-Maurice d'Agaune (Canton Valais, Switzerland)—be delivered to the cathedral. In 1220 he demanded that Maurice's skullcap be delivered by the dukes of Andechs-Merania under duress from the Emperor himself. Having the relics idealistically endorsed and promoted the cathedral.[30]

25. *Eadem* and Lieselotte E. Saurma-Jeltsch, "Der Zackenstil als ornatus difficilis," *Aachener Kunstblätter* 60 (1994) (Festschrift Hermann Fillitz), 257–266.

26. Wilhelm Schlink, *Der Beau-Dieu von Amiens: das Christusbild der gotischen Kathedrale* (Frankfurt a.M., 1991); Michael Camille, *Gothic Art: Visions and Revelations of the Medieval World* (London, 1996); Roland Recht, *Le croire et le voire, l'art des cathedrals XIIe–XVe siècles* (Paris, 1999); Christof L. Dietrichs, *Vom Glauben zum Sehen. Die Sichtbarkeit der Reliquie im Reliquiar. Ein Beitrag zur Geschichte des Sehens* (Berlin, 2001).

27. Ernst Schubert, "Imperiale Spolien im Magdeburger Dom," in *idem*, *Dies diem docet. Ausgewählte Aufsätze zur mittelalterlichen Kunst und Geschichte in Mitteldeutschland*, (Cologne, Weimar, Vienna, 2003), 458–474, here 458.

28. Robert Suckale (as in note 14), 271–281.

29. For the wider context, see Reiner Haussherr, *Dombauten und Reichsepiskopat im Zeitalter der Staufer*, Akademie der Wissenschaften und Literatur, Abhandlungen der geistes- und sozialwissenschaftlichen Klasse, Nr. 5, (Mainz/Stuttgart, 1991).

30. Bernd Nicolai, "Überlegungen zum Chorbau des Magde-

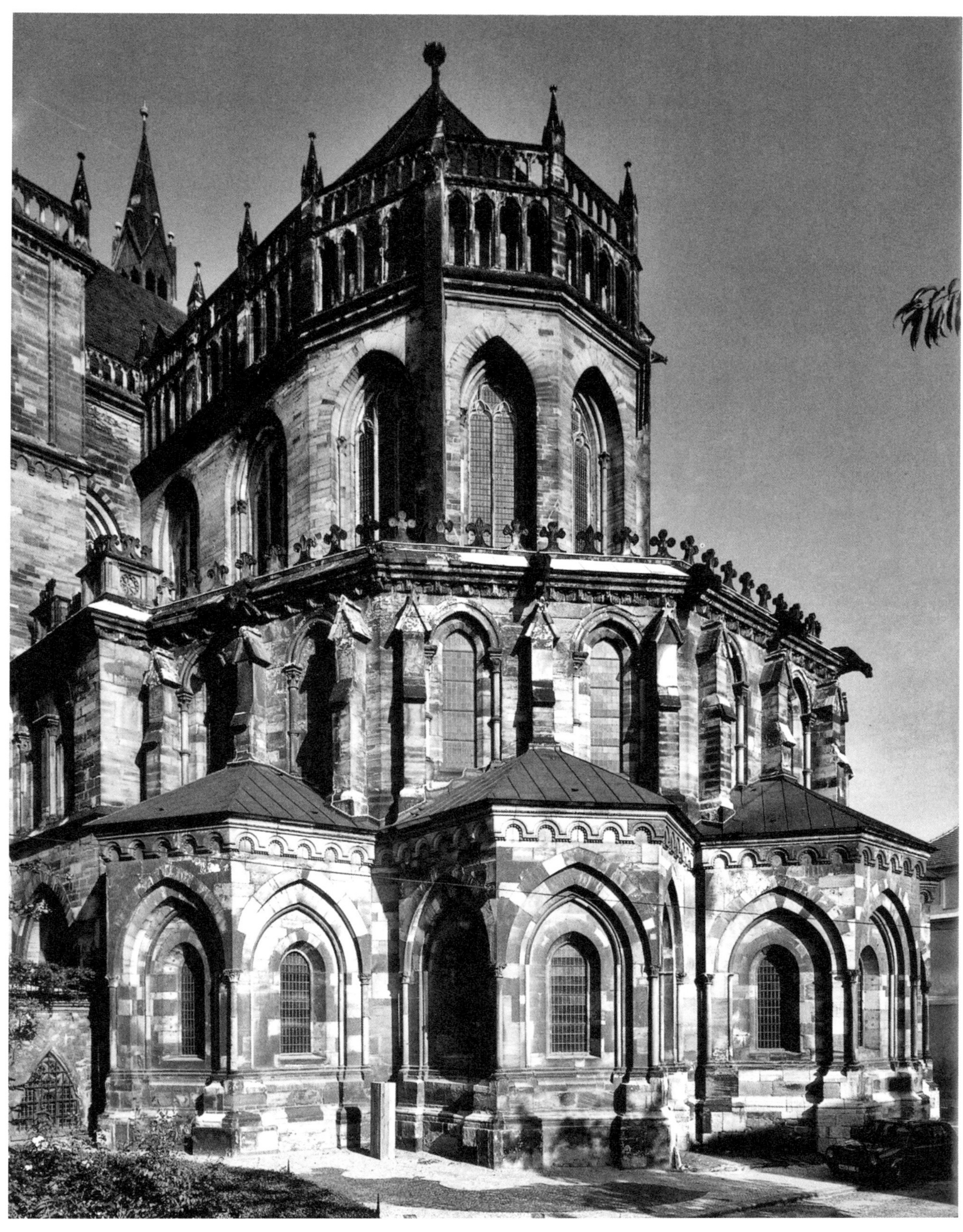

FIGURE 4. Magdeburg Cathedral, view from east (photo: Ernst Schubert, *Der Magdeburger Dom* [Leipzig, 1994], p. 14).

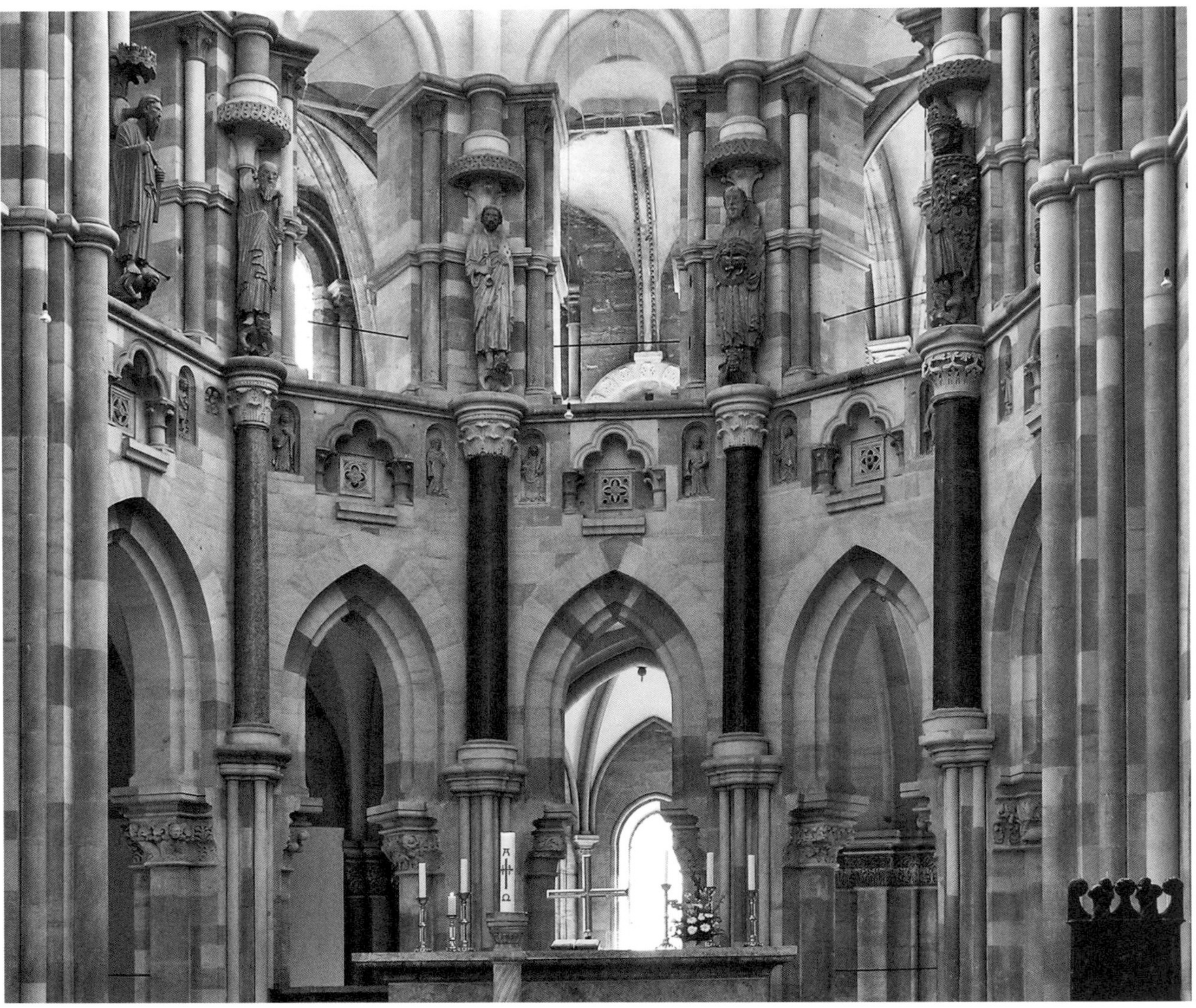

FIGURE 5. Magdeburg Cathedral, choir, looking eastwards (photo: T. Kaffenberger, Mainz).

In 1209 Albrecht traveled from Rome back to Magdeburg via St.-Maurice d'Agaune to the Burgundian part of the Empire with its sees of Lausanne (Fig. 6) and Basel. Both of these cathedrals had unusual ambulatory plans for that time. They did not have radiating chapels but had eastern flanking towers, which is a hallmark of cathedrals of the Empire. In this respect, Magdeburg did not have the first cathedral choir ambulatory in the northern Holy Roman Empire. The question is why the ambulatory was built. There is no simple or clear answer. The sanctuary at Lausanne, which is referenced as early as 1212, used French Burgundian models, such as the cathedrals of Langres and Canterbury. On the other hand, Basel developed an unorthodox ambulatory

burger Doms unter Albrecht II. (1209–1232)," in *Der Magdeburger Dom. Ottonische Gründung, staufischer Neubau*, ed. Ernst Ullmann (Leipzig, 1989), 147–157, and recently, *idem*, "'Noblili structura et opere sumptuoso.' Der Chorbau des Magdeburger Doms als Neuformulierung der 'Reichskathedrale' im Spannungsfeld baulicher Modelle der Romania und der Gotik der Ile-de-France um 1200," in *Aufbruch in die Gotik. Der Magdeburger Dom und die späte Stauferzeit*, Exhib. Cat., ed. Matthas Puhle and Stephan Weinfurter, vol. 2, essays (Mainz, 2009), 70–83, and the article on Albrecht's career in Bologna and Paris by Martin Kintzinger, *ibid.*, 290–299.

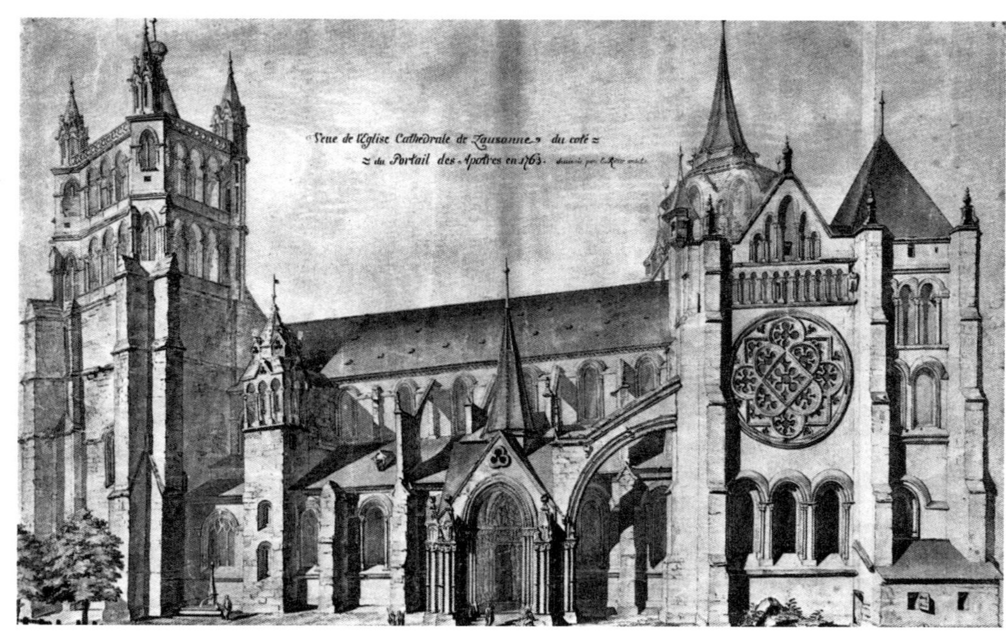

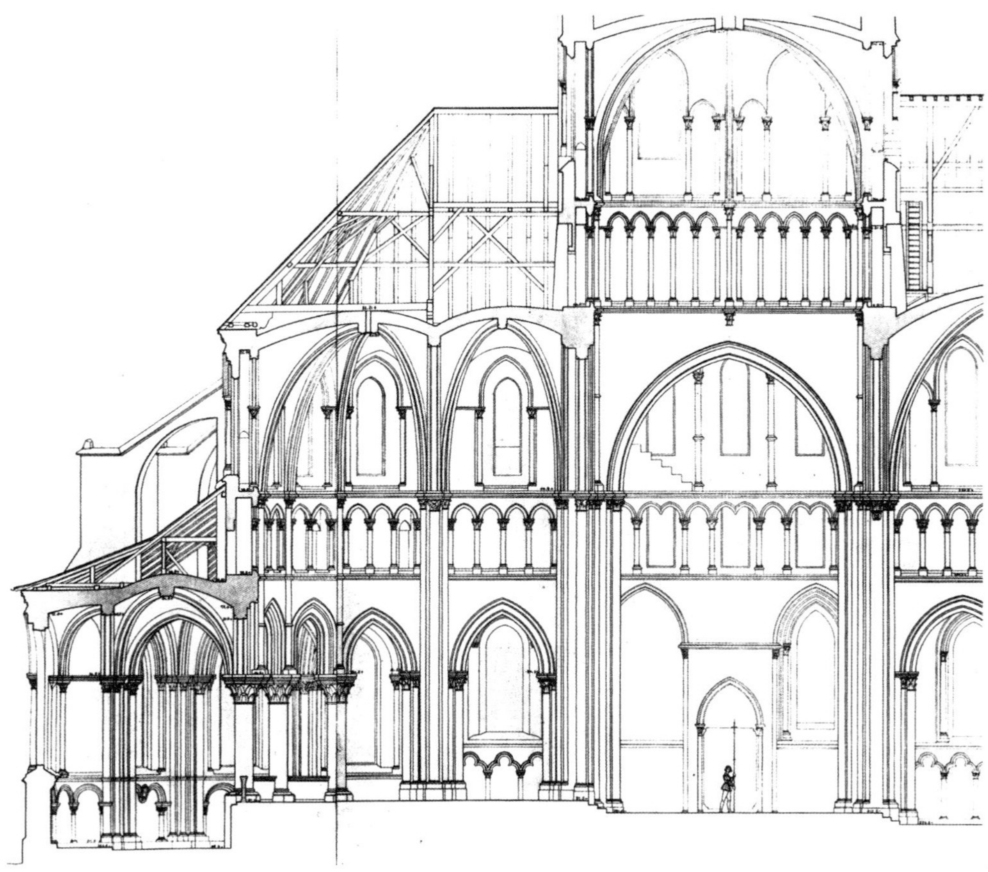

FIGURE 6. Lausanne Cathedral, painting showing the southern elevation, after Erasmus Ritter, 1763 (photo: *La cathédrale de Lausanne* [Lausanne, 1975], p. 62).

FIGURE 7. Lausanne Cathedral, longitudinal section through the choir, after Recordon 1903/04 (photo: *La cathédrale de Lausanne* [Lausanne, 1975], p. 78).

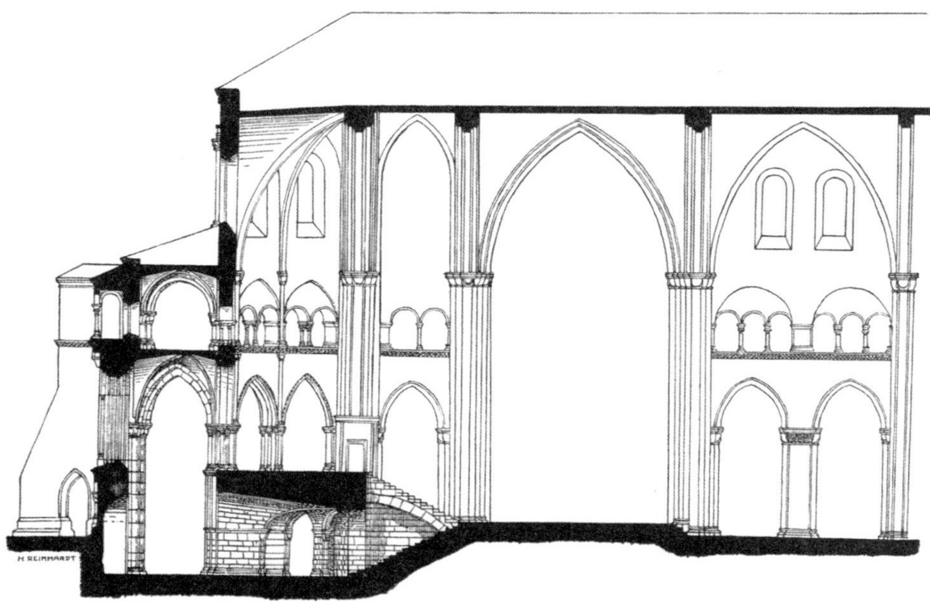

FIGURE 8. Basel Cathedral, reconstruction of the longitudinal section through the Romanesque choir (Photo: Hans Reinhard, *Das Baseler Münster* [Basel, 1926], p. 57).

scheme, combining an annular crypt with the visual impression of an ordinary ambulatory (Figs. 7, 8). The Basel ambulatory must be regarded as an elevated annular crypt, where the Ottonian and Hohenstaufen bishops were represented in murals. Such a concept was highly relevant for Albrecht, because he had the same objective—to emphasize the Ottonian tradition in order to justify his new building site. The austere ambulatory in Magdeburg served as a kind of crypt for Editha's tomb in the axial chapel. While Basel largely determined the elevation of the first Magdeburg plan, Lausanne provided the monumental eastern shape with two massive flanking towers as an extension of the transept. These two unique concepts were transferred to Magdeburg (Fig. 9). However, in terms of style, neither the early Gothic of Lausanne Cathedral, nor the late Romanesque architecture of Basel were to serve as a model. In all probability, Magdeburg's masons came from the western parts of the Empire, from the dioceses of Trier and Cologne. It is clear that the plan of this building was one thing, but its execution was an entirely different matter. The early parts of Magdeburg Cathedral, dating to 1209, were based on the ground plans of Basel and Lausanne, but were actually built by Rheninsh masons and artists.

This divergence came to an end when Albrecht acquired the relics of St. Maurice in 1220 and changed the entire internal structure. Albrecht had various formulas at his disposal that came from his personal and professional experience. Overriding all of these was his wish to have an up-to-date cathedral for the Holy Roman Empire. As a result, Magdeburg Cathedral used the most advanced cathedral models, such as that of Lausanne. In this respect, the first ground plan of Magdeburg was highly innovative for the Northern Empire.

It was to this first phase that Adolph Goldschmidt attributed, in 1899, a figured portal originally planned for Magdeburg Cathedral, which closely followed Parisian models such as the Ste.-Anne Portal of Notre-Dame de Paris (Fig. 10). Albrecht's personal knowledge of Notre-Dame before 1200 clearly served as a compelling link and likely model. It was never carved, however, and we don't even know for what part of the building it was intended.[31] It is possible that it might have been

31. Klaus Niehr, "Das Magdeburger 'Goldschmidt-Portal.' Geschichte der Pariser Skulptur in der Provinz," in *Studien zur Geschichte der europäischen Skulptur* 1994, vol. 1 (as note 3), 311–320. Heiko Brandl, "Adolph Goldschmidt und das 'Goldschmidt-

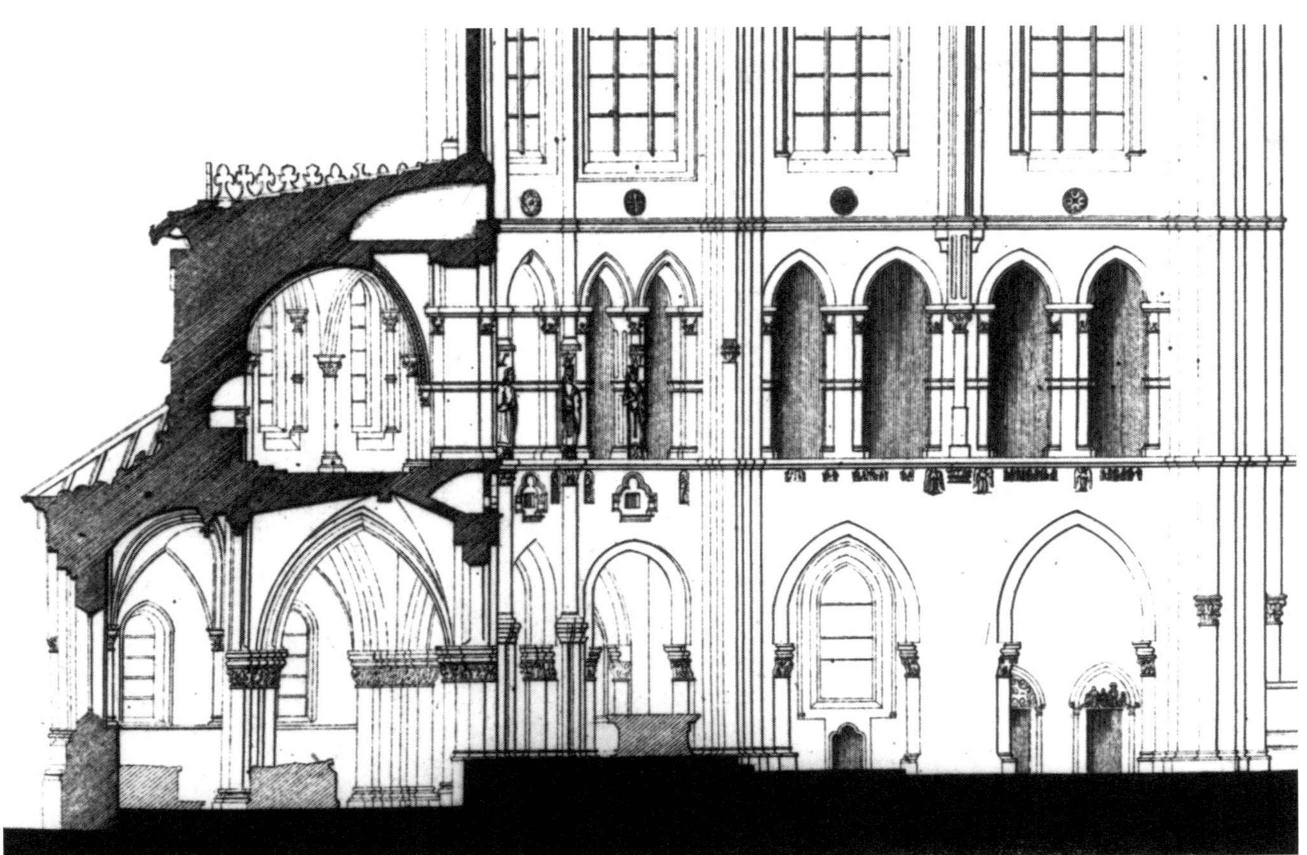

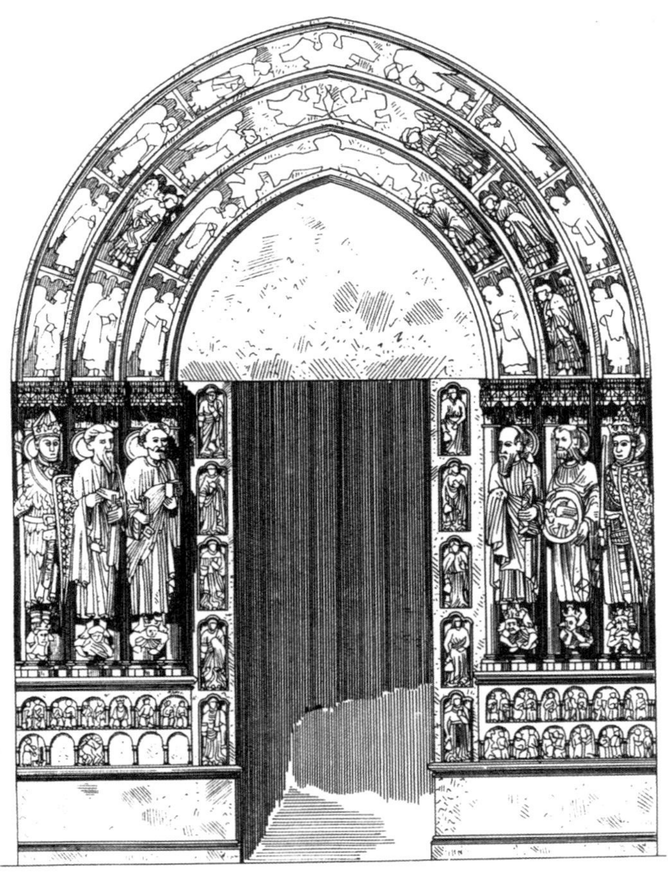

FIGURE 9. Magdeburg Cathedral, longitudinal section through the choir (after Clemens, Mellin, Rosenthal, *Der Dom zu Magdeburg* [Magdeburg, 1852–65], vol. 1, pl. 5).

FIGURE 10. Hypothetical reconstruction of the so-called "Golschmidt-Portal" undertaken in 1899 (Adolph Goldschmidt "Französische Einflüsse in der frühgotischen Skulptur Sachsens" in *Jahrbuch der Preuszischen Kunstsammlungen* 20 [1899], p. 292).

planned for the north transept, in front of the square of the bishop's palace. On the other hand, it could just as likely have been intended for the main entrance to the nave—similar to Bamberg's *Fürstenportal*. There is also the possibility that it was part of a more elaborate west façade, but it is modest in scale and has three figures on each side. It is not the sculptural program of a main portal but of a side or minor portal.

An equally difficult problem are the two statues that are now displayed in front of the gallery in the present choir. Here, the two saintly figures are dressed in knightly armor, but they are different in material and style. Matthias Friske has recently suggested that they date to the end of the twelfth century and are similar to figures found in illuminated manuscripts, such as the *Hortus deliciarum*.[32] These figures, as well as the Goldschmidt portal, need to be looked at again.

It must have been the impact of the acquisition of St. Maurice's relics, as well as Albrecht's involvement in the imperial coronation of 1220, that enabled him to develop a new design for the choir. There was no other authority or power that could cause such a dramatic change in the overall design, and one charged with political overtones—a change that combined imperial *memoria*, Roman Antiquity, and a representation of the cathedral's main saints within a unique setting. To this end he re-used four main porphyry and monolithic granite columns, the so-called Ravenna *spolia* (Fig. 11). These were a gift from Otto the Great for his newly founded diocese and were placed between the arcades of the sanctuary at the inner polygon. Pedestals were created for these monoliths, and, above the pointed arcades, triple-molded niches were carved in the upper parts of the wall to serve as repositories for relics. Small statues of the Wise and Foolish Virgins flanked the niches. The monumental figures of the saints in many ways extended the monoliths and formed a symbolic hierarchy and unity of Antiquity and Christianity, but even more so of *regnum* and *sacerdotium*. The balance of power between these two facets of the Holy Roman Empire was an important part of Albrecht's political concept.

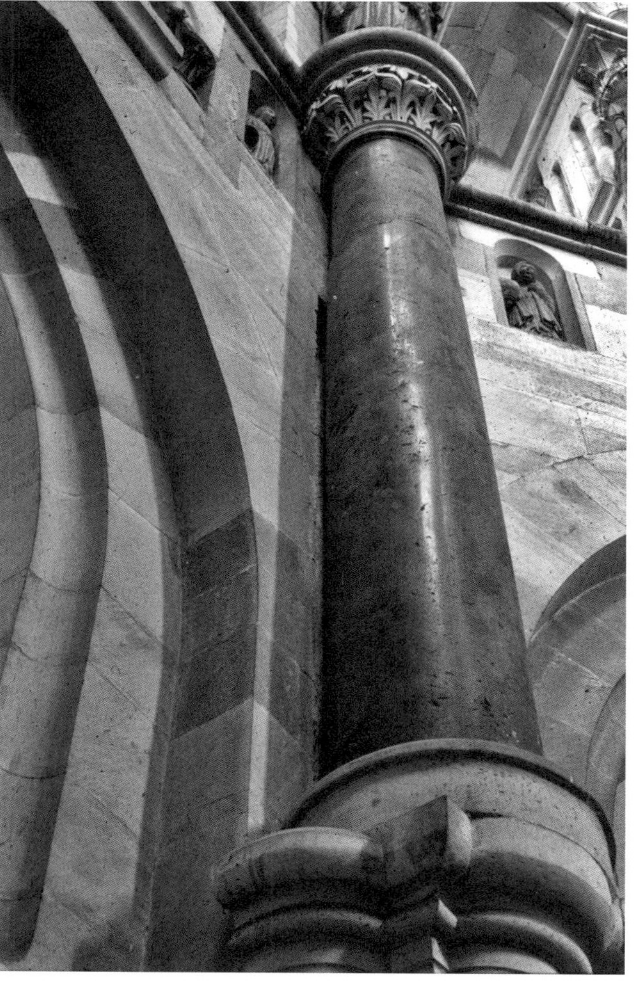

FIGURE 11. Magdeburg Cathedral, late antique porphyry column, possibly from Ravenna or Trier. The original location of the former shafts can be seen behind the column (photo: author).

The design was also changed to incorporate the sculpture on the vaulting, which is characteristic of the Cistercian order of around 1220. The south German abbey of Maulbronn and the nearby abbey of Walkenried, with its cathedral-like building (1209), are the main examples of this style. The near exclusive monopoly that

Portal,'" in *100 Jahre Kunstgeschichte an der Martin-Luther-Universität Halle-Wittenberg. Personen und Werke*, ed. Wolfgang Schenkluhn (Halle, 2004), 21–40.

32. Matthias Friske, "Überlegungen zur Datierung der Skulpturen im Chorhaupt des Magdeburger Doms," in *Theologie und Kultur, Geschichten einer Wechselbeziehung*, ed. Gerlinde Strohmaier-Wiederanders (Halle, 1999), 33–50.

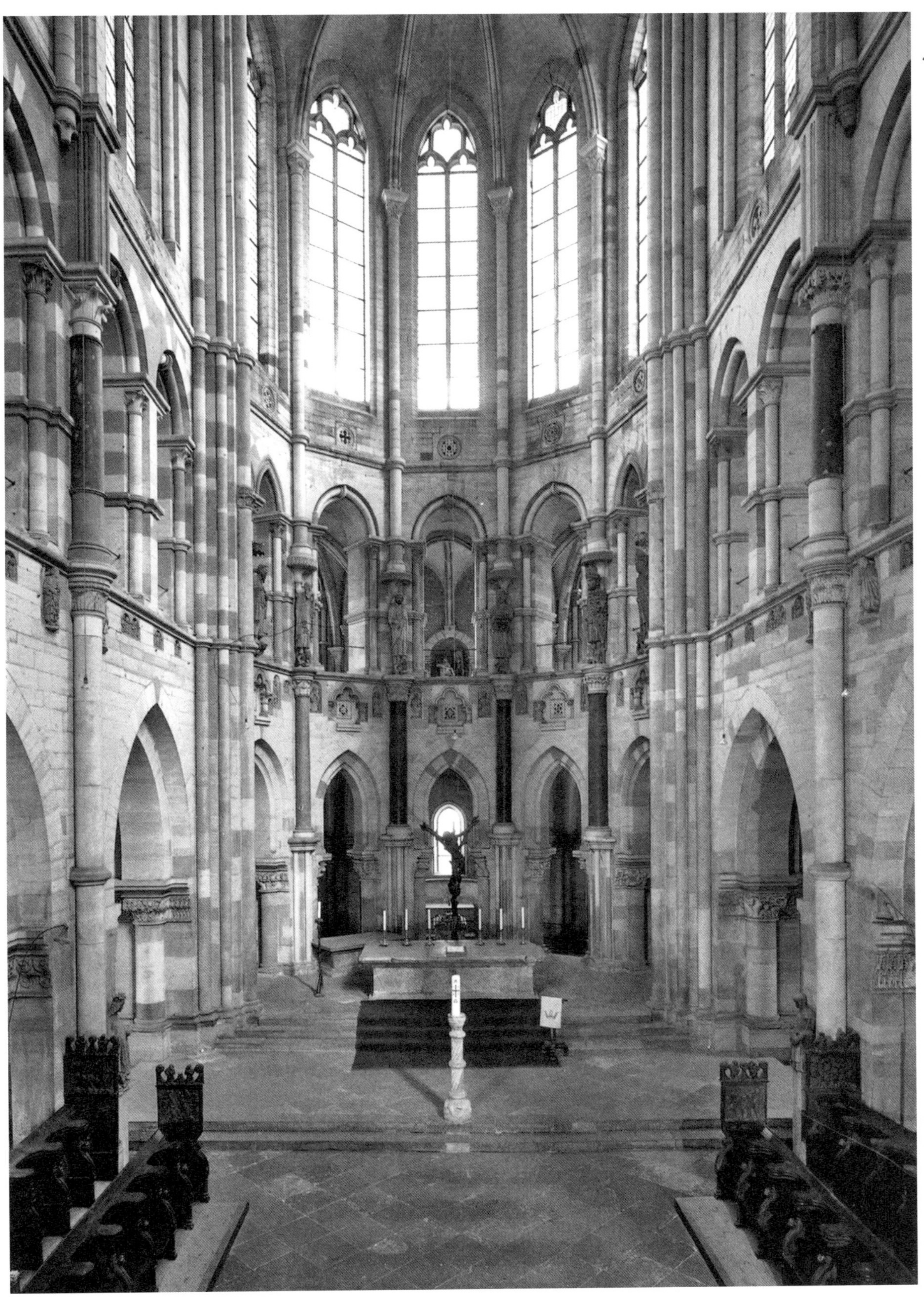

FIGURE 12. Magdeburg Cathedral, the choir looking eastwards (Ernst Schubert, *Der Magdeburger Dom* [Leipzig, 1994], p. 15).

the Cistercians had on this design is being questioned today. At the time of Magdeburg, this Cistercian design was wide-spread, stretching from Burgundy and the western parts of the Empire to central parts of the German territories, including Offenbach, Gelnhausen, Bamberg, and Magdeburg.[33] Ulrich Knapp has developed a model of a Hohenstaufen "Imperial Style," which refers strongly to Pinder's nationalist "Hohenstaufen Classic."[34] This model at the very least attempts to see evidence of an overarching program that does not seem to be borne out when the polycentric structure of the Holy Roman Empire is examined. On the other hand, these new forms and a sense for sculptural surface could be seen to demonstrate a specific *stylus sumptuosus*, a rich style.[35] Notwithstanding, such a sculptural program is often imbalanced against traditional architecture and a relatively plain building technique.

To conclude, Magdeburg Cathedral cannot be seen as a key building in the history of early Gothic architecture.[36] It does, however, show how the "gradual infiltration" and merging of Gothic formulae and Romanesque traditions in the *Regnum Teutonicum* of the Holy Roman Empire took place between 1200 and 1250. Magdeburg shows different stylistic idioms that were unified in the overall layout of the choir, which is typical of most of the cathedral buildings of the Hohenstaufen Age north of the Alps. Yet at Magdeburg the results were different. The dean of the cathedral, Wilbrand, Albrecht's step-brother, supervised the building site during his brother's many absences. From 1235 onwards, Wilbrand, then an archbishop, extended the programmatic approach with a second Magdeburg sculptural workshop. This involved the heightening of the clerestory, which clearly was undertaken as a reference to Reims Cathedral. Magdeburg around 1250 has to be seen as an advanced example of cathedral building under the rule of Frederick II of Hohenstaufen.[37] The building developed on a piecemeal basis and an entire Gothic structure was never envisaged from the beginning but new ideas and sculptural styles were introduced on a gradual basis.

The decline of the Hohenstaufen dynasty after 1250 and the parallel expansion of Rayonnant Gothic under Louis IX lead to a style that was adapted and transformed throughout the *Regnum Teutonicum* in buildings such as Cologne Cathedral or the nave of Strasbourg. But beyond national narratives we must also think that a changed Europe required a new kind of representation—one with a new sense of seeing and reading, compassion and perception, even if France was still the driving force until the commencement of the Hundred Years War.

33. This was examined by Bernd Nicolai, "Libido aedificandi," *Walkenried und die monumentale Kirchenbaukunst der Zisterzienser*, Quellen und Forschungen zur Braunschweigischen Geschichte, vol. 28 (Braunschweig, 1990), chapter on Magdeburg and concluding chapter.

34. Ulrich Knapp, "Zisterziensergotik oder Reichsstil? Zur Interpretation der frühgotischen Bauteile im Kloster Maulbronn," in *Maulbronn zur 850 jährigen Geschichte des Zisterzienserklosters*, Forschungen und Berichte der Bau- und Kunstdenkmalpflege in Baden-Württemberg, Bd. 7 (Stuttgart, 1997) 189–292.

35. A notion by Friedrich Moebius, "Kirchliche Architektur," in *Geschichte der Deutschen Kunst, vol. 2, 1200–1350*, ed. Friedrich Möbius and Helga Sciurie (Leipzig, 1989), 42.

36. Paul Frankl mentioned this in respect to the Gothic style, see *Gothic Architecture*, revised by Paul Crossley (New Haven, 2000) (first published 1962), 150.

37. A concise overview of the entire program is given by Helga Scurie, "Die Skulpturen des Magdeburger Domes," in *Geschichte der Deutschen Kunst, vol. 2* (as note 35), 322–332.

CAROLINE BRUZELIUS

From Empire to Commune to Kingdom: Notes on the Revival of Monumental Sculpture in Gothic Italy

THIS ESSAY will address the long tradition of scholarship on Italian sculpture in the late Middle Ages to consider a few aspects of the carved image as a public and rhetorical gesture.[1] The study will explore three topics that in some way relate to connections between the Kingdoms of Sicily and Tuscany: (1) Nicola Pisano, (2) the monumental free-standing pulpit, and (3) variations on the double-sided tomb or *arca*. Each of these, of course, is a field of study in itself, and has been the object of much research and reflection; each also spreads out across the map of Italy like an ink blot on soft paper, but always with our narratives precariously pinned in place by the threads of fragmentary remains and occasional documents. The modest intention of this article is to provide some glimpses into these three rich and complicated topics, with a special interest in connections north and south, but with no pretense of providing a comprehensive overview.

It is generally agreed that public sculpture in the thirteenth century was re-invigorated by the development of communal governments as well as by Frederick II's conscious revival of ancient precedent in using sculpture as a public and political instrument in the Kingdom of Sicily.[2] Both the communes in the north and the Kingdom in the south were institutions that needed to affirm their identity, independence, and authority, and one of the most visible public instruments with which to do this was sculpture, some of which was either antique, or imitated antique models (the *lupa romana* of Siena, the lion of Venice, for example). By the thirteenth century most ancient bronzes had probably been melted down,[3] but enough marble statuary must have survived, at least in broken fragments, to provide the medieval viewer with an idea of the ubiquity of Roman imperial political sculpture in urban settings (Fig. 1).[4] Exposure to the monuments of Constanti-

1. In writing this essay I have sought to preserve the somewhat informal nature of my talk at the symposium organized in March 2009 for the Index of Christian Art in Princeton, New Jersey. I thank Colum Hourihane for his invitation, and Dorothy Glass, Christine Verzar, Marilyn Lavin, and Giovanni Freni for their comments and suggestions. Because the literature on Italian Gothic sculpture is vast, I have kept the notes as succinct as possible.

2. See most recently Brendan Cassidy, *Politics, Civic Ideals and Sculpture in Italy, c. 1240–1400* (Brepols, 2007), esp. 23–41. For the Capuan Arch, see C. Shearer, *The Renaissance of Architecture in Southern Italy: A Study of Frederick II of Hohenstaufen and the Capua Triumphator Archway and Towers* (Cambridge, 1935); C. A. Willemsen, *Kaiser Friedrichs II. Triumphtor zu Capua* (Wiesbaden, 1953); P. C. Claussen, "Die Statue Friedrichs II vom Bruckentor in Capua (1234–1239)," in *Festshcrift für Hartmut Bierman*, ed. C. Andreas, M. Bückling, and R. Dorn (Weinheim, 1990), 19–39; E. Castelnuovo, "Il volto di Federico," in Calò Mariani and Cassano, eds., *Federico II: Immagine e potere* (Bari, 1995), 63–68; J. Meredith, "The Revival of the Augustan Age in the Court Art of Emperor Frederick II," in *Artistic Strategy and the Rhetoric of Power: Political Uses of Art from Antiquity to the Present*, ed. D. Castriota (Carbondale, 1986), 38–56, and J. Meredith, "The Arch of Capua: The Strategic Use of Spolia and References to the Antique," in W. Tronzo, ed., *Intellectual Life at the Court of Frederick II* (Washington, D.C., 1994), 109–26; Francis Ames-Lewis, *Tuscan Marble Carving 1250–1350: Sculpture and Civic Pride* (London, Ashgate, 2007), 207–209. In the fourteenth century there is also evidence of private collections that included antiquities, such as that of Oliviero Forzetta of Treviso, whose "shopping list" of 1335 included drawings and sculpture.

3. The Colossus of Rome was 100 feet tall.

4. See for example R. R. R. Smith on the ubiquity of ancient sculpture: "Late Antique Portraits in a Public Context: Honorific

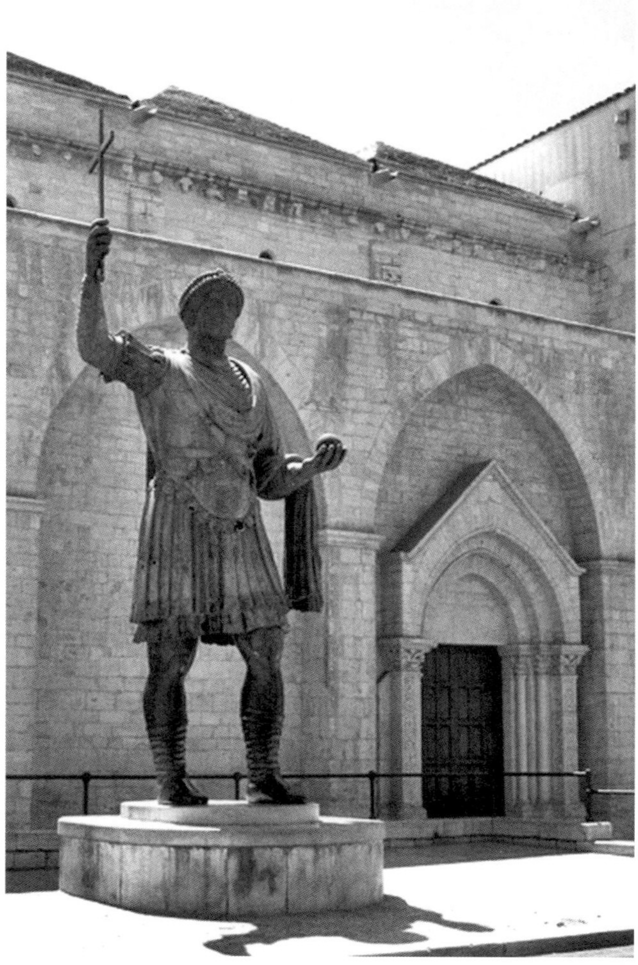

FIGURE 1. The Colossus of Barletta (Valentian?), late fourth century (photo: author).

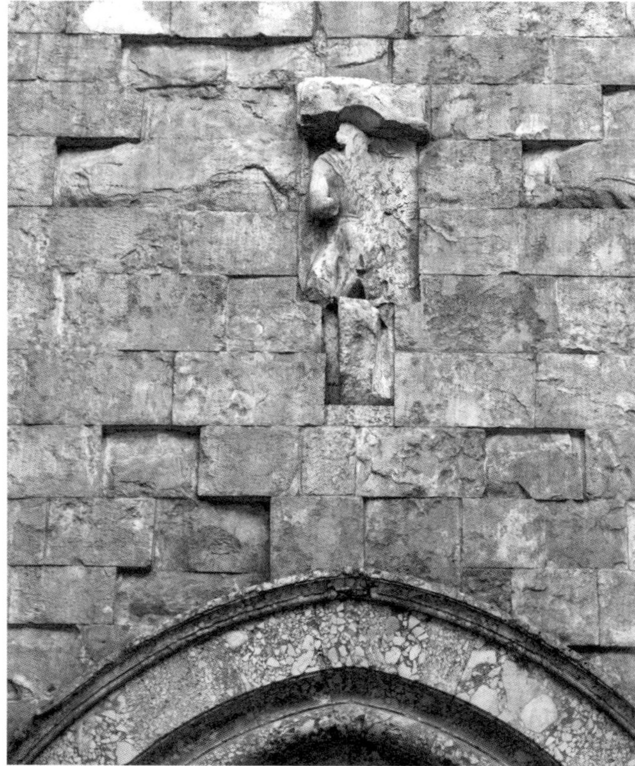

FIGURE 2. Castel del Monte, detail of side wall with fragment of ancient sculpture (photo: author).

nople must have been an especially vigorous reminder of the ways in which the ancient world populated its cities with sculpture: relief, free-standing bronze and marble statues, and equestrian or even chariot-riding rulers and heroes.[5] By the Middle Ages, statues that were not of obviously Christian emperors tended to be associated with paganism instead of the notion of the state, and much of this material had been defaced or destroyed, at least in the West,[6] but with Frederick II's re-use of ancient sculpture (Fig. 2) and imitation of antique models in various monuments, the artifacts of Antiquity came again to promote civic ideologies and abstract values, such as law and justice, as well as to suggest a pride in and emulation of Italy's Roman past. Indeed, only the classical world could provide a "non-Christian" model for such concepts, and it has been correctly observed that to do so Frederick II deliberately evoked the image of a pre-Christian, Augustan Rome.[7]

The vicissitudes of the last decades of Frederick II's reign, however, meant that the many builders and sculptors employed in his construction projects may have needed to look elsewhere for work. Some moved north in a diaspora of skilled labor.[8] The wealthy and ambitious communal cities of Tuscany, especially

Statuary at Aphrodisias in Caria, A.D. 300–600," *Journal of Roman Studies* 89 (1999), 155–189.

5. The importation of the bronze horses and the tetrarchs to Venice attest to the prestige of such items.

6. The equestrian Marcus Aurelius on the Capitoline was thought to represent Constantine, which accounts for the survival of this figure, and the statue of what may be Valentianus illustrated in Fig. 1 of this article carries a Christian cross.

7. Meredith, 1994, *passim*.

8. In my book on the Kingdom of Sicily under the Angevins, *The*

pro-Imperial Pisa, could provide refuge and employment for these artists and craftsmen, chief among them Nicola Pisano. In Pisa, Nicola would build on the innovations of such artists as Guido da Como and Fra Guglielmo to make the cathedral complex a center for ever more new and varied types of monumental sculptural programs, such as the polygonal pulpits and the decoration on the exterior of the baptistery. Pisan projects subsequently inspired some of the other thriving communes to initiate similar undertakings, in Genoa, Siena, Lucca, and Florence, for example. This essay examines two of these new types of monumental sculpture, the historiated pulpit and the *arca*, and explores the possible implications of *arche* for certain types of secular tombs.

Some seventy years after Nicola Pisano's purported move to Pisa, in the 1320s, several Tuscan sculptors reversed the process, moving south to the Angevin court of Naples to execute portals and tombs. At the end of this essay, I shall consider the anomalous tomb of Catherine of Austria (d. 1323) in the Franciscan church of San Lorenzo Maggiore as one of the first examples of the new Tuscan style imported in the south. In the works by Tino di Camaino in Naples, monumental sculpture in some sense came full circle, but in forms profoundly transformed by the Tuscan experiences of the second half of the thirteenth century.

It will seem banal to observe that in the Middle Ages, sculpture was in the deepest sense a public gesture, often outdoors, and usually aiming at ostentatious display. This was never an art for the lower classes: the very nature of sculpture—its expense and "display value"—made it a medium for the élite and appropriate for ideological purposes.

In the polemics of the thirteenth and fourteenth centuries, sculpture and its spoken equivalent, preaching, were among the most powerful tools available for the forceful expression of a wide variety of political values, among them the civic identity of communal governments and the authority of the Church.[9] I shall suggest that these were closely-related and inter-dependent phenomena, and both were intrinsically linked to notions of effective expression, or rhetoric.[10] There should be no wonder that pulpits are among the earliest and most prominent venues of this new "language of form," as they were literally the setting for the "performance" of preaching, an increasingly important enterprise in attempts to affirm issues of civic identity, convert heretics, and affirm the traditional role of the established Church, perhaps especially in relation to the challenges presented by the ever-more-popular mendicant orders, starting in the 1230s or so.[11]

One other general observation: Italian sculpture is usually of marble, which gave it a special valence in relation to the ancient world. As the remains of ancient statues were usually public and in open spaces, the polemical or political nature of monumental sculpture was understood as intrinsic to its very nature, and

---

Stones of Naples: Church Building in Angevin Italy, 1266–1343 (New Haven and London, 2004), I speculate on the apparent shortage of skilled labor in the Kingdom, 203–209.

9. For example, at the translation of Dominic's remains in 1267 to Nicola Pisano's new *arca*, the sermon by the Dominican Bishop Bartolomeo of Vicenza stated: "... if the audacious deeds of tyrants were sculpted on arches, columns, and gateways, deeds which were ephemeral and mostly harmful—how much more should the marvelous deeds and acts of this man be commended in a useful, delightful and healthy manner to the memory of his sons, since they are deeds that are going to live eternally?" Quoted in A. F. Moskowitz, "On the Sources and Meaning of Nicola Pisano's *Arca di San Domenico* in Bologna," in *Verrochio and Late Quattrocento Italian Sculpture*, ed. S. Bule, A. P. Darr, and F. S. Gioffredi (Florence, 1993), 277. Clearly the Dominican bishop had in mind the debris of ancient arches and other monuments that commemorated Roman emperors, but perhaps he knew the Capuan Gate as well.

10. Above, n. 9, in which the *gesta* of Dominic are compared with those of powerful (presumably imperial) rulers: A. F. Moskowitz, 1992, p. 275. See also Moskowitz, *Italian Gothic Sculpture, c. 1250–1400* (Cambridge, 2001), 4, who notes: "the function of language, according to Petrarch, was to 'accuse, to excuse, to console, to irritate, to placate souls, to move to tears and to remove them, to light fires of anger and to extinguish them, to color fact, to avert infamy, to transfer blame, to arouse suspicions—these are the proper work of orators.'" For preaching, communal politics, and civic identity, see A. Thompson, *Revival Preachers and Politics in Thirteenth-Century Italy: The Great Devotion of 1233* (Oxford, 1992).

11. As Max Seidel has observed in his important article of 1993, however, pulpits were not only for preaching, but also served a number of other functions, such as the display of relics and for knighting ceremonies. See "Die Kanzel als Bühne (Zur Funktion der Pisani-Kanzeln)," in *Gegegnunges. Festscrift für Petern Anselm Riedl zum 60. Geburtstab*, ed. K. Güthlein (Worms, 1993), 28–34.

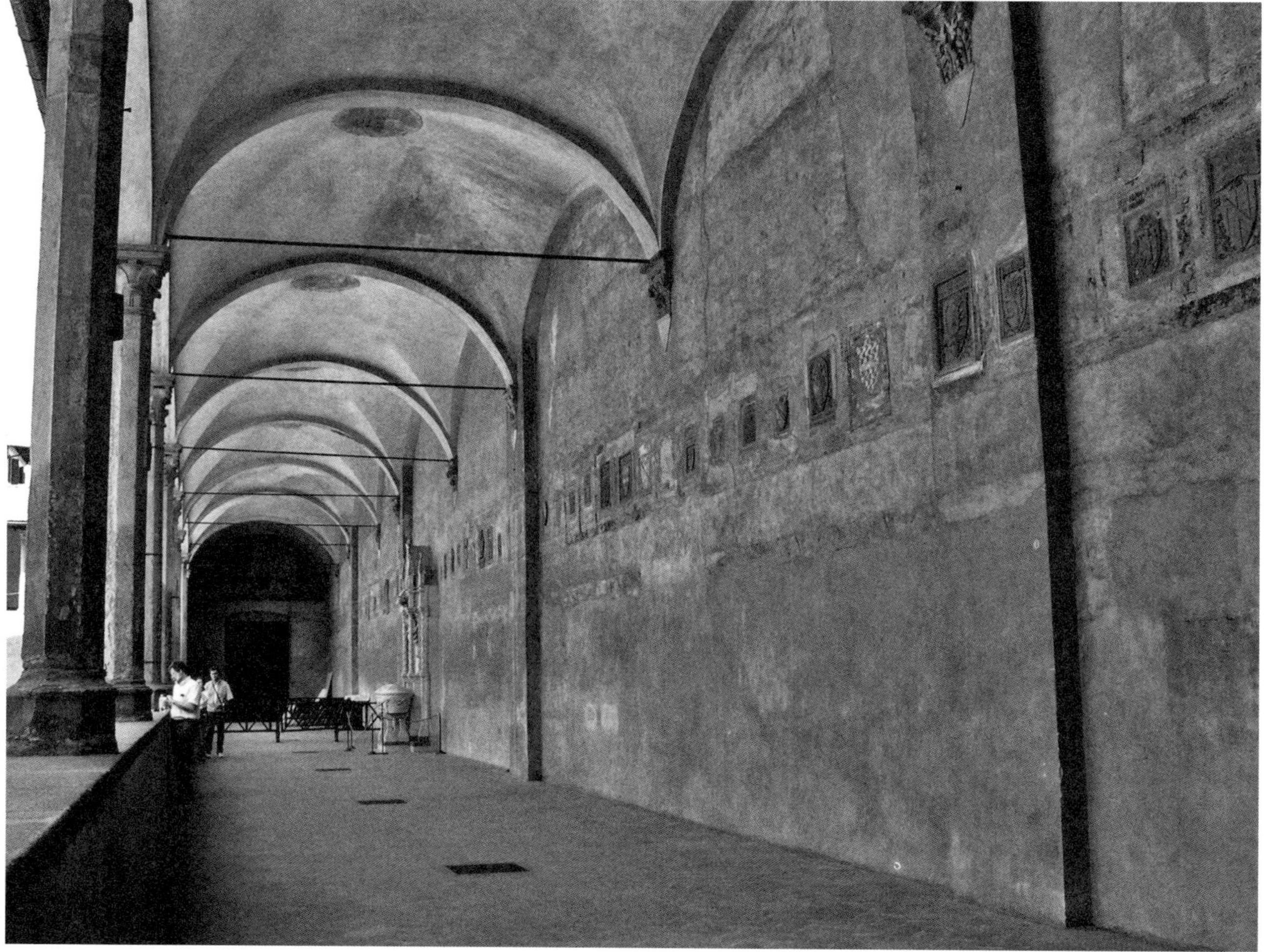

FIGURE 3. Florence, Sta. Croce, south gallery with memorial shields (photo: author).

indeed was eventually to lead to the phenomenon of ancient "talking statues," such as the Pasquino.[12] Medieval investment in public, political, and ideological sculpture may have developed almost simultaneously in the Kingdom of Sicily, the northern communes, and the papacy: for each, display and ostentation were at the heart of the matter.[13] When the extension of these ideas to large-scale tombs began in Italy after the middle of the thirteenth century, the earliest were, appropriately, the "public" ostentation of the bodies of saints (the *arca* of San Domenico, 1260s), and rapidly extended to tombs for prelates, princes and magnates, and finally, on a more modest scale, those of bankers and wealthy merchants. The adoption of incised sculpture on flat pavement slabs for private tombs represents the privatization of this medium and was part of a broader phenomenon of the colonization of church space by an economic élite of laymen.[14] There was some "trickle down" effect to the middle class, but this mostly consisted of the use of family shields to mark burial places, such as those on the exterior galleries of Sta. Croce in Florence (Fig. 3). Only very few of what must have been a stunning abundance of such monuments survive, however. The coats of arms that

12. In Rome, where the mutilated torso continues "to speak."
13. Cassidy, 2007, pp. 18–41.
14. See Bruzelius, "The Dead Come to Town: Preaching, Burying and Building in the Medieval Italian City," in *The Year 1300 and the Crearion of a New European Architecture* (Turnhout, 2007), 203–224.

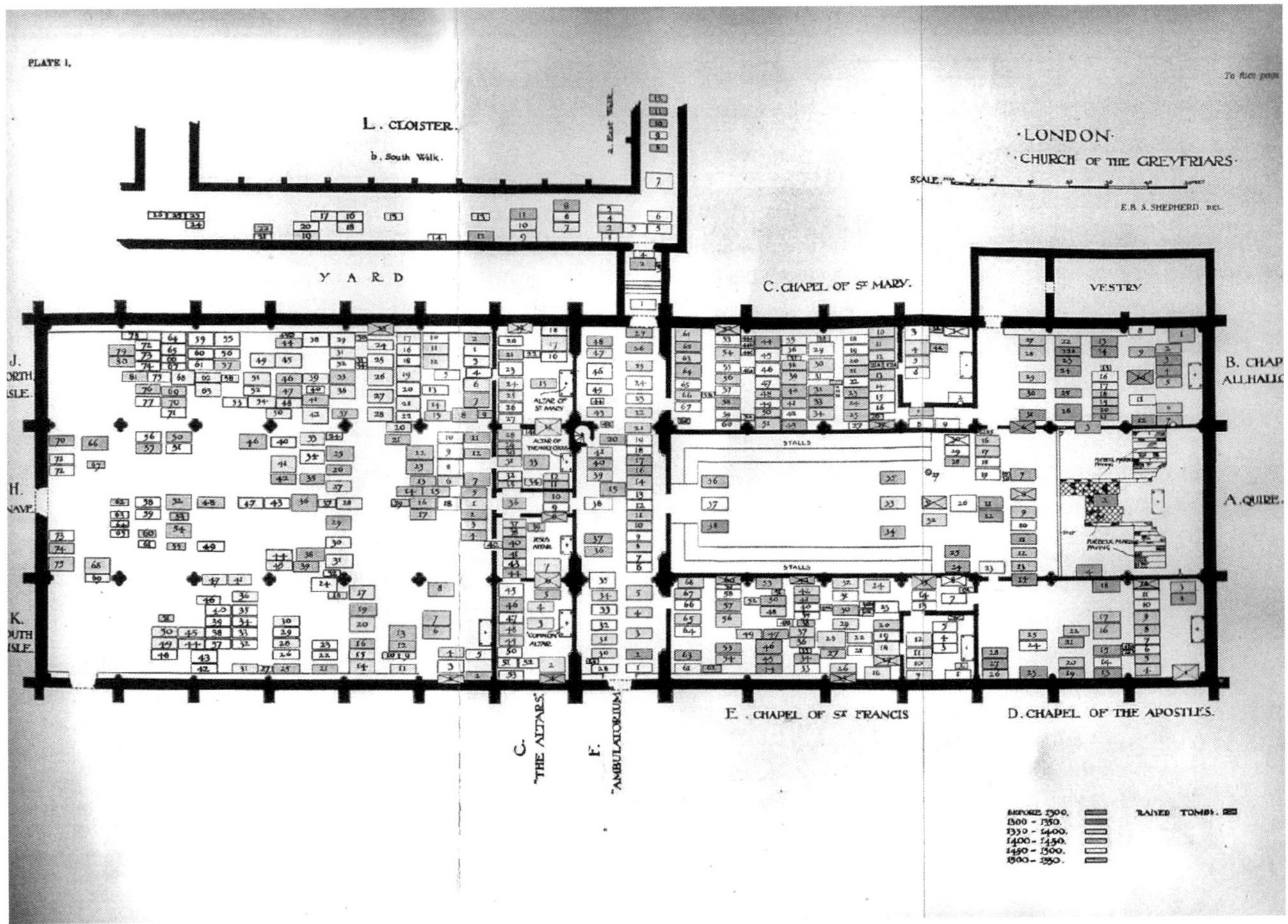

FIGURE 4. Reconstruction of the disposition of tombs at the Greyfriar's Church, London, by E. B. S. Sheperd, "The Church of the Friars Minor," *Archaeological Journal* 59 (1902), plate 1.

marked family tombs were also often accompanied by votive paintings, which covered churches like postage stamps.[15] The *sepultuario* of Sta. Croce of 1439, copied in 1596, lists 375 tombs within the church, but we should recall that tombs were collective, and many contained generations of family members.[16] Reconstructions of slab tombs in the pavement of churches, as at the Greyfriar's of London (Fig. 4), are a vivid reminder of the ubiquitous presence of the dead and their monuments in and around church space starting in the third and fourth decades of the thirteenth century.[17]

Sculpture produced for a religious context, such as portals, pulpits, altars, and tombs, has perhaps survived somewhat better than civic monuments, although the destruction of choir screens in the Counter-Reformation meant not only the loss of the screens themselves, but also the ancillary altars, tombs, shields, flags, and other decoration (panel paintings, for example) that were attached to them, some of which now fills our museums. Civic monuments, on the other hand, were particularly vulnerable to political change, factionalism, and vandalism,[18] and only a few, such as the tower of

15. On the proliferation of family memorials, see Michele Bacci, *Investimenti per l'aldilà. Arte e raccomandazione dell'anima nel Medioevo* (Bari, 2003), and *'Pro remedio animae.' Immagini sacre e pratiche devozionali in Italia centrale, secoli XIII e XIV* (Pisa, 2000).

16. On this see Bacci, 2000, 261, and Roberto Bartalini, *Scultura gotica in Toscana. Maestri, monumenti, cantieri del Due e Trecento* (Milan, Silvana, 2005), 197.

17. Bruzelius, 2007, pp. 203–224.

18. On this point, see Cassidy, pp. 23–30 in particular.

Florence Cathedral or the Fontana Maggiore in Perugia, are still partially intact. Others are known by fragments or copies. It is likely that the rates of survival give us the erroneous impression that more sculpture was religious than secular (or civic), and in the absence of the originals it is hard to demonstrate the contrary. But it was the fundamentally ostentatious and political nature of sculpture that made it an important and attractive medium for the Due and Trecento communes of Tuscany as well as for the papacy, and its potential to magnify and glorify the commissioner came directly from its use in Antiquity.[19]

A Few Words on Historiography

Modern scholarship tends to separate out the study of painting from that of sculpture and architecture, and has created systems of analysis that categorize each medium for specialized study.[20] In late medieval Italy, however, these media were often intended to form a united whole and meant to function together as an integrated program, as in the Bardi di Vernio Chapel.[21] Many of the individuals whom we classify as "sculptors," "painters," or "architects" switched roles to work on different aspects of a project, so we can imagine that flexibility of this type was normal procedure (our "disciplinary boundaries" were certainly not theirs).[22] A master was employed to produce a product, and it might or might not involve his own craftsmanship.[23] In addition, many churches of the thirteenth and fourteenth centuries, and especially those of the mendicant orders, were deliberately conceived as unobstructed settings for the episodic additions of donors' tombs and their painted and sculpted decoration (imagine, for example, Assisi, the Arena Chapel, or Sta. Croce without their tombs or frescoes).[24] While coherent programs were designed for the entire project at the Arena Chapel, and for much of the decoration of the upper church at Assisi, both with a highly specialized function, Sta. Croce in Florence is an excellent example of a mendicant church conceived for the successive interventions of lay patrons as they adopted existing chapels or commissioned new ones, or placed tombs in the nave, crypt, or external lateral galleries.[25] To the "monumental arts" in the form of sculpted tombs and frescoes in chapels and the church interior, we should add panel paintings large and small, hangings, coats of arms, and other objects. Consider for example the shrine of Margaret of Cortona, which consisted of Margaret's tomb and a cycle of frescoes (attributed to the Lorenzetti brothers) in a Franciscan church designed for her cult.[26] Of the original ensemble, only the tomb and some painted fragments remain. On a more modest scale, the tomb of Antonio Fissiraga, generous patron of the Franciscans in Lodi, also consisted of painting and sculpture in an architectural context; if only the austere tomb survived, we would miss out most of the full message of this "mixed-media" monument.[27]

The friars in particular came to conceive of their buildings as what can best be described as "hangars" for the interventions of their lay patrons, either as individuals or as confraternities.[28] Other types of institutions followed their example. Indeed, the "colonialization" of religious space by laymen is one of the

19. Ames-Lewis, pp. 6–16. Brendan Cassidy's recent book (2007) is fundamental for these issues.

20. Recent studies are more conscious of the need for the integration of these disciplines: see for example Giovanni Freni, "Spazio liturgico e luoghi sacri nella cattedrale e nella pieve," *Art in Terra D'Arezzo: il Trecento*, ed. A. Galli and P. Refice (Florence, 2005), 209–228; and by the same author "The Aretine Polyptich by Pietro Lorenzetti: Patronage, Iconography and Original Setting," *Journal of the Warburg and Courtauld Institutes* 63 (2000), 59–110; and Joanna Cannon and André Vauchez, *Margherita of Cortona and the Lorenzetti: Sienese Art and the Cult of a Holy Woman in Medieval Tuscany* (University Park, Pa., 1999); see also Cassidy, 2007, *passim*.

21. Roberto Bartalini 1, "'*Et in carne mea videbo Deum meum*:' Maso di Banco, la cappella dei Confessori e la committenza dei Bardi, a proposito di un libro recente," *Prospettiva* 98/99 (2000/01), 58–103.

22. For example, Arnolfo di Cambio's involvement with the Florence Duomo, or Tino di Camaino's role as building supervisor at San Martino in Naples.

23. Michelle O'Malley, *The Business of Art: Contracts and the Commissionig Process in Renaissance Italy* (New Haven and London, 2005), p. 3.

24. See Bacci 2000 and 2003, and Bruzelius, 2007.

25. As I have suggested elsewhere, we might view the character of mendicant churches and their vast dimensions as a sort of "investment" for the cultivation of lay patronage.

26. Cannon and Vauchez, 1999.

27. Bartalini, 2001, pp. 58–103.

28. Bruzelius, 2007, *passim*.

central features of late medieval art, and came to have profound implications for the design and conception of sacred space. Religious structures took on new shapes, and church architecture acquired a certain "malleability" to accommodate the desires and requests of patrons who left large bequests in their wills: spatial forms were developed in relation to a symbiotic relationship with the needs of laymen whose bequests, as is well known, often specified a votive painting along with a tomb marker, altar, or chapel. In the case of the wealthiest patrons, this could result in the production of a private and glamorously-decorated chapel by the best artists of the day, such as those of the Bardi and Peruzzi at Sta. Croce.[29] Although religious institutions attempted to "regularize" or "institutionalize" such lay interventions in order to maintain an appearance of coherence in church or cloister,[30] the aggregate effect was nonetheless one of churches pullulating with tomb monuments, memorials, family shields, votive paintings, flags, hangings, and other paraphernalia.[31] Even when the friars attempted to impose order,[32] the wealthiest patrons insisted on their rights to certain types of tombs and memorials. Money speaks.

The accidents of history have meant, however, that rarely do all three media survive as an active presence in church space, and our Linnaean systems of classification have tended to further divided sculpture, architecture, and painting into separate fields.[33] Issues of fragmentary survival and our systems of study hover everywhere in the background of the literature on medieval sculpture in Italy. Yet it is clear that the integration of sculpture and painting within the church or cloister was inherent in the design conception of each project, and buildings came to be conceived to provide space for increasingly extravagant tombs and altars as part of a process that was understood to be additive.[34]

Furthermore, most scholarship on Italian sculpture focuses on a region or city, in spite of the public nature and prominence of monuments that were of broad public and international importance. This approach has been important in building a body of knowledge, but has left out the "internationalism" of the artists, patrons, religious orders, or civic entities involved. Art-historical studies of the early twentieth century largely avoided this trap by their ambitious scope and broad frame (Adolfo Venturi and Pietro Toesca, for example).[35] Fundamental also are the studies of John Pope-Hennessy of 1955 and John White's *Art and Architecture in Italy 1250–1400* of 1966, to which can now be added Anita Moskowitz's, Joachim Poeschke's, and Brendan Cassidy's recent volumes on Gothic sculpture.[36] Almost always, however, Rome and the south receive less attention: the conceptual model of an artistic geography has remained Vasari,[37] and a great deal of

29. See for example the work of M. Bacci, 2000 and 2003, and Bartalini, 2001.

30. For example, Bruno Brevegliere, "Le aree cimiteriali di San Domenico a Bologna nel Medioevo (ricostruzini topografiche)," *Atti e memorie. Deputazione di Storia Patria per le Province di Romagna* 45 (1995), 179–223.

31. The purgation of medieval tombs and decoration date to different moments in different places, but generally can be associated with the Counter-Reformation and the removal of choir screens in the sixteenth century, various episodes of restoration and renewal in the eighteenth century, and modern restoration in the nineteenth and twentieth centuries. The Civil Code of 1804 required burial outside city walls in a revival of Roman practice and was applied in all territories under the control of Napoleon. These processes have expunged almost all the monuments associated with private patrons; the long-term effect was to "re-Christianize" church space.

32. There were efforts, for example, to create chapels that were consistent in scale and design even if not chronological in date.

33. An important exception is Bartalini's work on the Bardi di Vernio Chapel at Sta. Croce in Florence, republished as "'Monumenta laicorum:' I sepolcri della cappella Bardi in Santa Croce," in *Scultura gotica in Toscana* (2005), 179–203. See also the publications of Giovanni Freni cited in note 19.

34. Bartalini, Freni, and Cassidy have emphasized the need to consider the ensemble of painting and sculpture, although the architectural context is often given less consideration.

35. Adolfo Venturi, *Storia dell'arte italiana*, (Milan, 1901–1940); Pietro Toesca, *Storia dell'arte italiana* (Turin, 1927–), vols. 1 and 2.

36. Moskowitz, 2001, pp. 3–5 in particular, stresses the role of the mendicant orders in the proliferation of tombs and their fundamental importance in the development of new iconographic motifs for Italian art. John Pope Hennessy, *An Introduction to Italian Gothic Sculpture* (London and New York, 1969); John White, *Art and Architecture in Italy 1250–1400* (Baltimore, 1966); Joachim Poeschke, *Die Skulptur des Mittelalters in Italien. Gotik*, vol. 2 (Munich, 2000).

37. Although, as will be seen below, Francesco Aceto has de-

importance is given to the influence of French Gothic. A broad view of this topic, however, is fundamental, because everybody, especially the clergy, kept an eye out for precedent and models. The location and design of the tomb of Robert the Wise in Sta. Chiara of Naples, for example, must be considered in relation to that of Henry VII in Pisa.

The literature on Italian sculpture can be generally organized into four types of themes: studies of individual sculptors (for example the recent exhibition catalogues commemorating Arnolfo di Cambio);[38] books on the sculpture of a city or region (such as Carli, Seidel, or Kosegarten on Siena,[39] and Roberto Bartalini and Ames-Lewis on Tuscan marble carving); iconographic studies; and studies of categories of monuments, such as façades, pulpits, and tombs. A few scholars, such as Nicholas Penny, in *The Materials of Sculpture*,[40] have concerned themselves with materials, tools, and training. Sometimes research focuses on the work of one sculptor or one type of monument in a certain city—for example, Francesco Aceto's important articles on the tombs of Tino di Camaino in Naples (to which more reference will be made at the end of this essay), and Seidel's remarkable studies of the Pisani at Pisa and Siena. The *Enciclopedia dell'Arte Medievale* is now a fundamental resource for synthetic biographies of sculptors and individual projects with updated bibliographies. And recent scholarship has produced excellent studies on individual monuments, such as the Tarlati tomb in Arezzo and the *Arca* di San Cerbone at Massa Maritima.[41]

A focus on categories of sculpture has been extremely important for an understanding of the development new types of monuments, especially as so many exist only in fragmentary form.[42] The partially destroyed monuments of Henry VII in Pisa and Margaret of Brabant in Genoa have in particular stimulated important and interesting research and hypothetical reconstructions by Kosegarten and Kreytenberg.[43]

In the last few years several new books have addressed the political and civic aspects of sculpture. Ames-Lewis' *Tuscan Marble Carving 1250–1350: Sculpture and Civic Pride* and Cassidy's *Politics, Civic Ideals and Sculpture in Italy, c. 1240–1400* of 2007 are notable examples. Recent work has also emphasized the importance of the mendicants in the creation of distinctive types of monuments and their stimulus of patronage by the increasingly-wealthy lay public of the thirteenth and fourteenth centuries.[44]

As noted above, one striking feature of scholarship on Italian sculpture has been the interest in the influence of French models.[45] The question assumes a kind of cultural-artistic hegemony, which has set up a binary model of a French (by which is mostly meant the Gothic style of the Île de France) versus either Italian Romanesque or the "classicizing" idioms of Antiquity. In Italian scholarship in particular, the Cistercians have been given a starring role in notions of artistic exchange and the importation of "French" ideas, even though sculpture was to a large extent forbidden in their monasteries. The emphasis on "Cistercian" influence in Italian architecture and sculpture has surely

---

voted numerous important studies to the work of Tino di Camaino in Naples.

38. For example: *Arnolfo di Cambio. Una rinascita nell'Umbria medievale*, ed. Vittoria Garibaldi and Bruno Toscano (Milan, 2005).

39. Enzo Carli, *Gli scultori senesi* (Milan, 1980); Gerd Kreytenberg, *Die Werke von Tino di Camaino*, Liebighaus Monographie, 11 (Frankfurt, 1987); Antje Kosegarten, "Beiträge zur sienesischen Reliefkunst des Trecento," in *Mitteilungen des Kunsthistorischesn Institutes in Florenz*, vol. 12 (1966), 207–224; and Max Seidel, "Studien zu Giovanni di Balduccio und Tino di Camaino. Die Rezeption des Spätwerks von Giovanni Pisano," *Städel-Jahrbuch*, n.f. 5 (1975), 37–85.

40. Nicolas Penny, *The Materials of Sculpture*, (New Haven and London, 1993).

41. Enzo Carli, *Goro di Gregorio* (Florence, 1946), and Carli, *Gli Scultori Senesi* (Milan, 1980), 23 ff.; and Marco Pierini, *L'Arca di San Cerbone*, Quaderni del Centro Studi Storici (Siena, 1995).

42. For tombs, see for example in previous notes: Bartalini for Florence, Pincus for Venice, Seidel and Kosegarten for Siena, Gardner and Garms for Rome, and Moskowitz for the Pisani (as well as for her general study).

43. See above note 38.

44. See for example Moskowitz and Bartalani, *passim*.

45. For example, Cesare Gnudi, "Relations Between French and Italian Sculpture of the Gothic Period," *Romanesque and Gothic Art*, Acts of the 20th International Congress of the History of Art, v, 1 (Princeton, 1963), 161–167.

been exaggerated, especially in view of the almost endless to and fro of the upper clergy from northern Europe to Rome.[46]

The boundaries of our current nation-states have thus inflected our narratives about the Middle Ages, and it takes some effort to remember that not only was there was no "Italy" until after 1860, but also that what we consider "France" was in large measure put into final form under Louis XIV. The prelacy, on the other hand, was a medium for the constant movement and migration, and workmen as well as ideas flowed with and in the wake of priests, abbots, and bishops as they traveled back and forth to Rome. Perhaps we should simply generally assume that in large measure sculptors are from "somewhere else," except when there is evidence of a well-established *bottega*; itinerant workshops picked up new and sloughed off old members, and trained apprentices, in the course of their journeys. Sculptors went where there was work; the importance of access to high-quality materials as well as funding for projects meant that this was a profession that required the artist's mobility to sites with patrons and supplies. Later on, it is true, works were produced in a *bottega* and shipped out, but this practice seems to begin in the fifteenth century (such as Donatello's Brancaccio tomb in Sant'Angelo a Nilo in Naples) and not to have been a feature of medieval practice. In this context, how useful can regional studies really be?

Nicola Pisano & Sculpture in the Kingdom of Sicily

It is generally agreed that Nicola Pisano, "Nicola de Apulia," received his early formation in the Kingdom of Sicily, possibly in the workshops of Frederick II.[47] If this is so, several questions present themselves: what kinds of projects might Nicola have worked on before moving to Pisa sometime around 1245? How did access to marble in the south condition what he might have been able to produce while he was there? Might the availability of good marble as a result of the opening of new quarries have been a consideration in Nicola's move to the north?

The literature generally agrees that Frederick II's Arch of Capua on the northern border of the Emperor's domains included what may have been the first monumental stone portrait of a secular ruler since Antiquity.[48] The statue of the Emperor was flanked by re-used ancient figures of Apollo and Diana, and surrounded by busts and commemorative portraits of judges. The image of imperial dignity and authority rivaled those produced in ancient Rome; as Willibald Sauerländer put it, in the Arch of Capua the Emperor attempted to render an image of Frederick II in "Caesar's language."[49]

The location of the gate on the main artery towards Rome (the ancient Via Appia), was a gauntlet thrown down towards the papal states. As a symbol of the Emperor's sovereign authority and autonomy, it articulated a message not lost on either the papacy or the northern communal governments, ever more engaged in asserting their own power and image in monumental exterior declarations of authority.

It seems that the Frederick II's gate of the 1230s may have been one of the first examples of the integration of ancient marbles into a larger public project, although Frederick II also used ancient marbles in his palaces (Fig. 2). In this respect, he was emulating the monuments of Antiquity, which also incorporated older materials (the Arch of Constantine, for instance). But Frederick recalled ancient precedent not

46. For example, Carla Ghisalberti, "I legami culturali e stilistici tra la scultura architettonica federiciana dell'Italia meridionale e il mondo cistercense," *Intellectual Life at the Court of Frederick II Hohenstaufen*, Studies in the History of Art, 44, ed. W. Tronzo (Washington D.C., 1994), 41–62.

47. For a summary of Nicola Pisano's career and the literature up through about 1996, see the essay by M. Wundram, "Nicola Pisano," in *Enciclopedia dell'arte medievale*, VIII (1997), 687–695; M. L. Testi Cristiani, "La Toscana e Nicola 'Pisanus,'" *Federico II. Immagine e Potere*, ed. M. S. Calò Mariani and E. Cassano (Bari, 1995), 411–415; A. Venturi, in *Storia dell'arte italiana* (Rome, 1903), vol. III (*L'arte romanica*), 984 ff., was one of the first to affirm Nicola Pisano's Apulian origins.

48. Meredith, 1986, and Meredith, 1994.

49. W. Sauerländer, "Two Glances from the North: The Presence and Absence of Frederick II in the Art of the Empire; The Court Art of Frederick II and the *opus francigenum*," *Intellectual Life at the Court of Frederick II Hohenstaufen*, Studies in the History of Art, 44, ed. W. Tronzo (Washington D.C., 1994), 202.

only in the firmly secular and political nature of the program, but also in the placement of allegorical figures flanking the image of the ruler. In this purely secular program, the Emperor and accompanying figures were associated with abstract values, such as justice, concord, and peace. Sculpture had become a polemical tool in an increasingly intense conflict between papacy and empire: the Capuan Arch, by recalling the monumental gateways and arches of Antiquity, thus affirmed the autonomy of the Emperor to justice and authority within his domains. There were no elements of Christian iconography.

One of the striking features of Frederick's reign is the large number of secular projects patronized by the Emperor: castles, hunting palaces, gateways, etc., richly decorated with sculpture, and both Castel del Monte and the Capuan Arch are well-known monuments. But it is also important to note that there were also major ecclesiastical projects, especially in Puglia and Campania, independent of those commissioned by the Emperor: the on-going construction on S. Nicola in Bari, for example, as well as the cathedrals of Naples, Casertavecchia, and Sessa Aurunca in Campania. The Campanian projects are also often characterized by a strikingly classicizing idiom, as can be seen in the re-used amphitheater piers and fragments of ancient sculpture in the porch at Sessa,[50] and the towers of the 1230s at the cathedrals of Casertavecchia and Naples, both with pointed vaults embellished with coffering.[51] This interest in recreating elements of the classical style is a distinctive feature of Campanian art in the third and fourth decades of the thirteenth century, and can possibly be associated with the teaching at the episcopal school of Capua.[52]

But, as I noted above, marble in the south was re-used Greek and Roman material that had in imperial times been imported from elsewhere, either Carrara, Greece, Asia Minor, or North Africa.[53] When marble was used in the south (and it was particularly favored first for rood screens and pulpits, then royal and noble tombs), it was always recycled from ancient monuments. This must have constrained the scale and dimensions of what could be produced.[54] Prior to the Angevins and their pillage of marble from Rome, the use of marble in the Kingdom therefore tended to be "discreet interventions," isolated elements inserted into larger contexts, often imported to the Kingdom of Sicily with great trouble and expense. Think of Desiderius and the marbles brought from Rome to Montecassino: these were vitally important to his project, but immensely expensive and moved to the building site with great trouble and effort.

As noted above, the ancient statues integrated intact into the Capuan Arch were part of the ostentatious display of both medieval and classical images to convey the idea of the majesty of empire and notions of continuity with the historic Roman past. In liturgical furniture, however, figural elements tended to be restricted to the supports of lecterns in pulpits and candelabra; for the body of the pulpit itself there was a preference for intarsia designs of lavish materials (Salerno, Ravello), or, at most, the symbols of the evangelists.[55] In the South there was little interest in the types of richly historiated pulpits that can be found, for example, in the pulpit of Guido da Como in San Bartolomeo in Pantano, Pistoia, of 1250. Pulpits in the south tended to be visually inarticulate and there is no surviving evidence of richly historiated pulpits with biblical scenes,

50. Venturi, pp. 539 ff., was perhaps the first to point this out.

51. C. Bruzelius, "A Note on the 1233 Tower of Archbishop Peter of Sorrento and the Topography of Naples," in *Architektur und Monumentalskulptur des 12.–14. Jahrhunderts*" (Bern, 2006), 225–235.

52. *Ibid.*

53. As Nicolas Penny reminds us, marble was rarely available between the decline of the Roman Empire and the late fourteenth century (Penny, 1993, p. 35), and suggests that the use of the quarries between Pisa and La Spezia was already in decline by the late third century C.E., because of the declining market for monumental statuary, though quarrying continued in the Proconnesos.

54. For example, for the tomb of Queen Mary of Hungary, commissioned after her death in March 1325, Robert the Wise ordered his vicars in Rome to obtain marbles there. See H. W. Schulz, *Denkmäler der Kunst des Mittelalters in Unteritalien* (Dreden, 1860), vol. 4, p. 146, doc. CCCLXVIII. This was standard operating practice in Angevin Naples, where marble was used in the portals of the cathedral and mendicant churches (San Lorenzo, Sta. Chiara, San Domenico) as well as the profusion of royal, noble, and ecclesiastical tombs.

55. On liturgical sculpture and Easter candlesticks in Southern Italy, see Nino Zchomelidse, "Der Österleuchter im Dom von Capua: Kirchenmobiliar und Liturgie im lokalen Kontext," *Mededelingen van het Nederlands Instituut te Rome* 55 (1996/97), 18–43.

such as those of Tuscany. Even ambitious pulpits in the south, such as that of Sta. Maria Maggiore in Teggiano by Melchiorre in 1279, confine themselves to images of the evangelists (Fig. 5).[56] Could this be because old (re-used) marble, like limestone, becomes harder and more friable, so that the materials used in the south would have been harder to work than newly quarried stone?

An ambitious young sculptor like Nicola Pisano might therefore have been severely limited not only by the availability of marble in the south but also by local taste in marble carving, at least in ecclesiastical projects. Futhermore, as the Kingdom became increasingly submerged in the titanic struggle against the papacy, Frederick's building activity slowed; by the mid-1240s work on the Emperor's projects would have been encumbered by his deposition by the papacy (1245) and the fact that the Kingdom was intermittently under interdict from 1230 onwards.[57] The difficult political and economic circumstances that ensued would also have affected any ecclesiastical enterprises such as cathedral pulpits and choir screens. Sculptors and builders may well have had difficulty finding work. So it would have been natural enough for Nicola Pisano to move to the stoutly Ghibelline city of Pisa, where perhaps he had good pro-Imperial connections. Pisa was rich, had grand ambitions for its cathedral, and, perhaps most importantly, there was good marble available that was newly accessible. Ancient quarries had recently been re-opened, and as early as 1157 a canal had been constructed from Monte Pisano to Pisa for the transport of blocks intended for the city walls. This canal also provided the materials for more luxurious projects like pulpits and buildings.[58] Marble had immense value as a prestige material, and its use in ecclesiastical and civic monuments evoked exactly the kind of conspicuous display and ostentation vital in conveying the image of the city. As Penny has observed, the construction of the great cathedrals and abbeys of Tuscany, beginning with the cathedral of Pisa in the mid-eleventh century and followed by Siena, Lucca, and other sites, required a large supply of marble for columns, capitals, and the revetment of walls, all of which resonated with ideas of the splendors of ancient Rome. Although some of these materials, as at Pisa, were brought from Rome itself, there was also a need for a local supply of stone, and the cathedrals no doubt acted as a stimulus for the re-opening of the quarries.[59]

At the same time that quarries were re-activated, and roads and canals were created or improved for the transportation of these heavy materials, there were also important technical advances in the development of iron tools, as Ames-Lewis has pointed out.[60] Pisa was an important center of iron production, and perhaps because of the city's broad trading contacts, the Pisans acquired at an early date new smelting and tempering techniques developed in Syria for making weapons and armor. As early as 1228, Pisa was celebrated for the skill of its armorers,[61] and the technology that developed new types of armor also helped the sculptor with his tools.

The pulpits of Pisa presented several major innovations: the production of ambitious new shapes (octagons, hexagons), the monumentalization of New Testament scenes in a classicizing idiom, and the introduction of pulpits in a baptistery setting.[62] These appear first in Nicola Pisano's pulpit for the baptistery, which in scale and regularity would have been difficult to achieve without new marbles quarried on demand.

It is no doubt overly simplistic to observe that the polygonal shapes of Nicola's pulpits mimic the plan of Castel del Monte, but if Angiola's thesis that the pulpit is a "pro-Ghibelline" structure promoted by Archbishop Visconti is correct, this resemblance might not be entirely fortuitous. Particularly striking are the triple porphyry shafts used in the angles between each sculpted panel in the Pisa Baptistery pulpit, which

56. Francesco Gandolfo, *La scultura normanno-sveva in Campania* (Bari, 1999), 120–121.

57. Peter D. Clarke, *The Interdict in the Thirteenth Century: A Question of Collective Guilt* (Oxford, 2007), 61, 83, 118, esp. notes 160 and 191.

58. Ames-Lewis, p. 23.

59. Penny, pp. 51–53.

60. Ames-Lewis, p. 111; Penny, 1994, pp. 84–91; and M. Ayrton, *Giovanni Pisano* (London, 1969), 31–32.

61. Ames-Lewis.

62. As noted by Ames-Lewis, pp. 70–71; see especially Eloise M. Angiola, "Nicola Pisano, Federigo Visconti, and the Classical Style in Pisa," *Art Bulletin* LIX (1977), 1–27. See also Max Seidel, 1993, pp. 28–34.

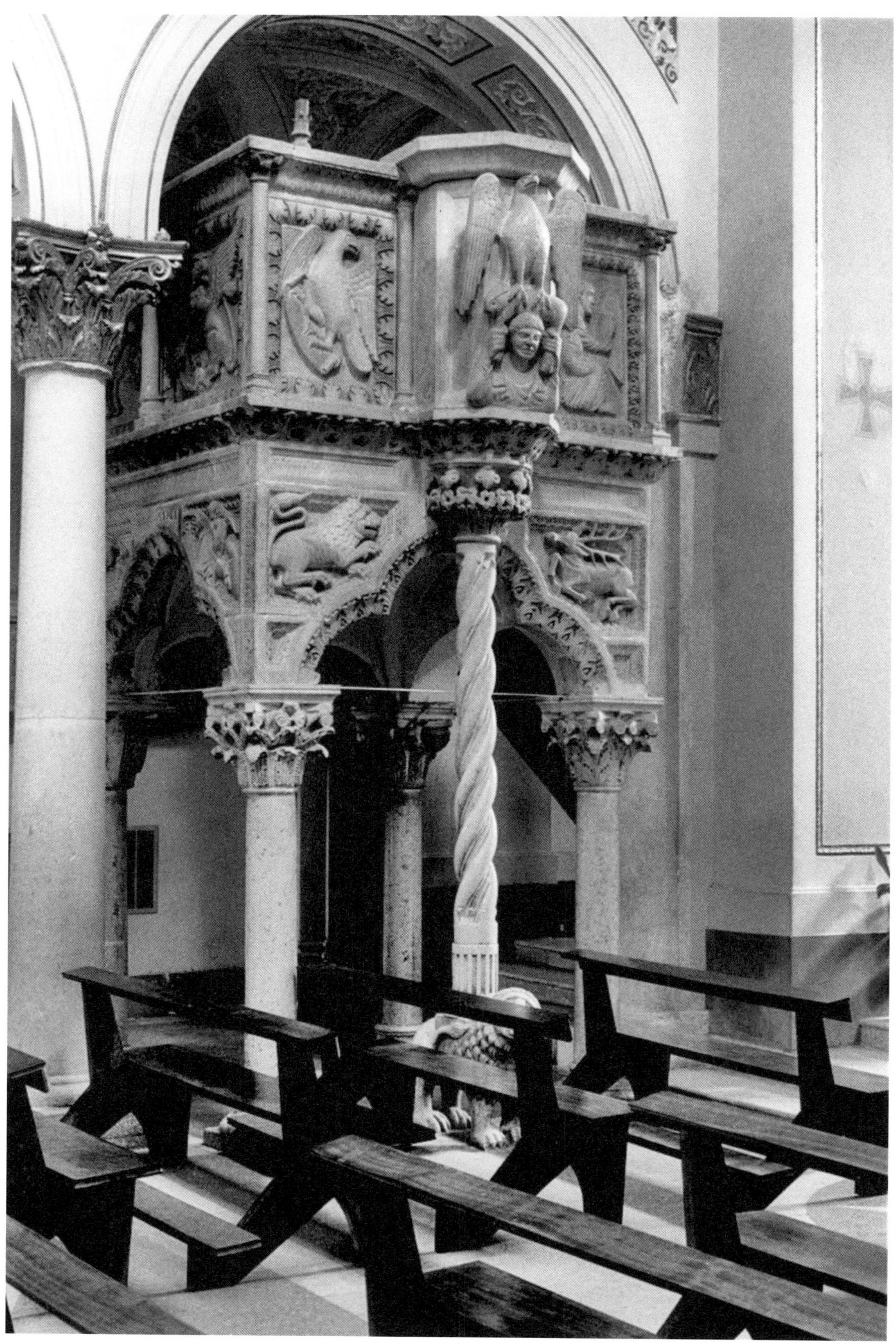

FIGURE 5. Teggiano, Sta. Maria Maggiore, the 1279 pulpit by Melchiore (photo: Chester Brummel).

recall the triplets of shafts in precious marbles placed in the corners of the upper rooms at the Apulian castle, a decorative motif that also appears at Frederick's Castel Maniace in Syracuse.

Preaching & Pulpits

The explosion in the production of monumental marble pulpits in the thirteenth century is a striking phenomenon, and we might wish to consider why they became so important and why such pulpits were so prominent in the Ghibelline cities of Tuscany (Pistoia, Pisa, and Siena).

One aspect of the profusion of monumental pulpits may be related to the debate concerning who had authority to preach, and where they could do so. The profusion of twelfth- and thirteenth-century reform movements, some promoting a new "apostolic" vision of the faith and others directed at a more general revitalization of the Church, used preaching as their primary tool.[63] Preaching was the central instrument for promoting new ideas, either by reformers or various heretical groups. Eventually, although some laymen were given permission to preach (the Umiliati), they were only allowed to offer moral exhortations, and forbidden to touch upon matters of doctrine.[64]

Canons Regular and Benedictine monks had also come into serious conflict with the secular clergy over the right to preach, especially in parishes under their jurisdiction where they claimed the right to the *cura animarum*.[65] Although Jerome states that the task of monks is penitence, not preaching, nonetheless ordained monks insisted upon the right to do so, and thus played a central role in promoting the aims of the Gregorian reform. To this end the papacy extended to certain individuals the right to "preach anywhere" (*ubique predicare*), as for example Gregory VII did for Abbot William of Hirsau in the third quarter of eleventh century.[66] As part of the attempt to press the goals of the reform against episcopal resistance, this Pope and some of his successors (Urban II and Gelasius II) deliberately enlisted itinerant preachers to drum up support against a resistant episcopacy.[67]

The decretals of Gratian of *c.* 1140 attempted to clarify the fraught distinction between ordained clergy with the responsibility for the *cura animarum* versus those who had received special authorization by the local bishop to preach and administer the sacraments. Nevertheless, a typical feature of medieval religion was the charismatic itinerant preacher, such as Robert d'Arbrissel (*c.* 1060–1115), who wandered from village to village in rough clothing, a clear and obvious imitation of Christ and the apostles long before the friars came along.[68]

In the long struggle over who could preach, no pope exceeded Innocent III's utilization of itinerant preachers to swing public opinion against a conservative and obdurate episcopacy. So it is no surprise that in 1210 he allowed Franciscans, and five years later, Dominicans to preach on the condition that they had the permission of the local bishop. Indeed, the mendicants thus addressed the tenth canon of the fourth Lateran Council, which emphasized the importance of preaching in spreading the word of God, even as it recognized that many bishops were too busy, or not well enough trained, to be effective preachers.[69]

Virulent controversy between the friars and secular clergy over the right to preach erupted in the middle of the thirteenth century,[70] however, and at issue were in part the additional rights that the friars had acquired to hear confession (1221) and administer the sacraments.[71] Indeed, by the 1230s friars were conducting "full ser-

63. Jean-Pierre Rénard, *La formation et la designation des prédicateurs au début de l'Ordres des Precheurs (1215–1237)*, Ph.D. Diss. (Fribourg, 1977), 34–60.

64. See Mulchahey, p. 9.

65. Rénard, pp. 37–44.

66. *Ibid.*, p. 42.

67. *Ibid.*, pp. 43–44.

68. *Ibid.*, pp. 41–42.

69. On mendicant preaching in general, see *La predicazione dei frati dalla metà del '200 alla fine del '300*, Atti del XXII Convegno internazionale, Assisi 13–15 ottobre, 1992 (Spoleto, 1995), *passim.*

70. Rénard, pp. 59 ff.

71. Mulchahey, p. 53. On the role of the friars as confessors, see *Dalla penitenza all'ascolto delle confessioni: il ruolo dei frati mendicanti*, Atti del XXII Convegno internazionale, Assisi, 12–14 ottobre, 1995 (Spoleto, 1996). See also R. Rusconi, "I Francescani e la confessione nel secolo XIII," in *Francescanesimo e vita religiosa dei laici nel '200*, Atti dell' VIII convegno internazionale di studi francescani (Assisi, 1981), 251–309, esp. 261–267.

vice" sacramental operations,[72] and these often, at least in Italy, occurred outside, in the campo, piazza, and market (though the Dominicans didn't consider markets appropriate venues for preaching the word of God).[73] It should be noted that preaching in combination with the sacraments had important financial implications, as this meant that the customary oblations offered to the clergy now passed to the friars.

Towards the middle of the thirteenth century, the challenge presented by the mendicants to the secular clergy erupted in the fracas with the cathedral of Paris.[74] These tensions in turn placed pressure on the friars to build their own large churches and move their ministries indoors to their convents.[75]

I would like to suggest that monumental marble pulpits may have emerged in part as an element of this discourse, and were perhaps a way for the secular clergy to reaffirm its vital role in the *cura animarum* and administration of the sacraments to the lay public. The fundamental themes of contrition, confession, penitence, redemption, and salvation are implicit in the New Testament scenes executed in prestigious materials on the new pulpits of the thirteenth century.[76] The 1260 pulpit of the baptistery in Pisa would have presented a powerful contrast to the rustic portable wooden pulpits of the friars, giving authority to the role of baptism as a central ritual of membership in both church and commune. So it is entirely fitting that the Nicola's baptistery pulpit was erected in the space that specifically focused on the fused notions of concept of entry into the Christian community and entry as a citizen to the city.[77]

The advent of the historiated pulpit may also relate to new types of "visual aids" used by preachers. There is some evidence that visual props or tools, such as paintings on linen, may have been part of preaching, and it may be that the series of linen paintings in Naples of scenes from the Crucifixion, a seated Virgin, and Francis receiving the stigmata, are examples of these.[78] For later periods there is more evidence, such as prints (the illustrations in the *Rhetorica Christiana* by Valadés, for example, that illustrate friars pointing to images as part of their sermons),[79] and in the fifteenth century Bernardino da Siena was famous for preaching outdoors with a plaque on which was inscribed the holy name of Christ. As is well known, the friars preached in the *volgare* in order to communicate effectively with the lay public, a departure from the tradition of the Latin sermon that was inaccessible to the broad range of the lay public.[80] The use of vivid every-day stories from the lives of saints, codified in the *Legenda aurea*, brought preaching into a direct and accessible "story" mode for the lay public.[81] Although there is little surviving evidence, either light-weight portable images, in the form of scrolls like the *exultet* rolls, or larger linen paintings that could be rolled out, can be imagined.

With the mendicant orders the art of preaching had taken on special importance as a tool for conversion and

72. Although as Rusconi, 1981, pp. 260–262, notes, there was considerable regional variation.

73. Humbert of Romans: "Nor is it appropriate to preach in undignified places, as some people do, preaching in market places and busy streets and at fairs ... men are already busy in such places, and busy with worldly occupations, so it would be liable to undermine their respect for the word of God to preach there." Published in *Early Dominicans: Selected Writings*, ed. S. Tugwell (Mahwah, N.J., 1982), 250.

74. There is a great deal of literature on the controversy; see, among other sources, Rusconi 1981, pp. 279–289. The classic study is M.-M. Dufeil, *Guillaume de Saint-Amour et la Polémique universitaire Parisienne, 1250–1259* (Paris, 1972).

75. Which, as Rénard, p. 71, notes, were built *ad capiendos homines in praedicationibus*.

76. Angiola, 1977, esp. 9–19.

77. Augustine Thompson, *Cities of God: The Religion of the Italian Communes, 1125–1325* (University Park, Pa., 2005), 309–320 and 326–335. See now Andrea Longhi, ed., *L'Architettural del battistero. Storia e progetto* (Geneva, Milan, 2003), especially Longhi's essay, "Battisteri e scena urbana nell'Italia comunale," 105–127.

78. These were first published by Ferdinando Bologna in *I pittori alla corte Angioina di Napoli* (Rome, 1969), 235–245.

79. See Jaime Lara, *Christian Texts for Aztecs: Art and Liturgy in Colonial Mexico* (Notre Dame, Ind., 2008), 51–52. On the market for paintings on linen for the new world, see James Bloom, "Why Painting?" in N. De Marchi and H. J. Van Miegroet, eds., *Mapping Markets for Paintings in Europe, 1450–1750*, Urban History 6 (Turnhout, 2006), 28–29.

80. Moskowitz, 2001, p. 287, for example.

81. As is well known, these types of narratives on the lives of saints, as well as the Concordance, were developed by the mendicant orders as aids in preaching.

penitence, and the Dominicans were in the forefront of developing an educational system oriented towards the creation of effective preachers. Fundamental to their concept of preaching was the idea of *gratia:* that the gift of eloquence and grace was a fundamental prerequisite for effective preaching.[82] Archbishop Federico Visconti of Pisa, in lamenting the woeful morals and education of his own clergy, urged his priests to emulate and take advantage of a free education with the friars, whose goal was to produce a *gratiosos praedicator*. Dominican prayers for the community, for example, asked for "the ability to speak with grace and eloquence."[83]

For the secular clergy, the ostentatious pulpit within sacred space could therefore have represented an affirmation of their right to preach and administer the sacraments; the representation of New Testament scenes in the context of a permanent and monumental pulpit took on significance as part of the "voice" of the clergy in affirming its traditional rights to the *cura animarum* in the tradition of an apostolic succession embedded in the New Testament. It also placed the cathedral in the center of civic rituals. The classical language that Nicola Pisano encountered in southern Italy, as well as in the ancient sarcophagi of the Camposanto, forcefully addressed the issues of ecclesiastical authority and visual "eloquence" for the clergy, and provided a monumental form of "illustration" for sermons in the same way that portable paintings might have done for the friars. The images produced by the cathedral were, however, in the majestic, dignified, and noble material of marble,[84] a material that as we have seen conveyed venerable tradition as well as vague notions of antiquity.

Ames-Lewis and Angiola have suggested that the baptistery pulpit may have reflected Archbishop Visconti's desire to assert the pre-eminence of Pisa as a mainstay of Imperial strength in Central Italy,[85] and this may explain the importance of pulpits in the Ghibelline cities of Tuscany. Ames-Lewis goes further to describe the pulpit as an "unconventional" vehicle for political statements.[86] However, if we consider baptism as the "hinge" of civic and religious identity, serving as the special marker of the rights and obligations of the secular clergy in relation to the lay public, the pulpit in the baptistery takes on a political valence.[87] A pulpit in the baptistery gave particular emphasis to the themes of salvation and redemption through Christ and within the commune as effected through baptism, and had thereby an important civic and communal role as well as a Christian one. It is therefore no wonder that a splendid pulpit was later erected in Sant'Andrea in Pistoia by Giovanni Pisano, which, as a *pieve*, had the much valued right to baptize.

Arche, *the Promotion of Saints*, *and Some Royal Tombs*

Antique and early Christian sarcophagi were usually three-sided: with a front and short sides. The *Arca* of San Domenico however, is a sarcophagus "in the round" that commemorates a saint and is intended to be viewed on all sides.[88] The type is closely associated with the divided interior spaces of thirteenth-century mendicant churches, where lay public and friars had separate zones.

Several studies, and Moskowitz's in particular, have pointed out the importance of architectural context for monuments like the *Arca* of San Domenico. Located in the south aisle of the lay church, perhaps with one long

82. See Rénard, 159ff., on *gratia* as fundamental to preaching; he quotes Humbert of Romans, who remarks that those who have "grace" in preaching ought to do more of it: *illi qui in hoc habent gratiam, ab habentibus gratiam in hoc*...; and should devote themselves to preaching: *gratia praedicandi et inter homines conversandi*.

83. Rénard, p. 163. A Dominican prayer states, "Accord to your servants, Lord, the ability to speak with grace (or eloquence)"— *verbum tribue graciosum*. As Rénard notes, p. 163, Humbert of Romans states that each convent should have several *praedicatores gratiosi*, and the General Chapters stated that preaching should be done by friars *de bene dotatus*, and by friars who are *praedicatores gratiosi*.

84. I tend therefore to agree with Angiola's suggestion, p. 26, that the Pisa pulpit is essentially retrograde in style.

85. Ames-Lewis, p. 70, also wonders whether the pulpit was developed in response to mendicant fresco cycles, but the date of the Pisa pulpit, 1259–1260, may be too early for this.

86. Ames-Lewis, p. 70.

87. See Seidel, 1993, pp. 28–34.

88. Anita Moskowitz, 1992, pp. 271–281. On the tombs of saints, see Jörg Garms, "Gräber von Heiligen und Seiligen," in *Skulptur und Grabmal des Spätmittelalters in Rom und Italien. Akten des Kongresses 'Scultura e monumenta seplcrale del tarde medioevo a Roma e in Italia': Rom 4.–6. Juli 1985* (Vienna, 1990) 83–105.

side facing the friars' choir and the other the lay public, the iconography has been interpreted as addressing two distinct populations, with scenes of "The Raising of Napoleone Orsini" and the "Burning of the Heretical Books" towards the public and pilgrims, while those of "Reginald of Orléans" and the "Establishment of the Order of Friars Preachers," more institutional in nature, were for the religious community.[89]

The free-standing tomb seems a form largely reserved for saints, and the monumental sculpted tomb was a particularly Dominican preference. So it is interesting to reflect upon the *arca* in relation to the promotion of saints in the new religious orders with recently-deceased founders, and it is perhaps no coincidence that these programs emerged in the wake of the controversy with the secular clergy. The Franciscans, like the Benedictines before them (at Subiaco), preferred large-scale fresco narratives. Even though the first cycle of the early 1260s in the lower church of Assisi is badly damaged, the basic outlines of the ideological program promoting the cult of Francis were clearly already well-established. Prominent among them was the concept of Francis as *alter Christus*, a theme played out in the broadly-paced parallel scenes down the length of the lower basilica.[90]

The *Arca* of San Domenico was begun in 1264, about the same time as the Assisi frescoes, and it seems probable that the impulse to commemorate founders in the Assisi lower church and the new monument of Bologna may be related.[91] The sarcophagus for Dominic was carved in the round and supported by caryatid figures of virtues, in imitation of classical atlantids. The virtues of the Bologna tomb raised the tomb chest to unprecedented heights (they are almost one meter high), so that it could become the visual focus for pilgrims down the length of the crowded church, who, moving forward, could also touch its base (this is evoked in the image of the tomb of Peter Martyr in the Spanish chapel at Sta. Maria Novella, for example).

Why do the Dominicans seem to prefer sculpted commemorations of their founding saints? The first and most obvious thing, of course, was the desire to ostentatiously display the bodies of Dominic and Peter Martyr, which needed to be simultaneously commemorated, contained, protected, and exalted. The reader will recall that once the new Basilica di San Francesco was sufficiently complete, Francis' body had been interred in a tomb well below the altar of the lower church, where it still remains.[92] As a result, there was no visible "body" of Francis to enshrine in a monumental tomb. By contrast, the model of the ancient historiated sarcophagus served the needs of the Dominicans because it exalted the on-going active presence of the saint in the church. In addition, the sculpted tomb evoked late antique and early Christian sarcophagi, thereby conveying the idea of *renovatio*, a concept key to the Dominican reform. The *arca* as a form was both more traditional and, at the same time, affirmed the tangible presence of the saint in the church.

On the other hand, fresco painting, developed so prominently in Franciscan contexts, had a more powerful narrative structure as well as a popularizing quality; large-scale painted cycles could "surround" the pilgrim and serve as a mirror of perfection and as a point of reference for the religious community and pilgrims.[93] In contrast, the program of the Dominican *Arca* conferred upon the remains of the saint the grandeur and majesty of ancient monuments; it "competed" with or perhaps even challenged a specifically Christian model of virtue as against the "deeds of tyrants sculpted on arches, columns, and gateways," as Bishop Bartolomeo of Vicenza noted in the sermon of 1267 that inaugurated the new tomb.[94]

The double-sided tomb monument associated with

89. For the significance of Reginald's conversion, see Mulchahey, pp. 29–31.

90. Chiara Frugoni, *Francesco e l'invenzione delle stimmate* (Turin, 1993), 105–136.

91. Moskowitz, 1992, p. 274. Barbara Dodsworth, "Dominican Patronage and the Arca of San Domenico," in *Verrochio and Late Quattrocento Italian Sculpture*, ed. S. Bule, A. P. Darr, and F. S. Gioffredi (Florence, 1992), 284, also suggests an environment of competition between the Dominicans and Franciscans.

92. Most recently, Donal Cooper, "'*In loco tutissimo et firmissimo*': The Tomb of St. Francis in History, Legend, and Art, in *The Art of the Franciscan Order in Italy*, ed. William R. Cook (Leiden, Boston, 2005), 1–39.

93. D. Rigaut, "Ordini monastici e mendicanti," in *Enciclopedia dell'Arte Medievale*, VIII (1997), 826.

94. Moskowitz suggests that the "tyrant" and the "sculpted arches" in this text may refer to Frederick II and the Capuan Gate (1992, p. 277). As she notes, Prince Enzo was a prisoner in Bologna

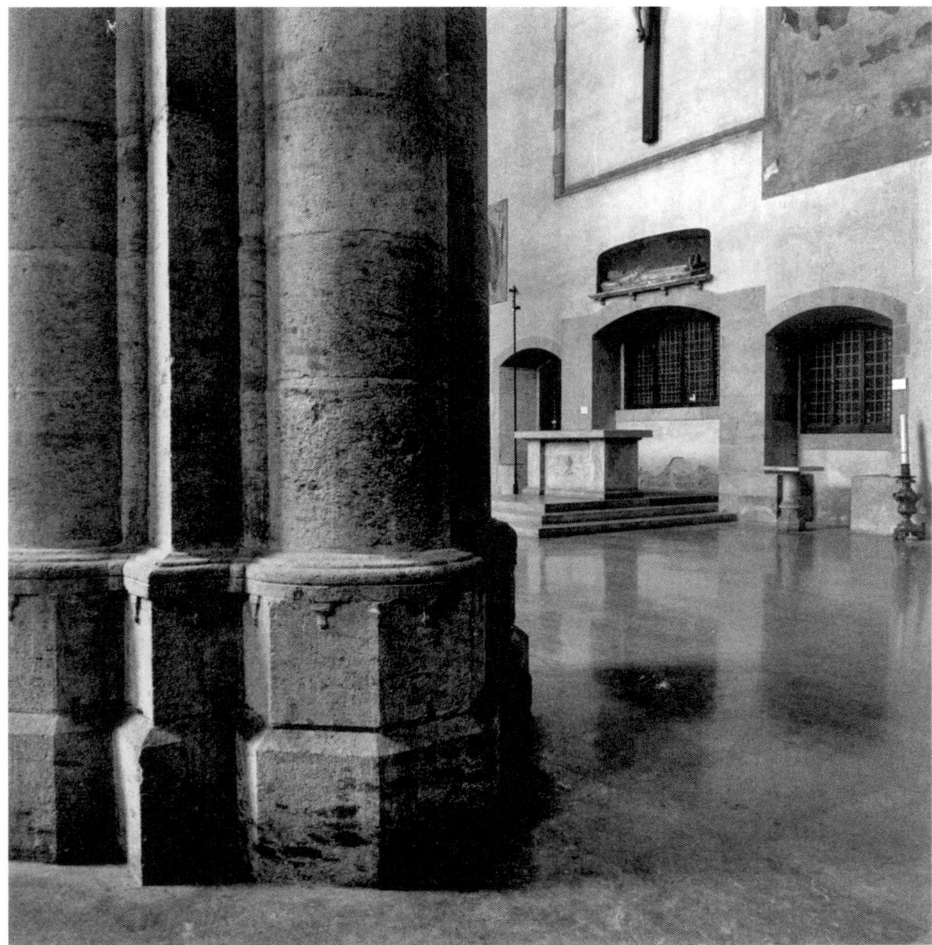

FIGURE 6. Sta. Chiara, Naples, nuns' choir, with the effigy of Robert the Wise (photo: Massimo Velo).

the divided interior spaces of mendicant architecture is in effect a "bilingual" monument that could address two hierarchical groups.[95] A variation of this concept was used in two prominent royal tombs in the Clarissan churches of Sta. Chiara and Sta. Croce (now destroyed) of Naples,[96] both of which had strictly enclosed communities of religious women and were founded by Queen Sancia of Mallorca. The tombs of Robert the Wise and Sancia were incorporated in each church into the dividing walls between the enclosed choir and the altar area, so that they faced the two audiences (monastic and public), as well as the main altar in front of the tombs. Tomb and consecrated host were at the spatial "hinge" of the main altar (Fig. 6).

The tomb of Robert the Wise (d. 1343) in the nuns' choir at Sta. Chiara has a simple niche with a second effigy of the King (Fig. 7), a "dislocated" version of a double-sided sarcophagus. Although the second effigy has often been described as a first provisional monument made for the King while his "primary" tomb by

---

until his death in 1271, and Bologna was a stoutly anti-imperial city. This author also notes that perhaps the tomb was actually inspired by pulpits (Moskowitz, 1992, p. 280), which I find less convincing.

95. Moskowitz, 2001, pp. 32–33.

96. On these tombs, see Tanja Michalsky, *Memoria und Repräsentation. Die Grabmäler des Könighauses Anjou in Italien* (Göttingen, 2000), 149–152, 169–171, and 342–345; Lorenz Enderlein, *Die Grablegen des Hauses Anjou in Unteritalien. Totenkult und Monumente 1266–1343* (Worms am Rhein, 1997), 35–38, 49–53, 65–71, 101–105, 115–118, and 125–130, 137–139, 141–143, 150–153, and 167–188.

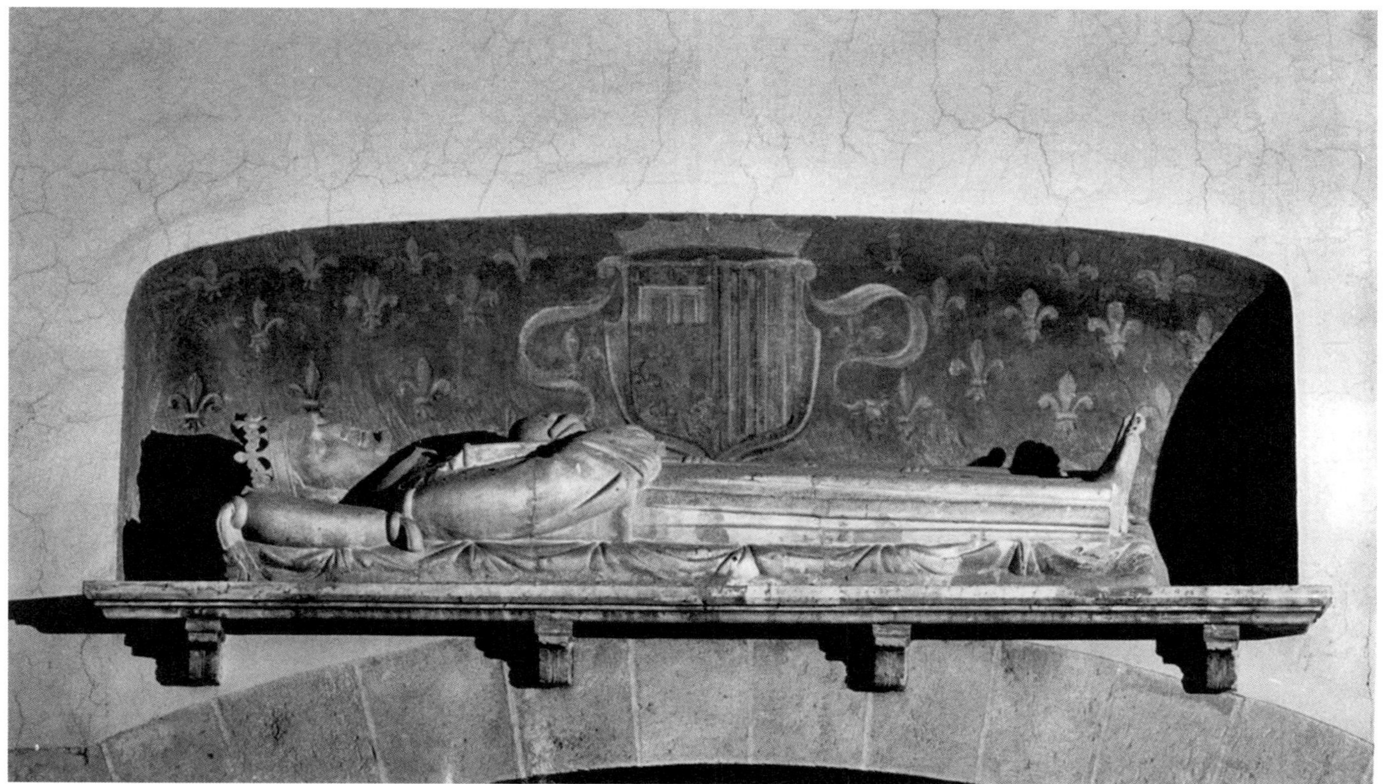

FIGURE 7. Sta. Chiara, Naples, detail of the effigy of Robert the Wise (photo: Massimo Velo).

Giovanni and Paccio Bertini was being carved, it is far more likely that the single recumbent figure of the King dressed in Franciscan habit was intended to evoke and receive intercessory prayers from the nuns in *clausura*: it was intended from the start as an effigy for the Clarissan community.

The tomb of Sancia of Mallorca at her later foundation of Sta. Croce survives only in drawings by Seroux D'Agincourt (Fig. 8), and is clearly a more austere and completely-resolved double-faced tomb.[97] On the public side, the Queen is flanked by members of the first and second orders; on the other, she presides at a sort of "last supper" flanked by Clarissan nuns.

In both of the Clarissan convents, the nuns worshiped in a choir on axis behind the main altar, so that they had a direct and privileged view of the Mass through the grating below the tombs;[98] as noted above, the images of the two rulers were both visually and physically associated with the Eucharist. In some measure, both were "passage tombs," not in the literal sense of physical movement, but rather in the metaphorical and spiritual sense of movement via the Eucharist from the world of the living to the enclosed community of prayer beyond.[99] The concepts of these Neapolitan tombs were therefore intimately associated with the architectural character of the divided space.

The concept of the "passage tomb" for sarcophagi carved in the round was coined by Julian Gardner for

97. See Francesco Aceto, "Tino di Camaino a Napoli: una proposta per il sepolcro di Caterina d'Austria e altri fatti angioni," *Dialoghi di Storia dell'Arte* I (1995), 10–27.

98. Caroline Bruzelius, "Hearing is Believing: Clarissan Architecture, 1212–1340," *Gesta* 31 (1992), 83–92; and Bruzelius, "Nuns in Space: Strict Enclosure and the Architecture of the Clarisses in the Thirteenth Century," in *Clare of Assisi: A Medieval and Modern Woman*, ed. Ingrid Peterson (St. Bonaventure, N.Y., 1996), 41–62.

99. Julian Gardner, "A Princess among Prelates: A Fourteenth-Century Neapolitan Tomb and Some Northern Relations," *Römisches Jahrbuch für Kunstgeschichte* 23–24 (1988), 31–60.

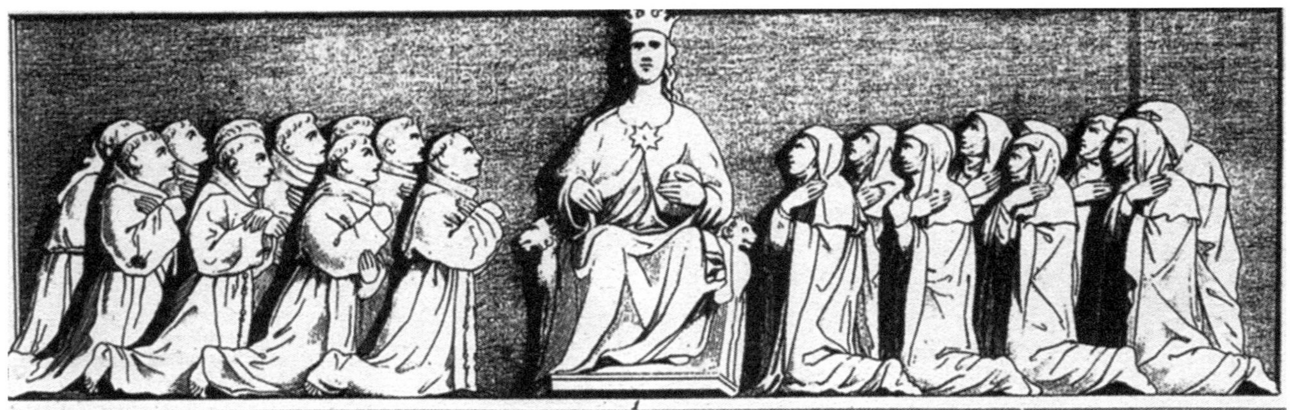

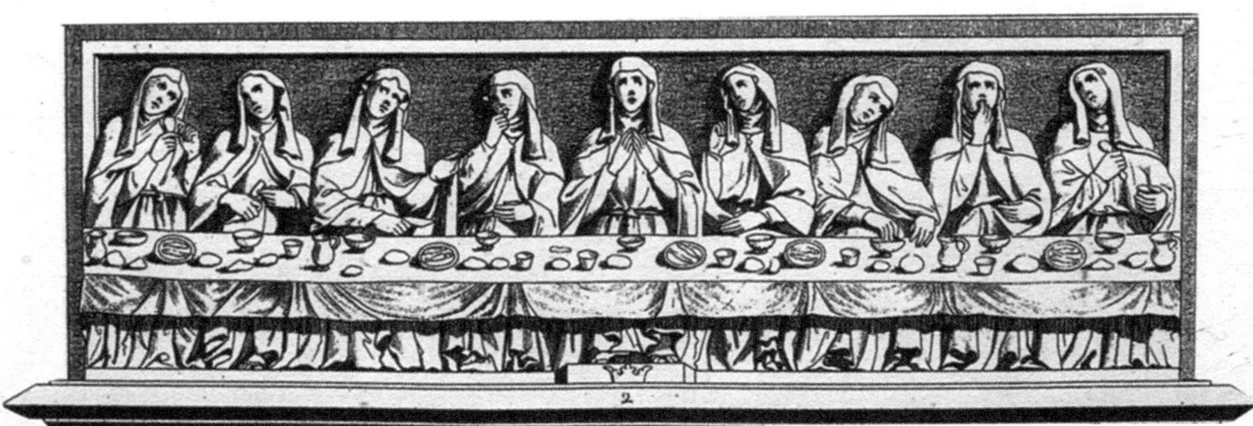

FIGURE 8. Seroux D'Agincourt, the tomb of Sancia of Mallorca at Sta. Croce, Naples.

the fascinating and enigmatic monument of Catherine of Austria (d. 15 January, 1323) at San Lorenzo Maggiore in Naples (Fig. 9).[100] This striking tomb is placed between two compound piers on the last bay of the south side of the chevet. As is well known, the tomb presents numerous anomalies, however: it is visibly squeezed and adjusted to fit into its present location, with the bases of the four saints that stand beside the effigy projecting off the top and the base is indented to fit between the shafts of the compound piers.[101] A comparison with Tino di Camaino's contemporary monument for Mary of Hungary (d. March 25, 1323), suggests the extent of the contraction of forms in the tomb of Catherine.[102] It is unlikely that Tino di Camaino, who had just arrived in Naples to begin a major new phase of his career in service of the Angevin court, would have willingly executed a tomb as awkwardly placed and designed as Catherine's, a project that Francesco Aceto described as "un tentativo quasi disperato" to create a harmonious monument within tight physical constraints.[103]

100. Francesco Aceto, "Tino di Camaino a Napoli. Una proposta per il sepolcro di Caterina d'Austria e altri fatti angioini," *Dialoghi* 1 (1995), 11–26, and more recently Aceto, "Le memorie angioine in San Lorenzo Maggiore," in *La chiese di San Lorenzo e San Domenico. Gli ordini Mendicanti a Napoli*, Atti della giornata di Studio su Napoli, Losanna, 13 dicembre 2001, ed. S. Romano and N. Bock (Naples, 2005), 67–94, esp. 84–88.

101. Aceto, 1995, pp. 11–12, and 2005, pp. 85–87, discusses the peculiar qualities of the tomb.

102. Marbles for the tomb were commissioned from Rome by Robert the Wise in February 1325, and payment of 154 *once* was made to Gagliardo Primario and Tino on 31 March 1326. See Aceto, 1995, p. 14.

103. As Aceto, 1995, p. 12, notes, the perplexity provoked by this tomb has been such that various art historians, among them De Rinaldis, suggested that it could not have been executed by Tino di Camaino.

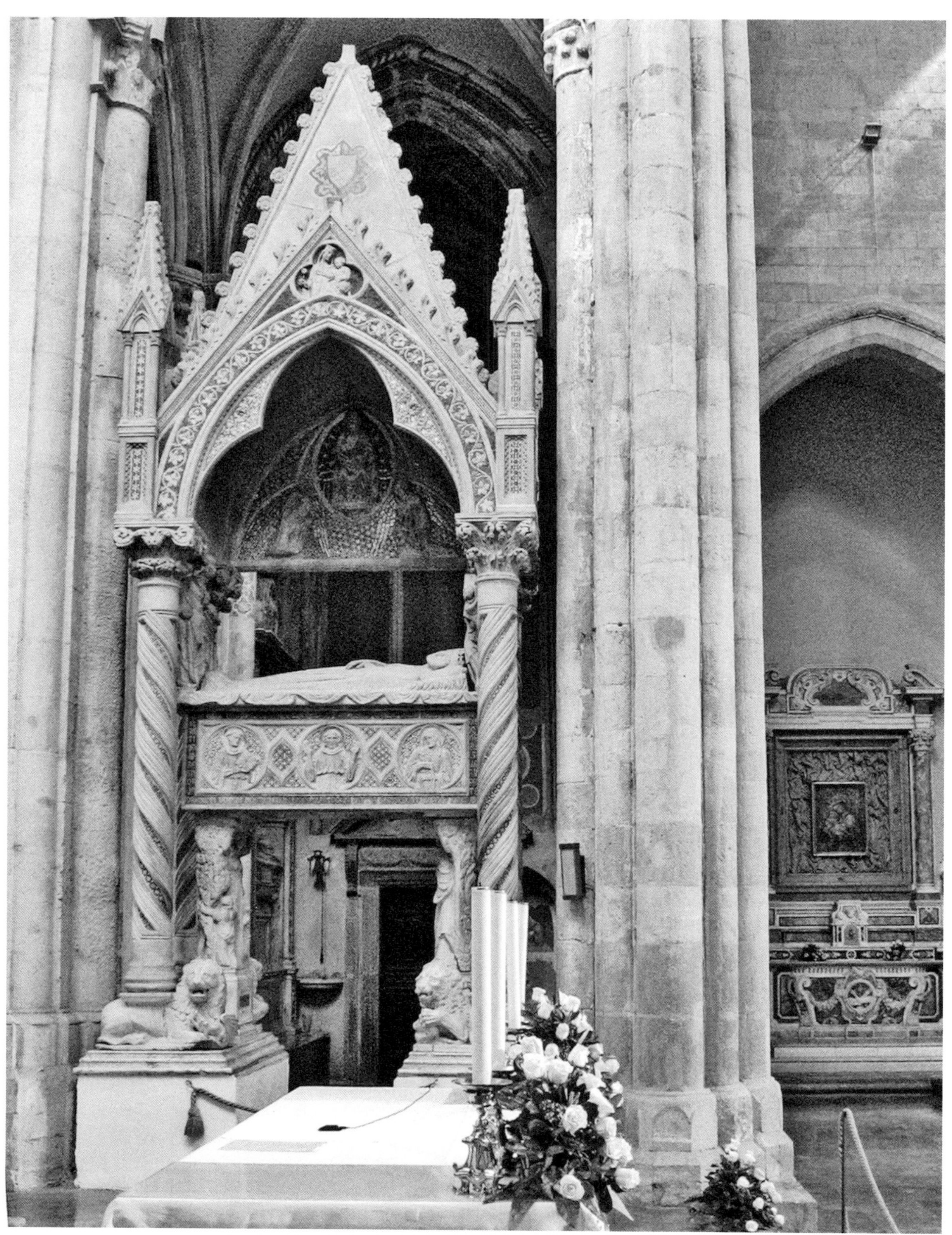

FIGURE 9. Tino di Camaino, tomb of Catherine of Austria, d. 1323. (photo: Peter Goltra).

As previously noted, free-standing and double-sided tombs were exceptional monuments usually associated with the cult of saints (Dominic and Peter Martyr). Catherine's tomb has therefore been explained as a "transalpine tradition," i.e., an element of "Frenchness" introduced by the Angevin régime.[104] But Aceto has now proposed a radically different narrative, one that suggests that the structure was originally intended as a wall-tomb in the south transept arm and reconceived and re-sculpted for its present location. As I have shown in my book on Naples, the interior of San Lorenzo underwent radical change shortly after Catherine of Austria's death in 1323, a project perhaps in part funded by her donations.[105] When Catherine's tomb was first commissioned, the church had double aisles in the area of the transept (the foundations of the piers are visible under the pavement), and the bays on the south side formed a necropolis for members of the royal family, in particular the tomb of Robert's son Louis and his brother, Raymond Berengar. This was a prized zone for burial near the passage of the friars from the cloister to the choir.[106] The royal tombs of the princes were destroyed long ago, but perhaps the surviving fragments of frescoes by Montano d'Arezzo on the east and west walls of this area attest to royal patronage and may possibly have been part of the monuments.[107] Aceto and I believe that Catherine's tomb was originally intended and partially carved as a wall-tomb for this area of the (now destroyed) double aisles.

The princess left a substantial bequest to San Lorenzo in her will.[108] Later the same year, another "big death," that of Giovanni di Capua (d. Dec. 12, 1323), grandson of the great *Protonotario* and *Logoteta* of the realm, Bartolomeo di Capua, stimulated the construction of a family chapel in the Franciscan church.[109] The decision in 1324 to reconfigure the church by extending it to the west (Fig. 10), absorbing the old porch and a free-standing tower on the south, made possible the construction of multiple Di Capua chapels on this side.[110]

The tomb of Catherine was thus originally conceived and partially carved as a wall-tomb in the area of the (now missing) double aisles on the south side. With the reconfiguration of the interior, which began a year or so later, the tomb was redesigned for its new location to the right of the main altar. What had been a wall-tomb became a free-standing "passage tomb," incorporating already-completed bits and adding new ones probably executed by (perhaps a slightly cross) Tino himself, in order to adjust the partially completed tomb to the new architectural context. The standing saints intended for the back of the tomb against the wall were flipped to the ends of the top slab, and hang out over the edge. These modifications were most likely Tino's, so this work was probably accomplished before the artist's death around 1337. If this is the case, the modifications to the interior of the church may also have been roughly complete by that time.

The odd squeezed shape of Catherine's tomb, which has led scholars in the past to doubt its attribution to Tino di Camaino, can now be understood as a response to changes to the church in which it is located, interventions that took place while the tomb was being prepared. The monument therefore exists in a dialectic with the transformed space, and the sculptor was forced to squeeze and severely contract his original composition between the two columns of the apse.

104. Reference is often made to the tomb of Dagobert at St.-Denis, for example in Michalsky, p. 116; I am not persuaded.

105. See Bruzelius, 2004, pp. 63–73.

106. Michalsky, pp. 268–277.

107. San Lorenzo was badly damaged by several earthquakes, one in 1349 and another in 1456.

108. Enderlein, pp. 76–81. See also his discussion of Tino di Camaino, pp. 82–89.

109. The fragments of his tomb are discussed by Francesco Aceto: "Per l'attività di Tino di Camaino a Napoli: le tombe di Giovanni di Capua e di Orso Minutolo," *Prospettiva*, 53–56 (1988), 134–142, esp. 135–139.

110. Around this time, the old basilica was demolished and moved to the side walls between the chapels to create the vast interior space we see today. In this process, the nave columns were moved to between the chapels on the side walls, where the responds were re-cut to absorb them. The columns and their ancient capitals, in turn, supported a second arch over each chapel to thicken the upper walls and create the more substantial structure for the vast single nave building. See Bruzelius, 2004, pp. 65–67. The Di Capua chapels were abandoned in 1539 when Pietro Antonio di Capua, Duke of Termoli, restored the *jus patronatus* to the friars of San Lorenzo.

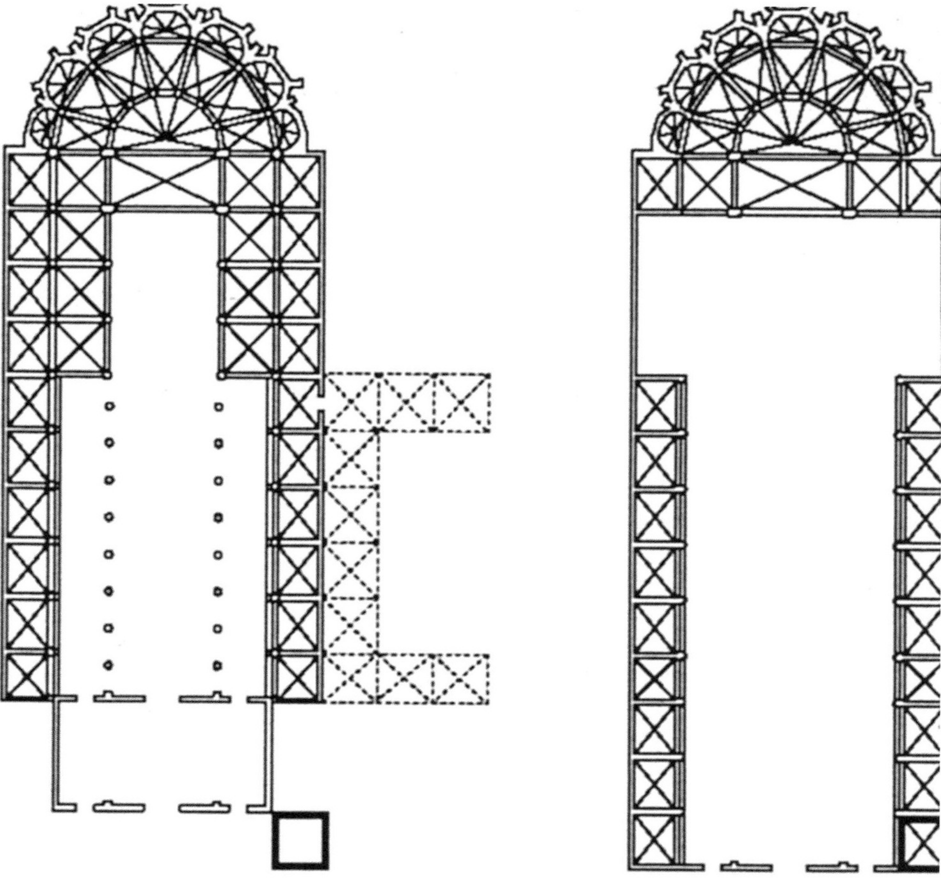

FIGURE 10. San Lorenzo, schematic plans of the church with extensions and additions of chapels (author).

The tomb of Catherine of Austria reminds us that monuments must be considered in relation to (the often complicated history of) a site. It is striking that these changes and compromises occurred in spite of the prominence of the patron, the artist, and the setting.

The study of this tomb is also a reminder of the importance of collaborative and interdisciplinary research in understanding medieval art. Although scholarship in our fields tends to be the work of individuals working alone, along the lines of the "Lone Ranger" model, this practice often constrains our understanding of the monument and its site. Works of art are no more "islands" than are we ourselves, and the stories that large-scale medieval sculpture can tell us may be best expressed within the broad frame of the larger architectural or urban setting.

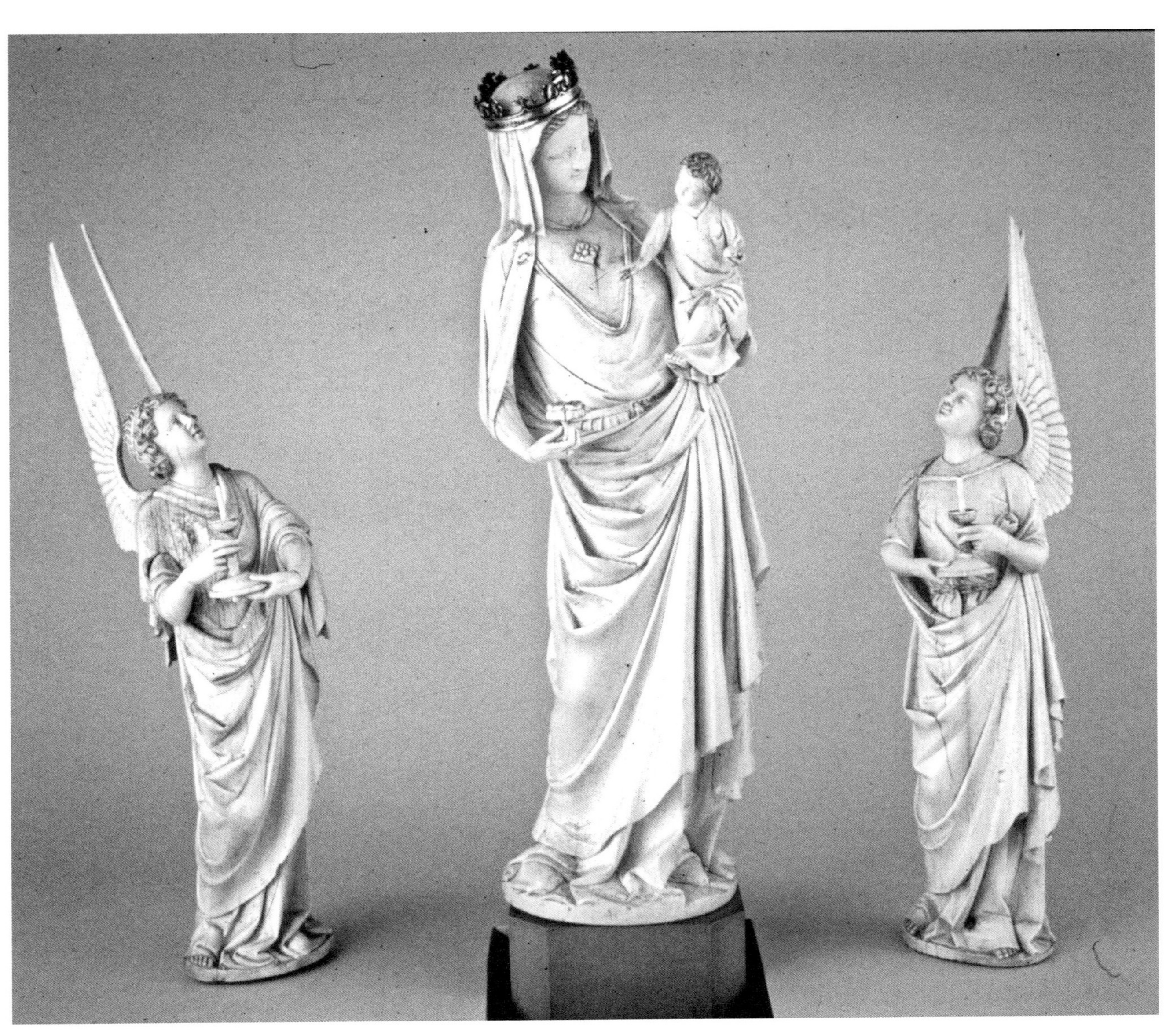

FIGURE 1. Virgin and Child with Angels from the treasury of St.-Denis (H.: 34, 8, and 25 cm.), Paris, *c.* 1250–1270 (Cincinnati, Taft Museum and Rouen Cathedral).

DANIELLE GABORIT-CHOPIN

Gothic Ivories: Realities and Prospects

IN THE history of Gothic art, ivory carving forms an important chapter, even if its place is sometimes insignificant—in relative scope—in most of the general books dealing with the period. Sculpture in ivory developed consistently from the beginning of the thirteenth to the end of the fifteenth century; and this period is remarkable for the diversity of its works, their number, scale, and artistic quality. During the thirteenth century, statuettes in the round appeared—mainly of the Virgin and Child, some of a surprisingly large scale, such as the Virgin in the Musée des Beaux-Arts de Caen, which is more than forty centimeters high, or the Virgin of the Musée national du Moyen Âge, which is more than fifty centimeters in height.[1] In these works, the Virgin is either standing or sitting on a throne. Groups of statuettes that may originally have been set in architectural displays are also found. These include the Virgin and angels mentioned in the inventories of the treasury of the abbey of St.-Denis (the Virgin is now in Cincinnati, Taft Museum, and the angels are in the treasury of Rouen Cathedral) (Fig. 1).[2] A number of ivory *figures d'applique*, tabernacles, triptychs and diptychs, crosiers, etc., are also found in this period, as well as secular objects, including caskets, mirror cases, handles for knives, writing tablets, combs, and so on, which are some of the most attractive works of the whole Gothic period.

Ivory comes from the elephant's tusks, and the fact that all these works were carved in that material supposes that a large amount of this precious raw material was available. Paris is recognized as the main center of production. However, we still don't understand the journey or routes that the tusks made from Africa or Asia to Paris and to other western centers. Neither do we fully understand how the craft was organized.

Raymond Koechlin

The fundamental work on Gothic ivories is the volumes written by Raymond Koechlin (Fig. 2), which were published in 1924.[3] This corpus in many ways stopped all research on this subject until 1970. Even today, the first question posed by anyone studying or looking at an ivory is to enquire whether it is mentioned in Koechlin, and if not, why not?

Raymond Koechlin (1860–1931) was born into a wealthy family from Alsace, but was based in Paris from 1870. He was a collector of impressionist paintings, an expert on Japanese art, and was president of the Union des arts décoratifs and of the Amis du Louvre. It was during the Universal Exhibition of 1900 that he first became attracted to Gothic ivories, at which stage he began to gather documents and photographs of such works.[4] It is interesting and unusual that he himself made the photographs for his research and publications. He collected around 2,000 negatives covering public and private collections throughout Europe.

His publication of *Les ivoires gothiques français* is in three volumes. The first of these encompasses his text: his methodology and categorization of various work-

1. R. Koechlin, *Les ivoires gothiques Français*, 3 vols. (Paris, 1924), vol. II, no. 67, pl. XXV (H.: 42 cm.). V. Huchard, *Images in Ivory: Precious Objects of the Gothic Age*, Exhib. Cat., The Detroit Institute of Arts and The Walters Art Gallery, Baltimore, 1997–1998 (Detroit, 1997), no. 4 (H.: 52 cm.).

2. *Le trésor de Saint-Denis*, Exhib. Cat., Musée du Louvre (Paris, 1991), nos. 45–46, pp. 231–237.

3. See note 1.

4. P. Alfassa, *Raymond Koechlin. Notice lue à l'assemblée générale des Amis du Louvre le 30 avril 1932* (Compiègne, 1932), 20.

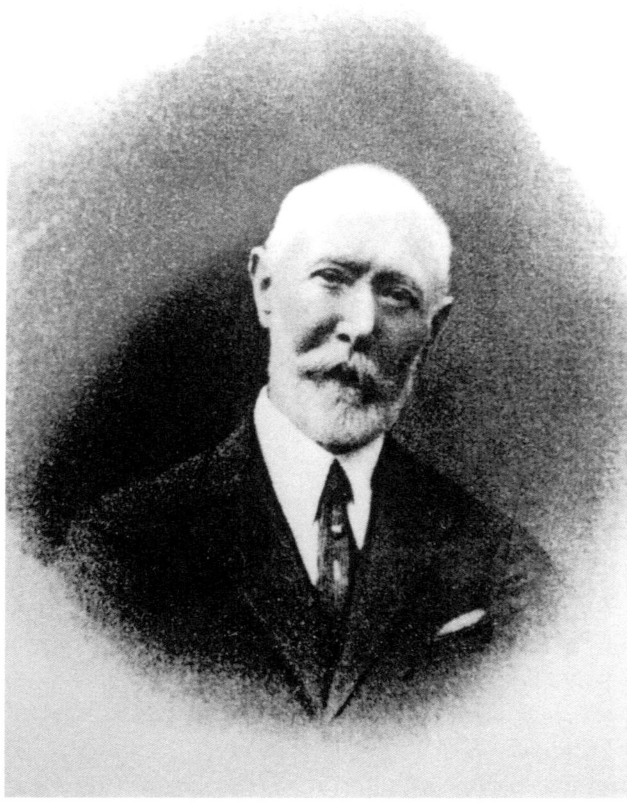

FIGURE 2. Raymond Koechlin (1860–1931). Author of *Les ivoires gothiques français*, Paris, 3 vols., 1924.

shops, as well as supporting archival documentation. The second volume is a catalogue of 1,328 entries, in which the ivories are classified into groups or large workshops. The third volume is devoted to the illustrations, most of them from Koechlin's own photographs. This work, remarkably comprehensive for the beginning of the twentieth century, has exercised a major influence. Since this pivotal study, many Gothic ivories have been discovered, published, and reconsidered, and the Courtauld Institute, London, is developing a new electronic version of Koechlin's original work that collates new additions and new research.

Despite these early and continuing initiatives, the fundamental question for scholars is still to see what avenues of research remain in the whole field of Gothic ivories and how such work can be undertaken. In his work, Koechlin asserted that he intended to "file the monuments logically, in regard to their degree of mannerism."[5] He was slightly obsessed by the necessity to impose order on the corpus and was determined to develop a linear structure that showed stylistic evolution. He despised mannerism. This may explain, for example, why he thought the ivory Virgin of the Sainte-Chapelle in Paris (Musée du Louvre, Fig. 3) to be too elegant and too gracious, "trop maniérée," to be a work of what he calls the "pure Gothic" of the second half of the thirteenth century.[6] He decided, because of its "mannerism," that the Virgin had to be dated later, to *circa* 1300.

Thanks to the decisive publication of *French Gothic Sculpture* by Willibald Sauerländer in 1970, we were able to get a new and clearer idea of the whole chronology of French Gothic art, and we now believe that the Virgin in the Louvre is the one mentioned in the inventory of the treasury (the "memorial") of the Sainte-Chapelle in Paris, dating to before 1279, and that in fact it was carved some years before.[7] Thus it is that a large part of the chronology suggested by Koechlin needs be reconsidered. In much the same way, Koechlin defined various "workshops," such as the "tabernacles" workshop, the "series of arcades" workshop (regarding diptychs), the workshop "with bands of rosettes," the workshop "with Passion scenes," and so on—all of which were based on the typology and/or iconography of the ivories more than on stylistic aspects. It is now clear that in reality many Gothic ivories do not fit easily into such definitions and that the rules are rather too restrictive.

This is why some years ago books and articles (most of them referenced in the exhibition catalogue *Images in Ivory* [Detroit and Baltimore, 1997])[8] began to

5. M. Tomasi, "Remarques sur la méthode et les intérêts de Raymond Koechlin, historien de l'art," *Histoire de L'Art* 58 (2006), 133–159.

6. Koechlin, *Les ivoires gothiques* (as in note 1), vol. I, pp. 104–105, vol. II, no. 95, pl. XXXI: "Nous aurions plus de peine à reconnaître en elle, vu son style, celle du Mémorial de 1265–79" ... "fin XIIIe ou commencement XIVe."

7. D. Gaborit-Chopin, "La Vierge à l'Enfant d'ivoire de la Sainte-Chapelle," *Bulletin Monumental* 130 (1972), 215–224. D. Gaborit-Chopin, *Ivoires médiévaux. V^e–XVe siècle*, Exhib. Cat., Musée du Louvre (Paris, 2003), no. 100 (with bibliography).

8. See *Images in Ivory* (as in note 1): essays by P. Barnet ("Gothic Sculpture in Ivory: An Introduction"), E. Sears ("Ivory and Ivory Workers in Medieval Paris"), P. Williamson ("Symbiosis across

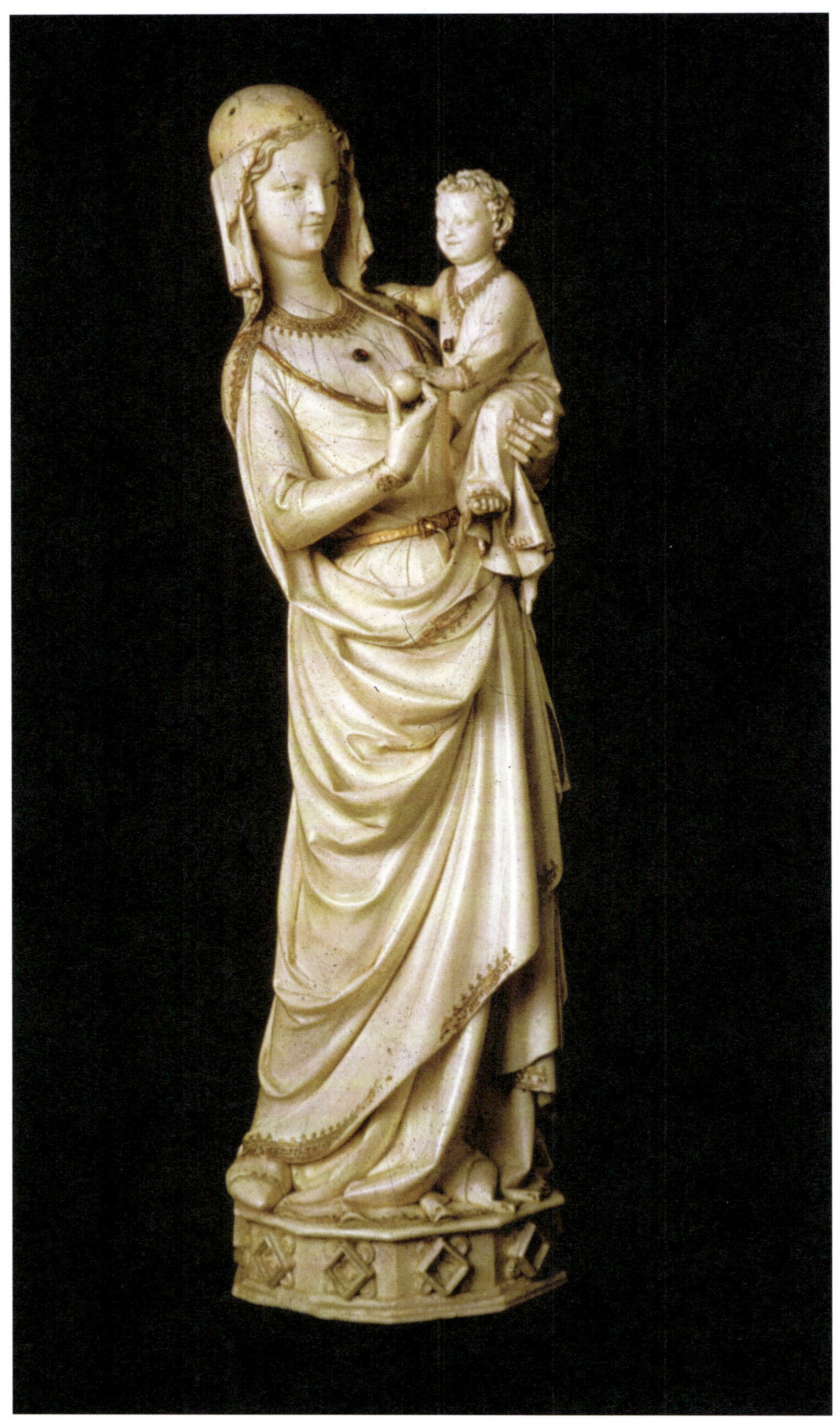

FIGURE 3. Virgin and Child from the treasury of the Sainte-Chapelle, Paris, *c.* 1260–1275 (Paris, Musée du Louvre).

reconsider Koechlin's contribution and to question both his methods and some of his conclusions. New research has focused on different aspects of the medium, involving interpretation of documentary sources and establishing connections between ivory and monumental sculpture, painting, and goldsmith work. It also includes re-examination of the use of polychromy in ivory and the raw material itself as well as the nature of workshops both in Paris, wider France, and elsewhere, and identification of new workshops. The field of secular ivories has also received considerable attention, as has the problem of forgeries and imitations. These are the subjects I should like to address in this paper.

Documents

Most of the documentary sources for French Gothic ivories were published by Koechlin, but the difficulty lies in their interpretation. Ivory carving in Paris is referred to in Étienne Boileau's *Livre des métiers*, written around the middle of the thirteenth century.[9] But the word "yvoirier" (meaning ivory carver) appears only in 1332, when Jean le Scelleur provided the countess Mahaut d'Artois with precious objects, not only ivories.[10]

We know that Parisian workshops that were allowed to carve ivory were located near the church St.-Germain l'Auxerrois, in the streets around the rue St.-Denis, the cloister Ste.-Opportune, and in the street of the Tabletterie. But the organization of the work, the relationship between different workshops, and the management of the stock of raw material are all still unknown. For the thirteenth century, the *Livre des métiers* lists the names of corporations that were allowed to carve ivory, as well as horn, bone, and wood. These made knife handles, rosaries, dice, combs, tablets, lanterns, and so forth, and they are also the "sculpteurs tailleurs d'ymages" that carved statues, crucifixes, handles for knives, etc., and the "paintres et ymagiers" who were painters and carvers of statues, workers in wood, stone, and ivory, and who accomplished every kind of painting.

Connection with Monumental Sculpture & Painting

It is evident, therefore, that Gothic ivories have to be studied in relation to monumental sculpture and painting. The links with sculpture, however, do not mean that we have "a small version of a monumental statue"; rather, that the ivory carver had to take into account the qualities and distinctive features of this precious material.

If we look once again at the Virgin of the Sainte-Chapelle, it is possible to see that this ivory is indeed related to monumental sculpture, such as the Virgin of the north portal of Notre-Dame de Paris, or the Virgin of St.-Amand-les-Pas.[11] But an even greater and more striking resemblance is found in a wooden statue, the Virgin of Wargnies (Paris, Musée du Louvre), where the technique of wood carving is closer to ivory carving than that of stone. Several other ivory Virgins, such as the one in the Rijksmuseum, Amsterdam, offer the same evidence. So, a similar date for this group of ivory statuettes of around 1260–1270 would appear to be justified, and perhaps can even be attributed to the same workshop, as suggested by Françoise Baron.[12]

Yet a comparison with monumental sculpture is not entirely conclusive. The Angel of the Annunciation in the Louvre (Fig. 4) is one of the most beautiful of Gothic ivories, but its date has been much debated. Charles Little related the Annunciation to a carving in Reims Cathedral, a figure of a deacon on the west portal, and dated it to around 1230–1240.[13] My publication

---

Scale: Gothic Ivory and Sculpture in Stone and Wood in the Thirteenth Century"), D. Gaborit-Chopin ("The Polychrome Decoration of Gothic Ivories"), R. H. Randall ("Popular Romance Carved in Ivory"), Charles T. Little ("Gothic Ivory Carving in Germany"), and H. Stahl ("Narrative Structure and Content in Some Gothic Ivories of the Life of Christ").

9. Étienne Boileau, *Le Livre des Métiers*, ed. R. de Lespinasse and F. Bonnardot (Paris, 1879). See also E. Sears, "Ivory and Ivory Workers in Medieval Paris" (as in note 7).

10. D. Gaborit-Chopin, in *L'art au temps des rois maudits. Philippe le Bel et ses fils 1284–1328*, Exhib. Cat., Paris, Grand-Palais (Paris, 1998), 139–140.

11. Fr. Baron, in *L'art au temps des rois maudits* (as in note 10), no. 15.

12. Fr. Baron, in *L'art au temps des rois maudits* (as in note 10), no. 18.

13. Charles T. Little, "Ivoires et Art Gothique," *Revue de l'Art* 46 (1979), 60, figs. 6, 7.

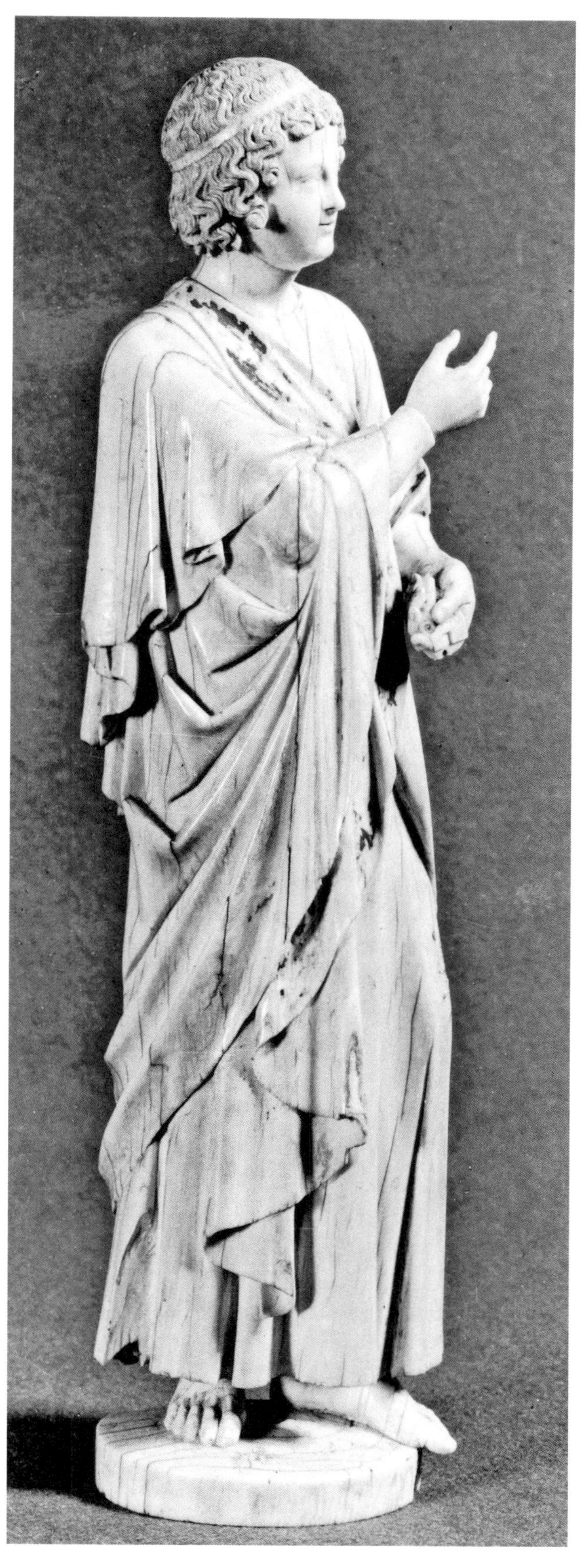

FIGURE 4. Angel of the Annunciation, Paris, *c*. 1240, or 1250–1260, or 1300? (Paris, Musée du Louvre).

in 1978 related this figure to carvings from around 1300, such as the tomb of the infant King John I, which comes from the time of Philip IV.[14] Paul Williamson, basing his theory on the new chronology proposed for Reims Cathedral, came to a compromise when he suggested a date of 1250–1260.[15] Yet, which proposal establishes the true date?

As the *Livre des métiers* indicates that "painters and carvers of statues" were amongst those allowed to carve ivory, this shows a connection between ivories and painting, above all manuscript illumination. Carvers of ivory diptychs and triptychs were certainly inspired by sketched or painted models. Koechlin identified a large atelier that he called the "workshop of the Passion Diptychs," whose work was characterized by a multitude of Passion scenes. Several fourteenth-century workshops, are, in fact, characterized by the use of this complex iconography, which also appears in such monumental sculpture as the example on the Portal de la Calende at Rouen Cathedral at the end of the thirteenth century. It is also found on ivories of the second half of the thirteenth and beginning of the fourteenth centuries (the "Soissons Diptych," or the St.-Sulpice du Tarn Triptych, for instance).

One of these workshops was studied by Richard Randall in an article based on the Minneapolis Diptych (Fig. 5).[16] Randall suggested dating this workshop to the last decades of the fourteenth century and based his arguments on the iconography. He distinguished two sequences produced in this workshop: the first with only Passion scenes, and the second, which included the Minneapolis Diptych, with Infancy as well as Passion scenes, which he dated to around 1380–1400.

Nevertheless, this date may be problematic. There is, in the Louvre, a small diptych that has images of the Ascension and the Pentecost, and that certainly came from the same workshop as the Minneapolis Ivory, which depicts similar scenes. The Louvre diptych is mentioned in an inventory of the treasury of the French king, Charles V, which dates before 1380. Stylistically, the Minneapolis Diptych appears to be of the same date.[17]

There is yet another diptych with Passion and Infancy scenes set within quatrefoils, also found in the Louvre.[18] This is a product of the same workshop, which is borne out when the same scenes, such as the Arrest of Christ, are compared (Fig. 6). The style of the figures, with their gestures and drapery, and the use of quatrefoils, are strikingly similar to the illuminations of the Petites Heures de Jean de Berry (Fig. 7), which were painted by Jean le Noir in 1375.[19] All of these works are part of the court circle of Charles V, and date to around 1360–1380.

Polychrome

The relationship between ivory carvers and painters is surely confirmed when the actual polychrome of the ivories is considered, a field not considered by Koechlin. Sometimes, scenes are directly painted onto ivory. Then, the problem is to decide if the painting was applied when the ivory was carved, or added later and perhaps even in another center. For example, the style of the painted scenes in a devotional booklet in the Victoria and Albert Museum confirms that it was indeed undertaken in a German workshop (Cologne, *c.* 1330–1340).[20]

The triptych in Lyon's Musée des Beaux-Arts is less clear. The central panel is attributed to the "group of the Soissons Diptych," probably from Paris or northern France in the last third of thirteenth century. But the painted scenes on the wings which are simpler and more sketchy in style, appear to be related to manuscript illumination of the north of France or Belgium (Fig. 8). Even if this triptych's painting and carving are of the same time and workshop (which seems possible), we

14. D. Gaborit-Chopin, *Ivoires du Moyen Âge occidental* (Fribourg, 1978), 146–147, fig. 217. Gaborit-Chopin, *Ivoires médiévaux* (as in note 7), no. 120.

15. P. Williamson, "Gothic Ivories in Detroit and Baltimore," *Apollo* (March 1997), 48–50.

16. R. H. Randall, "An Ivory Diptych," *The Minneapolis Institute of Arts Bulletin* (1991), 2–17.

17. Gaborit-Chopin, *Ivoires médiévaux* (as in note 7), no. 200.

18. Gaborit-Chopin, *Ivoires médiévaux* (as in note 7), no. 201.

19. Paris, BnF, MS. Lat. 18014. Jean le Noir worked in Paris between 1335 and 1380. See Charles Sterling, *La peinture médiévale à Paris, 1300–1500* (Paris, 1987), vol. 1, pp. 122–127, mainly figs. 125–127.

20. P. Williamson, in *Images in Ivory* (as in note 1), no. 40.

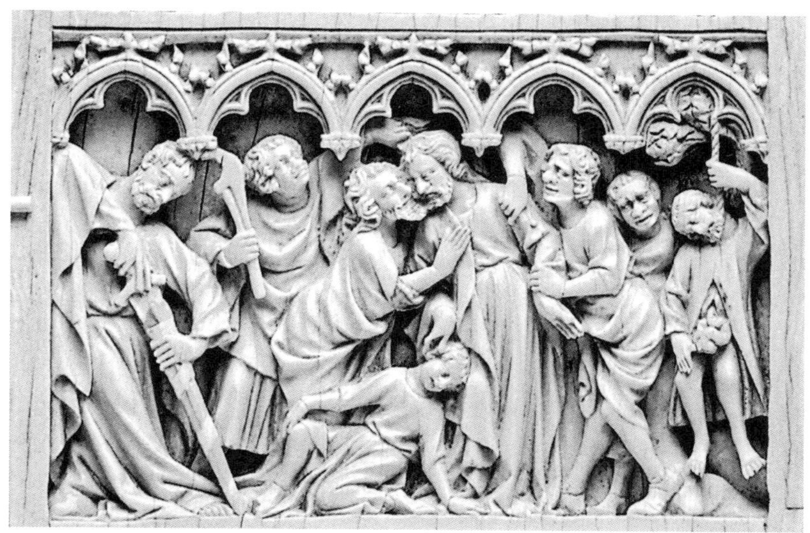

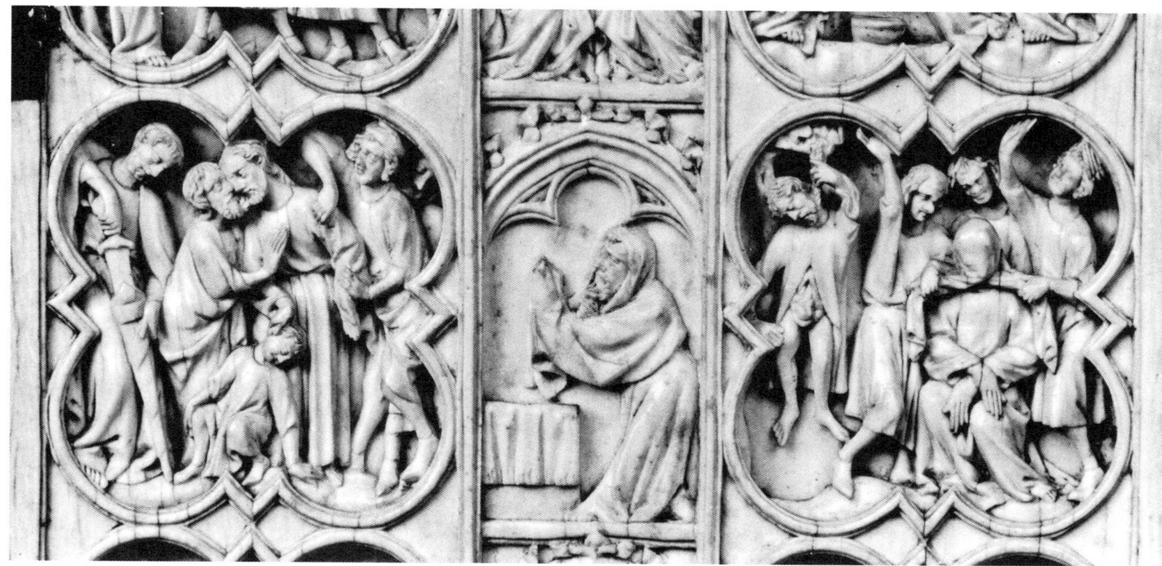

FIGURE 5. Passion Diptych: detail showing the Arrest of Christ, Paris, *c.* 1375–1400 or 1360–1380 (Minneapolis, Institute of Arts).

FIGURE 6. Passion diptych with quatrefoils: details of the Arrest of Christ and the Mocking of Christ, Paris, *c.* 1360–1380 (Paris, Musée du Louvre).

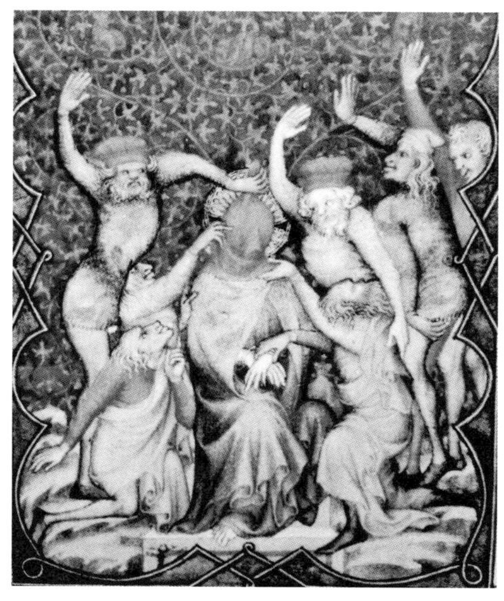

FIGURE 7. Petites Heures de Jean de Berry, illumination by Jean le Noir, 1375: The Mocking of Christ (Paris, BnF, MS.lat. 18.014, fol. 82).

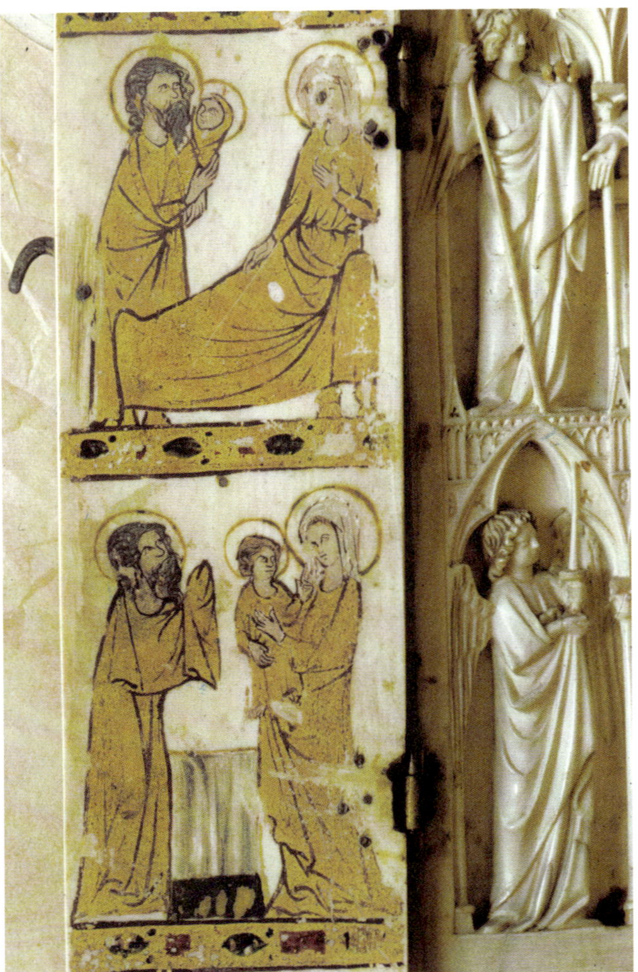

FIGURE 8. Triptych with painted wings: detail of the left panel, Paris or northern France, 1270–1300 (photo: Cascio-Levy; Lyon, Musée des Beaux-Arts).

are then faced with the problem of identifying where the "Soissons Diptych" workshop was actually based. It is perhaps time to re-examine other works from this workshop in greater detail.[21]

The study of the polychrome on statuettes or diptychs is a difficult task. Elephant ivory is appreciated for its whiteness, which symbolizes purity. This is one of the main reasons why so many Gothic statuettes of the Virgin were carved in ivory. It has to be remembered that the Virgin was compared to "the ivory throne" or "the ivory tower" (*turris eburnea*). Nevertheless, the medieval world was fond of colors and it is clear that a great number of Gothic ivories, particularly the most detailed statuettes, were highlighted with gilding and colors. Under the direction of Charles Little, Paul Williamson, Juliette Levy, and Agnès Cascio, careful examination and analysis has been undertaken on ivories in the Louvre Museum, the Metropolitan Museum, New York, the Victoria and Albert Museum, London, and on some works in French public collections.[22] Some statuettes, such as the Sainte-Chapelle Virgin (Fig. 9), the Deposition of Christ Group, or the little Virgin from the Timbal collection in the Louvre have traces of their original polychrome painting.[23] Polychromy never hides the ivory but rather enhances it, and it is usually applied to such selected areas as eyes, lips, girdles, collars, borders of mantles and dresses, inside parts of the mantels, thrones and so forth. Colors such as lapis lazuli, red, glazed green and red, and gilt on large orphreys (made of gold leaf on bole) are still found on a few examples. Light traces of colors are occasionally hidden in the inner folds of draperies and are sometimes invisible to the naked eye. Sometimes the gilding and the bole have disappeared completely and the design can only be seen in negative, as on the angels from St.-Denis, now in the Cathedral of Rouen (Fig. 10), or on the Angel of the Annunciation, mentioned above.

In many cases, the entire polychrome has been completely re-applied. In the best examples, the repainting reproduced the original, which it is still occasionally possible to see. Unfortunately, in other examples, it seems that nothing remains of the original painting, as on the group showing the Coronation of the Virgin (Louvre), whose painting was widely celebrated when it was acquired.[24]

A large number of Gothic ivories have been repainted, frequently on more than one occasion, and it

21. Gaborit-Chopin, in *Images in Ivory* (as in note 1), pp. 59–60, fig. IV–10; see also, S. M. Guérin, "Tears of Compunction: French Gothic Ivories in Devotional Practice" (University of Toronto, 2009).

22. A. Cascio and J. Levy, "Les ivoires peints. La polychromie des statuettes d'ivoire," *Coré* 5 (1998), 5–20. A. Cascio and J. Levy, "Ivoires gothiques: polychromie originale et repeints," *12th Triennal Meeting Lyon. 29 aug.–3 sept. 1999 (Comité de l'ICOM pour la conservation)* (1999), I, 429–433.

23. A. Cascio and J. Levy, "Nicodème travesti ...-Étude de la polychromie," *Revue de l'Art* 81 (1988), 45–46.

24. D. Gaborit-Chopin, *Ivoires médiévaux* (as in note 6), no. 99.

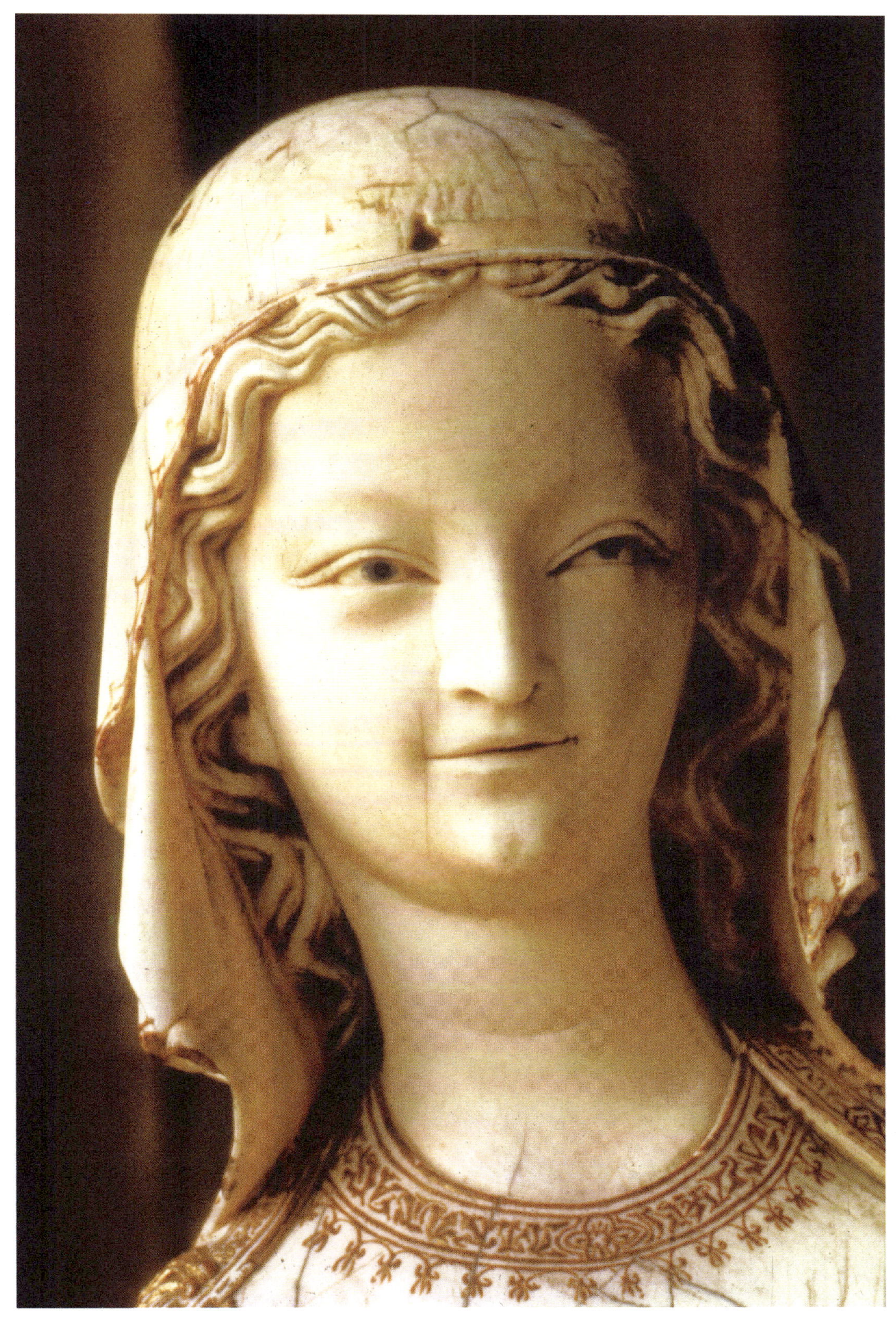

FIGURE 9. Head of the Virgin of the Sainte-Chapelle: gold on bole (orphrey bands), traces of lapis-lazuli blue (eyes), and of red glaze (lips).

is possible to find many layers of painting or gilding on a single work. One such work is the Virgin and Child from Villeneuve-les-Avignon, where successive layers of painting have been applied. Here it is difficult to identify which parts of the gilt borders are original. Its later re-working has a heavier line, and a crack in the ivory has been concealed by re-gilding a branch with leaves (Fig. 11).[25] The carving of St. Margaret triumphing over the dragon, now in the British Museum, London, has three layers of gilding, one with a brown base, another in ochre, and the third, the original, which is translucent.[26] Moreover, its branches with leaves were repainted along some cracks of the ivory.

As a general rule, traces of original polychrome are found infrequently, and overpainting is all too common. This hinders efforts to identify and accurately describe workshops or centers of production. It is clear, however, as these examples have shown, that microscopic examination is necessary.

Workshops in Paris & Beyond

The title of Koechlin's book refers to ivory as French-made, but it is clear that not all Gothic ivories are French. If more were known about the operations of the ivory trade in the Gothic period, the picture would be far clearer. Elephant tusks came mainly from Africa, and the crusades did not stop the trade. Italy was an important link between Africa (mainly through Egypt, but also beyond) and the West. We know also that some tusks (*dentes*) were shipped from Genoa to ports in southern France, or, by way of the Atlantic, to Flanders, England, and Normandy.[27] Even if we have no documented proof, it is still possible to believe, as Koechlin suggested, that ivory carving in Paris could be explained by the fact that tusks were unloaded in Rouen and shipped on the River Seine to Paris.

If it was possible to buy ivory in London or in Flanders, then, logically, it should also be possible to find ivory carvers in such cities, and not just in Paris. However, it is not possible to prove this fact and to identify such workshops, and thus the influence of the French style still dominates. Nevertheless, Richard Randall, Charles Little, Neil Stratford, Paul Williamson, Michele Tomas, and others in the course of their researches have all justifiably identified English, German, and Italian workshops, whose number will undoubtedly be increased over time.[28]

Koechlin himself identified some English workshops, one of which worked *c.* 1330–1340 for John Grandisson, bishop of Exeter, and another of which worked at the beginning of the fourteenth century and was responsible for carving the Salting Diptych, which has been attributed to Winchester.[29] Several other English works have been identified in the last few decades.[30] Questions of origin, however, still remain in such pieces as the Christ of Herlufsholm (Denmark), which has been dated to around 1230, where the body is made of elephant ivory but the arms are in walrus. Similarly, the Passion reliefs from Copenhagen, which are walrus, may be either English, as proposed by Neil Stratford,[31] or Danish, as their provenance suggests.

In addition, the figure of Christ's body in the Victoria and Albert Museum has been dated to *c.* 1300, but

25. Villeneuve-les-Avignon, treasury of the collégiale. See *L'Art au temps des rois maudits* (as in note 9), no. 108.

26. N. Stratford, in *Images in Ivory* (as in note 1), no. 27.

27. N. Stratford, "Gothic Ivory Carving in England," in *Age of Chivalry*, Exhib. Cat. (London, 1987), 107–113. P. Barnet, in *Images in Ivory* (as in note 8). D. Gaborit-Chopin, "Le commerce de l'ivoire en Méditerranée durant le Moyen Age," *Bulletin du Comité des Travaux historiques et scientifiques* 34 (2008), 23–33.

28. Several propositions for non-Parisian attributions were made, mainly in the catalogues of the exhibitions *Images in Ivory* (as in note 1) and *Age of Chivalry* (as in note 27), and also by R. H. Randall, *Masterpieces of Ivory from the Walters Art Gallery* (Baltimore, 1985); R. H. Randall, *The Golden Age of Ivory: Gothic Carvings in North American Collections* (New York, 1993); D. Gaborit-Chopin, *Ivoires médiévaux* (as in note 7); J. Lowden and J. Cherry, *The Thompson Collection at the Art Gallery of Ontario: Medieval Ivories and Works of Art* (Toronto, 2008). See also the bibliography in the following notes.

29. N. Stratford, in *Age of Chivalry* (as in note 27), 463–467, nos. 593–596; N. Stratford, in *Images in Ivory* (as in note 1), no. 38; P. Williamson, in *Images in Ivory* (as in note 1), no. 37.

30. P. Williamson, "An English Ivory Tabernacle Wing of the Thirteenth Century," *Burlington Magazine* (Dec. 1990), 863–866; P. Williamson, "Acquisitions of Sculpture at the Victoria and Albert Museum, 1992–1999," *Burlington Magazine* (Dec. 1999), 78.

31. N. Stratford, in *Age of Chivalry* (as in note 27), 11–112, fig. 76, and nos. 307–309.

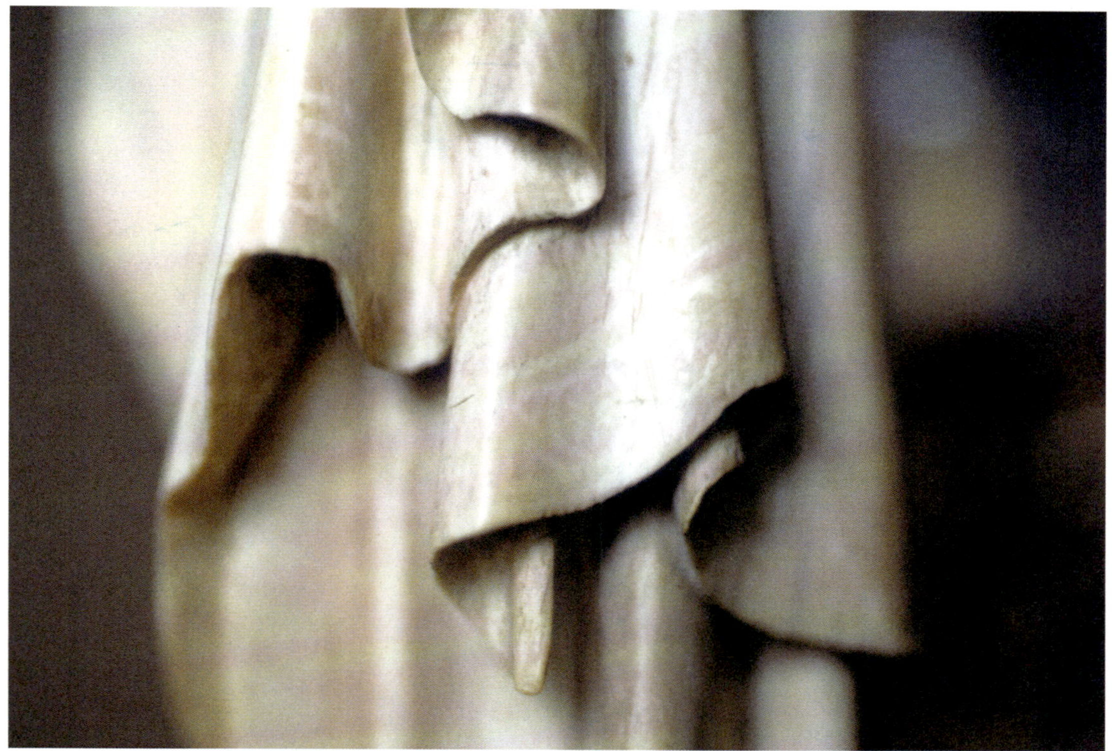

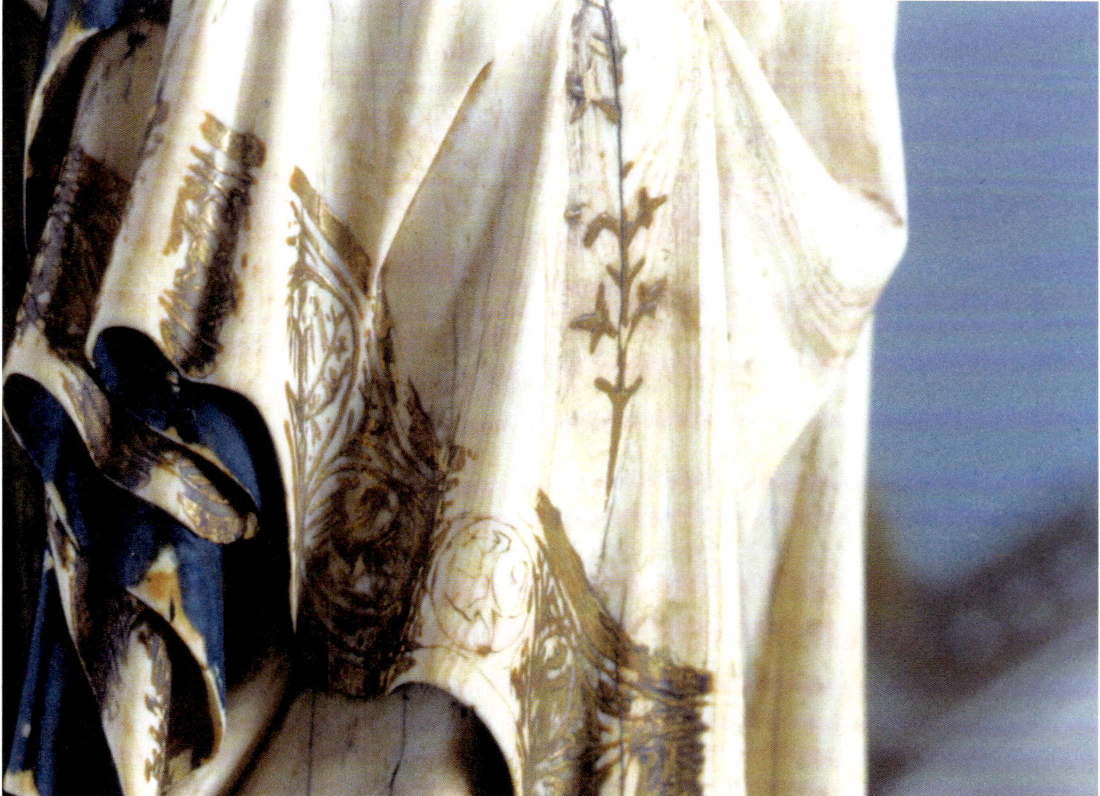

FIGURE 10. Orphrey bands on the Angel from St.-Denis, 1250–1275 (photo: Cascio-Levy).

FIGURE 11. Virgin of Villeneuve-les-Avignon (treasury of the church): detail of the mantel showing original motifs and those which have been re-gilded; the blue inside the folds is repainted. A branch hides a crack in the ivory on the left side (original re-gilded) (photo: Cascio-Levy).

its origin is not clear. Its similarities to and differences from contemporary French carvings of the dead Christ, such as those in the Bargello or the St.-Sulpice du Tarn triptych, are perplexing.[32]

Richard Randall and Charles Little have drawn attention to several German ivories from the Rhine area, such as Kremsmunster and Cologne. For example, the diptych of St. Martin and the Beggar, now in the Cleveland Museum (Fig. 12), is similar to a statue of a bishop made before 1350, now in the Diocesan Museum, Cologne.[33]

Another example concerns the secular casket in St. Ursula's Church in Cologne, showing lovers, charming and smiling, and crowned with headbands decorated with beads, which seem more German than French. It is possible to relate other secular ivories to this work, such as mirror cases like the one in the Victoria and Albert Museum. Both carvings have similar features, and they may come from the same German shop, perhaps specialized in secular ivories.[34] The carving of the Virgin and Child in the Nelson-Atkins Museum, Kansas City, points to the Mosan region of carvers, even if the differences with German workshops are not always clear.[35] It is hoped that further research in all these areas, as well as in relatively neglected countries, such as Spain, will in the future suggest new attributions and will enable us to better understand the reality of the situation.

Italian ivories are more complex. Italy was in the thirteenth and fourteenth centuries an important center for trading ivory, and it is surprising to find so few Italian Gothic works carved in elephant ivory. Two of the best known and most celebrated Italian pieces were carved in elephant ivory by Giovanni Pisano in 1299. These are the Virgin, or "la madonina," of the cathedral of Pisa, and the dead Christ, now in The Victoria and Albert Museum, both of which clearly show a relationship with Italian monumental sculpture.[36] Yet, curiously, the greatest number of Gothic Italian ivory carvings were made of bone. Although some big croziers, such as the example from Volterra now in the Victoria and Albert Museum, are made in ivory, others are made both of elephant ivory and bone, and some are completely carved in bone, and then enhanced with polychrome. Two examples of the last type are the croziers now in the Museo del Duomo in Siena, or the one in the Bargello.[37] Around 1400, the "bottega degli Embriachi," working in Florence, then mainly in Venice, made, with small plates of bone placed side to side, numerous triptychs, polyptychs, and oversize retables. Typical of these works are the retables in the Metropolitan Museum, the Louvre, or the Certosa di Pavia, as well as caskets with scenes from the legend of Paris, the Golden Fleece, the Griseldis, and so forth, which were exported all over Europe (Fig. 13). These works were not for mass consumption, for many of these objects were bought by kings and princes.[38] Venice was one of the main centers for trade with the Near East and Egypt, from where most of the elephants' tusks were imported. It is surprising to note, therefore, a large use of bone and not of elephant's ivory in this center.

It is also clear that workshops existed in France outside of Paris. Yet only a few provincial workshops have been recognized or identified. One such workshop, mentioned above, existed in the north of France and has been called the Soissons group. Another center is found in the east of France, in the Lorraine region. Here, in the first quarter of the fourteenth century, monumental stone carvings of the Virgin have a characteristic style with large face and silhouette, as well as elegant drapery. These same features are also found in ivory Virgins, such as the example formerly

32. P. Williamson, in *Images in Ivory* (as in note 1), no. 36. For Christ-figures of the Bargello and the Triptych of St.-Sulpice du Tarn, see D. Gaborit-Chopin, in *L'Art au temps des rois maudits* (as in note 9), nos. 85, 87.

33. R. Randall (as in note 28); R. Randall, in *Images in Ivory* (as in note 1), nos. 43–46. C. Little, in *Images in Ivory* (as in note 1), 81–93, nos. 41–42.

34. Gaborit-Chopin, *Ivoires du Moyen Âge occidental* (as in note 14), 157, no. 140.

35. R. Randall, in *Images in Ivory* (as in note 1), no. 47.

36. Gaborit-Chopin, *Ivoires du Moyen Âge occidental* (as in note 14), 159–162; P. Williamson, in *Images in Ivory* (as in note 1), no. 34.

37. P. Williamson, in *Images in Ivory* (as in note 1), no. 50. Gaborit-Chopin, *Ivoires du Moyen Âge occidental* (as in note 14), 162, fig. 252.

38. M. Tomasi, *La Bottega degli Embriachi. Museo Nazionale del Bargello* (Florence, 2001); M. Tomasi, "Baldassare Ubriachi, le maître, le public," *Revue de l'Art*, 134 (2001–4), 51–60.

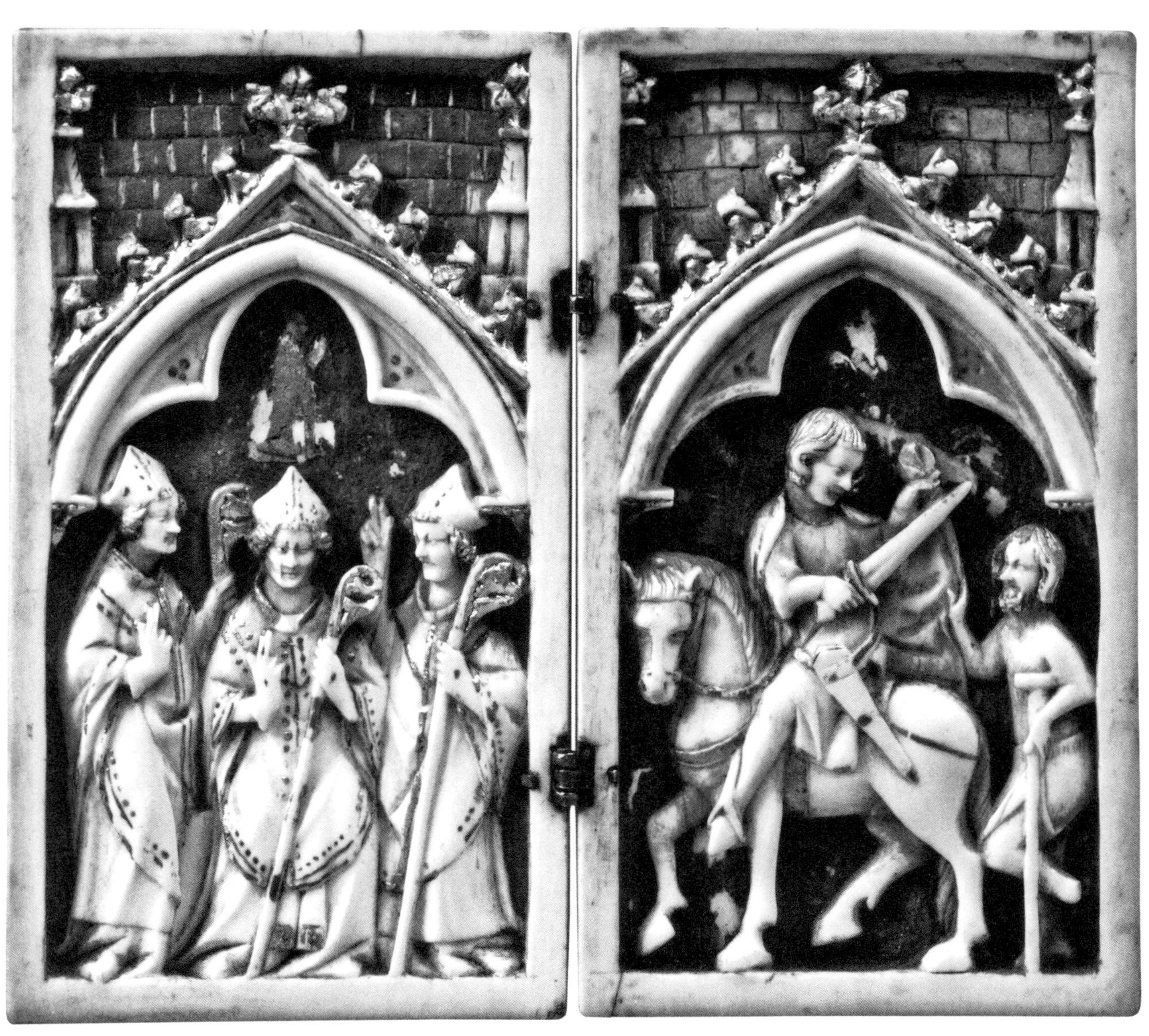

FIGURE 12. Cleveland, Diptych with St. Martin, Cologne, 1300–1350 (Cleveland, The Cleveland Museum of Art).

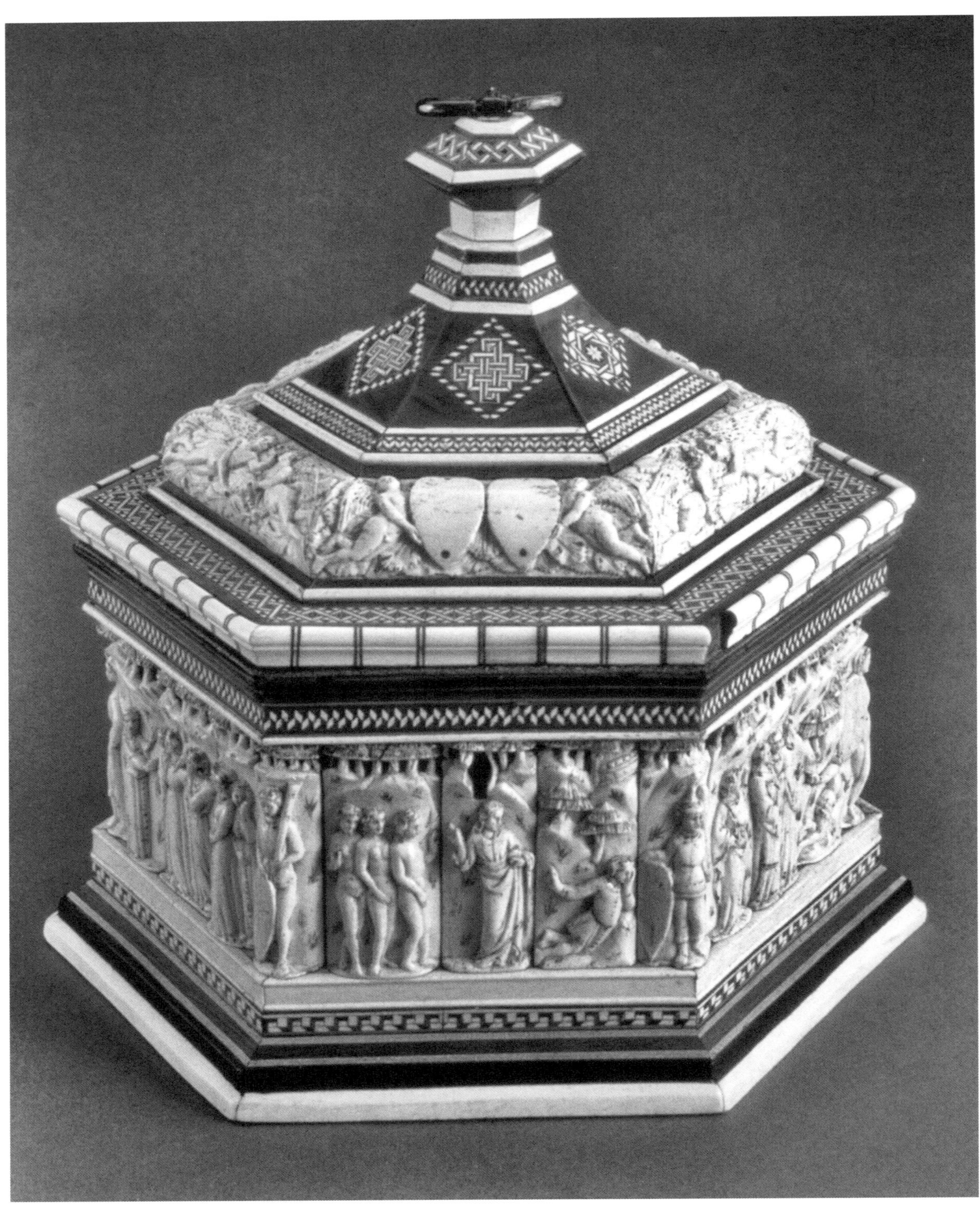

FIGURE 13. Wedding casket: Legend of Paris, Workshop of Embriachi, Venezia, *c.* 1400 (Paris, Musée du Louvre).

from the Mège Collection and now in the Louvre.[39] Another center was probably in the Loire Valley, where a fifteenth-century statuette of the Virgin and Child, originally from Laval and now in the Walters Art Museum, Baltimore, was carved possibly in the province of Touraine.[40] Its date—the first or second half of the fifteenth century—is still in discussion. But the whole question of fifteenth-century ivories remains complex and controversial, necessitating further research.

The Parisian Workshops

Another understandable but problematic aspect to Koechlin's catalogue is his classification of ivory diptychs according to their iconography and typology. For example, Koechlin identified a large workshop that was characterized by Passion iconography with all of the scenes separated by bands of rosettes. If this group is examined closely, it is possible to observe that the same iconography does not necessarily show the same style. A diptych now in the Detroit Institute of Art, which was carved in Paris in 1330, has Passion scenes separated by bands of rosettes. The same scenes separated by bands of rosettes are also found on a Passion diptych in the Louvre, for which the same origin and date have been suggested.[41] These two carvings show a general compositional similarity with some minor variations. However, the delicate rendering of the Detroit diptych is stylistically different from that of the stronger, more powerful Louvre carving. If the two ivories were inspired by the same iconography, they were certainly not carved in the same workshop. The "bands of rosettes workshop" suggested by Koechlin, thus, does not constitute stylistic criteria for a workshop. To proceed with this type of research from which a new classification of Gothic ivories might emerge, it is clear that the most minute photographs will be needed.

Secular & Religious Ivories

The *Livre des metiers* seems to indicate the separate existence of religious and secular workshops. This, however, may be doubted. Several religious diptychs from *circa* 1320–1330, such as the one in the Metropolitan Museum of Art,[42] have characteristic female figures with oval faces, long, sharp noses, and strong chins (Fig. 14). These similar facial features are found on the casket with romance scenes now preserved in the treasury of the Dommuseum in Krakow (Fig. 15).[43] Here, both secular and religious ivories were carved by the same workshop.

Another example that proves the same point is found in a casket of *circa* 1300–1325 with scenes from the life of St. Eustache, now in a private collection.[44] This religious casket is similar to other caskets with romance iconography, such as the one in the Walters Museum, or the casket in the Louvre that recounts the story of Perceval.[45] The latter is of great interest in this context, since its sides depict the story of Perceval while its lid shows saintly images, all carved by the same hand. It is clear, therefore, that the organization of the ivory craft mentioned in the *Livre des metiers* needs to be reconsidered.

Secular Ivories

The *Livre des metiers* points out that the guilds responsible for making combs, tablets, and handles are also

39. Gaborit-Chopin, *Ivoires médiévaux* (as in note 7), no. 180.

40. R. Randall, in *Images in Ivory* (as in note 1), no. 71.

41. *Images in Ivory* (as in note 1), no. 24–25.

42. New York, Metropolitan Museum, no. 17-190-167. For a survey of this "Workshop of the Casket of Krakow," see Gaborit-Chopin, *Ivoires médiévaux* (as in note 7), 394, nos. 158–161.

43. Koechlin, *Ivoires gothiques* (as in note 1), no. 1285.

44. R. Randall, *The Golden Age* (as in note 28), no. 180. The exhibition *L'Art au temps des rois maudits* (as in note 9) has shown that the style of this group of caskets and of others secular ivories (see notes 44, 45) reflect the soft and elegant art at the court of Philippe le Bel and his sons. So a date around 1300–1330 seems today more convenient than the date in the second quarter of the fourteenth century, first proposed for these secular pieces. See also Little, "L'art de l'ivoire au temps de Philippe le Bel," in *1300. L'art au temps de Philippe le Bel. Actes du colloque international, Paris, Grand Palais, 24–25 juin 1998* (Paris, 2001), 83–86.

45. Randall, *Masterpieces of Ivory* (as in note 28), no. 334; Randall, in *Images in Ivory* (as in note 1), no. 64; Gaborit-Chopin, *Ivoires médiévaux* (as in note 7), no. 132.

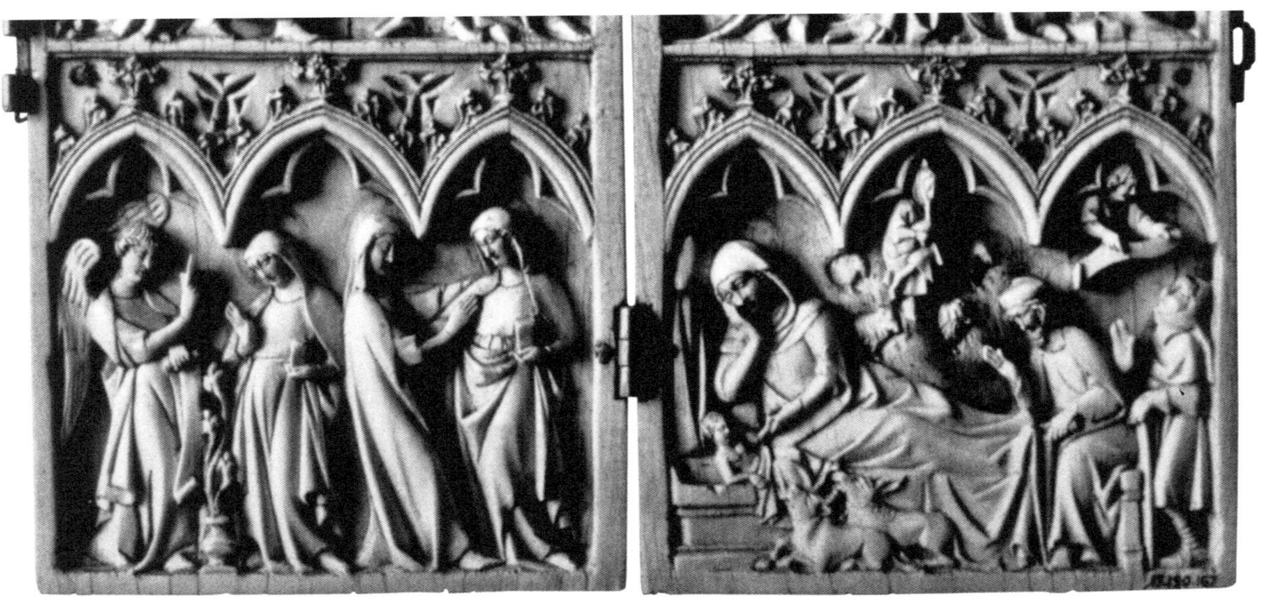

FIGURE 14. Detail of a diptych, Master of the Krakow casket, Paris, *c.* 1320–1340 (New York, Metropolitan Museum).

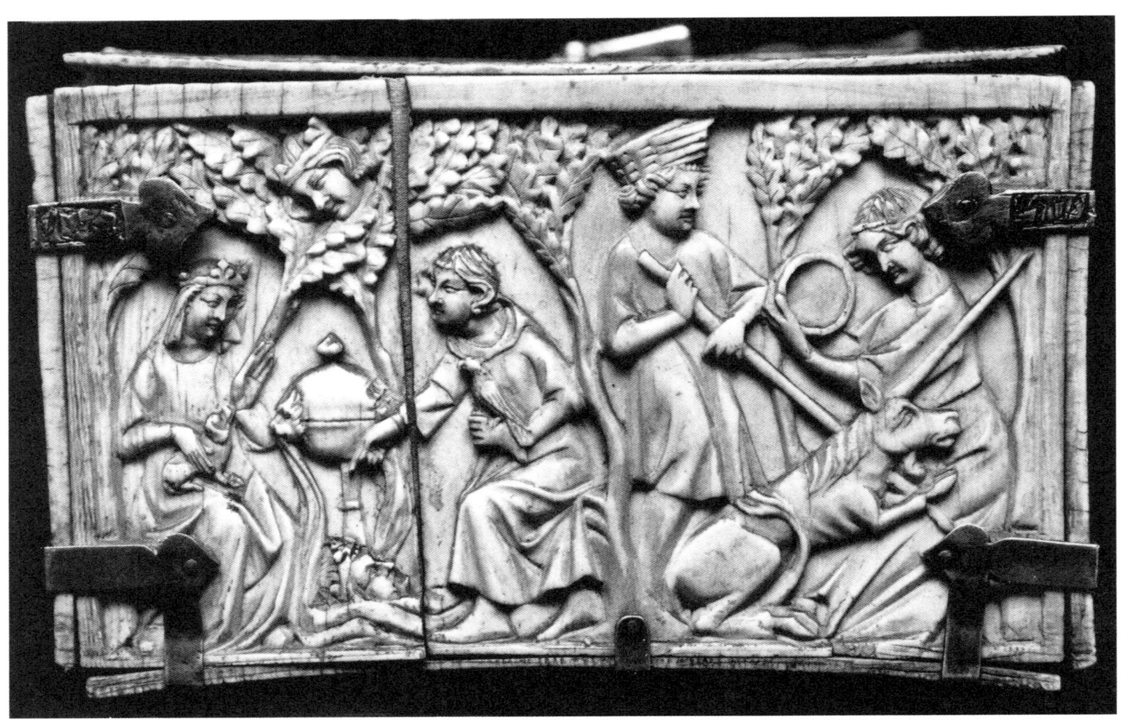

FIGURE 15. Panel from casket with romance scenes, Master of the Krakow casket, Paris, *c.* 1320–1340 (Krakow, treasury of the cathedral).

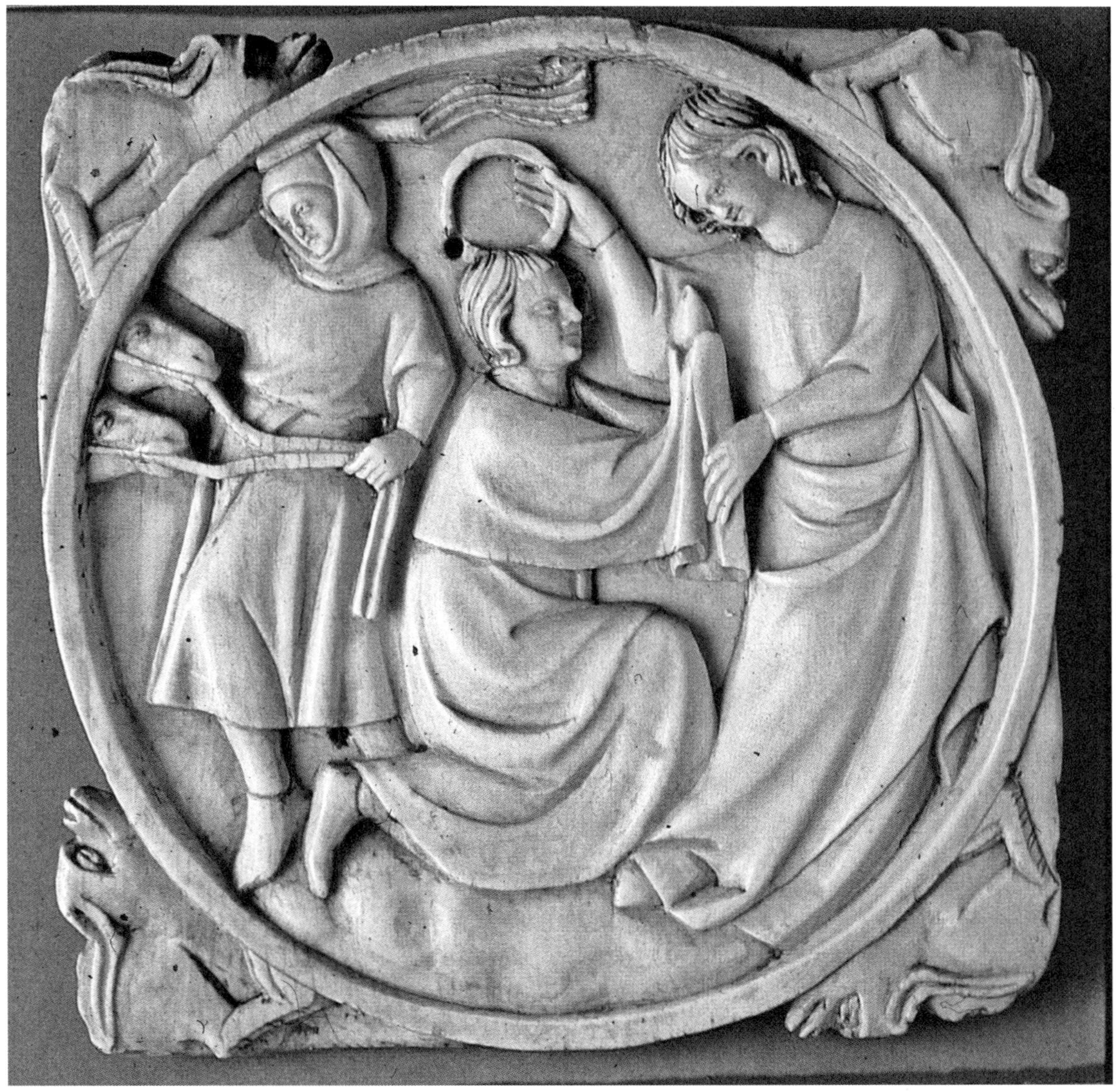

FIGURE 16. Mirror case: coronation of the lover, Paris, *c.* 1300 (London, Victoria & Albert Museum).

allowed to carve ivory. This does not necessarily mean that they made every handle, casket, or mirror case. When some of the secular ivories are examined, their links to religious ivories are apparent as to their technical qualities, compositional skills, elegance, and charm of the figures and subjects, all indicating artists of considerable skills. These can no longer be considered minor works. The mirror case with a royal couple now in the Musée du Moyen Âge in Paris (whose iconography is still the subject of much discussion),[46] or the example in the Victoria and Albert Museum with the coronation of the lover, clearly indicate the artistic excellence of this medium (Fig. 16).[47]

A document dating to 1377 from the accounts of the court of Burgundy is interesting in this context. It states that twenty-six pounds of ivory were bought in Paris, in the shop of Jehan Girost, "tablettier" (maker of tablets), for Jean de Marville, sculptor of the duke

46. Gaborit-Chopin, *Ivoires du moyen Âge occidental* (as in note 14), 207; Randall, in *Images in Ivory* (as in note 1), no. 54.

47. For example, in *Images in Ivory* (as in note 1), nos. 52–64.

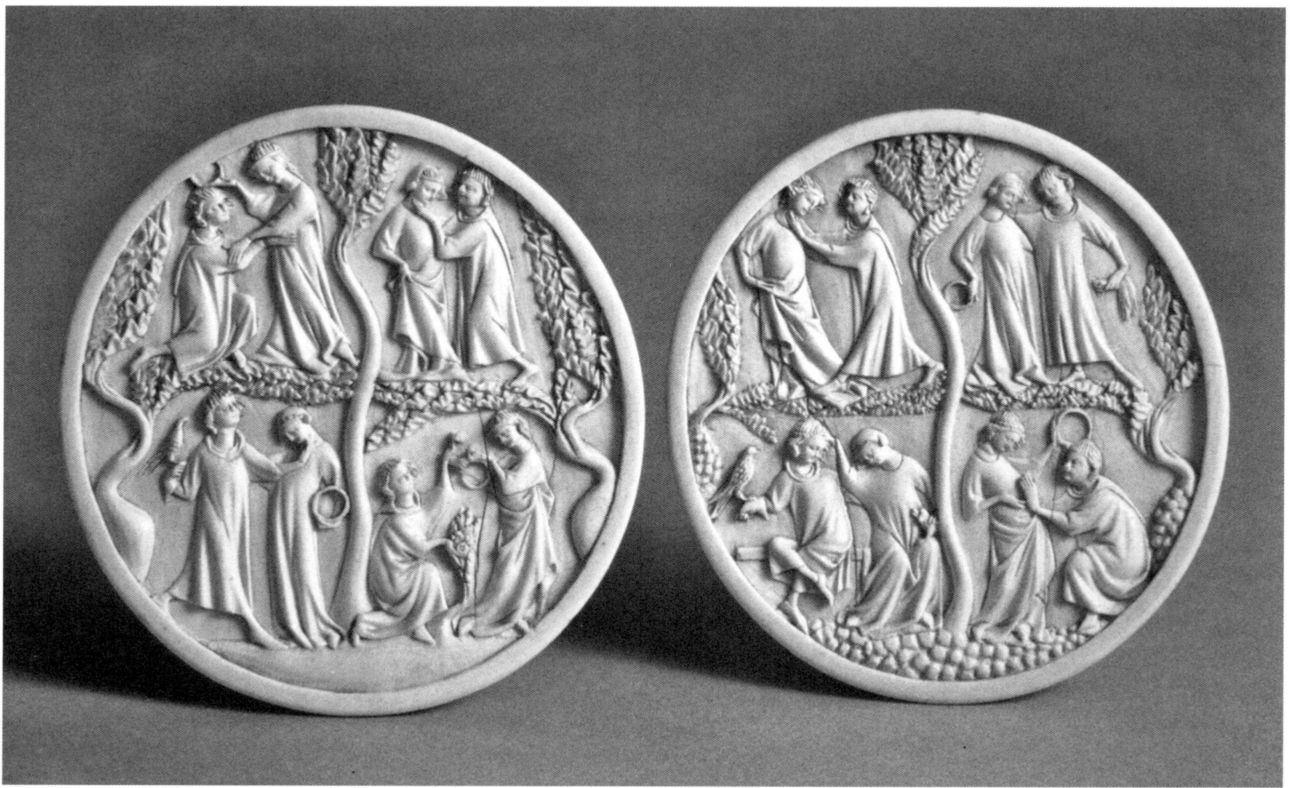

FIGURE 17. Pair of mirror cases: lovers in a garden (Paris, Musée du Louvre).

of Burgundy.[48] We can infer from this document that the "tablettiers" in Paris were not only makers of writing tablets or of caskets, but that they also worked the raw material, which they cut into blocks and panels and then sold to the sculptors and painters, "ymagiers" and "paintres et tailleurs d'ymages," who could later carve religious and secular objects. The strict distinction between religious and secular is a modern concept that did not exist in the medieval world. The medieval world was completely Christian, in all its manifestations, both religious and secular, and the profane was most certainly included in the religious context.

It is time to reconsider secular Gothic ivories. They are certainly not inferior to their religious counterparts and should be seen as an introduction or a key to the Gothic world. Mirror cases, caskets, writing tablets, handles, etc., can give us a perfect image of the ideal of chivalry or *amour courtois* (courtly love). An example is the pair of mirror cases showing lovers in a garden,[49] which are a kind of *gradus amoris*—a veritable booklet of courtly scenes with all the symbols and accessories of Love (crown, chapel of flowers, gloves, bird, small dog) (Fig. 17). Perhaps even more than religious works, they clearly reflect the yearnings and culture of their owners. Ivory caskets with scenes from the legend of the Round Table, the story of Perceval, or that of the "chatelaine de Vergy," and so on, were made for a public who could read these as books, that is to say, they were made mainly for women. Secular ivories reflect the quotidian life of the privileged classes. Several leaves from writing tablets show various games, including the frog and the "hautes coquilles" (a kind of "blind man's bluff"). Lilian Randall has shown how these games, which are also found in other media, can

48. Koechlin, *Les ivoires gothiques* (as in note 1), vol. 1, 213–214.

49. Paris, Musée du Louvre, MRR 197 (Paris, *c.* 1310–1320).

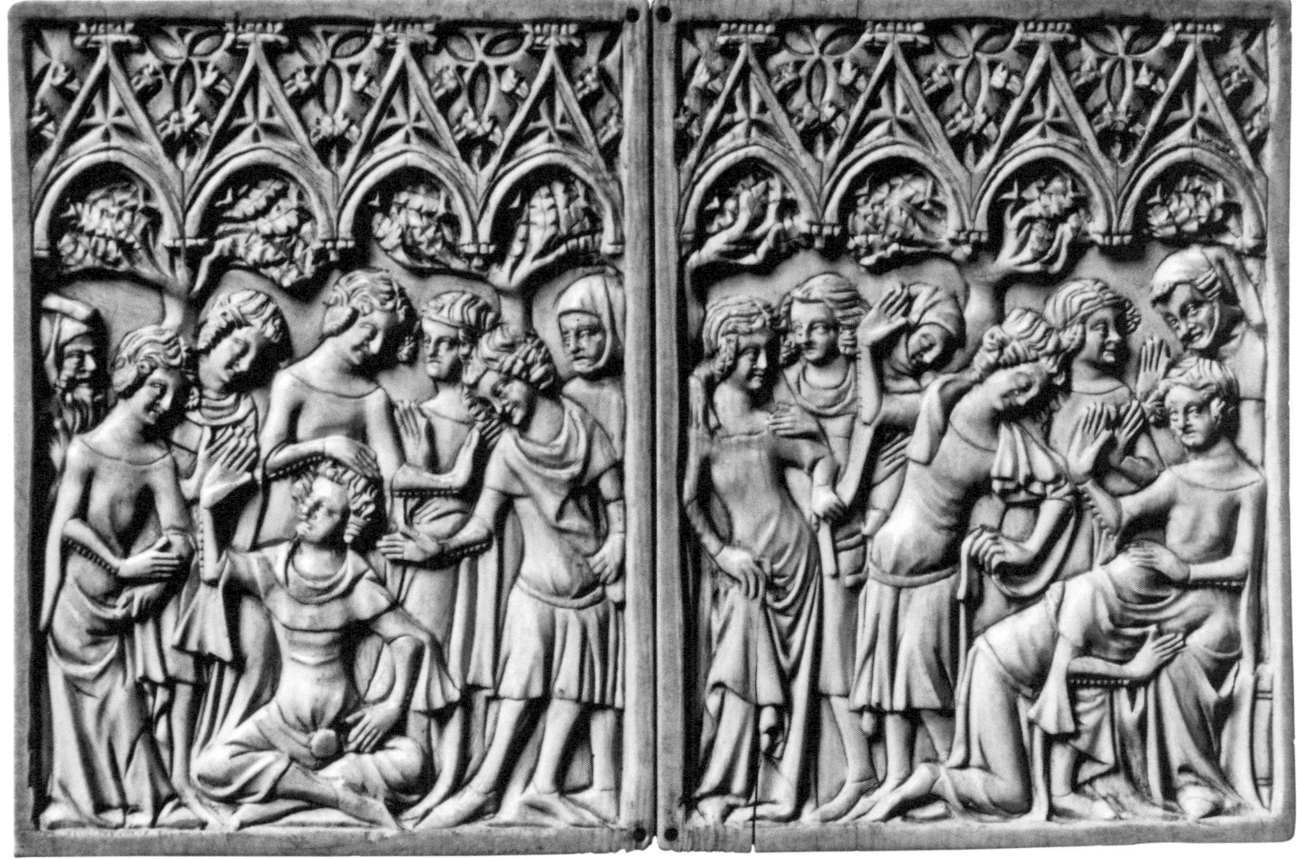

FIGURE 18. Leaves of writing tablets: the game of the frog and of the game of "hautes coquille," Paris, *c.* 1340–1350 (Paris, Musée du Louvre).

make reference to the Mocking of Christ.[50] But the secular aspect of this game on the two tablets in the Musée du Louvre is also significant (Fig. 18), since, instead of a date at the end of the fourteenth century, which was once given to these ivories, they can today be placed around the middle of the century, because the players wear short, tight tunics and dresses with a low neckline, which were fashionable clothes worn at the court of the French king Jean le Bon.[51] The chronology of secular ivories needs to be reconsidered.

As can hopefully be seen from this essay, the reality of Gothic ivories is quite complex, and the fields of sculpture and illumination offer a large and exciting area for future research. And yet ivories are not simply a reflection of monumental sculpture, but have their own meaning and status. It is also clear that they can no longer be considered as minor or merely precious items, but are in reality one of the most attractive and potentially revealing faces of Gothic art.[52]

50. L. Randall, "Games and the Passion in Pucelle's Hours of Jeanne d'Evreux," *Speculum* 47 (1972), 246–257.

51. These types of clothes can be observed for example in the manuscript of "Le remède de Fortune," by Guillaume de Machaut, around 1350. See Fr. Avril, *L'enluminure à la cour de France au XIVe siècle* (Paris, 1978), pls. 23–25; Gaborit-Chopin, *Ivoires médiévaux* (as in note 7), no. 177.

52. I am most grateful to the organizers and the persons in charge of this colloquium for their help, especially to Colum P. Hourihane for his strong confidence and his warm welcome, and to Charles T. Little for his friendly and efficient assistance. My thanks also to Agnes Cascio and Juliette Levy who allowed me to use their slides of polychrome ivories.

MADELINE H. CAVINESS

Gothic Glass Paintings: The Struggle for Survival

WILLIBALD SAUERLÄNDER's life-long work on European Gothic art, together with that of a handful of others, provided the twentieth-century foundations of our field.[1] It is an honor to be invited to contribute to this volume, and it has provided an occasion to think anew about a sub-field in which I was once a specialist.[2] When I was invited to contribute an essay on "stained glass," two historiographical issues that are interconnected came to mind. One is the fluctuating place of painted window glass in the canon and discourse of art history. The other is the history of destruction and restoration that has drastically reduced the surviving corpus of windows glazed in the Gothic period in Europe.

The conference in Princeton marked the fiftieth anniversary of an extremely important book, a collaborative study entitled *Le Vitrail Français*, published by Editions Deux Mondes in Paris in 1958.[3] The book immediately sold out, and copies have become rather rare. The cover dramatizes Romanesque painted glass, echoing decades of intense focus by Parisian scholars. Abbot Suger, drawn after his image in the window of St.-Denis, ushers the reader into the book from the flyleaf, but the endpapers celebrate a contemporary geometric glass painting.[4] These provide the visual and chronological framing of the text.

Among the contributors to that volume, Marcel Aubert and Jean Verrier were founding members of the French committee for the Corpus Vitrearum Medii Aevi (CVMA). Verrier and Jean Taralon were working in the Département des Monuments Historiques that had succeeded Malraux's Ministry of Beaux Arts.[5] Jean Lafond, who had studied with Émile Mâle, was a very knowledgeable elderly amateur—literally a lover of glass painting with a small collection in his Paris apartment—and he was an author of the first CVMA volume for France. His long-time friend, J.-J. Gruber, was a sensitive glass painter and restorer, with important insights into the materials and techniques of medieval glass painting (his daughter, Jeanette Weiss, is an accomplished creator in the medium). Louis Grodecki was a brash immigrant from Poland who insisted on

1. In recent decades, Willibald Sauerländer seemed like a permanent U.S. resident, a remarkably enthusiastic participant in many conferences, with a sharp eye and a keen mind ready to engage with others. It is doubly sad that he could not be in Princeton for the conference in his honor, both for his sake and because, selfishly, I regret that this paper could not benefit from his customary astute critique.

2. I want to extend my congratulations to Colum Hourihane for the extraordinary pace he keeps up, of conferences and publications, and for the great contributions on a variety of topics that these have made to medieval art history. Thanks also to Colum for digitizing all my Canterbury slides, which are now on the Index website. I also gratefully acknowledge the assistance of Ashley Beer Laverock with scanning and editing.

3. M. Aubert et al., *Le Vitrail français* (Paris, 1958). I cut my glass teeth on this book in Paris in 1960, while having the extraordinary opportunity to learn firsthand from its authors.

4. These motifs presage the work of Louis Grodecki in the following two decades, notably his studies of the windows of St.-Denis then in preparation, and his book on Romanesque painted glass: L. Grodecki, "Les vitraux allégoriques de Saint-Denis," *Art de France* 1 (1961), 19–46; L. Grodecki, *Les vitraux de Saint-Denis: Études sur le vitrail au XIIe siècle*, Corpus Vitrearum Medii Aevi, France, Études 1 (Paris, 1976); L. Grodecki, C. Brisac, and C. Lautier, *Le Vitrail Roman* (Freiburg, 1977).

5. The CVMA, founded in 1952, has as its goal to catalogue exhaustively all surviving medieval painted glass up to about 1480; it has since been extended (as the Corpus Vitrearum) to include works up to 1700. France published the third volume in the series: L. Grodecki, J. Lafond, et al., *Les Vitraux de Notre-Dame et de la Sainte*

testing every hypothesis against another, often playing the devil's advocate. He was also involved in forming the CVMA, and served as its International President from 1975 until his death in 1982.[6] When Grodecki moved to Strasbourg in 1961, he became a life-long friend of Willibald Sauerländer.

Some of the chapters in *Le Vitrail Français* are landmarks in our understanding of the medium of colored glass. Grodecki's contribution on its "Fonctions spirituelles" is still the basic text on the subject of the symbolic and metaphysical value ascribed by medieval theologians to light passing through glass: for instance, that the physical matter of light does not break solid glass is an allegory of the immaculate conception and birth, or that illuminating the interior of the church is comparable to illuminating the minds of the faithful. Significant subsequent contributions include Meredith Lillich's reinterpretation of the blue of St.-Denis as divine darkness (in view of early translations of the text of Dionysius the pseudo-Areopagite),[7] and, of wider import, is an overview by A. Vasiliu on the medieval meanings and significance of "diaphanous" and "translucent," terms that had fascinated Hans Jantzen and Hans Sedlmayr who claimed them as quintessential to the Gothic cathedral.[8]

Other chapters are divided between historical periods, with 1200 already identified as one divide, presaging other important contributions to the concepts surrounding that year.[9] The years 1260, 1380, and 1500 are also period markers. The historical account continued *à nos jours*, with a license to study the works of contemporary artists that was not granted then to students of literature at the Sorbonne. It was an exciting moment for glass painting when the work of replacing windows lost in World War II was still in full swing. Many of the glass artists commissioned to design new windows were also employed alongside other glass painters to repair and conserve medieval glass, at the behest of the Direction de l'Architecture of the Ministry. Max Ingrand, for instance, who was invited to design the Crucifixion window for the axial window of the Choir Clerestory of St.-Ouen Abbey Church of Rouen, was active in both areas, although most of the original medieval glass from St.-Ouen was restored in other major Parisian ateliers.[10] This exquisitely painted glass had not yet been returned to the windows after safe storage during the Second World War, and so it was available to examine from both sides on the benches, in order to chart earlier replacements and study the style of the authentic pieces (Fig. 1). While I was in Paris in 1960, a team made up of most of the authors of *Le Vitrail Français* agreed on the restoration charts to be used in the *Corpus Vitrearum Medii Aevi* volume; during weekly visits to the ateliers they also monitored cleaning and restoration procedures, and critiqued the new designs.[11] In Reims, where the Cathedral and St.-Remi had not yet been fully repaired from the First World War at the outbreak of the Second, Jacques Simon was still

---

Chapelle de Paris, Corpus Vitrearum Medii Aevi, France, 1 (Paris, 1959), following closely after E. J. Beer, *Die Glasmalereien der Schweiz vom 12. bis zum Beginn des 14. Jahrhunderts*, Corpus Vitrearum Medii Aevi, Switzerland, vol. 1 (Basel, 1956), and H. Wentzel, *Die Glasmalereien in Schwaben von 1250–1350*, Corpus Vitrearum Medii Aevi, Germany, vol. 1/1 (Berlin, 1958). *Le Vitrail français* was a celebration of the post-war project of the Monuments Historiques to photograph all France's windows, panel by panel on a decimal scale in black and white; much of this work was done before the windows were replaced in the churches, after storage during World War II.

6. M. H. Caviness, "Louis Grodecki (1910–1982)," in *Medieval Scholarship: Biographical Studies on the Formation of a Discipline*, 3: *Philosophy and the Arts*, ed. H. Damico (New York, 2000), 307–321.

7. M. P. Lillich, "Monastic Stained Glass: Patronage and Style," in *Monasticism and the Arts*, ed. T. G. Verdon (Syracuse, 1984), 222–225.

8. A. Vasiliu, "Le mot et le verre: Une définition médiévale du diaphane," *Journal des Savants* (Jan.–June 1994); L. Grodecki, "L'Interpretation de l'art gothique: Hans Sedelmayr, *Die Entstehung der Kathedrale*," *Critique* 65 (1952), 853, with reference also to H. Jantzen, *Ueber den gotischen Kirchenraum* (Freiburg-im-Breisgau, 1928).

9. Willibald Sauerländer served on the planning committee for the exhibition held at the Metropolitan Museum: J. Hoffeld, ed., *The Year 1200: A Symposium* (New York, 1975).

10. Pierre Gaudin, J.-J. Gruber, J. J. K. Ray, and the Labouret atelier. The conservators are acknowledged by J. Lafond, F. Perrot, and P. Popesco, *Les vitraux de l'église Saint-Ouen de Rouen*, vol. 1, Corpus Vitrearum Medii Aevi, France, I V/2 (Paris, 1970), 9.

11. Examination for the restoration charts and research continued in pace with the conservation. The CVMA volume was not published until a decade later: Lafond, Perrot, and Popesco, *Saint-Ouen Corpus* (as in note 10).

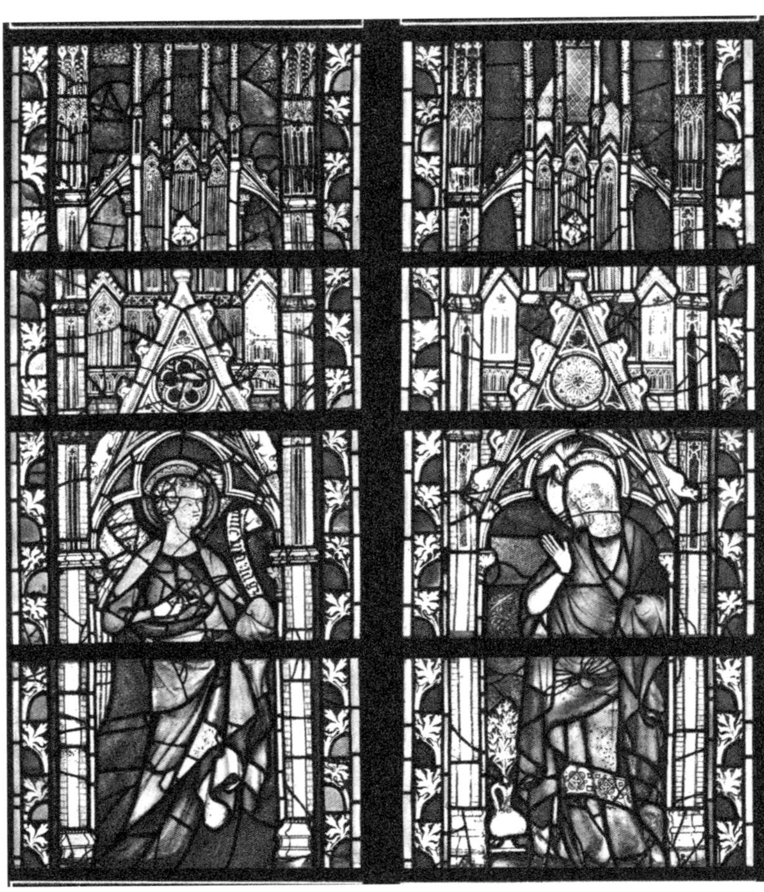

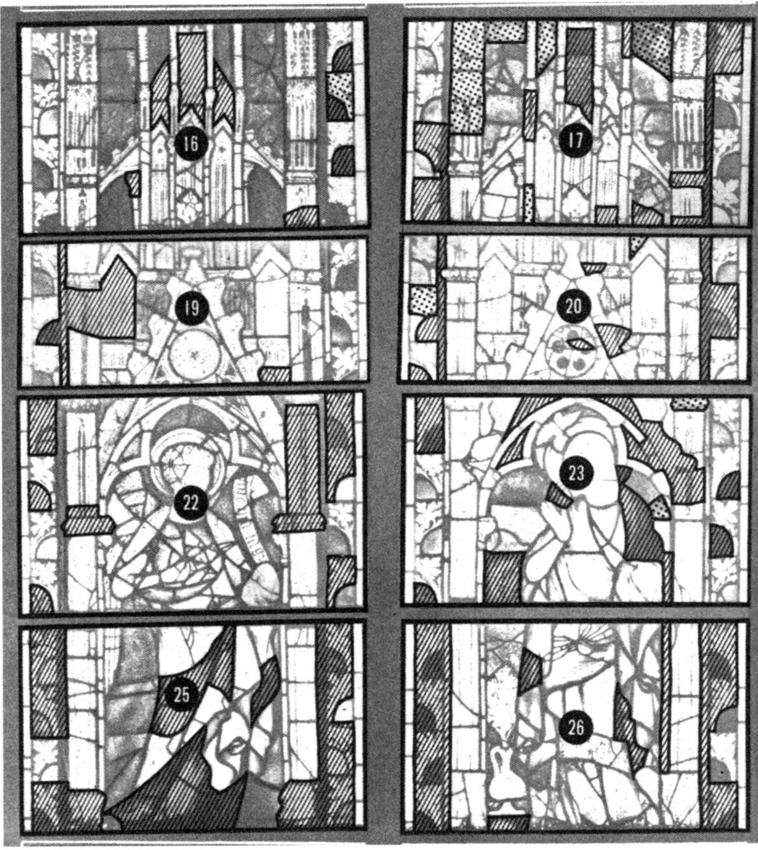

FIGURE 1. (a) The Annunciation to the Virgin, *c.* 1325; (b) Restoration chart indicating pieces replaced, Rouen, Abbey Church of St.-Ouen, Axial Chapel, window 39 (after the CVMA volume, as in note 10, by permission).

occupied with the medieval glass, while his son-in-law, Charles Marcq, executed Chagall's designs for the Cathedral and elsewhere.[12] Since most of the glass that was destroyed was from the second half of the nineteenth century, this was the first time in a hundred years that the glazing of medieval churches was fundamentally altered, and that the original glass was consolidated and restored.

Some of the modern designers, such as Georges Rouault, did not emulate medieval styles, yet they imitated aspects of medieval glass that in fact are due to corrosion and breakage. These include arbitrarily placed lead lines that interrupt color masses and resemble the leads used to repair breaks in old glass (as seen in the upper half of the annunciate angel, Fig. 1), as well as deliberate variation of hue and transparency in single pieces of glass, and very often complete absence of paint, both of which would be due to advanced deterioration in medieval glass.[13] In light of cubist painting, these effects were admired even in old glass paintings. This modernist aesthetic had a positive effect on the treatment of medieval glass, since nineteenth-century restoration practices that attempted to restore some imagined original appearance were largely abandoned in favor of conservation and protection to stabilize the condition.

This interweaving of art history, restoration, and creation already had a long history that had contributed to the survival of whatever is left of this fragile and vulnerable art form. It is that history that I trace here, followed by a case study of the dense pre-modern history of some dispersed panels. From available documents and the glass itself, I construct a dramatic story of survival, for some very finely painted English windows might have been lost to iconoclasm in the seventeenth century but for the determined actions of one family.

The title of my paper has a place in historiography, since it has long seemed necessary to me to reject the erroneous abbreviation of "stained and painted glass" to *stained* glass.[14] The term is inaccurate (the glass is not stained), whereas "painted glass," or glass painting, describes very well the practice of an art form that has endured from the ancient period to this day; even in English we speak of glass painters, not glass stainers. Very sensibly, in German *Glasmalerei* is the customary term. In French, *peinture sur verre* is commonly found, though in some contexts *vitraux* is preferred, since it carries the meaning of panels or windows. In fact, in England in the nineteenth century many authors preferred to use the term painted glass, though a few already chose the term stained glass.[15]

It is true that glass painters do not paint in the vivid colors of their medium. The colors are metal oxides imbedded in the glass when it is made.[16] The normative use of saturated blue as a ground color relies on its wavelength to push it into the distance, whereas yellow and red come forward. Twelfth- and thirteenth-century glass painters also knew how to choose a pale blue for the foreground (the optical rule is also reversed on canvas in Mark Rothko's "Blue over Red"). Eva Frodl-Kraft observed that medieval glass painters empirically used complementary colors in juxtaposition, such as yellow and blue, red and green.[17] Colors are

12. V. David and M. Hérold, "L'atelier Jacques Simon à Reims," in *Années folles, années d'ordre: L'Art Déco de Reims à New York* (Paris, 2006), 74–77. Chagall's windows for Jerusalem were exhibited at the Louvre before leaving France: J. Leymarie, *Chagall: Vitraux pour Jérusalem* (Paris, 1961).

13. Aubert et al., *Le Vitrail français*, (as in note 3), Pls. XXX, XXXI, XXXII, figs. 221, 224, 225, 227, 229, 233–236, in François Mathey's chapter, "Tendances modernes," 293–310.

14. Only when I was established in the field did an editor allow me to use painting in a book title: M. H. Caviness, *Paintings on Glass: Studies in Romanesque and Gothic Monumental Art*, Variorum Collected Studies, vol. 573 (Aldershot, 1997).

15. N. H. J. Westlake, *A History of Design in Painted Glass*, 4 vols., vol. 4 (London and Oxford, 1894); L. F. Day, *Windows: A Book about Stained and Painted Glass*, 3rd revised ed. (London, 1909); cf. L. F. Day, *Stained Glass*, 2nd ed., Victoria and Albert Handbooks (London, 1913); cf. P. Le Vieil, *L'Art de la Peinture sur Verre et de la Vitrerie* (Paris, 1774); É. Thibaud, *Considérations historiques et critiques sur les vitraux anciens et modernes et sur la peinture sur verre* (Clermont-Ferrand, 1842); E. Lévy, *Histoire de la peinture sur verre en Europe et particulièrement en Belgique* (Brussels, 1860).

16. Among many descriptions of techniques, see M. H. Caviness, *Stained Glass Windows*, Typologie des Sources du Moyen Âge Occidental 76 (Turnhout, 1996), 47–57.

17. E. Frodl-Kraft, "Die Farbsprache der Gotischen Malerei," *Wiener Jahrbuch für Kunstgeschichte* 20/21 (1977–78), 90–178.

very hard to control with light coming through a painting that is to be seen from a considerable distance and these selections clarified compositions. Natural light, however, constantly changes the chromatic values of glass. The Purkinje shift, whereby blue becomes more brilliant than red in reduced light, means that as the sun rose during Lauds and set at Vespers, figures in the painting would appear dark, silhouetted against a brilliant blue ground, unless they were clad in white or pale blue.[18] A transfiguration occurred at every dawn. Empirical observation of the dynamics of light and color may account for the common practice in northern Europe in the fourteenth and fifteenth centuries of painting figures on pale or colorless glass (grisaille) against a colored ground with dense painted decoration. The sculpturesque Virgin in the St.-Ouen Annunciation is dressed in bright blue, yellow, and white against a damasked red ground (Fig. 1a).

The effect of colorless figures was enhanced after the early fourteenth century, when glass painters could choose to apply silver oxide to selected areas; brushed on as a colorless liquid, it changed to yellow in the kiln to enliven haloes, crowns, hair, and the borders of mantles (Figs. 2, 6, 11, 12, 14b).[19] Known as silver stain, it is the only glass colorant referred to as a stain in modern English, though inaccurately. Normally glass painters use brushes charged only with a black or brown vitreous paint, built up in several separate layers, with highlights made by scraping away the paint before firing—the whites of the eyes are the only part that has no paint in a typical early fifteenth-century face from Hereford Cathedral (Fig. 2a). Each layer of paint might involve a separate firing, and silver stain has to be fired at a different temperature than paint. It was standard practice to apply modeling washes and other detail, such as brocade patterns, to the outer surface of the glass, where it unfortunately may disappear through corrosion; traces are still seen on the back of the same apostle's face (Fig. 2b).[20]

Painting was essential in the production of windows, a skill set constituting a large part of the craft that more than equaled objects produced with the richest materials, as alluded to in medieval assessments of art.[21] Glass painters are masters of the brush in a very similar way to Japanese *sumi* painters, but it is more relevant that they used graphic effects that are familiar in the West in printmaking (Fig. 2a). Yet they are masters of color as well, anticipating the effects of light of varying intensity and chromatic value streaming through their medium. They use the paint to modulate the amount of light that reaches the interior by using more paint on the colorless glasses to cut down the glare, and less on the denser glasses. The pure red acanthus leaves surrounding the apostle John from Hampton Court are only articulated by a central vein, but they stand out against a ground that was easily rendered black with a single wash (Figs. 6, 11).

One of the reasons I introduce a problem of nomenclature, which may seem quite irrelevant to the grand narrative of Gothic glass painting, is that the extraordinary temporal span of this way of producing windows has often taken precedence over periodicity in the writings on it. Many written histories that trace its development concentrate on changes in technique rather than on changes in style, and they tend to bring the tradition into the modern era. One reason may be that the materials and processes needed to produce a glass painting are complex—yet so are they for wall paint-

18. J. R. Johnson, *The Radiance of Chartres: Studies in the Early Stained Glass of the Cathedral*, Columbia University Studies in Art History and Archaeology 4 (New York, 1965), 16–20; M. H. Caviness, "Stained Glass Windows in Gothic Chapels, and the Feasts of the Saints," in *Kunst und Liturgie im Mittelalter*, ed. N. Bock et al. (Munich, 2000), 141.

19. C. Lautier, "Les débuts du jaune d'argent dans l'art du vitrail ou le jaune d'argent à la manière d'Antoine de Pise," *Bulletin monumental* 158, no. 11 (2000), 89–107.

20. E. Frodl-Kraft, *Die Glasmalerei: Entwicklung, Technik, Eigenart* (Vienna and Munich, 1970), 42–43, figs. 18–19; C. Lautier, "L'usage de la grisaille sur la face externe des vitraux de la cathédrale de Chartres," *Vitrea: Vitrail, verre, architecture* (*Revue du Centre International du Vitrail*) 5/6 (1990), 23–29.

21. Abbot Suger refers several times to the value of superb artistic execution, placing it before valuable materials when he refers to the painted glass of St.-Denis "quia magni constant mirifico opera sumptuque profuso virti vestiti et saphororum material ...:" G. Panofsky-Soergel and E. Panofsky, eds., *Abbot Suger: On the Abbey Church of St. Denis and its Art Treasures*, 2nd ed. (Princeton, 1979), 76–77.

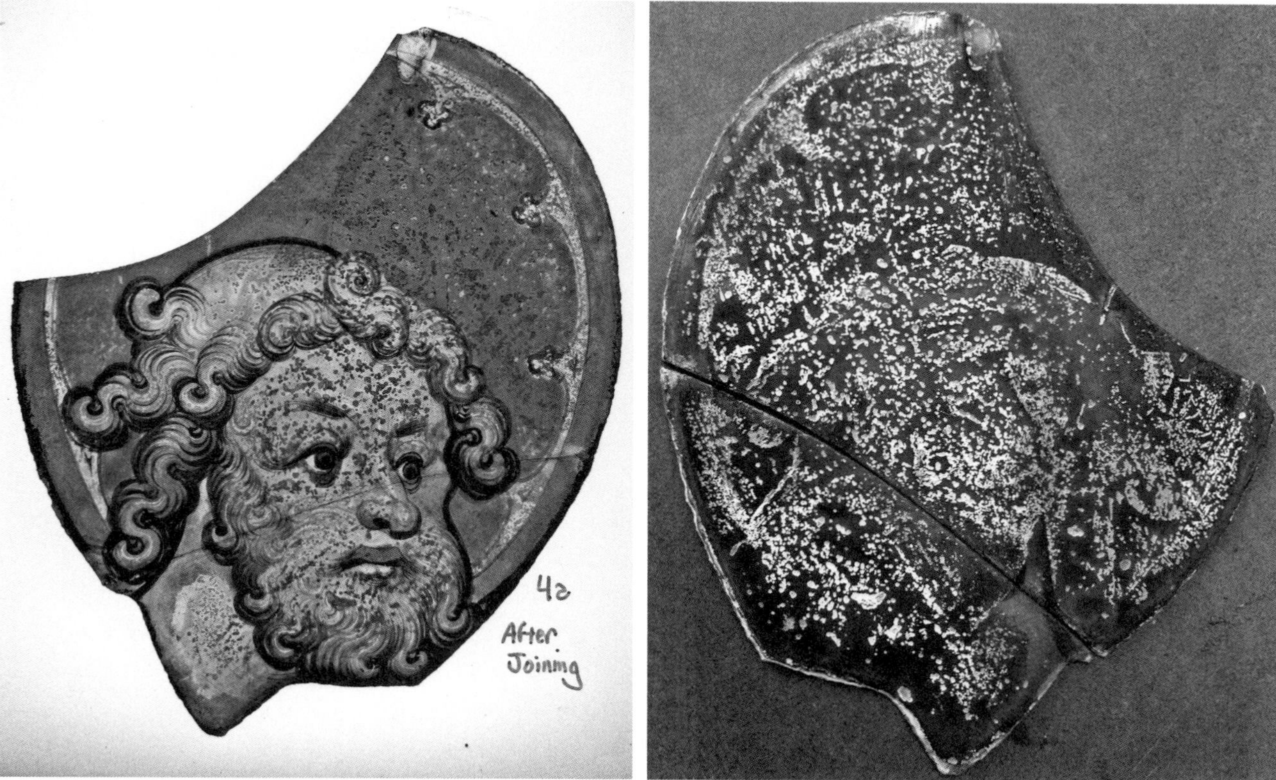

FIGURE 2. (a) Painted head of St. Peter from the Hereford Cathedral Creed Window (photo: Diane Rousseau); (b) back paint and corrosion on the same head (Museum of Fine Arts, Boston, 25.213; photo: author).

ings or textiles, and we are not so likely to find histories of either that span the ninth to the twentieth centuries. A rare monument of that kind is Herbert Read's *The Art of Sculpture*, a publication of the Mellon Lectures for 1954 in the prestigious Bollingen Series. The author skillfully cloaks his own motive for his lectures (to persuade an audience of the intrinsic qualities of sculpture) by giving agency to this art form when he sets out to show "with what difficulty the art of sculpture established its independence—its physical independence as an art separate from its architectural setting, and its aesthetic independence as an art with its own creative principles, and its own standards of appreciation."[22] And with that, he is off, bounding like André Malraux in his museum without walls, through modern Africa, ancient Greece, India, China, Egypt, and Europe, and the works of his contemporaries in England. The dedication, "to Naum Gabo, Barbara Hepworth, Henry Moore, Sculptors and Friends in Gratitude," explains much; Read was determined to find enduring aesthetic principles that could establish his friends' abstract and non-figural works as great sculptures. The relationships he sets out to forge between such diverse works are aesthetic; periodization, history, cultural context, and subject matter have no place in this critical discourse.

The claim to an independent art form was also made by many historians of glass painting, irked, no doubt, by the primacy given to architecture, and the relegation of painted glass to a decorative art. In the 1840s, Charles Cahier and Arthur Martin vociferously called for attention to the theology imbedded in the neglected thirteenth-century windows of Bourges Cathedral that had otherwise been mentioned only for their mystery

22. H. Read, *The Art of Sculpture* (London, 1954), 5.

and somber colors.[23] Other authors who singled out painted glass for publication had a more direct personal stake in the matter, as many were practicing glass painters, latter-day Giorgio Vasaris of their art, caught, as he was, between glorifying an apogee now past and wanting to claim even better things for the art of their own time.[24] Their narrow view served in the long run to isolate glass studies from the broader field of medieval art. This is one sense in which I make reference to a "struggle for survival," manifested in the effort to emancipate painted windows from a subsidiary category and to instate it in the canon. It is a condition from which painted glass has continued to suffer, judging by how little it is represented in our text books, whether in the older diachronic narratives of Gothic Art or in the synchronic and thematic treatments that are more in vogue now.[25] Among traditional survey books, the later editions of Gardner have even fewer illustrations of glass than before, and Michael Cothren informs me that Janson now has only one, as does the most recent edition of Marilyn Stokstad's history of medieval art.[26] In the late 1980s, Colette Manhès-Deremble with Paul Deremble, and especially Wolfgang Kemp, whose work encompassed other media too, attempted to main-line Gothic lancet windows for their systems of visual narratology—I use the metaphor for massive injections into the body of knowledge.[27] Yet the excitement of medieval storytelling in windows was negated by Norman Bryson, who resented having to read intertwined primary and secondary narrative modes in a typological window in Canterbury Cathedral. For him, the "visual pleasure" of "dazzling color and design" is interrupted by the "rigorous programme of religious instruction," resulting in "the supremacy of the *discursive* over the *figural*." [28] His evaluation reinstates the general aesthetic appreciation that the Fathers Cahier and Martin had struggled to displace.

Despite the long-term effect of isolating glass studies, the compulsion to write about glass paintings in the nineteenth century had a positive side. It not only served to make medieval windows known, but it also drove printers to higher and higher standards of color reproduction. The publication of the brilliant thirteenth-century windows of Bourges Cathedral in 1841–44, by Cahier and Martin, presents the first plates made by color lithography (Fig. 3).[29] One of the authors made watercolor drawings and rubbings of the glass, and even participated in etching the stone and copper, though most of the lithography was entrusted to F. Giniez, a young architect trained at the École des Beaux-

23. C. Cahier and H. Martin, *Monographie de la Cathédrale de Bourges*, 2 vols. (Paris, 1841–1844), i–ii.

24. Thibaud, *Considérations historiques* (as in note 15); C. Winston, *An Inquiry into the Difference of Style Observable in Ancient Glass Paintings, Especially in England with Hints on Glass Painting*, Part 2, illustrations (Oxford, 1846); H. Oidtmann, *Die Glasmelerei. Algemein verständlich dargestellt* (Cologne, *c.* 1892); L. Ottin, *Le vitrail: son histoire, ses manifestations à travers les âges et les peuples* (Paris, 1896); H. Arnold and L. B. Saint, *Stained Glass of the Middle Ages in England and France* (London, 1913); C. J. Connick, *Adventures in Light and Color: An Introduction to the Stained Glass Craft* (New York, 1937).

25. V. Sekules, *Medieval Art*, Oxford History of Art (Oxford, 2001), illustrates two whole stained glass windows (Lausanne Rose and Gloucester east), but no details that would show the painting, and no examples in France or Germany; M. Camille, *Gothic Art Glorious Visions* (Upper Saddle River, N.J., 1996), figs. 53, 75, 129: The anagogical window of St.-Denis, with 3 out of 5 panels largely original; a panel from the Erfurt Barfusserkirche; and a detail from the St.-Chéron window in Chartres Cathedral. W. Kemp, *Christliche Kunst: Ihre Anfänge. Ihre Strukturen* (Munich, 1994), does better, with a detail from the Prodigal Son Window of Bourges Cathedral on the cover.

26. H. Gardner et al., *Gardner's Art Through the Ages: The Western Perspective*, 12th ed. (Belmont, Calif., 2006); H. W. Janson, *History of Art*, 3rd ed. (New York, 1986); M. Stokstad, *Medieval art*, 2nd ed. (Boulder, Colo., 2004). I am grateful to Michael Cothren for this information; he is currently revising the short version of Stokstad's book. Among older textbooks for Gothic art are G. Henderson, *Gothic: Style and Civilization* (Harmondsworth, 1967), figs. 18, 31: the heavily restored Jesse Window in St.-Denis, and a general view of the upper windows in the north transept of Chartres Cathedral, and F. Deuchler, *Gothic Art* (New York, 1973), figs. 144, 145.

27. W. Kemp, *Sermo Corporeus: Die Erzählung der mittelalterlichen Glasfenster* (Munich, 1987), translated as W. Kemp, *The Narratives of Gothic Stained Glass*, trans. C. D. Saltzwedel (Cambridge and New York, 1997); C. Deremble and J.-P. Manhes, *Les Vitraux légendaires de Chartres: Des récits en images* (Paris, 1988).

28. N. Bryson, *Word and Image: French Painting of the Ancien Régime* (Cambridge, 1981), 1–28. Overall, and summarized p. 255 n. 31, he presents an oddly positivist progression of the visual sign, from glyph and sigil, through hieroglyph and ideogram, to Masacio and Piero della Francesca and ultimately to abstract expressionism and the painterly trace.

29. Cahier and Martin, *Bourges* (as in note 23).

Arts, Paris.[30] He worked up the prints from detailed models, and Lemercier of Paris printed them to scale on sheets of smooth but, unfortunately, acidic pulp paper, measuring 72 × 55 cm. (28½ × 21¼″). These combined efforts metaphorically aggrandized the windows in immense portfolio fascicles—with a pretentious text printed on quality rag paper introducing the plates—that offered an erudite iconographic analysis. The only way to read it is to put it on the floor and stand over it. Bound in two volumes, each weighs twenty-five pounds. As in most forms of nineteenth-century production, monumentality, if not always sheer size, assured its patrons and consumers of their own superiority. The technique of color reproduction caught on: in Berlin, Wasmuth published a volume of high-quality color lithographs, printed to scale and based on rubbings of the glass.[31] In 1860, Tircher in Brussels produced very fine color lithographs from watercolors by the glass painter and restorer Jean Baptiste Capronnier to illustrate Edmond Lévy's *Histoire de la peinture sur verre*.[32] Such rubbings were often used in the process of restoration of medieval glass, which set a trap for art historians, since we cannot assume they accurately represent a pre-restoration state. Grodecki used to say that we cannot know medieval glass painting until we understand how it has been mediated by the nineteenth-century glass painters and restorers. In fact, Belgium's medieval painted glass virtually disappeared in the hands of Capronnier, because he and his patrons preferred new lamps for old.

An unexpected bonus of Cahier and Martin's *Monographie de Bourges* is their presentation of all the "decorative" designs for borders and the so-called mosaic patterns that filled the interstices between the thirteenth-century medallions (Fig. 3b). These plates were arranged in a taxonomy that includes comparative material, and they immediately became patterns for the neo-Gothic and Crafts movements. Other illustrations of comparative material, especially of figural

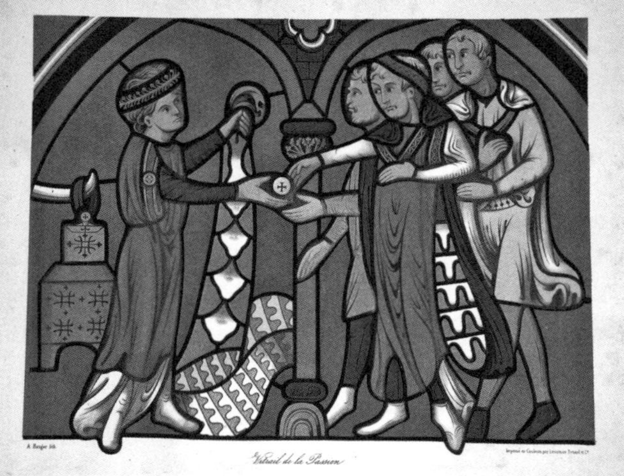

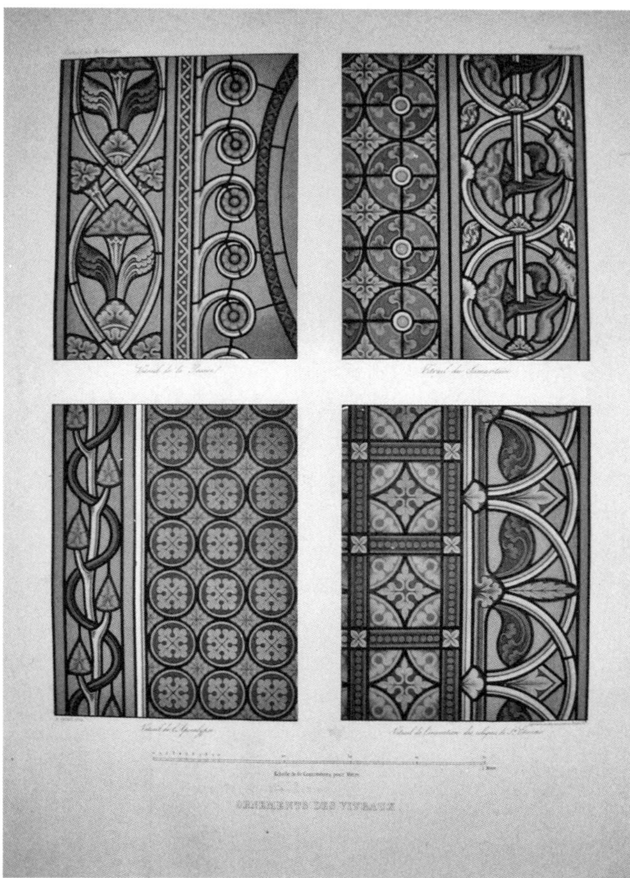

FIGURE 3. Color lithographs made for Cahier and Martin, *Bourges* (as in note 23), details of the Passion Window and of ornament (photo: author).

30. Cahier and Martin, *Bourges*, ii–iii, x (as in note 23). "Guiniez lith" appears in many captions; E. Hauger in a few.

31. C. Schaefer and A. Rossteuscher, *Ornementale Glasmalereien des Mittelalters und der Renaissance nach Original-Aufnahmen in Farbendruck* (Berlin, 1888).

32. Lévy, *Histoire* (as in note 15).

subjects—such as the Good Samaritan window in Sens—are line-drawings that show crisp contours but suppress most of the lead lines. Normally, in fact, less expensive books were illustrated in black and white in this way. An influential example is Nathaniel Hubert John Westlake's four-volume series, *A History of Design in Painted Glass*, 1881–1894, although he also used a few black-and-white rubbings.[33] My own copy has the bookplates of Frederic Leighton and Edward Burne-Jones, an indication of the interest this material held for artists at that time.

In more recent times, color reproduction has not advanced as we might have hoped. For instance, the frontispiece to Herbert Read's book on painted glass, published in 1926, is a far better color reproduction of the figure of Jared from the Canterbury clerestory than the plate made from a new large-format transparency for my *Corpus Vitrearum* volume nearly fifty-five years later.[34] The colors are shifted toward red in the *Corpus* plate, so that the purple hem of Jared's garment appears bright magenta and his chrysophase green mantle appears slightly yellow. The plate in Read's book is reproduced by the color collotype process, from a photograph made the previous year when the Victoria and Albert Museum was photographing all the Canterbury glass in black and white, using large glass plates that are fortunately preserved, but they apparently made some selected color transparencies as well. Photography comes up against the shifting chromatic values noted above, since there is no way to stabilize these effects in a monumental setting; even in a museum, a strip that supplies color standards when placed next to front-lit paintings is of no use in glass. Glass paintings are fraught with instability, not only changing like chameleons with the background and the light, but also changing with gradual destruction by the atmosphere. Close examination of Jared's white tunic reveals some loss of paint between 1926 and about 1975. Old photographs, and even lithographs, can help the art historian envisage the original condition and impact of the work. It is often the painted detail that is at issue, rather than the color of the glass, but since carbon and sulfur in the atmosphere can begin to separate the phosphates and silicates, the glass itself can loose transparency because of corrosion layers. If modern photographs are less satisfactory than old ones, it may well be due to the deteriorating condition of the glass itself, and this renders it unappealing to non-specialists, even those used to looking at damaged stone sculpture that has lost all its original polychromy.

The early twentieth century saw a burgeoning of research and publication on painted glass, but little use of new techniques for color reproduction. Black-and-white line-drawings or photographs became the norm for scholarly illustration in this new phase of historiography. Émile Mâle contributed chapters on painted glass to the first two volumes of André Michel's *Histoire de l'art depuis les premiers temps chrétiens jusqu'à nos jours* in 1905 and 1906, and to the fourth volume on the fifteenth and sixteenth centuries in 1911. He constructed a narrative in which Suger's St.-Denis was the dominant influence, and in which French glass maintained an autonomous development in the thirteenth and fourteenth centuries. Mâle also integrated glass painting into his highly influential volumes on French religious art, published in the decade following World War II, and reissued in many editions and translations.[35] Glass painting figures a good deal in the volumes on the twelfth and on the thirteenth century, but, whereas sculpture is reproduced from photographs, windows are reproduced in line-drawings, so that their artistic effects of color and brushwork are eliminated in favor of clarity of line. They are ideograms serving the purposes of iconography, and they attach glass to the archeological tradition of drawing damaged finds and the profiles of Greek pots. They are so reductive that they convey very little sense of the original works. It was in this visual form that Émile Mâle had introduced painted glass into the mainstream of medieval art history.

Periodization, more than continuity, was of great con-

33. N. H. J. Westlake, *A History of Design in Painted Glass* (London and Oxford, 1881–1894).

34. H. Read, *English Stained Glass* (London, 1926), pl. 1; cf. M. H. Caviness, *The Windows of Christ Church Cathedral, Canterbury*, Corpus Vitrearum Medii Aevi, Great Britain, II (London, 1981), pl. I.

35. É. Mâle, *L'art Religieux de la fin du moyen âge en France. Étude sur l'iconographie du Moyen Âge*, 5th ed. (Paris, 1949); É. Mâle, *L'art Religieux du XIIIe siècle en France. Étude sur l'iconographie du Moyen Age*, 6th ed. (Paris, 1953); É. Mâle, *L'art Religieux du XIIIe siècle en France. Étude sur l'iconographie du Moyen Age*, 9th ed. (Paris, 1958).

cern to art historians almost to the end of the twentieth century. Attempts to define and reify "Romanesque" and "Gothic" intensified, and, for many, this weird thing called stained glass did not fit comfortably. It is amusing to see how a young Herbert Read, working under Bernard Rackham in the Department of Ceramics at the Victoria and Albert Museum in 1926, kept tumbling over himself when he attempted to invent periods for *English Stained Glass*.[36] His survey goes up to the Pre-Raphaelites only to demonstrate "the gradual decline, checkered with various mutations and excrescences, but virtually lasting down to our own days" (apparently he had no glass-painter friends). He began, inexplicably, to define two periods of glass painting: "I. The rise and fall of Gothic art, 1000–1350, and II. The Rise and Fall of Humanistic art, 1350–1900." Next, he notes, as many have, that the terms and dates for the periodization of English medieval architecture proposed by Thomas Rickman (1776–1841), cannot be applied to the other arts.[37] In fact, even for English Gothic architecture, they are absurdly precise because the duration of each style is determined by the reigns of English monarchs: Early English 1189–1307, Decorated 1307–1377, and Perpendicular 1377–1546.[38] At that point, Read finds it necessary to turn from "surface appearances" to "lift our eyes above the immediate subject and survey the general drift of mind and expression." Despite that promise, he is far from anticipating the notion of *mentalités*, or introducing the thematic survey—or even generalizing from Émile Mâle's approach. With a whiff of Hegel (or more likely, Wilhelm Worringer), he announces three periods: "I. The Age of Reason ... generally known as the early Gothic period ... 1150–1350." For him, this ends precisely at the Black Death, although the illustrations inevitably have captions such as "middle of the 14th century."[39] And, "II. The Age of Sentiment ... humanistic ... romantic or late Gothic up to about 1500. III. The Age of Fancy... [characterized by] humanistic decadence ... [and] devoid of ... religious sentiment." He takes this third period to last until about 1900, but his terms are far more apt applied to the aggressive neo-Hun "Mod Gothic" of our own time.[40]

All in all, sculpture came off a great deal better than painted glass at the hands of Read. But he provides a *reductio ad absurdum* that allows us to see the preoccupation with Gothic labels as a pointless endeavor, or at least one with little intrinsic interest for our understanding of glass painting, seeming to touch more on nationalism and self-image. In a larger historiographical frame, despite its pejorative early use, "Gothic," was instated in the nineteenth century alongside "Classical" and "Renaissance," as a keystone of European civilization. E. S. de Beer in 1948, Wayne Dynes in 1973, and, more recently, Paul Crossley have provided very useful insights into its derivation and shifting meanings.[41] Many stronger minds than Herbert Read's have crumbled under the burden of seeking a rational and comprehensive definition of Gothic, which proves to be as elusive as the Grail. One would think that a term that is pure construction, a simulacrum with no signified existential referent (that is, once it was freed from the ethnological group called Goths), could be better defined, but of course referents exist in the minds of people who differ greatly in the way they receive the term and in the images in their memory bank.

The grand nineteenth-century project was to rescue "Gothic" from the valence of barbaric Goths, and instate it as one of the Great Periods in European Civilization and part of the patrimony of each nation. This

36. Read, *English Glass* (as in note 34), 6–8.

37. T. Rickman, *An Attempt to Discriminate the Styles of Architecture in England, from the Conquest to the Reformation: With a Sketch of the Grecian and Roman Orders*, 7th ed. (Oxford, 1881).

38. He cites a far more significant glass scholar, Westlake, as having tried to accommodate this system by sub-dividing it into five, but he omits to say that his basic division is by centuries, and that he allows for great variation between different places at the same time: N. H. J. Westlake, *A History of Design in Painted Glass*, 4 vols., vol. 1 (London and Oxford, 1881), 50.

39. Read, *English Glass* (as in note 34), pls. 17, 19–21.

40. Just Google Mod Gothic and surf.

41. W. Dynes, "Gothic, Concept of," in *Dictionary of the History of Ideas*, ed. P. P. Weiner (New York, 1973), 366–374; E. S. de Beer, "Gothic: Origins and Diffusion of the Term; The Idea of Style in Architecture," *Journal of the Warburg and Courtauld Institutes* 11 (1948), 143–162. Among many of his contributions to the historiography of Gothic are P. Crossley, "'The soldier of science': Paul Frankl and the Gothic Cathedral," in *Magistro et Amico amici discipulique: Lechowi Kalinowskiemu w osiemdziesiolecie urodzin (Festschrift*

trans-valued Gothic was quintessentially a product of colonialism, as demonstrated by Read's impulse to associate it with reason—after all, possessing an ancient, rational AND spiritual past is exactly what the Brits told the colonials they did not have.[42] Even in admitting an African building to the canon of art, Sir Herbert Read's condescension permeates the caption: "A native compound. Gold Coast, West Africa, XX century. Hand molded from mud."[43] Fathers Cahier and Martin had set out on a mission (I choose the word carefully) to combat the ignorance surrounding the windows of Bourges, and establish them as great Christian theological treatises, serving reason and spirituality; this they intended to make intelligible to a wide audience. The authors were opposed to art-historical periodization because it was tied to notions of "profane archeology" (the study of Classical art which they regarded as elitist), and the so-called Renaissance art that followed the Middle Ages.[44] Mâle's thirteenth century is also rational and spiritual. His book on the thirteenth century is dominated by scholastic texts in structure as well as in belief systems, but the original French titles that he gave his books do not mention Romanesque or Gothic art.

As if innocent of the grandiose colonial project, or perhaps because they were in step with the actual demise of colonial rule, many art historians in the middle of the twentieth century concerned themselves with splitting up a too-monolithic Gothic art. They perceived local trends, revivals and survivals of earlier forms, retardataire and avant-garde styles, a proto-Gothic phase that emerged from a twelfth-century renaissance around 1200, and so on. This discourse unified the high arts, since it could be applied equally to works in all materials, not least in painted glass. However, largely unconcerned about such terms, archeologists uncovered the dwellings and graves goods of people of all ranks, from village and town to castle. These secular works challenge (and demonstrate) the unspoken Christo-centricity of Gothic, and glass finds are rare in such contexts compared to pottery. Studies of popular and material culture were most often allied with the Annales School in France, and with socialism in Britain. "Gothic" thus became elitist, associated with such vague formulas as the "Court Style" of the late thirteenth century. The craze for marginalia, for obscenity and the sado-erotic, for grotesques and the grotesque, for the abject, and for street art such as the so-called pilgrim badges that has swept the medieval field, is antithetical to luxurious and sober works in glass. In church windows of the fourteenth century, just a few of the chimeras and apes that invaded contemporary manuscripts crept into tracery lights and borders where they are hard to see, and scarcely impinge on the sacred subjects that are in full view.[45] Sadly, with the exception of labors of the month and heraldic shields from the fifteenth century, there is so little left of glass created for private domestic spaces that we cannot know its range of subjects.

While some historians were expanding the canon, Louis Grodecki returned many times to pondering the origins of Gothic art, and particularly how to define the style in painted glass; after all, the very monument that had been instated as one where Gothic architec-

---

for Lech Kalinowski), ed. W. Bulsza and L. Sadko (Crakow, 2002), 23–24; and P. Crossley, "Salem and the Ogee Arch," in *Architektur und Monumentalskulptur des 12.–14. Jahrhunderts. Produktion und Rezeption. Festschrift für Peter Kurmann zum 65. Geburtstag;* and *Architecture et sculpture monumentale du 12ᵉ au 14ᵉ siècle. Production et réception. Mélanges offerts à Peter Kurmann à l'occasion de son soixante-cinquième anniversaire*, ed. S. Gasser, C. Freigang, and B. Boerner (Bern, 2006), 321–342.

42. In my teens I corresponded with a Masai "pen-pal" in Tanganyika (Tanzania). She told me that before Europeans came to her homeland her people had no religion.

43. Read, *Art of Sculpture* (as in note 22), pl. 1.

44. Cahier and Martin, *Bourges*, iii-vii (as in note 23), in the Preface to the plates.

45. Many chimeras are in the borders and tracery lights of the vast windows of St.-Ouen (Lafond, Perrot, and Popesco, *Saint-Ouen Corpus*, 41–42, pl. 41, as in note 10), and scattered to fill gaps in the windows of Saint-Père of Chartres (P. Biver and E. Socard, "Le vitrail civil au XIVᵉ siècle," *Bulletin Monumental* 77 [1913], 258–264). Other examples include the lower border in the Pilgrim Window of York Minster with scenes such as an ape's funeral (S. Brown, *Stained Glass at York Minster* [London, 1999], pl. 42); a knight-centaur from Jumièges (Aubert et al., *Le Vitrail français*, fig. 46, as in note 3), and excavated fragments published by A. De Schryver, Y. Vanden Bemden, and G. J. Bral, *Gothic Grotesques in Ghent: The Medieval Stained Glass Fragments Found in the Dominican Monastery* (Kortrijk, 1991).

ture came into being, St.-Denis, had windows made for it that were painted in distinctly Romanesque styles. The added conundrum was that the light they shed into the interior of Suger's choir was claimed as quintessentially Gothic light, as though Erwin Panofsky had reconsecrated the Abbey Church to Pseudo-Denis.[46] Attentive to works in other media, Grodecki proposed various solutions, one being that painted glass is best defined as Gothic if it was made for a Gothic building, on the assumption that the term had become a convention for certain structural systems and the spaces they define, and he noted that architecture and glass had a symbiotic relationship.[47]

More interestingly, in light of the way glass studies had risked isolating the medium, Grodecki argued that the Parisian Gothic style of French manuscript illumination was derived from the composition and structure of windows: the use of very firm black contours in manuscript and wall painting of the period stems from a structural necessity in painting on colored glass, since a lead came had to join the pieces of different colors. Even geometric framing devices that were structural elements, as the armatures for glass panels, were occasionally emulated by illuminators; this, however, is not exclusively relevant to Gothic compositions, because Romanesque manuscript painters also used round and quatrefoil frames to organize historiated initials, such as the "I" of *In principio*, and windows were similarly organized.[48] The claim that monumental glass painting drove developments in form and style in other media seems to be one of those semi-truths that itself is driven by a modernist concern with primacy, originality, and invention (after all, the 1950s and 60s witnessed the race to space). However, I am prepared to risk adding that the introduction of oil as medium for panel painting in northern Europe can be understood as a response to the more brilliant and precious material of painted glass. After all, in the fifteenth century a large painted altarpiece often partially covered the painted windows that had served as a retable for the altar. Whatever the validity of these truth-claims, observing communalities between the different media and pressing them into dialogue with each other breaks down the isolation of "glass studies."

It has been harder to break down the isolation of architectural studies. Despite Viollet-le-Duc's serious concern with monumental glass painting, twentieth-century research on Gothic buildings often neglected the glass made for window openings, as well as the figural sculpture, concentrating only on leafy capitals.[49] Yet the structural and design elements involved in the development of glass painting on a monumental scale constitute as much of a novelty in the twelfth century as did the new forms of vaulting and buttressing. Iron armatures (often 2 × 2 inches thick), slotted into the stone frame, lugs and pins to attach the glass, putty to waterproof the joints, lead cames to hold the edges of the glass securely, and stone tracery and mullions, all had to brace the surface against wind and weather. The west window of York Minster, for instance, is about the size of a tennis court. Opening up the Gothic wall did not come without masons and glaziers perfecting all these structural features. In this context, I dare to ask the very simple question: What drove these developments? Was it a love of high buildings and new engineering feats (the things that have driven our skyscraper culture for a century)? Or would it have been the spiritual functions, articulated for instance by

46. P. Kidson, "Panofsky, Suger and Saint-Denis," *Journal of the Warburg and Courtauld Institutes* 50 (1987), 1–17.

47. L. Grodecki, "Le vitrail et l'architecture au XIIème et au XIIIème siècle," *Gazette des beaux-arts* 36 (1949), 5–24. He was also interested to define an early Gothic style in sculpture: L. Grodecki, "La 'première sculpture gothique.' Wilhelm Vöge et l'état actuel des problèmes," *Bulletin monumental* 117 (1959), 265–289.

48. L. Grodecki, "Les problèmes de la peinture gothique," *Critique* 11 (1955), 611–612; L. Grodecki, "Les problèmes de l'origine de la peinture gothique et le 'Maître de Saint Chéron' de la cathédrale de Chartres," *La Revue de l'Art* 40–41 (1978), 43–64. He endorsed Arthur Haseloff's term for the Bibles Moralisées as "vitraux de poche."

49. E. E. Viollet-le-Duc, "Vitrail," in *Dictionnaire raisonné de l'architecture française du XIème au XVIème siècle*, 9 (Paris, 1868; repr., 1870), 373–462. A. Prache, "Stained Glass and Architecture at Saint-Remi of Reims and at Braine: Distinct or Complementary Disciplines?" in *The Four Modes of Seeing: Approaches to Medieval Imagery in Honor of Madeline Harrison Caviness*, ed. E. C. Pastan, E. S. Lane, and E. Shortell (Aldershot, 2009), 151–156, has reviewed the relationship between the two branches of study, in relation to my work and hers.

Durandus? Or the liturgical and cult needs of more chapels on the main level where they were easily connected by processions? Long ago Stephen Murray had the misfortune to suggest publicly that stained glass is the hole in the doughnut, and I remember replying that Gervase of Canterbury stated that he did not want to write about "the mere disposition of stones" at Canterbury, but did so to explain the positions of the various shrines. Instances may be rare in which a whole program of subjects was planned for windows and sculpted portals, although it does happen, as in the west façade of Chartres Cathedral. Yet we might at least reflect that the designers kept coming up with the right number of lights in a rose window for the twelve apostles, twenty-four elders and so on, or four rivers, four seasons, twelve months, twelve zodiac signs as in Lausanne Cathedral. Perhaps the hole in the doughnut was larger than Murray imagined, and the design of the stonework inside the opening in the wall was the province of the glass designers. As in manuscript studies, quarrels over hierarchy are moot if we take a more holistic view. Especially welcome are many recent studies of whole buildings, and of interconnected functions and programs, whether with plural authorship or monographs. Complementary volumes, like those of Stephen Murray and Michael Cothren for Beauvais Cathedral, also demonstrate interconnections.[50]

Despite all these positive changes in the field, why do I still feel uneasy about the possible neglect of painted glass? For those of us who share a passion for medieval painted glass, and for that glorious symbiosis of architecture, sculpture, and glass that is accepted as quintessentially Gothic, there should be no doubt. In 1984, Meredith Lillich stated as a given that "medieval stained glass ... is identified in the popular imagination as the 'cathedral art.' There is no question that stained glass plays a major role in the Gothic esthetic and that stained glass windows, especially rose windows became a hallmark of Cathedral Gothic."[51] Yet what hope is there that this claim will be believed when it is embedded in a book on painted glass that is largely illustrated by poor black-and-white photographs? This is not the fault of the author. Lucky as we are if an archive such as the Direction de l'Architecture can provide photographs printed to scale, we are dependent ultimately on the physical condition of the glass when the photograph was taken. Lillich's dazzling study of windows in the east of France, titled *Rainbow Like an Emerald*, has ONE color plate as frontispiece—this despite an application to the Meiss Fund of the College Art Association for a subvention to pay for more color photography. Her fascinating exposition of the cult of the Holy Face of Christ had to rely on very poorly preserved glass panels that might have been more legible in color; the thirteenth-century images painted in the glass of St.-Gengoult have escaped the attention of scholars outside the field, even though her study encompasses works in other media.[52] Despite the present explosion of digital images that make color reproduction so easy, the university presses are doing no better; I look jealously at the flower catalogues that come in the mail, and think what we could do with commercial resources. Who knows but that scholarly books that encompass painted glass might even sell.

Poor photographs confront the viewer with the struggle for survival of the glass itself. Its physical condition is not unconnected with scholarly reception. Whether or not painted glass has been integrated into the mainstream of our modernist history of art is ultimately a question of the value placed on it—aesthetic, iconographic, innovative, or so on. Whether or not it has been destroyed, neglected, over-restored or con-

50. S. Murray, *Beauvais Cathedral: Architecture of Transcendence* (Princeton, 1989), and M. W. Cothren, *Picturing the Celestial City: The Medieval Stained Glass of Beauvais Cathedral* (Princeton, Oxford, 2006).

51. Lillich, "Monastic Stained Glass: Patronage and Style," (as in note 7), 302. Reprinted in M. Lillich, *Studies in Medieval Stained Glass and Monasticism* (London, 2001), 302.

52. M. P. Lillich, *Rainbow Like an Emerald: Stained Glass in Lorraine in the Thirteenth and Early Fourteenth Centuries*, College Art Association Monographs on the Fine Arts, 47 (University Park and London, 1991), 42–47, pls. III, 2–8. Her study is not mentioned by G. Wolf, "From Mandylion to Veronica: Picturing the "Disembodied" Face and Disseminating the True Image of Christ in the Latin West," in *The Holy Face and the Paradox of Representation. Papers from a Colloquium Held at the Bibliotheca Hertziana, Rome and the Villa Spelman, Florence, 1996*, ed. H. L. Kessler and G. Wolf, (Villa Spelman Colloquia, vol. 6) (Bologna, 1998), nor by other authors in the same collection.

served, is also a result of the qualities ascribed to it in changing social contexts. And the two, as we have seen, are interconnected: glass in a derelict, neglected state is unlikely to be regarded as worthy of mainstream art, and objects that do not stir viewers' imaginations are not worth the effort and expense of conservation. In the roughly 800 years since its installation as a weatherproof membrane, painted glass has been reviled and over-valued, in alternating cycles. Oddly enough, at the extremes, both attitudes have caused destruction. One led to iconoclasm, the other to over-restoration.

The drone in the background all this time has been the gradual breaking down of the glass, its paint, its metal supports of lead and iron, its wooden and stone frames; there can be no benign neglect for this medium. Such deterioration has contributed to the frustration of many modern viewers, who may appreciate the general ambience of colored light, but complain that they cannot see the paintings, especially when they are at some distance. Legibility may be severely impacted by multiple breaks in the glass that have traditionally been mended with additional lead cames (Fig. 1). The distance of many windows from the ground contributes to their decay, since if they are high up they are more exposed to the weather, and the difficulty of access means that their condition can be overlooked. The dilapidations found a decade ago in the huge early fourteenth-century oculus over the main altar of Siena Cathedral risked its very existence (Fig. 4). It is in large part its status as a work attributed to Duccio that has ensured that this glass will remain in a secure space in the Museo dell'Opera della Metropolitana, where the full effects of color and paint can be appreciated, and a copy will replace it in the building itself (Fig. 5).[53] Yet even museums cannot ensure that the process of deterioration does not continue: fifteenth-century glass from Milan Cathedral, installed for many years in the Isabella Stuart Gardener Museum in Boston, visibly suffered from condensation pouring down its outer surface because the protective glazing was installed right up against it, and the wooden frame created an acidic atmosphere that encourages the separation of phosphates and silicates in the glass.

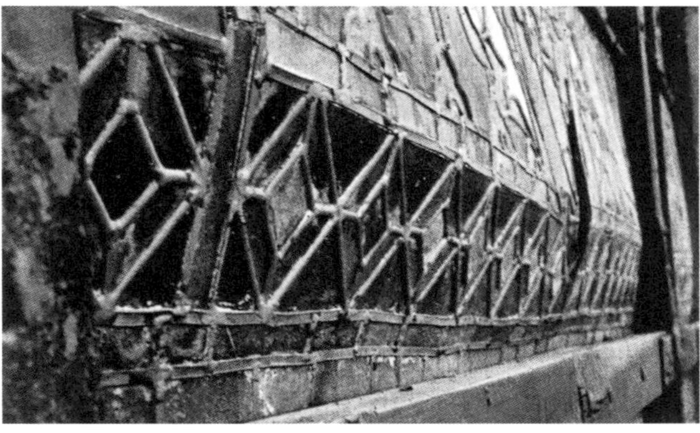

FIGURE 4. Corroded detail of Siena Cathedral oculus, iron and wood giving way (photo: see below).

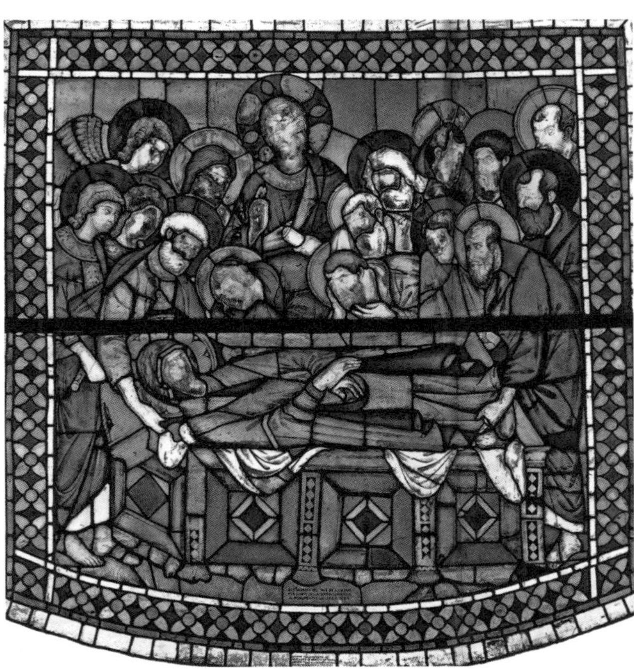

FIGURE 5. The Assumption of the Virgin, detail of the oculus from Siena Cathedral, now in the Museo del Opera del Duomo (Opera della Metropolitana Siena, aut. n. 558/09, by permission).

53. M. Borgogni, "La luce ricomposta. La ricostruzione dalla vetrate nella Sala delle Statue nel Museo dell'Opera della Metropolitana," in *Oculus Cordis: La Vetrata di Duccio. Stile, Iconografia, Indagini tecniche, Restauro*, ed. M. Caciorgna, R. Guerrini, and M. Lorenzoni, (Atti del Convegno internazionale di studi, Siena, Spedale di Santa Maria della Scala, Sala Santa Caterina, 29 settembre 2005) (Siena, 2007); S. Strobl, "The Challenge of Conserving an *Oculus* Window," in *Oculus Cordis: La Vetrata di Duccio. Stile, Iconografia, Indagini tecniche, Restauro*, fig. 6.

Some caretakers of the Gothic period got off to a good start in making allowance for the maintenance of this precious and highly-valued medium, beginning from the time it was installed. For instance, financial arrangements were made for the regular repair of the Sainte-Chapelle windows, Paris.[54] For Chartres Cathedral, Claudine Lautier has identified the hand of a restorer who replaced glass in several of the windows not long after they were made—perhaps replacing pieces broken in a hail storm.[55] There are also instances of fourteenth- and fifteenth-century repairs of this kind, and Françoise Perrot documented the very extensive repairs made to the mid-twelfth-century glass in the west windows of Chartres after the fire of 1194.[56] An unwillingness to part with glass paintings from a previous generation is evident in numerous sites where old panels have been set into a later surround. The *Belle Verrière* window of Chartres is a famous example: This Virgin and Child of about 1180–1190 was also apparently salvaged from the fire and put into a Gothic lancet window, with a complement of censing angels and narrative scenes that give the original image the appearance of a precious icon.[57] Many twelfth-century panels in fact have been similarly preserved—whether moved up from the crypt of St.-Denis to an upper chapel in the thirteenth century for liturgical reasons, or releaded and repaired after a fire in Troyes and installed with new borders to fill larger windows. The list is long, and in some cases it would have been easier to start over with new designs, indicating that material values did not govern the decision. On the other hand, there are also cases where a window or two were sacrificed at the will of a wealthy patron, in order to build a chantry chapel. In some cases, such as the mid-fifteenth-century Jacques Coeur Chapel in the Cathedral of Bourges, the new glass is so resplendent it makes up for the loss.

The immediate post-medieval phase was much more destructive.[58] Throughout northern Europe, beginning in England in the early sixteenth century, and growing in violence at the peak of Protestant iconoclasm in the seventeenth, painted windows were smashed, or simply disappeared from abbey ruins; it was by great good fortune that such panels survived, only to be over-restored for a growing market in the nineteenth and twentieth centuries. During the Reformation, a great many small devotional works were destroyed as idols, but it was possible to hide some of them. Painted glass was harder to take out and hide, though equally, iconoclasts could not reach all of it. Fairly systematic iconoclasm in Canterbury Cathedral, during the Civil War between the Parliamentarians and the Royalists, is carefully documented in a painting by Thomas Johnson, "Canterbury Quire as in 1657;" it shows soldiers with pikes standing on the sills of windows at all levels and beating out the lower panels of glass, as they would have done in 1642–1643.[59] Lying behind the orchestrated action is iconophobia, a fear of the power that the image could have over people, and perhaps even of the possibility that images did have supernatural powers. The destruction of "papist idols" is character-

54. Foundation charters, dated 1246 and 1248, when the windows must have been glazed, specify the chapter's fiscal duties concerning the repair and maintenance of the glass; cited Grodecki, Lafond, et al., *Les Vitraux de Notre-Dame et de la Sainte Chapelle de Paris* (as in note 5), 73, n. 1.

55. C. Lautier, "Les vitraux de la cathédrale de Chartres à la lumière des restaurations anciennes," in *Künstlerischer Austausch / Artistic Exchange. Akten des XXVIII. Internationalen Kongresses für Kunstgeschichte, Berlin, 15.–20. Juli 1992*, ed. T. W. Gaehtgens (Berlin, 1993), 413–424.

56. F. Perrot, "Les verrières du XIIe siècle de la façade occidentale [de la cathédrale de Chartres]: Études archéologique," *Les monuments historiques de la France*, no. 1 (1977), 37–51.

57. C. Brisac et al., "La Belle-Verrière de Chartres," *Revue de l'Art* 46 (1979), 16-24; C. Bouchon, "Regards sur le vitrail de Notre-Dame de la Belle-Verrière de Chartres au travers de ses restaurations," in *Le vitrail roman et les arts de la colour. Nouvelles approches sur le vitrail du XIIe siècle*, ed. J. F. Luneau, *Revue d'Auvergne 570* (Cleremont-Ferrand, 2004), 169–182. Mary B. Shepard, "Memory and *Belles Verrières*" in *Romanesque Art and Thought in the Twelfth Century*, (University Park, 2008), 291–302.

58. Many studies of iconoclasm have appeared recently, among them J. Phillips, *The Reformation of Images: Destruction of Art in England, 1535–1660* (Berkeley, 1973).

59. D. Ingram Hill, "The Iconoclasts in Canterbury Cathedral," *Canterbury Cathedral Chronicle* (1974), 20–22; Caviness, CVMA, *Canterbury*, (as in note 32), 38, 10, 152; M. Sparks, "The Refitting of the Quire of Canterbury Cathedral, 1660–1716: Pictorial and Documentary Evidence," *Journal of the British Archaeological Association* 154 (2001), fig. 1.

istically defiantly staged through verbal and pictorial rhetoric (often prints), and these records themselves could shock or delight later audiences. Such iconoclastic exchanges are often referred to now as "iconoclash," since they are at the intersection of conflicting belief systems; one man's idol is another man's icon.[60]

Canterbury Cathedral narrowly escaped being torn down in 1652 in order to sell the fabric to fund the war against the Netherlands.[61] It was put back into use and gradually refurbished after the Restoration of 1660. In these circumstances, glass was needed immediately to fill the gaping holes in the windows, and the easiest way to obtain it was to gather up the fragments from the floor and sills, arrange them in a virtually non-representational (or unintelligible) kaleidoscope, and put these made-up panels in the windows to keep out the rain and wind (Fig. 7). There the fragments of figures usually awaited a "rational" restoration in the late eighteenth, nineteenth, or even twentieth centuries—unless, of course, the canons elected to glaze the whole window with unpainted, colorless quarries, a condign action of the Enlightenment.

Leaving aside the well-known iconoclasms of the French Revolution and the Napoleonic wars, since these mimic in many respects the events of the English Civil War, we come full circle to the reception history of thirteenth-century stained glass more or less at the very beginning of modernity, when the Fathers Cahier and Martin and their color lithographs were enthusiastically heralding the age of mechanical reproduction. The fervor that drove such laborious enterprises, and the restoration of the cathedrals with their sculpture and painted glass, is often credited to a Gothic Revival movement. Yet the preface to the *Monographie* makes quite clear that the Fathers' declared agenda was to correct the ignorance of their clerical predecessors, and with it the neglect of the windows that had allowed the destruction of some panels in the winter of 1841. They appear to believe fervently in the notion that such windows were the bibles of the laity, and should be explicated to them. The spirit is that of a Catholic Revival; Gothic is nowhere in their philosophy.

This brief review of the material fate of medieval painted glass, and of its reception through time, is followed by a case study. I have recently discovered an event during another Catholic Revival that involves important painted glass from an English cathedral having been salvaged during the Civil War. It was presumably hidden in the 1640s and eventually—after the Restoration—installed in the private chapel of a Royalist. Both acts involved the personal risk of being accused of Papacy. Such survivals are almost unknown, because there was no collectors' market of the kind that scooped up glass from the French Revolution, so most often painted glass simply disappeared.

The glass had been taken out of Hereford Cathedral, which appears to have suffered as much as Canterbury from the Parliamentarians, though few records have come to light other than the fabric's lingering scars. For instance, sculpted tombs were defaced by literally hacking off the nose of a bishop's effigy and decapitating the angels that surround his bier. The destruction of stone images is laborious, but decapitation is relatively easy and it constitutes a symbolic act; by collapsing the sign so that the likeness in stone is elided from its referent, revenge is taken on the image as a surrogate. The decapitated bodies remain to tell the tale, like corpses on a gibbet.[62] Hereford's cult statue of the Virgin Mary, a particular target by Protestants, was utterly destroyed. Evidence of damage to the windows is still seen in the nave aisle of Hereford Cathedral, with the hasty re-glazing mentioned above that is typical of repairs after the Civil War of the 1640s (Fig. 7).

The convergence of several circumstances has enabled me to confirm a hypothesis that I had pondered for forty years.[63] I was especially lucky to have a dialogue

60. B. Latour and P. Weibel, eds., *Iconoclash: Beyond the Image Wars in Science, Religion and Art*, Exhib. Cat., Karlsruhe, Zentrum für Kunst und Medientechnologie (Cambridge, Mass., 2002).

61. Sparks, "Quire of Canterbury Cathedral," (as in note 59), 188.

62. M. H. Caviness, "Iconoclasm and Iconophobia: Four Historical Case Studies," *Diogenes* 50, no. 199 (2003), 99–114. A classic case is the commissioned beheading of the statues of kings on the west façade of Notre-Dame de Paris.

63. M. H. Caviness, "Fifteenth Century Stained Glass from the Chapel of Hampton Court, Herefordshire: The Apostles' Creed and Other Subjects," *The Walpole Society Publications* 43 (1968–70),

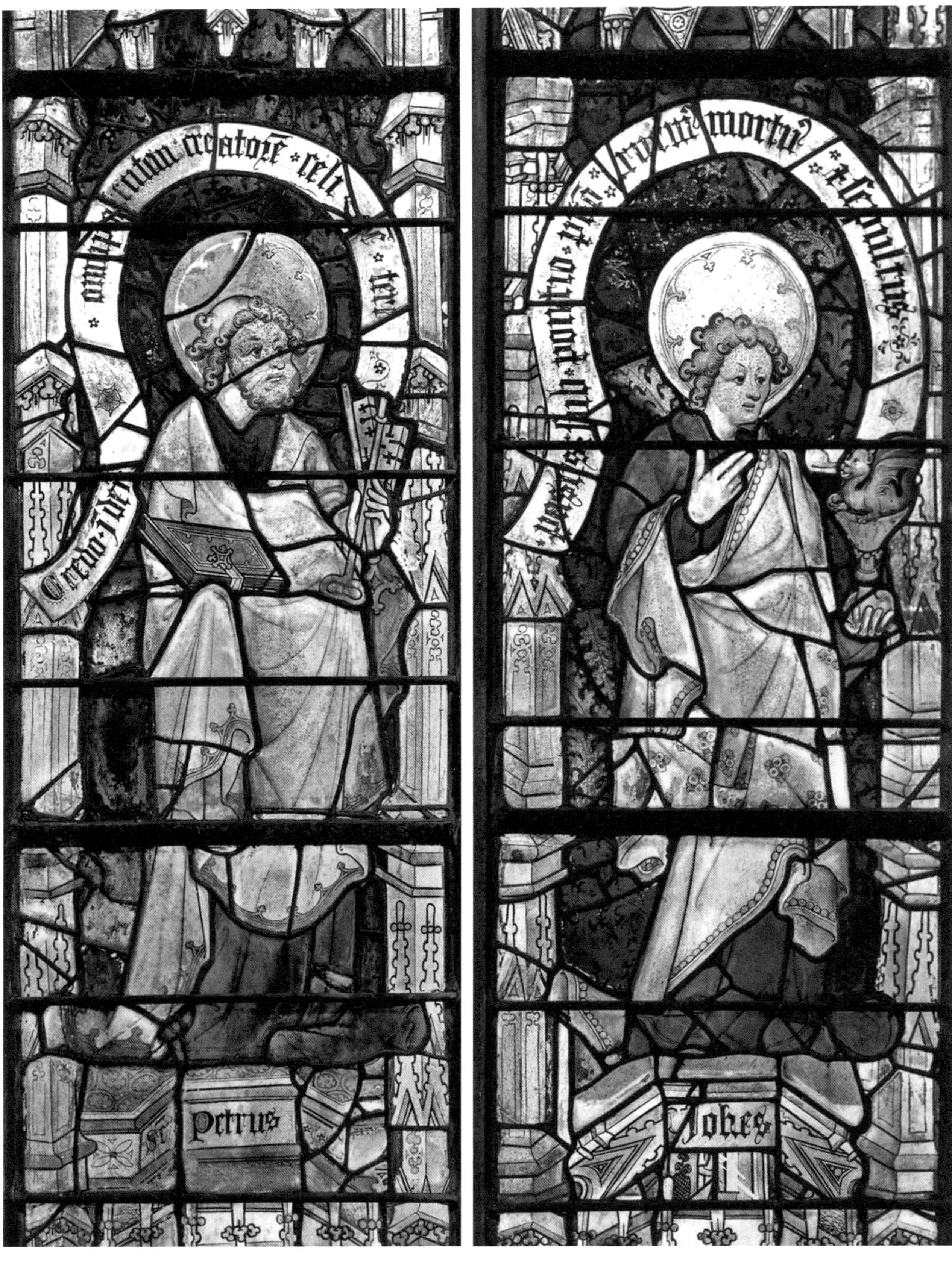

FIGURE 6. Two Apostles with Creed inscriptions from Hereford Cathedral: Window with Eight Apostles, the Pietà, and other Saints—details: St. Peter and St. John (Museum of Fine Arts, Boston; photo © 1970).

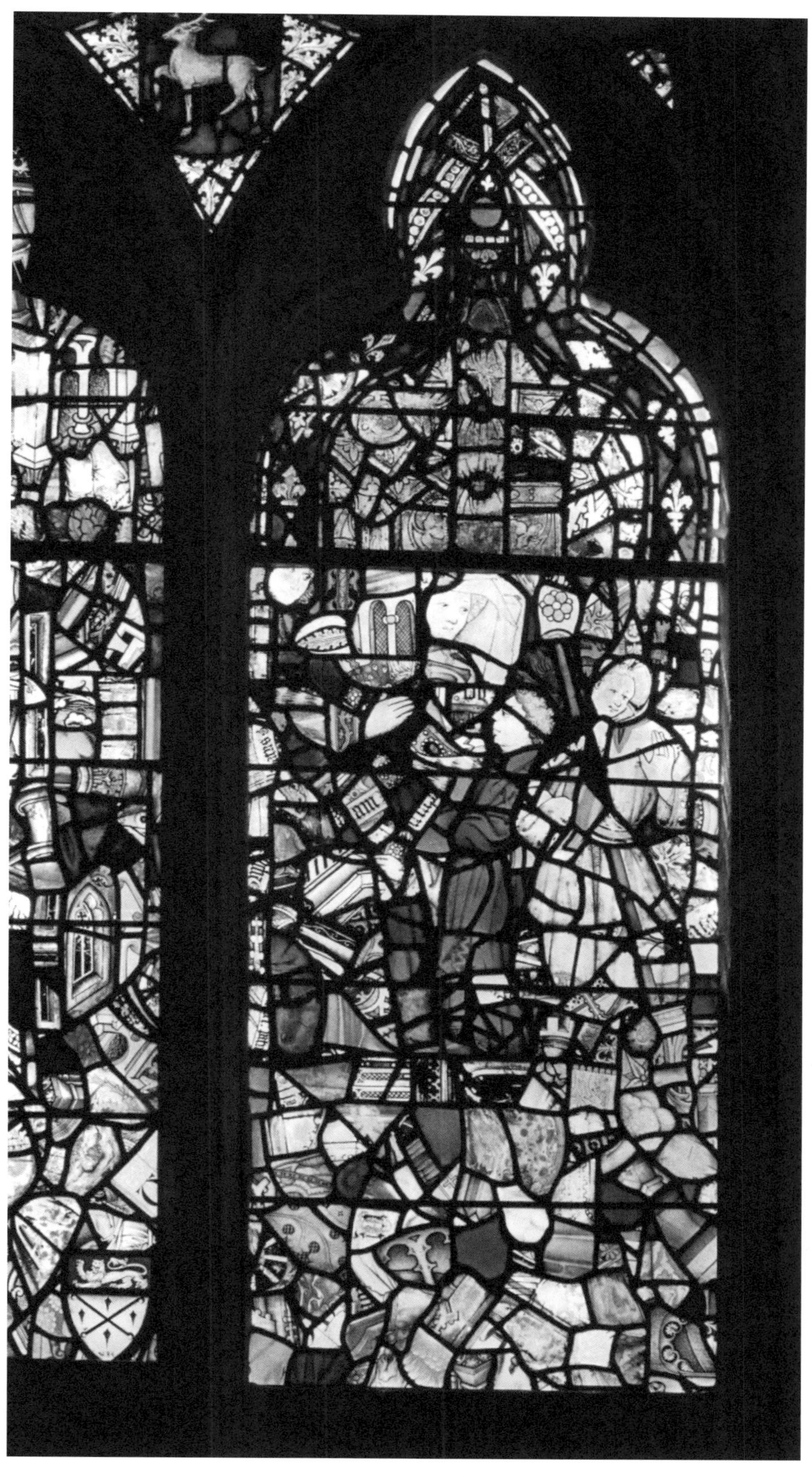

FIGURE 7. Hereford Cathedral, south choir aisle, fragments of glass leaded up after iconoclasm (photo: Roger Rosewell, by permission).

with the restorer Diane Rousseau during her on-going conservation of the Apostles' Creed that belongs to the Museum of Fine Arts, Boston. Each of us made new observations, sometimes helped by Marilyn Beaven as well, that led to a clear understanding of ways in which the late seventeenth-century glass painters adapted the glass to its new setting.[64] In Hereford, study of accounts of the local events of the English Civil War, and of archival documents, confirmed the struggle on the part of a single Catholic family, beginning at the time of the Civil War, to preserve these beautifully painted remnants of early fifteenth-century glass (Figs. 2, 6, 11, 12). At the same time, thanks to very accurate laser measurements of some early fifteenth-century stonework in Hereford Cathedral, taken for me by the cathedral architects, I can now be certain these panels perfectly fit the perpendicular window openings in the southwest transept (Figs. 10, 13).[65]

All that was previously certain about these figures was that they had been seen in the Chapel of Hampton Court, Herefordshire, not far from Hereford, in 1683, and that Grosvenor Thomas and Wilfred Drake, dealers in painted glass, bought them from the owner of the house in 1923.[66] Grosvenor Thomas' inventory of his purchases coincides very closely with the subjects seen in the chapel windows in 1683.[67] The fifteenth-century owner of the manor house, Sir Rowland Lenthall, had received license from the King to crenellate in 1435, and parts of the existing structure date from that period (Fig. 8); it had been assumed that the glass originated in the chapel and therefore dated from the 1430s, although I was uneasy with that date on stylistic grounds, as was David O'Connor.[68] Seen today, the house appears to be dominated by early nineteenth-century renovations (which the chapel and gate-tower escaped), but John Cornforth found evidence of extensive work on parts of the house towards the end of the seventeenth century and into the eighteenth.[69]

When they removed the fifteenth-century glass, Thomas and Drake glazed the chapel windows with largely modern quarries and the heraldic shields of previous owners, leaving some seventeenth-century heraldic glass and other fragments in the tracery lights of the north side. Examination of the stonework last year revealed that parts of the window embrasure on the interior show the kind of extreme rain damage that could only have happened with exposure to the elements. I conclude that the chapel was abandoned and in ruins for a period, and repaired with stone from other parts that were better preserved. The timber roof—or vaults—was not restored, and instead a wooden ceiling was installed that is too short for the chapel. Architectural

35–60, reprinted in Caviness, *Paintings on Glass*, ch. XV. All the glass known to have come from Hampton Court is described and illustrated.

64. Much thanks to the selection committee of the ICMA and my British hosts, who enabled me to see some of this glass in London and Glasgow, and to my brother and sister-in-law, Michael and Jennifer Harrison, who put up with me while I worked in Hereford, near their home. Catherine Beale and Roger Rosewell arranged a visit to Hampton Court together. I am also grateful to the curators and conservators of the Victoria & Albert Museum in London, to the Burrell Collection of the Glasgow Museums, and to the Boston Museum of Fine Arts, for allowing me to examine the panels on the bench.

65. I am very grateful to Mr. Kilgour for providing these studies.

66. T. Dingley, *History from Marble compiled in the Reign of Charles II*, ed. J. Gough Nichols, printed in photolithography by Vincent Brooks, from the Original in the Possession of Sir Thomas E. Winnington, Bart., with an introduction and Descriptive Table of Contents by John Gough Nichols, F.S.A. ed., *Camden Society 94* (London, 1867), 35, no. 33; his entry for Hampton Court is dated January 1683, those for Hereford, 1684. The files in the Boston Museum of Fine Arts from the time of the purchase of one window in 1925 include a typed list from the dealers. The panels are also recorded in their sale books: M. M. Beaven, "Grosvenor Thomas and the Making of the American Market for Medieval Stained Glass," in *The Four Modes of Seeing: Approaches to Medieval Imagery in Honor of Madeline Harrison Caviness*, ed. E. C. Pastan, E. S. Lane, and E. Shortell (Aldershot, 2009), 481–496.

67. The Boston Museum has a typed list provided by the dealers. The Sales Books are now in the Library of the Society of Antiquaries in London.

68. C. J. Robinson, *A History of the Mansions and Manors of Herefordshire* (London, 1873; repr., Logaston Press, 2001), 145; Caviness, "Glass from Hampton Court," 35–60; D. O'Connor, "Bishop Spofford's Glass at Ross-on-Wye," in *Medieval Art, Architecture and Archaeology at Hereford*, ed. D. Whitehead, British Archaeological Association Conference Transactions, XV (London, 1995), 143.

69. J. Cornforth, "Hampton Court, Herefordshire—The Property of Captain the Hon. Philip Smith," *Country Life* (1973), 450–453 and 518–451.

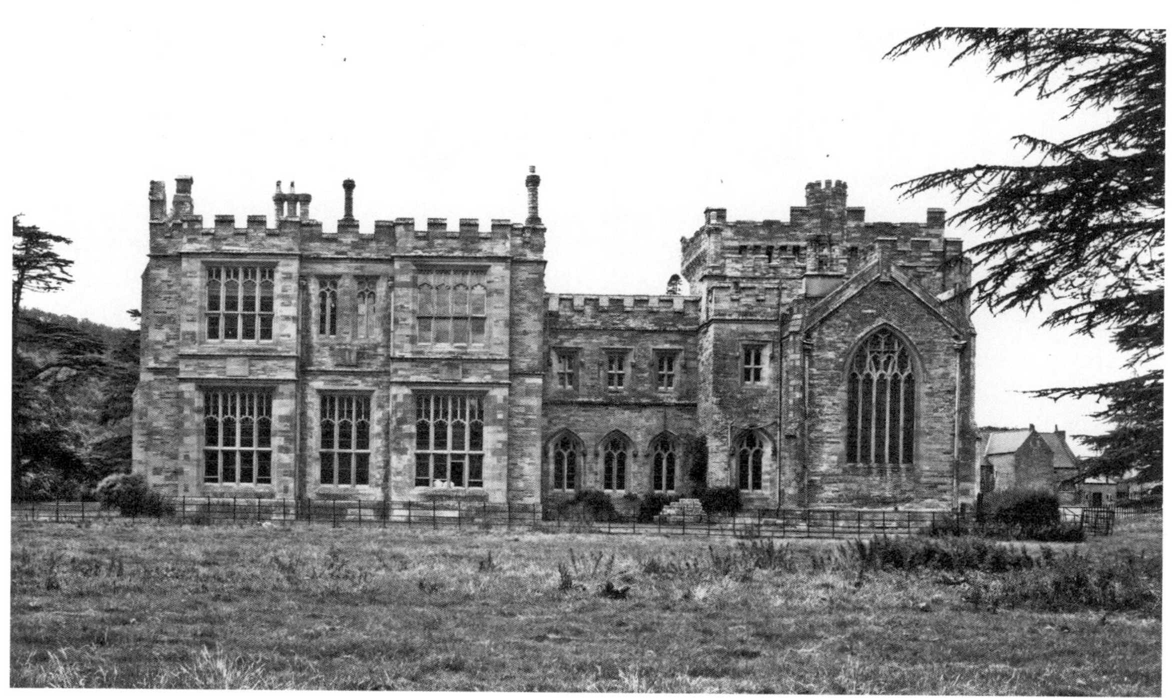

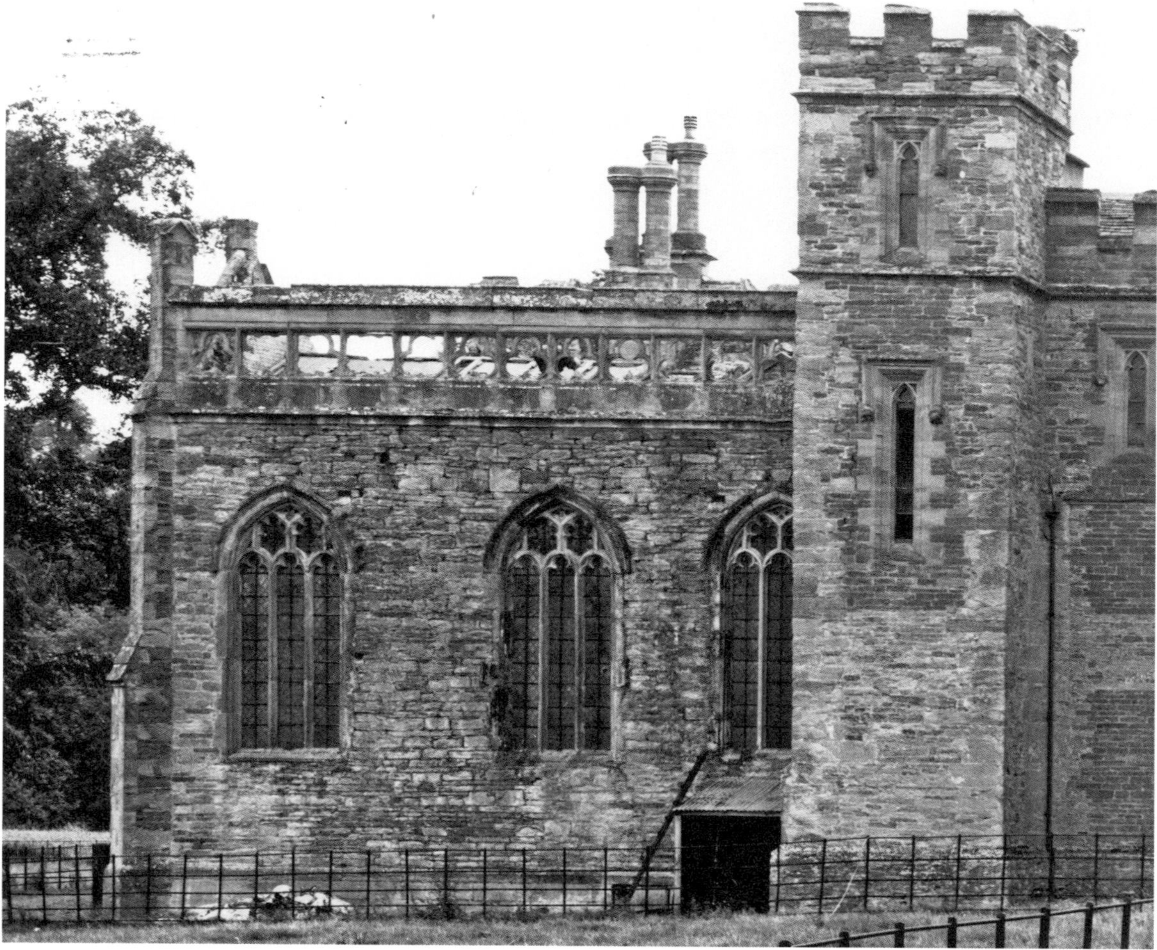

FIGURE 8. Hampton Court, Herefordshire: (a) Photographed from the east, with the chapel on the right; (b) The chapel from the north, both 1975 (National Monuments Record, by permission).

historians have concluded that it was taken from some other space, perhaps the hall. A distant view by a little-known painter called Leonard Knyff, dated 1699, shows a completely restored house in magnificent formal gardens. John Cornforth has convincingly argued that Thomas Lord Coningsby began some of this work about 1680, just before Dingley's description; he had inherited the house in 1666 but did not come of age until 1679.[70]

My narrative returns to Hereford to find out what happened to the "Hampton Court" glass between the early fifteenth century and 1683, and, specifically, how it might have been saved during the Civil War. As the Parliamentarian army approached Hereford in 1642, there was fear in the town that the militia would burst in and "burn bibles," but it turned out to have a period of grace; having entered in October, the Earl of Stamford withdrew from Hereford in December. But he had captured Lord Scudamore, Governor of Herefordshire. The Royalists then held the city until December 1645. The Sheriff of Herefordshire, Fitzwilliam Coningsby, was in charge of its defense, and managed to hold off a siege by the Scottish army. For his staunch defense of the King and the Catholic Church he became known to his enemies as one of the Nine Worthies.[71] During those three years, Coningsby would have had time to hide some religious images, perhaps already damaged, possibly sequestering them in his house. He owned Hampton Court and a good deal of land round it at the time, but he was captured when Hereford fell, eventually being freed and continuing his fight in Ireland. Parliamentarian revenge on these leaders was severe after 1645—one of the Nine had his manor house burned down. It was common for the troops to demolish buildings for their lead roofs or timbers—the lead roof was stripped off the Cathedral Chapter House in 1645, and it still stood in ruins in 1799.[72] Bishop Coke was imprisoned in 1641 and again in 1645.[73] The seventeenth-century engraving published in 1718 in Dugdale's *Monasticon Anglicanum* shows a tidy cathedral; presumably most of the fabric was left intact, or hastily repaired after 1646 when Parliament decided on the new liturgy and preaching ministers were appointed to replace the chapter. Fitzwilliam Coningsby and Hampton Court did not fare as well. His lands were seized and he went into debt, from which he had not fully recovered at his death in 1666.[74] During his absence, his wife was reduced to begging friends for help to pay the rent to live elsewhere; in 1652, Parliamentary troops occupied Hampton Court.[75] This is surely when the chapel fell into ruin, probably from a combination of stripping lead from the roof and iconoclasm. Any painted glass that Sir Rowland Lenthall had installed in the windows would have been broken, but it is entirely possible that the panels from the cathedral remained securely hidden in the very extensive cellars that run under the house; an area could even have been walled off.

There is no indication of glass in Hampton Court Chapel before 1683. It is hard to know how to interpret Thomas Dingley's statement in that year that the "Chapel is considerable and hath been for its curious painted glass," but he goes on to mention many of the subjects he saw in it. His list corresponds very closely with the pieces that passed through the hands of Thomas and Drake and are recorded in their Sales Book, which is now in the Society of Antiquaries Library in London. However, they made no mention of prophets, and there are other discrepancies. It is very unlikely that Dingley saw all twelve Apostles with creed scrolls, since only eight were in the east window in 1923; and the five-light window could never have held twelve. Thomas and Drake found Marian scenes in the fifth light of the east window (Fig. 8).

We have to turn to the glass to tell its own tale. It is evident that borders have been trimmed off, and the architectural canopies cut down and jumbled (Figs. 6, 11).

70. Cornforth, "Hampton Court,"(as in note 69), 451–453.

71. J. Webb, *Military Memoir of Colonel John Birch Sometime Governor of Hereford in the Civil War between Charles I. and Parliament written by Roe, his Secretary*, *Camden Society*, N.S. 7 (London, 1873), 107.

72. G. Aylmer and J. Tiller, eds., *Hereford Cathedral: A History* (London and Rio Grande, 2000), 102, pl. 111b.

73. Robinson, *Mansions of Herefordshire* (as in note 65), 103.

74. Cornforth, "Hampton Court" (as in note 66), 451.

75. Robinson, *Mansions of Herefordshire*, (as in note 62), 146–147.

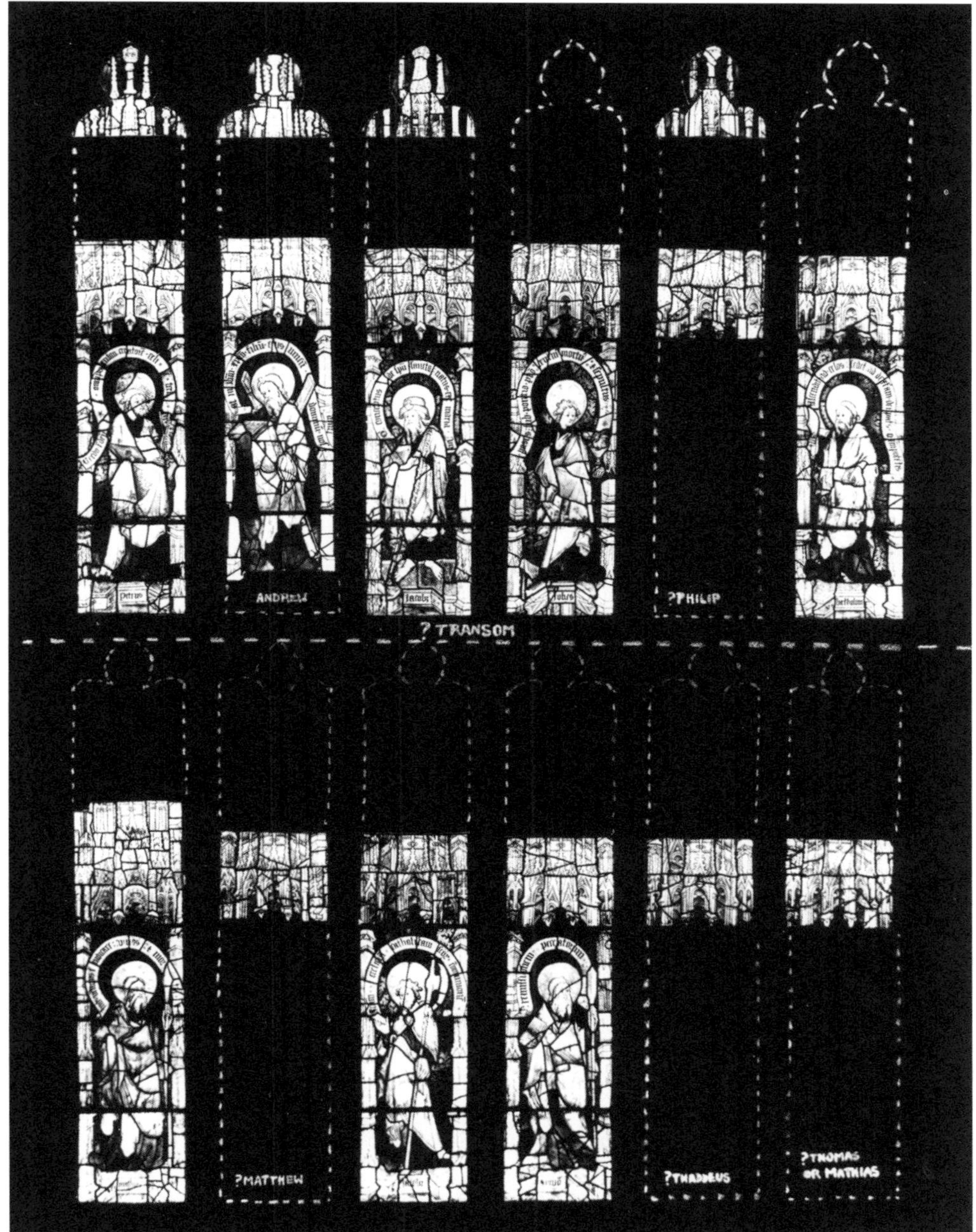

FIGURE 9. Schematic reconstruction of the Apostles' Creed Window (author, 1970).

Fragments of glass from other panels of the series were used in quantities to replace missing pieces. As I argued in 1970, the full Creed required a window of six perpendicular lights, and the abbreviated canopies indicate that they were much higher than the ones in the chapel (Fig. 9). At least two more large windows are needed for the other subjects. The new, accurate measurement of three perpendicular windows in the south transept of Hereford Cathedral prove that all the Hampton Court glass must have been made for them. A complete reconstruction of the Apostles' Creed, including high canopies, is a comfortable fit in the larger of two windows in the west wall (Fig. 10, right).

Three standing saints—the deacons Stephen and

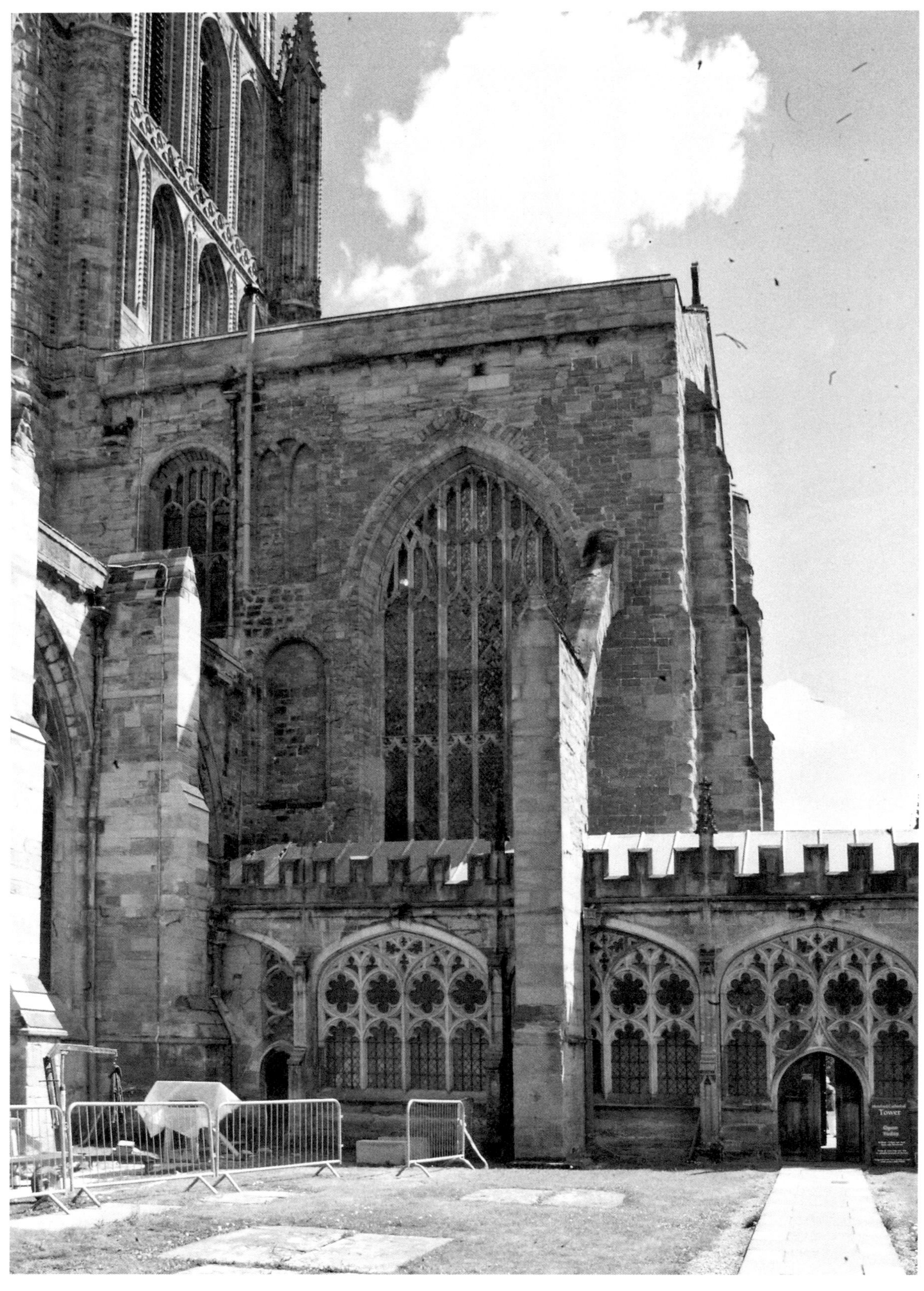

FIGURE 10. Hereford Cathedral, exterior of the southwest transept, two perpendicular windows in the west side (photo: Roger Rosewell, by permission).

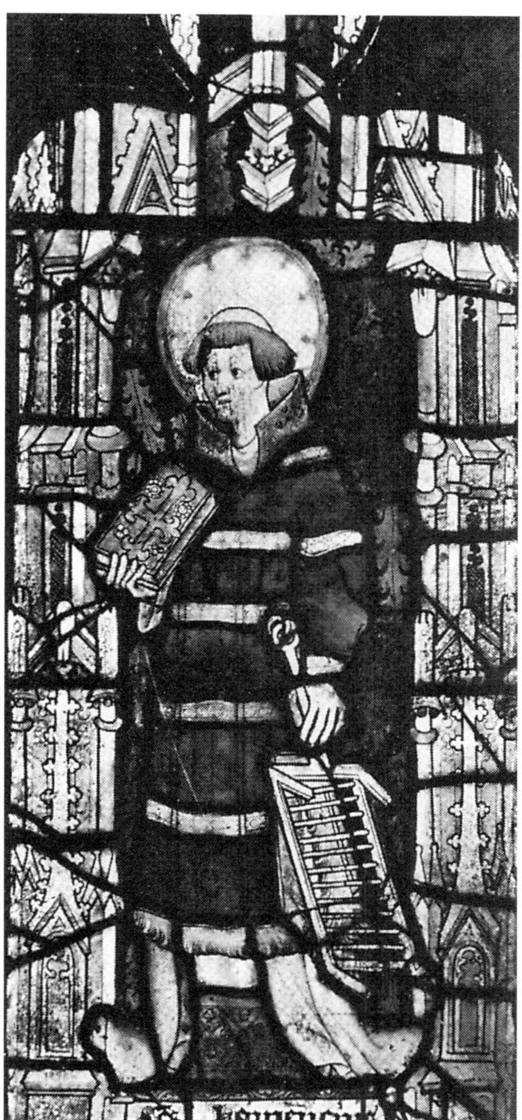

FIGURE 11. St. Lawrence from Hereford Cathedral (London, Victoria & Albert Museum, C.237-1931, by permission).

Lawrence now in the Victoria and Albert Museum in London, and one in Washington, most probably Benedict—would have been designed for the smaller west window over the aisle roof, which would have accommodated three more figures of this size (Figs. 10, left, and 11). Three smaller hagiographic subjects with canopies are now in the Montreal Museum of Fine Arts: St. Anne teaching the Virgin, St. Winifred, and St. Thomas Becket, would fit the tracery lights of the same window, and the John the Baptist and the *Pietà* squeezed into the tracery of the Boston window may have been there as well.

Two magnificent Marian scenes—the Annunciation and Assumption—now in the Burrell Collection in Glasgow, must have been part of a larger series with the Seven Joys, or the whole life, of Mary (Fig. 12). These two panels fit the width of the lights in the south window of the transept, and even the present interval of the iron bars, but they appear to be a tiny fraction of a series extensive enough to have included the Life of St. Anne as well as of Mary (Fig. 13).[76] Or, like the later window in the transept of Canterbury, it could have had a central Crucifixion, with saints and kneeling donors. Another complication is that Dingley said of this window, over the tomb of Bishop Trefnant in the south transept, "in the Glass are the remains of the figures of Saint Thomas of Cantelupe, the blessed virgin, King Ethelbert in his royal robes, St. Dennis the patron of France with his head in his hands, and that of the holy Apostle St. Paul."[77] I surmise that either these saints were in the lower part of the window, perhaps presenting donors to a central figure, or they had been gathered up from elsewhere in the building when it was refurbished in 1660. The stonework of this window was apparently entirely replaced when the nineteenth century glass was put in, but it fills the original exterior frame, and on the interior it is commensurate with the blind tracery that frames the tomb of Bishop Trefnant and extends up on each side of the window to prolong the window tracery into the apex. It is possible that the original glazing was complete about the time of his death in 1404, which is close to the time John Thornton of Coventry was contracted to paint the immense Great East Window in York Minster with narrative subjects.

With the full history of the "Hampton Court" glass in mind, we were able to make some detailed observations in the conservation workshop that reveal some

76. I am grateful to Marie Stumpff, Senior Conservator for Objects, Glasgow Museums, for pointing out that the compositions, and possible wealth of subjects, are found in English alabaster carvings.

77. Dingley, *History from Marble* (as in note 60), clxxxiv.

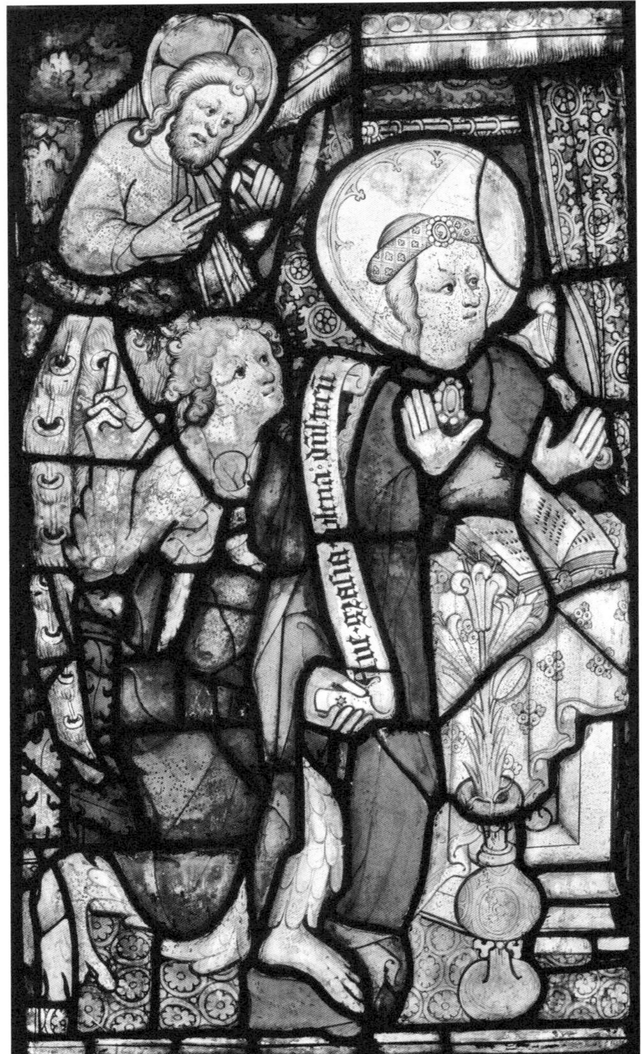

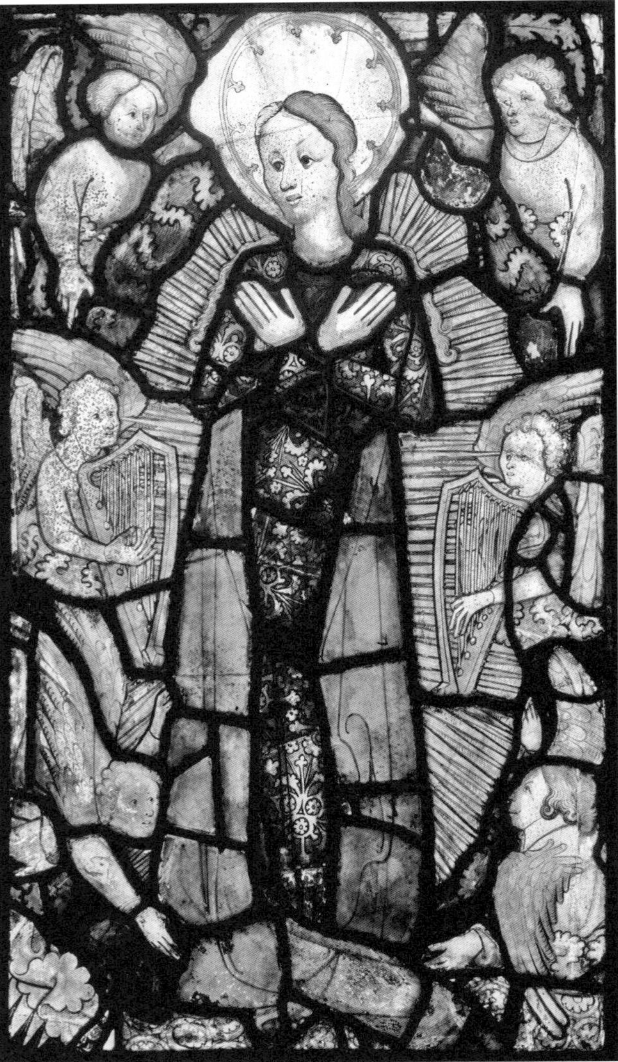

FIGURE 12. Two scenes from the Life of the Virgin Mary: (a) The Annunciation; (b) The Assumption (Glasgow Museums, Burrell Collection, 45.588 and 45.589, photos by permission).

very unusual aspects of the restoration that was carried out for Thomas Coningsby *c.* 1680. With some pieces of glass out of the leads we could see how they had been trimmed down, and we found instances of the use of palimpsest glass. The head of St. Peter was marred by a mending lead that sealed a crack; this has been removed so the mended crack will be scarcely perceptible (Fig. 2). Elsewhere, when Diane Rousseau took mending leads out to make new repairs, she sometimes found the imprint of an unusual type of lead, unlike others in the window that had been supplied in 1923. When modern leads are extruded from a mill, they have an indent that is very regular and closely spaced, like the edge of a coin. But some of the old mending leads left a very different imprint in the putty on the edge of the glass—one I could only characterize as post-medieval and premodern (medieval cames are cast, not extruded).

A part of the nimbus of St. Peter is not original, and we were interested to ascertain its age (Fig. 14a). The glass proved to be medieval, and cut with more or less medieval tools, but the edge does not have the corrosion layers of the original pieces in the window. We found the same kind of ragged edges where the panels had been cut down to fit the Hampton Court windows.

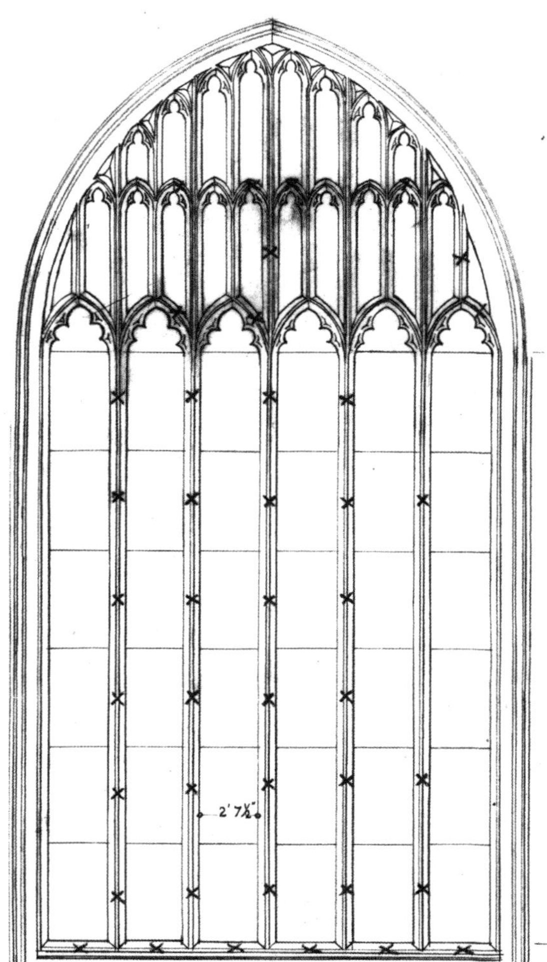

FIGURE 13. Hereford Cathedral, South Window of the South West Transept, scale drawing of the stonework by E. A. Rosier, 1956 (photo: Dean and Chapter of Hereford, Cathedral Archives 6425/450/31, by permission).

In those cases, it was clear that the restorer cut through painted areas. The replacement piece in St. Peter's nimbus was cut by our pre-modern restorer. It turned out to be reused fifteenth-century glass made for a quite different design—a palimpsest, with original paint and silver stain wiped off with acid, and new stain applied to fit the nimbus. This is a technique often used in twentieth-century forgeries, but it has never been observed in such an early restoration. By tracing the faint original design, and working from a small straight edge that was cut in the fifteenth century, we found that the piece had been a typical early to mid-fifteenth-century decorative quarry. Thomas and Drake put back some quarries of this exact type in the east window of Hampton Court Chapel (Fig. 14b).

Much more subtle are some replacements in the Creed inscriptions that are only detectable through the use of palimpsest quarries, and the cutting of the

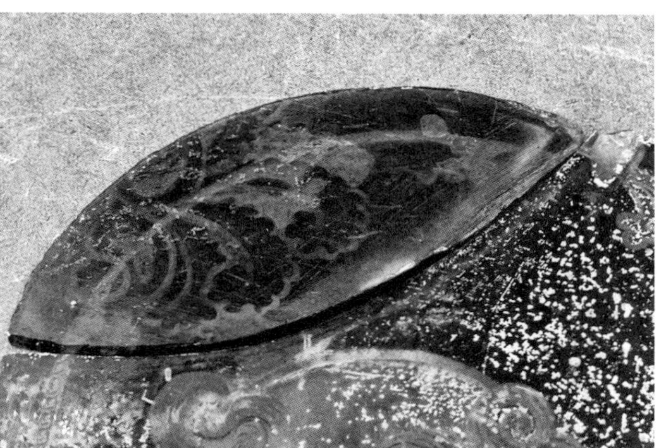

FIGURE 14. (a) Replacement in the nimbus of St. Peter, painted on a fifteenth-century quarry that has been cut down and cleaned off (detail of Fig. 6a; photo: author); (b) A fifteenth-century quarry (or copy) placed in the east window of Hampton Court Chapel in 1923 (photo: Roger Rosewell, by permission).

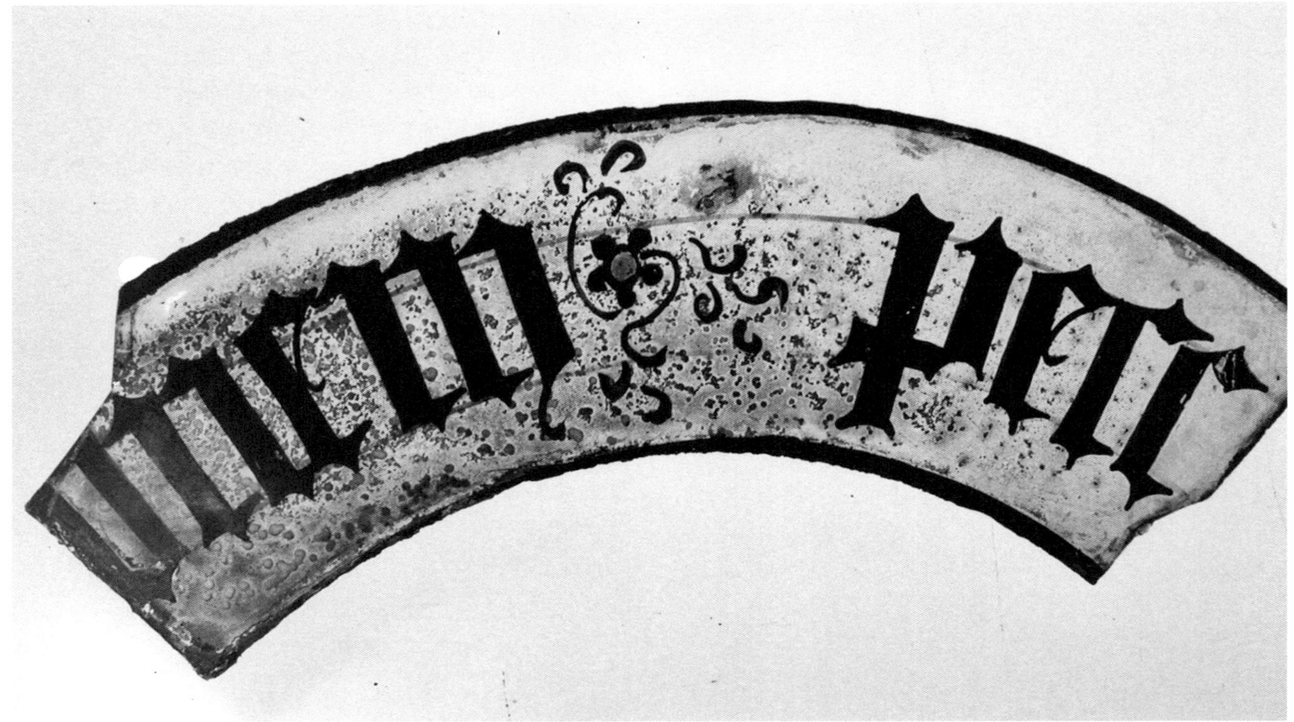

FIGURE 15. Replacement piece in the Creed inscription "*remissionem peccatorum*" held by St. Simon; new letters painted on palimpsest glass about 1680 (Museum of Fine Arts, Boston, 25.213; photo: author).

edges. The letters use the same template for ascenders and serifs as elsewhere—either traced from shattered originals or composed on the basis of other parts. The *om* and *entem* of *Omnipotentem* and the *cre* of *creatorem* are reconstructed on palimpsest glass (Fig. 6). The restorers were less fortunate with a phrase that had great import at the time: belief in the holy Catholic Church. *Ecclesiam* must have been so damaged that the restorer read an *i* for the *e*. He filled in the forgiveness of sins impeccably, one might say, supplying the end of *remissionem* and the beginning of *peccatorem* (Fig. 15). This verse of the Creed smacks of Papacy because of its association with the granting of indulgences.

In fact, all the figures that Fitzwilliam Coningsby salvaged from Hereford Cathedral during the Civil War would have qualified as Papist idols; the Parliamentarians called people who were devoted to them "Baalists," among other things. The other side of iconoclash is that, for the same reason, Thomas Coningsby would have been as ardently determined to restore them, using whatever glass could be found that more or less matched the old. He referred to Oliver Cromwell's troops as Rebels. John Cornforth argued that Coningsby was a precursor of the antiquarians whose passionate interest in England's past led to the early beginnings of a Gothic revival. I see him as a man driven by pride in his family's adherence to Catholic traditions, and the determination not to waver from them that makes a recidivist.

Although the Restoration monarch, Charles II, tried to instate freedom of religion to Catholics, Parliament forced him to withdraw from that policy in 1679, and he agreed to the Test Act that instead forced public officials to adhere to the Anglican liturgy, and denounce some teachings as superstitious and idolatrous. A very strong anti-Catholic movement among the public, inflamed by reports of a Papist plot against the King, had led to several killings in 1678. Thomas Coningsby's installation of the Hereford glass in his private chapel must have taken place in these uncertain years immediately after he came of age. It was a daring act, since no doubt by 1679 the Apostles with the Creed and especially the Marian scenes would have been considered as idolatrous and superstitious as they had been in 1645. Coningsby might have felt more secure for a time with James II on the throne (1685–1688), and he rose to high office in the ensuing years. However, he was not without taint when the Anti-Papacy laws were re-enforced: letters in the County Archives, dated 1715, suggest that as Lord Lieutenant of Herefordshire he did not bring cases against people suspected of being recusants—that is, who practiced Catholicism despite having taken the mandatory oath of loyalty to the Anglican Church.[78] He was reminded that this offence carried mandatory sentencing.

The struggle to observe Catholicism, openly or clandestinely, had a long history by 1715. The story is usually told in battles and acts of Parliament, but I have retold it here as the survival of a work of art in an era of iconoclasm. The south transept window of Hereford Cathedral must have been one of the most resplendent given to the cult of the Virgin in the Middle Ages. Despite its height, iconoclasts may have been very determined to destroy it, and these surviving panels more than many—the Annunciation has the image of God as well as the angel, and belief in the Assumption of the Virgin was completely rejected by the Protestants (Fig. 12). Richard Culmer's account of the subjects smashed in 1642 in the great Perpendicular "Idolatrous" window of the northwest transept of Canterbury Cathedral includes God the Father, Christ on a large crucifix, the dove of the Holy Spirit, the Apostles, and the seven joys of the Virgin Mary. He took especial note that the Minister had to climb nearly sixty steps on a ladder when he was "rattling down proud Beckets glassy bones."[79] And, above all, he was delighted with the symmetry, "as that window was the superstitious glory of the Cathedrall ... so now it is more defaced than any window in the Cathedrall." The great Marian window of Hereford Cathedral would have had the same appeal to iconoclasts. Fitzwilliam Coningsby sheltered the remnants from the Parliamentarians at great risk, and paid a price for his overall resistance.

This case history indicates the extent to which most historians who accepted modernist constructions of Gothic and Gothic Revival movements underestimated—or suppressed—the role of Christian religious belief systems in their own thinking. It is possible that these beliefs are at the core of the canon that art historians had, until recently, accepted as consonant with artistic practices in Europe in the period between the Lateran Council of 1215 and the Reformation. In the mid-nineteenth century, Cahier and Martin, and later Émile Mâle, expressed this notion openly, probably unaware that such an attitude did the ideological work of advancing colonial agendas. In the mass media of the contemporary neo-colonial United States, a digitally manipulated image, purportedly showing iconoclastic damage to a sixteenth-century window with the Virgin and Child, has been presented as a metonymy for "Christian persecution" (Fig. 16).[80] Apparently, smashing religious painted glass is still associated with the suppression of the values and beliefs of one Christian sect by another.

The modernist notion of "Gothic art" has excluded a great deal of material culture that is in the secular realm, as we have seen. Insight into this ideology has been rare, and exceptionally revealing statements may strike us as eccentric. In 1962, trying to disrupt Hegel's *Zeitgeist*, yet claiming that there had been a whole civilization of the "Gothic Age," Paul Frankl stated that "The answer to the old problem of the parallelism of the immanent processes lies in the fact that the different spheres of activity, for all their differences, were intended to find their common harmony in the hearts of men; and it was there that they had their common root, which lay in the personality of Jesus. From this root we can understand every one of the many spheres, including

78. QRO/31/xx in card file, with ref. to Charles Coningsby, papist, 1679 = QR/31/xx in black book.

79. Caviness, *CVMA Canterbury* (as in note 34), 253 cited in full.

80. "The Rage over Christian Persecution," *The New York Times Magazine*, front cover, 21 December 1997, photographic manipulation by Dalton Portella/Magic Graphics. See: Caviness, "Iconoclasm and Iconophobia: Four Historical Case Studies," 111–112, fig. 118.

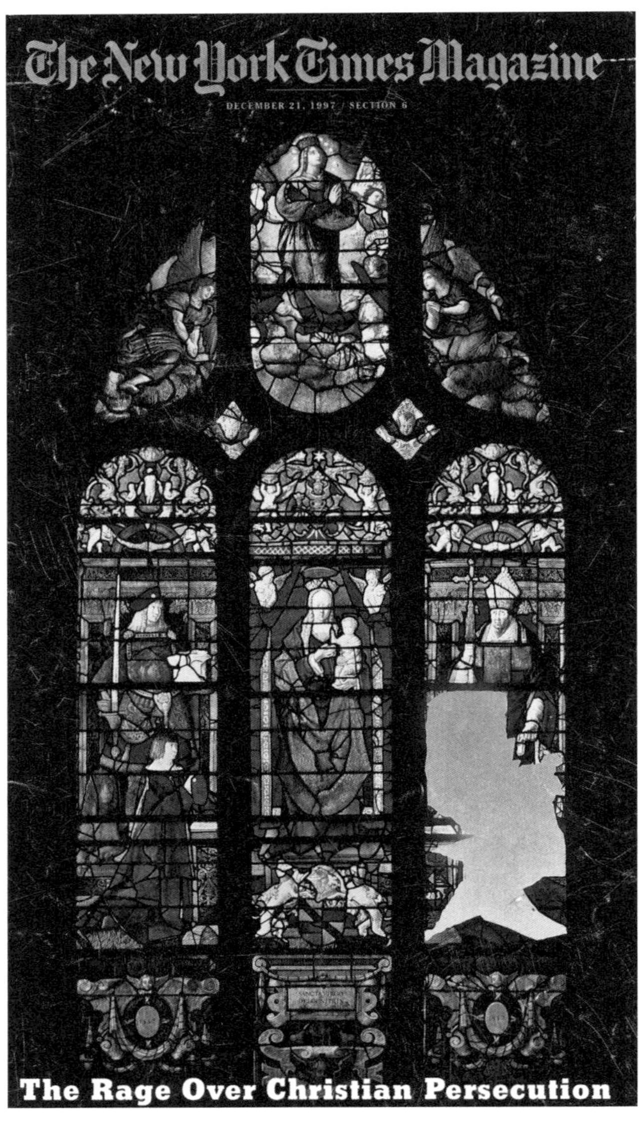

FIGURE 16. "The Rage Over Christian Persecution," manipulated digital image by Dalton Portella/Magic Graphics, *New York Times Magazine*, December 1997, front cover (by permission).

architecture, and we can understand why they all became Gothic."[81] The term Gothic has become less and less relevant as medievalists explore the Jewish, Islamic, and secular visual works of Europe. Such a welcome expansion of the canon, and the recognition of "Gothic" as a historicist label, may present a new jeopardy to the study of painted glass, since accidents of its survival so clearly identify it with Christian places of worship where the metaphysics of light played an essential role.

81. P. Frankl, *Gothic Architecture*, 1st ed. (Harmondsworth and Baltimore, 1962), 300.

MICHELLE P. BROWN

What Does 'Gothic' Mean in the Context of the Medieval Book? Goths at the Gates

THE Codex Argenteus in Uppsala is the first truly Gothic manuscript.[1] Made in the early sixth century in the Ravenna of the Ostrogothic ruler Theodoric, it is a translation of the Gospels into the Gothic vernacular—establishing it as a *lingua sacra* in succession to Hebrew, Greek, and Latin. It was undertaken by Ulfilas of Constantinople and used to help convert his own people, the Goths of Moesia.[2] The volume is one of the most imposing examples of a late antique *codex purpureus*, its purple-dyed pages, inscribed with gold and silver inks, exuding the imperial dignity—*porphyrygenitus*. It proclaimed the Goths as heirs of imperial Rome in the West, and sought to ally them to its eastern successor, Byzantium. Yet the Goths converted to the wrong brand of Christianity, Arianism, which led to their ostracization and eventual disappearance.

What has all this to do with high medieval "Gothic" art and culture? It was during this period of transition, in which the early Middle Ages were forged, that ethnic labels such as "Goth," "Hun," and "Vandal" came to be imbued with the negativity that they retain to this day. The cultural sophistication of Gaiseric's Vandal kingdom of Carthage, of Visigothic Spain, and of Theodoric's Ostrogothic Italy has been downplayed in favor of the image of Attila at the gates of Rome—even if this impetus did allow Leo, Bishop of Rome, to assume a new leadership in the West, *faut-de-mieux*, as Pope. To the chroniclers and apologists of papacy and Byzantium alike, these "barbarians" became the antithesis to the civilization of Graeco-Roman Antiquity, although at the time they were the real protectors and perpetuators of that civilization. The crux of the term "Gothic" is not so much a denigration of quality as a distinction from the religious and cultural orthodoxy of Greece or Rome. It is, therefore, highly appropriate that when the Italian humanists later sought to revive and reinterpret the antique past, at the period of transition from the Middle Ages to the early Modern world, they should have alighted upon the term "Gothic" as a catch-all for the prevailing cultural and political primacy of medieval northern Europe—for what lay beyond the bounds of a civilization orientated towards the classical past.[3]

The term Gothic stems ultimately from the terminology used by Greek and Roman authors from the first century C.E. onwards to describe a Germanic grouping

1. This paper brings to bear the perspective of a book historian and early medievalist upon the "Gothic" phase of book production. This was undertaken at the behest of the conference organizers in order to stimulate discussion of the wider context of this important period of illumination. It is hoped that it will be received in this spirit and that no pejorative intent will be adduced, as this is far from the author's intent.

2. For the missionary context of production of the Codex Argenteus (Uppsala, Universitetsbibliotek, DG 1), see M. P. Brown, ed., *In the Beginning: Bibles Before the Year 1000*, Exhib. Cat., Freer and Sackler Museum, Smithsonian Inst. (Washington, D.C.: Smithsonian Institution, 2006), p. 60. For a facsimile, see O. von Friesen and A. Grape, *Codex Argenteus Uppsaliensis* (Uppsala and Malmö: Almquist and Wiksell, 1927).

3. L. D. Reynolds and N. G. Wilson, *Scribes and Scholars: A Guide to the Transmission of Greek and Latin Literature*, 3rd ed. (Clarendon Press: Oxford, 1991); M. Baxandall, *Giotto and the Humanists* (Oxford: University Press, 1971).

of peoples, the *Gutones*.[4] The Ostrogoths and Visigoths were amongst the most successful participants in the barbarian invasions that stimulated the demise of the Roman Empire in the fifth century. In the late ninth-century translation into Old English of Boethius' *Consolation of Philosophy*, originally composed during the Empire's death throes, they are *Gota* (the Goth), and in Chaucer's Middle English version of that same work an 'h' was added to form Goth. The adjectival form, Gothic, first occurred in English in 1611, in the preface to the King James Bible, in reference to the Gothic language, but later in the seventeenth century a continental usage became current in which Gothic was synonymous with Germanic. A pejorative humanist use was also adopted, in which, as part of the conceptualization of history as three phases—Antiquity, the Middle Ages, and the Modern period—which still persists today, responsibility for the end of Antiquity and the consequent decline into the early Middle Ages was ascribed to the barbarian Goths. Gothic accordingly described anything that the humanists disliked about the period that intervened between the classical world and their own perceived revival of its values and material culture. Humanist philologist Lorenzo Valla, for example, applied the term to the old-fashioned "monkish" script, and in seventeenth-century England it was applied to Gothic typefaces, also known as blackletter.

The use of the term Gothic in a specifically art-historical context, however, stems from Vasari's *Lives of the Architects, Painters and Sculptors* (1550), in which he wrote dismissively of all medieval architecture as Germanic, and blamed it upon the Goths (*Goti*):[5]

> There are works of another sort that are called German, which differ greatly in ornament and proportion from the antique and the modern. Today they are not employed by distinguished architects but are avoided by them as monstrous and barbarous ... This manner was invented by the Goths, who, after the destruction of the ancient buildings and the dying out of the architects because of the wars, afterwards built—those who survived—edifices in the manner: these men fashioned the vaults with pointed arches of quarter circles, and filled all Italy with these damnable buildings.

In eighteenth-century England, a bastion of neoclassical "modernism," Gothic likewise came to refer to anything outmoded or crude. Yet before the century was out, these very features were becoming virtues in the Gothic architectural revival and the "Gothick" novel, with its preoccupation with the mysterious and macabre.[6] An implicit dualism of religiosity and its subversion endures still in the subculture of today's Goths—"Gothic" first being used of a particular type of punk music in 1979.[7]

To turn to a consideration of the use of the term "Gothic" in respect to books, it is significant that the origins of modern bibliophile connoisseurship lie within the orbit of nineteenth-century "Gothick" and the Arts and Crafts revival of medieval and early Renaissance aesthetics and craftsmanship espoused by Ruskin and Morris. This led, from inception, to a focus amongst book collectors upon the high Middle Ages at the expense of earlier medieval and humanist works. The balance has only been addressed over the past fifty years to form a more integrated view of the development of medieval illumination and of book history.

Humanism had found its principal mode of expression in its books, and it was to an earlier age that scholar-scribes such as Petrarch initially looked for inspiration—both textual and stylistic. The manuscripts

4. The Roman cartographer Ptolemy wrote of the Guti in the mid-second century C.E.

5. Giorgio Vasari, *The Lives of the Artists*, ed. G. Bull (Harmondsworth and New York: Penguin, 1987).

6. Tina Waldeier Bizzarro, "Gothic," in Paul F. Grendler, ed., *Encyclopedia of the Renaissance*, vol. 3 (New York: Scribner, 1999); Joseph Bosworth and T. Northcote Toller, *An Anglo-Saxon Dictionary Based on the Manuscript Collections of the Late Joseph Bosworth* (Oxford: Clarendon, 1882); Wayne Dynes, "Concept of Gothic," in Philip P. Wiener, ed., *Dictionary of the History of Ideas: Studies of Selected Pivotal Ideas*, vol. 2 (New York: Scribner, 1973); Paul Frankl, *The Gothic: Literary Sources and Interpretations through Eight Centuries* (Princeton, N.J.: Princeton University Press, 1960); Louis Grodecki, *Gothic Architecture*, trans. Mark Paris (New York: Rizzoli, 1985, with additions, 1993).

7. *Wikipedia*, *Punk*, http://en.wikipedia.org/wiki/Punk (24 April 2006); *Herwig Wolfram*, *History of the Goths*, trans. Thomas J. Dunlap (Berkeley, Calif.: University of California Press, 1987); Pete Scathe, *History of Goth*, http://www.scathe.demon.co.uk/histgoth.htm (24 April 2006).

of twelfth-century northern Italy, with their rounded Caroline minuscule and elegant vine-scrolls, would inspire the humanist cursive and formal bookhands—and subsequently italic and roman typefaces—and the classic humanist *bianchi girari* (white-vine) ornament.[8] Ironically, the origins of these very features lay within the Carolingian Empire—the ninth-century epitome of the usurpation of Mediterranean centrality by the "barbarian" kingdoms of the North and their appropriation of *imperium*.[9]

Experimentation with the cultural expression of local identities that often characterizes a reaction to the perennial obsession with naturalistic classicism and concepts of empire (be it Byzantine, Carolingian, Ottonian, Angevin, Holy Roman or, latterly, Victorian or Third Reich) can be observed from the early Middle Ages, embodied in works such as the Lindisfarne Gospels and the Silos Apocalypse.[10] The culmination of both trends came together in what we now term "Gothic," as a period and as a broad stylistic vocabulary within which there are many local permutations and certain unifying ingredients. Classicism is undoubtedly one of them, despite the "Gothic" label of otherness.

The so-called "Transitional Style" that, around 1200, marked a shift in figural art towards three-dimensional modeling and more naturalistic proportions, represented something of a rediscovery of the classical artistic canon—one of the periodic renascences that punctuate the history of art. The proportions and modeling of the sculpted figures adorning the façades of Reims and Chartres cathedrals and the Pisani pulpits, or the painted forms of the Westminster Psalter, Maître Honoré's *La Somme Le Roy*, and John Siferwas' Lovel Lectionary are more attuned to the classical Roman idiom than those of so-called "Romanesque" art.[11] For, as is well known, the stylistic terms Romanesque and Gothic derive their primary relevance from architectural styles and structural techniques and have been extended to embrace other media over a wide chronological and regional spread.[12]

Anti-classical northern "otherness" is evidently not, then, a prerequisite of "Gothic" art. Nor is stylistic homogeneity, for Sir Geoffrey Luttrell's Psalter is a far cry from the Très Riches Heures of Jean, Duc de Berry.[13] And what are we to call Flemish works such as the Prince of Nassau's copy of the *Roman de la Rose* (London, British Library, Harley MS. 4425), penned around 1490–1500 in a hand that fuses Gothic textualis and secretary features, and painted in northern Renaissance fashion? The palaeographical term *bâtarde*, used of its script, is apt and could apply to the work as a whole, however attractive a love-child it might be.[14] What, then, is distinctive about Gothic art and the societies that produced it, especially as expressed in the illuminated manuscripts of the thirteenth to fifteenth centuries?

In the study of book history, it is primarily the shift towards a specialized urban context of production and patronage accompanying the growth of universities with their impetus to book consumption that marks the transition into the high medieval production phase that lies between the "monastic period," pre-1200, and humanism and the early printed book.[15] This

8. J. Wardrop, *The Script of Humanism* (Oxford: Clarendon, 1963).

9. B. Bischoff, *Latin Palaeography: Antiquity and the Middle Ages*, trans. D. Ó Cróinín and D. Ganz (Cambridge: Cambridge University Press, 1990); M. P. Brown, *Guide to Western Historical Scripts from Antiquity to 1600* (London: British Library Publications, 1990); R. McKitterick, *The Carolingians and the Written Word* (Cambridge: Cambridge University Press, 1989).

10. London, British Library, Cotton MS. Nero D.iv, and Add. MS. 11695.

11. London, British Library, Royal MS. 2.A.xxii, Add. MS. 54180, and Harley MS. 7026.

12. For an early example of its application in twentieth-century art history, see É. Mâle, *The Gothic Image: Religious Art in France of the Thirteenth Century*, Eng. trans. of 3rd ed. (London: Collins, 1913), 165–8. On further applications of the term, see P. Frankl, *The Gothic: Literary Sources and Interpretations Through Eight Centuries* (Princeton, N.J.: Princeton University Press, 1960); E. Panofsky, *Gothic Architecture and Scholasticism* (New York: Meridian, 1957); W. Worringer, *Form in Gothic* (New York: Schocken Books, 1964); A. Martindale, *Gothic Art* (New York: Thames and Hudson, 1967); W. Swaan, *The Gothic Cathedral* (Garden City, N.Y.: Doubleday, 1969); J. Harvey, *The Master Builders: Architecture in the Middle Ages* (New York: McGraw-Hill, 1971).

13. London, British Library, Add. MS. 42130, and Chantilly, Musée Condé, MS. 65.

14. On *bâtarde*, see Brown, *Historical Scripts*, no. 42.

15. L. J. Bataillon et al., eds., *La production du livre universitaire au moyen âge* (Paris: Éditions CNRS, 1988).

period broadly corresponds to the Gothic era. Of course, monastic scriptoria did not down tools in 1200, and a significant proportion of patrons and craftspeople involved in the medieval urban book-trade were mendicants or clerics in minor orders (the latter office even earning tax breaks for craftsmen such as William de Brailes). Nonetheless, there was undoubtedly greater lay participation in the commissioning and making of books after 1200 than before, with even female ownership escalating in respect to devotional texts.

These trends are not unprecedented, however. Current scholarship is, for example, reappraising the levels of earlier lay literacy and involvement. Scholar-king Alfred the Great's mother and wife are both known to have owned decorated books, and the later Anglo-Saxon period also witnessed significant high-level aristocratic female patronage.[16] The Gospelbook (New York, Pierpont Morgan Library, MS. M. 709) commissioned *c.* 1051 by Judith, Countess of Flanders, wife of Tostig Godwinson, Earl of Northumbria, is a masterly display of status and cultural affiliation. Its treasure binding is one of the most opulent of its age, in true imperial Ottonian and Byzantine fashion, and endows the book with all the overt sacrality of those carried in procession during the liturgy—as potent a symbol of devotion as the Book of Hours in its chemise held by Rogier van der Weyden's Magdalene.[17] The Judith of Flanders Gospels' image of the Crucifixion (fol. 1^{v}) is colored with gold and costly pigments, as effective an expression of visible consumption of wealth as its later medieval counterparts. Clinging to the rood is a woman —either the earliest such iconography of the Magdalene, or perhaps Judith herself as repentant recipient of salvation, an intercessory patronage statement akin to later medieval images, such as the poignant depiction of Joanna "the Mad" before the Virgin.[18]

Christine de Pizan is rightly lauded as a seminal figure in women's history, authorship and publication, but her contribution can also be set in the context of the wider role of women in book production, commencing with figures such as the nun Lidia of Thessaloniki, who received spiritual instruction from Abbot Macarius in Egypt and won renown as "a scribe writing books and living in great asceticism in the manner of men," and the English eighth-century nun Abbess Eadburh of Minster-in-Thanet, who supplied books for St. Boniface's German mission, dripping with gold to wow the natives, as well as the teacher-poetess Leoba of Tauberbischofsheim and Hugeberc of Heidenheim, who wrote (sometime before 787) the lives of Sts. Wynnibald and Willibald, declaring "It may seem very bold on my part to write this book when there are so many holy priests capable of doing better."[19] The contribution of women to medieval book production was such that only in this trade sector could they inherit businesses from husbands and fathers, as in the case of Parisienne Marguerite de Sens, who, in 1275, inherited her stationer's business on Rue St. Jacques from her husband, Guillaume, and perpetuated its near-monopoly of the publication of Aquinas. By the end of the Middle Ages, women such as Genevieve Pelletier, the daughter of a bookbinder who inherited his shop on Rue Neuve and married the libraire-printer-binder Simon Vostre, were playing a prominent role in the publishing industry and preparing the way for successors such as Yolande Bonhomme, who printed some 200 titles in Paris between 1525–1557.[20]

Of course, not all book production was urban-based

16. T. A. Heslop, "The production of *de luxe* manuscripts and the patronage of King Cnut and Queen Emma," *Anglo-Saxon England* 19 (1990), 151–95; R. Gameson, "The Gospels of Margaret of Scotland and the Literacy of an Eleventh-Century Queen," in J. H. M. Taylor and L. Smith, eds., *Women and the Book: Assessing the Visual Evidence* (London, Toronto: British Library, University of Toronto Press, 1997), 148–171; P. McGurk and J. Rosenthal, "The Anglo-Saxon Gospel Books of Judith, Countess of Flanders," *Anglo-Saxon England* 24 (1995), 251–308.

17. Rogier van der Weyden, *The Magdalen Reading*, National Gallery, London.

18. The Book of Hours of Joanna La Loca, London, British Library, Add. MS. 11852, fols. 287^{v}–288^{r}.

19. On this and the foregoing, see M. P. Brown, "Female Book-Ownership and Production in Anglo-Saxon England: The Evidence of the Ninth-Century Prayerbooks," in C. Kay and L. Sylvester, eds., *Lexis and Texts in Early English: Papers in Honour of Jane Roberts* (Amsterdam: Brill, 2001), 45–68.

20. On the role of these and other women in the Parisian book-trade, see R. and M. Rouse, *Manuscripts and their Makers: Commercial Book Producers in Medieval Paris, 1200–1500*, 2 vols. (London: Harvey Miller, 2000).

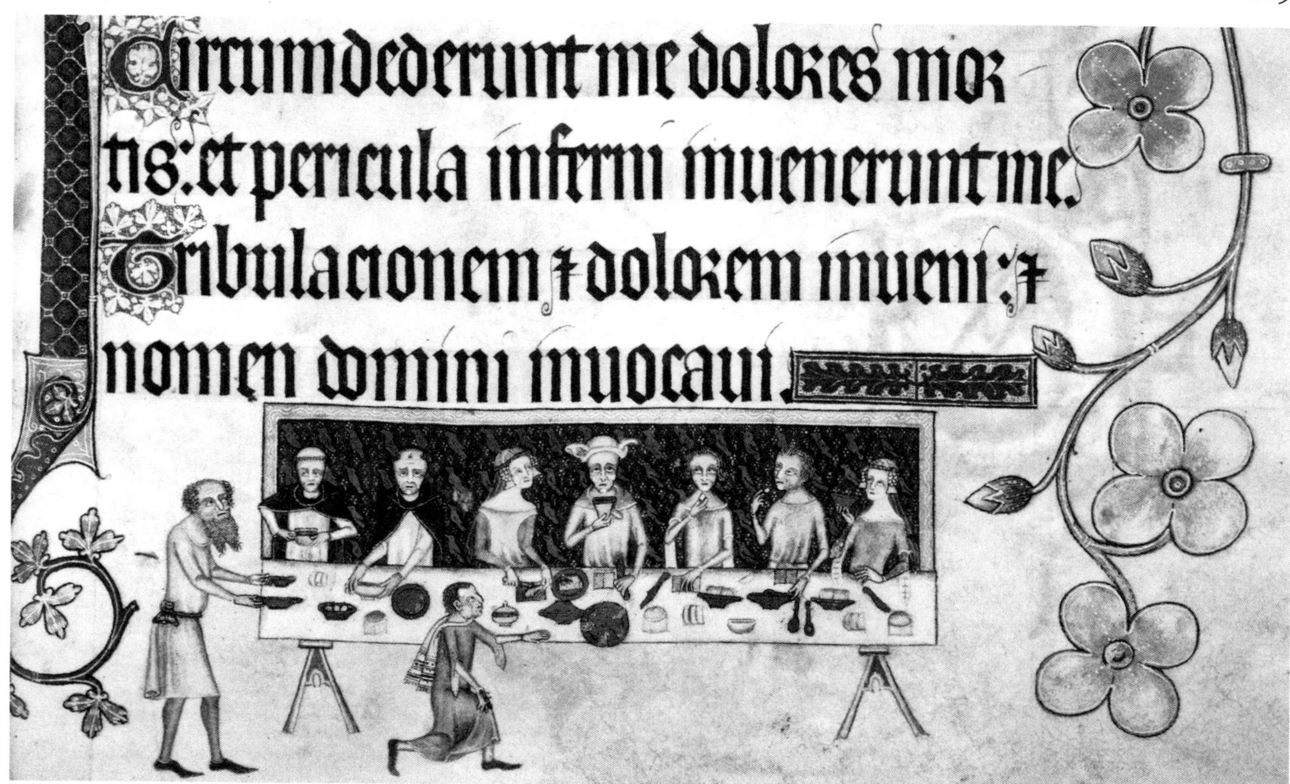

FIGURE 1. Feast scene showing either Dominicans or Augustinians dining with members of the Luttrell family. Detail from the Luttrell Psalter, English, *c.* 1325–1335, (British Library, Add. MS. 42130, fol. 208r).

from 1200. During the fourteenth century, the bibliophile Bohuns kept an Austin friar, John de Teye, as their illuminator at Pleshey Castle.[21] The Dominicans or Augustinians who dine with the Luttrells (Fig. 1) may likewise have earned bed and board for their part in the spiritual conceptualization and/or illumination of the family's great Psalter.[22] In 1383–4, Abbot Nicholas Lytlington commissioned the Abbey's new Missal (the Lytlington/Litlyngton Missal, Westminster Abbey Library, MS. 37). The bought-in scribe and project manager for the other parts of the work, Thomas Preston, was paid £4 of the overall cost of £34. 14 *s.* 7 *d.*, plus a liveried clothing allowance of £1, and given board and lodging in the abbey for the project's two-year duration. The materials and specialist tasks were subcontracted out: the 156 sheets of vellum (*percamenti vitulini*) cost £4. 6 *s.* 8 *d.*, the act of binding 21 *s.*, its cover 8 *s.* 4 *d.*, and its embroidery 6 *s.* 10 *d.*, the musical notation 4 *s.*, the Crucifixion miniature 10 *s.*, plus £22. 3 *d.* for fifty illuminated initials and the pigments.[23] The cost of the Luttrell Psalter project (by analogy with that of the Litlyngton Missal) would have exceeded by some £3 the sum of the rents paid on 28 booktrade shops in Old Chaunge near St. Paul's Cathedral in the 1350s,[24] and the annual value of a major baronial estate.[25]

Abbot Lytlington's cipher and arms frequently occur

21. L. F. Sandler, "A Note on the Illuminators of the Bohun Manuscripts," *Speculum* 60 (1985), 364–372.

22. The feast scene occurs on fol. 208r of the Luttrell Psalter; see M. P. Brown, *The Luttrell Psalter* (London: Folio Society and British Library Publications, 2006).

23. The list of *Expense novi missalis* occurs in the Westminster Abbey Treasurer's Roll of 1383–4, see Sandler, *Gothic Manuscripts*, no. 150.

24. C. P. Christianson, *Memorials of the Book Trade in Medieval London* (Woodbridge: Brewer, 1987).

25. See Brown, *Lutrell Psalter*.

in his missal, proclaiming his personal patronage, as do Robert Bruyning's in the Sherborne Missal.[26] Likewise, Abbot Bruyning looked beyond Sherborne Abbey's own scriptorium, wherein the gifted Benedictine scribe John Whas labored—a local lad, his father probably having been a cottar nearby—to recruit charismatic itinerant Dominican John Siferwas as master-illuminator of the Sherborne Missal. And yet, the mechanics of the urban economy prevailed. Work on these projects was undertaken by composite teams assembled for the project in hand, their contributions carefully costed in monetary terms as well as in *opus dei*. Yet these are the exceptions that prove the rules, for the broad trends bear witness to important shifts in urbanized patterns of production, distribution, and reception of books during the thirteenth to fifteenth centuries.

Is Gothic a truly international style, or just a catch-all label of convenience for an evolutionary stage in the production and consumption of art in the various regions of Europe during the high Middle Ages? Regionalism was the product of many centuries of exploration of national identities expressed in language, literature, and the arts, during which time vernacular vocabularies were developed visually as well as linguistically. German Gothic is as different from Spanish or Italian Gothic as are their languages. Even International Gothic, a term coined to denote greater stylistic affinity across Europe, is not devoid of vernacular dialects. The growing internationalization of communications during the high Middle Ages did mean that certain features of book production rapidly achieved international diffusion, much as Latin remained the unifying *lingua franca*. For example, the shift from writing the first line of text on the page above the top line to below it to contain the text within frame rulings of ever increasing complexity, spread throughout the European university publishing industry in the period 1220–1240, expedited by the rapid movement of books, book-makers, and book-owners from one city to another. The Smithfield Decretals (London, British Library, Royal MS. 10.D.iv), for example, which was written in the early fourteenth century in a town specializing in law (possibly Bologna or Avignon), was destined for use in Paris, but, within a decade or so, had traveled to London, where its illumination was completed by an artist in Paternoster Row for John Batayle, canon of Smithfield Priory.[27]

Such international relations also transformed the early medieval palette to one enriched by artificially manufactured copper blues, fostered by university experimental sciences, and the dyestuffs of the textile trade (red lakes from brazilwood, crocus-stamen saffron, and woad blue).[28] This palette transformation occurred in the fourteenth century, yet thirteenth-century illumination is still "Gothic." It is also salutary to note that in early eighth-century Britain, whose usual palette was restricted to red, green, and yellow, the ninety or so colors in the Lindisfarne Gospels were made from only six locally available plants and rocks, by a monk immersed in his environment and fully aware of its potential. He knew, for example, of lapis lazuli from the Himalayas and imitated the appearance of ground lapis by boiling woad and suspending particles of hoof and horn gum within it. What does this say concerning international communications?[29] In the *Admonitio Generalis* of 789, Charlemagne was already limiting woad growers who were leaving tracts of Europe fallow in their wake (woad exhausts the soil), predicting late medieval civic ordinances regulating this disruptive—and smelly—industry.

What other factors characterize book production during the three centuries in question? One is a will-

26. M. P. Brown, "The Sherborne Missal and 'Roddoke Robertus': The Anatomy of a Major Manuscript Commission," in a forthcoming *festschrift* for Christopher de Hamel, ed. by W. G. Noel et al.

27. A. Bovey, "A Pictorial Ex Libris in the Smithfield Decretals," in A. S. G. Edwards, ed., *Decoration and Illustration in Medieval English Manuscripts*, English Manuscript Studies 1100–1700, vol. 10 (2002), 60–82, and *The Smithfield Decretals: Image, Text and Audience in Fourteenth-Century England* (London and Toronto: British Library Publications and Toronto University Press, forthcoming).

28. D. V. Thompson, *The Materials and Techniques of Medieval Painting* (New York: Dover, 1956); J. J. G. Alexander, *Medieval Illuminators and Their Methods of Work* (New Haven: Yale, 1992); C. de Hamel, *Scribes and Illuminators* (London: British Museum, 1992).

29. M. P. Brown, *The Lindisfarne Gospels: Society, Spirituality and the Scribe* (London, Lucerne, and Toronto: British Library, Faksimile Verlag, and Toronto University Press, 2003), 275–298 and Appendix.

ingness to step beyond the boundaries of the age-old creative tension between *traditio* and *innovatio*. In the early eighth century, Bede, the foremost scholar of his day, was accused of the heresy of innovation. His ecclesiastical peers deemed his work to have transgressed the subtle relationship whereby new learning was distilled from, or glossed, that of the past, rather like law of precedence. And yet this was exactly what Bede had done, troping upon the work of such figures as Gregory Nazianzen, Augustine, Jerome, Gregory, Isidore, and Pliny. His critics were less well-read and did not recognize the allusions. In refuting them, Bede effectively invented footnotes.[30] A visual parallel is the early eleventh-century Old English Hexateuch (London, British Library, Cotton MS. Claudius B.iv), which conflated vernacular biblical paraphrases with picture cycles of Early Christian origin, adapted to reflect the interests of contemporary "communities of reading," including women, and emphasized the Anglo-Saxon people's sense of journey from their homelands to England. Innovative details of dress and artifacts were updated to reflect contemporary society, and details exploring theological nuance were introduced, but within a traditional compositional and narrative structure. Thus, Pharaoh hanging his baker becomes the English monarch and his witan dispensing legal judgement. The English thereby asserted their own cultural and linguistic identity and set themselves within the biblical landscape.[31] In the Hexateuch, Ælfric instructed the lay patron of his Old English paraphrase of the Torah on how to excavate the hidden treasures of Scripture by employing spiritual understanding, illustrating this by typological examples, such as Joseph saving the people from starvation being a type of Christ who saves humanity from the hungers of hell, a strategy later used to maximum effect in the *Bible moralisée*.[32] John Fifhide, who may have been the enterprising maker of the Holkham Bible Picture Book (London, British Library, Add. MS. 47682), likewise adapted conventions of pictorial narrative, casting himself as "everyman," a witness to the biblical action and an empathetic guide to the viewer.[33] His apocalyptic scene of internecine conflict amongst the ranks of the mighty and the commons during the last days is updated by costume, weaponry, and heraldic detail to allude to the social unrest of the early fourteenth century and the turmoil surrounding the deposition of Edward II. Fifhide himself even dons a costume, in the manner of guild-workers participating in contemporary mystery plays, dressing up as the smith who avoids making nails for the Crucifixion by hitting his thumb and proferring his wife to undertake the detestable task (Fig. 2). Such devices serve to reframe the text and reprise authorial intention, much like Bernstein's *West Side Story* and Baz Lehrmann's film *Romeo and Juliet*.

By the twelfth century, texts and picture cycles of late antique pedigree were already being supplemented by new knowledge and new images. A late twelfth-century Durham copy of an herbal (London, British Library, Sloane MS. 1975), descended from such classical authors as Dioscorides and Pseudo-Apuleius, includes at its end some new images, fully painted like the main cycle, depicting for the first time cautery and a cataract operation, learned from Islam during the Crusades, and incorporated into traditional western medical lore. The rise of scholasticism also led many texts that had not previously been illustrated to receive diagrams or picture cycles (as in the late twelfth-century Durham copy of Bede's prose *Life of St. Cuthbert* [London, British Library, Yates Thompson MS. 26]). However, it was the thirteenth century, with its universities and a taste for entertainment and edification amongst an urban elite, that witnessed the burgeoning of new compositions, both literary and visual.

The copies of Gerald of Wales' works "published" by himself to court the favor of the great and the good

30. M. P. Brown, "Bede's Life in Context: Materiality and Spirituality," in *The Cambridge Companion to Bede*, ed. Scott De Gregorio (Cambridge: Cambridge University Press, forthcoming).

31. See C. R. Dodwell and P. Clemoes, *The Old English Illustrated Hexateuch*, Early English Manuscripts in Facsimile 18 (Copenhagen: Rosenkilde and Bagger, 1974); R. Barnhouse and B. Withers, eds., *The Old English Hexateuch: Aspects and Approaches* (Kalamazoo and Ann Arbor: University of Western Michigan, 2000); B. Withers, *The Illustrated Old English Hexateuch* (London: British Library Publications, 2007).

32. J. Lowden, *Beauty or Truth? Making a 'Bible Moralisée' in Paris around 1400* (Louvain: Peeters, 2006).

33. M. P. Brown, *The Holkham Bible Picture-Book* (London: Folio Society & British Library, 2008).

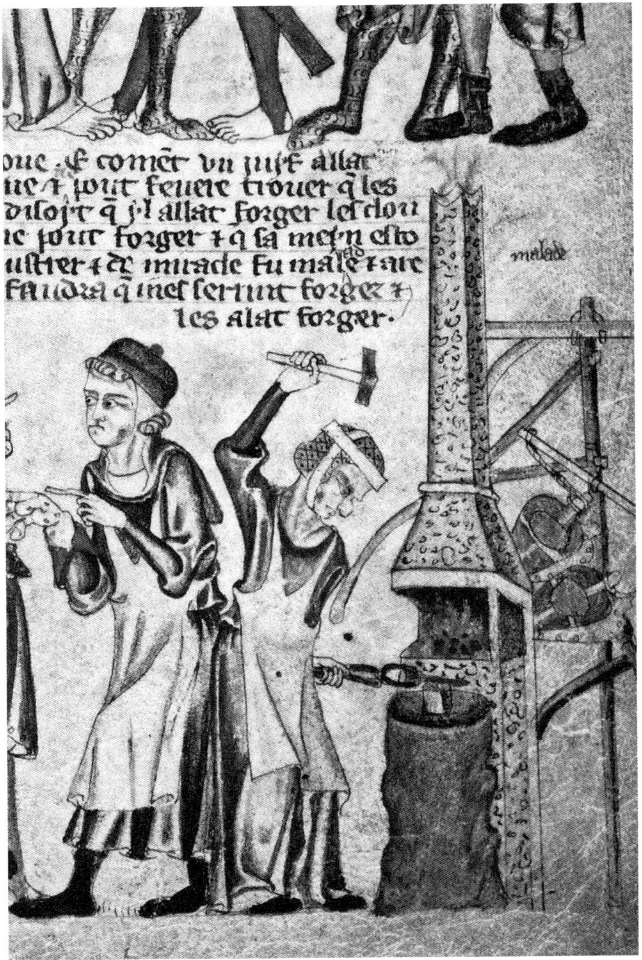

FIGURE 2. Fifhide dressed as a smith avoiding making nails for the Crucifixion by hitting his thumb and proffering his wife for the task. Detail from the Holkham Picture Book, *c.* 1320–1340, (British Library, Add. MS. 47682, fol. 31r).

during the first quarter of the thirteenth century, represent perhaps the first instance of an author devising illustrations. Gerald did not actually paint the lively images in the margins of his *Topographia Hibernica*, his account of his journeys in Ireland, but he stood at the shoulder of the artists and scribes of the Lincoln Cathedral scriptorium, making authorial emendations to text and image.[34] He probably demonstrated the latter by drawing upon wax tablets, a process he relates when describing the making of the Book of Kells, a book so wondrous that you would think it the work not of man but of angels, whose artist is instructed by a stylus-wielding angel. By mid-century, St. Alban's chronicler-monk, Matthew Paris, was regularly illustrating his work with marginal tinted drawings, easier to produce by the non-professional than full illumination.[35] Yet even the role of desktop publisher was not new. In his autobiographical note, Bede had described himself as author, notary, and scribe, in the pursuit of monastic humility.[36]

In the mid-thirteenth century, the maker of the Hereford Mappa Mundi sought to encapsulate knowledge of the world, its places and peoples (real and mythical) in the abbreviated visual encyclopaedia of a map, perhaps designed to be displayed as an altar reredos. Its information was derived from antique and early Christian texts, such as the geographical works of Ptolemy and Isidore, and the Marvels of the East. Some sixty years later, the artist of another such map, destined to serve as a reredos at Aslake Abbey in Norfolk, had apparently encountered a sailor familiar with the new portolan charts, depicting coastlines charted during trading voyages.[37] New experimental knowledge found itself in potential confrontation with the received wisdom of centuries, in the face of which the artist opted to conflate both sets of data, rather than choose. Thus, the Canary Islands and other features were depicted twice, in their variant locations. *Traditio* and *innovatio* were already in active dialogue. Together, they helped to form strategies of reading, of both text and image, that prepared the way for modern concepts of intertextuality and hypertext, exploring the relationships between word, sound, and image in ways that we are only now beginning to exploit again in the electronic environment. Once again, such strategies were not exclusive to the central Middle Ages. Multivalent

34. M. P. Brown, "Gerald of Wales and the 'Marvels of the East': The Role of the Author in the Development of Marginal Illustration," in *English Manuscript Studies*, Vol X: *Decoration and Illustration in Medieval English Manuscripts*, ed. A. S. G. Edwards (London: British Library, 2002), 34–59.

35. S. Lewis, *The Art of Matthew Paris in the Chronica Maiora* (Berkeley, Calif. and Cambridge, University of California Press and Corpus Christi College, 1987).

36. Brown, "Bede's Life in Context: Materiality and Spirituality."

37. M. P. Brown and P. Barber, "The Aslake World Map," *Imago Mundi* 44 (1992), 24–44.

reading of text and image had also been a feature of early medieval book culture, fostered by intellectuals such as Bede who favored an almost kabbalistic approach to the excavation of meaning through a literal exegesis and numerous allegorical and metaphorical constructs.

To other than the learned scholar, well-versed in exegesis, such layered meaning might be difficult to "read"—art rendered it more accessible. In the Book of Cerne, made in Lichfield in the 820s, an exegetical approach is adopted in the openings of its Passion narratives by employing a visual exploration of the complementary aspects of the human and divine natures of Christ expounded in each Gospel.[38] Luke focuses upon Christ's humanity and sacrifice, symbolized by the bovine immolatory victim, an association reinforced by the image's inscription "forman accepit vituli" which is an oblique reference to the "formam serui accipiens" in Philippians 2.7, which says that Christ "... made himself nothing, taking the very nature of a servant, being made in human likeness. And being found in appearance as a man, he humbled himself and became obedient to death—even death on a cross!" This is the authoritative statement of the relationship between Incarnation and Atonement, read on Passion Sunday. Such a reading of the image is grounded in assumptions of intertextuality and the ability of keywords and iconographic elements to stimulate mental connections with texts stored in the viewer's inner library. The image becomes not only a visual exegetical meditation, but also a sacred *figura*, or schemmatic representation, of the divine. A less complex, but equally inter-textual, device in Cerne is the major initial commencing St. Matthew's Passion narrative (fol. 3r). The bow of the *e* is inhabited by a manticore, the harbinger of death in the Early Christian Physiologus—a herald of the Passion and a *memento mori*. Use of symbolic creatures within the menagerie of later medieval marginal grotesques is well known, but its appearance here is one of the earliest in art.[39]

In the fourteenth century, similarly multi-layered meaning was deployed in the Luttrell Psalter.[40] For example, on fols. 159v–160r (Fig. 3), Sir Geoffrey is depicted as one of four men rowing a boat backwards. As Lucy Sandler recognized, this image is triggered by keywords in the adjacent verse, "You created the waters and the sea" (Ps. 89:12–13).[41] Sir Geoffrey is propelled backwards by his sins (his fellow oarsmen), whilst Truth and Mercy (who go before the face of the Lord in the accompanying Psalm), appearing in the form of two men hauling ropes, impel him towards humility. This is symbolized by the snail in the lower margin, which not only leaves a sticky trail, reflecting the words "in lumine" above (as Michael Camille noted), but which serves as a sign of humility, for it pulls in its horns when touched by proper authority, itself signified by the bull which symbolizes both Christ's sacrifice and his royal strength—"Taurus" being Edward I's nickname. Proper use of authority leads to elevation, commemoration, and good fame, signified by the Eleanor Cross, memorial to Edward I's saintly spouse, elevated heavenward by its mason beside the phrase: "For who in the skies above can compare with the Lord? Who is like the Lord among the heavenly beings?" (Ps. 89:6). I have suggested that, in addition to the meanings inherent in the individual vignettes, a unified reading across the entire opening forms a statement concerning Sir Geoffrey's views on authority and service, and their rewards.[42] The similarities and differences in approach in Cerne and Luttrell are instructive of visual authorial intent and reception, but there are few occasions for scholars to look beyond boundaries of period or place to examine both.

What was different, however, were the communities of reading within which such works operated.[43] Even

38. M. P. Brown, *The Book of Cerne: Prayer, Patronage and Power in Ninth-Century England* (London and Toronto: British Library and Toronto University Press, 1996).

39. Brown, *Book of Cerne*, 118.

40. Brown, *Luttrell Psalter*; M. Camille, *Mirror in Parchment: The Luttrell Psalter and the Making of Medieval England* (London, 1998).

41. L. F. Sandler, "The Word in the Text and the Image in the Margin: The Case of the Luttrell Psalter," *Journal of the Walters Art Gallery, Essays in Honour of Lilian M. C. Randall* 54 (1996), 87–97, and "The Images of Words in English Gothic Psalters," in *Studies in the Illustration of the Psalter*, ed. B. Cassidy and R. Muir Wright (Stamford: Shaun Tyas, 2000), 67–86.

42. Brown, *Luttrell Psalter*.

43. R. McKitterick, *The Uses of Literacy in Early Medieval Europe* (Cambridge: Cambridge University Press, 1990); M. P. Brown, *The Book and the Transformation of Britain, c. 550–1050: A Study in Orality*

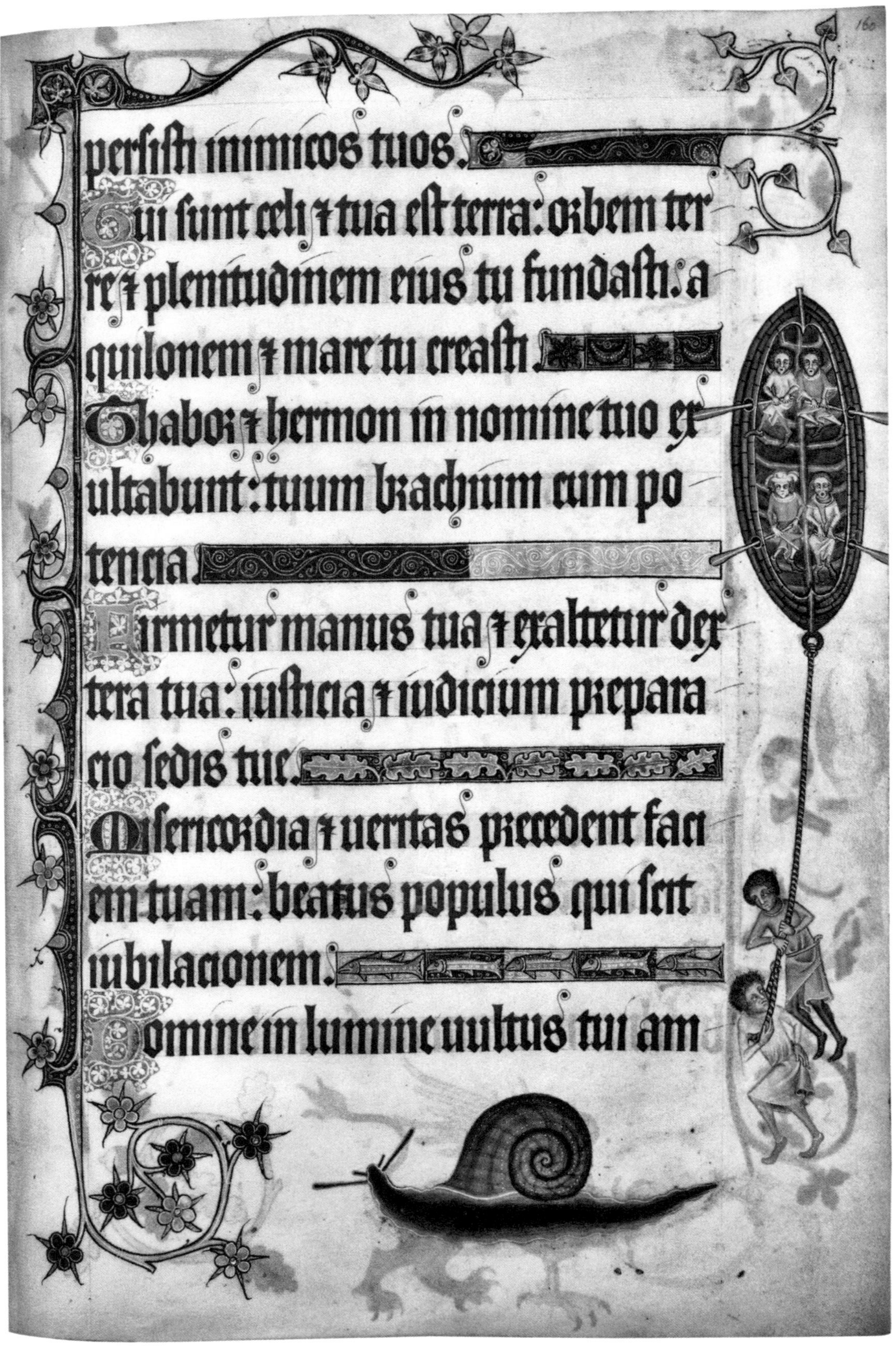
persisti inimicos tuos.
Tui sunt celi ⁊ tua est terra: orbem ter
re ⁊ plenitudinem eius tu fundasti: a
quilonem ⁊ mare tu creasti.
Thabor ⁊ hermon in nomine tuo ex
ultabunt: tuum brachium cum po
tencia.
Firmetur manus tua ⁊ exaltetur dex
tera tua: iusticia ⁊ iudicium prepara
cio sedis tue.
Misericordia ⁊ ueritas precedent faci
em tuam: beatus populus qui scit
iubilacionem.
Domine in lumine uultus tui am

FIGURE 3. Sir Geoffrey Luttrell shown as one of four men rowing a boat backwards. The Luttrell Psalter, English, *circa* 1325–1335, (British Library, Add. MS. 42130, fol. 160[r]).

that monastic scholar par excellence, Bede, was attributed with a love of the vernacular song that cheered the mead hall and, on occasion, the monastic refectory. The performance arts had entertained countless generations of men, women, and children alike. Now, in the central Middle Ages, books assumed the potential of doing likewise. Just as it had during the early stages of the development of the codex, vernacular language began once more to assume a crucial role in the dissemination of written thought. The homogeneity of a Latinate high church culture, fostered by emperors and popes to cultivate unity, gave way to multi-lingual societies with rising levels of lay literacy and more fluid social structures. The drift of rural populations to the towns began in earnest during the thirteenth century, and escalated in the traumatic fourteenth. More people than at any time since the Roman Empire were seeking specialized craft skills and mercantile opportunities and had more disposable income.[44] The middle classes and lower upper classes could now emulate the fashions and habits of the court and church elites. Perhaps the essence of "Gothic" is that, like the movements sparked by latter-day design gurus such as William Morris and Terence Conran, it was a social phenomenon that promoted art for the masses.

The masses might indeed be able to marvel at the glories of carved church façades and glittering, multi-colored interiors—but they had been able to do that during earlier ages, if fortunate enough to live near a major church or to go on pilgrimage, where they would have seen cult-books such as the Lindisfarne Gospels. Their pots and other accoutrements of daily life might sometimes be adorned with grotesques and other imagery that had escaped from the menageries of high culture—but so had been those of their ancestors. The principal currency of communication remained oral and visual, in the orbit of public display and "vulgarized" emulation. But for the first time ever, people other than royalty and the wealthy laity and religious might also own books, however rudimentary. A plethora of secular romances, poetry and prose literature, didactic works of moral exemplification and social mores, legal handbooks, and encyclopaedic and historical writings joined the canon of Scripture, the patristics, and the ancients.

The height of such bibliophilic aspiration for most moderately well-off people was a book of hours or a primer—equivalent to the family Bible—which was a sign of popular piety and the desire of the laity to participate in their own salvation.[45] The creation of a "must have" book, viewed as a sign of spiritual and social status, as a form of edification and entertainment, or of devotion and diversion, was another defining feature of the Gothic period. Prayerbooks and Psalters had fulfilled this function previously, but, although these could be owned by laypeople as well as religious, and could be for personal as well as for public use, they were few and far between. And, as in the other Abrahamic faiths, the emphasis was upon mnemonic retention and recitation, with priests being required to become *psalteratus*, capable of reciting the Psalms from heart. At the time of the production of one of the first fully fledged Book of Hours, illuminated by William de Brailes in Catte Street near the Bodleian in Oxford in the mid-thirteenth century,[46] the texts would still have been recited by readers who were not necessarily Latinate. By the fifteenth century, however, vernacular versions abounded.

Such works were amongst the first to be printed in any numbers later that century. Nor did the advent of printing immediately put an end to the "Gothic" book. Deluxe illuminated vellum manuscripts, such as the Psalter of King Henry VIII (London, British Library, Royal MS. 2.A.xvi), continued to be produced, whilst the early typefaces, woodcuts or hand-decoration, layout and aids to assembly and navigation (running heads, initials, catchwords, and the like) were a semi-mechanized perpetuation of manuscript practices and devices. These were often produced by craftspeople

and Visual and Written Literacy, The Sandars Lectures in Bibliography, 2009 (London: British Library Publications, forthcoming).

44. G. Cavallo and R. Chartier, eds., *A History of Reading in the West* (Oxford: Oxford University Press, 1999).

45. For an introduction to Books of Hours, see R. J. Wieck, *Time Sanctified: The Book of Hours in Medieval Art and Life* (New York and Baltimore: Braziller and Walters Art Gallery, 1988).

46. C. Donovan, *The de Brailes Hours: Shaping the Book of Hours in Thirteenth-Century Oxford* (London and Toronto: British Library Publications and University of Toronto, 1991).

who had transformed themselves from stationers, scribes, limners, or binders into printers, such as Peter Schoeffer who had worked as a scribe in Paris as a student and later became a prominent Mainz printer.[47] The end of the "Gothic" period came at different times in different places, and in a variety of ways that have still to be fully examined and defined.

The boundaries of the "Gothic" book are therefore extremely fluid. High medieval book production was the heir of late antique and early medieval attitudes and practices, and it conditioned and shaped that of the humanists and the early Modern age. Perhaps most significantly, this was a transitional time of profound social change and renewed international exchange, of which changes in the creation and reception of the book are symptomatic and in which they played a crucial role.[48]

What then is the current validity of the term Gothic? If, for scholarly purposes, it is best broken down into smaller components that are qualified by vocabularies indicating time, place, and medium—early Gothic, Italian Gothic, Gothic sculpture, and the like—does the term nonetheless retain any useful function as a shorthand in the popular imagination for a period characterized by courtly chivalric ideals? Publishers and the marketers of exhibitions obviously have no doubts in this respect, hence *The Age of Chivalry* title for the first of the two seminal London exhibitions devoted to the art of the high Middle Ages, leaving the second to rejoice in the title *Gothic: Art for England*, although it covered 1400–1547, the end of the period.[49] Clearly, there remains a broad stylistic vocabulary that traverses the boundaries of the media and that transcends the differences of period and place that preoccupy the academic mind.

With specific regard to the decorated book, however, we may do well to recognize that not only should illumination be viewed against the wider backdrop of art in other media, but also against that of palaeography, codicology, textual studies, and socio-historical contextualization. Although in-depth studies of particular manuscripts and groupings are essential in order to deepen our understanding and construct an overview, it is worthwhile stepping back to survey the period as a whole and to see how decorated books sit amongst non-illuminated books of their age, as well as how the issues they raise evolved across the entire Middle Ages. Thus, the controlling impetus of early connoisseurship, exhibition, and auction-house trade that has hyped "Gothic" illumination as art for art's sake, and as the epitome of "medieval" can increasingly be overcome, allowing illuminated manuscripts to assume their proper place in the continuum of book history and of human communication, enabling us to question not just what they are, but what they might ultimately mean.

47. C. P. Christianson, *A Directory of London Stationers and Book Artisans, 1300–1500* (New York: Bibliographical Society of America, 1990), and *Memorials of the Book Trade in Medieval London* (Woodbridge: Brewer, 1987).

48. For an overview of the medieval book and its relevance to wider book history, see S. Eliot and J. Rose, eds., *The Blackwell Companion to the History of the Book* (Oxford: Blackwell, 2007).

49. J. J. G. Alexander and P. Binski, eds., *Age of Chivalry: Art in Plantagenet England, 1200–1400* (London: Royal Academy, 1987); R. Marks and P. Williamson, eds., *Gothic: Art for England, 1400–1547*, Exhib. Cat. (London: Victoria and Albert Museum, 2003).

GIUSEPPA Z. ZANICHELLI

The Historiography of Italian Gothic Manuscripts

I DO NOT believe that, after the Princeton Conference on Romanesque art in 2006,[1] it is necessary to justify the use of such a "mega-term" as Gothic, even if in the Italian context it is more ambiguous than ever; its usefulness more than compensates for the flimsiness of its definition. It is in this context that I should like to remind you that the critical debate on Italian Gothic has focused, more than in other European countries, on architecture and architectural sculpture. Analyzed from an evolutionistic perspective, Italian Gothic was compressed between the more important periods of the Romanesque and the Renaissance.[2] Illuminated manuscripts were almost completely ignored in subsequent debates, even if, as Xenia Muratova pointed out, it is precisely within the realm of book production that the term Gothic acquired a specific meaning. This term emerged in the humanistic era in connection with the angular script used in the Pre-Carolingian and Post-Romanesque periods.[3] In the realm of book production, however, the deep-rooted exegetical method of the Maurists and of Mabillon removed any aesthetic connotation from the word.[4]

In order to understand Italian Gothic manuscripts, it is necessary to analyze three types of problems. The first issue is geographic, because, as Willibald Sauerländer observed in 1994,[5] it is necessary to consider the peculiar situation of Italian culture in the thirteenth and fourteenth centuries. In the Italian Peninsula, the geopolitical and cultural situation was regional, with differing degrees of connection to internal and transalpine models, depending on location and strength of political power. In northern Italy, the Lombardy area was dominated by communal cities during the twelfth and early thirteenth centuries, but thereafter the power shifted from municipality to principality, with the Della Torre family, and, after 1277, with the French-oriented Visconti family. Piedmont, on the other hand, was dominated by the House of Savoy, and was also connected to the French Royal dynasty. In the eastern sector, the oligarchic power of Venice became the connecting axis between western-central Europe and Constantinople. In central Italy, the myriad small cities governed by local rulers became centers of diversified patronage, while Bologna, seat of the first university, established itself as *alma mater librorum*. In Tuscany, the communal power was held mainly by bankers and merchants belonging to the middle and upper classes. The situation in Rome was unstable because of the continuous struggle between the aristocratic families and the papal court, which was frequently obliged to relocate elsewhere and eventually moved to Avignon. In southern Italy, Frederick the Second and his son, Manfred, were

1. *Romanesque Art and Thought in the Twelfth Century, Essays in Honor of Walter Cahn* (Index of Christian Art, Occasional Papers X), ed. C. Hourihane (Princeton, 2008).

2. The entry by P. Kidson, "Gotico," in *Enciclopedia dell'arte medievale*, vol. 7 (Rome, 1996), 41–54, is still completely dedicated to the architectural context; see also G. German, "Dal Gothic Taste al Gothic Revival," in *Arti e storia del Medioevo*, vol. 4, Il Medioevo al passato e al presente, ed. E. Castelnuovo and G. Sergi (Turin, 2004), 391–438.

3. X. Muratova, "Questa maniera fu trovata dai Goti . . .," in *Il Gotico europeo in Italia*, ed. V. Pace and M. Bagnoli (Naples, 1994), 23–47, 29–30. Cf. M. Baxandall, *Giotto and the Orators: Humanist Observer of Painting in Italy and the Discovery of Pictorial Composition, 1350–1450* (Oxford, 1971).

4. G. Bickendorf, *Die Historisierung der italienischen Kunstbetrachtung im 17. und 18. Jahrhundert* (Berlin, 1998), 225–314.

5. W. Sauerländer, "Dal Gotico europeo in Italia al Gotico italiano in Europa," in *Il Gotico europeo* (as in note 3), 7–21, 7.

conquered by the Angevins in 1261, who were later replaced by the Aragonese dynasty.

The second issue is chronological, as the Italian Gothic period is not seen as a continuum. The problem is Giotto, who divides the period in half, and creates what could be called "pictorial space," as Panofsky argued.[6] Giotto's legacy conditioned the overall analysis of Italian Gothic, because of the identification of his paintings as the end of Byzantine influence and the beginning of the Renaissance.[7]

The third issue is historiographic—that is, just exactly when does the historical awareness of Gothic as a meaningful term in relation to Italian manuscript illustration actually begin? The first studies of Italian illuminated manuscripts rigorously followed a deep-seated Italian tradition in artistic historiography, rooted in the *Vite* of Giorgio Vasari. Gaetano Milanesi,[8] the editor of Vasari's works, made some observations, printed as notes to his critical edition. He later added his observations as part of his *Storia della miniatura italiana*, in which he limits his analysis to fifteenth-century artists cited in documents related to choir-books. In it, Milanesi asserts that in the thirteenth and fourteenth centuries these volumes "were few, and lacking in illuminated ornaments."[9] In 1871, Milanesi offered a more developed analysis, in which he correlated his observations with the different pictorial schools determined by Vasari. He firmly established the connection between painting and illumination, whereby thirteenth-century illumination was determined to be Cimabuesque and Byzantine, and that of the following century Giottoesque, although Milanesi maintained that the connection between painting and illumination was not binding, due to the differences in techniques and materials. He also reinforced the superiority of Tuscan culture over the rest of Italy.

Italian historiography must be contextualized within the cultural politics of the newly unified government that followed the wars of the Risorgimento. An extensive program of cataloguing the cultural heritage started in order to promote national identity.[10] At the same time, as well as in the last decades of the nineteenth century, the Deputazioni di Storia Patria were founded in most towns that were formerly capitals of independent states, in order to safeguard local cultural traditions. These cultural associations promoted the publication of local studies on their autonomous, glorious pasts. In 1885, in Milan, the documentation collected by Gerolamo D'Adda on late medieval and Renaissance illumination ("this very curious branch of art," whose study "remains till now a wish"), was published.[11] D'Adda claims, for example, in analyzing the *Canzone* written by Bartolomeo di Bartolo for Bruzio Visconti, that the illuminator was a Milanese pupil of Giotto, who worked in 1336 for Azzone Visconti in Milan.[12] At the same time, the *Chronicle* of Pietro Bescapé was deemed to be interesting as a vernacular text, rather than as an illuminated one.[13] The method used is clearly based solely on the need to document and is not interpretative. As such, it is closely linked to the domi-

6. E. Panofsky, *Renaissance and Renaissances in Western Art* (Stockholm, 1960), 143.

7. S. Romano, *La O di Giotto* (Milan, 2008).

8. G. Vasari, *Le Vite de' più eccellenti pittori, scultori, ed architetti*, 9 vols. (Florence, 1878–1885).

9. G. Milanesi, "Storia della miniature italiana," in G. Vasari, *Le Vite* (as in note 8), vol. 6 (Florence, 1850), 161–352, 163.

10. G. Z. Zanichelli, "The Role of Stylistic Analysis in the Cataloguing of the Illuminated Manuscripts," in *Kataguisirung mittelalterlicher Handschriften in internationaler Perspektive*, ed. Bayerische Staatsbibliothek (Wiesbaden, 2007), 99–111, 100.

11. G. Mongeri, "L'arte del minio nel ducato di Milano dal secolo xiii al xvi. Appunti tratti dalle memorie postume del marchese Gerolamo d'Adda," *Archivio Storico Lombardo* 12 (1885), 330–356, 528–557, and 759–796, 336.

12. G. Mongeri, "L'arte del minio" (as in note 11), 350: for this manuscript (Chantilly, Musée Condé, MS. 599), see now P. Stirnemann, "Entry 2," *Enluminures Italiennes Chefs-d'oevres du Musée Condé*, Exhib. Cat., Chantilly, Museum Condé (Paris, 2000), 12–17.

13. Milan, National Library Braidense, MS. AD.XIII.48. See L. Galli, "Entry 20," in *Miniatura a Brera 1100–1422. Manoscritti dalla Biblioteca Nazionale Braidense e da collezioni private*, Exhib. Cat., Braidense National Library, ed. M. Boskovits (Milan, 1997), 130–145. Others manuscripts thought to be representative of the Milanese production are: the Pliny of Pietro da Pavia (Milan, Ambrosiana Library, MS. E 24 inf.), see L. Armstrong, "The Illustrations in Pliny's 'Historia Naturalis': Manuscripts before 1430," *JWCI* 46 (1983), 19–39; the *Beroldo* of Giovannino de' Grassi (Milan, Trivulziana Library, MS. 2262); see M. Bollati, "Breviario ambrosiano," in *Biblioteca Trivulziana, Milano* (Florence, 1995), 70–71.

nant historical methodology of the period.[14] Another characteristic of Italian culture is its rigorous links to the Roman Catholic tradition, which were made apparent in the exhibition held in Turin in 1898. This was formerly the location for national exhibitions of industrial art, which were modeled on the great European exhibitions, such as that of London in 1851. The *Esposizione d'Arte Sacra Antica e Moderna* was followed with the publication of the lavishly illustrated *Atlante Paleografico-Artistico*.[15] Of the 115 religious codices exhibited, only thirteen were of the Gothic period, mainly from the fourteenth century. The exhibition had reproduced the illuminated pages, although the interest was on paleographic problems. Against such a background, and supported by a general interest in medieval life, the great success of Ludwig Volkman's study of the *Divine Comedy*,[16] which was published in German in 1898 and translated into Italian and English the following year, can be easily understood. Once more the author complains that illumination is a "field not adequately cultivated," but his interest remains mainly literary. Even if he does put together a very impressive collection of illuminated manuscripts of the fourteenth and fifteenth centuries, he shows no interest in the obviously different styles of the two periods.

During the last years of the nineteenth century and the beginning of the following, three very important studies, produced by scholars of the Vienna School, signaled the first awareness of the existence of Gothic Italian illumination; the studies at the time appeared revolutionary. In 1887, Alois Riegl recognized the Book of Hours of Joan of Anjou as Neapolitan, underlining the Tuscan and French connections.[17] In 1895, Julius von Schlosser[18] used the *Tacuinum sanitatis* of Vienna[19] to illustrate the *höfische Kunst*, the international and secular style expressed mainly in decorative arts. This study was ignored by the majority of scholars and was not translated into Italian until 1965.[20] In 1901, Max Dvořák[21] shifted attention to the stylistic and formal analysis of Gothic Italian manuscripts, pointing to the key role of French and Byzantine illumination in shaping the Italian ornamentation of the page, as well as identifying the cultural links between Avignon, Siena,[22] and Naples, and the decorative and technical characteristics of the artistic development of each school.[23]

The year 1901 also saw the beginning of the monumental publication of Adolfo Venturi's twenty-five volume *Storia dell'arte italiana*, covering art from the early Christian period to the sixteenth century. Through Venturi, Morellian connoisseurship entered the history of art in Italy, and for the first time local traditions

14. Characterized by the same documentary method are the studies of Francesco Malaguzzi Valeri on contemporary illuminated manuscripts of Bologna: F. Malaguzzi Valeri, "I codici miniati da Niccolò da Bologna e dalla sua scuola in Bologna," *Atti e Memorie della Deputazione di Storia Patria per le Antiche* 11 (1893), 1–41; *idem*, "La miniatura a Bologna dal XIII al XVI secolo," *Archivio Storico Italiano* 18 (1896), 242–315.

15. F. Carta, C. Cipolla, and C. Frati, *Atlante Paoleografico-Artistico compilato sui manoscritti esposti alla mostra de Arte Sacra nel 1898* (Torino, 1899). See F. Crivello, "L'*Esposizione di'Arte Sacra* di Torino del 1898 e lo sviluppo degli studi sulla miniatura in Italia," *Annali della Scuola Normale Superiore di Pisa—Classe di Lettere e Filosofia* 2 (1997), 97–142.

16. L. Volkman, *Iconografia dantesca. Die bildlichen Darstellungen zur Göttlinchen Komödie* (Leipzig, 1897; Eng. trans., London, 1899; Ital. trans., Florence, 1899).

17. A. Riegl, "Ein angiovinisches Gebetbuch in der Wiener Hofbibliothek," *Mitteilungen des Instituts für Österreichische Geschichtforschung* 8 (1887), 430–454.

18. J. von Schlosser, "Ein veronesisches Bilderbuch und die höfische Kunst des XIV. Jahrhunderts," *Jahrbuch der Kunsthistorischen Sammlungen in Wien* 16 (1895) 144–230.

19. Vienna, National Library of Austria, MS. Series nova 2644; now see facsimile edition *Tacuinum sanitatis in medicina: Codex Vindobonensis S.N. 2644*, ed. F. Unterkircher, J. Stummvoll, and G. Barbieri (Rome, 1986).

20. Julius von Schlosser, *L'arte di corte nel secolo decimo quarto*, ed. G. L. Mellini (Milan, 1965).

21. M. Dvořák, "Byzantinische Eifluß in Italienische Buchmalerei," *Mitteilungen des Instituts für Österreichische Geschichtforschung* 6 (1901), 792–820; see also his "Die Illuminatoren des Johann von Neumarkt," *Jahrbuch der Kunsthistorischen Sammlungen in Wien* 22 (1901), 35–126.

22. Meanwhile, Siena was studied by F. Hermanin, "Il miniatore del Codice di San Giorgio nell'Archivio Capitolare di San Pietro in Vaticano," in *Scritti vari di filosofia in onore di Ernesto Monaci* (Rome 1901), 445–453.

23. This was researched by A. von Erbach-Fürstenau, "Pittura e miniatura a Napoli nel secolo XIV," *L'Arte* 8 (1905), 1–17.

were examined as part of a consistent context.[24] Venturi's primary interest was in the Renaissance, and his analysis of the Middle Ages did not produce a coherent system. The illuminated manuscripts of the thirteenth century (which he classified as Romanesque) were introduced to demonstrate the weight of Arabic models in *De arte venandi cum avibus*, while the *Vitae Sanctorum patrum* from the Vatican Library was seen as an example of Byzantinism,[25] a very topical issue in Italian Roman-oriented culture.[26] The same year that the *Exposition des primitifs Français* in Paris revealed Gothic painting and illumination of the thirteenth century to be the origin of French culture,[27] the Italian Dugento in this field was considered mainly in the context of *bizantinische Frage*. In Venturi's fifth volume, which was dedicated to Trecento painting,[28] the intellectual setting changes and illumination appears to be an expression partly of the Romanesque tradition, but mostly as a forerunner to the Renaissance, the true national style.[29]

The problem of Gothic illumination, although perceived as alien, was posed in 1912 by Pietro Toesca, a scholar aware of the European debate on the relationship between codex and cultural context.[30] Having undertaken postgraduate work in Rome under Venturi, and following in the footsteps of Courajod and Schlosser, Toesca brought together German philology, Viennese formalism, and a few borrowings from Mâle's iconographic methods in his study of thirteenth-century French art.[31] Toesca felt particularly close to the aesthetics of Benedetto Croce and his theory of art as poetic achievement. He underlined the differences between painting and illumination in the Duecento, pointing out the presence of French elements in manuscripts, which was a unique characteristic that was to linger on during the first half of the following century, while Florentine and Byzantine influences weakened. It was, however, only in the second half of the Trecento, he believed, that it was possible to reconstruct great corpora of works connected to important personalities based in court,[32] craftsmen whose work was characterized by fine colors, elegant forms, pleasing narratives, and honest realism, even if constricted by "many gothic clichés," which were perceived as foreign intrusions. Giovannino de' Grassi, architect, sculptor, painter,

24. G. C. Sciolla, *La critica d'arte del Novecento* (Turin, 1995), 50–56; A. Iacobini, "Adolfo Venturi pioniere di una disciplina nuova: la Storia della miniatura," in *Adolfo Venturi e la storia dell'arte oggi*, ed. M. D'Onofrio (Modena, 2008), 269–286.

25. Vatican City, Vatican Library, MS. Lat. 375; the illuminator is thought to be a follower of the artist of the Greek codex of John Climacus: Vatican City, Vatican Library, MS. Gr. 1754.

26. A. Venturi, *Storia dell'Arte Italiana*, vol. 2, Dall'arte barbarica all'arte romanica (Milan, 1902), 486–490; *idem*, Storia dell'arte italiana, vol. 3, L'arte romanica (Milan, 1904), 756–769. See X. Barral i Altet, Review: M. Brnabò, "Ossessioni bizantine e cultura classica in Italia. Tra D'Annunzio, fascismo e dopoguerra," *Arte Medievale* 4/1 (2005), 139–143.

27. F. R. Martin, "L'administration du génie national. L'*Exposition des primitifs français* de 1904, in *Medioevo e Medioevi. Un secolo di esposizioni d'arte medievale*, ed. E. Castelnuovo and A. Monciatti (Pisa, 2008), 93–108.

28. A. Venturi, *Storia dell'Arte Italiana*, vol. 5, La pittura del trecento e le sue origini (Milan, 1907), 1003–1049.

29. In this volume, Bologna is presented as the main center of book production, and the manuscripts are assembled in homogeneous groups, over which hang the shadows of Oderisi da Gubbio and Franco Bolognese, quoted by Dante, and the research of personalities grants extended space to Niccolò di Giacomo. In addition, the schools of Siena are considered with the Ambriosian Vergil of Simone Martini, the codices of the Master of the Codex of St. George, the illuminator of *Documenti d'Amore* of Francesco da Barberino (Vatican City, Vatican Library, MS. Barb. Lat. 4076 and MS. Barb. Lat. 4077), and other illuminators of liturgical manuscripts. From this school descends the Neapolitan one, illustrated with the Statutes of Order *Saint Esprit aux trios désirs* (Paris, BnF, MS. Lat. 4274) and the *Hamilton Bible* (Berlin, Kupferstichkabinett, MS. 78 E 3); the Florentine school is represented by the *Biadaiolo Codex* (Florence, Laurenziana Library, MS. Tempi 3); and, meanwhile, few words are reserved for the production in Milan, Verona, and Venice. This division is to be maintained in the following studies.

30. P. Toesca, *La pittura e la miniature in Lombardia dai più antichi monumenti alla metà del Quattrocento* (Milan, 1912). See E. Castelnuovo, "Nota introduttiva," in P. Toesca, *La pittura e la miniature in Lombardia dai più antichi monumenti alla metà del Quattrocento* (Turin, 1968), xxxix–lxi; G. Romano, "Pietro Toesca a Torino," *Ricerche di Storia dell'arte* 59 (1996), 5–19; G. Mariani Canova, "La storia della miniatura negli studi del XX secolo: l'orizzonte internazionale e quello italiano," in *Medioevo: arte e storia* (Milan, 2008), 131–145, 132.

31. É. Mâle, *L'art religieux de la fin du moyen âge en France, étude sur l'iconographie du moyen âge et sur ses sources d'inspiration* (Paris, 1908).

32. As Giovanni of Benedetto da Como, the Master of MS. 757 in Paris, Pietro da Pavia.

illuminator, and draftsman, stands out among them, as he was aware of new research in three-dimensional art and was an expert on naturalistic drawing—the illuminator rightfully became an artist. The identification of preëminent codices with courtly ones is more than obvious in Paolo D'Ancona's research on Florentine illumination.[33] Given that Florentine production at the time was religious and not secular,[34] he recognized its slower development compared to workshops in Milan, Bologna, Siena, and Naples.

In the period between the two World Wars, illuminated codices appear only in general studies, such as *Il Medioevo* by Toesca,[35] or the Parisian exhibition *Livre Italien* in 1926 by Seymour de Ricci;[36] or the extraordinary corpus of Florentine painting begun by Richard Offner, a disciple of Berenson, in 1930;[37] or in the systematic cataloguing of important libraries, such as the National Library of Austria, for which Julius Hermann wrote three volumes on Italian fourteenth-century codices.[38] It is clear that in Italy there was no realization that Gothic illumination, as such, existed, rather there was the idea of a Duecento Byzantinizing style and a Trecento style, which was perceived as new. This was not because of its naturalistic interest, but mainly because it looks back at Italian classical tradition, and, on this basis, could be called a national style.[39] Such a perception also prevailed in the analysis of forty-two miniatures and twenty-four manuscripts that were displayed in the Giottoesque exhibition of 1937, in Florence.[40] Two years before that, in 1935, Panofsky had posed the question: "By what right do we call a Gothic miniature Gothic?" His answer being: "The Gothic style may be considered as a synthesis of all Western currents present in previous Medieval art from which all Eastern elements have been excluded."[41] Byzantinizing Italy was necessarily out, and this exclusion would also weigh heavily in the Parisian Exhibition of 1968[42] and in New York's *The Year 1200* exhibition of 1970,[43] even if scholars of Byzantine art had begun in the interim to underline the role of Eastern tradition in the formation of the Gothic style.[44]

After the Second World War, interest in Gothic manuscripts escalated, although Italian art historians focused almost exclusively on the visual and formal

33. P. D'Ancona, *La miniatura fiorentina (secoli XI–XVI)* (Florence, 1914).

34. The absence of strong personalities induces the author to divide the manuscripts on the basis of content: sacred, literary, and popular; for the first section, there are the important choir-books of Sta. Maria Novella, for the other, the *Pater noster*, in which operate two models, French and popular.

35. P. Toesca, *Il Medioevo* (Turin, 1927); *idem*, *Il Trecento* (Turin, 1951).

36. *Catalogue de l'exposition du Livre Italien: Manuscrits—Livre imprimés—Reliures*, Exhib. Cat., Bibliothèque Nationale (Paris, 1926). Sixty-nine codices of the fourteenth century and 162 of the fifteenth were exhibited.

37. R. Offner, *Studies in Florentine Painting: The Fourteenth Century* (New York, 1927).

38. H. J. Hermann, *Die italienische Handschriften des Dugento und Trecento, bis zur mitte des XIV. Jahrhunderts*, vol. 1 (Leipzig, 1928); vol. 2. *Oberitalienische Handschriften des zweiten Hälfte des XIV. Jahrhunderts* (Leipzig, 1929); vol. 3. *Neapolitanische und Toskanische Handschriften des zweiten Hälfte des XIV. Jahrhunderts* (Beschreibendes Verzeichnis des Illuminierten Handschriften in Österreich, VIII, V) (Leipzig, 1930).

39. W. F. Volbach, *Le miniature del codice Vatic. Pal. Lat. 1071 "De arte venandi cum avibus*," "Rendiconti della Pontificia Accademia Romana di Archeologia," 15 (1939), 145–175, 174.

40. *La mostra giottesca* (Florence, 1937); see A. Monciatti, "La *Mostra giottesca* del 1937 a Firenze," in *Medioevo e Medioevi* (as in note 26), 141–168, 150.

41. E. Panofsky, *Gothic and Late Illuminated Manuscripts (with a special reference to manuscripts in the Pierpont Morgan Library)* (Fine Arts 336, New York University) [London, Warburg Library, CHF 175, typescript], (New York, 1935) 23, 30.

42. In the exhibition *L'Europe Gothique, XIIe–XIVe siècles*, Musée du Louvre (Paris, 1968), only eleven Italian manuscripts were exhibited, mainly from central Italy and without photographic documentation in the catalogue. W. Sauerländer, "L'Europe Gothique, XIIe–XIVe siècles. Point de vue critiques à propos d'une exposition," *RevArt* 3 (1969), 83–92.

43. W. Sauerländer, "*Review: 'The Year 1200' A Centennial Exhibition at the Metropolitan Museum of Art. February 12–May 10, 1970*," *Art Bulletin* 53 (1971), 506–516. The only interest in manuscripts of this period is for iconographic purposes: L. Eleen, "A Thirteenth-century Workshop of Miniature Painters in the Veneto," *Arte Veneta* 39 (1985), 9–21; *eadem*, "New Testament manuscripts and their lay owners in Verona in the thirteenth century," *Scriptorium* 41 (1987), 221–236.

44. W. Koehler, "Byzantine Art in the West," *Dumbarton Oaks Papers* 1 (1941), 61–87; O. Demus, *Byzantine Art and the West* (New York, 1970), 108–118, 163, who pointed out the arrival in the West from Byzantium of the two revolutionary ideas of "articulated body and animated figure" around 1150.

aspects of the image. This is evident in the exhibition of the Bolognese Trecento of 1950,[45] in which Roberto Longhi, connoisseur and philologist, author of the anti-Byzantine *Giudizio sul Duecento*,[46] and also one of the main exponents of Renaissance studies during the Fascist era, characterized the very complex picture of this illumination as "local, but not provincial." Longhi described Bolognese art as realistic and poetic and found in the illuminator, referred to as "Illustratore," an affirmation that perhaps "Giottoesque in Trecento was only Giotto himself."[47] Four years later, Mario Salmi,[48] the primary organizer of the Paris and Rome exhibitions on Italian illuminated manuscripts of 1950[49] and 1953 to 1954,[50] wrote an essay, largely influenced by Toesca,[51] on Gothic Lombard illumination. He also wrote "La miniatura gotica fiorentina,"[52] which, although indebted to Offner's research, showed an interest in texts and their relationship to illumination. The methodology was based on documentation but also included stylistic analysis. Longhi's main thesis was the reassertion of the solid classicism of Florentine culture versus the poetic linearism and colorism of the Sienese model. This stress on regional dimensions is also relatively strong in the Milanese exhibition of 1958,[53] a show of courtly masterpieces, which focused on single personalities, artists, and aristocratic patrons. The ensuing publication by the librarian and biblio-economist Emma Pirani of the first volume that was dedicated to Italian and European Gothic illumination does not come as a surprise. This booklet focused on masterpieces, which were lavishly reproduced in color. It belonged to a popular artistic series and followed, but also simplified, Salmi's methodology.[54]

In the following years, two codices were the subject of study within this new Italian-Gothic perspective, signaling the beginning of a new critical approach in Italy. The first codex was the so-called Conradin Bible,[55] a luxury manuscript formerly attributed to Aquileia, the Veneto, or Northern Italy, but located in Sicily (Fig. 1). The attribution by Daneu Lattanzi[56] was based on a series of comparisons with manuscripts and mosaics. This Mediterranean connection was used in Buchthal's pioneering research,[57] in which he analyzed the Perugia *Missal* for the first time in a study of Italian Gothic illumination that was part of the international debate on Crusader culture, and placed a Venetian illuminator in an atelier in Jerusalem. In 1966, Longhi identified the illuminator of the Conradin Bible with the Dantesque Oderisi da Gubbio, and his antagonist, Franco Bolognese, as the illuminator of the Bible 18 of the Bibliothèque Nationale de France.[58] The cultural location of the Conradin Baltimore Bible was a golden opportunity, not only for the discovery of other illuminated codices in the same style, but also for a survey of unknown Gothic codices of the Dugento. The second manuscript was the *Epistolary* of Giovanni di Gaibana,[59] which until then had been firmly located in Padua (Figs. 2, 3). It was Sergio Bettini, one of the

45. R. Longhi, "Prefazione," in *Guida alla mostra della pittura bolognese del Trecento* (Bologna, 1950), 11–24.

46. R. Longhi, "Giudizio sul Duecento," *Paragone* 2 (1948), 5–57.

47. L. Bellosi, "Roberto Longhi e l'arte del Trecento," in *L'arte di scrivere sull'arte. Roberto Longhi nella cultura del nostro tempo*, ed. G. Previtali (Roma, 1982), 27–36, 34.

48. M.G. Duprè Dal Poggetto, "Il contributo di Mario Salmi agli studi sulla miniatura italiana: un primo resoconto generale," in *Studi di storia dell'arte sul Medioevo e il Rinascimento nel centenario della nascita di Mario Salmi* (Florence, 1992), 151–162.

49. *Trésors des bibliothèque d'Italie*, Exhib. Cat., Petit Palais (Paris, 1950).

50. *Mostra storica nazionale della miniatura*, Exhib. Cat., Rome, Palazzo Venezia, by G. Muzzioli and M. Salmi (Florence, 1953).

51. M. Salmi, "La pittura e la miniatura gotica in Lombardia," in *Storia di Milano*, vol. 4 (Milan, 1954), 541–574.

52. M. Salmi, *La miniature gotica fiorentina*, Quaderni di storia della miniatura 1, (Rome, 1954). Strangely enough, on the book cover is drawn the image of a Paduan calligrapher, Giovanni di Gaibana, and not a Florentine one.

53. *Arte lombarda dai Visconti agli Sforza*, Exhib. Cat., Castello Sforzesco (Milan, 1958).

54. E. Pirani, *La miniatura gotica* (Milan, 1966).

55. Baltimore, The Walters Art Gallery, MS. 152.

56. A. Daneu Lattanzi, *I manoscritti e incunaboli miniati di Sicilia*, vol. 1, *Biblioteca Nazionale di Palermo* (Rome, 1965), 49–55; *eadem*, *Lineamenti di Storia della Miniatura in Sicilia* (Florence, 1966), 58–64.

57. H. Buchthal, *Miniature Painting in the Latin Kingdom of Jerusalem* (Oxford, 1957), 48–51.

58. R. Longhi, "Apertura sui trecentisti umbri," *Paragone* 17 (1966), n. 191, 3–7; *idem*, "Postille all'apertura sugli umbri," *Paragone*, n. 195, 1–12.

59. Padua, Chapter Library (Biblioteca Capitolare), MS. E2.

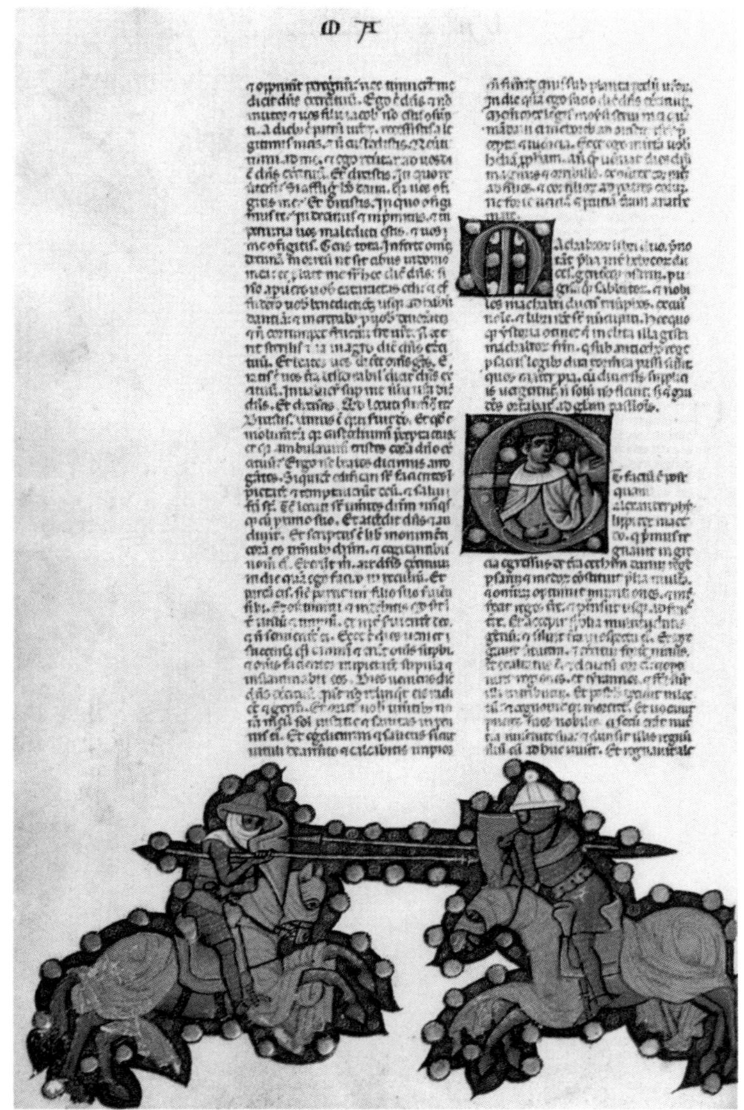

FIGURE 1. *Maccabees I* from the *Conradin Bible*, Baltimore, The Walters Art Museum, MS. 152, fol. 29v.

first Italian scholars to embrace the new methodologies of Weitzmann and Demus, who defined different Gothic cultures of academic Padua and oligarchic Venice, where he conjectured that the illuminator was trained.[60] It was during these years that Padua University became one of the leading centers for the study of Gothic illumination,[61] together with Pisa University where Ragghianti's pupils were based.[62] The history of illumination became a university discipline in 1968, when the first chair was founded at Naples

60. S. Bettini, "Le miniature dell'Epistolario di Giovanni di Gaibana nella storia della pittura veneziana del Duecento," in C. Bellinati and S. Bettini, *L'epistolario miniato di Giovanni di Gaibana* (Vicenza, 1968), 69–120. For this school, see G. Mariani Canova, "La storia della miniatura negli studi del XX secolo (as in note 29), 138.

61. G. Folena and G. Mellini, *Bibbia istoriata padovana della fine del Trecento: Pentateuco, Giosuè, Ruth* (Padua, 1962); G. Mariani Canova, *Miniature dell'Italia settentrionale nella Fondazione Giorgio Cini* (Vicenza, 1978).

62. G. Dalli Regoli, *Miniatura pisana del Trecento*, Raccolta pisana

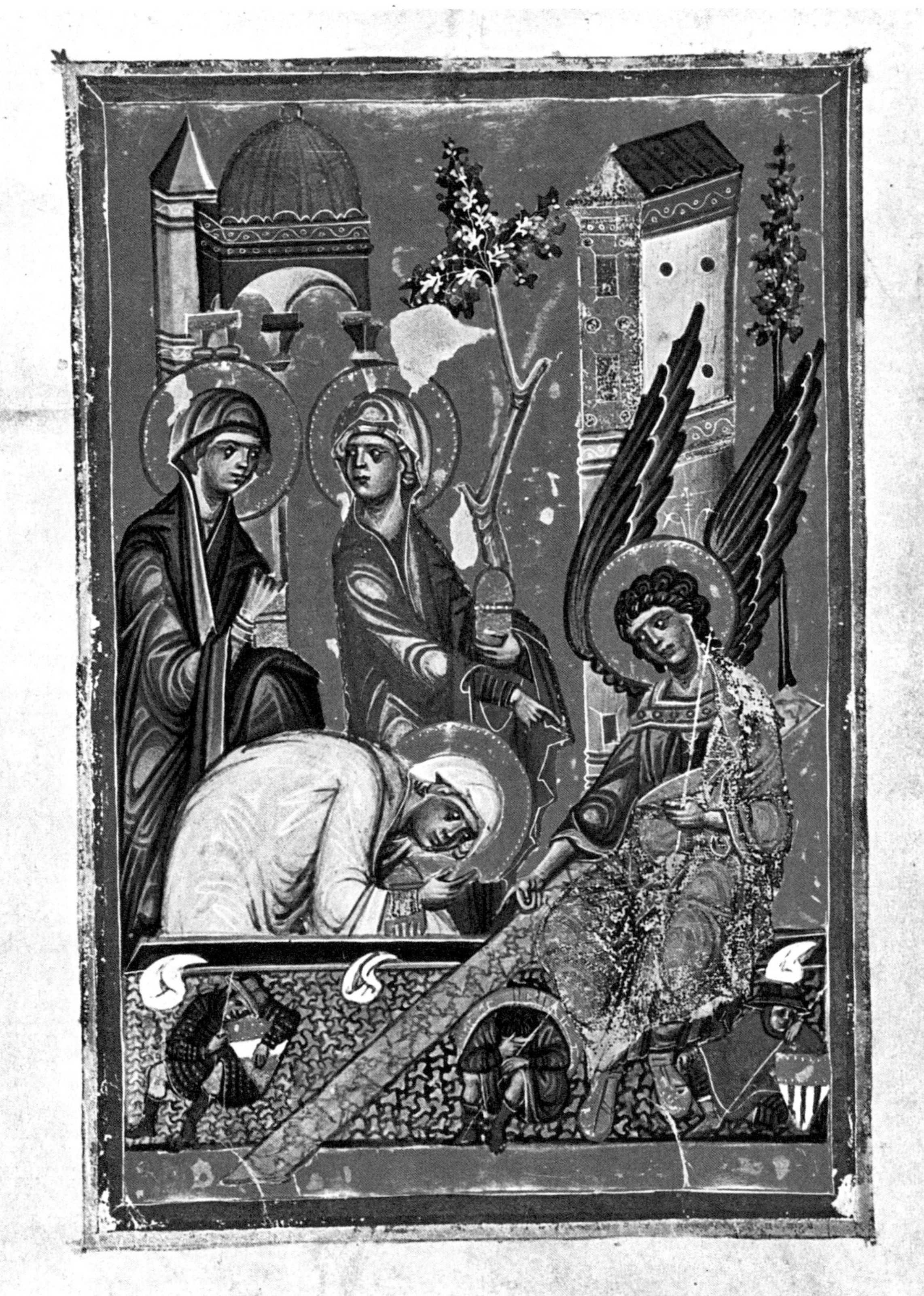

FIGURE 2. *Three Women at the Sepulchre*, from the *Epistolary* of Giovanni di Gaibana, Padua, Biblioteca Capitolare, MS. E2, fol. 48v.

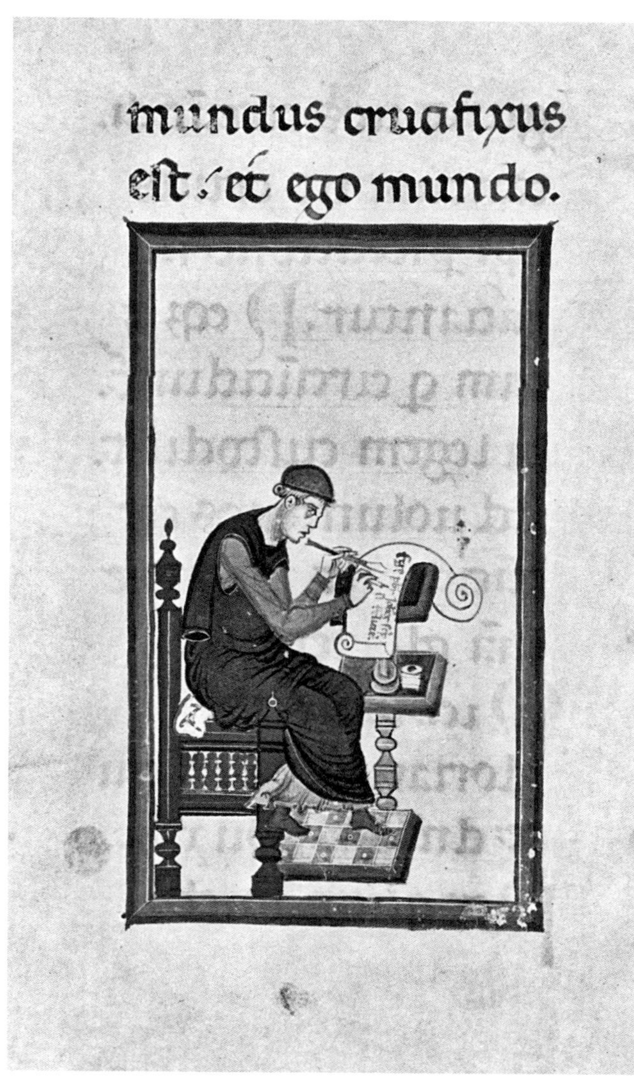

FIGURE 3. *The Scriptor Giovanni di Gaibana*, from the *Epistolary* of Giovanni di Gaibana, Padua, Biblioteca Capitolare, MS. E2, fol. 98ᵛ.

University.[63] It was held by Mario Rotili, a disciple of Ferdinando Bologna,[64] and author, in 1968–1969, of two little volumes titled "La miniatura gotica in Italia."[65] This was a synthetic survey that presented for the first time an analysis of the critical debate, as well as a formal and cultural evaluation of the characteristics of the Italian Gothic book in relation to the European context, and a close examination of contemporaneous treatises, technical and artistic, on illumination.[66]

Italian researchers endeavored to classify correctly the bulk of discovered manuscripts by means of the systematic cataloguing of public and private libraries, and, in doing so, made important contributions to our knowledge of the stylistic aspects of production. However, non-Italian scholars applied an iconological methodology to the study of Gothic Italian manuscripts, which started in 1961 with the observations by Rosalie Green and Isa Ragusa on the *Meditations on the Life of Christ*, as editors of MS. Italian 115 of the Bibliothèque Nationale de France.[67] Two publications by Millard Meiss, who is also known to Italian scholars for his controversial essay on Tuscan painting after the Black Death,[68] were seminal in laying out a new Italian approach to the study of illuminated Gothic manuscripts. In 1967, *French Painting in the Time of Jean de Berry*[69] identified the Bolognese Master of the Brussels Initials as one of the foremost artists in Parisian illumination at the end of the fourteenth century. In 1969, in his two weighty volumes on the *Divine Comedy* (co-

di arte e studi 9 (Venice, 1963); A. Caleca, *Miniatura in Umbria* (Florence, 1969); A. Calderoni Masetti and G. Dalli Regoli, *Sanctae Hildegardis Revelationes: manoscritti 1942* (Lucca, 1973); A. Caleca, "Un codice pisano della fine del Duecento," in *La miniatura italiana in età romanica e gotica* (Florence, 1979), 207–221.

63. Naples was an intellectual *milieu* particularly open to the problem of illuminated manuscripts, as witness the formation of the Società della miniature, established in 1882: see A. Perriccioli Saggese, "I 'Capitoli per la promozione dell'arte della miniature a Napoli' e la 'fortuna' della miniature nella seconda metà dell'Ottocento," in *Storie di artisti, storie di libri. L'Editore che inseguiva la Bellezza. Scritti in onore di Franco Cosimo Panini* (Rome, 2008), 431–439.

64. F. Bologna, *La pittura italiana delle origini* (Rome, 1962), 83–94; *idem, I pittori alla corte angioina di Napoli, 1266–1414, ed un riesame dell'arte nell'età federiciana* (Rome, 1969): in the analysis of the painting of the thirteenth century appear frequent references to contemporary illuminations.

65. M. Rotili, *La miniatura gotica in Italia* (Naples, 1968–1969): the beginning of Gothic production was firmly located in Naples in the time of Frederick II and the chronological limits of the phenomenon are fixed between 1250 and 1400.

66. See also M. G. Ciardi Dupré, "La miniatura gotica in Toscana," in *Civiltà delle arti minori in Toscana* (Arezzo, 1971, Florence, 1973), 53–63; and O. Mazal, *Buchkunst der Gotik* (Graz, 1975), 96–105.

67. *Meditations on the Life of Christ: An Illustrated Manuscript of the 14th Century, Paris, Bibliothèque Nationale, Ms. ital. 115*, by I. Ragusa and R. B. Green (Princeton, 1961).

68. M. Meiss, *Painting in Florence and Siena after the Black Death* (Princeton, 1951, Italian trans., 1982).

69. M. Meiss, *The French Painting in the Time of Jean de Berry*, I: *The Late XIV Century and the Patronage of the Duke* (London, 1967).

edited with Peter Brieger and Charles Singleton),[70] Meiss clarified the problem of the image, by declaring that it was the product of design as well as of poetry.

The result was that, in the following years, Italian universities emphasized a new approach toward different methodologies, studying, for example, the relationship between the transmission of texts and of illustrative cycles, such as in chivalric romances.[71] Or, as another example, focus had been on the problem of patronage of the mendicant orders, the latter study coinciding with the 1982 celebrations of the eighth centenary of the birth of Francis of Assisi.[72] If Gothic illumination was by then perceived as an entity, it continued to walk a fine line between Romanesque and Renaissance.[73] To understand this changing context, new methodologies, such as iconography and workshop organization, were essential.[74]

In the following years, interest in Gothic Italian illumination increased, generating a richness of methodological options, as shown by two studies on Bolognese illumination in 1980. The study by Elly Cassee on the *Missal* of Bertrand de Deux,[75] with its in-depth examination of theological issues relating to the images, and *La miniatura Bolognese*, by Conti in 1981,[76] which focused on the technical and stylistic differences between ateliers; both were important. This second study is comparable with the work of Branner[77] on Parisian ateliers, which, with its numerous appendices on the division of work between illuminators in codices and iconographical cycles, shows a different methodology and a keen interest in interaction between workshops. In Italy, however, stylistic analysis, albeit with variants, still predominates in scholarship, as is clearly evident in the dispute on the origins of the Master of the Codex of St. George. In 1981,[78] Maria Grazia Ciardi Dupré Dal Poggetto proposed a Roman origin for this illuminator, adding to suggestions previously made by Hélène Toubert that this was also the home of the Master of the Conradin Bible,[79] and, as such, making it a center of book production while analyzing the patronage of Cardinal Stefaneschi. This hypothesis was rejected in the catalogue of the exhibition *Il gotico a Siena* in favor of Florentine training,[80] where the premise was to promote Siena as "the capital in Tuscany, of the new western style, gothic, that is French,"[81] and thus to eliminate the Byzantine shadow from Duccio's style.[82] It is enlightening to compare the contemporaneous book by Susan Partsch, a disciple of Hans Belting, on the

70. P. Brieger, M. Meiss, and C. Singleton, *Illuminated Manuscripts of the Divine Comedy* (London, 1969), vol. 2.

71. A. Perriccioli Saggese, *I romanzi cavallereschi a Napoli* (Naples, 1979); *eadem*, "Le illustrazioni di storia nei codici miniati a Napoli tra Duecento e Trecento: riflessioni sullo stato degli studi," in *Medioevo: il tempo degli antichi* (Milan, 2006), 547–556.

72. M. G. Ciardi Dupré Dal Poggetto, "La miniatura e l'ordine francescano nei secolo XIII," "La miniatura nei libri francescani," "La miniatura francescana dalle origini alla morte di san Bonaventura," "La nascita dei cicli corali umbri," "Il ciclo corale di San Francesco a Bologna," "Il primo papa francescano Niccolò IV (1288–1293), e il suo influsso sulla miniatura umbra," in *Francesco d'Assisi: Documenti e Archivi—Codici e Biblioteche—Miniature*, Exhib. Cat., Foligno, Palazzo Trinci (Milan, 1982), 295–298, 323–330, 331–337, 338–350, 351–357, 358–365.

73. The difficulty of forging a cultural, chronological, and geographical definition of Gothic illumination is shown clearly in the first two congresses of History of Italian Illumination: the first was dedicated to the Romanesque and Gothic production, *La miniatura in età romanica e gotica*, by G. Vailati Schoenburg Waldenburg (Florence, 1979); the second to the Gothic and the Renaissance, *La miniatura italiana tra Gotico e Rinascimento*, by E. Sesti (Florence, 1985).

74. D. D'Arcais, "L'organizzazione del lavoro negli *scriptoria* laici del primo Trecento a Bologna," in *La miniatura in età* (as in note 71), 357–369; G. Mariani Canova, "Gli antifonari di S. Domenico in Bologna," *La miniature in età*, 371–393.

75. E. Cassee, *The Missal of Cardinal Bertrand de Deux: A Study in 14th-Century Bolognese Miniature Painting* (Florence, 1980).

76. A. Conti, *La miniatura bolognese. Scuole e botteghe 1270–1340* (Bologna, 1981).

77. R. Branner, *Manuscript Painting in Paris During the Reign of Saint Louis* (Berkeley, Los Angeles, London, 1977).

78. M. G. Ciardi Dupré Dal Poggetto, *Il Maestro del Codice San Giorgio e il Cardinale Jacopo Stefaneschi* (Florence, 1981).

79. H. Toubert, "Autour de la Bible de Conradin: trois nouveaux manuscrits enluminé," *Melanges de l'Ecole Francaise de Rome* 91/2 (1979), 729–284.

80. L. Bellosi, "Il 'Maestro del Codice di San Giorgio,'" in *Il Gotico a Siena: miniature, pitture, oreficerie, oggetti d'arte*, Exhib. Cat., Siena, Palazzo Pubblico (Florence, 1982), 166–170.

81. G. Previtali, "Ragioni e limiti di una mostra," in *Il Gotico a Siena* (as in note 78), 13–17, 14.

82. This term is absent also in the catalogue of the more recent exhibition: *Duccio: alle origini della pittura senese*, Exhib. Cat., Siena, Santa Maria della Scala (Milan 2003).

Florentine *Profane Buchmalerei*, with its strong iconographic interest, which was aimed at reconstructing symbolic, cultural, and social meanings of the image (Figs. 4, 5).[83]

In terms of contextual studies, one of the main topics has certainly been the contribution of Italian illuminators to Crusader art. The already mentioned study by Buchthal[84] was expanded by Jaroslav Folda's work on St. Jean d'Acre,[85] by Belting's idea of *lingua franca*,[86] and by Buchthal's essay on the Wolfenbüttel sketchbook.[87] The main Italian contributor to this debate, Valentino Pace,[88] did not see the presence of Italian illuminators in the East, but instead saw the presence of eastern models in Italy.[89] Other scholars, who, like Pace, spoke at the C.I.H.A. Congress of 1978 were more interested in examining the impact of Byzantine models in Italy than in the presence of Italian illuminators in the Holy Land. Michael Jacoff,[90] for example, emphasized the presence of Paleologian models in the Gerona Master and in codices made in Bologna, rather than in Crusader art. In the *Supplicationes variae* (Fig. 6), Amy Neff[91] studied the iconographic models and the interaction between two different systems of images (devotional and *drôleries*) and techniques (miniatures and drawings), while Rebecca Corrie[92] discussed the localization of the Conradin Bible in Messina, and gave a dynamic insight into the cultural models circulating in the Hohenstaufen *scriptoria*.

The unceasing discovery and publication of illuminated manuscripts[93] in the following decades prevented the construction of a comprehensive picture of the study of Gothic illumination in Italy. The question of identity has never been critically addressed, and the problem of the relationship between the Eastern and Western worlds remains unsettled, as many studies deal only with single manuscripts or single centers of production.[94] Furthermore, Italian manuscripts only rarely enter into the more complex analysis of the relationship of illuminated texts and the history of mentality, and marginally at that. Alison Stone's research on manuscripts of the Legend of St. Margaret,[95] undertaken in 1991, is an exception.

83. S. Partsch, *Profane Buchmalerei der Bürgerlichen Geselschaft im spätmittelalterlichen Florenz. Der Specchio Umano des Getreidehändlers Domenico Lenzi*, Heidelberger Kunstgeschichtliche Abhandlungen, 16 (Worms, 1981). This topic was widely developed: see V. Molleta, "The 'Somme le roi' from French Court to Italian City-State," in *Patronage and public in the Trecento*, ed. V. Moleta (Florence, 1986), 125–158.

84. H. Buchthal, *Miniature Painting* (as in note 56).

85. J. Folda, *Crusader Manuscripts Illuminated in Saint Jean d'Acre, 1275–1291* (Princeton, 1976).

86. H. Belting, "Zwischen Gotik und Byzanz. Gedanken zur Geschichte der sächsischen Buchmalerei im 13. Jahrhundert," *Zeitschrift für Kunstgeschichte* 41 (1978), 217–257.

87. H. Buchthal, *The "Müsterbuch" of Wolfenbüttel and its Position in the Art of the Thirteenth Century*, Byzantina Vindobonensia, 12 (Vienna, 1979).

88. V. Pace, "Italy and the Holy Land: Import-Export. I. The Case of Venice," in *The Meeting of Two Worlds: Cultural Exchange Between East and West During the Period of the Crusades* (Studies in Medieval Culture, 21), ed. V. P. Goss and Ch. Verzar Bornstein (Kalamazoo, 1986), 331–345.

89. V. Pace, "La Bibbia bizantina di S. Daniele del Friuli," in *La miniatura in età* (as in note 71), 131–157; *idem*, "Icone di Puglia, della Terra Santa e di Cipro: appunti preliminari per un'indagine sulla ricezione bizantina nell'Italia meridionale duecentesca," in *Il Medio Oriente e l'Occidente nell'arte del XIII secolo* (Comité International d'Histoire de l'Art, 2), ed. H. Belting (Bologna, 1982), 181–192.

90. M. Jacoff, "The Bible of Charles V and Related Works: Bologna, Byzantium, and the West in Late Thirteenth Century," *Il Medio Oriente* (as in note 87), 163–179.

91. A. Neff, "A New Interpretation of the *Supplicationes Variae* Miniatures," in *Il Medio Oriente* (as in note 87), 173–179. See also "Byzantium Westernized, Byzantium Marginalized: Two Icons in the *Supplicationes variae*," *Gesta* 38 (1999), 81–102; *eadem*, "'Palma dabit palmam': Franciscan Themes in a Devotional Manuscript," *Journal of the Warburg and Courtauld Institutes* 65 (2002), 22–66.

92. R. Corrie, "The Conradin Bible: East Meets West at Messina," in *Il Medio Oriente* (as in note 87), 295–307; see also *eadem*, *The Conradin Bible, ms. 152, The Walters Art Gallery: Manuscript Illumination in a Thirteenth-Century Italian Atelier* (Ann Arbor, 1986), with in-depth analysis of the atelier and the iconographic cycles in use.

93. An important example not focused only on masterpieces, is the extraordinary catalogue of the exhibition organized by François Avril in 1984 in Paris: see F. Avril, *Dix siècles d'enluminure italienne, (VIe–XVe siècles)* (Paris, 1984).

94. See, for example, the essays published in *La miniatura in Italia*, vol. 1, *Dal tardo antico al Trecento con riferimenti al Medioe Oriente e all'Occidente europeo*, ed. A. Putaturo Murano and A. Perriccioli Saggese (Naples, 2005), 131–246.

95. M. A. Stones, "Le ms. Troyes 1905, le recueil et ses enluminures," in Wace, *La vie de Sainte Margherite*, ed. H.-E. Keller (Tübingen, 1990), 185–239.

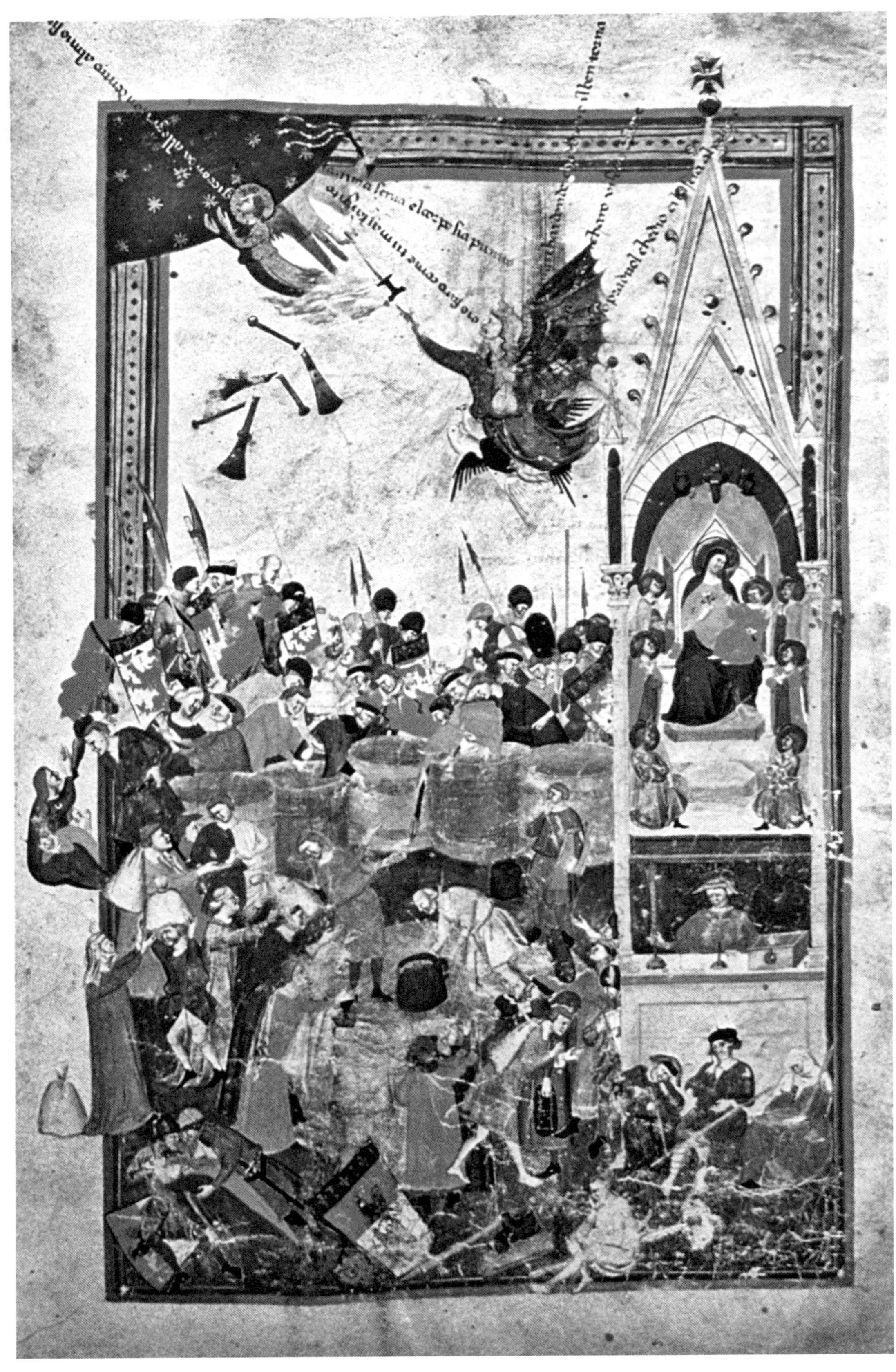

FIGURE 4. *Wheat Market at Orsanmichele in Florence* from the *Speculum Humanae* by Domenico Lenzi, Florence, Laurentian Library, MS. Tempi 3, fol. 79^{r}.

The studies of the last two decades are too numerous to attempt a complete survey of them and are characterized in Italy by a progressive accentuation of the French origin of Gothic Italian illumination,[96] as well as by an emphasis on the unbreakable link between material support, text, images, and artistic context. This approach offers the best opportunity for recovering the works of secondary scriptoria and centers, and consequently the restitution of the connective tissue in which to contextualize the masterpieces. This approach is more than evident in research linked to the great exhibitions of 1994, celebrating the eighth centenary of the birth of Frederick the Second,[97] an occasion not only for defining and legitimizing the function of luxury, courtly, scientific, and chivalric codices, but also for establishing relations with new acquisitions and identifying less elaborated copies.[98] In the commentaries attached to facsimiles, the focus is usually on a single work in which not only style and iconography is studied, but also patronage and context. As such, the illuminated manuscript becomes part of a larger cultural system, no longer relegated to the margins as "minor" art.

Another characteristic of Italian studies is the cooperation between art historians and philologists, which has meant that the analysis of images does not only reveal semiotic properties,[99] but also stylistic ones, which are the specific concerns of art historians as well. In

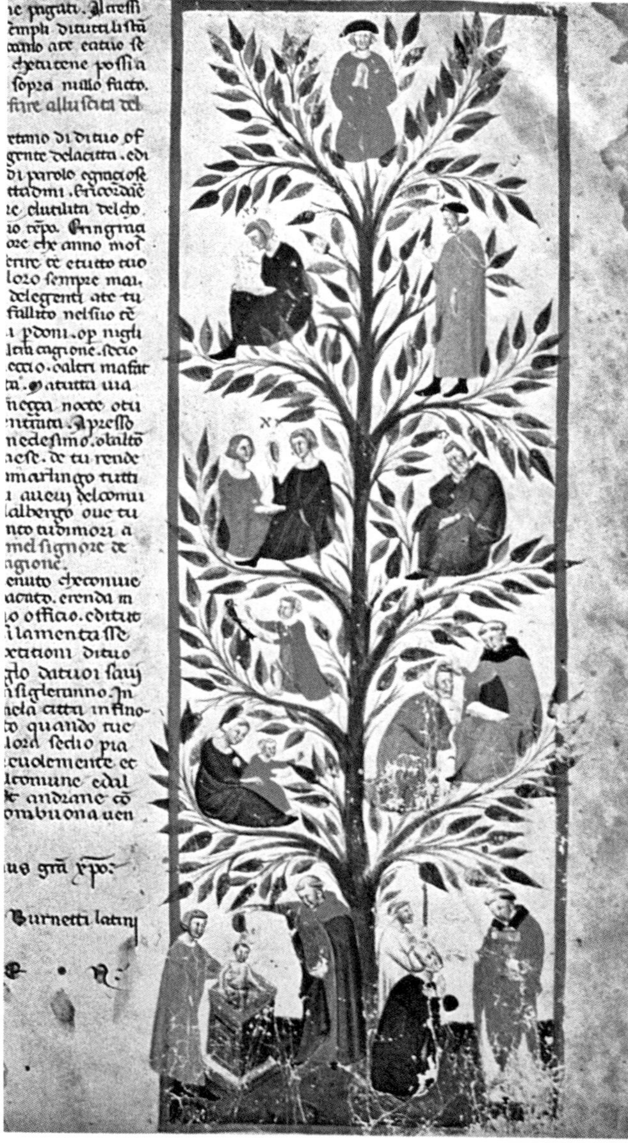

FIGURE 5. *The Ages of Man*, by Brunetto Latini, Il Tesoro, Florence, Laurentian Library, MS. Plut. XLII, 19, fol. 96^{r}.

96. See the contributions collected in *Il Gotico europeo* (as in note 3), such as P. Supino Martino, "Il libro nuovo," 351–357, and L. Ayres, "Bibbie italiane e bibbie francesi: il XIII secolo," 361–371; G. Orofino, "Cavalleria e devozione. Libri miniati francesi a Napoli e Bari in età protoangioina," *Ibid.*, 375–385.

97. F. Gandolfo, "Le celebrazioni dei personaggi storici attraverso le mostre d'arte medievale," in *Medioevo e Medioevi* (as in note 31), 441–454.

98. G. Orofino, "Il rapporto con l'antico e l'osservazione della natura nell'illustrazione scientifica di età sveva in Italia meridionale," in *Intellectual Life at the Court of Frederick II Hohenstaufen*, ed. W. Tronzo (Washington, D.C., 1994), 129–149; *eadem*, "Solatiosus homo fuit: i 'piaceri del principe' nella miniatura sveva," in *Mezzogiorno—Federico II—Mezzogiorno*, ed. C. D. Fonseca (Rome, 2000), 777—793; *eadem*, "Il contributo di Federico II all'iconografia profana: le illustrazioni del Romanzo di Alessandro," in *Federico II e le nuove culture* (Spoleto, 1995), 393–415.

99. Centers such as the Institut de Recherche et Histoire de Textes in Orléans and the Institut für Frümittelalterforschung in Münster study the images as iconography and sign language, but not as style, missing in this way a fundamental component of the image; in Italy this exclusive "philological" use of image is more reduced, focused mainly on Dante: L. Ricci Battaglia, "Il commento figurato alla Commedia: *schede di iconografia dantesca*," in *Bilanci e prospettive degli studi danteschi alle soglie del nuovo millennio*" (Verona and Ravenna, 1999; Rome, 2001), 601–640; or scientific manuscripts: *Le parole della scienza, Scritture tecniche e scientifiche in volgare (secoli XIII–XV)* (Lecce, 1999; Galatina, 2001); and *Lo scaffale della biblioteca scientifica in volgare (secoli XIII–XVI)* (Matera, 2004; Florence, 2006).

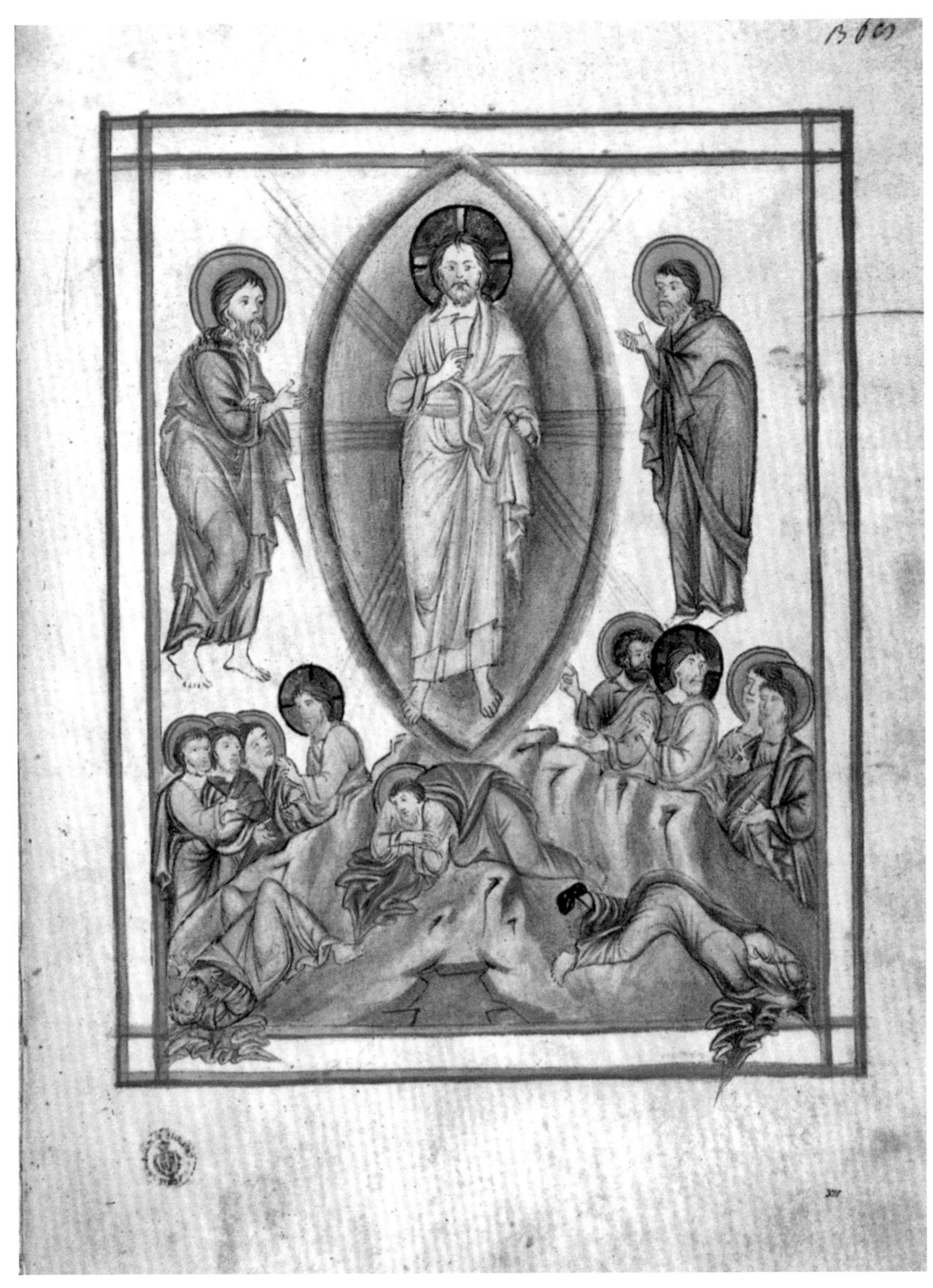

FIGURE 6. *The Transfiguration* from the *Supplicationes variae*, Florence, Laurentian Library, MS. Plut. 25.3, fol. 371^{r}.

this respect, it is sufficient to note the fundamental research by Mariani Canova on scientific manuscripts,[100] or those of Ciardi Dupré on Boccaccio and Dante.[101]

The focus on stylistic problems, on the interaction between text and images and between codex and intellectual and/or artistic context, enables us to understand Italian Gothic book production in single centers, but many questions remain unanswered. Jonathan Alexander, in his pivotal book on the methods employed by illuminators,[102] points to the lack of information on Italian workshops, particularly the relations between painters and illuminators. This is true even for Bologna, the most studied center. Recent publications and exhibitions deal mainly with biblical and legal codices, but different texts were illustrated in these Bolognese ateliers, sometimes following rigorously stabilized traditions, but frequently inventing illustrative systems for new texts. Typical works are such codices as the *Alexander Romance* in Venice (Fig. 7) and *De arte venandi cum avibus* in Bologna,[103] which were illuminated around 1285; or the three copies of the *Histoire de Troie* dated to 1315;[104] or the contemporary *Fiore di Virtù*;[105] or Pliny (Fig. 8);[106] and last but not least, the two oldest copies of the illustrated *Divine Comedy* (Figs. 9, 10).[107] The last were the only manuscripts with a complete illustrative system due to the economic power of Bolognese workshops, which were able to finance and produce illuminated codices for the market. The Florentine

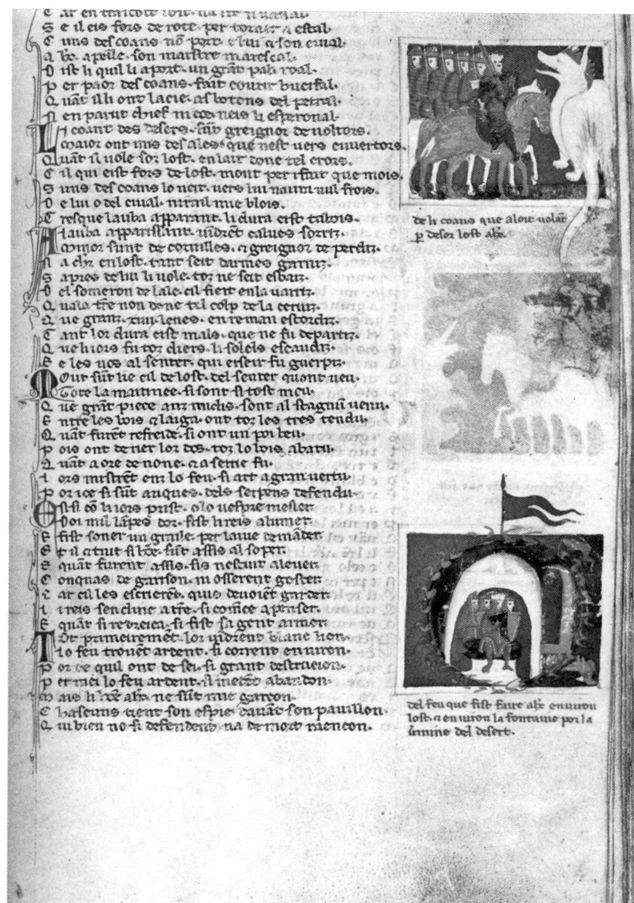

FIGURE 7. *Roman d'Alexandre*. Venice, Correr Museum, MS. 1493, fol. 45r.

100. G. Mariani Canova, "La tradizione europea degli erbari miniati e la scuola veneta," in *Di Sana Pianta. Erbari e taccuini di sanità* (Modena, 1988), 21–28; *eadem*, "Duodecim celestia signa et septem planete cum suis proprietatibus: l'immagine astrologica nella cultura figurativa e nell'illustrazione libraria a Padova tra Trecento e Quattrocento," in *Il Palazzo della Ragione di Padova. Indagini preliminari per il restauro. Studi e ricerche*, ed. A. M. Spiazzi (Treviso, 1998), 23–61; *Miniatura a Padova dal Medioevo al Settecento*, ed. G. Mariani Canova (Modena, 1999).

101. The proposal to identify in Boccaccio the illustrator of Paris, BnF, MS. It. 482, was made by V. Branca, "Per il testo del Decameron. La prima diffusione del Decameron, I, Composizione dell'opera e testimonianze fino alla morte di Boccaccio," *Studi di filologia italiana* 8 (1950), 100; see M. G. Ciardi Dupré Dal Poggetto, "L'iconografia dei codici miniati boccacciani dell'Italia centrale e meridionale," in *Boccaccio visualizzato: narrare per parole e immagini tra Medioevo e Rinascimento*, ed. V. Branca, I (Turin 1999), 3–152, 66–72. See also *eadem*, "*Narrar Dante* attraverso le Immagini: le prime illustrazioni della *Commedia*," in *Pagine di Dante: le edizioni della Divina Commedia dal torchio al computer* (Milan, 1989), 81–102.

102. J. J. G. Alexander, *Illuminators and Their Methods of Work* (London, 1992).

103. Venice, Museo Correr, MS. Correr 1493, and Bologna, University Library, MS. 717: see A. Conti, "Il codice Correre del *Roman d'Alexandre* e il primo stile della miniatura bolognese," in *Le Roman d'Alexandre. Riproduzione del ms. Venezia, Biblioteca Museo Correr, Correr 1493*, ed. R. Benedetti (Udine, 1998), 57–67.

104. H. Buchthal, *Historia Troiana: Studies in the History of Medieval Secular Illustration* (London, 1971), 14, 39.

105. G. Freuler, "Manifestatori di cose miracolose," Arte italiana del '300 e del '400 da collezioni in Svizzera e nel Lichtenstein (Lugano, 1991), 140–142.

106. L. Armstrong, "The illustration of Pliny's 'Historia naturalis': manuscripts before 1430," in *Journal of the Warburg and Courtauld Institutes*, 46 (1983), 19–39.

107. London, British Library, MS. Egerton 943, Florence, Ric-

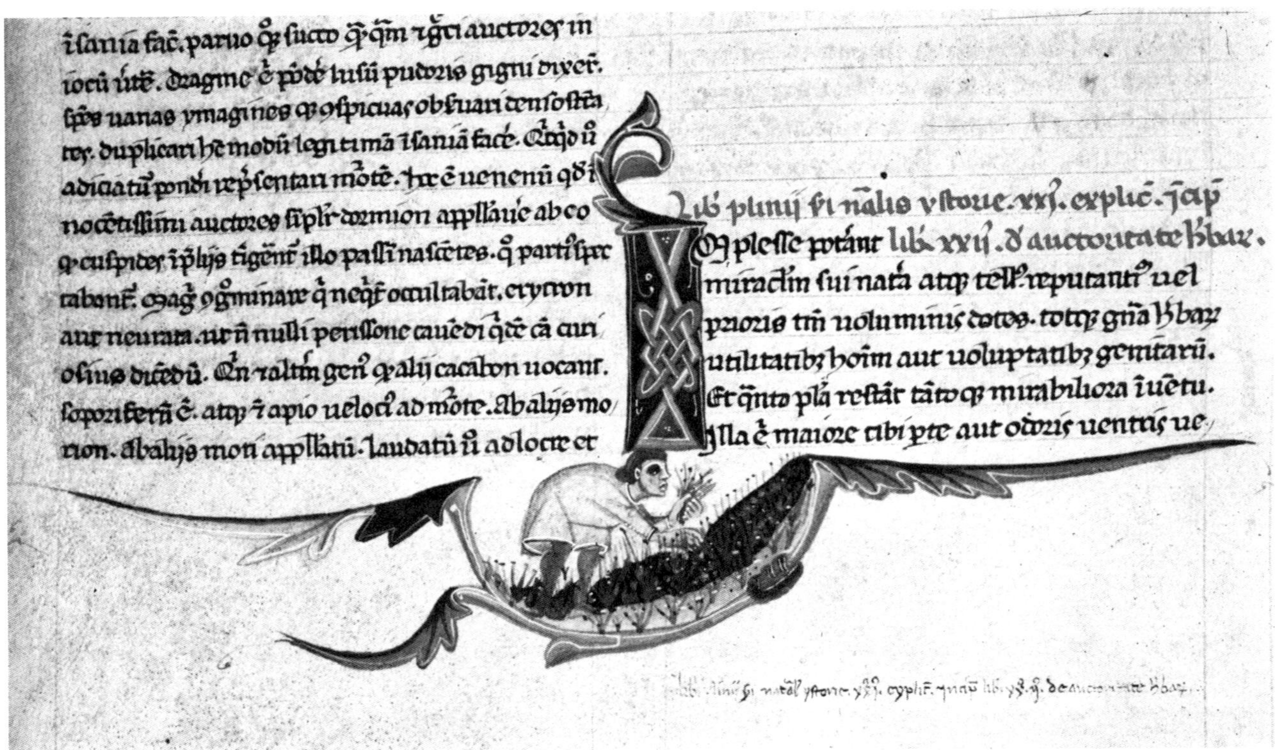

FIGURE 8. C. Pliny, *Naturalis Historia*, Book XXII. El Escorial, Royal Library of the Monastery of San Lorenzo, MS. R.I.5. fol. 163[r].

ateliers were quite different, as they worked only on commission and were not financially able to complete a job without a patron. For this reason, many Florentine illuminated manuscripts survived with only partial decoration, such as the *Chronicle* of Giovanni Villani.[108] A related problem is the mobility of Bolognese workshops and the interaction with minor scriptoria and local religious communities. The alternative attributions of some manuscripts to Padua and Bologna exemplify the difficulty of judging on a stylistic basis

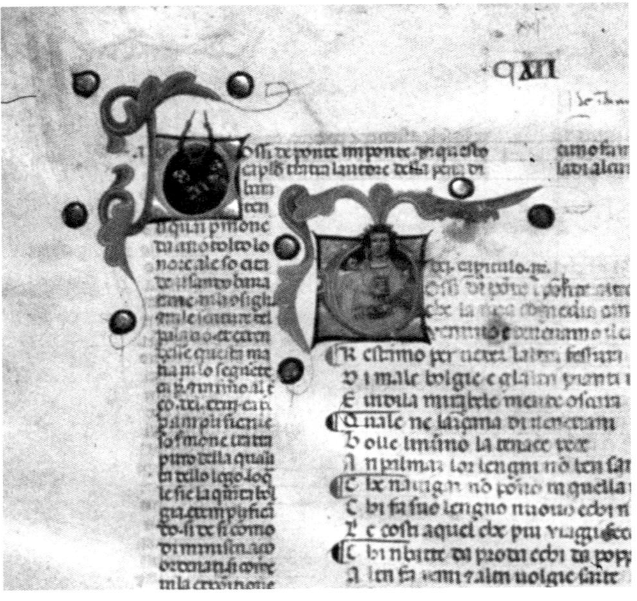

FIGURE 9. Dante Alighieri, *Divina Commedia*, *Inferno*, Canto XXI, *Avarice*. Florence, Riccardiana Library, MS. 1005, fol. 62[v].

cardiana Library, MS. 1005 (Hell and Purgatory), and Milan, Brera National Library, MS. AG.XII.2 (Paradise): see G. Z. Zanichelli, "L'immagine come glossa. Considerazioni su alcuni frontespizi miniati della Divina Commedia," in *Dante e le arti visive* (Milan, 2006), 109–148.

108. G. Z. Zanichelli, "La *Cronica* di Giovanni Villani e la nascita del racconto storico illustrato a Firenze nella prima metà del Trecento," in *Il Villani illustrato. Firenze e l'Italia medievale nelle 253 immagini del ms. Chigiano L VIII 296 della Biblioteca Vaticana*, ed. C. Frugoni (Florence, 2005), 59–76.

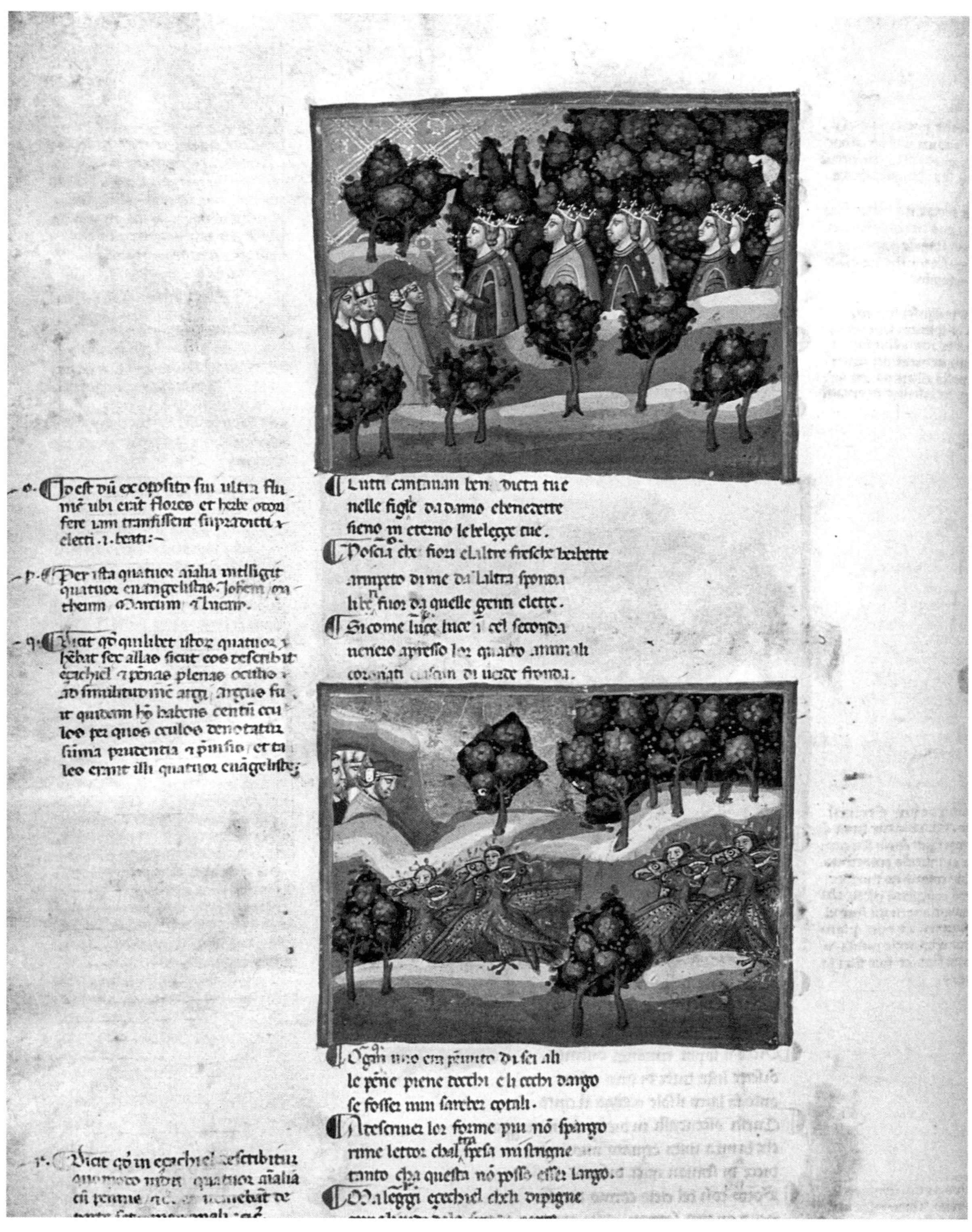

FIGURE 10. Dante Alighieri, *Divina Commedia*, *Purgatorio*, Canto XXIX, *Earthly Paradise*. British Library Board. MS. Egerton 943, fol. 116v (All Rights Reserved).

only. A problem that has been completely neglected is the relationships between illuminators, metalworkers, and glyptic artists for works such as the Lombard *Pax* of the Master of the Hours Book of Modena (Fig. 11),[109] and the Venetian reliquaries.[110]

The relationship between reader and illustrated book in Italian society, and the role of images in the creation of *volgare illustre*, that is, the literary vernacular language, are topics that are still open to research. A recent acquisition casts new light on the problem of the origins of the devotional codex. The author of this manuscript, the *Offiziolo* (Fig. 12), was Francesco da Barberino, an intellectual notary who wrote the text in Padua in the same years in which Giotto was painting for Enrico Scrovegni,[111] and was used to match word and image as a means of philosophical and poetic communication.[112] This remarkable codex, together with the *Supplicationes variae*, seems to indicate a cultured origin for devotional booklets.[113] Certainly in Italy, the Church's strict control on nunneries by Boniface VIII, and their submission to the male branch of each religious order, strongly constrained female literacy, but the regular clergy was also strictly controlled. This situation favored secular production, which is individual, and reflects, more than elsewhere, a single *Weltanschauung*. In the *Offiziolo*, to give an example, the cyclical time of the daily prayers is illustrated with images of the ages of man (Fig. 13), symbolizing linear time, and, in this way, the image gives new meaning to the text.[114] The execution of the illustrative system by a profes-

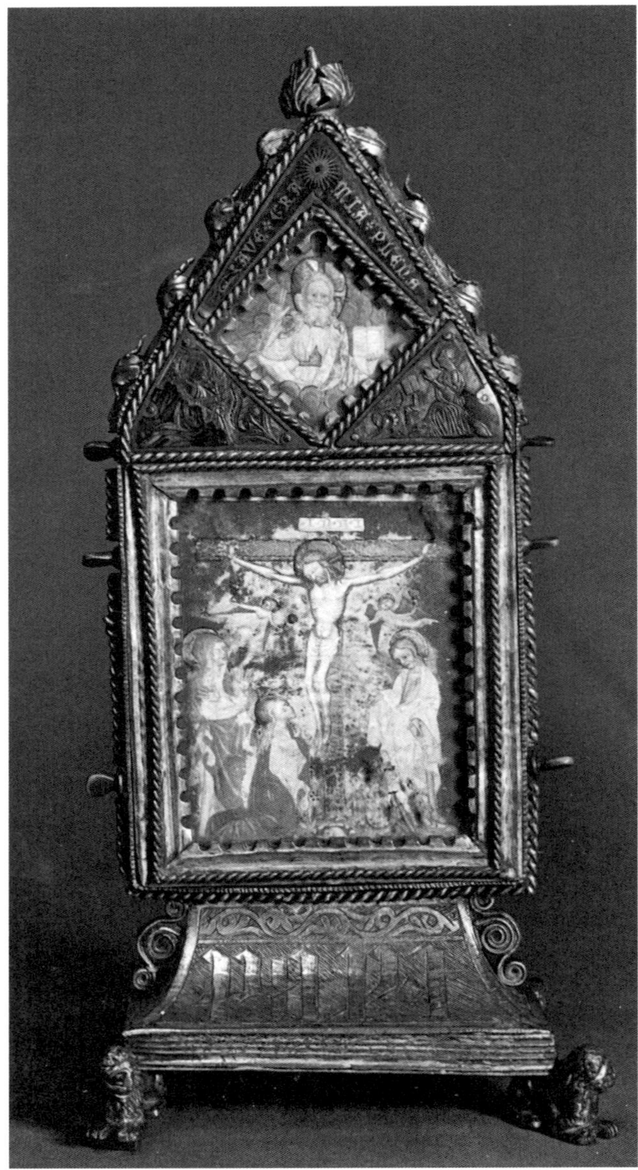

FIGURE 11. *Pax* of the Master of Hours Book of Modena (private collection).

109. M. Bollati, "Tra oreficeria e miniature: una pace per il Maestro del Libro d'ore di Modena," in *Arte lombarda del secondo millennio. Saggi in onore di Gian Alberto Dell'Acqua* (Milan, 2000), 41–46; G. Z. Zanichelli, "Le immagini della preghiera: il libro d'ore di Modena," in *Libro d'ore di Modena, ms. Lat. 842 = α.R.7.3—Biblioteca Estense Modena* (Modena, 2006), 29–96, 57, 68.

110. A. Laiou, "Venice as a Centre of Trade and of Artistic Production in the Thirteenth Century," in *Il Medio Oriente* (as in note 87), 11–26.

111. K. Sutton, *L'Officiolum di Francesco da Barberino*, Christie's, Rome, December 5th 2003; *eadem*, "The lost 'Officiolum' of Francesco da Barberino rediscovered," *Burlington Magazine* 147 (2005), 152–164.

112. D. Golden, "Testo e immagine nei 'Documenti d'Amore' di Francesco da Barberino," *Quaderni di Italianistica*, 1 (1980), 125–138; A. Petrucci, "Minima barberiniana. I. Note sugli autografi dei *Documento d'Amore*," in *Miscellanea di studi in onore di Aurelio Roncaglia a cinquant'anni dalla sua laurea* (Modena, 1989), 1005–1009.

113. G. Z. Zanichelli, "Le immagini della preghiera (as in note 106); *eadem*, "Santi e immagini: il ms. 1853 di Verona," in *Preghiera alla Vergine con le leggende di San Giorgio e Santa Margherita* (Modena, 2007), 19–82.

114. The same iconography reappears also in the *Documenti d'Amore*, written by Francesco da Barberino between 1309 and 1313, as underlined by E. Sears, *The Ages of Man: Medieval Interpretations of the Cycle* (Princeton, 1986), 104–107, figs. 40–41.

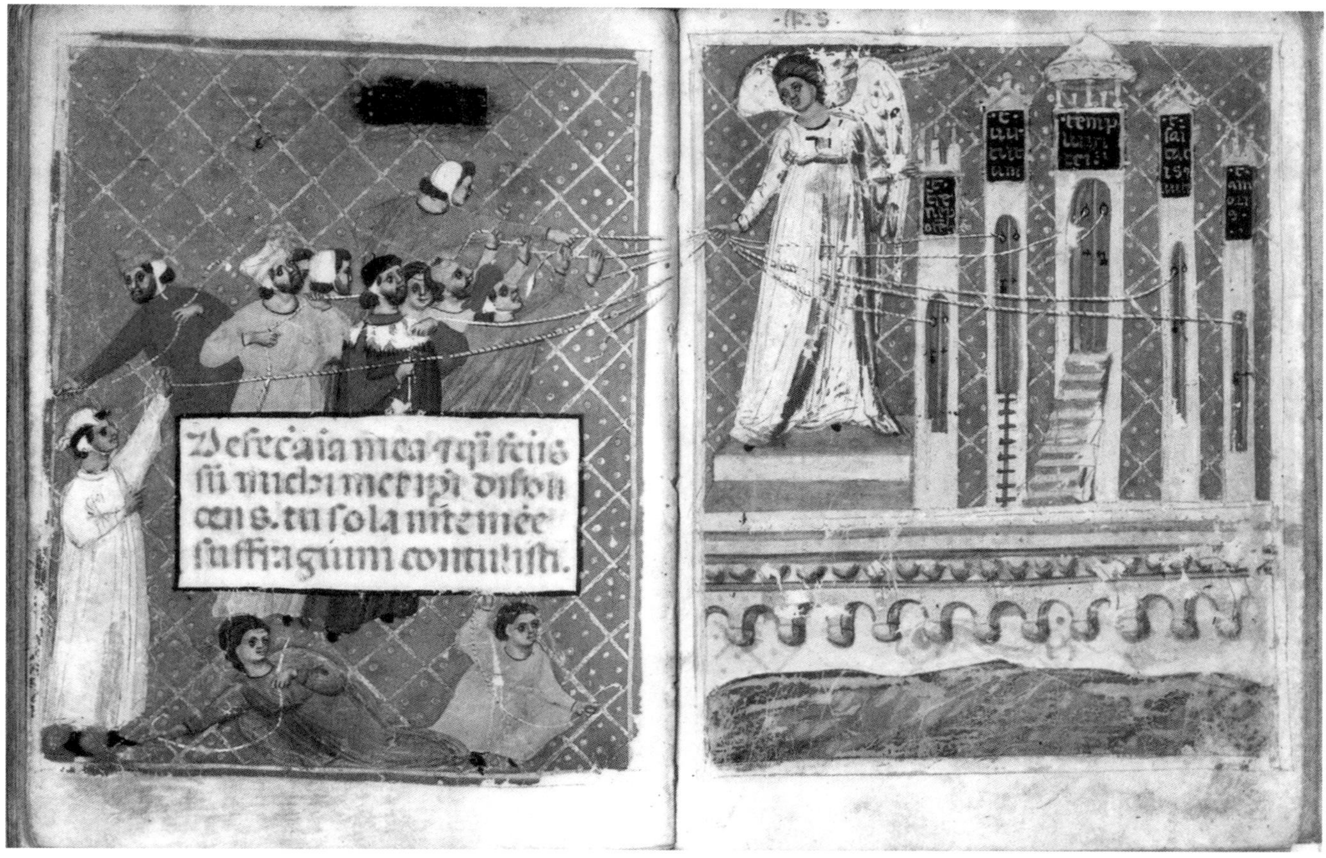

FIGURE 12. *Book of Hours* of Francesco da Barberino, *Hope* (private collection).

sional illuminator forces us to question the traditional identification of the person who made the images with the person who wrote the text, which was proposed for the other work of Francesco, the *Documenti d'Amore*, as well as for Boccaccio. This compels future scholars to look again at the role of the adviser and the choice of drawing, whether at a preparatory level or as a finished work. This intellectual aspect to illustration, shared also by such secular texts as the Morgan Museum and Library's *Canzoniere*,[115] or the *Carmina Regia* by Convenevole da Prato (Fig. 14),[116] differs fundamentally from the use of images in a Franciscan context, this context being the only field of Italian Gothic production so far examined in an effort to understand the impact of the image on the reader.[117]

Other kinds of books need to be studied from this perspective. Books such as the Pseudo-Agar in Paris,[118] the *De creatione mundi* in Siena,[119] and vernacular texts

115. S. Huot, "Vizualization and Memory: The Illustration of Troubadour Lyric in a Thirteenth-Century Manuscript," *Gesta* 31 (1992), 3–13.

116. Convenevole da Prato, *Regia Carmina dedicati a Roberto d'Angiò re di Sicilia e di Gerusalemme*, ed. C. Grassi (Milan, 1982).

117. H. Flora, *Imaging Gender, Poverty, and Spirituality in the Trecento: The "Meditationes vitae Christi"* (Ann Arbor, 2005); C. Frugoni and F. Manzari, *Immagini di San Francesco in uno* 'Speculum humanae salvationis' *del Trecento* (Padua, 2006).

118. Paris, BnF, MS. Lat. 2688: F. Avril, *Dix siècles* (as in note 91), n. 37, 48–49; H. Kessler, n. IV.5, in *Il volto di Cristo*, Exhib. Cat., Rome, Palazzo delle Esposizioni, ed. G. Morello and G. Wolf (Milan, 2000), 173–174.

119. Siena, Communal Library, MS. H.VI.31. G. Freuler, "La miniatura senese degli anni 137–1420," in A. Labriola, C. De Benedictis, and G. Freuler, *La miniatura senese 1270–1420* (Milan, 2002), 177–353, 272–273, and 278–279.

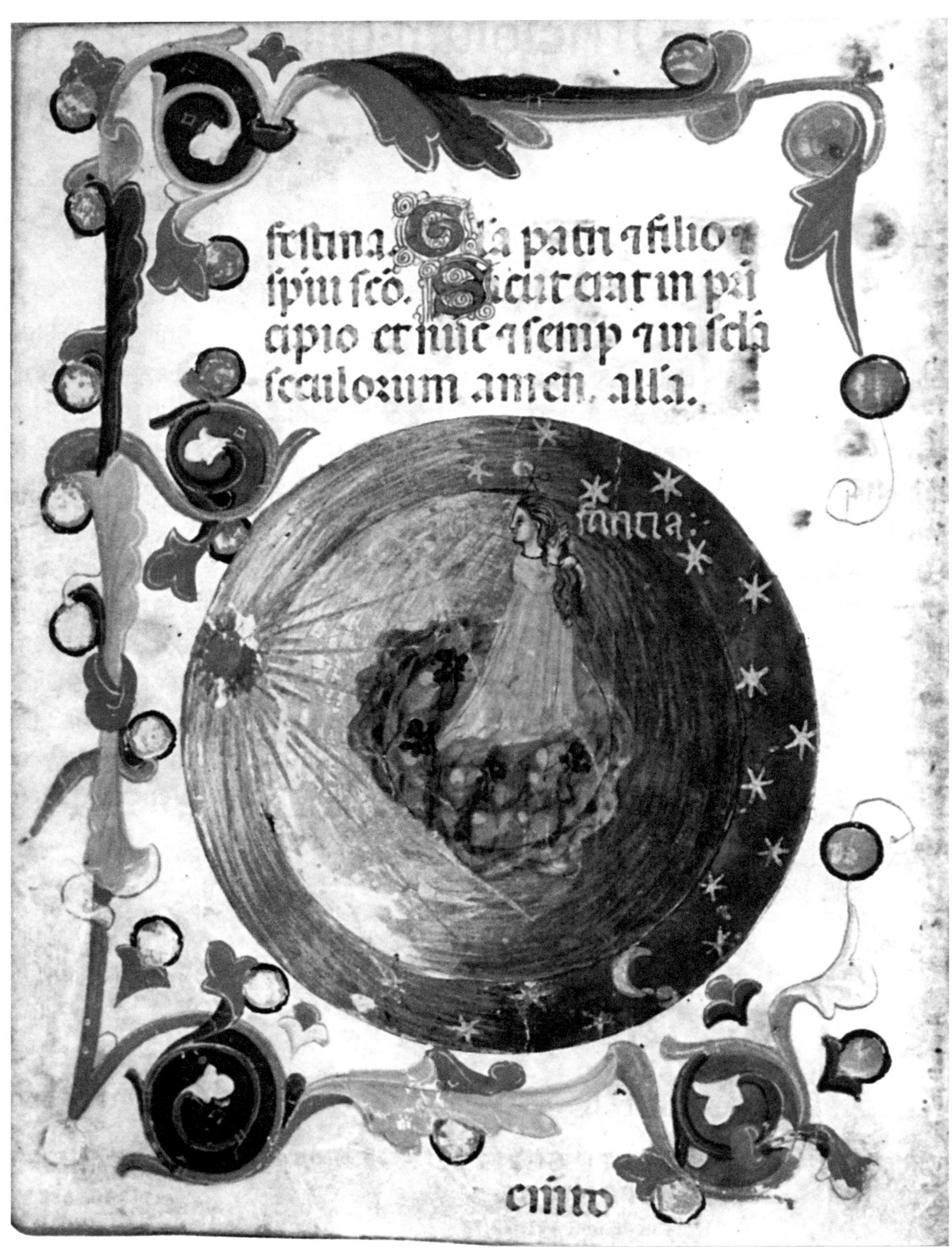

FIGURE 13. *Book of Hours* of Francesco da Barberino, *Prima* with *Infancia* (private collection).

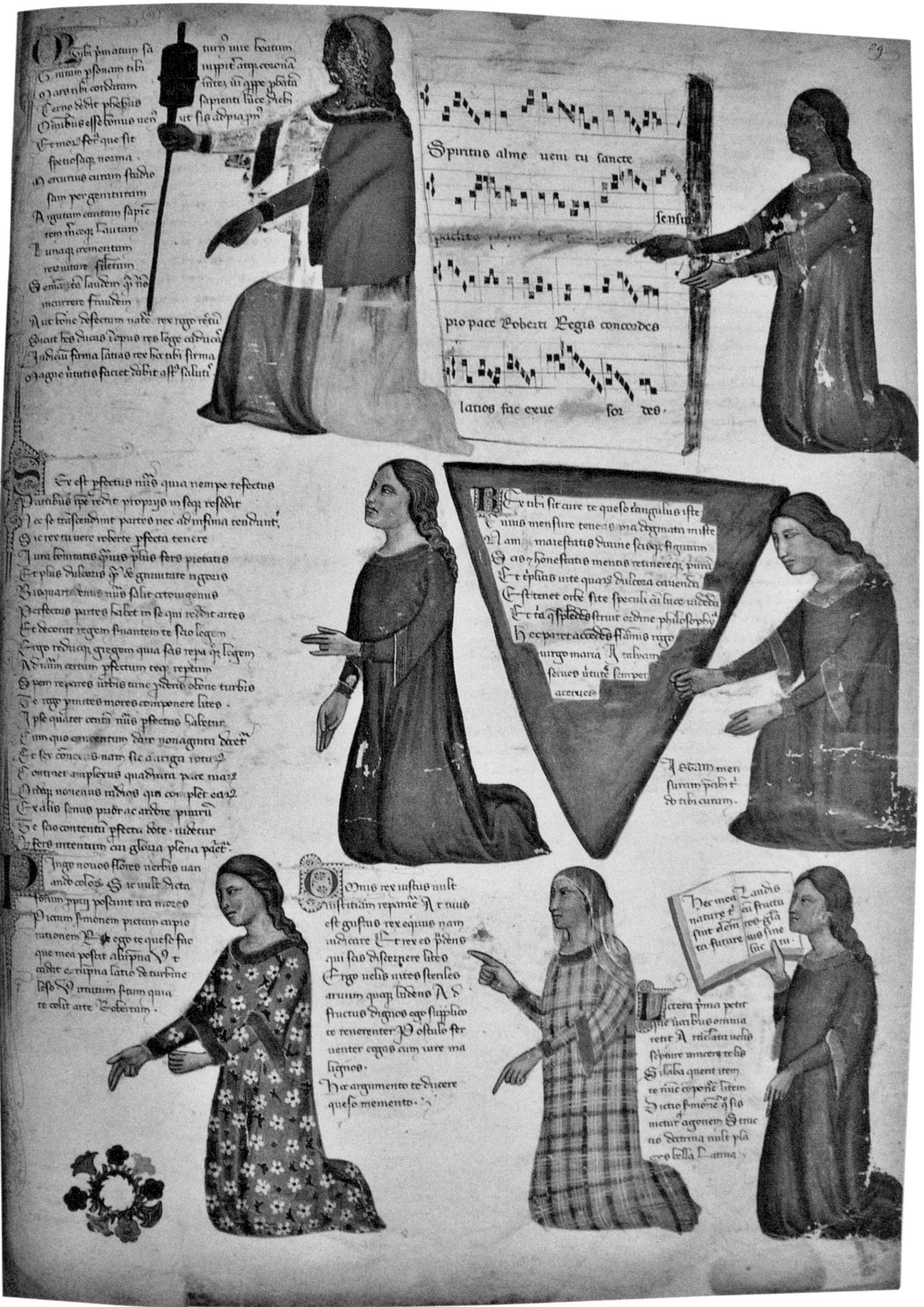

FIGURE 14. Convenevole da Prato, *Carmina Regia*. British Library Board. MS. Royal 6.E.IX, fol. 29r (All Rights Reserved).

in particular. It is possible that devotional texts and the lives of saints addressed a female audience—but who programs the images, and how are they related to the verbal visions of preachers, the liturgical furnishings, and the material images in churches? It is also important to remember the development of literacy in Italian city-states, that is, with full literacy for notaries and physicians, and partial literacy for merchants and craft workers. This notion opens the question as to how widespread the diffusion of texts illustrated by drawings and watercolors for these different *milieux* actually was. Sketches found in the rough copies of notary acts (Fig. 15), depicting chivalric and courtly scenes, are evidence of a considerable interest in subjects normally linked to the aristocracy.[120]

Old and new studies have underlined the presence of Italian illuminators in foreign ateliers,[121] but new documents offer new directions for research. In some of the most recent exhibitions and online catalogues, a growing number of bibles have surfaced whose origins are in monastic Veneto (Fig. 16). They are characterized by a merging of local, French, and Byzantine elements, and it is my belief that, after a complete examination of the texts and illustrative cycles, it will be possible to revisit the problem of Crusader art or *lingua franca* and its relations with the Veneto. To this end, I should like to mention a little Book of Hours that was certainly produced in the Holy Land for Hospitaller use, with minor initials made by an English or French illuminator and major initials made by a Venetian one (Fig. 17).[122] This book is not only proof of the presence of Venetian illuminators in the Holy Land, but it also provides the missing elements with which to reconstruct one of the main routes into Italy that was traveled by more traditional books of hours, and not such aristocratic ones as

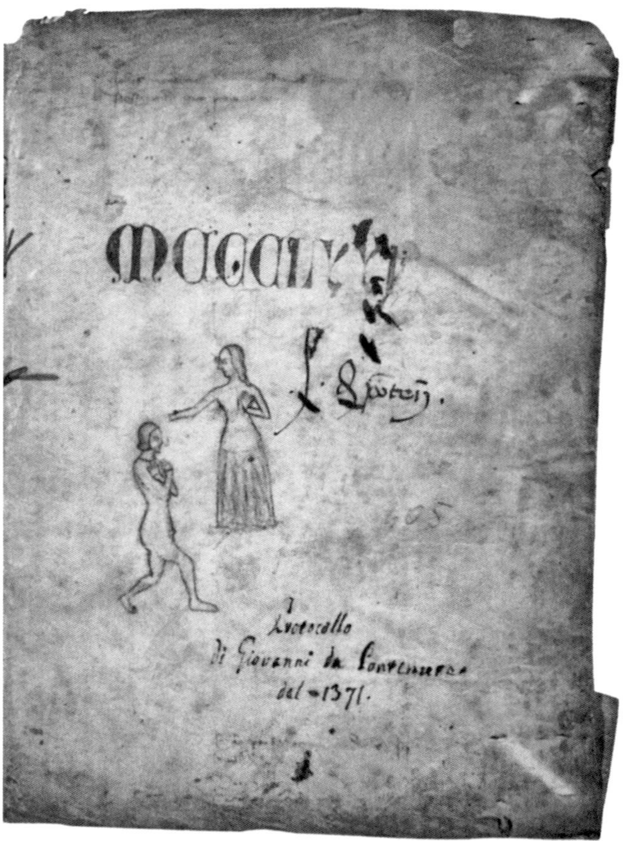

FIGURE 15. Notary Giovanni da Pontenure, b. 405. Piacenza, Public Archive.

the *Offiziolo* and *Lamentationes*. This route was through the Adriatic Sea, in so far as it is possible to see that the first devotional manuscripts of this kind seem to be have been produced in this area.[123] It was not only the meeting point for Angevin-Hungarian and Emilia illuminators,[124] but also for the Bohemian court, another topic that is now open to research thanks to the newly discovered *Dalimilova Chronicle* (Fig. 18).[125]

120. G. Z. Zanichelli, "Codici miniati a Piacenza tra XIV e XV secolo," in *Il Gotico a Piacenza* (Piacenza, Palazzo Gotico), ed. P. Ceschi Lavagetto and A. Gigli (Milan, 1998), 73–79, and 199–221, 206–207.

121. G. Schmidt, *Die Malerschule von St. Florian: Beiträge zur südd. Malerei zu Ende des 13. und im 14. Jahrhundert* (Graz, 1962); F. Manzari, *La miniature ad Avignone al tempo dei papi* (Modena, 2006), 137–145.

122. G. Z. Zanichelli, "Between Byzantium and Europe: Problems of Iconography and Style in the Image Production in Northern Italy," in *Mediaeval Book Centers: Local Tradition and Inter-Regional Connections* (Moscow, 2005).

123. B. C. Stocks, "The Illustrated Office of Passion in Italian Books of Hours," in *The Art of the Book: Its Place in Medieval Worship*, ed. M. M. Manion and B. J. Muir (Exeter, 1998), 111–152.

124. S. L'Engle, "Maestro del Leggendario Angioino," in *Dizionario biografico dei miniatori italiani*, ed. M. Bollati (Milan, 2004), 562–564.

125. Prague, National Library, MS. XII.E.17, Dalimilova chron.: *Précieux manuscrits, livres ancien set modernes*, Paris, Druot-Richelieu,

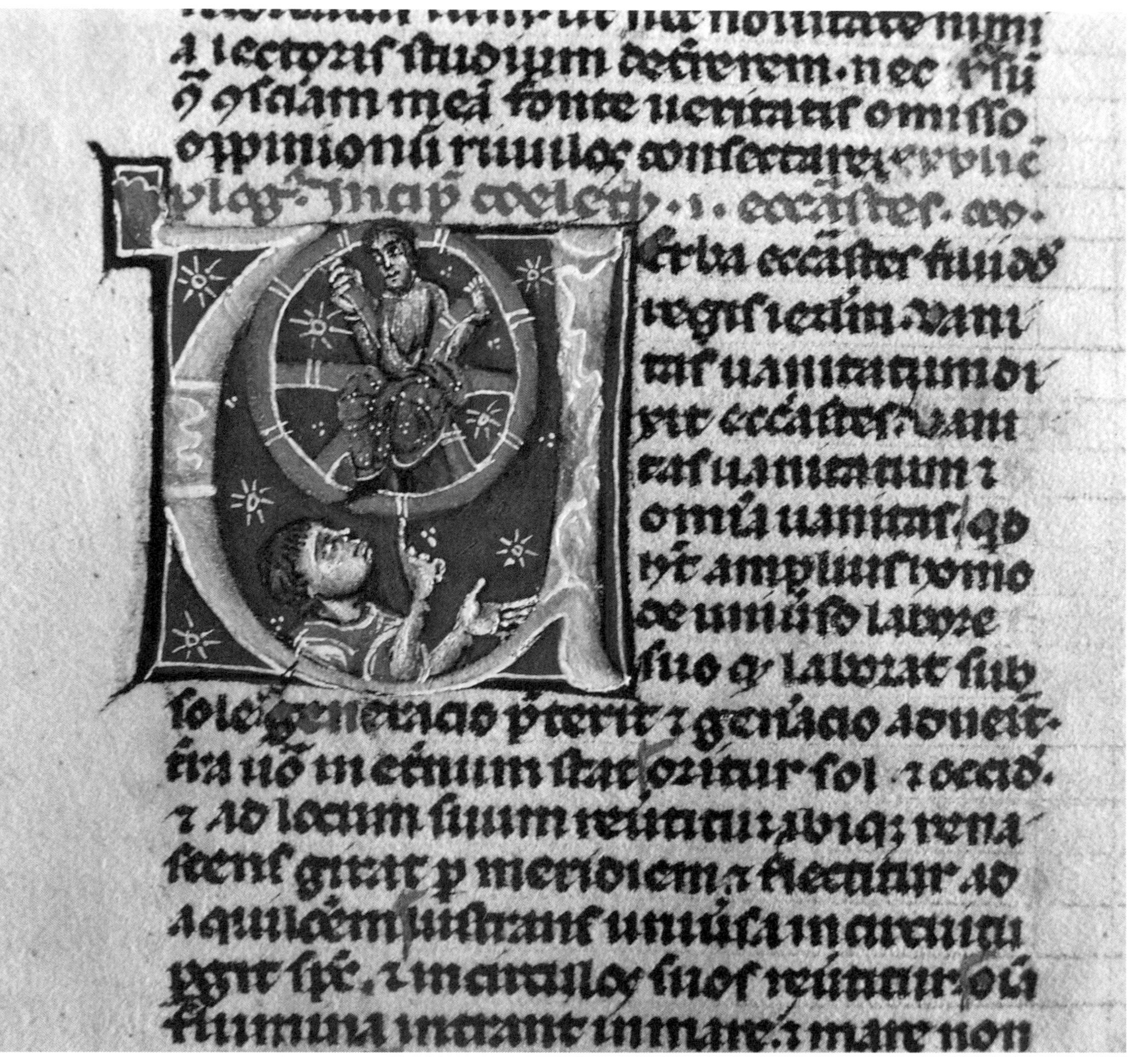

FIGURE 16. *Bible*, *Ecclesiastes*. Parma, Biblioteca Palatina, MS. 2791, fol. 166v.

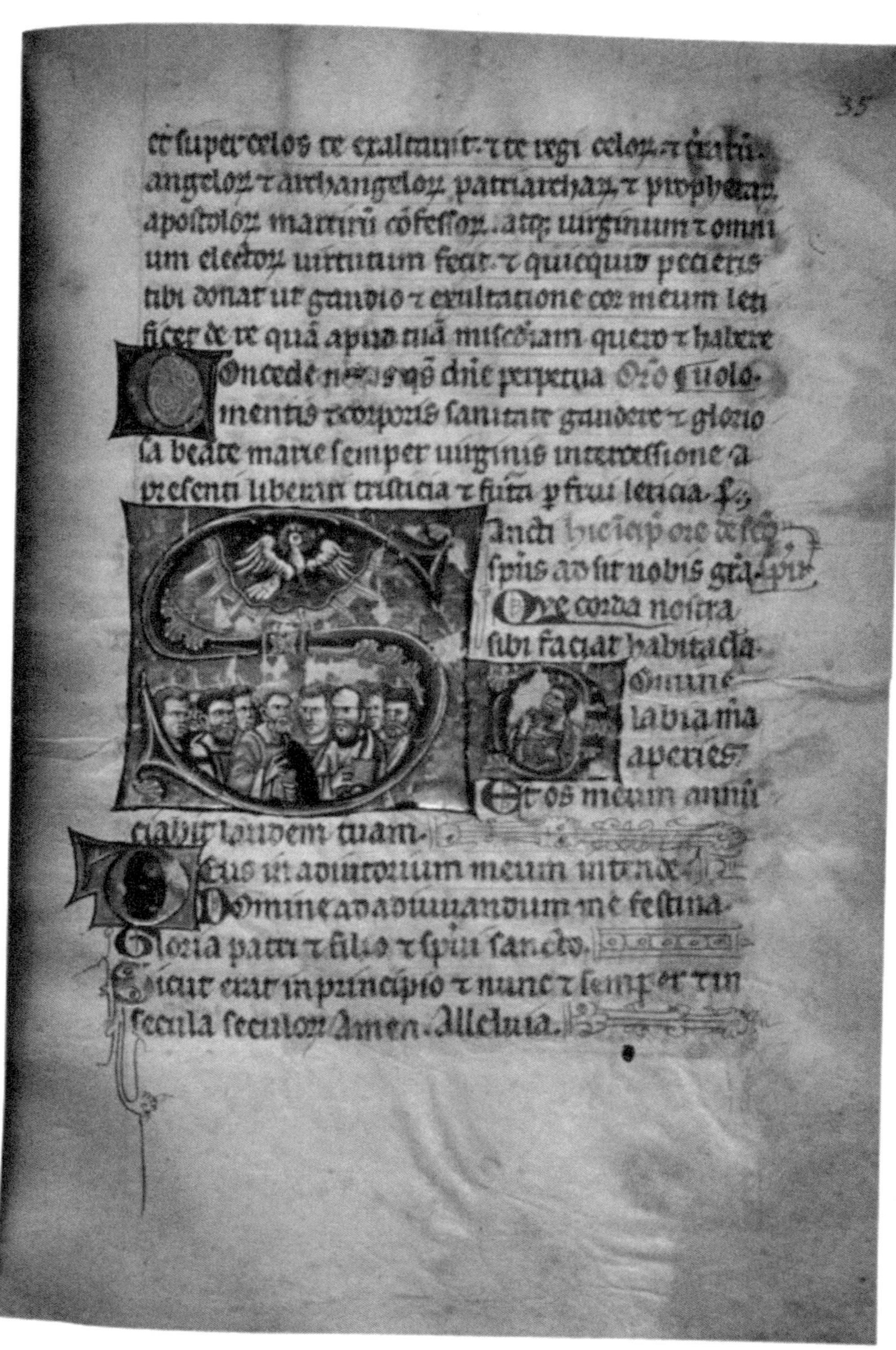

FIGURE 17. *Book of Hours* from Holy Land. British Library Board. MS. Add. 14061, fol. 35r (All Rights Reserved).

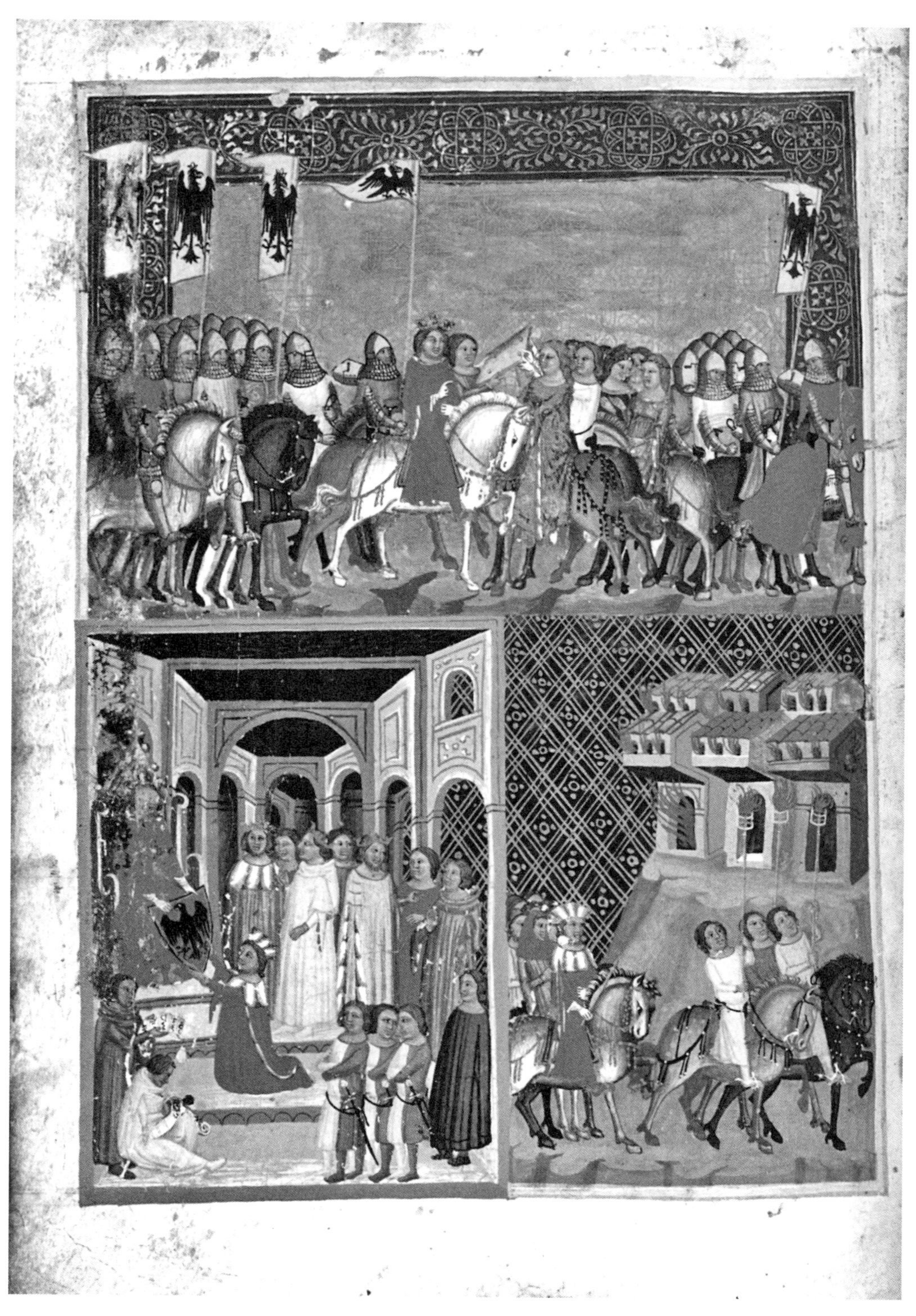

FIGURE 18. *Dalimilova kronika*. Prague, National Library of the Czech Republic, MS. XII.E.17, fol. 3v.

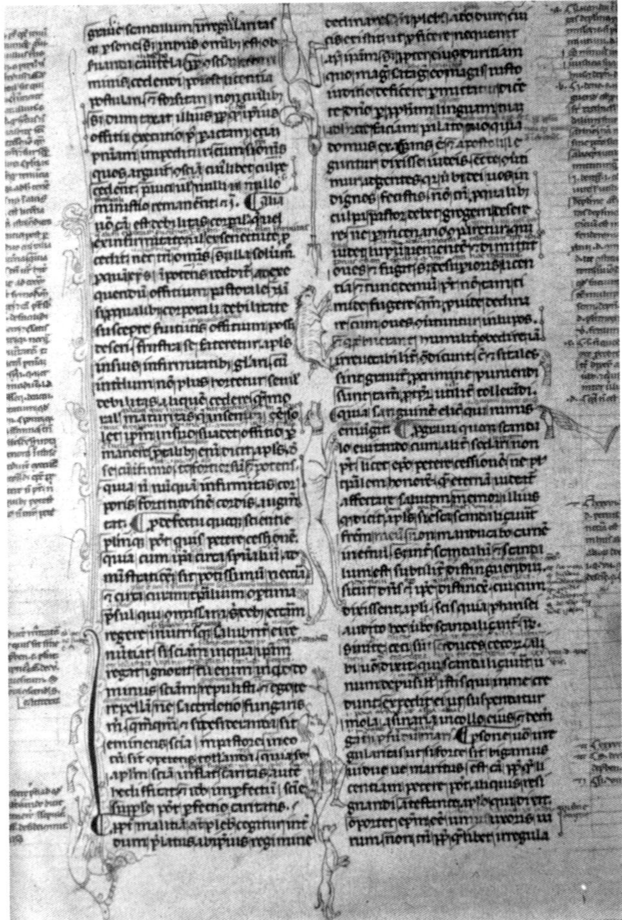

FIGURE 19. *Decretales*. Oxford, Bodleian Library, MS. Lat. Th. B. 4, fol. 23v.

In conclusion, I should like to recall an important observation made in 1967 by Carl Nordenfalk in his review of Lilian Randall's book on Gothic marginal decoration.[126] He singled out the first attempt of Gothic marginal decoration in the use of *drôleries* from a papal *Registrum* produced in Rome between 1207 and 1213. This observation, which occasionally resurfaced during the critical debate,[127] has not received the attention it deserves. It is evidence—together with the extraordinary and unknown *venatio* in the *Decretales* that was written in Modena in 1241 (Fig. 19)[128]—of the strong capacity of Italian illuminated manuscripts to renew its linguistic strategy, and it opens future paths for a fresh evaluation of the Italian contribution to the European Gothic book.

March 17th 2005, 18–22 n. 60; *Dalimilova kronika, pařížský zlomek latinského překladu* (Prague, 2005).

126. C. Nordenfalk, Review of "Lilian M. Randall, *Images in the Margins of the Gothic Manuscripts* (Berkeley, 1966)," *Burlington Magazine* 109 (1967), 418–421.

127. V. Pace, "Cultura dell'Europa medievale nella Roma di Innocenzo III: le illustrazioni marginali del Registro Vaticano, 4," *Römisches Jahrbuch für Kunstgeschichte*, 41 (1985), 45–61; A. Iacobini, "La pittura e le arti suntuarie: da Innocenzo III a Innocenzo IV (1198–1254)," in *Roma nel Duecento. L'arte nella città dei papi da Innocenzo III a Bonifacio VIII*, ed. A. M. Romanini (Turin, 1991), 237–320, 300–304; A. Bräms, "L'évolution de la mise en page et du décor marginal," in J. Wirth, *Les marges à drôleries des manuscrits gothiques (1250–1340)* (Genève, 2008), 45–77, 50.

128. Oxford, Bodleian Library, MS. Lat. Th. B. 4, Gregorius papa IX, *Decretales cum glossis Bernardi parmensis*: O. Pächt and J. J. G. Alexander, *Illuminated Manuscript in the Bodleian Library, Oxford*, vol. 2, *Italian School* (Oxford, 1970), 8. n. 73.

LUCY FREEMAN SANDLER

One Hundred and Fifty Years of the Study of the Illuminated Book in England: The Bohun Manuscripts from the Nineteenth Century to the Present

THE GROUP of richly illuminated manuscripts produced during the second half of the fourteenth century for members of the Bohun family has been the subject of numerous articles and monographs, beginning in 1852,[1] the first time any of them was mentioned in print, up to the present day. The history of the study of these books is pertinent not only to research on Bohun material per se, but also offers evidence of changing concepts of the study of English Gothic manuscripts in general, and, implicitly, offers guidelines for the directions of future research, directions that are themselves open to challenge and change.

The essay that follows does not provide a chronological account of publications on the Bohun manuscripts but instead is intended to evaluate research on these books under a number of methodological headings, first, the approach to the study of illuminated manuscripts that can be called "cataloguing," or, in its wider ramifications, "mapping," and in some of its more technical details, "codicology." Its aim is description of manuscript "facts"—format, contents, decoration—in order to determine original ownership, place of production, and date. The usefulness of this approach is self-evident, and I would estimate that most of the research on English Gothic manuscripts over the last 150 years has been devoted to cataloguing, mapping, and codicological description.

The Bohun manuscripts may be used as case studies of the descriptive approach. The term "Bohun manuscripts" refers to a group of about ten richly illuminated psalters and books of hours produced in England during the second half of the fourteenth century for individuals of the Bohun family, whose male members were earls of Hereford, Essex, and Northhampton, constables of England, and knights of the garter, and in two generations were related by marriage to the royal family.[2] The chief illuminators of these manuscripts were house artists, who worked only for the Bohuns and practiced their craft over a period from about 1360 to 1390 in the family castle at Pleshey, Essex. From documents that I connected with the surviving manuscripts in the mid-1980s, we now know the names of two of the artists, John de Teye, and Henry Hood, who was John's apprentice from 1384 onward. Both were Augustinian Friars allowed by their order to live and work in the Bohun household at Pleshey.[3]

The Bohun manuscripts are distinctive in a number of ways: the books themselves comprise the largest cohesive group of illuminated manuscripts produced in England during the second half of the fourteenth

1. H. O. Coxe, *Catalogus codicum MSS. qui in collegiis aulisque Oxoniensibus hodie adservantur* (Oxford, 1852), 1 (Codices MSS collegii Exoniensis), 17–18.

2. For a list with principal bibliography, see appendix.

3. On the Bohun artists, their dates, names, patrons, and worksite, see L. F. Sandler, "A Note on the Illuminators of the Bohun Manuscripts," *Speculum* 60 (1985), 364–72, with revised views on the identification of the artists' hands; L. F. Sandler, *The Lichtenthal Psalter and the Manuscript Patronage of the Bohun Family* (London, 2004), 126–29

century; they are exceptionally lavishly illustrated and exceptionally interesting for their innovative programs of illustration; and the circumstances of their production, that is, the employment of Augustinian friars as illuminators, the venue in which the books were illuminated, and the status of the clerical illuminators as members of the Bohun *familia*, are unique survivals of a production system that might once have characterized the making of manuscripts for other noble households in England, for which, however, little other evidence survives.

The first manuscript that was recognized in modern times as made for a member of the Bohun family was a psalter in Exeter College, Oxford,[4] described by H. O. Coxe in 1852 in his catalogue of manuscripts in Oxford colleges.[5] The Exeter Psalter may serve as an example of what these books look like. The psalter is relatively large in format, about 286 × 190 millimeters, and was illustrated in two stages, first by John de Teye and an anonymous associate between *c.* 1360 and 1373, and then, following the original pictorial program, by a different group of artists, during the 1390s. Every psalm opens with a historiated initial whose frame is extended into the margin with spiraling finials and foliated branches, the marginal extensions often populated just outside the initial with human, animal, and hybrid figures. Heraldic shields identify the Bohuns as owners of the book. The psalms at the main divisions of the text, of which only two remain (Fig. 1), have larger historiated intials, and full borders. The program of the historiated initials is a continuous cycle of Old Testament subjects drawn from the first four books of the Pentateuch in the Vulgate version, from Creation (Fig. 2) to the numbering of the children of Israel (Fig. 3), literally translating the verbal text into detailed images, of which originally there were more than two hundred in the manuscript.

Among the Bohun manuscripts are two more psalters of similar size and format, one, executed mainly in the 1360s and early 1370s and completed in the 1380s, and now in the Egerton Collection at the British Library,[6] with a cycle of historiated initials whose subjects are drawn from the first three books of Kings, covering the lives of Saul, David, and Solomon (Fig. 4). The Egerton manuscript also includes an Hours of the Virgin and Office of the Dead, whose historiated initials have subjects closely following the account of the life of Christ in the Gospel of Luke (Fig. 5). The other large-format Bohun psalter, begun as early as the period of the Black Death in 1348, but mainly illustrated in the 1360s, is now in the Austrian National Library in Vienna.[7] It contains a cycle of historiated initials responding directly to the words of the text, that is, word-illustrations (Fig. 6).

A second set of Bohun manuscripts, consisting of psalters and books of hours, sometimes in combination, is smaller in format, and generally later in date, executed in the 1380s for a younger generation female, Mary, daughter of Humphrey de Bohun, the seventh and last Bohun earl of Hereford, and/or her spouse, Henry of Bolingbroke, later Henry IV.[8] These books are illustrated with historiated initials and sometimes miniatures too—*bas-de-page*, half-page, or full page. All the figural illustrations are concentrated at the main divisions of the text. The themes of the psalter illustrations are biblical (Figs. 7, 8), and the cycles are selective versions of those of the large-format Exeter and Egerton psalters, while the Hours of the Virgin are illustrated with standard cycles of the life of Christ and the Virgin, to which are added sequences of miracles of the Virgin (Fig. 9).

How has our present map of the Bohun manuscripts been drawn and redrawn? The early efforts, and indeed many since, were focused on identifying the owners on the basis of the profuse heraldry that characterizes the manuscripts. Coxe, for example, in 1852, noting that the Exeter College Psalter bore the arms of the Bohun family and the ruler of England on alternate pages at the beginning of the text, and that later calendrical insertions referred to Henry VII and Henry VIII, concluded that the book had been made for the use of Thomas of Woodstock, earl of Gloucester and sixth son of Edward III, who married Eleanor de Bohun, elder sister of Mary, in the mid-1370s, and that it had descended in the royal

4. See appendix, no. 3.
5. See note 1.
6. See appendix, no. 4.
7. See appendix, no. 2.
8. See appendix, nos. 6–11.

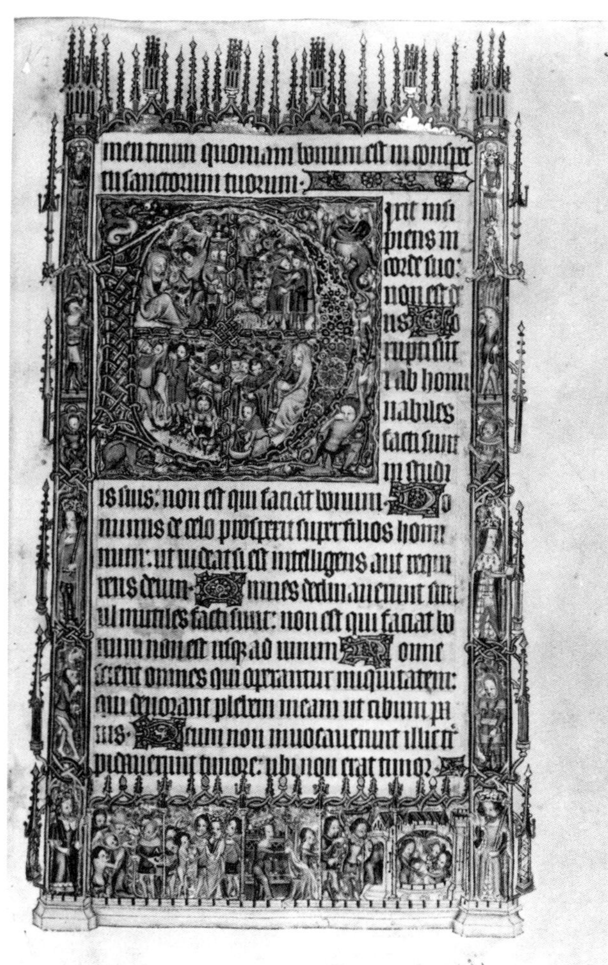

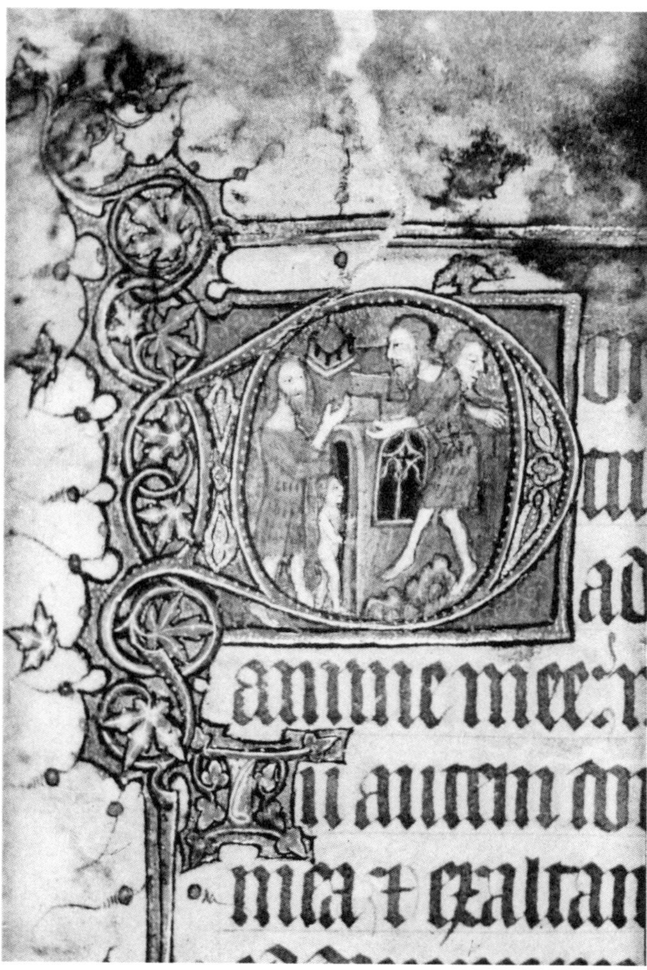

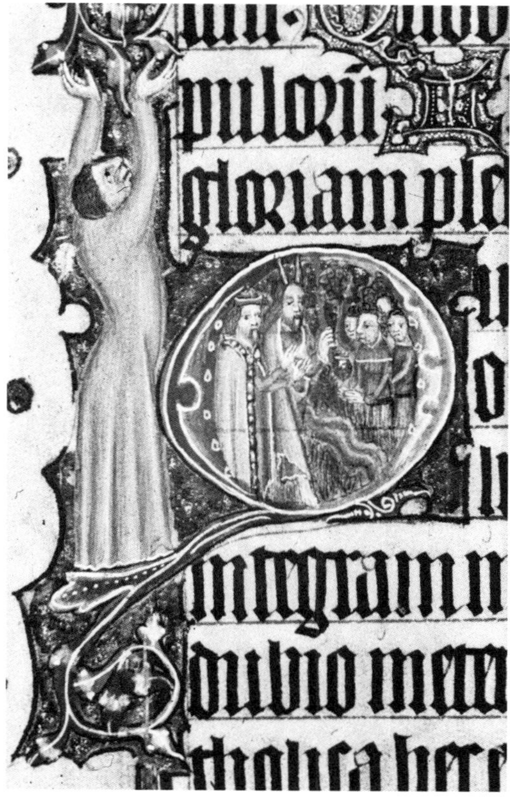

FIGURE 1. Exeter College Psalter, Psalm 52, Joseph scenes. Oxford, Exeter College MS. 47, fol. 32 (new numbering) (photo: Exeter College).

FIGURE 2. Exeter College Psalter, Psalm 3 (first remaining psalm), Cain, Enoch, and the city built by Cain (Gen. 4:17). Oxford, Exeter College MS. 47, fol. 7 (photo: Exeter College).

FIGURE 3. Exeter College Psalter, Athanasian Creed, Moses and Eleazar numbering the children of Israel by the River Jordan (Num. 26:63). Oxford, Exeter College MS. 47, fol. 110^{v} (photo: Exeter College).

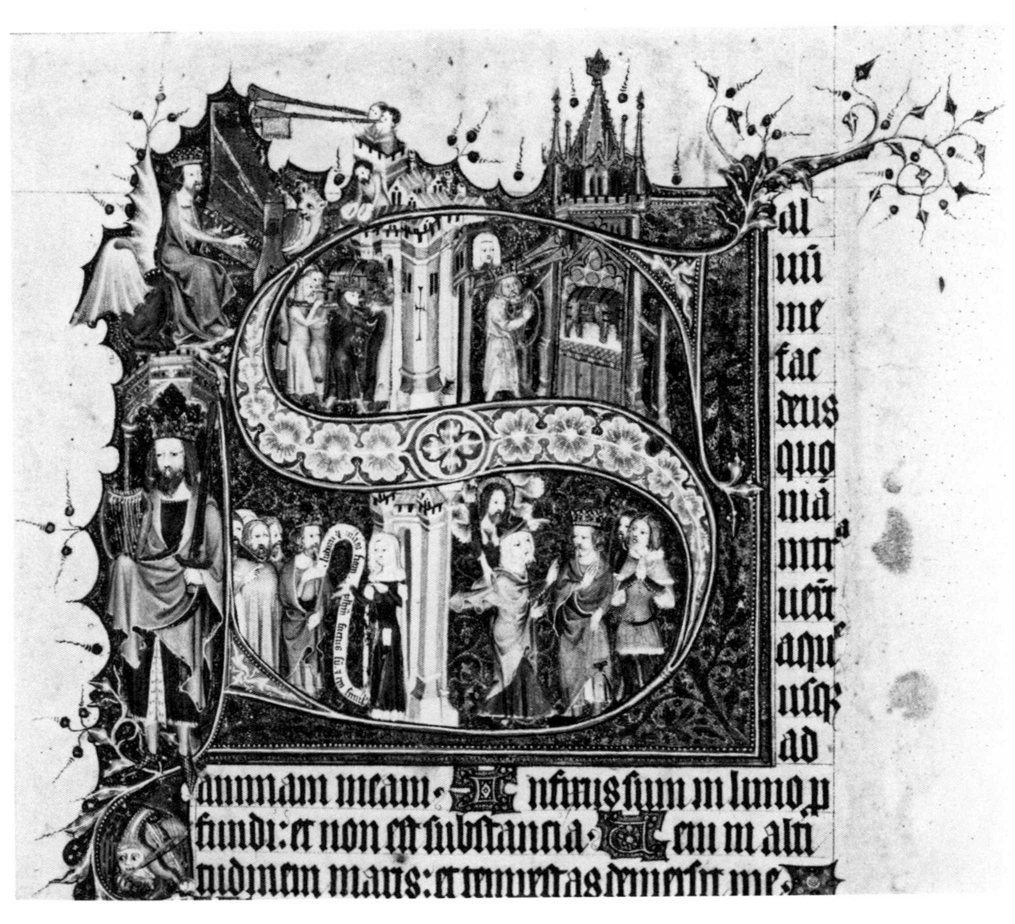

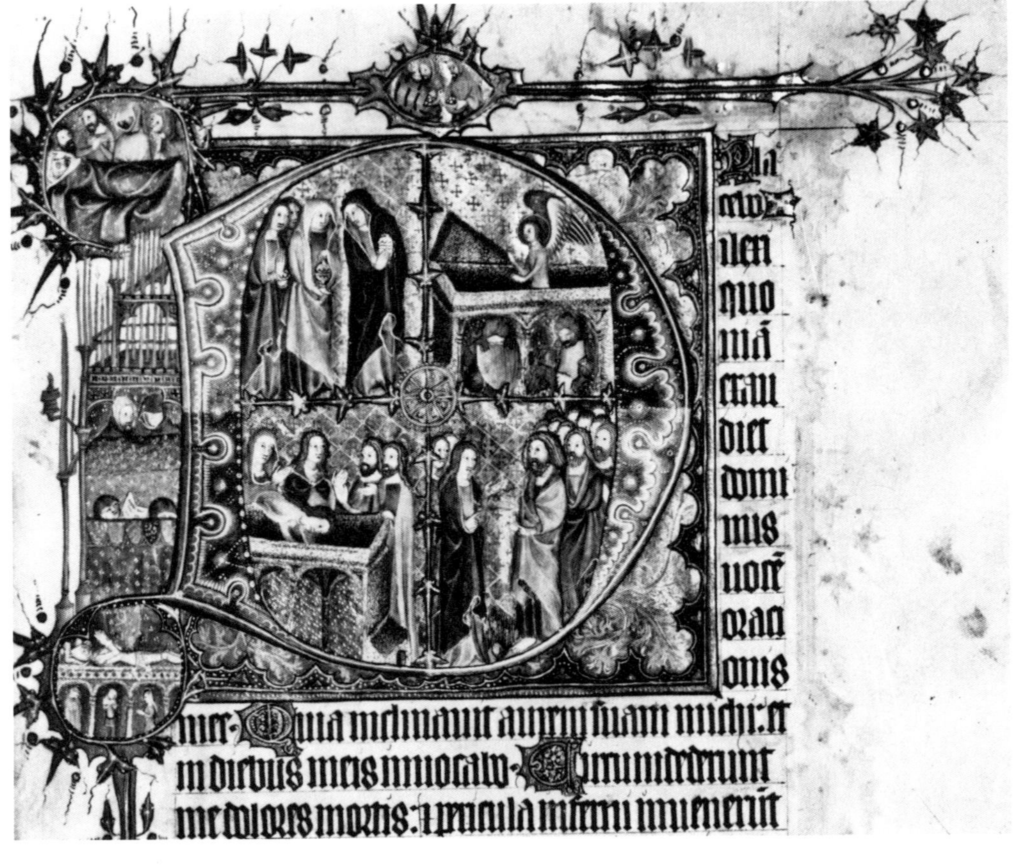

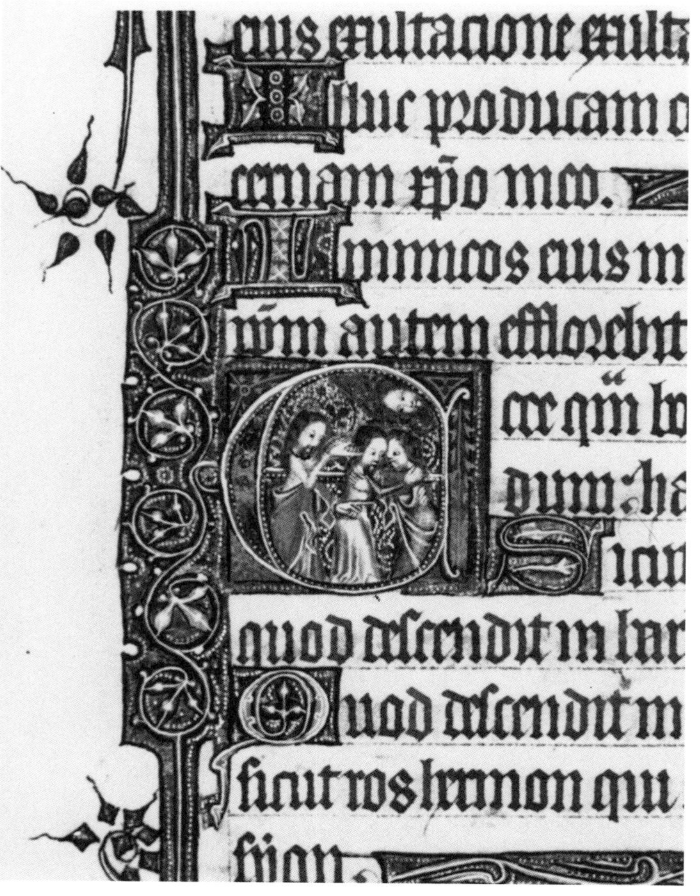

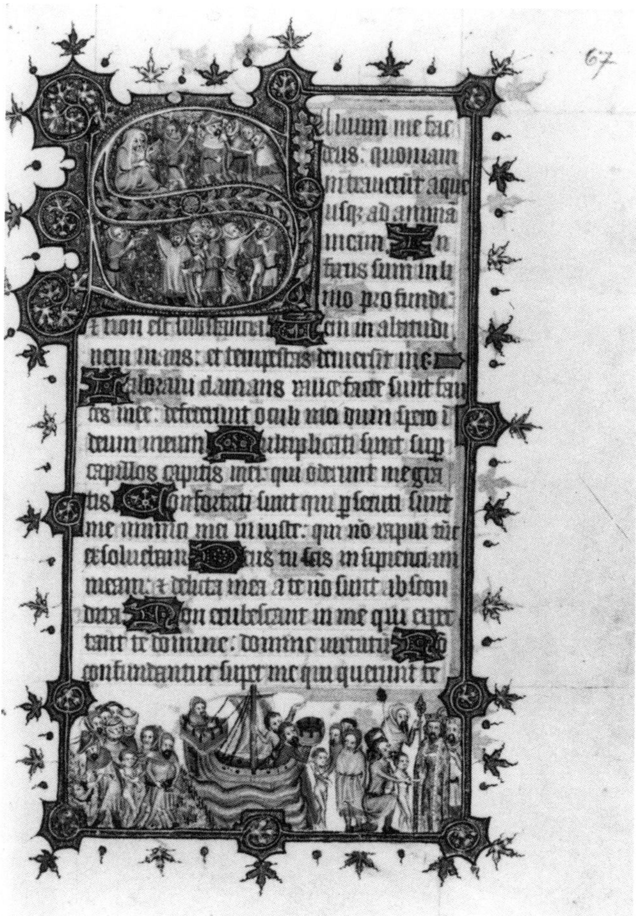

Above:

FIGURE 6. Vienna Psalter, Psalm 132, "Behold how good and how pleasant it is for brethren to dwell together in unity." Vienna, Österreichische Nationalbibliothek cod. 1826*, fol. 116v (photo: Österreichische Nationalbibliothek).

FIGURE 7. Lichtenthal Psalter, Psalm 68, Joseph scenes. Baden-Baden, Lichtenthal Abbey Archiv MS. 2, fol. 67 (photo: author).

Opposite:

FIGURE 4. Egerton Psalter, Psalm 68, David scenes. London, British Library MS. Egerton 3277, fol. 46v (photo: British Library).

FIGURE 5. Egerton Psalter, Office of the Dead, Marys at the Tomb; in the margin, death and funeral of a nobleman. London, British Library MS. Egerton 3277, fol. 142 (photo: British Library).

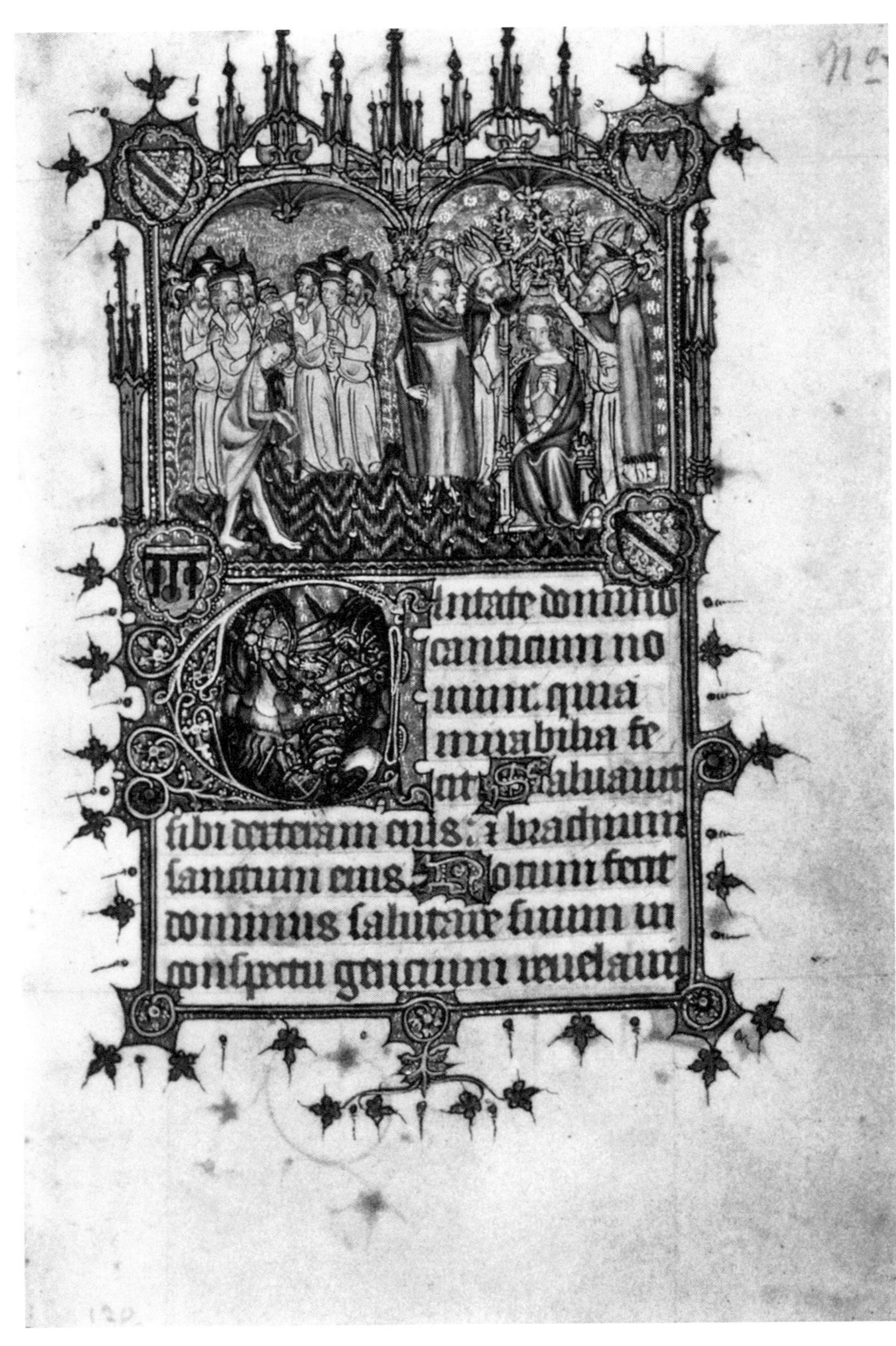

FIGURE 8. Fitzwilliam Psalter, Psalm 97, David scenes. Cambridge, Fitzwilliam Museum MS. 38-1950, fol. 120 (photo: Fitzwilliam Museum).

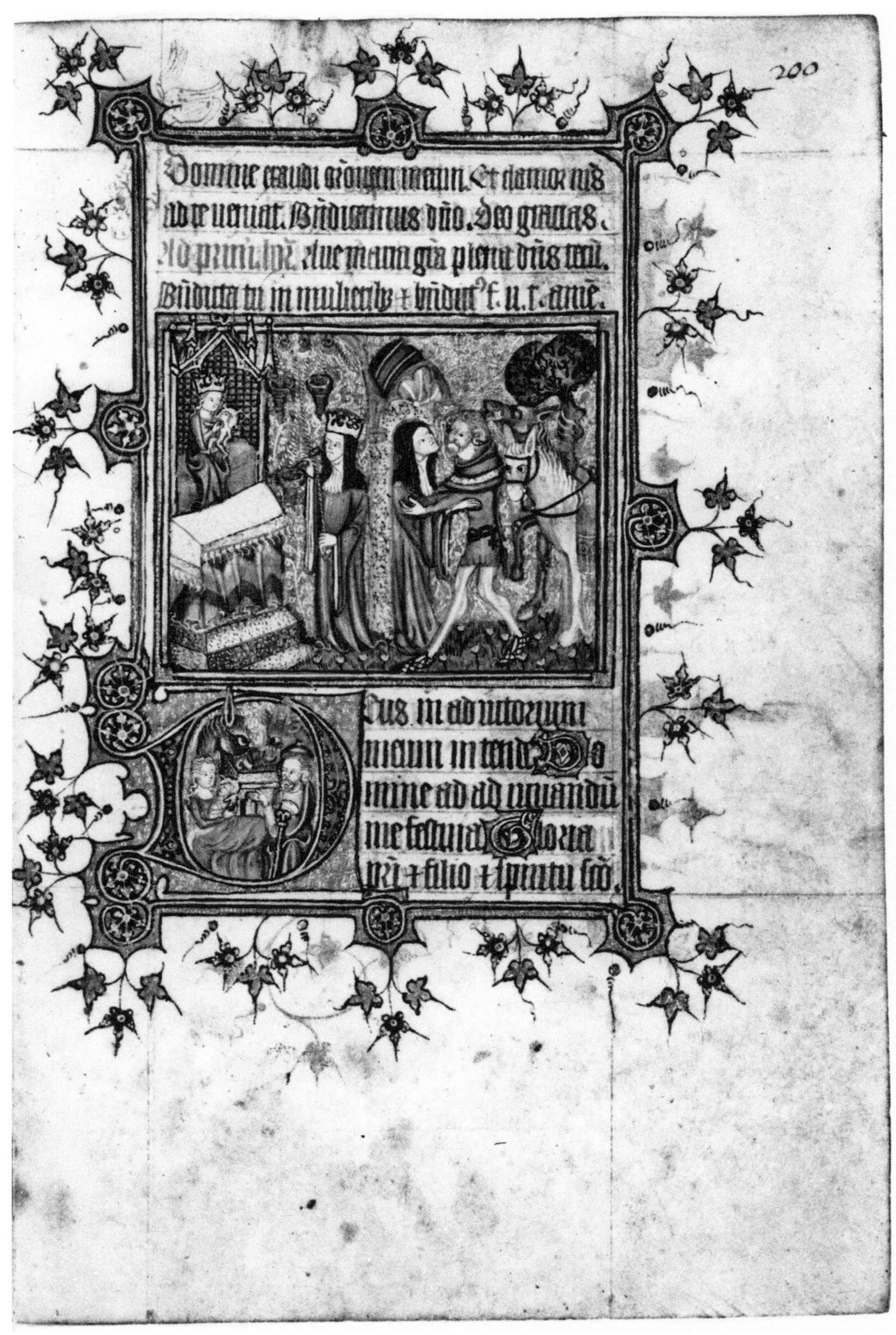

FIGURE 9. Bodleian Psalter and Hours, Prime, the errant nun-sacristan replaced by the Virgin; in the initial, the Nativity. Oxford, Bodleian Library MS. Auct. D.4.4, fol. 200 (photo: Bodleian Library).

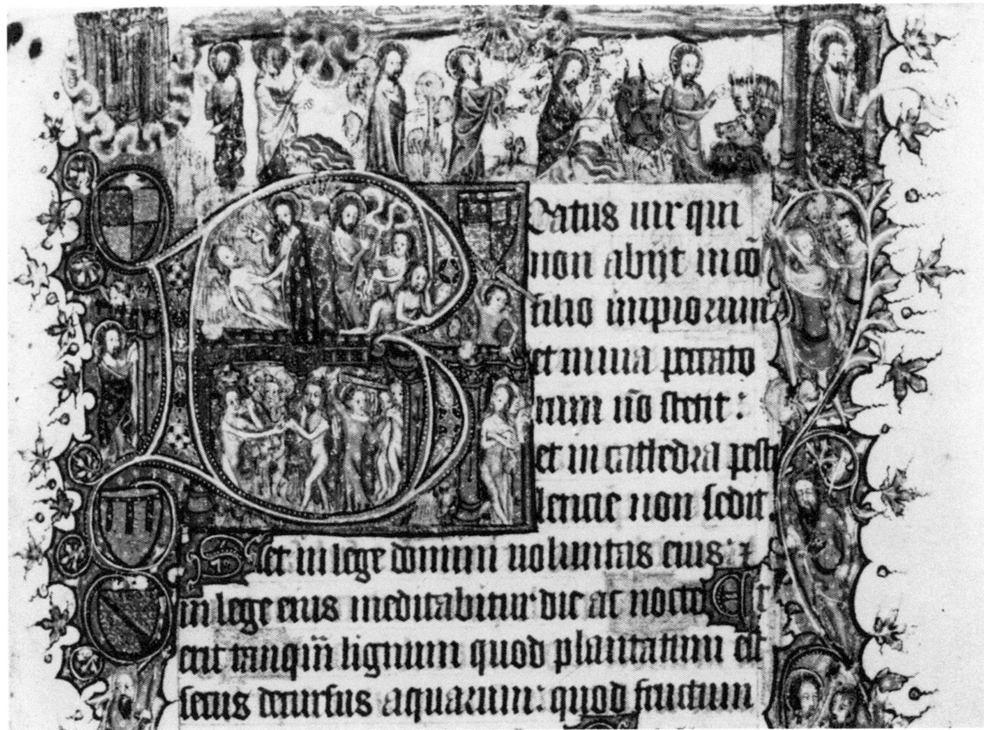

FIGURE 10. Lichtenthal Psalter, Psalm 1, creation scenes, arms (counter-clockwise) of England, Lancaster, Bohun, and heir apparent. Baden-Baden, Lichtenthal Abbey Archiv MS. 2, fol. 8 (photo: author).

family.[9] It is little wonder that interest was focused on ownership of the manuscript, since the heraldry made it clear that it was a ducal, if not a royal book. And, all the other Bohun manuscripts have been initially identified on the basis of heraldry too, although with many differences of opinion about the individuals to whom the same armorials should be attributed, and even differences in the description, and, consequently, identification of the armorials themselves.[10]

The process of identification of Bohun manuscripts on the basis of heraldry continues to the present. In 1987, for instance, Felix Heinzer recognized that an almost unknown psalter in the Cistercian convent of Lichtenthal near Baden-Baden (Figs. 7, 10), then thought to be a fifteenth-century French book, was in fact a Bohun manuscript.[11] Once Heinzer noticed that the Lichtenthal Psalter included the arms of England and Bohun, he consulted the fourteenth-century volume of the Survey of Manuscripts Illustrated in the British Isles series and was able to confirm the original ownership and date of the manuscript from the entries on the Bohun manuscripts included there.[12]

Heraldic identification has not been the only means used to determine the original owners of the Bohun manuscripts. As early as 1908, in the catalogue of the historic manuscript exhibition at the Burlington Fine

9. Coxe, *Catalogus* (as in note 1), 17–18.

10. On armorial identifications and controversies, especially in regard to the smaller size Bohun manuscripts, see L. F. Sandler, "Lancastrian Heraldry in the Bohun Manuscripts," in *The Lancastrian Court*, *Proceedings of the 2001 Harlaxton Symposium* (Harlaxton Medieval Studies 13), ed. J. Stratford (Donington, 2003), 221–32.

11. F. Heinzer and G. Stamm, *Die Handschriften von Lichtenthal*, Die Handschriften der Badischen Landesbibliothek in Karlsruhe, 11 (Wiesbaden, 1987), 350–52; and in further detail, F. Heinzer, "Un témoin inconnu de 'Bohun Manuscripts': Le ms. 2 des archives de l'abbaye de Lichtenthal," *Scriptorium* 43 (1989), 259–66. On the earlier identification of the Lichtenthal Psalter as fifteenth-century French, see Sandler, *Lichtenthal Psalter* (as in note 3), 152.

12. L. F. Sandler, *Gothic Manuscripts 1285–1385*, A Survey of Manuscripts Illuminated in the British Isles 5, ed. J. J. G. Alexander (London, 1986), I, figs. 354–75; II, 147–63, nos. 133–41.

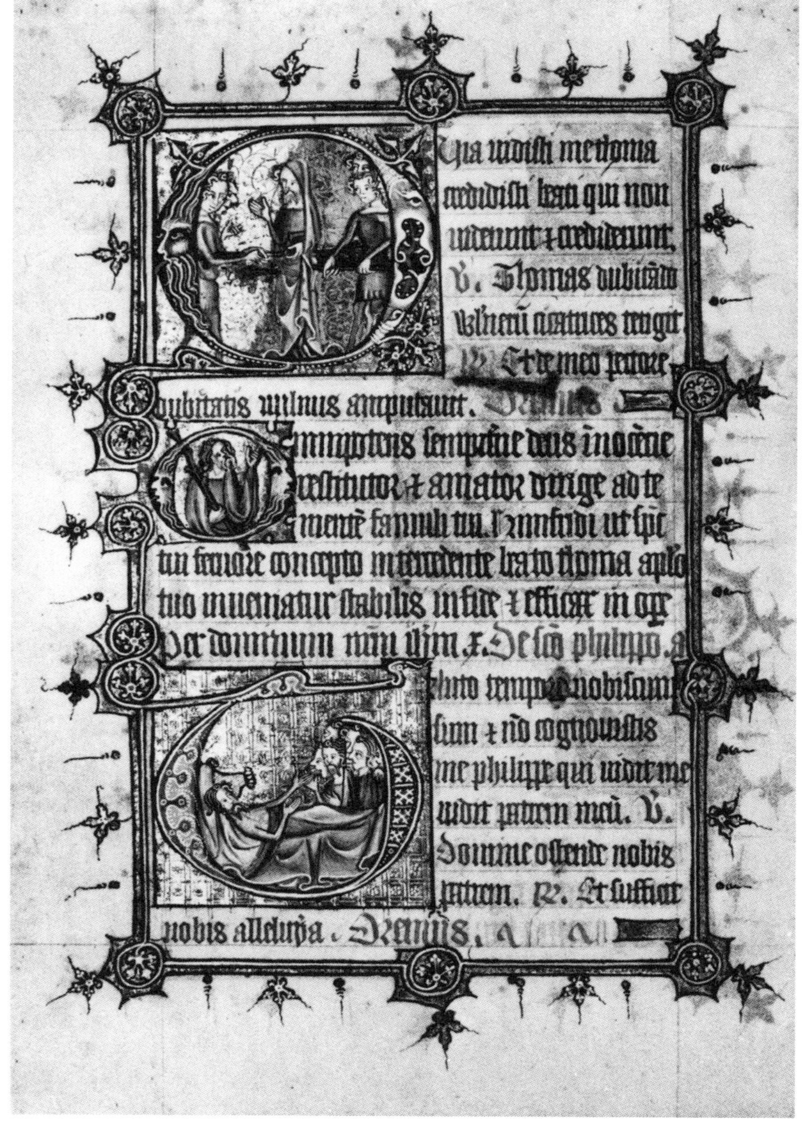

FIGURE 11. Pommersfelden Memoriae, memorials of Apostles Thomas and Philip, with prayer for Humphrey. Pommersfelden, Graf von Schönborn Schlossbibliothek MS. 348 (2934), fol. 3v (photo: Graf von Schönborn Schlossbibliothek).

Arts Club,[13] Sydney Cockerell observed that the Exeter College Psalter included not only the Bohun arms, but also textual prayers naming "Himfridus," whom he identified as Humphrey de Bohun, the seventh earl of Hereford, Essex, and Northampton. Consequently, in opposition to Coxe, Cockerell attributed the ownership to this Humphrey rather than to Thomas of Woodstock. He dated the manuscript *c.* 1370, during the lifetime of Humphrey, who died in 1373. Subsequently, the same prayers on behalf of Humphrey were found in four other manuscripts with Bohun heraldry (Fig. 11),[14] and most scholars have identified the Humphrey in question as the seventh earl.

Humphrey, however, was a favorite Bohun family

13. London, Burlington Fine Arts Club, *Exhibition of Illuminated Manuscripts* (London, 1908), 35–36, no. 73.

14. A second manuscript with textual references to Humphrey (see appendix, no. 7) was noted by E. G. Millar, *English Illuminated Manuscripts of the XIVth and XVth Centuries* (Paris, 1928), 63–65; a third (appendix no. 2) was added by M. R. James, in M. R. James and E. G. Millar, *The Bohun Manuscripts* (London, 1936), 33; a fourth (appendix no. 4) by M. Rickert, *The Reconstructed Carmelite Missal* (London, 1952), 74 n. 2; and the fifth (appendix no. 8) in the typewritten *Katalog der Handschriften der Gräflich von Schönbornischen Bibliothek zu Pommersfelden*, IV, n.d.

name, passed down to eldest sons in four generations from *c.* 1200 to 1373.[15] The immediate predecessor of Humphrey, the seventh earl, was his uncle, another Humphrey, the sixth earl, who died in 1361, and indeed, in my entries on the Exeter Psalter and the Bohun psalters in Vienna and London in the fourteenth-century volume of the Survey of Manuscripts Illuminated in the British Isles series, I suggested that the textual references to "Himfridus" in these and other Bohun manuscripts could have referred initially to Humphrey the sixth earl, no matter that in several cases they might have been written much later than 1361.[16]

Apart from heraldry and text, the importance of other codicological aspects of manuscripts in providing clues to original ownership and provenance has recently been underscored in discoveries made about the two smaller Bohun volumes now in Copenhagen, the Hours of Mary de Bohun (Fig. 12), and the lives of the Virgin, St. Margaret, and St. Mary Magdalene (Fig. 13).[17] It has long been thought that these manuscripts were bequeathed to Mary de Bohun's daughter Philippa and must have reached Copenhagen through Philippa's marriage in 1406 to Erik, king of Denmark, Sweden, and Norway.[18] Indeed, this "fact" led me to try to reconstruct the possible connection between Mary de Bohun's other daughter, Blanche, who married Ludwig, count palatine of the Rhine, in 1403, and the Bohun psalter now at Lichtenthal Abbey, my hypothesis being that just as with Philippa, the Lichtenthal Psalter was inherited by Blanche and brought to Germany when she married Ludwig.[19]

I continue to believe that my hypothesis about the Lichtenthal Psalter is credible, but a simple observation about the bindings of the two Copenhagen manuscripts has shown that the accepted idea of their provenance is no longer supportable. The bindings (Figs. 14, 15) are of red morocco tooled in gold, and fall into the general category of "modern," a category usually passed over without further notice in manuscript descriptions.[20] A few years ago, however, the Copenhagen-based manuscript scholar Marina Vidas pointed out to me that the bindings of the Copenhagen Bohun volumes appeared to be similar to those of a number of incunabula in the Royal Library that had been discussed by Ruth Bentzen in an essay titled "Lord Harley og Grev Thott, en studie i nogle af det Kongelige Biblioteks bind og bøger fra Harleys og Thotts bogsamlinger."[21] Bentzen's article is concerned primarily with printed books acquired by Count Otto Thott (1703–1785) from the collection of Edward Harley, sec-

15. For Bohun genealogy, see G. E. Cokayne, *Complete Peerage of England*, rev. ed., ed. V. Gibbs et al. (London, 1910–59), s.v. Essex, Hereford, Northampton. "Humphrey" was preserved as the name of Humphrey of Gloucester (1390–1447), the fourth and youngest son of Mary de Bohun and Henry of Bolingbroke.

16. Sandler, *Gothic Manuscripts*, II (as in note 12), 148, 150, 153. In the entry on the Bohun Psalter and Hours in the Bodleian Library (appendix no. 7), *Gothic Manuscripts*, II, 158, I suggested that the textual reference to Humphrey in a manuscript with arms of Mary de Bohun and Henry of Bolingbroke "might refer to the text model rather than the intended owner of this particular book," and since then have concluded that such textual memorials are dynastic rather than personal; see Sandler, "Lancastrian Heraldry" (as in note 10), 227.

17. See appendix, nos. 10–11.

18. Proposed at the end of the nineteenth century by J. H. Wylie, *History of England under Henry the Fourth*, II (London, 1894), 454, and already implied by C. Bruun, *De illuminerede Haandskrifter fra Middelalderen i det Store Kongelige Bibliotek* (Copenhagen, 1890), 192; Bruun identified the arms as Bohun, Lancaster, and the king of England, suggested the connection with Mary de Bohun, mother of Queen Philippa, and Henry of Bolingbroke, and dated the volume to the second half of the fourteenth century. His identification of the Lancastrian arms (as borne by John of Gaunt) was a mis-reading of a heraldic shield actually representing the arms of the royal heir-apparent (as borne by Edward the Black Prince), and his error has been repeated regularly; see Sandler, "Lancastrian Heraldry" (as in note 10), 222, 225, 227–28.

19. Sandler, *Lichtenthal Psalter* (as in note 12), 151–53.

20. E.g., the descriptions in N. C. L. Abrahams, *Description des manuscrits français du moyen âge de la Bibliothèque royale de Copenhague* (Copenhagen, 1844), 9 (on Thott MS. 517.4°), and Bruun, *De illuminerede Haandskrifter*, 197, on both manuscripts, noting the similarity of the bindings. The binding of Thott MS. 517.4° is viewable on line at http://www.kb.dk/permalink/2006/manus/242/eng/Binding—without further description, however.

21. R. Bentzen, "Lord Harley og Grev Thott, en studie i nogle af det Kongelige Biblioteks bind og bøger fra Harleys og Thotts bogsamlinger," *Fund og Forskning I det Kongelige Biblioteks samlinger* 44 (2005), 277–63. I am most grateful to Dr. Vidas for providing me with provisional photos of the bindings, and to Dr. Erik Petersen of the Kongelige Bibliotek for arranging to supply the fine-quality digital images reproduced here.

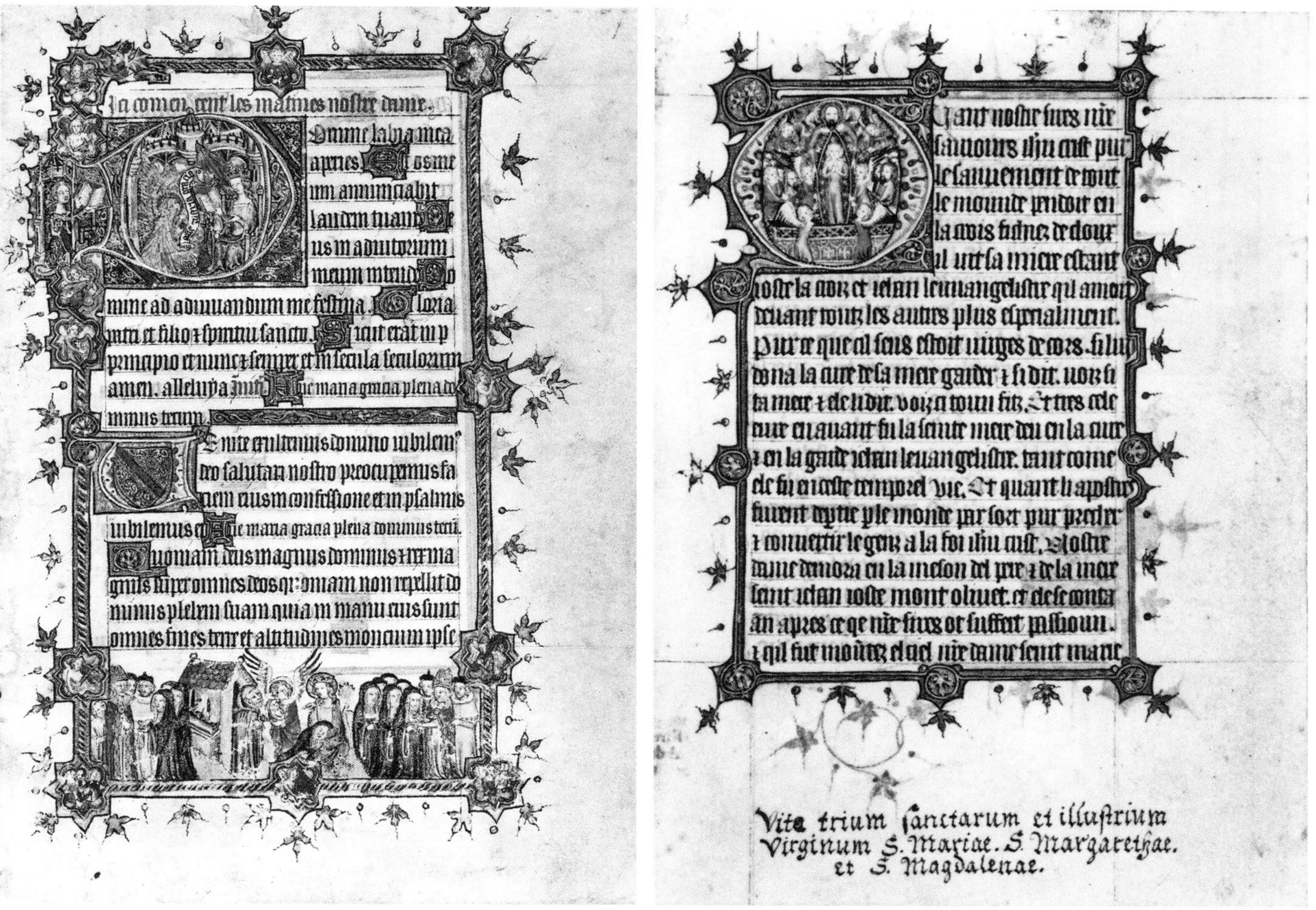

FIGURE 12. Cophenhagen Hours, Matins, Annunciation; in the margin, Mary de Bohun; in the small initial, Bohun arms; in the *bas-de-page*, Miracle of the Fallen Abbess. Copenhagen, Kongelige Bibliotek MS. Thott 547.4°, fol. 1 (photo: Kongelige Bibliotek).

FIGURE 13. Copenhagen Lives of Saints, Assumption of the Virgin. Copenhagen, Kongelige Bibliotek MS. Thott 517.4°, fol. 1 (photo: Kongelige Bibliotek).

ond earl of Oxford (1689–1741), and his father, Robert Harley, first earl of Oxford (1661–1724). Edward Harley had many of these bound in so-called Harley Bindings, a term used for the work of a number of eighteenth-century London binders of both books and manuscripts, including many manuscripts of the Harley collection at the British Library.[22] Some of the incunabula bindings discussed by Bentzen, however, were classified as of unknown provenance, and it is with a small group of these that the bindings of the two Copenhagen Bohun manuscripts can be identified, rather than the clearly English bindings.[23]

22. On "Harley Bindings," see H. M. Nixon, "Harleian Bindings," in *Studies in the Book Trade in Honour of Graham Pollard* (Oxford, 1975), 153–94; also *idem*, *Five Centuries of English Bookbinding* (London, 1978); H. M. Nixon and M. M. Foot, *The History of Decorated Bookbinding in England* (Oxford, 1992); and D. Pearson, *English Bookbinding Styles 1450–1800* (London, 2005). Manuscripts with "Harleian bindings" are identified as such in the British Library online Digital Catalogue of Illuminated Manuscripts, http://www.bl.uk/catalogues/illuminatedmanuscripts.

23. See Bentzen, "Lord Harley" (as in note 21), 356–58 and figs. 28–30.

FIGURE 14. Copenhagen Hours, upper cover. Copenhagen, Kongelige Bibliotek MS. Thott 547.4° (photo: Kongelige Bibliotek).

FIGURE 15. Copenhagen Lives of Saints, upper cover. Copenhagen, Kongelige Bibliotek MS. Thott 517.4° (photo: Kongelige Bibliotek).

In fact, three bindings scholars—Philippa Marks, Jan Storm van Leeuwen, and Mirjam Foot—have identified the Bohun bindings as Dutch, not English,[24] and Storm Van Leeuwen and Foot have both attributed them to an early eighteenth-century Hague binder of the so-called Magnus Group V, the "Drawer-Handle Binder" or the "Fleuron Binder" (perhaps two names for a single binder or bindery).[25] It turns out—and for this I have to thank Mirjam Foot in particular—that in all likelihood the Copenhagen manuscripts were bound for an early eighteenth-century Dutch collector, as yet unnamed in print, and were acquired by Count Thott

24. I am most grateful to Dr. Philippa Marks for her advice on the Copenhagen bindings, and to Dr. Jan Storm van Leeuwen and Dr. Mirjam Foot for their help, which was offered generously and graciously in countless e-mail exchanges.

25. See M. M. Foot, *The Henry Davis Gift: A Collection of Bookbindings* (London, 1978–83), 1, *Studies in the History of Bookbinding*, 250–51, 257–58, identifying 38 bindings in "Magnus Group V," a group later expanded by Foot to at least 66 in "An Eighteenth-Century Incunable Collector in The Hague," in *Incunabula, Studies in Fifteenth-Century Printed Books Presented to Lotte Hellinga*, ed. M. Davies (London, 1999), 371–87. This group of bindings has since been treated by Foot's colleague Jan Storm van Leeuwen as the work of two binderies in The Hague, the "Drawer Handler Bindery" and the "Fleuron Bindery," whose period of operation extended from the end of the seventeenth century to *c.* 1730; see J. Storm van Leeuwen, *Dutch Decorated Bookbinding in the Eighteenth Century*

from this source.[26] Thus, we have to conclude that two Bohun manuscripts were not in Denmark before 1728, the date at which Thott began making his major purchases, and could not have come to Denmark with Mary de Bohun's daughter, Philippa.[27] The lesson in this is that we medievalists overlook "modern" manuscript bindings at our peril, reminding us that all aspects of codicology are worth attention, and that their study can contribute to the expansion and clarification of the map of medieval manuscripts.

How was it that Cockerell, and others since, linked the Bohun manuscripts with one Humphrey de Bohun, namely the seventh earl (1342–1373), rather than another? Of course, the inclusion in the manuscripts of the arms of England in their particular post-1340 form would have eliminated the several Humphreys prior to Humphrey, the sixth earl (1309–1361).[28] But, essentially, it was a matter of style, whether of image or of script. To the connoisseur's eye, the books simply "looked" as if they had been executed closer to 1370 than to 1360, although no dated *comparanda* were introduced, nor would that have been possible, since there is a paucity of firmly dated English material between 1345, the *terminus ante quem* of a deluxe psalter made for Simon de Montacute, bishop of Ely,[29] and 1383–1384, the date of the well-known missal of Nicholas Litlyngton, abbot of Westminster.[30]

Stylistic description and analysis is, of course, one of the chief tools of the art historian. What we call "style" can be concerned with the visual character of individual artists or works of art, or with groups—be they workshops, cities, regions, nations, or even periods, such as The Gothic, the topic of the present collection of essays.[31] Scholars of English manuscripts have usually focused narrowly, for instance, avoiding characterizations of Gothic as a period style, much as quite a few studies have included the term "Gothic" in their titles, but only as shorthand for a range of dates. To return to the Bohun manuscripts, and to go back to Coxe in 1852, typical of eighteenth- and nineteenth-century cataloguing practices, he described only the textual components of the Exeter College Psalter, remarking almost offhandedly that the manuscript was "optime illuminatus deauratusque" (most finely illuminated and gilded).[32]

In the Burlington Fine Arts Club exhibition of 1908, the Exeter College Psalter and the Bohun psalter now in the Fitzwilliam Museum, Cambridge, were shown side-by-side in the same case, and Cockerell described them as works by the same artist.[33] Subsequently, in the first survey of fourteenth- and fifteenth-century English manuscripts, published in 1928, Eric Millar identified a group of five Bohun manuscripts, those in the Fitzwilliam, in Exeter College, in the Bodleian, in Vienna, and in Copenhagen.[34] Millar grouped them together because they were related in heraldry, in textual refer-

(Utrecht, 2006), IIA, 22–38, III, 154–59. In correspondence, Dr. Storm van Leeuwen identified the tools used in the binding of the Copenagen Bohun Hours (MS. Thott 547.4°) as belonging to the Drawer Handle Bindery and those of its sister volume (MS. Thott 517.4°) as belonging to the Fleuron Bindery.

26. See Foot, "An Eighteenth-Century Inunable Collector" (as in note 25). A paper by Dr. Foot identifying this collector is forthcoming in a collection of essays in memory of Jos Hermans.

27. Bentzen, "Lord Harley" (as in note 21), 277.

28. The preceding Humphrey, the fourth earl of Hereford and Essex, had died in 1322. His first surviving son, John (d. 1336), became the fifth earl, followed by his next son, Humphrey the sixth.

29. Cambridge, St. John's Coll. MS. D.30; see Sandler, *Gothic Manuscripts* (as in note 12), I, figs. 291–93, II, 125–26, no. 112.

30. London, Westminster Abbey MS. 37; see Sandler, *Gothic Manuscripts* (as in note 12), I, figs. 393, 402–05, II, 172–74, no. 150.

31. See Meyer Schapiro, "Style," in *Theory and Philosophy of Art: Style, Artist, and Society. Selected Papers* (New York, 1994), 51–102, reprinted, with revisions from *Anthropology Today: An Encyclopedic Inventory*, ed. A. L. Krober (Chicago, 1953), 287–312.

32. Coxe, *Catalogus* (as in note 1), (Codices MSS collegii Exoniensis), 17.

33. Burlington Fine Arts Club (as in note 13), xiii (Cockerell), 34–35, no. 72, and 35–36, no. 73 (catalogue entries by George Warner). The Fitzwilliam Psalter (see appendix, no. 6) was called the "Psalter of John of Gaunt" by Warner, who analyzed the armorials carefully, and subsequently made a full description of the manuscript when it belonged to Henry Yates Thompson; see G. F. W[arner]., *A Descriptive Catalogue of Fourteen Illuminated Manuscripts Nos. XCV to CVI and 79A Completing the Hundred in the Library of Henry Yates Thompson* (Cambridge, 1912), 45–52, no. XCIX, reprinted with slight revisions in James and Millar, *Bohun Manuscripts* (as in note 14), 51–59.

34. Millar, *English Illuminated Manuscripts* (as in note 14), 25–27; see appendix, nos. 2, 3, 6, 7, 11.

ences to Humphrey, and, as he put it, "in a peculiar and very interesting style."[35] Later, in a Roxburghe Club volume of 1936, in which he and M. R. James described these same five Bohun manuscripts in great detail,[36] Millar characterized their style in more specific terms. As salient features, he picked out the architectural pinnacles in the borders, the backgrounds of delicately patterned punctured gold, the use of red-tinted liquid gold over burnished gold, the delicately drawn faces with considerable modeling of features, and the large black dots for eyes. He then ventured beyond "group style" to locate the manuscripts more generally in the history of style, observing that the figure-drawing recalled that of the Douai and St. Omer psalters, examples of the East Anglian "school" of the first half of the fourteenth century, and he related the decorative motifs to East Anglian manuscripts too. Finally, Millar went on to list later manuscripts "claiming some degree of relationship," such as the well-known Litlyngton Missal.[37]

In defining a "Bohun style," and in positioning the Bohun manuscripts within a historical development by specifying their ancestry and their descendants, Millar introduced into the discourse on English illumination a concept that had long been common currency among European scholars.[38] Although in general art historians have often based stylistic development on a biological model of birth, maturity, and decay,[39] it would be more accurate to call Millar's schema genealogical. He was, however, party to a view that English illumination "declined" with the onset of the Black Death, and was "revived" with the Bohun manuscripts.[40]

In the same year—1936—that James's and Millar's Roxburghe Club volume was published, the Bohun psalter in Vienna was described in detail by Hans Julius Hermann.[41] Familiar with the lists of Bohun manuscripts compiled earlier by Cockerell, Millar, and others, Hermann's own contribution was to distinguish several illuminators of the historiated initials. Although he commented that separation of these hands was difficult, using handling of color, figures, and drapery as criteria, Hermann identified three artists in the Vienna manuscript, one of whom he named as the chief illuminator of the Exeter College Psalter, which he, following Cockerell and others, dated *c.* 1370.[42] Hermann's effort to distinguish the "style" of individual artistic personalities reflected the connoisseur's approach that had normally been employed to study Old Master drawing and painting. Although European scholars had long discussed and argued about the *oeuvres* of named Continental illuminators such as Jean Pucelle or the Limbourgs, and constructed bodies of work of anonymous "masters" such the "Master of Mary of Burgundy,"[43] Hermann was the first to treat the then-anonymous craftsmen who produced the illustrations of the Bohun manuscripts as individual artistic creators. His identification of the illuminators of the Vienna Psalter laid the foundation for subsequent as-

35. *Ibid.*, 25.

36. James and Millar, *Bohun Manuscripts* (as in note 14), with detailed descriptions of the subjects of the illustrations and the heraldry by M. R. James, and introduction by E. G. Millar; also hundreds of actual-size black-and-white reproductions of most of the illustrations in each manuscript.

37. E. G. Millar, in James and Millar, *Bohun Manuscripts* (as in note 14), 2–3.

38. See the pioneering survey of A. Haseloff, "La miniature dans les pays cisalpins depuis le commencement du xiie jusqu'au milieu du xive siècle," in A. Michel, *Histoire de l'art depuis les premiers temps chrétiens jusqu'à nos jours*, II, Formation, expansion et évolution de l'art gothique, pt. I (Paris, 1905), esp. 330–71. No comparable survey of later fourteenth- or fifteenth-century manuscripts appeared in Michel's multi-authored history.

39. Cf. Schapiro, "Style" (as in note 31) 69–81.

40. Millar, in James and Millar, *Bohun Manuscripts* (as in note 14), 1.

41. H. J. Hermann, *Die westeuropaïschen Handschriften und Inkunabeln der Gotik und der Renaissance*, Beschreibendes Verzeichnis der illuminierten Handschriften in Österreich, new series, VII, 2, Englische und französische Handschriften des XIV. Jahrhunderts der Nationalbibliothek in Wien (Leipzig, 1936), 17–38.

42. *Ibid.*, 17.

43. For example, see O. Pächt, *The Master of Mary of Burgundy* (London, 1947), 20 and n. 1, observing that the name was given to the anonymous illluminator by F. Winkler, for which see "Studien zur Geschichte der niederländischen Buchmalereі, etc.," in *Jahrbuch der Kunsthistorischen Sammlungen des allerhöchsten Kaiserhauses* 22 (Vienna, 1915), 279-306, and *idem*, *Die flämische Buchmalerei* (Leipzig, 1925), 103-13, where Winkler compiled the first *oeuvre*-list of the master.

sessments of the Bohun manuscripts primarily in terms of "hands," an approach whose chief current exponent is Lynda Dennison.

In her unpublished doctoral dissertation of 1988, and in numerous published articles, Dennison has devoted her attention to fixing an absolute chronology of the Bohun manuscripts, to identifying precisely, image by image, and decorative motif by decorative motif, the individual artistic contributors, and to outlining the development of their careers.[44] She has explained her criteria for identification of individual artistic personalities, in this way trying to verbalize and vindicate the "gut feeling" that two works, even those known to be separated by time, were painted by the same hand. The distinguishing criteria used are decorative format and motifs, figure proportions, poses, and facial types, and details of technique.[45] In the end, however, Dennison's verbal distinctions apply more to the Bohun manuscripts in general than to the identification of individual hands. This shows how difficult it is to use language precisely enough to convince others that Gothic artists, who indeed often seem to have been looking to immerse themselves in a "group style," can be separated out as individuals, much less understood in terms of the career development that Dennison attempted to trace.[46]

One of the most pervasive concepts used by manuscript scholars in discussions of style, and indeed by art historians in general, is that of "influence." "Under the influence" has come to connote general likeness of later to earlier, or foreign to native, work, and, as for manuscripts, this has been all too often the case in the absence of knowledge of the specifics of transmission, and with a modern sense of nationhood that would not have been recognized in the Middle Ages.[47] In his 1928 survey, for instance, Eric Millar considered the stylistic relationship of the Bohun manuscripts with those produced on the Continent—at least by implication—when he concluded, "I will only say that I can see no reason on stylistic grounds for supposing that the group is not entirely the work of English artists."[48] The reason the question of a foreign connection arose was that, as in treating other English Gothic manuscripts—the well-known early fourteenth-century Queen Mary Psalter, for instance—Millar had attributed its elegance and refinement to French influence.[49] And the question of "Frenchness" or "Englishness" in English manuscript illumination has continually resurfaced in the scholarly

44. L. Dennison, "The Stylistic Sources, Dating and Development of the Bohun Workshop, ca. 1340–1400," Ph.D. Thesis (London, 1988); "The Artistic Context of Fourteenth Century Flemish Brasses," *Transactions of the Monumental Brass Society* 14 (1986), 1–38 (published after 1988); "'The Fitzwarin Psalter and its Allies': A Reappraisal," in *England in the Fourteenth Century, Proceedings of the 1985 Harlaxton Symposium*, ed. W. M. Ormrod (Woodbridge, 1986), 42–66; "Oxford, Exeter College MS. 47: The Importance of Stylistic and Codicological Analysis in its Dating and Localization," in *Medieval Book Production: Assessing the Evidence*, Proceedings of the Second Conference of the Seminar in the History of the Book to 1500, July 1988, ed. L. L. Brownrigg (Oxford, 1990), 41–60; "The Dating and Localization of the Hague Missal (Meermanno-Westreenianum MS. 10 A 14) and the Connections between English and Flemish Miniature Painting in the Mid-Fourteenth Century," in *"Als ich can." Liber Amicorum in Memory of Professor Dr. Maurits Smeyers*, ed. B. Cardon et al. (Louvain, 2002), 505–36; "British Library, Egerton Ms. 3277: A Fourteenth-Century Psalter-Hours and the Question of Bohun Ownership," in *Family and Dynasty in Fourteenth-Century England*, ed. R. Eales and S. Tyas (Donington, 2003), 139–70; "Transformation, Interaction and Integration: The Career and Collaboration of a Fourteenth-Century Flemish Illuminator," in *Manuscripts in Transition, Recycling Manuscripts, Texts and Images*, Proceedings of the International Congress Held in Brussels (5-9 November 2002), ed. B. Dekeyzer and J. Vander Stock (Leuven, 2005), 173–92.

45. See Dennison, "Stylistic Sources" (as in note 45), 45–47, 133–34, 184–87.

46. See, for instance, Dennison's construction of the individual development of one of the early artists of the Vienna Bohun Psalter (Dennison's "Vienna Hand B"). To this artist Dennison attributed all or portions of four other extant volumes made for non-Bohun owners, none, however, datable either by internal or external documentation; "Stylistic Sources" (as in note 45), 59–67. Dennison evidently believes that it is possible to determine the stylistic development of an individual artist in the absence of documentary guideposts.

47. For the question of influence in relation to English Gothic manuscripts before the mid-fourteenth century, see L. F. Sandler, "Illuminated in the British Isles: French Influence and/or the Englishness of English Art, 1285–1345," *Gesta* 45 (2006), 177–88.

48. Millar, in James and Millar, *Bohun Manuscripts* (as in note 14), 3.

49. Millar, *English Illuminated Manuscripts* (as in note 14), 14–15.

discourse, its most recent expression being Michael Camille's characterization of the Luttrell Psalter, of the second quarter of the fourteenth century, as "a work of resolutely English insularity," and his observation that the manuscript "would have appeared rather coarse and even crude to the courtly tastes of the patrons of ... the Queen Mary Psalter with its Parisian grisaille style."[50]

The concept of foreign influence on the Bohun manuscripts was first introduced specifically by Margaret Rickert in the 1952 publication of her painstaking reconstruction of the dismembered Carmelite Missal,[51] a giant-sized work of the end of the fourteenth century, which had been listed by Millar as a stylistic descendant of the Bohun manuscripts. In this study, and in her subsequent survey, *Painting in Britain: The Middle Ages*, Rickert wrote that Italian influence "completely transforms" what she characterized as the "debased version of the East Anglian style" that she found in the earliest work in the Bohun manuscripts, and attributed such newer features as strong modeling of faces and drapery to sources in Lombard, Sienese, or possibly Avignonese illumination. Rickert concluded that there was some indication of the "presence of English illuminators or manuscripts in Italy," and that "it would not be unreasonable to expect an exchange of influences between English and Italian styles."[52]

Rickert also mentioned in passing the possible influence of "some version of French or possibly Flemish style, with small, linear figures and a formal border of one particular kind of cinquefoil leaf" in the manuscripts made for Mary de Bohun.[53] Rickert's implicit rejection of Millar's conception of the "Englishness" of the Bohun artists, and her conclusions about the impact of Italian and Flemish art on the Bohun manuscripts, were themselves influential, and in various degrees provided a framework for the stylistic analysis of subsequent scholars, in particular, Amanda Simpson and Lynda Dennison.

Amanda Simpson discussed the Bohun manuscripts in her Courtauld Institute doctoral thesis of 1978, *The Connections between English and Bohemian Painting during the Second Half of the Fourteenth Century*, which was published in 1984.[54] Although in fact she rejected earlier claims of a "Bohemian connection," the study made an important contribution to the question of foreign influence on the artists of the Bohun manuscripts. Against the *continuo* of the East Anglian tradition, the Bohun style was divided by Simpson in two, the Italian-influenced and the Flemish-influenced, and sections of each manuscript were assigned to artists operating in tandem under one or the other influence.[55] Simpson found the sources of the Italianate Bohun style in Lombard works of the 1370s and 1380s, and she compared the Flemish Bohun style to that of illuminators she identified as working in the 1360s for Louis de Male, count of Flanders. As Rickert had, Simpson sought to determine the channels through which Italian and Flemish influences reached the Bohun artists, concluding that Humphrey the seventh earl's foreign travel offered one plausible explanation, since, as he was known to have been a bibliophile, he might well have collected books in Flanders and in Italy.[56] And because of the range of connections with Continental manuscripts, Simpson suggested that the place of execution of the Bohun books could have been London, the most cosmopolitan

50. M. Camille, *Mirror in Parchment: The Luttrell Psalter and the Making of Medieval England* (Chicago, 1998), 330.

51. London, British Lib. MSS. Add. 29704–29705, and 44892. M. Rickert, *The Reconstructed Carmelite Missal* (London, 1952).

52. M. Rickert, *Painting in Britain: The Middle Ages* (Harmondsworth, 1954), 243, and *Carmelite Missal*, 75.

53. Rickert, *Painting in Britain* (as in note 53), 149.

54. A. Simpson, *The Connections between English and Bohemian Painting during the Second Half of the Fourteenth Century* (New York, 1984). Simpson (p. 120) added one manuscript, a series of *memoriae* from a book of hours, now in Pommersfelden, to the Bohun group (see appendix, no. 8). She expressed concern about the dating of all the Bohun manuscripts to *c.* 1370, since it was "unlikely that about that date, at the age of twenty-eight, he [Humphrey the seventh earl] should have ordered a large number of books, and it is reasonable to suppose that some of the books were executed during the 1360s" (p. 121), and consequently she constructed a relative chronology, the earliest work being the Vienna Psalter begun in the 1360s and the latest the Copenhagen Hours, after Mary de Bohun's marriage in 1380/81, the dates and positions of the rest within the chronology not specified.

55. Simpson, *Connections* (as in note 55), 119–32.

56. *Ibid.*, 121, 130.

center in England.[57] She did not as yet know of the documents identifying the place of production as the Bohun residence at Pleshey Castle.

Lynda Dennison then moved the sources of the Italianate Bohun style away from direct contact with Italy and back to earlier English manuscripts in which Italianisms can be traced, namely East Anglian books of the 1320s and 1330s, such as the Gorleston Psalter and the St. Omer Psalter. She also saw the hand of the earliest illuminator of the Vienna Psalter in two Italian-influenced psalters she dated to the early 1340s, one in the Douce collection in the Bodleian Library, and the other in the Biblioteca Queriniana in Brescia.[58]

Dennison also reformulated the hypothesis of Flemish influence on the Bohun artists. What to Simpson had been Flemish influence on an indigenous artist, to Dennison became the active participation of an actual Flemish immigrant to England, whom she identified as one of the very same individuals who had first worked in Flanders for Louis de Male, and then, in Dennison's view, had moved to the Bohun household in England and become first the assistant, and then the chief associate of John de Teye, the native English illuminator.[59]

Dennison's characterization of the Bohun artists keeps alive questions both of influence and how we define it, and of individual artistic style and how we recognize it. In particular, her conclusion that one of the Bohun artists was actually a Fleming whose hand can be found in surviving manuscripts made for Louis de Male returns us to the question of individual artistic identity. Here, Dennison, like Millar before her, based her conclusions on separate and discrete motifs and details of technique, in particular, physiognomies, hair styles, achitectural framing elements, and animated initial frames.[60] No account was taken of pictorial *gestalt*, that is, the relation between part, parts, and whole that would also characterize the work of an individual illuminator. Consequently, the subtle conception of style as a set of formal *relationships* that we find in the manuscript studies of such scholars as Meyer Schapiro[61] and Otto Pächt[62] did not and does not affect Dennison's thinking. To my mind, a more holistic view of what constitutes the style of an individual artist would disengage the Bohun artist from the artist of the manuscripts of Louis de Male. And yet the undoubted parallels would encourage thinking about the significance of all the visual parallels in manuscripts produced across Europe in the years from *c.* 1350 to *c.* 1390, whether in England, in Flanders, in Paris, in Avignon, or in Prague.

In view of their extraordinary length, iconographic description has played an important role in the study of the pictorial cycles in the Bohun manuscripts. For the Roxburghe Club volume on the Bohun manuscripts, James, in the tradition of detailed textual and pictorial description he himself had established at the end of the nineteenth century,[63] undertook the task of identifying

57. *Ibid.*, 131.

58. Dennison, "Stylistic Sources" (as in note 45), 50–57.

59. *Ibid.*, 133–34, arguing that this artist came to England *c.* 1345–1350 and became John de Teye's assistant *c.* 1355–1360; had this been the case, he would have accepted a lower rank than he had held in Flanders—a situation open to question. Dennison re-dated the Louis de Male manuscripts to *c.* 1345–1350. Their traditional dating, accepted by Simpson, *Connections* (as in note 55), 129, was *c.* 1360; see C. Gaspar and F. Lyna, *Les principaux manuscrits à peintures de la Bibliothèque royale de Belgique* (Paris, 1937), I, 346–47, who, however, based their chronology in part on a mis-dating of the marriage of Louis de Male and Margaret de Brabant to 1357, whereas the correct date was 1347 (see Dennison, 120). It was the correction of the dating that made it possible for Dennison to propose not only a pre-1360 date for the manuscripts of the Louis de Male group, but also a move on the part of their chief illuminator to England as well as his participation in the illumination of the Bohun manuscripts as early as 1355. See also Dennison, "Transformation, Interaction and Integration" (as in note 45), 173, re-dating the arrival of the Louis de Male artist in England to 1355.

60. Dennison, "Stylistic Sources" (as in note 45), 107–34.

61. In addition to Schapiro's essay "Style" (as in note 31), which is not specifically concerned with manuscript illumination, see his *Words and Pictures: On the Literal and the Symbolic in the Illustration of a Text* (The Hague, 1973), and *The Language of Forms, Lectures on Insular Manuscript Art*, intro. J. Rosenthal (New York, 2005), the publication of a series of lectures given at the Pierpont Morgan Library in 1968.

62. See, O. Pächt, *Book Illumination in the Middle Ages* (London, 1986), and *The Practice of Art History: Reflections on Method* (London, 1999).

63. See M. R. James' earliest catalogues of the manuscripts of Eton College, and the Fitzwilliam Museum, Jesus, Kings and Sidney Sussex Colleges, Cambridge, all of 1895; see also L. Dennison,

more than five hundred pictorial subjects, supplying where possible biblical chapter and verse or the words of the psalms to which the illustrations corresponded. James rejected the idea that the artists were following pictorial models; instead, they "seem to have invented their own compositions and read the [Bible] text for the purpose,"[64] a claim that runs counter to the received view, now I think widely associated with the name of Kurt Weitzmann, that illuminators depended on iconographic sources that can be diagrammed like textual stemmata.[65] Nevertheless, James's claim is valid for the Bohun artists, who were as thoroughly familiar with the biblical texts themselves as they were with pictorial traditions for their illustration.[66]

Do we stop with James's site-map of iconography, as staggering an accomplishment as it was, or with identification of patronage, or with definition of style? The Bohun manuscripts apart, certainly methods that go beyond the descriptive have been applied widely to the study of English manuscripts ever since the 1930s. Concepts drawn from social, anthropological, psychological, and literary theory have directed study from outward to inward, and in the opposite direction, ever more intense analysis that starts from the word, the line, the page in all of its visual, verbal, and aural aspects has aimed to expose what Joyce Coleman, Mark Cruse, and Kathryn Smith, the editors of a forthcoming volume of essays, are calling the "social life of illumination."[67]

As an example of the way I have been employing these concepts in a recent series of studies of the Bohun manuscripts, I cite here a recent article, titled "Rhetorical Strategies in the Pictorial Imagery of Fourteenth Century Manuscripts: The Case of the Bohun Psalters,"[68] in which some of the illustrations of the Exeter College Psalter and the Lichtenthal Psalter are discussed. One of the pictorial subjects in these manuscripts is the marriage of Moses and Zipporah (Exodus 2:21). In both cases, the artist, John de Teye, departed from the conventional representation of marriages, which is axial,[69] to show the event at an oblique angle, heightening the illusion of a spatial setting, and facilitating the narrative flow from one scene of the biblical cycle to the next. In the Exeter College Psalter (Fig. 16), the dominant figure in the marital couple is Moses, his body almost completely hiding that of Zipporah. But in the Lichtenthal Psalter (Fig. 17), Zipporah is clearly in the foreground, taking, in fact, the superior position, on the right of Moses.

What accounts for these compositional differences? I believe that we have to recognize the sensitivity of John de Teye—who, as an Augustinian friar, was his own scholarly adviser—to the expectations and needs of his patrons, the intended owners of the two manuscripts: on the one hand, the adult male earl of Hereford, Humphrey the sixth or seventh, and on the other hand, the newly married ten-year-old Mary de Bohun. In particular, Zipporah, in the Lichtenthal Psalter, with her long, pale, unbound hair and gold princess' chaplet, provided a visual model for the young bride who owned the manuscript.

My interest in these, and indeed, in all Bohun images, lies in the interpretation of form—that is, the way the images look—in the light of my understanding of historical circumstances. To me, "historical circumstances" includes an assessment of reception as well as

---

ed., *The Legacy of M. R. James, Papers from the 1995 Cambridge Symposium* (Donington, 2001), esp. Introduction, 1–10, J. Backhouse, "Manuscripts on Display: Some Landmarks in the Exhibition and Popular Publication of Illuminated Books," 37–52, and A. J. Piper, "Cataloguing British Collections of Medieval Western Manuscripts, 1895–1995," 53–64. On the development of James as a cataloguer, see also R. W. Pfaff, *Montague Rhoades James* (London, 1980), 172–208.

64. James and Millar, *Bohun Manuscripts* (as in note 14), 8.

65. See, for example, K. Weitzmann, *Ancient Book Illumination* (Cambridge, Mass., 1959), and *Illustration in Roll and Codex: A Study of the Origin and Method of Text Illustration* (Princeton, 1970).

66. See L. F. Sandler, "The Illustration of the Psalms in Fourteenth-Century English Manuscripts: Three Psalters of the Bohun Family," in *Reading Texts and Images, Essays on Medieval and Renaissance Art and Patronage in Honour of Margaret M. Manion*, ed. B. J. Muir (Exeter, 2002), 123–51.

67. *The Social Life of Illumination*, ed. J. Coleman, M. Cruse, and K. Smith (Turnhout, forthcoming).

68. In *Rhetoric without Words: Delight and Persuasion in the Medieval Arts*, ed. M. Carruthers (Cambridge, 2010), 96–123.

69. For many examples, see A. Melnikas, *The Corpus of the Miniatures in the Manuscripts of Decretum Gratiani* (Rome, 1975), III, *Causae* XXVII–XXXVI.

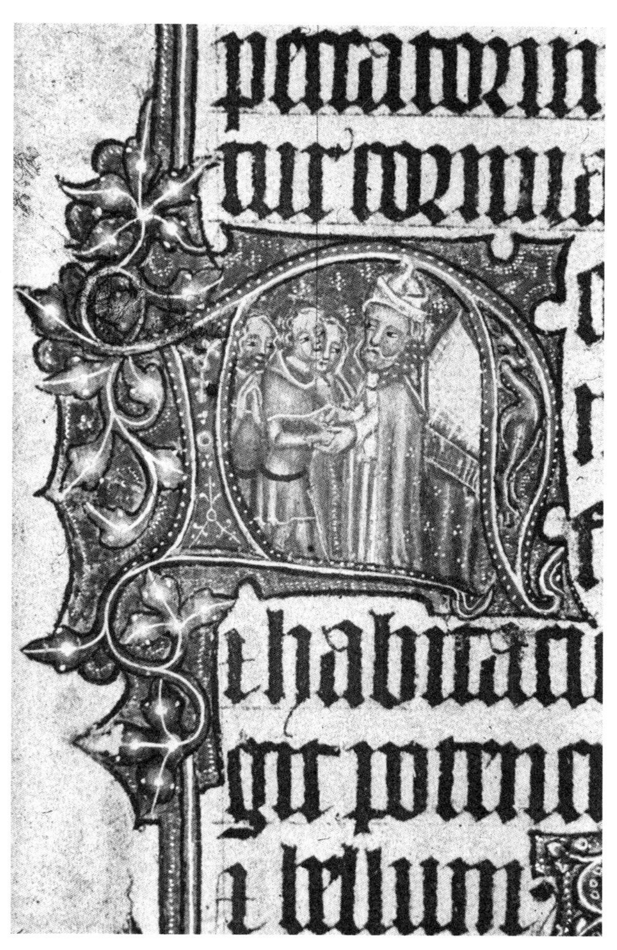

FIGURE 16. Exeter College Psalter, Psalm 75, marriage of Moses and Zipporah. Oxford, Exeter College MS. 47, fol. 49v (photo: Exeter College).

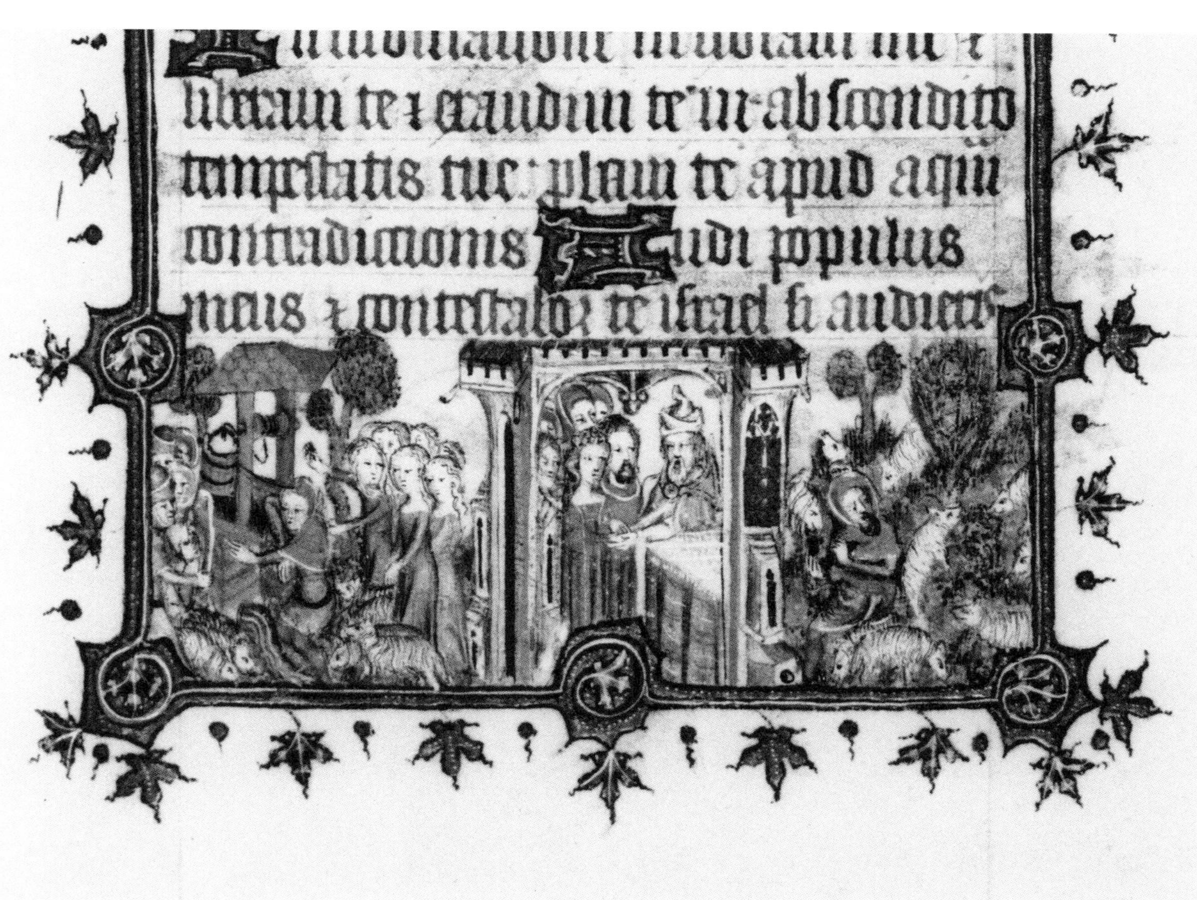

FIGURE 17. Lichtenthal Psalter, Psalm 80, *bas-de-page*, Moses scenes. Baden-Baden, Lichtenthal Abbey Archiv MS. 2, fol. 83 (photo: author).

production, and the artistic and socio-political status of individual makers of these manuscripts as well as that of their recipients. How artists responded, or did not respond, to texts, who devised programs of illustration and how, how manuscripts were used, how looking at images in a textual setting affected book-owners, how artists "voiced" their own social personae, and how they provided social mirrors as well as models for the patrons—these are among the questions that are of current interest, not only in my work on the Bohun manuscripts, but in that of other scholars of English Gothic manuscripts. It seems to me that for the last two decades and more, scholarship that is at once broadly contextual and sharply probing of the very nature of artistic processes has made important contributions to shaping and re-shaping our views of English illuminated manuscripts of the Gothic period, and, indeed, in the end, to our understanding of the term "Gothic."

APPENDIX

The Bohun Manuscripts

The list that follows includes, in rough chronological order, all the manuscripts that have been associated with Bohun ownership to date, together with the chief bibliography for each, starting with the first published reference. The date ranges given here are those accepted or proposed by the author.

1. Private owner, fragmentary Hours with Bohun arms, *c.* 1345–1350.

   C. de Hamel, "A New Bohun," in *The English Medieval Book: Studies in Memory of Jeremy Griffiths*, ed. A. S. G. Edwards, V. Gillespie, and R. Hanna (London, 2000), 19–26.

2. Psalter, Vienna, Österreichische Nationalbibliothek Cod. 1826*, begun *c.* 1350, completed by 1373?

   H. J. Hermann, *Die westeuropaïschen Handschriften und Inkunabeln der Gotik und der Renaissance*, Beschreibendes Verzeichnis der illuminierten Handschriften in Österreich, new series, VII, 2, Englische und französische Handschriften des XIV. Jahrhunderts der Nationalbibliothek in Wien (Leipzig, 1936), 17–38; M. R. James and E. G. Millar, *The Bohun Manuscripts* (London, 1936), 33–46; L. F. Sandler, *Gothic Manuscripts 1285–1385*, A Survey of Manuscripts Illuminated in the British Isles, 5, ed. J. J. G. Alexander (London, 1986), II, 147–9; L. F. Sandler, "Word Imagery in English Gothic Psalters: The Case of the Vienna Bohun Manuscript (ÖNB, cod. 1826*)," in The Illuminated Psalter, ed. F. O. Büttner (Turnhout, 2004), 281–90.

3. Psalter, Oxford, Exeter College MS. 47, begun *c.* 1360, completed *c.* 1390.

   H. O. Coxe, *Catalogus codicum MSS. qui in collegiis aulisque Oxoniensibus hodie adservantur* (Oxford, 1852), I (Codices MSS collegii Exoniensis), 17–18; London, Burlington Fine Arts Club, *Exhibition of Illuminated Manuscripts* (London, 1908), 35–36, no. 73; James and Millar, *Bohun Manuscripts*, 5–22; Sandler, *Gothic Manuscripts*, II, 149–51; L. Dennison, "Oxford, Exeter College MS. 47: The Importance of Stylistic and Codicological Analysis in Dating and Localization," in *Medieval Book Production, Assessing the Evidence*, ed. L. L. Brownrigg (Los Altos Hills, Calif., 1990), 41–60; A. G. Watson, *A Descriptive Catalogue of the Medieval Manuscripts of Exeter College, Oxford* (Oxford, 2000), 79–82.

4. Psalter and Hours of the Virgin, London, British Library MS. 3277, begun after 1361? Completed in the 1380s.

   M. Rickert, *The Reconstructed Carmelite Missal* (London, 1952), 74 n. 1; British Library, *Catalogue of Additions to the Manuscripts 1936–1945* (London, 1970), 376–81; Sandler, *Gothic Manuscripts*, II, 151–54; L. Dennison, "British Library, Egerton MS. 3277: a Fourteenth-Century Psalter-Hours and the Question of Bohun Family Ownership," in *Family and Dynasty in Late Medieval England, Proceedings of the 1997 Harlaxton Symposium*, ed. R. Eales and S. Tyas, Harlaxton Medieval Studies, IX (Donington, 2003), 122–56; L. F. Sandler, "Bared: The Writing Bear in the British Library Bohun Psalter," in *Tributes to Jonathan J. G. Alexander, The Making and Meaning of Illuminated Medieval & Renaissance Manuscripts, Art & Architecture*, ed. S. L'Engle and G. B. Guest (London, 2006), 269–80.

5. London, British Library MS. Royal 20. D. IV, Romance of Lancelot, Flanders or Artois, *c.* 1300, two repainted miniatures with Bohun arms, *c.* 1360–1380.

G. F. Warner and J. P. Gilson, *Catalogue of Western Manuscripts in the Old Royal and King's Collections* (London, 1921), II, 378; 83–84; F. Wormald, "Afterthoughts on the Stockholm Exhibition," *Konsthistorisk Tidskrift* 22 (1953), 82–83; Sandler, *Gothic Manuscripts*, II, 154–55; A. Stones, "A Note on the 'Mâitre au Menton Fuyant,'" in *"Als Ich can," Liber amicorum in Memory of Professor Dr. Maurits Smeyers*, ed. B. Cardon et al. (Leuven, 2002), 1263.

6. Psalter, Cambridge, Fitzwilliam Museum MS. 38-1950, *c.* 1380–1394, with fifteenth-century additions.

Burlington Fine Arts Club, 34–35, no. 72; G. F. W[arner], *A Descriptive Catalogue of Fourteen Illuminated Manuscripts Nos. XCV to CVI and 79A Completing the Hundred in the Library of Henry Yates Thompson* (Cambridge, 1912), 45–52, no. XCIX, reprinted with slight revisions in James and Millar, *Bohun Manuscripts*, 51–59; F. Wormald and P. M. Giles, *A Descriptive Catalogue of the Additional Illuminated Manuscripts in the Fitzwilliam Museum Acquired between 1895 and 1979 (Excluding the McClean Collection)* (Cambridge, 1982), II, 431–36; Sandler, *Gothic Manuscripts*, II, 159–61; L. F. Sandler, "Gone Fishing: Angling in the Fitzwilliam Bohun Psalter," in *Signs and Symbols*, Proceedings of the 2006 Harlaxton Symposium, ed. J. Cherry and A. Payne (Stamford, 2009), 168–79.

7. Psalter and Hours of the Virgin, Oxford, Bodleian Library MS. Auct. D.4.4, *c.* 1380–1394, with fifteenth-century additions.

F. Madan et al., *Summary Catalogue of Western Manuscripts in the Bodleian Library at Oxford*, II (Oxford, 1922), 85–66; James and Millar, *Bohun Manuscripts*, 23–32; Sandler, *Gothic Manuscripts*, II, 157–59.

8. Memoriae and Gospel Sequences from a Book of Hours, Pommersfelden, Gräflich Schönbornische Bibliothek MS. 348, *c.* 1380–1394.

Katalog der Handschriften der Gräflich von Schönbornischen Bibliothek zu Pommersfelden, IV (typewritten copy at Monumenta Germaniae Historica, Munich); Sandler, *Gothic Manuscripts*, II, 155–57; *Andachtsbücher des Mittelalters aus Privatbezitz*, ed. J. Plotzek (Cologne, 1987), no. 12.

9. Baden-Baden, Lichtenthal Abbey Archive MS. 2, Psalter (in Latin) and Short Office of the Cross (in Anglo-Norman), *c.* 1380–1394.

F. Heinzer and G. Stamm, *Die Handschriften von Lichtenthal*, Die Handschriften der Badischen Landesbibliothek in Karlsruhe, II (Wiesbaden, 1987), 350–52; F. Heinzer, "Un témoin inconnu de 'Bohun Manuscripts': Le ms. 2 des archives de l'abbaye de Lichtenthal," *Scriptorium* 43 (1989), 259–66; *Mittelalterliche Andachtsbücher*, ed. H.-P. Geh and G. Römer (Karlsruhe, 1992), 88–90; *Faszination eines Klosters, 750 Jahre Zisterzinserinnen-Abtei Lichtenthal*, ed. H. Siebenmorgan (Karlsruhe, 1995), 260–61; L. F. Sandler, *The Lichtenthal Psalter and the Manuscript Patronage of the Bohun Family* (London, 2004); L. F. Sandler, "The Anglo-Norman Office of the Cross of the Lichtenthal Psalter," in *Cultural Performances in Medieval France, Essays in Honor of Nancy Freeman Regalado*, ed. E. Doss-Quinby, R. L. Krueger, and E. J. Burns (Cambridge, 2007), 153–62.

10. Legends of the Virgin Mary, St. Margaret, and St. Mary Magdalene (in Anglo-Norman), Copenhagen, Kongelige Bibliotek MS. Thott 517.4°, *c.* 1380–1394.

N. C. L. Abrahams, *Description des manuscrits français du moyen âge de la Bibliothèque royale de Copenhague* (Copenhagen, 1844), 9; C. Bruun, *De illuminerede Haandskrifter fra Middelalderen i det Store Kongelige Bibliotek, Copenhagen* (Copenhagen, 1890), 197; E. Jorgensen, *Catalogus codicum latinorum medii aevi Bibliothecae Regiae Hafniensis* (Copenhagen, 1926), 232–33; Wormald, "Afterthoughts," 83–84; Sandler, *Gothic Manuscripts*, II, 162–63; L. F. Sandler, "Mary de Bohun's *Livret de saintes* in Copenhagen," in *Tributes to Nigel J. Morgan*, ed. J. Luxford and M. A. Michael (London, 2010), 65–76.

11. Hours of the Virgin, Copenhagen, Kongelige Bibliotek MS. Thott 547.4°, *c.* 1380–1394.

C. Bruun, *De illuminerede Haandskrifter*, 192–6; Jorgensen, *Catalogus*, 232–33; James and Millar, *Bohun Manuscripts*, 47–52; Sandler, *Gothic Manuscripts*, II, 161–62; E. Petersen, "Illuminatio, Texts and Illustrations of the Bible in the Royal Library, Copenhagen," in *International Association of Bibliophiles XVth Congress, Copenhagen 20–26 September 1987, Transactions*, ed. P. A. Christiansen (Copenhagen, 1992), 75–79; *Living Words and Luminous Pictures: Medieval Book Culture in Denmark*, ed. E. Petersen (Copenhagen, 1999), no. 20; N. Damsholt, "Women and Book Culture," in *ibid.* [Essays], 113–15.

12. Hours of the Virgin and Psalter of Eleanor de Bohun, Edinburgh, National Library of Scotland MS. Adv. 18.6.5, *c.* 1389–1397.

Burlington Fine Arts Club, 73–74, no. 150; Sandler, *Gothic Manuscripts*, II, 163–5; L. F. Sandler, "The Last Bohun Hours and Psalter," in *Tributes to Kathleen L. Scott*, ed. M. V. Hennessy (Turnhout, 2009), 231–50.

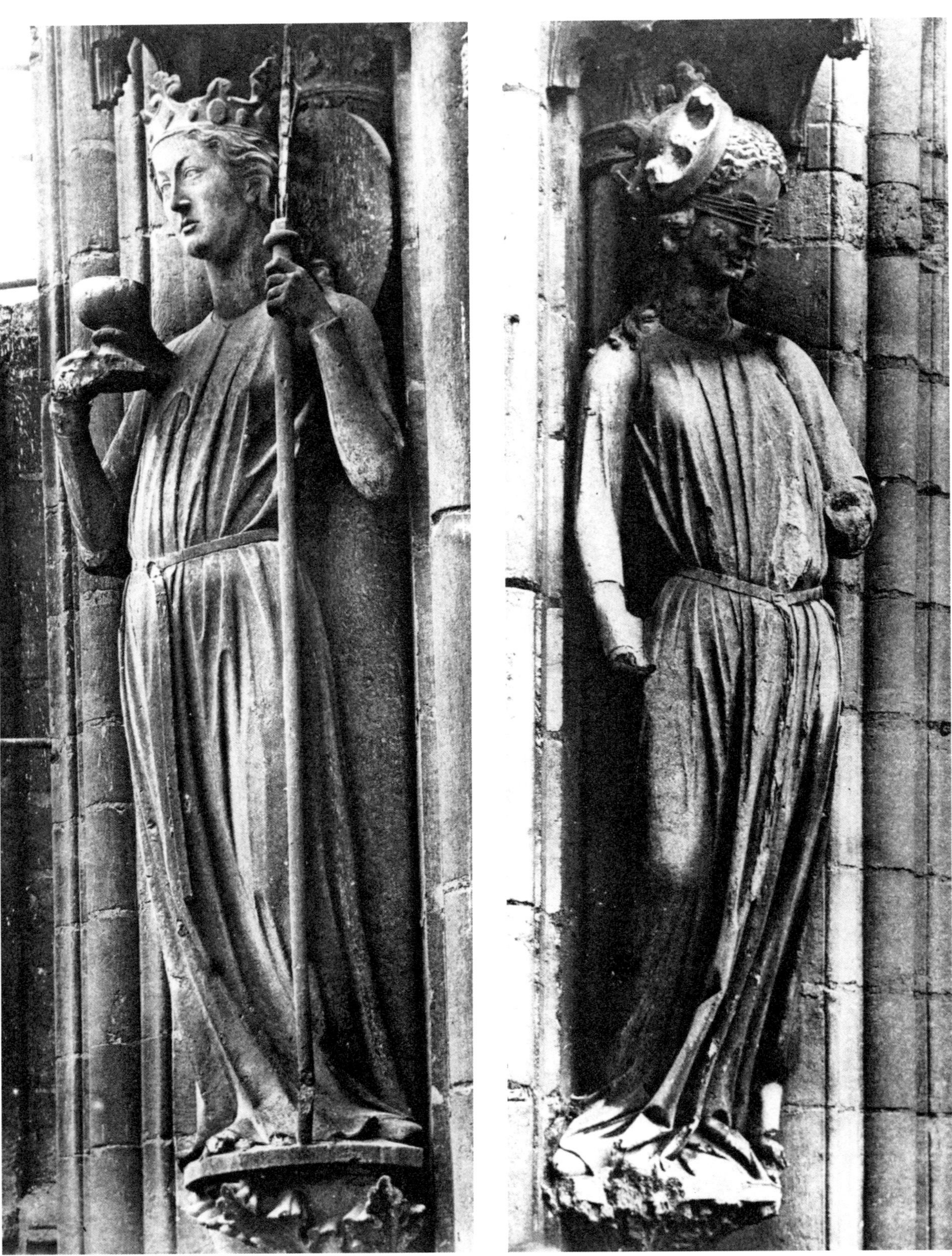

FIGURE 1. Ecclesia, south façade, Reims Cathedral (photo: Foto Marburg / Art Resource, N.Y.).

FIGURE 2. Synagoga, south façade, Reims Cathedral (photo: Foto Marburg / Art Resource, N.Y.).

NINA ROWE

Rethinking Ecclesia and Synagoga in the Thirteenth Century*

SCHOLARS and students of Gothic art are well familiar with the iconographic motif of Ecclesia and Synagoga. The paired female personifications of Church and Synagogue recur in manuscript illuminations, carved ivories, enamels, stained glass, sculpture, and panel paintings from the late twelfth century to the end of the Middle Ages to such an extent that they can be considered a favored theme of the Gothic era. In such contexts, this elastic motif can signify the harmony of the Old and New Testaments, the triumph of the Church, the backwardness of Judaism, or the hope for Jewish conversion, among other theological and societal notions. The theme is so prevalent and has been referenced so extensively in scholarship that many may wonder whether there is anything new to say about it at all. But there are key aspects of both the origins and effects of Ecclesia and Synagoga that have been overlooked and that suggest now-lost resonances of the figures pertinent specifically to the Gothic period.

My departure point for this discussion is the observation that in the years around 1225–1240, Ecclesia and Synagoga came to be a motif that was particularly favored by designers of sculpted façade programs on cathedrals across northern Europe. A consideration of the figures in this era, within the sole medium of monumental sculpture, allows for examination of the theme in the years that it was first introduced to broad urban audiences, making possible an assessment of the motif's reception in both sacred and social terms. The three best surviving exemplars from this period are the paired sculptures on cathedral entrances at Reims, Bamberg, and Strasbourg, all created around 1225 (Figs. 1, 2, 3, 4, 5 and 6).[1] What unites the figures at these sites is that in each instance the female personifications of Church and Synagogue are affiliated with images of ideal male rulership. At Reims Cathedral, colossal figures of Ecclesia and Synagoga are installed high up on the cathedral's south façade, where they flank a rose window and are surrounded by seven images of kings—part of a larger program around the building's east end featuring fourteen kings in total. At Bamberg Cathedral, over-lifesized images of Ecclesia and Synagoga stand atop the two pillars at either side of the *Fürstenportal* at the building's northern flank. Thus installed, the female personifications greet visitors entering the space dominated by the celebrated Bamberg Rider

* This essay previews some of the conclusions in my forthcoming book, *The Jew, the Cathedral, and the Medieval City: Synagoga & Ecclesia in the Thirteenth Century* (Cambridge University Press). Research for this project was made possible by a Sylvan C. Coleman and Pamela Coleman Memorial Fund Art History Fellowship from The Metropolitan Museum of Art (2007–2008). I thank the members of the Medieval Department of the Metropolitan Museum for support and guidance during my fellowship year. A grant from the Ames Fund for Junior Faculty, Fordham University, covered the costs of photographs and permissions. Thanks are also due to Libby Parker for reading my work in multiple versions and to Glenn Hendler for proofreading, technical assistance, and all around good humor.

1. Ecclesia and Synagoga also were included among the sculpted figures on the north porch at Chartres and at the west façade of Notre-Dame de Paris (both *c.* 1220), but these have now been destroyed. At Notre-Dame, replicas apparently following late medieval models were installed in the nineteenth century on the west façade. The larger iconographic contexts of these façades accord in general terms with the ensembles at Reims, Bamberg, and Strasbourg, supporting my overall thesis about the use of the Ecclesia–Synagoga motif in public settings in the first half of the thirteenth century. On the figures at Chartres and Notre-Dame, see P. C. Claussen, *Chartres-Studien: zur Vorgeschichte, Funktion und Skulptur der Vorhallen* (Wiesbaden, 1975), 135–140; and W. Sauerländer, *Gothic Sculpture in France, 1140–1270* (London, 1972), 450–457.

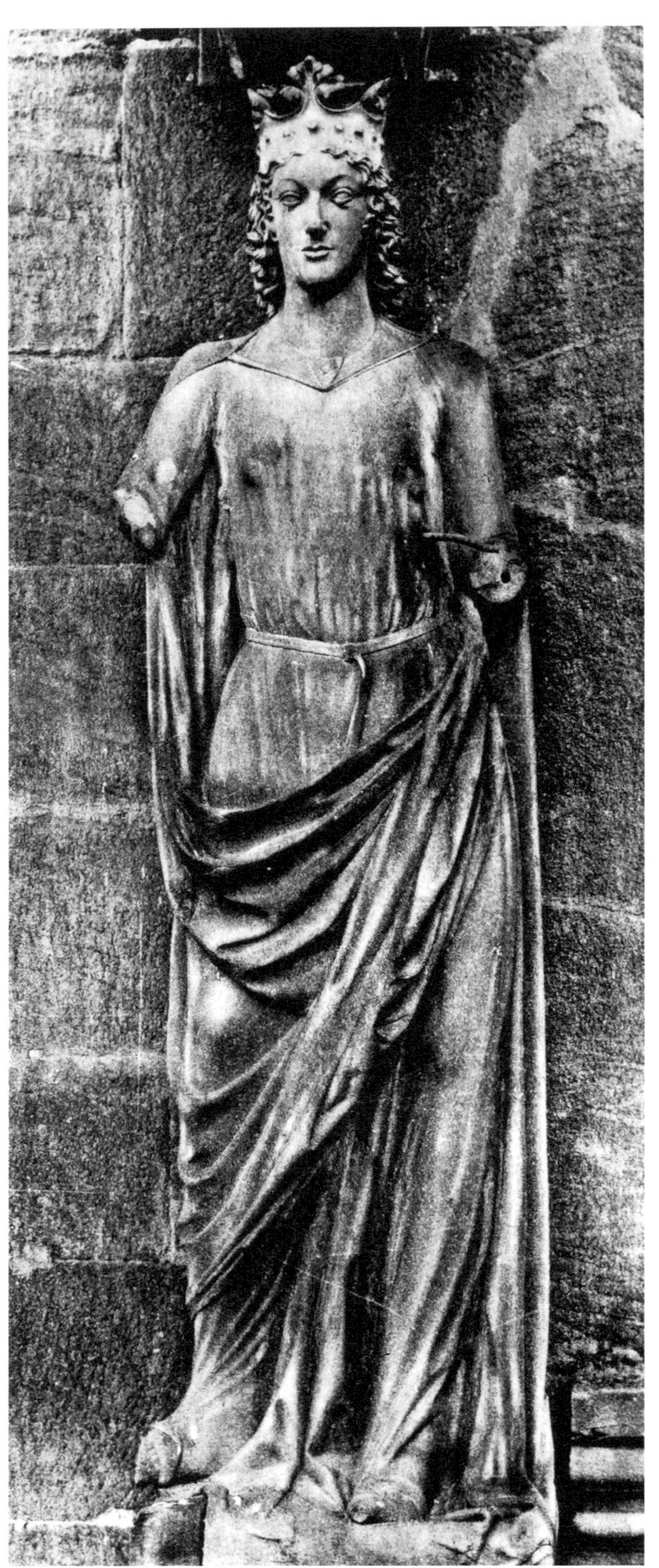

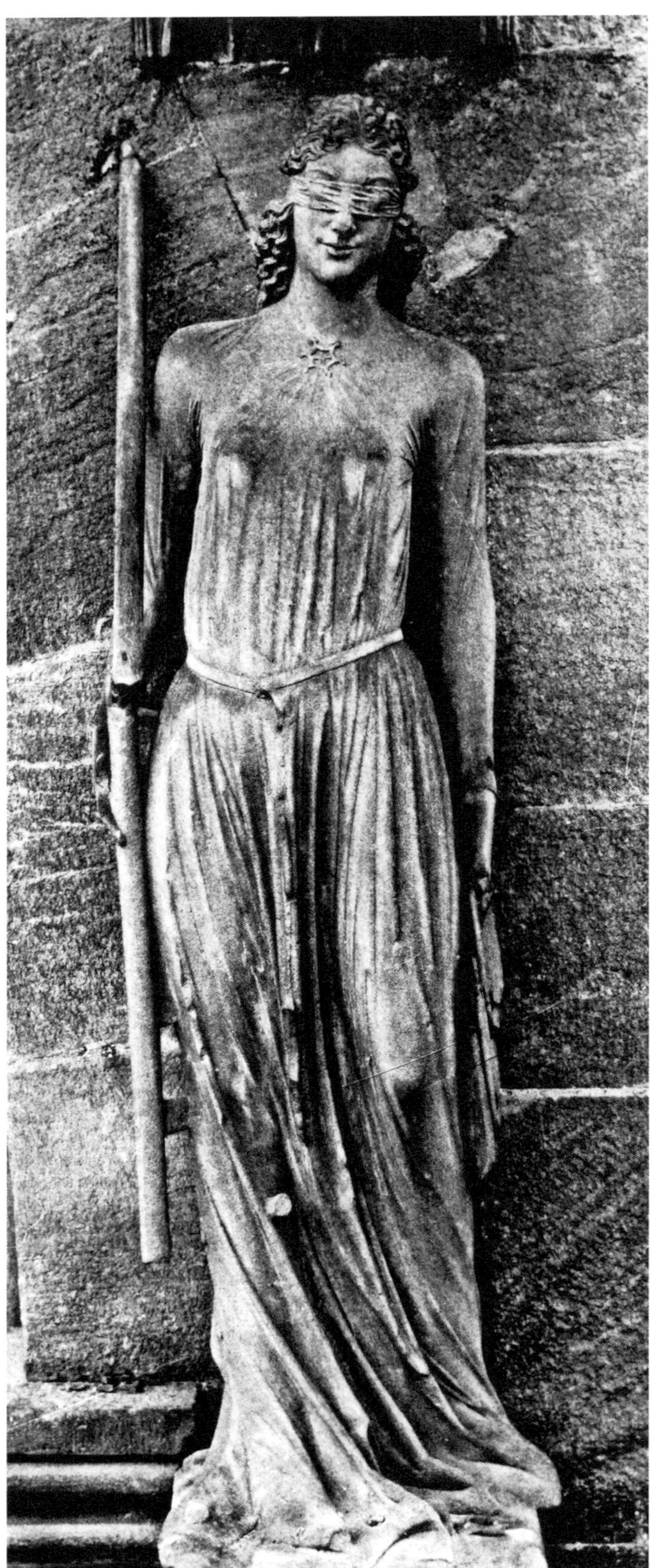

FIGURE 3. Ecclesia, north façade, Bamberg Cathedral (photo: Foto Marburg / Art Resource, N.Y.).

FIGURE 4. Synagoga, north façade, Bamberg Cathedral (photo: Foto Marburg / Art Resource, N.Y.).

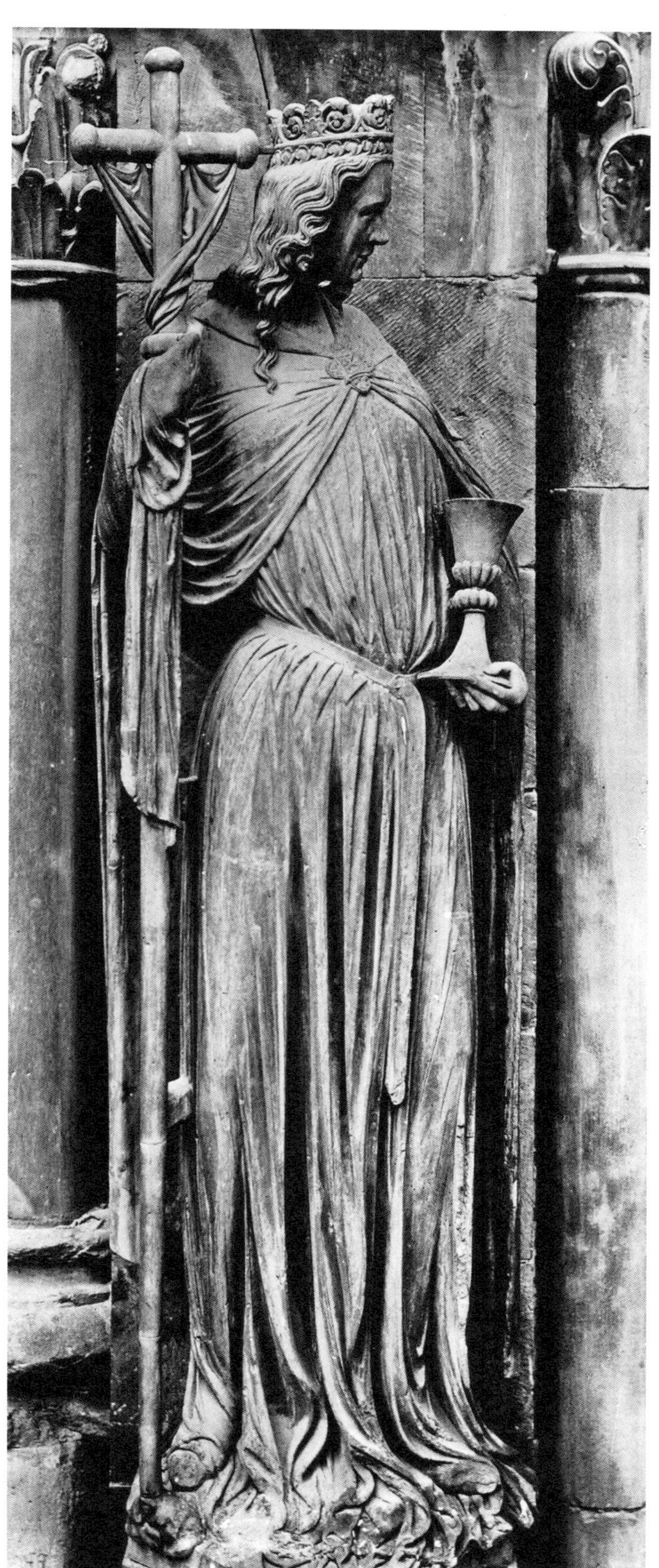

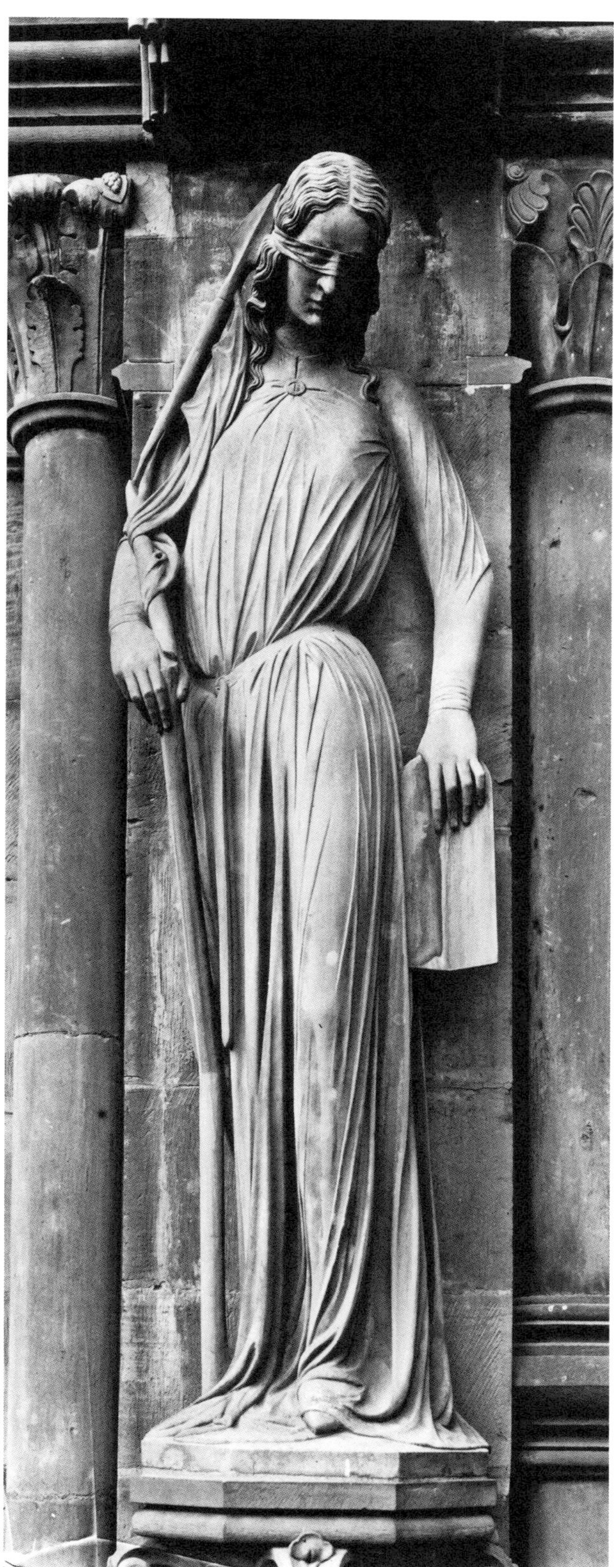

FIGURE 5. Ecclesia, south façade, Strasbourg Cathedral (photo: Foto Marburg / Art Resource, N.Y.).

FIGURE 6. Synagoga, south façade, Strasbourg Cathedral (photo: Foto Marburg / Art Resource, N.Y.).

sculpture. At Strasbourg, personifications of Church and Synagogue, again over-lifesized, enter the space of the viewer, appearing low down and bracketing the cathedral's south façade, dominated at the center by a sculpture of King Solomon (see Fig. 12).

Focusing on monumental, public representations of Ecclesia and Synagoga in the second quarter of the thirteenth century, I concern myself with two principal questions. First, why was it that this motif suddenly became popular as a hinge element in some of the most lavish and ambitious cathedral façade programs of the day? And second, what did these works teach their audiences of urban viewers about the position of Jews in an ideally ordered Christian realm? To address these issues, I investigate what I take to be the antique origins of both the Ecclesia–Synagoga theme and its association with images of male rulership, considering as well how the figures exemplify a vogue for classicizing stylistic trends in the early thirteenth century. I assess the enthusiasm for the motif as a response to new anxieties about the status of Jews in Christian society, and thus argue that, in their monumental and public form, the figures had an emphatically political meaning. I round out my discussion with an examination of the figures of Ecclesia and Synagoga on the south façade of Strasbourg Cathedral, considering the reception of the sculptures within their urban *milieu*. Ultimately, I hope that my analysis contributes to our understanding of Gothic visual programs as ensembles that, through the exploitation of naturalistic style, insisted on the legitimacy of concocted images of order, images that often stood in opposition to realities on the street.

Ecclesia & Synagoga in the Scholarship

To begin this investigation, it is worthwhile to review briefly the historiography of the Ecclesia–Synagoga motif, and thus to demonstrate how this essay builds on, but departs from, existing scholarship. The foundational study of the theme is Paul Weber's *Geistliches Schauspiel und kirchliche Kunst* of 1894.[2] In this groundbreaking book, Weber seeks to demonstrate the influence of sacred dramas on visual production by reviewing texts dating from the early through the late Middle Ages and matching their descriptions of Ecclesia and Synagoga to various artistic representations. Weber's study is a gold mine, an indispensable compendium of textual treatments of the theme. And Weber is admirably forthright in his conviction that together Ecclesia and Synagoga functioned as a tool through which clerics sought to foster enmity toward Jews, thereby demonstrating that the spread of this motif contributed to society-wide hostilities. Weber's study invites reflection on the particular historical contingencies surrounding the sites under discussion, although this author stops short of considering relevant political, social, or economic factors in any sustained way. Other studies have focused more specifically on textual instances of Ecclesia and Synagoga, addressing pictorial representations only in passing.[3] More accessible to Anglo-American audiences is Wolfgang Seiferth's *Synagogue and Church in the Middle Ages: Two Symbols in Art and Literature*, published in English after the German original in 1970.[4] Addressing images dating from the Early Christian period to the Reformation in media, including carved ivories, manuscript illumination, enamels, monumental sculpture, and painting, and discussing theological and liturgical texts, as well as the general history of Jewish-Christian relations throughout the Middle Ages, this book is valuable in its expansive sweep. But while Seiferth's study has become a standard reference for scholars in a variety of disciplines, the breadth of the material covered in it precludes tenable conclusions about the production or reception of many of the works discussed.[5] Beyond these studies, encyclopaedias of iconography catalogue a range of

2. P. Weber, *Geistliches Schauspiel und kirchliche Kunst in ihrem Verhältnis erläutert an einer Ikonographie der Kirche und Synagoge* (Stuttgart, 1894).

3. H. Pflaum, *Die religiöse Disputation in der europäischen Dichtung des Mittelalters*, pt. 1, *Der allegorische Streit zwischen Synagoge und Kirche* (Geneva and Florence, 1935). Observations in this and Weber's text (as in note 2) are reformulated in A. Oepke, *Das neue Gottesvolk in Schrifttum, Schauspiel, bildender Kunst und Weltgestaltung* (Gütersloh, 1950), chapters 10 and 11.

4. W. Seiferth, *Synagogue and Church in the Middle Ages: Two Symbols in Art and Literature*, trans. L. Chadeayne and P. Gottwald [c1964] (New York, 1970).

5. Propositions in Weber's *Geistliches Schauspiel* and Seiferth's *Synagogue and Church* (as in notes 2 and 4), as well as related scholar-

images of Ecclesia and Synagoga and introduce corresponding written sources.[6] Typically, these discussions note that images of Synagoga became increasingly defamatory as animus toward Jews quickened across Europe from the late eleventh century on. General surveys of images of Jews in medieval art likewise review a range of instances of the motif, identifying and grouping image types.[7] A recent exhibition catalogue devoted just to representations of Ecclesia and Synagoga supplements such surveys by offering a useful compilation of images.[8]

But for those committed to interrogating the uses and effects of cultural productions in specific historical *milieux*, most of the previous scholarship on the Ecclesia–Synagoga motif leaves gaps because the figures tend to be isolated from both their larger iconographic and historical contexts. Tracking gestures, attributes, and, only occasionally, the visual settings of the figures, questions regarding medium, scale, style, patronage, and particularly viewership tend to be unexplored. Exceptions to these trends are found in recent analyses of the monumental sculptures that most concern me. Helga Sciurie recognizes that renderings of Ecclesia and Synagoga on high medieval cathedral portals both responded to and helped shape urban conceptions of virtue and justice, although her discussion is brief and general, and contemporary ideas about Jews fall out of her analysis altogether.[9] Annette Weber takes on more directly the conditions for viewing monumental figures of Ecclesia and Synagoga, specifically at the cathedral of Strasbourg.[10] Her suggestive discussion runs parallel to some of the insights I offer below, but Weber gives little consideration to the local status of Jews and the regional political scene—issues at the heart of my analysis. Other recent studies consider works in the specific media of illumination and painting, recognizing, if only implicitly, the effects of scale and medium.[11]

Jews in a Christian World

To explain the tight correlation between early thirteenth-century public sculpted renderings of Ecclesia and Synagoga and contemporary political and social concerns regarding Jews requires a brief overview of the fundamental elements of the Christian idea of the Jew in the Middle Ages, and an understanding of how these conceptions began to be tested in the twelfth and thirteenth centuries. In the simplest terms, Christianity conceives of Judaism as a tradition it has superseded.[12] In this understanding, Hebrew scripture recounts the history, customs, and prophecies of God's

---

ship discussed below, is reassessed and summarized in F. Böhmisch, "Exegetische Wurzel antijudaistischer Motive in der christlichen Kunst," *Das Münster* 50, no. 4 (1997), 345–358.

6. Iconographic encyclopedias include A. Weis, "Ekklesia und Synagoge," in *Reallexikon zur deutschen Kunstgeschichte*, ed. E. Gall and L. H. Heydenreich (Stuttgart, 1958), Vol. 4, 1189–1215; W. Greisenegger, "Ecclesia und Synagoge," in *Lexikon der christlichen Ikonographie*, ed. E. Kirschbaum (Rome, 1968), Vol. 1, 569–578; and G. Schiller, *Ikonographie der christlichen Kunst* (Gütersloh, 1976), Vol. 4, Pt. 1, 45–68.

7. For example, B. Blumenkranz, *Le juif médiéval au miroir de l'art chrétien* (Paris, 1966), 59–66 and 105–115; R. Mellinkoff, *Outcasts: Signs of Otherness in Northern European Art of the Late Middle Ages*, 2 vols. (Berkeley, 1993), Vol. 1, 48–51 and 217–220; H. Schreckenberg, *The Jews in Christian Art: An Illustrated History* (New York: Continuum, 1996), 31–73; and J.-F. Faü, *L'Image des juifs dans l'art chrétien médiéval* (Paris, 2005), 29–60 (worth note is Faü's incorrect identification of a drawing of Synagoga at Bamberg as the lost figure from Chartres, fig. 23, among other errors).

8. H. Jochum, ed., *Ecclesia und Synagoga: Das Judentum in der christlichen Kunst—Ausstellungskatalog* (Essen and Saarbrücken, 1993).

9. H. Sciurie, "Ecclesia und Synagoge an den Domen zu Straßburg, Bamberg, Magdeburg und Erfurt: Körpersprachliche Wandlungen im gestalterischen Kontext," *Wiener Jahrbuch für Kunstgeschichte* 46–47 (1993–1994), 679–687 and 871–874. Less developed observations in the same vein are found in *idem*, "Ecclesia und Synagoge: Bilder von Sinnlichkeit und Gewalt am deutschen Kirchenportal des 13. Jahrhunderts," in *Blick-Wechsel: Konstruktionen von Männlichkeit und Weiblichkeit in Kunst und Kunstgeschichte*, ed. I. Lindner et al. (Berlin, 1989), 243–250.

10. A. Weber, "Glaube und Wissen—Ecclesia et Synagoga," in *Wissenspopularisierung: Konzepte der Wissensverbreitung im Wandel*, ed. C. Kretschmann (Berlin, 2003), 89–126.

11. Noteworthy examples are A. Timmermann, "The Avenging Crucifix: Some Observations on the Iconography of the Living Cross," *Gesta* 40/2 (2001), 141–160; and S. Lipton, "The Temple is my Body: Gender, Carnality and Synagoga in the *Bible moralisée*," in *Imagining the Self, Imagining the Other: Visual Representation and Jewish-Christian Dynamics in the Middle Ages and Early Modern Period*, ed. E. Frojmovic (Leiden, 2002), 129–163.

12. Recent studies have taken this key aspect of Jewish-Christian relations as a departure point. See K. Biddick, *The Typology of*

original "chosen" people, but with the incarnation, the laws of Leviticus, Numbers, and Deuteronomy are abrogated, and the text that records them is considered an "Old" Testament, a shadowy precursor to the New. Paul articulates this notion forcefully in his letter to the Romans where he invokes the Genesis story of the twins Jacob and Esau (Gen. 25:21–34). The brothers emerged from Rebecca's womb already struggling with one another, a contest explained by the voice of God as a presage for a future defined by conflict: "Two nations are in your womb," says the Lord to Rebecca. "Two peoples, born of you, shall be divided" (Gen. 25:23).[13] Esau, emerging from the womb first, held the family birthright. But, foolishly, he did not value this divinely-granted preëminence, and in exchange for a lowly bowl of lentils, ceded his privileged position to Jacob, who eventually gained the blessing from their father, Isaac. Paul invokes this tale as a prophecy of the relationship of Judaism and Christianity: "The elder shall serve the younger" (Rom. 9:12). Although the Jews were God's original chosen people, in the new Christian age these "children of the flesh" who still cling to ancient laws are rejected in favor of the "children of the promise," now deemed to be the true descendants of Abraham (Rom. 9:8).

Augustine's conception of Jews and their place in history and society built on Paul and set standards and expectations that were to prevail in the early Middle Ages. By the time that this church father wrote in the late fourth and early fifth centuries, Christians could take it as a given that God had abandoned his original chosen people, and that now followers of Christ constituted the "True Israel" (*verus Israel*).[14] In this schema, Jews get cast as outdated representatives of the earlier age—old folks who stick around to remind others to revel in the vigor of a youth that has discovered a more righteous way. "Why," asks Augustine in his *Tractatus adversus Iudaeos*, "do the Jews not realize that they remained stationary in useless antiquity [*in vetustate supervacanea*], rather than hurl charges against us, who hold fast to the new promises ...?"[15] But for Augustine, Jews still had a critical role in Christian history and hermeneutics. Understood as living testaments to the pre-history of the church, and thus the longevity of the tradition, Jews were sanctioned keepers of the Old Testament, living witnesses who could "carry" the books for the good of Christians, but who failed to understand the meaning therein. "Our librarians are what they have become," as he puts it.[16] Augustine could also conceptualize these keepers of the Old Testament as minions in service to Christian truth: "[J]ust as it is customary for servants [*capsarii*] to carry books behind their masters, so that those who carry faint and those who read profit," so too the Jews carry the books for Christians.[17]

Such notions of the Jew—preserved in Christian society to protect Old Testament scripture for the benefit of Christians—held sway in northern Europe

---

the Imaginary: Circumcision, Technology, History (Philadelphia, 2003); and K. Stow, *Jewish Dogs: An Image and its Interpreters—Continuity in the Catholic-Jewish Encounter* (Stanford, Calif., 2006).

13. I. J. Yuval takes this tale as the principal framing device for his examination of the Jewish-Christian encounter in *Two Nations in Your Womb: Perceptions of Jews and Christians in Late Antiquity and the Middle Ages*, trans. B. Harshav and J. Chipman (Berkeley, 2006).

14. The foundational studies on Augustine and the Jews are B. Blumenkranz, *Die Judenpredigt Augustins* [c1946] (Paris, 1973); and *idem*, "Augustin et les juifs: Augustin et le judaïsme," *Recherches augustiniennes* 1 (1958), 225–41. Blumenkranz's conclusions have been augmented and refined in the works of Cohen, cited below, and P. Fredriksen, *Augustine and the Jews: A Christian Defense of Jews and Judaism* (New York, 2008), as well as other discussions by this author, cited within her bibliography. Fredriksen's book offers an exacting analysis of the development of Augustine's conceptions of Jews in relation to the spiritual climate of his day. As such, she presents a nuanced exposition of the ideas that I cast here in broad terms. For a key assessment of the historiography, see J. Cohen "'Slay them Not': Augustine and the Jews in Modern Scholarship," *Medieval Encounters* 4, no. 1 (1998), 78–92.

15. Augustine, *Tractatus adversus Iudaeos* 6:8, Migne PL 42: 56. Translation in: Augustine, *The Fathers of the Church*, Vol. 27, *Treatises on Marriage and Other Subjects*, trans. C. Wilcox et al. (New York, 1955), 400.

16. Discussed in J. Cohen's important work, *Living Letters of the Law: Ideas of the Jew in Medieval Christianity* (Berkeley, 1999), 35–41. For the librarian formulation, see, for example, Augustine, *Enarrationes in Psalmos* 56:9 *CCSL* 39, 700. ("*Librarii nostri facti sunt, quomodo solent serui post dominos codices ferre, ut illi portando deficient, illi legendo proficiant.*")

17. "*Maior seruiet minori modo impletum est; modo, fratres nobis seruiunt Iudaei, tanquam capsarii nostri sunt, studentibus nobis codices portant.*" Augustine, *Enarrationes in Psalmos* 40:14 *CCSL* 38, 459. See discussion by Cohen (section cited in note 16).

throughout the early Middle Ages, in large part, it seems to me, because the intellectual lights of the age had few encounters with actual Jews. Certainly there were some churchmen, notably Isidore of Seville in the seventh century and Agobard of Lyons in the ninth, who railed against the Jews, but their objections did not ignite broad social reconceptualizations of the idea of the Jew.[18] It was only when Christians began to concern themselves with the reform of society, seeking to echo heavenly perfection in the earthly realm, and when Jews and Christians started to live side by side in northern European urban centers, that Christians became aware of Jews on a broad scale in social and not just theological terms, and started to recognize that Augustinian ideals for Jewish status did not match reality.[19]

In the era between *c.* 980 and 1200, hundreds of Jews, it seems, migrated from southern European and Middle Eastern centers and settled in the kingdoms of Germany, France, and England to take advantage of the new economic opportunities in the North.[20] Many of the initial communities were established at the invitation of secular rulers who identified Jews as a force that could jump-start local fiscal expansion because of their storied mercantile acumen.[21] When they got there, Jews often settled in streets at the center of town, living collectively but by no means cut off from the larger Christian society. Christians and Jews would encounter one another in city squares daily, and Christians regularly turned to Jewish moneylenders for loans large and small.[22] Jewish dominance in the high medieval money trades is well known, though the reasons for it are sometimes little understood. In the simplest terms, scripture prohibited the charging of interest to one's co-religionists,[23] and so, in principle, Jews were the only population within European society on hand and warranted to participate in the credit market. Jews, thereby, quickly became intimately associated with moneylending in the popular imagination, despite the fact that Jews wrangled among themselves over the propriety of the practice and economic intercourse with Christians in general.[24] In the mid-twelfth century, Bernard of Clairvaux, for example, could complain in this oft-quoted excerpt: "wherever there are no Jews, we lament that Christian moneylenders ... behave Jewishly in a manner even worse [*peius iudaizare*]."[25] Secular and ecclesiastical lords protected the Jewish monopoly on the money trades, relying on the ready flow of capital borrowed from Jews and accrued through taxing Jewish gains to support building projects, wage wars, and sustain lavish courts. Jews thus became an essential cog within the economic machinery of the high Middle Ages.

Some clerical Christians also had intellectual con-

18. See B. Blumenkranz, *Juifs et chrétiens dans le monde occidental, 430–1096* [c1960] (Paris, Louvain, and Dudley, Mass., 2006), 213–279; and Cohen, *Living Letters* (as in note 16), 95–145.

19. For a broad formulation of this development, see R. I. Moore, *The Formation of a Persecuting Society: Power and Deviance in Western Europe, 950–1250* (Oxford, 1987).

20. Under the leadership of Alfred Haverkamp, a team of scholars at the Arye Maimon-Institüt für Geschichte der Juden at the University of Trier has made revolutionary contributions to the study of Jewish settlement and life in western Europe. Any examination of the medieval Ashkenazim should begin with A. Haverkamp and R. Barzen, eds., *Geschichte der Juden im Mittelalter von der Nordsee bis zu den Südalpen: Kommentiertes Kartenwerk*, 3 vols. (Hannover, 2002).

21. For an overview (with some historical errors), see the classic L. K. Little, *Religious Poverty and the Profit Economy of Medieval Europe* (Ithaca, 1978), 42–46. More reliable general discussions are: K. R. Stow, *Alienated Minority: The Jews of Medieval Latin Europe* (Cambridge, Mass., 1992), 210–230; and R. Chazan, *The Jews of Medieval Western Christendom, 1000–1500* (Cambridge, 2006), 129–198.

22. On Jewish-Christian interaction in cities, see I. Marcus, "A Jewish-Christian Symbiosis: The Culture of Early Ashkenaz," in *Cultures of the Jews: A New History*, ed. D. Biale (New York, 2002), 448–516; and the essays in C. Cluse, ed., *The Jews of Europe in the Middle Ages (Tenth to Fifteenth Centuries): Proceedings of the International Symposium held at Speyer, 20–25 October 2002* (Turnhout, 2004).

23. Exodus 22:25, Deuteronomy 23:19–20, Leviticus 25:35–37, and Luke 6:34–35.

24. See J. Katz, *Exclusiveness and Tolerance: Studies in Jewish-Gentile Relations in Medieval and Modern Times* (Oxford, 1961), 27–36.

25. Cohen, *Living Letters* (as in note 16), 234–236, at 236. For further equations of Jews with the money trades, see S. Lipton, "The Root of all Evil: Jews, Money and Metaphor in the *Bible moralisée*," *Medieval Encounters* 1, no. 2 (1995), 301–322; *idem*, *Images of Intolerance: The Representation of Jews and Judaism in the Bible moralisée* (Berkeley, 1999), 30–53; K. Stow, "Papal and Royal Attitudes toward Jewish Lending in the Thirteenth Century," *AJS Review* 6 (1981), 161–184, at 179; and R. Chazan, *Medieval Stereotypes and Modern Antisemitism* (Berkeley, 1997), 105–109.

tacts with Jews, turning to leading rabbis for guidance in the study of scripture, a phenomenon notably explored by Beryl Smalley in *The Study of the Bible in the Middle Ages*, and chronicled in dialogue such texts as Gilbert Crispin's well-known "Disputation of a Jew with a Christian."[26] When Christians got to know actual Jews, they learned that the population did not conform to the characterization of timid librarians or servants conceived by Augustine. First, Christians discovered that Jewish theological traditions had not stagnated with the formation of the church, and that the Talmud—that post-biblical compendium of midrash, custom and folklore—and not simply the so-called "Old" Testament, stood at the center of Jewish intellectual and ritual life. Moreover, contemporary Jewish religious and social practices were determined by an impressive body of rabbis, leading figures among whom were the celebrated Rashi and other members of his family.[27] Jews, it turned out, were not blindly keeping to the customs and rituals of the ancient Israelites for the good of Christians, but instead were undergoing a scholarly renaissance that rivaled the intellectual and reformist revival of contemporary Christians in the long twelfth century. Likely more surprising was the discovery that some Jews composed anti-Christian polemics, ridiculing Christian interpretation of Hebrew scripture and the fundamentals of church doctrine—these texts being a counter to the *adversus Iudaeos* tracts found in Christian theology from the patristic era on.[28]

I offer a few examples from this genre that is only just beginning to be explored by scholars.[29] One work, known as the *Book of the Covenant*, by rabbi Joseph Kimhi of twelfth-century Narbonne, exemplifies a multitude of denunciations of the core Christian belief that Mary of Nazareth was a Virgin when she gave birth to Jesus. The critical passage of Isaiah 7:14, of course, refers to an *almah*, a "young girl" in Hebrew, not a virgin. Kimhi thus mocks what he deems to be Jerome's mistranslation which "led you [Christians] astray and caused you to err."[30] Another text, the *Nizzahon Vetus* (Old Book of Polemic), a late thirteenth-century Ashkenazic work that draws upon earlier traditions, observes ironically that in other cases Christians turn to Jews for their authoritative experience with the Hebrew of biblical scripture, the book of Isaiah being, "after all, in our possession."[31] Jewish polemicists further observe the lack of any overt association between the Isaiah text and Mary of Nazareth: "The prophet said that an *almah* would give birth to a son. So what? ... [H]ow do you know this [girl] is Mary? Where do you find her name ... ?"[32] And the texts cast further aspersions on the motivations behind Mary's claims to virginity while in a chaste marriage: "To say that a virgin will give birth [would seem] dubious to people, for they will not believe that she did not play the harlot."[33] Christian ritual is consistently derided as well. In these polemical texts baptism, for example, is sometimes likened to a satanic dousing in "impure waters," and the

26. B. Smalley, *The Study of the Bible in the Middle Ages*, 3rd ed. (Oxford, 1983), 149–172; A. S. Abulafia and G. R. Evans, *The Works of Gilbert Crispin Abbot of Westminster* (Oxford, 1986).

27. For good introductions to high medieval Jewish intellectual life, see Stow, *Alienated Minority* (as in note 21), 135–156; and Chazan, *Jews of Medieval Western Christendom* (as in note 21), 243–283.

28. A useful overview is G. Dahan, *The Christian Polemic against the Jews in the Middle Ages*, trans. J. Gladding (Notre Dame, Ind., 1998).

29. Scholarship analyzing Jewish anti-Christian invective has long been available to readers of Hebrew, but until recently English-language publications on the phenomenon have been limited. Earlier contributions are: E. I. J. Rosenthal, "Anti-Christian Polemic in Medieval Bible Commentaries," *Journal of Jewish Studies* 11, nos. 3–4 (1960), 115–135; Katz, *Exclusiveness and Tolerance* (as in note 24), 106–113; D. Berger, *The Jewish-Christian Debate in the High Middle Ages—A Critical Edition of the Nizzahon Vetus* [c1979] (Northvale, N.J., 1996). Recent work that has inspired my own approach is R. Chazan, *Fashioning Jewish Identity in Medieval Western Christendom* (Cambridge, 2004); E. Horowitz, *Reckless Rites: Purim and the Legacy of Jewish Violence* (Princeton, 2006); P. Schäfer, *Jesus in the Talmud* (Princeton, 2007). In the art-historical realm, see the important study K. Kogman-Appel, "The Tree of Death and the Tree of Life: The Hanging of Haman in Medieval Jewish Manuscript Painting," in *Between the Picture and the Word: Manuscript Studies from the Index of Christian Art*, ed. C. Hourihane (Princeton, 2005), 187–208, figs. 262–273.

30. J. Kimhi, *The Book of the Covenant*, trans. F. Talmage, Medieval Sources in Translation, 12 (Toronto, 1972), 54.

31. *Nizzahon Vetus*, no. 86: Berger, *The Jewish-Christian Debate* (as in note 29), 103.

32. *Nizzahon Vetus*, no. 86: Berger, *The Jewish Debate-Christian* (as in note 29), 103.

33. Kimhi, *The Book of the Covenant* (as in note 30), 54.

rite of confession is deemed just a ruse so that priests can learn the names of loose women with whom they might later pursue their own sinful couplings.[34]

Jewish expressions of scorn for Christ could become more pointed still. An important recent study by Peter Schäfer examines rare manuscript and early printed versions of the Talmud to discern that medieval versions of the text were peppered with denunciations of Jesus and his mother, mocking those aspects of the Christian story at the heart of Christian belief.[35] Jesus is said to be the bastard child of an adulteress, the farthest thing from the son of God; he appears as a disobedient and a sexually lewd student; his power to heal is mocked; his execution is presented as righteous punishment for his idolatry and dereliction; and rather than resurrected, Jesus is said to be punished eternally in hell, boiling in excrement. Similar mocking tales, elaborated further, appear in the parodic polemical work *Toledot Yeshu* (History of Jesus), written in western Europe in the early Middle Ages and broadly circulated thereafter.[36] New awareness of the contents of the Talmud spread with the theological explorations of Peter Alfonsi and Peter the Venerable and culminated in the infamous Talmud Trial in Paris in 1240.[37] Of course, self-protection required that Jews keep denunciations of Christianity to themselves, and there is limited (though still compelling) evidence of public outbursts expressing such opinions.[38] Nonetheless, with Jews and Christians living side by side in cities and encountering one another regularly through economic, intellectual, and perhaps social interactions, not to mention the confidences revealed by Jewish converts to Christianity, it is apparent that Christians got word of Jewish contempt for key aspects of Christian dogma and tradition. With such revelations, Christians were confronted with the fact that the Jews of twelfth- and thirteenth-century Ashkenaz were far from the docile librarians and servants that Augustine had promised. Northern European communities of this era were proud, financially successful, creative, and sometimes obstreperous—a people who, in the eyes of Christian authorities of the day, needed to be kept in their place.

As I see it, the early thirteenth-century institutionalization of identifying dress for Jews, initiatives aimed at limiting Jewish profiteering in the money trades, and the Talmud Trial, with its subsequent burning of twenty-four cartloads of Jewish books at the center of Paris, can all be understood as developments parallel to the installation of images of Synagoga on cathedral façades in the same era across northern Europe.[39] Both action and image materialized a drive to reconfigure the Jew to fit the Christian mold. Synagoga, as an embodiment of the Jewish tradition, is shown as downtrodden, weakened, and contained (see Figs. 2, 4, and 6). But she

34. *Nizzahon Vetus*, nos. 231 and 236: Berger, *The Jewish-Christian Debate* (as in note 29), 219–220 and 223–224.

35. Schäfer, *Jesus in the Talmud* (as in note 29).

36. For texts and analysis, see S. Krauss, *Das Leben Jesu nach jüdischen Quellen* (Berlin, 1902); and G. Schlichting, *Ein jüdisches Leben Jesu: Die verschollene Toledot-Jeschu-Fassung Tam u-mu'ad: Einleitung, Text, Übersetzung, Kommentar, Motivsynopse, Bibliographie* (Tübingen, 1982). An English translation of one version is in: H. W. Basser, "The Acts of Jesus," in *The Frank Talmage Memorial Volume*, ed. Barry Walfish (Hanover, N.H., 1993), 273–82. A new edition is being prepared using a manuscript recently acquired by Princeton University (Schäfer, *Jesus in the Talmud* [as in note 29], 145, n. 3). See also W. Horbury, "The Trial of Jesus in the Jewish Tradition," in *The Trial of Jesus: Cambridge Studies in Honor of C. F. D. Moule*, ed. E. Bammel (Naperville, Ill., 1970), 103–21; D. Biale, "Counter-History and Jewish Polemics against Christianity: The 'Sefer toldot yeshu' and the 'Sefer zerubavel,'" *Jewish Social Studies* 6, no. 1 (1999), 130–45; and J. Dan, "Toledot Yeshu," in *Encyclopaedia Judaica*, 2nd ed. 20 (Detroit, 2007), 28–9.

37. For introductions to Peter Alfonsi and Peter the Venerable on Jews, see the discussion in A. S. Abulafia, *Christians and Jews in the Twelfth-Century Renaissance* (London and New York, 1995). Key examinations of the Talmud trial—discussions that feature an internal scholarly debate of their own—are found in J. Cohen, *The Friars and the Jews: The Evolution of Medieval Anti-Judaism* (Ithaca, N.Y., and London, 1982), 60–76; *idem*, *Living Letters* (as in note 16), 317–363; R. Chazan, "The Condemnation of the Talmud Reconsidered (1239–1248)," *Proceedings of the American Academy for Jewish Research* 55 (1988), 11–30; *idem*, *Daggers of Faith: Thirteenth-Century Christian Missionizing and Jewish Response* (Berkeley, 1989), 25–37 and 170–181.

38. See Horowitz, *Reckless Rites* (as in note 29), 149–185; and Marcus, "A Jewish-Christian Symbiosis" (as in note 20), 478–484.

39. Introductory discussion of such constraints are found in Stow, *Alienated Minority*; and Chazan, *Jews of Medieval Western Christendom* (both as in note 21).

is also beautiful, a figure who is patently part of the Christian system. This aestheticization of the defeated Synagogue draws directly on ancient classical conventions, an issue I turn to presently.

Antique Origins & Political Resonances

The tendency to personify abstract concepts in female forms, of course, was a mainstay of antique pictorial programs and texts. The Romans harnessed the approach and exploited it particularly in visual assertions of imperial power. On the Arch of Titus, Roma, a Tyche figure—embodying the luck or spirit of a city or domain—leads the emperor's quadriga, while the ruler is crowned by a personification of Victory. Antique artists equally could use female personifications of conquered territories to convey Roman dominance over such lands. The Sebasteion at Aphrodisias (Asia Minor, first century C.E.), a temple sanctuary complex erected to honor the Julio-Claudian emperors, presented a series of standing female figures in relief, each representing a province or peoples (*ethne*) conquered by Rome.[40] Personifications of the Dacians, the Egyptians, the Judaeans, and others in the company of rulers and deities, lined the temple portico, demurely taking position as obedient subjects to the divine order orchestrated by the gods and delivered by the Emperor. Elsewhere on the monument, Roman dominance over the colonized territories was visualized more overtly. In the relief of Claudius subjugating Britannia, for example, the emperor is shown at the peak of his strength dominating a flailing personification of the province (Fig. 7).[41] Here, the Emperor wedges his right knee against Britannia's thigh as he pulls her back by her hair. Britannia reaches up her right arm, seeking to stay Claudius' blow, while with her left hand she flounders to keep her chiton from falling off, though its slippage has already exposed her full breast. The artist here took pains to convey the grace and beauty of the moment, evident in the idealized faces and bodies of both figures, the balletic engagement of masculine and feminine forms, and in the fluttering drapery of Claudius' cloak, carved in delicate relief. Here, a female personification participates in the long-standing Greco-Roman tradition of insisting on the righteousness of defeat through aestheticized form.

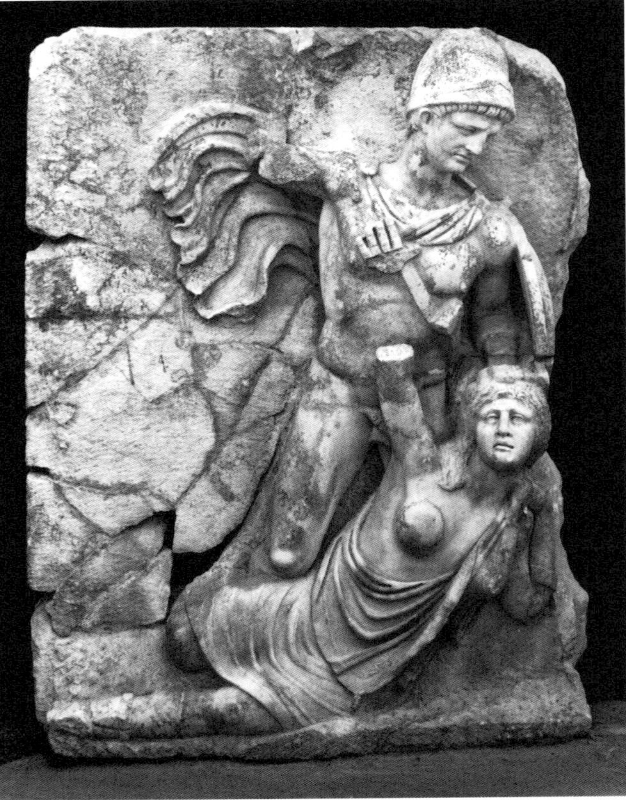

FIGURE 7. Claudius defeats Britannia, relief from Sebasteion, Aphrodisias (photo: New York University Excavations at Aphrodisias).

Just as female personifications could be used to convey the variety of peoples subsumed within the empire, they equally could be used to represent an imagined homogeneity across the domain through the medium of coinage. This was particularly the case as imperial cohesion began to break down in the fourth century. In the decades following the establishment of Constantinople as an imperial residence in 323, and its subsequent elevation to the status of second capital of the empire, there emerged a new sister Tyche for Roma,

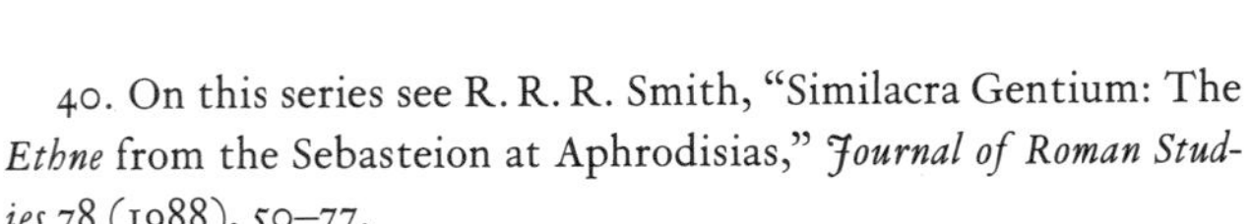

40. On this series see R. R. R. Smith, "Similacra Gentium: The *Ethne* from the Sebasteion at Aphrodisias," *Journal of Roman Studies* 78 (1988), 50–77.

41. See R. R. R. Smith, "The Imperial Reliefs from the Sebasteion at Aphrodisias," *Journal of Roman Studies* 77 (1987), 88–138, at 115–117.

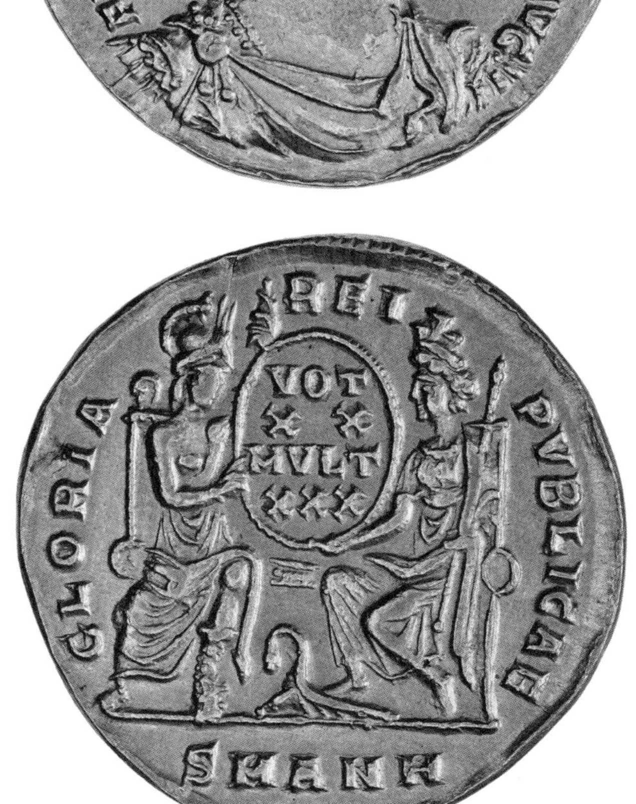

FIGURE 8. Solidus of Constantius II with Roma and Constantinopolis on reverse. New York: American Numismatic Society, Acc. 1961.42.1 (photo: Courtesy of the American Numismatic Society).

the figure of Constantinopolis.[42] Constantinopolis and Roma appear side by side on imperial coins beginning in the 340s, and persist to the end of the century. Typically, the obverse of such coins features the bust of the emperor, while the reverse shows Rome and Constantinople personified as sister-queens, sometimes both enthroned and together holding a shield, as on a solidus of Constantius II from around 350 (Fig. 8).[43] Roma faces front, wears a military helmet and holds a scepter. Constantinopolis, also holding a scepter, bears a turreted city-wall crown, has one foot on a boat's prow, and turns deferentially toward her senior companion. This coin was reissued several times under Constantius II's successors, was minted at centers across both the eastern and the western portions of the Empire, and became one of the most common of late imperial coins.[44] Other coins show the enthroned sisters bearing symbols of victory, as in a double gold solidus minted by Gratian, but based on models established under Constatius II.[45] In subsequent coins, Roma is sometimes left out altogether, and the upstart Constantinopolis is shown as the sole consort to the imperial likeness on the coin's obverse, as in a gold solidus struck for Theodosius II and subsequent rulers.[46] More luxurious works, such as manuscripts, consular diptychs, and jewelry, similarly feature Tyche figures for Rome, Constantinople, and other imperial centers,[47] but the rivalry between the two imperial capitals in the fourth century as depicted on coins makes most vivid the development of a widely circulating image-type presenting older and younger feminized embodiments of temporal power,

42. See J. M. C. Toynbee, "Roma and Constantinopolis in Late-Antique Art from 312–365," *Journal of Roman Studies* 37 (1947), 135–144; and G. Bühl, *Constantinopolis und Roma: Stadtpersonifikationen der Spätantike* (Kilchberg and Zurich, 1995), esp. 10–78, for the following discussion.

43. J. P. C. Kent, *Roman Imperial Coinage*, Vol. 8, *The Family of Constantine I: A.D. 337–364* (London, 1981), 39–40 and 504–507.

44. See discussion of related coins in Toynbee, "Roma and Constantinopolis" (as in note 42), 139–141, esp. n. 30; and H. Cohen, *Description Historique des monnaies frappes sous l'empire romain—Médailles impériales* (Paris, 1888), Vol. 7, 456–458, nos. 108–126. The same figures with slight variations appear on other mid-fourth century coins: *ibid.*, Vol. 8, 34–35, nos. 22–27; 44–46, nos. 8, 22–24 and 26–30.

45. J. C. P. Kent, *Roman Coins* (New York, 1978), 338, no. 708.

46. Kent, *Roman Coins* (as in note 45), 342, no. 749.

47. Some are discussed in K. J. Shelton, "Imperial Tyches," *Gesta* 18/1 (1979), 27–38.

one often subservient to the other, and both bound intimately with images of the male sovereign.

The motif of Ecclesia and Synagoga, I argue, grew directly out of this imperial vocabulary of forms. It was thinkers who were accustomed to seeing female personifications of fortune or civic authority in official imperial contexts who first inserted feminine embodiments of Church and Synagogue into theological texts. Certainly, there had been a long tradition in Judeo-Christian texts of using female personae to materialize notions of defeat or triumph. We need think only of the downtrodden Jerusalem, assimilated to a dejected woman, in the Book of Lamentations (Lam. 1 : 1–2; 1 : 8–9; and 5 : 16–17), or the Israelites celebrated as a queenly figure by Zacharaiah (Zach. 9 : 9)—figures that drew upon larger literary and pictorial trends of the ancient world. Church fathers transferred such traditions to the Christian realm, developing Ecclesia and Synagoga as characters to be integrated within larger theological speculations. So Augustine, for example, in his exegesis on Psalm 44, could invoke the Church as a bride mystically united with Christ, while the Synagogue appears as a worn out matron: "Indeed, Ecclesia is the new bride, Christ the bridegroom.... Who then gave birth to the son of God in the flesh? Synagoga. He will leave father and mother ... And who is the mother he leaves? The Jewish people, Synagoga."[48]

But in the era of the Christianization of the Roman empire, one thinker apparently recognized that the two characters had their own triumphal story to tell. Drawing upon a long tradition of debate literature, this unknown writer composed a dialogue between Ecclesia and Synagoga arguing over which one has the right to rule the earth. This text, known as the *Altercatio Ecclesiae et Synagogae*, was composed in Spain or north Africa sometime between 438 and 476, and was popular throughout the Middle Ages, in part likely because of its misattribution to Augustine.[49] In the text, Ecclesia and Synagoga are presented as aristocratic matrons, rivals each making the case for her claim to sovereignty before a judge.

The narrator of the dialogue introduces the players, explaining that now that the emperor has embraced Christianity, it is evident that the "lady who is the Synagogue, once powerful and wealthy" no longer has rights to her possession.[50] Of course, the Synagogue and her people the Jews never had such authority within the empire. But the author here casts the contest in absolute and strikingly politicized terms. So, for example, the struggle between Jacob and Esau, from the time of Paul interpreted typologically as a reference to the struggle between Christianity and Judaism, as discussed above, here gains a patently imperial cast:

> *The Church*: Read what was said to Rebecca: The elder shall serve the younger. And when you ask how you [Synagoga] serve, look at the legions' standards ... bear in mind that the emperors are worshippers of Christ.... No Jew may be emperor, prefect, comes, may enter the senate, be admitted to military service.... You have lost the rank of membership of the higher nobility.[51]

Indeed, in 418, Emperor Honorius banned Jews from holding public office, thereby inscribing theological conceptions of Jewish ignominy into a practical legal code.[52] Within the *Altercatio*, putatively a work of theology, in turn, imperial law decides spiritual merit. The contest between Church and Synagogue makes vivid Christological notions of scriptural typology and historical progression, but the terms of the debate are decidedly administrative.

Questions of worldly authority do not alone inform each character's defense of her right to sovereignty. When the characters' barbs turn vicious and more personal, their mutual denunciations still often are

48. "*Etenim sponsa Ecclesia est, sponsus Christus ...*" and "*Unde enim natus est filius dei secundum carnem? Ex illa synagoga. Ille qui dimisit patrem et matrem, ... Quomodo dimisit et matrem? Gentem Iudaeorum, synagogam....*" *Enarrationes in Psalmos* 44:3 and 44:12, *CCSL* 38, 495 and 502.

49. A new edition of the *Altercatio* text is found in *CCSL* 69A. English translation from the Migne PL edition of the works of Augustine is found in A. Lukyn Williams, *Adversus Judaeos: A Bird's Eye View of Christian Apologiae until the Renaissance* (Cambridge, 1935), 326–338. Translations given here are from Lukyn Williams with slight alterations.

50. Lukyn Williams, *Adversus Judaeos* (as in note 49), 327.

51. Lukyn Williams, *Adversus Judaeos* (as in note 49), 328.

52. A. Linder, ed., trans., and commentary, *The Jews in Roman Imperial Legislation* (Detroit, Mich., 1987), 76–77. Such laws, though, seem to have been ignored in many cases.

founded upon claims of relative social status: "I knew the king when you [Gentiles] were but barbarians; I ruled great nations when you were mere herdsmen," asserts the Synagogue dismissively. "Yes, you were mistress of the world," rejoins the Church, "but now are only maid."[53] Throughout the rest of the text, this maid is repeatedly indicted as a miserable, unhappy, murderous, foolish woman (*misera*, *infelicissima*, *mulier parricida*, *stulta*). After a series of exchanges over points of Christian doctrine, Ecclesia seems to weary of invoking repeated theological justifications for her authority and lashes out:

> Listen, Synagoga, listen and see thou widowed and forsaken woman! I am what you have not been able to be. I am the queen who has removed you from your throne.... My bridegroom is fair beyond the sons of men, the king of kings, who has set the marriage crown on my head and has clothed me with purple...[54]

Ecclesia gained her status because she won the love of a regal Christ. She is the favored consort at the celestial court, while superseded Synagoga looks on, dashed from the throne. Christ's queenly bride continues to debate her dejected predecessor, and the text ends with the Church's declaration of triumph.[55]

Pictorial representations of Ecclesia and Synagoga, for their part, enter the lexicon of the medieval artist only in subsequent centuries, usually in small-scale luxury works. The earliest instances are in ivory plaques, carved in the late Carolingian era to adorn manuscripts. In these pieces, personifications of Church and Synagogue appear standing to either side of the crucified Christ, as in an ivory from the Victoria and Albert Museum (Fig. 9).[56] Here, as in other related works, Ecclesia catches the blood emerging from Christ's side as Synagoga retreats from the scene. I suggest that the formulation of the pictorial motif of Ecclesia and Synagoga in the ninth century was an element within a broader Carolingian cultural phenomenon—a taste for things antique. In many of these ivory Crucifixion plaques, Ecclesia and Synagoga appear along with personifications of Oceanus and Terra (Sea and Earth), and Sol and Luna (Sun and Moon), that is, figures drawn from the vocabulary of Roman official art.[57] Frequently, moreover, acanthus leaf ornamental borders, an additional borrowing from the antique visual realm, frame the ensembles. It is a commonplace of art-historical literature to speak of the Carolingian fascination with antique imperial culture as a type of rebirth, a notion notably elaborated by Erwin Panofsky.[58] Recently, scholars have complicated Panofsky's conceptualizations, demonstrating the subtle ways that Antiquity could serve alternately as a model and a negative exemplum in the interrelated political, theological, and cultural spheres, and further, that Carolingian borrowings from the past involved reformulations driven by contemporary contingencies, rather than blind adaptations.[59] In the case of the Crucifixion plaques with Ecclesia and Synagoga, it seems that the female personae function as modified Tyche figures, included within a constellation of classicizing forms surrounding the crucified Christ that collectively celebrate Christian, rather than imperial, triumph.

In the twelfth century, as Jews moved to the intellec-

53. Lukyn Williams, *Adversus Judaeos* (as in note 49), 327.

54. Lukyn Williams, *Adversus Judaeos* (as in note 49), 331.

55. Some manuscripts break at line 540, others continue to 597 (see *Altercatio* in *CCSL* 59A [as in note 49], 17–18). But both versions end with Ecclesia claiming victory for herself.

56. London: V & A, 250–1867. See A. Goldschmidt, *Die Elfenbeinskulpturen aus der Zeit der karolingische und sächsische Kaiser, VIII.–XI. Jahrhundert* (Berlin, 1914), Vol. 1, no. 88; and D. Gaborit-Chopin, *Ivoires du moyen-âge* (Fribourg, 1978), 70, fig. 86.

57. Another similar work also featuring Oceanus and Terra is London: V & A, 251.1867. Related Crucifixion plaques with Ecclesia and Synagoga as well as Sol and Luna, though without Oceanus and Terra, are: Paris: BnF MS. lat. 9453; Gannat: Church of Saint-Croix; and New York: Cloisters 1974.266 with Paris: Louvre OA 10652. See Goldschmidt, *Elfenbeinskulpturen* (as in note 56), Vol. 1, nos. 85, 86, and 89; Gaborit-Chopin, *Ivoires du moyen-âge* (as in note 56), 70–71 and 190 (no. 85); and *idem*, *Ivoires médiévaux Ve–XVe siècle* (Paris, 2004), no. 38.

58. E. Panofsky, "Renaissance and Renascences," in *Renaissance and Renascences in Western Art* (New York, 1972), 42–113, esp. 43–54 on the Carolingians. For application of Panofsky to Carolingian ivories, see R. Melzak, "Antiquarianism in the Time of Louis the Pious and its influence on the Art of Metz," in *Charlemagne's Heir: New Perspectives on the Reign of Louis the Pious (814–840)*, ed. P. Godman and R. Collins (Oxford, 1990), 629–640, at 634–636.

59. A noteworthy discussion is L. Nees, *A Tainted Mantle: Hercules and the Classical Tradition at the Carolingian Court* (Philadelphia, 1991), 3–17, for a review of historiography.

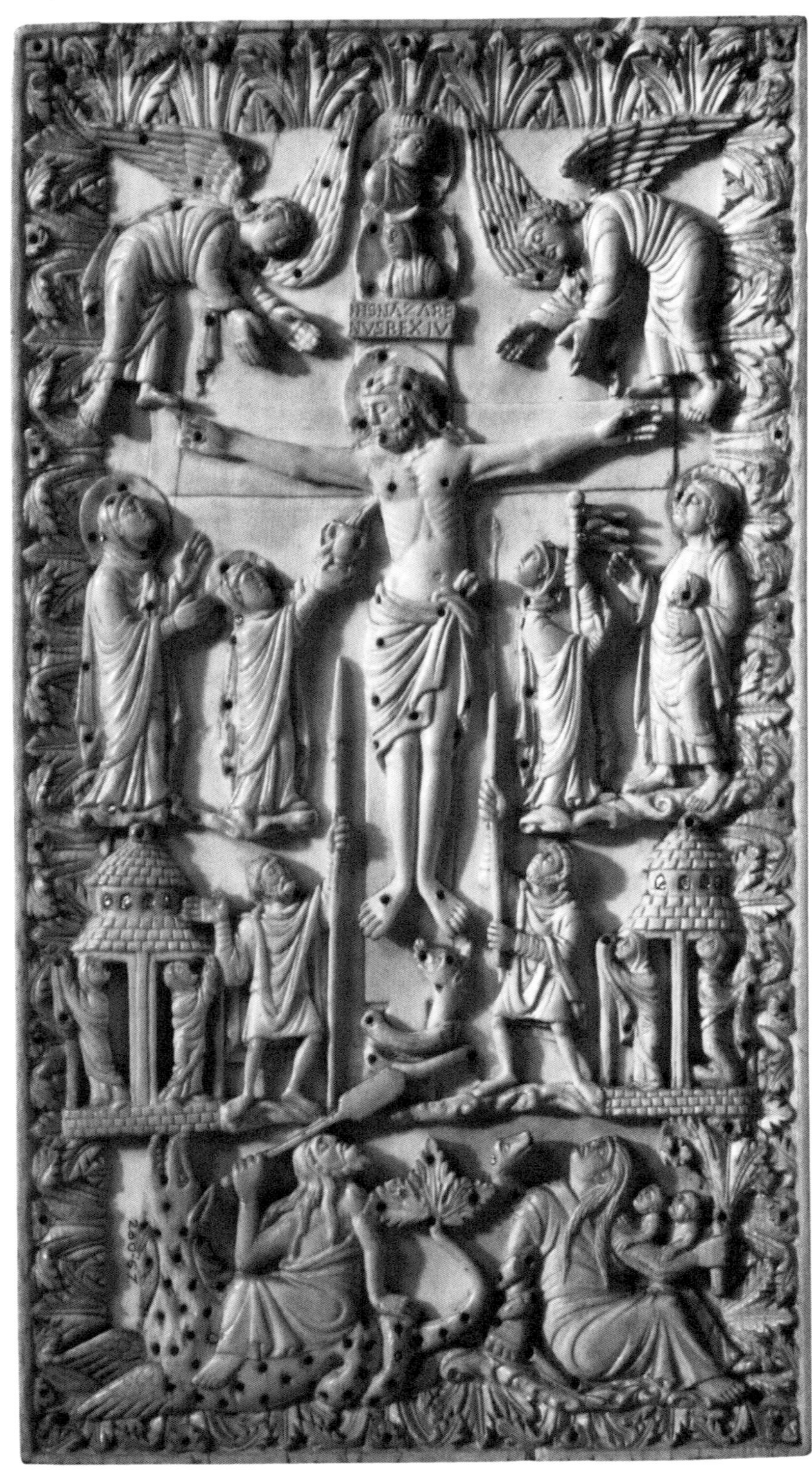

FIGURE 9. Crucifixion Ivory. London: Victoria & Albert Museum, 250.1867 (photo: © Victoria & Albert Museum, London).

tual and cultural centers of Europe, depictions of Synagoga in luxury pieces took on a decidedly more defamatory tone. Now, on works like the Stavelot altar, for example, Synagoga appears with a lance and blindfold, emblems of her enmity toward Christ and blindness to his message. Around the same time, artists also began to depict Ecclesia and Synagoga within public pictorial cycles, as on the right tympanum of the abbey church of St.-Gilles-du-Gard. In that relief, Synagoga gets her due for rejecting Christ, standing to the right of the cross and being shoved down, dashed from the scene by a vengeful angel.

Ecclesia, Synagoga & Triumph

Yet it was in the thirteenth century, in the era when ecclesiastical and lay rulers were increasingly uneasy about Jewish denunciations of Christian belief, Jewish profiteering at the expense of Christians, and the liberty with which Jews circulated unrecognized throughout Christian cities, that the Ecclesia–Synagoga motif was adopted in monumental, lifelike form as a key element within the decorative programs of the most ambitious urban building projects of the day. Here I return to the three examples that I introduced at the beginning of this essay. In each of these three monumental instances of the motif, the female personifications of Church and Synagogue are joined to an image (or images) of masculine, divinely-sanctioned rulership. At Reims, they appear with seven colossal images of kings, hovering in the top storey of the cathedral's south façade.[60] At Bamberg, as I have argued in a recent article, Ecclesia and Synagoga are best understood in relation to the celebrated Bamberg Rider sculpture, a Christian prince, directly inside the portal they adorn.[61] And at Strasbourg, they bracket an ensemble dominated at the center by a figure of Solomon.[62] As discussed above, in the very years that these programs were being created, secular and ecclesiastical rulers were instituting new legal and administrative codes designed to constrain the Jew within Christian society. And so it appears that while the Ecclesia–Synagoga motif in these contexts was intended to convey a general theological message of the ascendancy of the Church, it also projected an ideal of Jewish docility and submission in a correctly ordered Christian realm.

Style, in part, was the carrier of this message. In the opening decades of the thirteenth century, artists experimented with idealized naturalistic styles long rejected in monumental works perhaps because of their association with idolatrous paganism. Sculptors at Reims, Bamberg and Strasbourg participated in this classicizing revival, drawing inspiration either indirectly through forms transmitted in metalwork, or directly from antique ruins scattered about northern Europe or viewed on journeys south of the Alps.[63] Such analogies are evident, for instance, when comparing the faces of Ecclesia and Synagoga at Reims with Roman

60. For (often limited) discussions of Ecclesia and Synagoga within the key scholarship on Reims Cathedral, see: H. Reinhardt, *La cathédrale de Reims: son histoire, son architecture, sa sculpture, ses vitraux* (Paris, 1963), 156; and B. Decrock and P. Demouy, "La Sculpture," in *Reims: La cathédrale*, ed. P. Demouy (La Pierre-qui-Vire, 2000), 212–283, at 224–225. P. Kurmann, *La façade de la cathédrale de Reims: architecture et sculpture des portails—étude archéologique et stylistique*, 2 vols. (Paris and Lausanne, 1987), 173, n. 53, 179, 182, and 184; and A. Erlande-Brandenburg, *La cathédrale de Reims: chef-d'œuvre gothique* (Arles, 2007), 76, address only the style, not the iconography, of the figures.

61. See my "Synagoga Tumbles, a Rider Triumphs: Clerical Viewers and the Fürstenportal of Bamberg Cathedral," *Gesta* 45/1 (2006), 15–42, with further references.

62. Pertinent scholarship cited in discussion below.

63. On antique formulas at Reims, see especially: Panofsky, "Renaissance and Renascences" (as in note 58), 59–63 and 101–102; and W. Sauerländer, "*Antiqui* et *Moderni* at Reims," *Gesta* 42/1 (2003), 19–37; as well as *idem*, "Les statues royales du transept de Reims," *Revue de l'art* 27 (1975), 9–30; Richard H. L. Hamann-MacLean, "Antikenstudium in der Kunst des Mittelalters," *Marburger Jahrbuch für Kunstwissenschaft* 15 (1949-50), 157–250, at 228–230; *idem*, "Die Kathedrale von Reims: Bildwelt und Stilbildung," *Marburger Jahrbuch für Kunstwissenschaft* 20 (1981), 21–54, at 31–34; P. C. Claussen, "Antike und gotische Skulptur in Frankreich um 1200," *Wallraf-Richartz-Jahrbuch* 35 (1973), 83–108, at 88–94; Reinhardt, *La cathédrale* (as in note 60), 148–150; and Kurmann, *La façade* (as in note 61), 165–166. For the influence of the antique at Bamberg, see Hamann-MacLean, "Antikenstudien" (cited previously in this note), 183–184; and R. Baumgärtel-Fleischmann, "Das Papstgrab im Bamberger Dom," and "Bauforschung zum Grabmal Papst Clemens II.," in *Clemens II. Der Papst aus Bamberg, 24. Dezember 1046–9. Oktober 1047* (Bamberg, 1997), 31–44 and 45–79. For discussions relevant to Strasbourg see: Claussen, "Antike und gotische

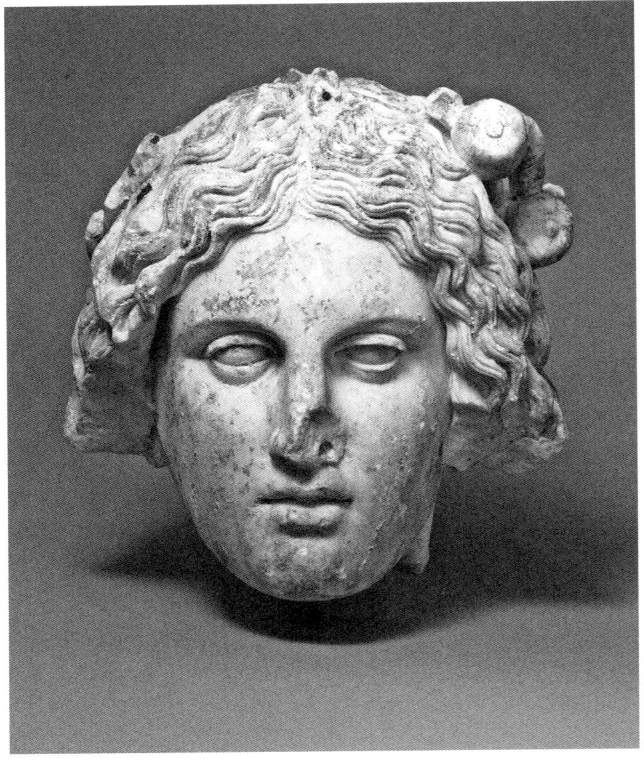

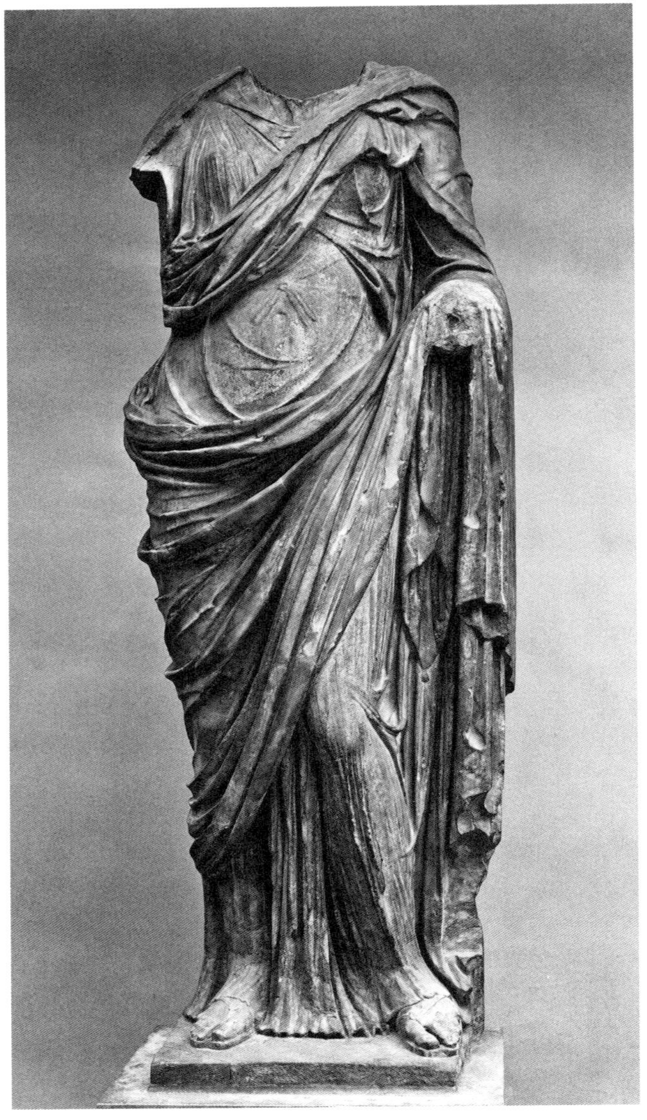

FIGURE 10. Marble Head of a Deity, Roman, Imperial, first half of the 2nd century C.E., The Metropolitan Museum of Art, Fletcher Fund, 1927, 27.122.1 (photo: © The Metropolitan Museum of Art).

FIGURE 11. Marble Statue of a Woman, Roman, Imperial, 1st or 2nd century C.E., The Metropolitan Museum of Art, Gift of Mrs. Frederick F. Thompson, 1903, 03.12.10a (photo: © The Metropolitan Museum of Art).

examples (compare Figs. 1 and 2 with 10), or the damp drapery of the figures at Bamberg and Strasbourg with that of an imperial Roman female figure (compare Figs. 4 and 5 with 11), to invoke two among hundreds of possible classical points of comparison. In an era when both an imperious church and ambitious lay leaders sought to evoke the grandeur of ancient Rome in emphatically Christian terms, this long-rejected triumphalist representational mode was embraced, although of course it is impossible to prove a causal connection between the two phenomena.

The idealized naturalism of Ecclesia and Synagoga at Reims, Bamberg, and Strasbourg, moreover, confirms the status of the personae as figures that mediate between the lived and the ideal realms. The works are carved with a dramatic lifelikeness—limbs and joints

Skulptur" (cited previously in this note), 100–102; and Hamann-MacLean, "Antikenstudium" (cited previously in this note), 228 and 236–238. For general discussions in addition to citations above see: W. Sauerländer, "Art antique et sculpture autour de 1200: Saint-Denis—Lisieux—Chartres," and "Intentio vera nostra est manifestare ea, que sunt, sicut sunt: Bildtradition und Wirklichkeitserfahrung im Spannungsfeld der staufischen Kunst," in *Cathedrals and Sculpture* (London, 1999), Vol. 1, 339–365 and 369–392.

adhere to the rules of anatomy, faces and gestures mimic human expressions, gravity seems to weigh down drapery. Such elements place the figures in dialogue with the natural world. Their status as personifications and their idealized beauty, however, make plain that they are representatives of a transcendent heavenly order. So Synagoga defeated, linked with the mighty Ecclesia, conveys the virtue of a Judaism that maintains a docile presence within the Christian sphere, but the figures stop short of presenting any kind of blueprint for actual administration.

Case Study: Christians and Jews around the South Façade of Strasbourg Cathedral

Examination of Ecclesia, Synagoga, and their larger architectonic and iconographic context at Strasbourg brings to light the social and political meanings that the figures projected in the second quarter of the thirteenth century (Fig. 12). The south façade at Strasbourg was created around the year 1230, an addition augmenting the Romanesque incarnation of the cathedral, which had been built in the eleventh century.[64] This southern portal is on the side of the building facing the bishop's palace, and it functioned not only as a ceremonial entrance to the church, but also as the locale for convening the bishop's municipal court.[65] That is, the bishop of Strasbourg also bore the title of count, and this portion of the cathedral seems to have been conceived as an arena for the performance of his secular as well as his sacred authority. Over the course of the thirteenth century, the rest of Strasbourg Cathedral was rebuilt in the Gothic style, and this portal was integrated within that new structure, but at the outset, both stylistically and functionally, this region of the building often operated as an autonomous site.

The south portal at Strasbourg has been altered since its inception, victim to vandalism during the French Revolution and changes in taste. Originally, the sculpted ensemble at Strasbourg south was protected by a roof and enclosed at the front by a gate, so that the whole space had the feeling of a loggia, a coherent and enclosed space, though one open to the city. Indeed, one can still see the consoles that initially supported the roof on the façade, below the string course at the base of the building's triforium. In addition to the removal of the porch's roof, some of the original sculpture has been lost. Isaac Brunn's well-known engraving of *circa* 1617 shows that when the portal was created, twelve figures of apostles adorned the jambs, raised up to the level of the Solomon figure at the center (Fig. 13). The thirteenth-century Solomon figure was destroyed and a nineteenth-century replica now sits in its place. The same is true for the bust-length figure of Christ behind the Old Testament king, as well as the scenes in the lintels, though the celebrated tympana of the Death of the Virgin and her Coronation are original.[66]

In 1972, Otto von Simson published an article explaining the complicated iconography of this portal that integrates figures of Solomon, Christ, and apostles, Marian scenes, and Ecclesia and Synagoga.[67] In brief, von Simson explains the ensemble as a manifestation of the Christian understanding of the putatively Solomonic text of the Song of Songs. Building upon earlier

64. The authoritative discussion of this region of the cathedral long was: E. Fels, "Le chœur et le transept de la cathédrale de Strasbourg: étude architecturale," *Bulletin de la Société des Amis de la Cathédrale de Strasbourg* 2 (1932), 65–96. Those observations were revised in L. Grodecki and R. Recht, "Le bras sud du transept de la cathédrale: architecture et sculpture," *Bulletin monumental* 129, no. 1 (1971), 7–38; republished in *Bulletin de la Société des Amis de la Cathédrale de Strasbourg* 10 (1972), 11–32. Updated discussions, both with reviews of earlier scholarship on chronology, are: H. Krohm, "Das Südquerhaus des Straßburger Münsters—Architektur und Bildwerke," in *Meisterwerke mittelalterlicher Skulptur*, ed. H. Krohm (Berlin, 1996), 185–203, at 187; and J.-P. Meyer, "La construction du portail sud du transept à la cathédrale de Strasbourg," *Bulletin de la Société des Amis de la Cathédrale de Strasbourg* 26 (2004), 93–110, at 97–99. For the history of the whole cathedral, see the monographic study, H. Reinhardt, *La cathédrale de Strasbourg* (Paris, 1972).

65. See A. Erler, *Das Straßburger Münster im Rechtsleben des Mittelalters* (Frankfurt am Main, 1954). Erler admits that the sources are silent about the precise circumstances under which the Strasbourg south façade would have staged legal proceedings (p. 52), but collectively he garners sufficient evidence of the use of the site for this function.

66. For the latest assessment of the construction of the south façade with a discussion of alterations, see Meyer, "La construction" (as in note 64).

67. O. von Simson, "Le programme sculptural du transept méridional de la cathédrale de Strasbourg," *Bulletin de la Société des Amis de la Cathédrale de Strasbourg* 10 (1972), 33–50. Key elements of this

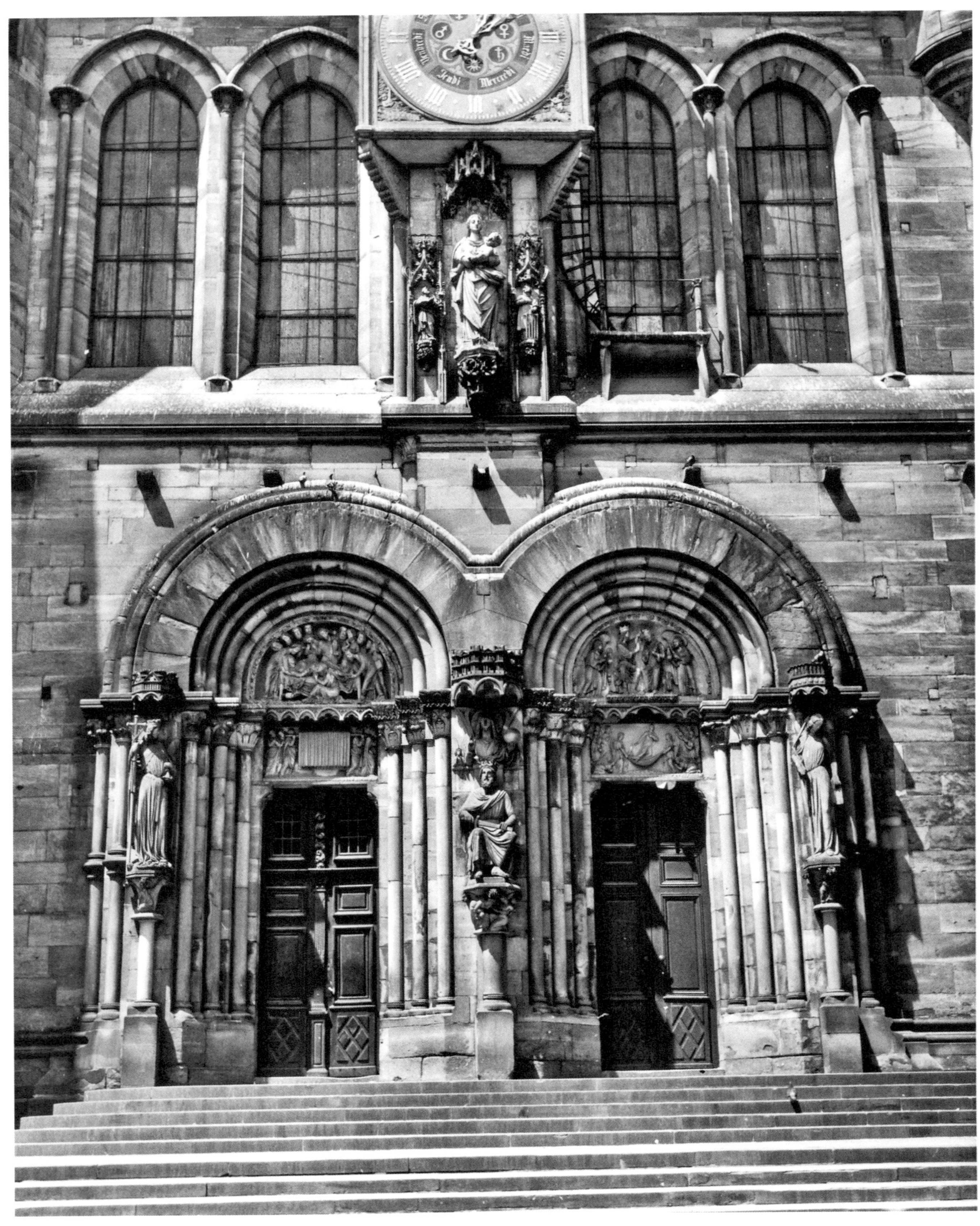

FIGURE 12. Strasbourg Cathedral, south façade (photo: Foto Marburg / Art Resource, N.Y.).

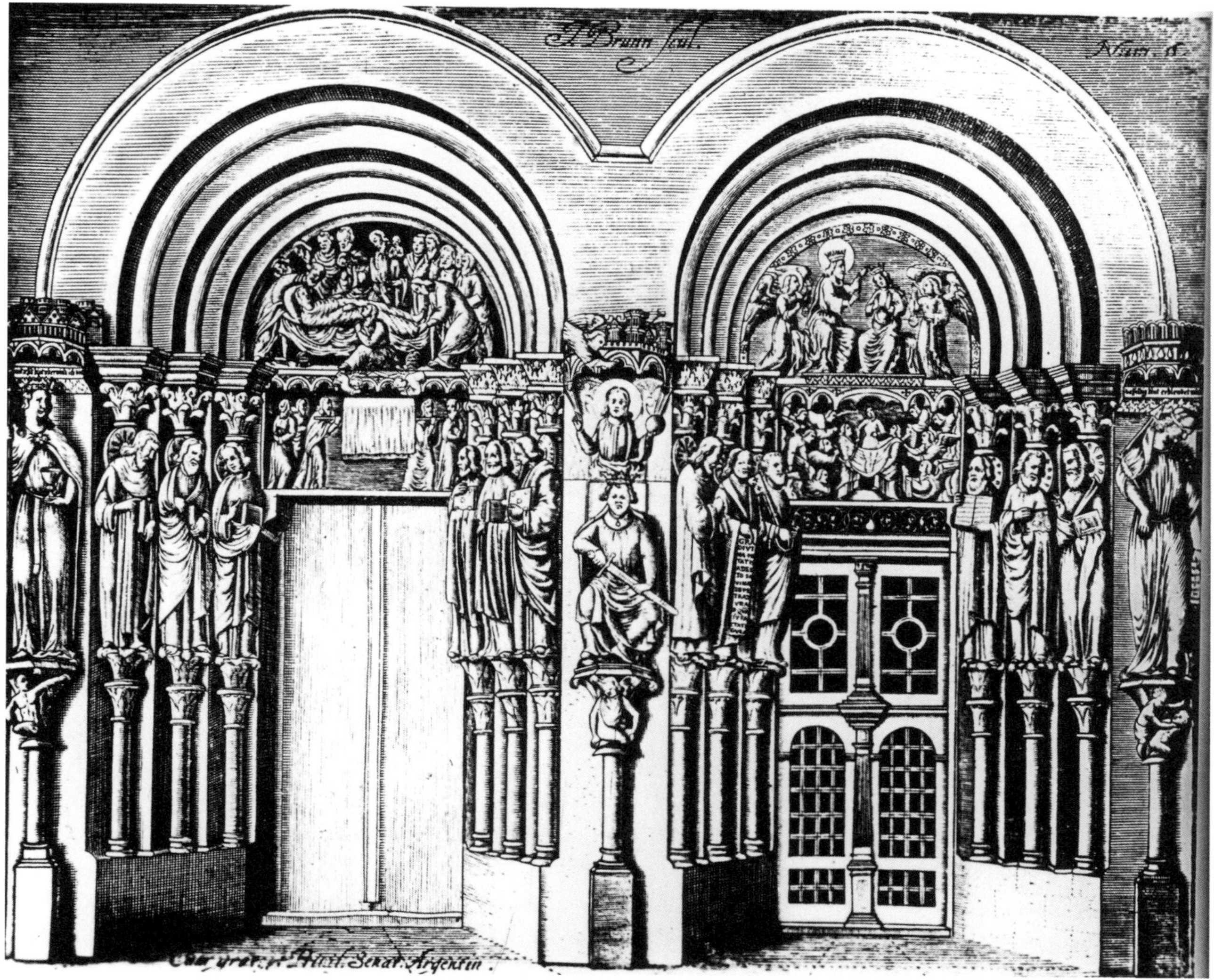

FIGURE 13. Isaac Brunn. Strasbourg Cathedral, south façade, before modern damage and alterations. Engraving, *c.* 1617. Originally in Oseas Schadaeus, *Summum Argentoratensium Templum, das ist Aussfürliche und Eigentliche Beschreibung des viel künstlichen, sehr kostbaren und in aller Welt berühmten Münsters zu Straßburg* (Strasbourg, 1617), pl. 6 (image: Foto Marburg / Art Resource, N.Y.).

hermeneutics, twelfth-century exegetes saw the poem as an allegorization of Christ's union with the Church and the Christian soul, the lovers (the *sponsus* and *sponsa*) in the dialogic Song then functioning as figures for Christ and his beloved Ecclesia. The Ecclesia figure in turn was taken to allude to the Virgin, crystallizing in a triune figure of Bride-Church-Mary. Christian exegetes further associated the scorned bride, the Sulamite (or Sunamite) woman of the Song, with Synagoga or the Jews. Ultimately, von Simson sees the Strasbourg ensemble, along with the Pillar of Angels, a structure at the interior of the Strasbourg south transept, as an expression of Honorius Augustodunensis' eschatological vision for the salvation of the Christian soul, as well as

argument are reiterated and amplified in L. Asch, "L'Eglise et la Synagogue de la cathédrale de Strasbourg," *Société d'Histoire des Israelites d'Alsace et de Lorraine—XXIe colloque, Strasbourg 27 et 28 février 1999*, ed. A. Bloch et al. (Strasbourg, 2000), 13–22; and B. Nicolai, "Orders in Stone: Social Reality and Artistic Approach. The Case of the Strasbourg South Portal," *Gesta* 40/2 (2002), 111–128.

the Jews. Honorius anticipates that at the end of days, just as the lovers in the Song call the Sulamite woman to turn toward them, so too the call of the Church would be heard by the Jews, who would finally turn toward Christ. For von Simson, the corkscrew posture of Synagoga on the Strasbourg façade manifests that idea—or ideal—of turning (see Fig. 6).[68]

The clerics of Strasbourg may well have looked upon the figure of Synagoga on their new south façade and reflected on both the ideal and the reality of Jewish conversion. In March of 1229, there had been a celebrated local case in which a Jewish man converted to Christianity, renounced his Jewish wife, and demanded custody of their four-year-old son.[69] As overlord of the city's Jews, the local bishop had the authority to adjudicate in this case, weighing the child's prospect of life with a Christian father and no mother against a future in the Jewish community. Apparently it was not an easy decision, because after considering the matter before a diocesan synod, the bishop took the case all the way to Pope Gregory IX. The Pope ruled that it was better for the child to live motherless than to put his soul in danger by leaving him with the Jews, a judgment that was later enshrined in Gregory IX's *Decretals*.[70] Further evidence of Jewish conversion to Christianity in Strasbourg in the second quarter of the thirteenth century is found in the local use of the surname "Judeus" among people who apparently were Christian. One Burchardus Judeus, for example, served as a witness to a document concerning the property of Strasbourg's collegiate church of St. Thomas.[71]

But a closer look at the figures of Ecclesia and Synagoga at Strasbourg suggests that the message of the ensemble was one of Christian triumph more than anticipation of ultimate union, a point recently made by Willibald Sauerländer in an article on the portal.[72] At the left extreme is the Church (Fig. 5). Legs oriented outward and upper body turned to the right, she has just noticed Synagoga over at the other end of the porch. The triumphant Queen Ecclesia thrusts her shoulders back and twists around to confront her predecessor. With her right hand she grasps the staff of a labarum, and with her left she cradles a chalice. Crown planted firmly on her head, the Church extends her neck slightly outward so as to better her view across the portal complex. Her eyes are wide open and her lips are parted as if she has just called out. Synagoga across the way is the weak subject of this direct address (Fig. 6). Physically, she is the antithesis of the Church. While Ecclesia's luxuriant robe provides stability, Synagoga's diaphanous drapery slithers down her thighs and weaves around her ankles. While Ecclesia's mantle unifies her upper body, arms, and attributes, Synagoga has no mantle and her arms jut out to either side. Her spear is broken and tangled in a banner, and she holds the tablets of the law tentatively, hiding them behind her body. The Church calls out, but, blindfolded and weakened, the Synagogue is not up to the fight. She turns away, mournfully absorbed in her own defeat.

The docile and decrepit Synagoga of Strasbourg cathedral's south façade had little in common with the actual Jewish population living in the streets directly to the north of the cathedral, running alongside the residence of the cathedral chapter.[73] Jews had come to the city of Strasbourg beginning in the twelfth century, joining other communities in the Rhineland region. Local rabbis became leaders among the Jews of Alsace, and local pawnbrokers and creditors dominated the money trades. This scholarly, spiritual, and fiscal success found expression in the rapid establishment

68. Worth note is the recent article that recognizes that Honorius did offer a remarkably mild assessment of the place of Jews in Christian salvation history: J. Cohen, "*Synagoga conversa*: Honorius Augustodunensis, the Song of Songs, and Christianity's 'Eschatological Jew,'" *Speculum* 79, no. 2 (2004), 309–340.

69. J. Aronius, *Regesten zur Geschichte der Juden im fränkischen und deutschen Reiche bis zum Jahre 1273* (Hildesheim, 1970), 196 (no. 445); A. Hessel and M. Krebs, *Regesten der Bischöfe von Straßburg*, Vol. 2, *Regesten der Bischöfe von Straßburg vom Jahre 1202–1305* (Innsbruck, 1928), 53 (no. 947).

70. S. Grayzel, *The Church and the Jews in the XIIIth Century*, rev. ed. (New York, 1966), 180–183 (no. 59); and S. Simonsohn, *The Apostolic See and the Jews—Documents: 492–1404* (Toronto, 1988), 128–129 (no. 124).

71. I. Elbogen, A. Freimann, and H. Tykocinski, eds., *Germania Judaica*, Vol. 1, *Von den ältesten Zeiten bis 1238* [c1934] (Tübingen, 1963), 370.

72. W. Sauerländer, "Strasbourg, cathédrale: le bras sud du transept: architecture et sculpture," *CAF* 162, Strasbourg, 2004 (2006), 171–184.

73. The authoritative study on Jews in medieval Strasbourg is found in: G. Mentgen, *Studien zur Geschichte der Juden im mittelalter-*

of the community in a cluster of streets at the center of town, housing a synagogue, a community bakery, a *mikveh* (ritual bath), and luxury homes.[74] This Jewish district was nested right at the center of the city, the main artery of the *vicus iudaeorum* (today's *rue des juifs*) running parallel to the cloister of the cathedral canons and terminating at a short street (today's *rue du dome*) leading directly to the north façade of Strasbourg Cathedral (Fig. 14).

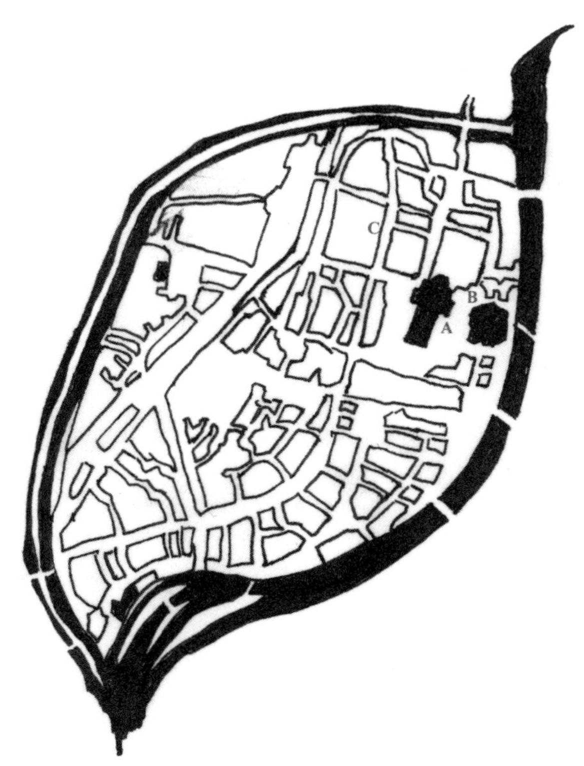

FIGURE 14. Map of Strasbourg, after Speklin's map of 1577 (reproduced in K. Achtnich, *Der Bürgerstand in Straßburg bis zur mitte des XIII. Jahrhunderts* [Leipzig, 1910]). Key: A = Cathedral; B = Bishop's Palace; C = Street of the Jews.

Beyond this physical integration within the civic milieu, administratively the Jews of Strasbourg seem to have been considered integral members of urban society. Around 1214, the Strasbourg bishop and the leading burghers of the city negotiated the terms of a document known as the Second Municipal Charter. Among the rulings of this agreement was a provision that the local Jews were to be keepers of the city banner, while seven nearby monasteries were to outfit the civic militia with horses to pull the war chariot.[75] The Jews, thus, were entrusted with the most important symbol of the city's military strength, a vexillum possibly adorned with an image of the Virgin and Child.[76] The Jews of Strasbourg, moreover, may have fought alongside the civic militia in defense of the city. The *vicus iudaeorum* lay close to the city wall, and at the edge of this district was a tower, once known as the "Judenturm," from which soldiers could stave off hostile forces. There is no firm evidence that Jews themselves were charged with the defense of this region, but evidence from other Rhineland cities suggests this possibility.[77] These were Jews with good reason to feel proud and self-assertive. They had established themselves quickly, were thriving financially and spiritually, and constituted a valued component of the larger civic structure. Moreover, there are no reports of attacks on Jews within Strasbourg during the whole of the thirteenth century.

---

lichen Elsaß (Hannover, 1995), 29–33 and 125–136. Earlier studies are C. T. Weiss, *Geschichte und rechtliche Stellung der Juden im Fürstbistum Straßburg* (Bonn, 1896); A. Glaser, *Geschichte der Juden in Straßburg* (Strasbourg, 1924); Elbogen et al., *Germania Judaica* (as in note 71), 367–372; and Z. Avneri, ed., *Germania Judaica*, vol. 2, *Von 1238 bis zur Mitte des 14. Jahrhunderts*, pt. 2 (Tübingen, 1968), 798–806.

74. See M.-D. Waton, "Des bains juifs à Strasbourg," *Cahiers Alsaciens d'archéologie d'art et d'histoire* 29 (1986), 53–55 and figs. 1–6; and J.-P. Rieb, "Un ensemble medieval urbain exceptionnel, rue des juifs à Strasbourg," *Archéologie médiévale en Alsace—Bulletin de la Société Industrielle de Mullhouse* 3, no. 806 (1987), 149–169.

75. W. Weigand, *Urkundenbuch der Stadt Strassburg*, Vol. 1, *Urkunden und Stadtrechte bis zum Jahr 1266* (Strasbourg, 1879), 481 (no. 617). For commentary, see Mentgen, *Juden im mittelalterlichen Elsaß* (as in note 73), 125.

76. On the banner, see P. Martin, "Das große Straßburger Stadtbanner," *Zeitschrift für historische Waffen- und Kostümkunde* 7 (1942), 185–189. On its significance, see A. Haverkamp, "'Concivilitas' von Christen und Juden in Aschkenas im Mittelalter," in *Jüdische Gemeinden und Organisationsformen von der Antike bis zur Gegenwart*, ed. R. Jütte (Vienna, Cologne, and Weimar, 1996), 103–136, at 127–128.

77. See Mentgen, *Juden im mittelalterlichen Elsaß* (as in note 73), 125–126. On the right of Jews to bear arms up until around the mid-thirteenth century, see G. Kisch, *The Jews in Medieval Germany: A Study of their Legal and Social Status* (Chicago, 1949), 111–128.

When clerics looked at the figure of Synagoga on the south façade of Strasbourg cathedral, they encountered a weak and broken figure that gainsaid the status of the prosperous and esteemed local Jewish community. Moreover, if the portal's iconographic program was inspired by Christian exegesis on the Song of Songs, as von Simson and others would have it, clerics who were in the know might have equally reflected on Jewish interpretations of the Solomonic text—interpretations that undermined and even mocked Christian hermeneutics, in the manner of the examples reviewed earlier in this essay. For, in distinction to the Marian allusions that Christian exegetes discerned in the Song of Songs, Jewish thinkers long had taken the poem's nuptial imagery as a figuration of God's relation to the Jews before and under the Diaspora.[78] The commentaries often take the form of a historical narrative, tracking the relationship between the Lord as bridegroom and his bride, the people of Israel, progressing from Exodus through the time in the kingdom of Judea, to the Roman occupation and the current exile, with an anticipation for future redemption with the coming of the Messiah. Rashi, for example, explains the Solomonic text as a dialogue between God and his estranged beloved, Israel, who together look back to a time of union in the Promised Land before the Diaspora. While Christian exegetes likened the Jews to the Sulamite woman of the Song who was alienated from the bridegroom-Christ, Rashi assured his Jewish readers that the exile referenced in the text does not bespeak a rejection of Israel nor is it an annulment of Israel's chosen status, but rather, it is simply a temporary separation—Israel is still God's wife and God is still Israel's husband.[79] The well-known opening line of the Song, in which the bride longs for the "kiss of his mouth" (1 : 1), according to Rashi, anticipates the Lord's reunion with Israel, when God will stop covering his face and renew the covenant.[80] Rashi instructs his readers not to be discouraged by their current exiled state, and even warns them not to submit to the temptations of Christians keen to convert Jews—an ideal that, indeed, was central to Christian exegesis on the Song as discussed above. The passage "Your throat [is] like the best wine | worthy of my beloved to drink" (7 : 9), Rashi explains, is an admonishment to be careful in dialogues with Christians: replies to Christians who seek debate or conversion should be like good wine.[81]

The Song of Songs held a particularly prominent place for Jewish exegetes, since it was read during the Passover Shabbat celebration. With hermeneutical texts like those of Rashi circulating widely, with the intellectual stature of the Strasbourg community and with the remarkably close proximity of the *vicus iudaeorum* to the cathedral district, it is easy to imagine that the canons of Strasbourg Cathedral would have been aware of Jewish scholarship on the Song of Songs—if not Rashi's in particular, then other similar pronouncements.[82] When they looked at the south façade of Strasbourg Cathedral, these clerics could be reassured that Solomon was a hero of Christian, not Jewish, history, who ruled the earth in anticipation of Christian triumph. If Jews insisted that their Diaspora was simply a temporary episode of exile, the clerics could find evidence of Jews' patent estrangement from the Lord in the figure

78. See E. E. Urbach, "The Homiletical Interpretation of the Sages and the Expositions of Origin on Canticles, and the Jewish-Christian Disputation," in *Studies in Aggadah and Folk Literature*, ed. J. Heinemann and D. Noy, Special Issue of *Scripta Hierosolymitana* 22 (1971), 247–275; and G. Stemberger, "Midraschim zum Hoheslied und Geschichte Israels," in *Rashi, 1040–1990: Hommage à Ephraïm E. Urbach*, ed. G. Sed-Rajna (Paris, 1993), 313–319.

79. Y. Nevo, "Jewish-Christian Polemics as Reflected in Medieval Commentaries of Twelfth-Century Northern France," in *Studies on Our Heritage* [in Hebrew], ed. Z. Betzer, Sh. Z. Havlin, and Sh. Vargon (Rehovot, 1999), 29–54 at 38. I am grateful to Eli Gutwirth for tracking down this article and to Irit Ziffer for her painstaking translation of the Hebrew for me.

80. Nevo, "Jewish-Christian Polemics" (as in note 79), 39–40.

81. Nevo, "Jewish-Christian Polemics" (as in note 79), 39.

82. For evidence of Jewish-Christian reciprocal influence in the understanding of the Song of Songs, see V. I. J. Flint, "Anti-Jewish Literature and Attitudes in the Twelfth Century," *Journal of Jewish Studies* 37 (1986), 39–57 and 183–205; A. Green, "The Shekhinah, the Virgin Mary and the Song of Songs: Reflections on a Kabbalistic Symbol in its Historical Context," *AJS Review* 26, no. 1 (2002), 1–52; and S. Shalev-Eyni, "Iconography of Love: Illustrations of Bride and Bridegroom in Ashkenazi Prayerbooks of the Thirteenth and Fourteenth Century," *Studies in Iconography* 26 (2005), 27–57.

of the defeated Synagoga with broken spear and drooping banner. Clerics who knew that Jews found in the Song of Songs defenses against Christian proselytizing, rather than Honorius' call for Jewish conversion, could note Synagoga's silence in the face of her Christian opponent. As Ecclesia twists her head toward Synagoga and opens her mouth in debate, Synagoga turns away, lips sealed—hardly proffering the spiritual and intellectual "good wine" that Rashi recommends Jews harness in conversation with Christians.

Other Jewish texts offered more mocking assessments of the Christian understanding of the Song of Songs. The *Nizzahon Vetus*, mentioned previously, for instance, notes the confused identities of Christ and his mother-bride in the Christian hermeneutics on Song of Songs 5:1.[83] The text of the biblical passage reads: "I have come into my garden, my sister, my beloved." Aware of the Christian assimilation of the beloved to Mary, the Jewish polemicist observes that Christ entered the "garden" of heaven on the day of his death without his mother, and so the Christian take on the verse does not make sense. The polemicist observes, in the same passage, a further snarl of implied kinship ties: "If this were said of Jesus it would prove that he had a sister." Further, "they [Christians] maintain that Jesus said ... he has no father or mother, no son or daughter, but Israel." This (albeit inexact) paraphrase of Matthew 12:48–50 points to the illogic of exegesis that casts the bride of the Song of Songs as mother, beloved, and sister, and that considers this composite figure to be a companion to the bridegroom-as-Christ, himself said to be free from the ties of such earthly relations.[84] The analysis moreover points to an apparent inversion of roles found in Christian exegesis on Song of Songs 3:11:

> The heretics [Christians] speak defiantly concerning the verse, ... "[B]ehold King Solomon with the crown wherewith his mother crowned him in the day of this wedding." They say that every "Solomon" in the Song of Songs is sacred and that this verse refers to the mother of Jesus. This is how you should answer them [in a debate]: "What was the crown with which his mother crowned him? If anything Jesus crowned his mother and not she him."

By the thirteenth century, Jews in cities across northern Europe were accustomed to seeing sculpted tympana and likely other ephemeral church adornments featuring the motif of the Coronation of the Virgin, Christ crowning his mother as Queen of Heaven.[85] An image of this very moment was depicted in the right tympanum of Strasbourg south (Fig. 12). How then, the Jewish polemicist asks, can Christians justify exegesis that casts the Virgin as the crowner and Christ as the crownee? Strasbourg's clerics, looking at the right tympanum of the south façade, might have wondered at this inversion themselves before reflecting on exegesis such as that of Alan of Lille, which explicates the Song of Songs' invocation, "come from Lebanon | come, you will be crowned" (4:8), as a reference to the Coronation of the Virgin.[86] They likely also remembered typological interpretations that explained the importance of Christ's ultimate crown, the crown of thorns, held by an angel in the top tier of the Pillar of Angels within the south transept.

Thus we can understand the south façade of Strasbourg as an ensemble that stood at the intersection of a range of theological and social discourses in which Jews and Christians variously cooperated with and confronted one another on matters spiritual and municipal. The Strasbourg sculptural program, of course, indicates none of the intellectual confidence of northern European Jews in the thirteenth century, nor does it suggest more immediately the vitality of the local Jewish community. That is, if the Strasbourg bishop created an atmosphere for relatively peaceful coexistence in Strasbourg's city streets, up on the site where the bishop held court and where ceremonial entrances were performed, the Synagogue was presented as

83. *Nizzahon Vetus*, no. 153: Berger, *The Jewish-Christian Debate* (as in note 29), 166.

84. For the Gospel reference, see Berger, *The Jewish-Christian Debate* (as in note 29), 309, note to p. 166.

85. See the key study P. Verdier, *Le couronnement de la Vierge: Les origines et les premiers développements d'un thème iconographique* (Paris, 1980).

86. A. Matter, *The Voice of My Beloved: The Song of Songs in Western Medieval Christianity* (Philadelphia, 1990), 166–167.

utterly bested—allowed to remain in Ecclesia's realm only thanks to ecclesiological fiat. With this observation, I finally turn from the realm of abstract intellectual debate to the more concrete terrain of the larger imperial orbit.

Beyond the interests of the church, around the time of the construction of Strasbourg Cathedral's new south façade, Emperor Frederick II was instituting a new legal code that defined Jews as subservient within an ordered Christian society. This imperial action was driven by an outbreak of violence against Jews. In the mid-1230s, there was a wave of attacks on Jewish communities in the German heartland following the circulation of rumors that Jews slaughtered Christian children and gathered the blood for ritual use—that is, the blood libel.[87] Frederick II adjudicated on the blood libel accusations from his court at Hagenau, just twenty-eight kilometers north of Strasbourg. After both Jewish and Christian plaintiffs made appeals to Frederick, the Emperor launched an inquiry to settle the question. Like a new Solomon, the emperor weighed testimony from both sides, listening to witnesses, including Jews who recently had converted to Christianity. After two rounds of deliberations, Frederick issued his Privilege and Judgment in Favor of the Jews (*Privilegium et Sententia in Favorem Iudaeorum*), which declared the charges of ritual murder to be libelous and outlawed their perpetuation. Further, the Emperor assigned Jews a new official status within the realm, deeming them to be *servi camere nostre* or Servants of the Royal Chamber—special property of the Emperor and thereby off limits to attack.[88] These protections, of course, came at a price. Jews now were constrained to make yearly payments to the Emperor's coffers. What Frederick's ordinances effectively did was transform the antique theological notion of Jews as docile stewards to Christians into a policy for temporal administration. Those "librarians" and "servants" of Augustine now were obligated to the royal chamber as appurtenances within a larger imperial system of social control. Jews would not inspire riotous outbreaks of violence. They would be Frederick's special property, quietly kept in their place.

The south façade of Strasbourg Cathedral does not directly manifest the specific aspects of either imperial or episcopal policies on Jews. Cathedral decorative programs were too expensive, and intended to last for too long, to respond to the particular contingencies of a given decade, in my view. But by the early thirteenth century, ecclesiastical and lay rulers had reason to be disquieted by what we might call the uppity Jewish communities of Ashkenaz. And, as just discussed, Jewish presence in Christian lands sometimes ignited murderous riots, anathema to Augustinian justifications for Jewish survival, to say nothing of more general ideals for maintaining terrestrial order. The figure of Synagoga defeated was one means through which to project an ideal of a Judaism that persisted but knew its subordinate place within Christian society. Artists harnessed this motif, and, echoing antique devices for depicting imperious power, joined it to figurations of both Ecclesia triumphant and ideal masculine rulership. These ensembles, then, were presented in monumental naturalistic form and placed in city centers, proclaiming that earthly order is effected through the ascendance of the Church and the defeat of her forerunner.

Afterlife

By way of conclusion, I observe that the triumphalist political meanings of the Ecclesia–Synagoga motif that I discern at Strasbourg—as well as at Reims and Bamberg—were only in vogue for a short period. From the mid-thirteenth century through the fourteenth, monumental sculpted personifications of Church and Syna-

87. For thorough discussions of the attacks and their aftermath with further bibliography, see G. Langmuir, "Ritual Cannibalism," in *Toward a Definition of Antisemitism* (Berkeley, 1990), 263–281; and B. Diestelkamp, "Der Vorwurf des Ritualmordes gegen Juden vor dem Hofgericht Kaiser Friedrichs II. im Jahr 1236," in *Religiöse Devianz: Untersuchungen zu socialen, rechtlichen und theologischen Reaktionen auf religiöse Abweichungen im westlichen und östlichen Mittelalter*, ed. D. Simon (Frankfurt, 1990), 19–39.

88. On this ruling, see F. Lotter, "Geltungsbereich und Wirksamkeit des Rechts der kaiserlichen Judenprivilegien im Hochmittelalter," *Aschkenas* 1 (1991), 23–64, esp. 36–37; and A. Patschovsky, "Das Rechtsverhältnis der Juden zum deutschen König (9.–14. Jahrhundert)," *Zeitschrift der Savigny-Stiftung für Rechtsgeschichte* 110 (1993), 331–371, at 355–366.

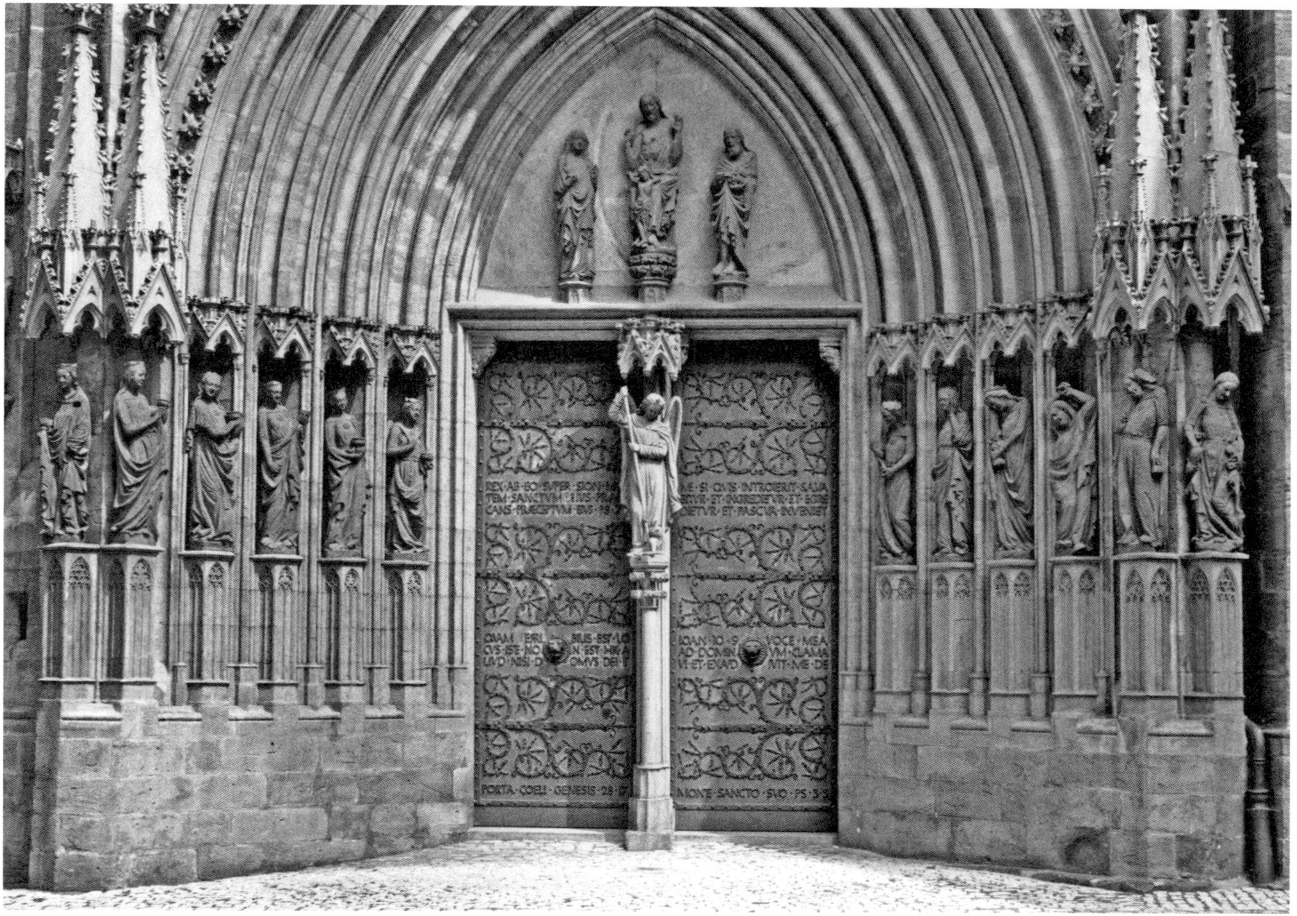

FIGURE 15. Erfurt Cathedral, north façade, "Triangular Portal," western side with Ecclesia, Synagoga and the Wise and Foolish Virgins (photo: Foto Marburg / Art Resource, N.Y.).

gogue began to be seen alongside generalized embodiments of Virtue and Vice rather than with images of masculine power.[89] A favored iconographic setting for the figures was among figures of the Wise and Foolish Virgins, as they appear at Erfurt (Fig. 15), as well as other sites.[90] This change in iconographic context, I posit, was driven in part by the rituals carried out before monumental public sculptures of Ecclesia and Synagoga, at sites such as those addressed in this essay. Burghers were entreated to participate in penitential rituals below the hovering figures of Ecclesia and Synagoga at Strasbourg and perhaps at Reims.[91] The bishops

89. See Sciurie, "Ecclesia und Synagoge an den Domen" (as in note 9).

90. At the Trier Liebfrauenkirche, Ecclesia, and Synagoga are on the west façade (*c.* 1240) with Peter as fisher of souls, John the Evangelist with chalice triumphing over evil, and Adam and Eve. At the northern "Paradise Portal" of Magdeburg Cathedral (*c.* 1250; installed thus *c.* 1330–1335), the west porch of the cathedral at Freiburg im Breisgau (*c.* 1290), and the western "Triangular" portal of Erfurt Cathedral (*c.* 1330), Ecclesia and Synagoga accompany the Wise and Foolish Virgins. Large-scale sculptures of Ecclesia and Synagoga figure within related programs at the cathedrals of Minden (*c.* 1250–1280) and Worms (*c.* 1300–1310), and at the church of St.-Seurin in Bordeaux (*c.* 1300).

91. See P. Desportes, *Reims et les rémois aux XIIIe et XIVe siècles* (Paris, 1979), 167; B. Abou-El-Haj, "The Urban Setting for Late Medieval Church Building: Reims and its Cathedral between 1210 and 1240," *Art History* 11, no. 1 (1988), 17–41, esp. 25–28; *idem*, "Program and Power in the Glass of Reims," in *Radical Art History:*

of Strasbourg and Bamberg carried out legal proceedings before the sculpted figures, and at Bamberg it seems that accused criminals were bound to the post beneath Synagoga.[92] For generations, lay people and clerics participated in and oversaw rituals of atonement and the exercise of legal justice performed in front of personifications of Church and Synagogue. For these audiences, the figures appear to have accrued a generalized meaning, conveying the contest between good and evil in broad social terms—this being an index of the larger spiritual developments of the late thirteenth and fourteenth centuries, where new emphasis was put on the internal spiritual battle of the laity rather than on a corporate plan for earthly order.

As cathedral decorative programs used the Ecclesia–Synagoga motif to convey a general opposition between morality and immorality, the actual Jewish populations of northern Europe increasingly were expelled from and exterminated within Christian society. French King Philip IV's general expulsion of 1306 compelled the Jews of Reims and the region to leave.[93] Although some Jews were readmitted to the kingdom in 1315 under Louis X, and more returned around 1359, the communities never re-established their previous vibrancy, and Jews were expelled from the French crown lands once and for all in 1394.[94] Farther east, in the region of the empire, meanwhile, deadly riots were decimating Jewish populations on a scale not seen since the infamous Rhineland slaughters of the First Crusade. In the 1280s and '90s, rumors of Jewish ritual murder of Christian children began to circulate, despite Frederick II's denunciation of the claim in 1236. Such tales, along with the newly developed calumny of Jewish host desecration, inspired mobs of Christians in 1298 to join the retinue of a German knight named Rindfleisch who launched widespread massacres, killing thousands of Jews at 146 centers throughout Franconia, Swabia, Hesse, and Thuringia. Between 1336 and 1339, gangs known as the Armleder, after the leather bands that these low estate marauders wore on their arms instead of knightly armor, swept through cities in Franconia and Alsace, assaulting and killing Jews for their putative enmity toward Christians.[95] And, as is well known, accusations that Jews caused the plague by poisoning wells and other water sources inspired mobs to slaughter countless Jews across Europe.[96]

We have unusually rich information on the extermination of the Jews of Strasbourg.[97] Strasbourg had the largest population of Jews in the upper Rhine at the time; according to some reports, 2,000 in total. Here,

---

Internationale Anthologie, Subject: O. K. Werckmeister, ed. W. Kersten (Zurich, 1997), 22–33 and 226–33; and my, "Idealization and Subjection at the South Porch of Strasbourg Cathedral," in *Beyond the Yellow Badge: Anti-Judaism and Antisemitism in Medieval and Early Modern Visual Culture*, ed. M. Merback (Leiden, 2008), 179–202, esp. 197–202, with further references.

92. Erler, *Das Straßburger Munster im Rechtsleben* (as in note 65), 30–32; and R. Neumüllers-Klauser, "Der Bamberger Dom als Stätte mittelalterlicher Rechtspflege," *Bericht des Historischen Vereins Bamberg* 102 (1966), 177–189.

93. See W. C. Jordan, *The French Monarchy and the Jews: From Philip Augustus to the Last Capetians* (Philadelphia, 1989), 214–223.

94. See E. A. R. Brown, "Philip V, Charles IV, and the Jews of France: The Alleged Expulsion of 1322," *Speculum* 66, no. 2 (1991), 294–329; R. S. Kohn, "Les juifs en France du nord dans la seconde moitié du XIVe siècle—un état de la question," in *L'expulsion des Juifs de France—1394*, ed. G. Dahan (Paris, 2004), 13–29; and, for general discussions, see Stow, *Alienated Minority* (as in note 21), 281–308; R. Chazan, *Medieval Jewry in Northern France: A Political and Social History* (Baltimore, 1973), 181–196; and Jordan, *The French Monarchy and the Jews* (as in note 93), 150–213.

95. Both campaigns are addressed in F. Lotter, "Hostienfrevelvorwurf und Blutwunderfälschung bei den Judenverfolgungen von 1298 ('Rintfleisch') und 1336–1338 ('Armleder')," in *Fälschungen im Mittelalter: Internationaler Kongreß der Monumenta Germaniae Historica, München, 16.–19. September 1986*, ed. W. Setz (Schriften der Monumenta Germaniae Historica 33, I–V), 5 vols., Vol. 5, 533–583.

96. Key discussions are: F. Graus, *Pest, Geißler, Judenmorde: Das 14. Jahrhundert als Krisenzeit* (Göttingen, 1987), 155–389; and A. Haverkamp, "Die Judenverfolgungen zur Zeit des Schwarzen Todes im Gesellschaftsgefüge deutscher Städte," in *Zur Geschichte der Juden im Deutschland des späten Mittelalters und der frühen Neuzeit*, ed. A. Haverkamp (Stuttgart, 1981), 27–93.

97. For a thorough analysis of the sources, see Mentgen, *Juden im mittelalterlichen Elsaß* (as in note 73), 364–85. See also Lazare Landau, "La condition des Juifs au moyen-age: le massacre de la Saint-Valentin (Strasbourg, 14 février 1349), *Rencontre Chrétiens et Juifs* 6 (1972), 251–7; and Philippe Dollinger, "L'émancipation de la ville et la domination du patriciat (1200–1349)," in *Histoire de Strasbourg des origines à nos jours*, ed. Georges Livet and Francis Rapp (Strasbourg: Éditions des Dernières Nouvelles, 1981), 39–94, at 89–91.

on Friday, 13 February 1349, the Jews of the city were gathered together and prepared for their deaths. Meanwhile, the Jewish street was barricaded and those Jews hiding in their homes were hunted down. The following day, on the feast of St. Valentine, the Strasbourg Jews were led in a massive procession toward the site prepared for their collective incineration. While the Jews marched, Christians of the city tore at their clothes, leaving the community members half-naked as they headed toward execution. At the site, a great pyre, or perhaps a wooden house built for the occasion, was set aflame. Children who consented to baptism, and apparently particularly attractive Jewish women, were spared from the conflagration, but some seem to have chosen death over conversion. The burning is reported to have gone on for six days, though it may be that it took this much time to catch all the Jews who sought refuge in the *vicus iudaeorum*.

By the mid-fourteenth century, the once-vibrant Jewish communities of France and Germany had been silenced—expelled from their homes and executed in widespread and systematic slaughters. Pockets of Jews re-established themselves in these regions during the generations following the Black Death, but the former strength of Jewish intellectual and economic life in northern Europe was never to be recovered. All the while, images of Ecclesia and Synagoga stood at the heart of the region's economic and cultural centers. Inserted into new iconographic and social contexts, they were now drained of any reference to Jewish history and contemporary Jews. In the late thirteenth and fourteenth centuries, as urban dwellers shuffled past cathedral entryways, personifications of Church and Synagogue bespoke a general opposition between upright and amoral interior life—the political imperatives of an earlier age, when vigorous populations of Jews needed to be contained and controlled within the Christian system, now were but a faint memory. Jews themselves had been wiped out of Europe's cities, and Synagoga, a now anodyne symbol, stood dutifully, amongst an array of good and evil forces, a fantasy of a docile deviance cut to ecclesiological specifications, and contained within an ordered Christian realm.

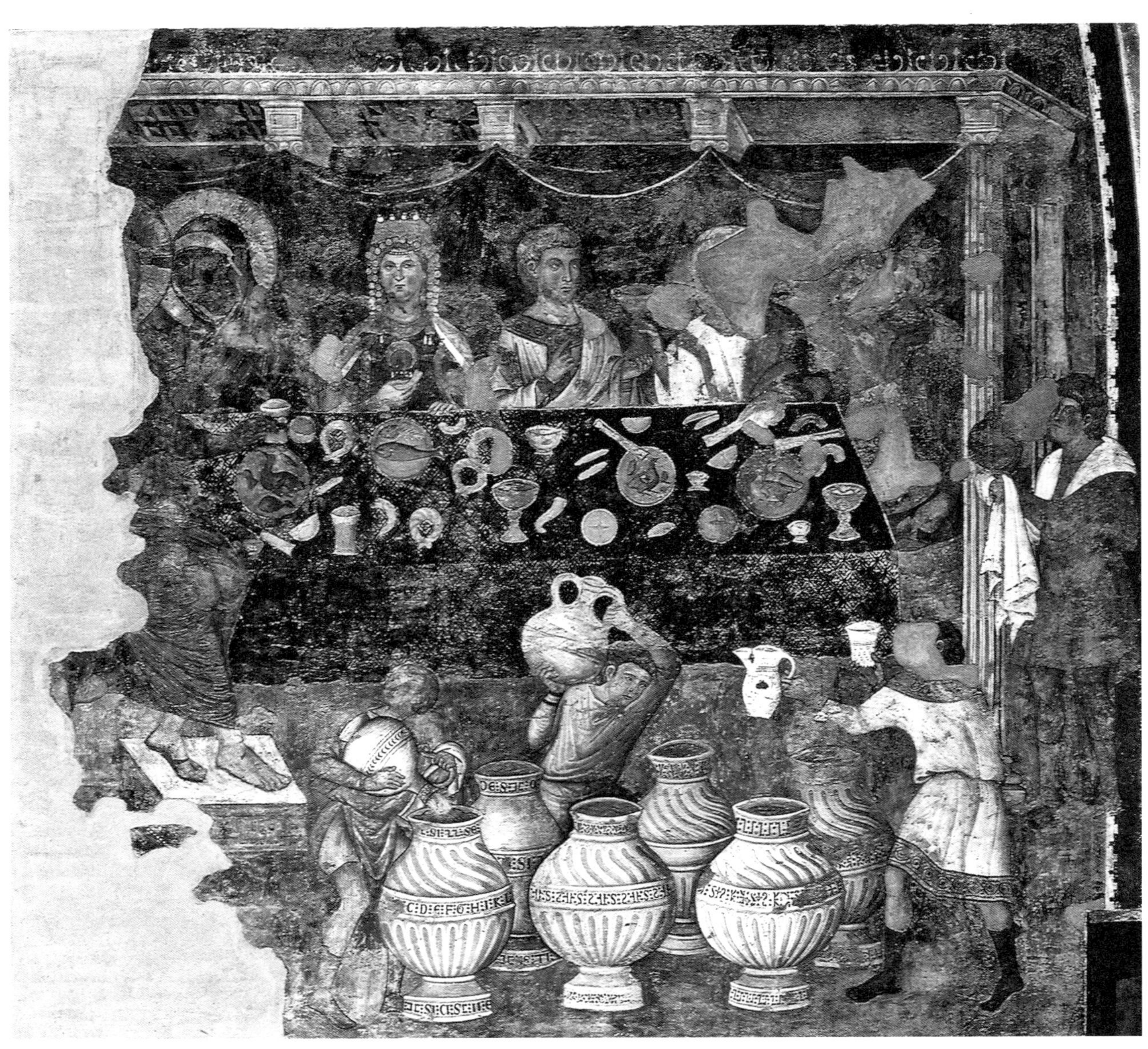

FIGURE 1. Assisi, San Francesco, nave of the Upper Church, Miracle at Cana, late thirteenth century (photo © Stefan Diller).

AMY NEFF

The Humble Man's Wedding: Two Late Thirteenth-Century Franciscan Images of the *Miracle at Cana**

CHRIST PERFORMED his first public miracle at Cana in Galilee, the transformation of water into wine. John, the only evangelist to record the event, gives it considerable importance: this was the first of Christ's signs that "manifested his glory, and his disciples believed in him" (John 2:11). Despite this heady endorsement, it seems that the *Miracle at Cana* was not typically included in thirteenth-century Italian narratives of Christ's life, which most often focus on the Infancy and Passion, the core subjects of thirteenth-century piety.[1] Certainly, Franciscan art fits this profile, for the emotional appeal of Infancy and Passion scenes effectively served the Order's ministry of Christian renewal, by kindling the viewer's empathy and compassion, stimulating the ardent piety of religious commitment.[2] Moreover, theologically, narratives of the Infancy and Passion were particularly well suited to visualize the Franciscans' emphasis on Christ's humanity, a self-humbling begun as a helpless, needy child and completed in suffering and humiliation. Thus, when the *Miracle at Cana* appears in two Franciscan monuments of the late thirteenth century, this fact should not be taken for granted. The scene had not been a standard component of Duecento Christological cycles and does not conform in any obvious way to the affective character or the missionary goals often seen in Franciscan images of Christ's life. Precisely because they are not "standard" Franciscan images, analysis of two Franciscan depictions of the *Miracle at Cana*, a fresco in the Upper Church of San Francesco, Assisi, and a miniature in the *Supplicationes variae*, might contribute to a broader understanding of the large and diverse phenomenon known as Franciscan art.

In the nave of the Upper Church of San Francesco, Assisi, the *Miracle at Cana* is part of the Christological cycle painted, in all likelihood, *c.* 1290.[3] The New Testament scenes occupy the top two registers of the south wall, above the *Legend of St. Francis*, with the story of Christ's infancy and childhood at the top of the wall (Figs. 1, 2). The second register focuses on the Passion but includes two miracle scenes, *Cana* and the *Raising of Lazarus*. Placed near the apse of the church, the *Miracle at Cana* initiates this sequence. The tinted drawing of the *Miracle at Cana* in the *Supplicationes variae* is nearly

* An earlier version of this paper was presented at the International Congress of Medieval Studies at Western Michigan University; there and at Princeton, I have benefited greatly from many colleagues' comments. I would also like to gratefully acknowledge the University of Tennessee, Exhibit, Performance, and Publication Expenses Fund, for its generous support.

1. A. Derbes and M. Sandona, *The Usurer's Heart: Giotto, Enrico Scrovegni, and the Arena Chapel in Padua* (University Park, 2008), 74, also note the small number of Cana scenes in this period. A few Italian examples dating *c.* 1180–1210 will be discussed in this essay.

2. See A. Derbes, *Picturing the Passion in Late Medieval Italy: Narrative Painting, Franciscan Ideologies, and the Levant* (Cambridge, 1966); A. Derbes and A. Neff, "Italy, the Mendicant Orders, and the Byzantine Sphere," in *Byzantium: Faith & Power (1261–1557)*, ed. H. Evans, Exhib. Cat., New York, Metropolitan Museum of Art (New Haven, 2004), 449–61.

3. For the date of the Assisi fresco, see D. Cooper and J. Robson, "Pope Nicholas IV and the Upper Church at Assisi," *Apollo* 157 (2003), 31–35.

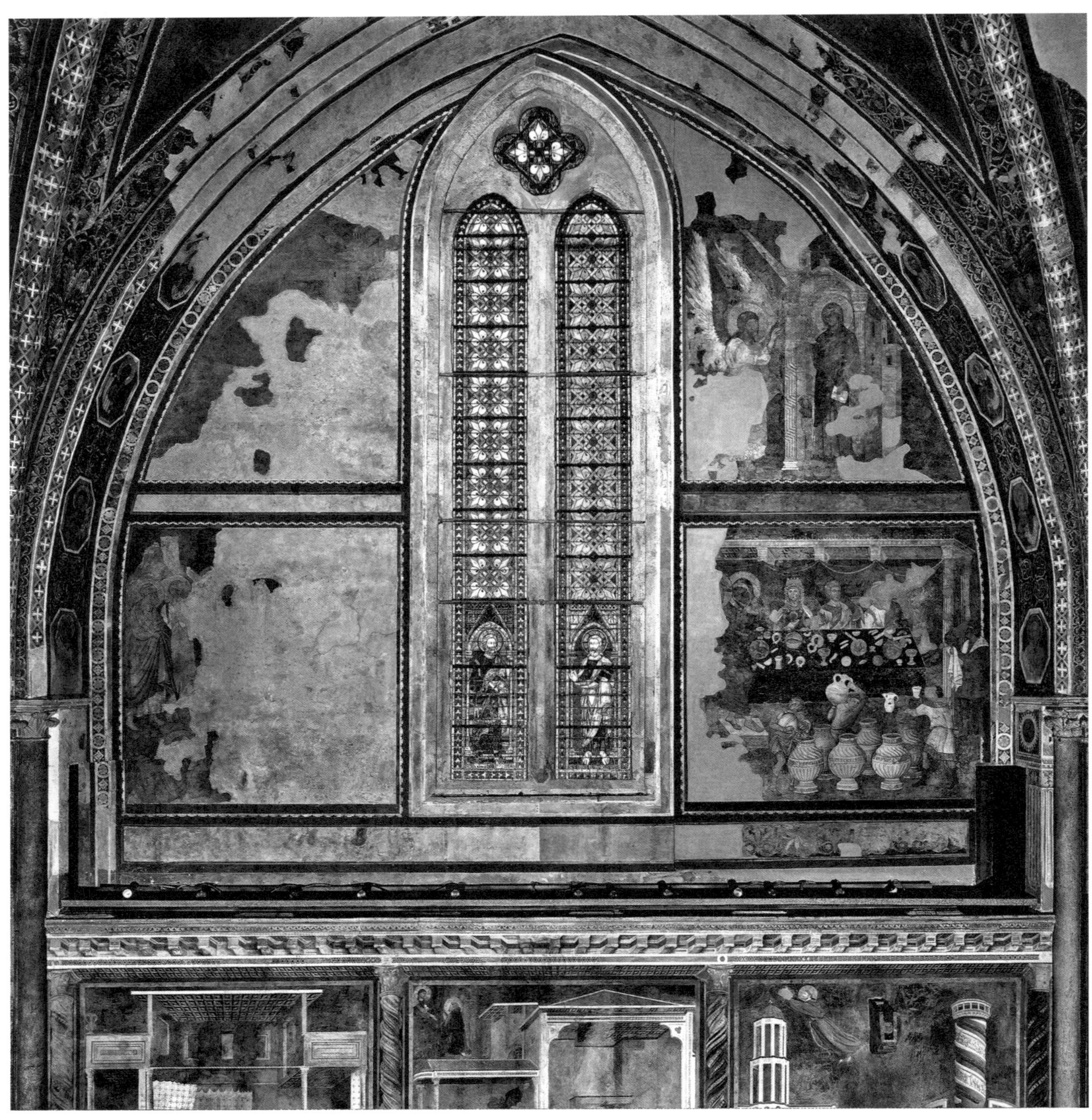

FIGURE 2. Assisi, San Francesco, nave of the Upper Church, first bay of south wall, Annunciation and Miracle at Cana (photo © Stefan Diller).

contemporary, dated 1293 (Fig. 3).[4] This exceptionally lavish manuscript, intended for use as a private prayer-book, was probably not owned by a Franciscan friar; it seems, rather, to have been the possession of a wealthy patron, most likely a young man, in Genoa, the city indicated in the manuscript's calendar. Yet a friar must have planned the thematic content of the *Supplicationes*, for the book's contents reveal a profound understanding of the theology of St. Bonaventure, minister general of the Order from 1257–1274, and its preëminent theologian.[5] As mentor or confessor to the book's owner, a Franciscan friar could have designed the *Supplicationes* to be used in his student's spiritual education and practice—a practice that included visual meditation on the life of Christ. At the end of the *Supplicationes* are thirty-three drawings telling this narrative, including the *Miracle at Cana*. In significant ways, this essay's two Franciscan depictions of *Cana* are different—one a large-scale fresco in a public space, one a drawing in a privately-viewed manuscript—but both are in monuments intended to teach the Gospel and inspire devotion.

The Gospel of John tells the story: Christ and his disciples were invited to a wedding, and Christ's mother was there (John 2:1–11). When there is no more wine at the feast, Mary tells Christ of the lack. At first, Christ seems to rebuke Mary, saying that the hour has not yet come, but he commands servants to fill six stone jugs with water, to draw from the jugs, and to take what is drawn to the host, or steward of the feast, the Architriclinus. It is discovered that the water has been changed into wine, a fact that puzzles the Architriclinus; the disciples, however, recognize the miracle and believe. This narrative weaves together a number of strands, not all readily understood. And although illustrations of Cana were rare in Duecento Italy, medieval exegesis of Cana is plentiful, explicating the timing of the feast, the invitation, Christ's seeming rebuke, the wedding, the water, the transformation, the jars, the groom, the Architriclinus, and more.[6] It is therefore important to look carefully at the selection of elements included in the two images to determine what might correspond to Franciscan interests. To represent Franciscan thought on Cana, I take St. Bonaventure, whose profound influence on Assisi and on the *Supplicationes* is well documented.[7] His two main writings on the Gospel of John, a *Commentary* and a *Collation*, demonstrate a particular interest in the subject, a solid grounding in earlier exegesis, and a selective bias that is arguably mendicant.[8]

Both Franciscan scenes of *Cana* show Christ seated at a table with Mary next to him, while servants carry in jars, pouring liquid into the stone *hydriae*—six at Assisi, three in the *Supplicationes variae*. The Architriclinus holds up a cup of wine. In the drawing, he is crowned; at Assisi, enough remains of his damaged face to show that he was white-haired and not crowned. And nearly everything else is different in the two scenes. In the fresco at Assisi, Christ sits at the left of the table; his halo and his feet on a footstool are still visible. In the

4. Florence, Biblioteca Medicea Laurenziana, Plut. 25.3, fol. 370^{v}. The manuscript's date is inscribed on a leaf pasted inside its front cover. For its drawings, see B. Degenhart and A. Schmitt, *Corpus der italienischen Zeichnungen, 1300–1450*, I-1 (Berlin, 1968), 7–16; for the manuscript's Franciscan thematic program, A. Neff, "'*Palma dabit palmam*:' Franciscan Themes in a Late Thirteenth-Century Italian Devotional Manuscript," *JWarb* 65 (2002), 22–66.

5. The manuscript also contains a few Dominican texts and one image of a Dominican friar; these, however, are far outnumbered by Franciscan items; see the listing in A. Neff, "Byzantium Westernized, Byzantium Marginalized: Two Icons in the *Supplicationes variae*," *Gesta* 7/1 (1999), 96–7.

6. The enormous complexity possible in the exegesis of Cana is exemplified in J. Leclercq, "Textes et images dans l'explication d'un symbole," in *Hommages à André Boutemy*, ed. G. Cambier (Brussels, 1976), 231–43, which, for all its multiple levels of interpretation, shares little common ground with the iconography of Cana in the two monuments discussed in this essay. See also the varied interpretations in the sermons published by D. L. d'Avray, *Medieval Marriage Sermons: Mass Communication in a Culture without Print* (Oxford, 2001).

7. While Bonaventure's exegesis is fundamental, future research on these images should also consider other Franciscan authors, especially John of Wales and Matthew of Aquasparta, whose writings have been associated with the decoration of the Upper Church at Assisi.

8. Bonaventure, *Collationes in Evangelium Ioannis* (hereafter, *Coll Jn*), in *S. Bonaventura Opera Omnia*, vol. 6, ed. PP. Collegii a S. Bonaventura, 10 vols. (Quaracchi, 1882–1902), 535–634; *Commentarius in Evangelium Ioannis* (hereafter *Comm Jn*), in *idem*, 237–532; trans. R. J. Karris, *Commentary on the Gospel of John* (Saint Bonaventure, N.Y., 2007). Translations from the *Coll Jn* are mine.

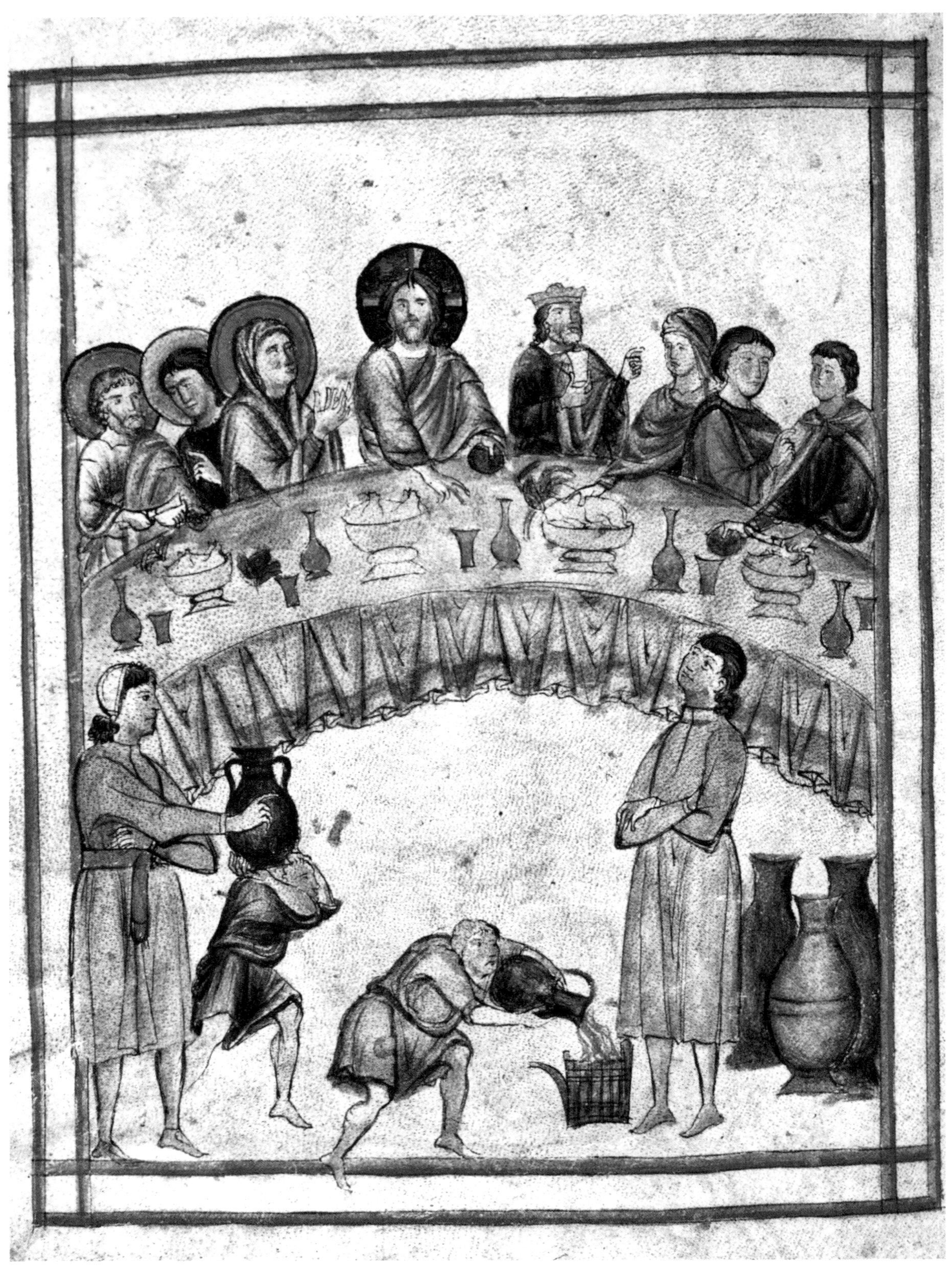

FIGURE 3. *Supplicationes variae*, Miracle at Cana, 1293. Florence, Biblioteca Medicea Laurenziana, Plut. 25.3, fol. 370v (by permission of the Ministero per i Beni e le Attività culturali).

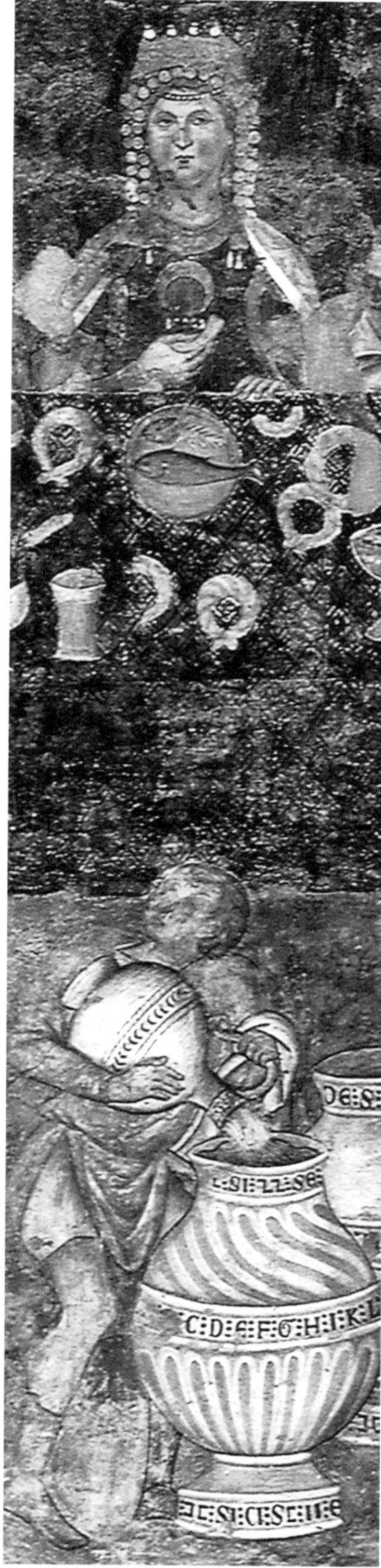

FIGURE 4. Assisi, San Francesco, nave of the Upper Church, Miracle at Cana, detail (photo © Stefan Diller).

Supplicationes, Christ is near the center. Both scenes include the bride, who is not mentioned in the Gospel text, but only at Assisi is she resplendent in a turquoise-blue gown and red tunic with gold borders, a yellow-gold mantle over her shoulders (Fig. 4). Gems or pearls top her golden crown and frame her face, while a large pendant hangs from a necklace or golden collar. In contrast, the bride in the *Supplicationes* is utterly plain, in a yellow-brown turban and drab brown cloak. She does not look happy. The groom, seated to her right, turns away from her, as he does in the Assisi fresco, although there the bride seems unconcerned. According to a frequently repeated legend, the bridegroom at Cana was John the Evangelist, who, converted to belief on his wedding-day, abandons his bride to follow Christ.[9] In the *Supplicationes*, John speaks to a wedding guest, while at Assisi, he addresses the Architriclinus; the goblet of miraculous wine rests in his hand. Evidently, there was no single Franciscan iconography for the *Wedding at Cana*. Although not every detail is accounted for, a brief survey reveals that a variety of earlier models were used to design the two Franciscan scenes.

It is well established that the biblical program in the Upper Church at Assisi was self-consciously modeled after the decoration of Rome's apostolic churches.[10] Whether the *Miracle at Cana* was included at St. Peter's is uncertain, since most of the New Testament cycle had already been lost by the seventeenth century, when Giacomo Grimaldi recorded the medieval nave paintings in drawings and brief descriptions.[11] And the

9. Bonaventure notes that although not all agree, the testimony of "great authorities" confirms that the bridegroom was indeed John; *Comm Jn* 2.15, 272; trans. Karris, 151.

10. See especially H. Belting, *Die Oberkirche von San Francesco in Assisi. Ihre Dekoration als Aufgabe und die Genese einer neuen Wandmalerei* (Berlin, 1977); and S. Romano, "La redazione del programma e lo svolgimento del cantiere della navata," *La basilica di San Francesco ad Assisi. Pittori, botteghe, strategie narrative* (Rome, 2001), 179–206.

11. For the New Testament cycle at St. Peter's, see W. Tronzo, "The Prestige of Saint Peter's: Observations on the Function of Monumental Narrative Cycles in Italy," in *Pictorial Narrative in Antiquity and the Middle Ages* (Studies in the History of Art 16), ed.

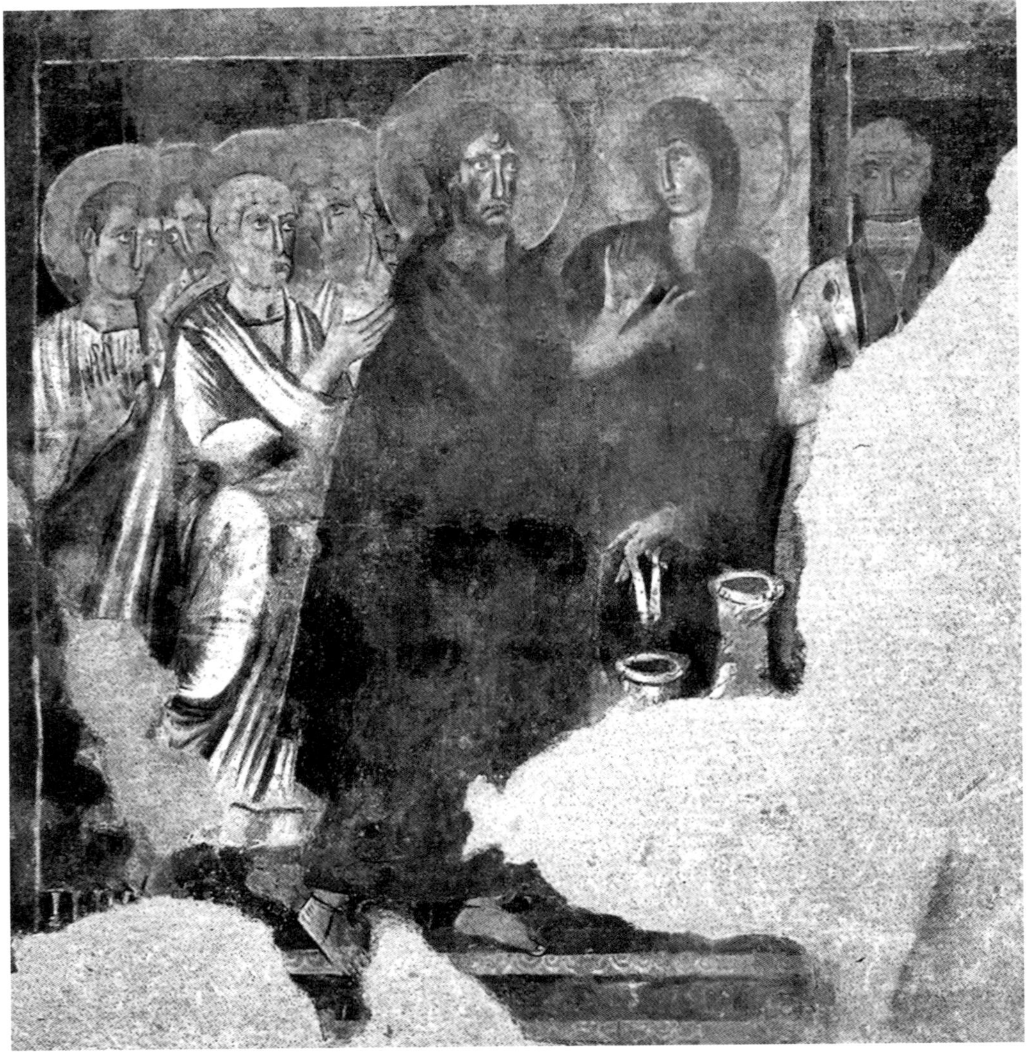

FIGURE 5. Ferentillo, Abbey Church of S. Pietro in Valle, Miracle at Cana (after Tamanti, *Gli affreschi di San Pietro in Valle* [as in note 12], pl. 35).

subject is rare among medieval naves that were modeled to a significant extent after St. Peter's. The *Cana* scene painted in the late twelfth century at San Pietro in Valle at Ferentillo is exceptional in this respect (Fig. 5).[12] But if the wall-painting at Ferentillo reflects an earlier scene at St. Peter's, that model had little in common with the Assisi fresco. Instead of picturing guests seated at a wedding-feast, the scene at Ferentillo follows Early Christian iconography that focuses on Christ, who stands near the water-jars, making a commanding gesture, enacting the miracle.[13] Close by is Mary, whose presence is unusual but not unknown in early

H. L. Kessler and M. S. Simpson (Hanover, N.H., 1985), 93–112; and H. L. Kessler, "L'antica basilica di San Pietro come fonte e ispirazione per la decorazione delle chiese medievali," in *Fragmenta picta. Affreschi e mosaici staccati del Medioevo romano*, ed. M. Andaloro, A. Ghidoli, et al. (Rome, 1989), 45–64.

12. O. Demus, *Romanesque Mural Painting* (New York, 1970); G. Tamanti, ed., *Gli affreschi di San Pietro in Valle a Ferentillo: Le storie dell'antico e del nuovo testamento* (Naples, 2003).

13. The limited space available at the right of the damaged painting seems inadequate for a table or guests; see the wall diagram in Tamanti, *Gli affreschi* (as in note 12), 233.

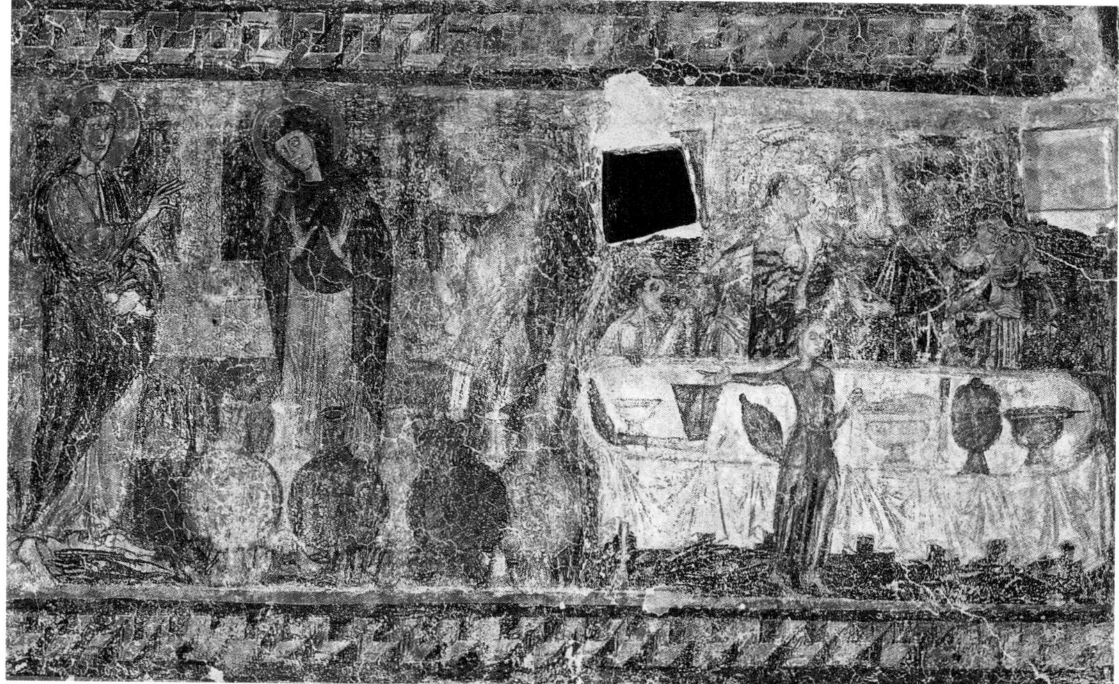

FIGURE 6. Castel Appiano, Chapel, Miracle at Cana (photo: after Stampfer and Steppan, *Die Burgkappelle* [as in note 15], fig. 58).

Christian representations of the scene.[14] From the Carolingian period on, Mary is often pictured requesting or reacting to Christ's miracle; at Ferentillo she draws back with a gesture of acclamation or astonishment. Similar iconography appears in the southern Italian Tyrolean Alps, at Castel Appiano, *c.* 1200–1210, where the scene of the wedding-feast is added, as was common in medieval representations of *Cana*, again, starting in the Carolingian period (Fig. 6).[15] Still, Christ and his miraculous power are dominant, as Mary pulls back slightly, reacting with reverence and awe. Neither sits at the rather rowdy wedding-table. The iconographic focus on Christ's performance of the miracle continues in some examples well into the Trecento, as in a miniature by Pacino di Bonaguida from a narrative sequence of Christ's life (Fig. 7).[16] The only suggestion of the wedding-feast is the servant at the right, who carries a knife as he turns to leave the room; the banquet itself is not pictured.

The artist of the Assisi fresco selected an altogether different model, known in Byzantine iconography from about the mid-tenth century, and in south Italy at Sant'Angelo in Formis, *c.* 1070–1080, where, unfortunately, little of the scene survives.[17] In its

14. For the iconography of *Cana*, see U. Nilgen, "Hochzeit zu Kana," in *LCI*, vol. 2, col. 299–305; for the early medieval period, E. Thunø, *Image and Relic: Mediating the Sacred in Early Medieval Rome* (Analecta Romana Instituti Danici, Supplementum 32; Rome, 2002), 92–4. The unusual prominence of St. Peter among the witnesses at Ferentillo's *Cana* must reflect the Abbey Church's dedication.

15. See H. Stampfer and T. Steppan, *Die Burgkappelle von Hocheppan* (Bolzano, 1998), 56, for a dating between 1204–10; Demus, *Romanesque* (as in note 12), dates the paintings to the late twelfth or early thirteenth century.

16. New York, Pierpont Morgan Library MS. M.643, fol. 6; H. Flora, *Cimabue and Early Italian Devotional Painting* (New York, 2006), 29, 33, 46. For a full description of the manuscript, see the Morgan Library's online database, *Corsair*. The manuscript's owner had a special devotion to the Third Order Franciscan, Gerard of Villamagna. Another Trecento example omitting Cana's banquet scene is the miniature in the Lombard *Sermone* of Pietro da Barsegapé, *c.* 1300–1310; see L. Galli, in *Miniature a Brera 1100–1422: manoscritti dalla Biblioteca Nazionale Braidense e da collezioni private*, Exhib. Cat., ed. M. Boskovits (Milan, 1997), 130–45; fig., 131.

17. See C. Minott, *The Iconography of the Frescoes of the Life of Christ*

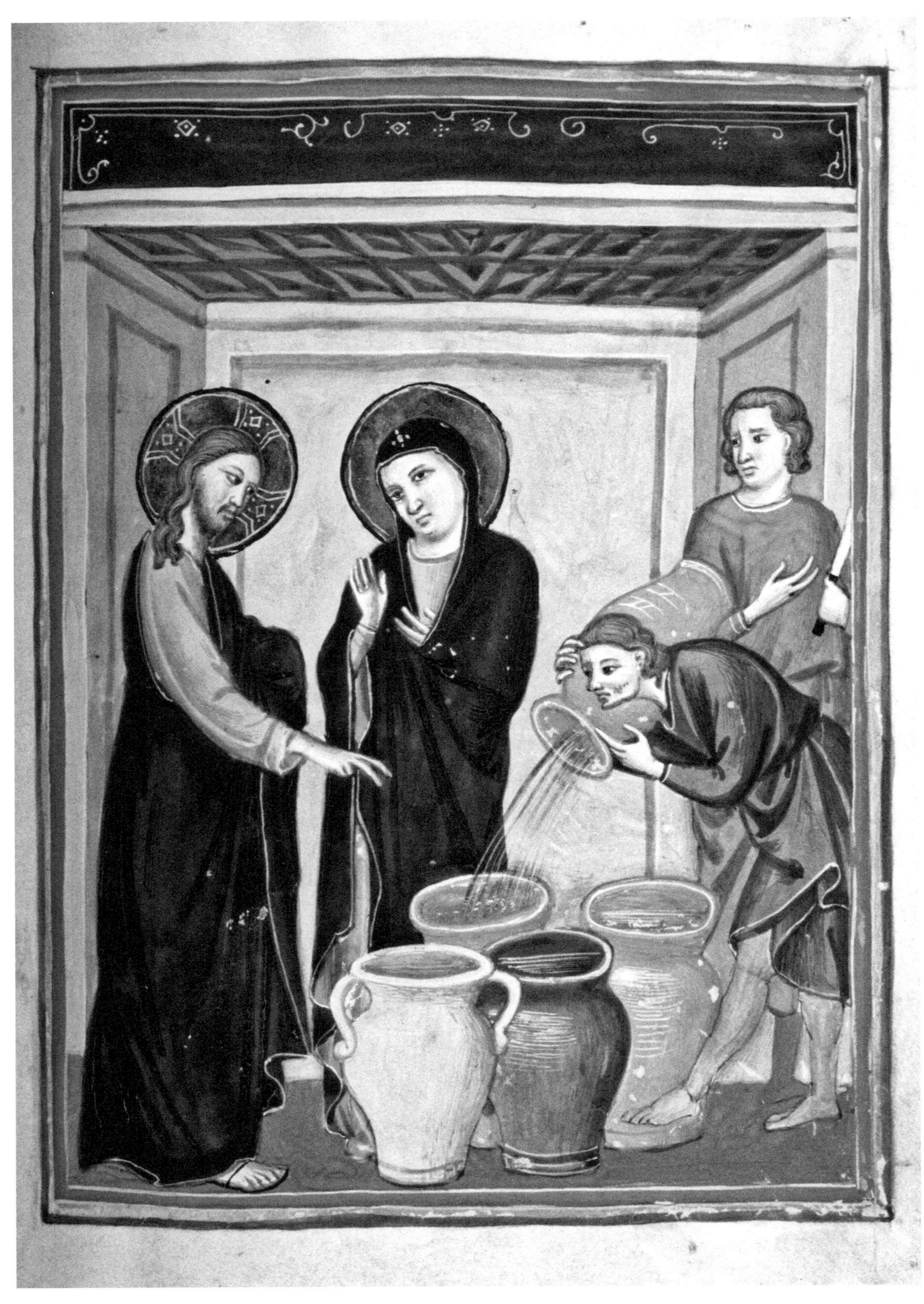

FIGURE 7. Pacino di Bonaguida, the Miracle at Cana, *c.* 1320; New York, Morgan Library and Museum, MS. M. 643, fol. 6r.

general lines, the wall-painting at Sant'Angelo probably resembled the late twelfth-century mosaic at the Cathedral of Monreale, which, although heavily restored, preserves its original Byzantine iconography (Fig. 8).[18] There are several points of similarity to Assisi: an architraved portico behind the table, Christ seated with Mary, who turns toward him, and the bride, crowned and central, facing the viewer. Some of the servants—the only twelfth-century figures to have survived intact—are also comparable. One pours water into the *hydria*; his pose, except for the head and his hitched-up tunic, is very much like that of his counterpart at Assisi. Another servant, in both scenes, approaches the table from the right, holding a covered dish, a long white cloth draped over his shoulder. Similarities to the Assisi fresco can also be found in more contemporary Byzantine iconography. In the thirteenth-century Gospel Book at Mount Athos (Iviron 5) the feast's table is rectangular, and the sumptuously dressed bride wears a crown and jewels around her face, though these seem sewn to her veil rather than attached to her crown (Fig. 9).[19]

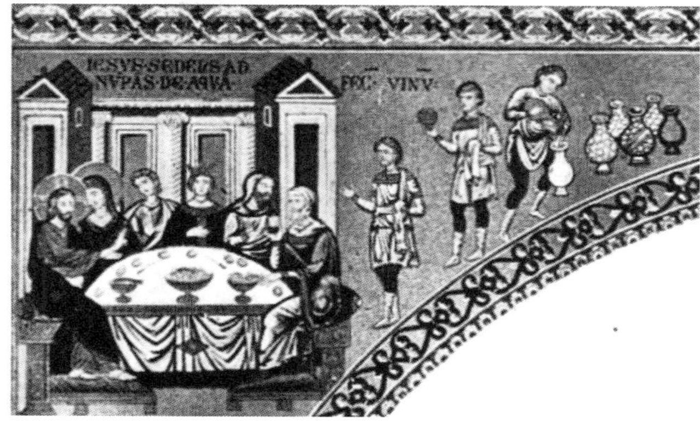

FIGURE 8. Monreale Cathedral, Miracle at Cana, from the lithograph by D. B. Gravina, 1859 (after Demus, *Mosaics* [as in note 19], pl. 66a).

The artists of the *Supplicationes variae* adapted many

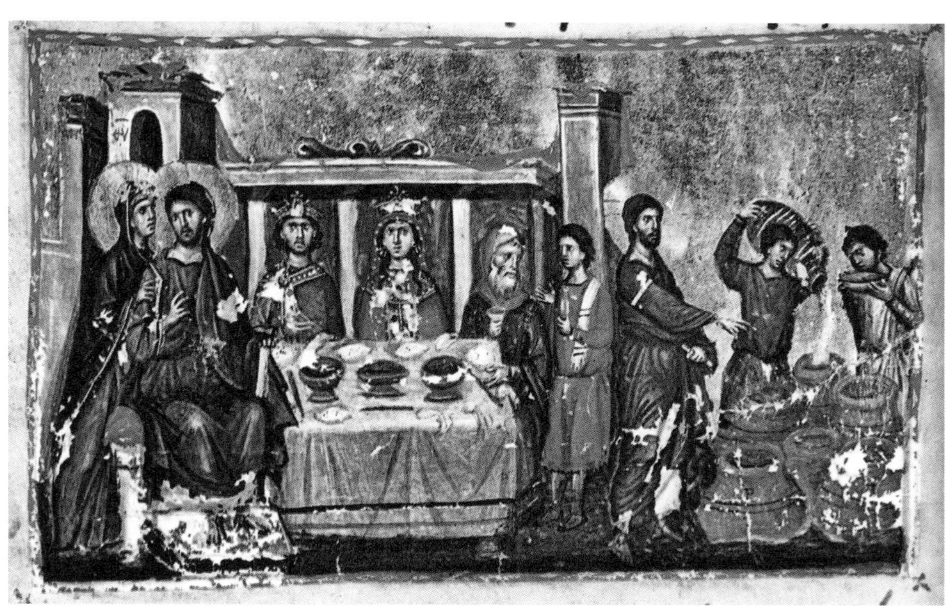

FIGURE 9. Gospel Book, thirteenth century; Mount Athos, Iviron 5, fol. 363v, Miracle at Cana (after *Treasures of Mount Athos*).

in the Church of Sant'Angelo in Formis (Ph.D. Diss., Princeton University, 1967), 87–91.

18. O. Demus, *The Mosaics of Norman Sicily* (New York, 1950), 108-12, discusses the restorations. A closely related contemporary scene of *Cana* survives from the bronze doors of Benevento Cathedral, with an apsidal structure in the background instead of a portico; F. Avril, X. Barrel i Altet, D. Gaborit-Chopin, *Il tempo delle crociate* (Milan, 1983), 79, 244, fig. 362.

19. Mount Athos, Iviron 5, fol. 363v. For the manuscript, see K. Maxwell, "Paris, Bibliothèque Nationale de France, Codex Grec 54: Modus Operandi of Scribes and Artists in a Palaiologan Gospel Book," *DOP* 54 (2000), 119–21.

Byzantine models in their narrative images, but not for the *Miracle at Cana*. Compositionally, the scene most resembles German examples of the twelfth and thirteenth centuries. As in the Book of Pericopes of St. Ehrentraud, Salzburg, *c.* 1140, Christ is formal and hieratic at the center of the table (Figs. 3, 10).[20] He does not acknowledge Mary, who addresses him, and the bride is undistinguished, at the far right. Comparison to the *Last Supper* and institution of the Eucharist is evident in the scene's emphatic symmetry and Christ's exaggerated gesture of blessing; Cana's transformation of water prefigures the Last Supper's transubstantiation of wine, an iconography plausibly developed in response to the Eucharistic concerns of the period. Similarly, in the *Supplicationes* drawing, Christ ceremoniously displays a disk of bread as he gestures toward the transformed wine, and the unusual shape of the curved table is like that of the *Last Supper* (Fig. 11).

However, in patristic and medieval exegesis on the miracle at Cana, Eucharistic reference is significant but not the sole or even the primary focus. Interpreters of the event often followed the lead of John's Gospel, with a strong focus on the miracle's manifestation of Christ's glory and its consequences. In this vein, Bonaventure begins his account of Cana by explaining the nature of Christ's revelation at the wedding, that it was "made by the Word and about the Word Incarnate."[21] Cana is about the incarnation, the divine Word joined to flesh. The significance of any historical, earthly wedding pales in light of the true wedding, which is that of Christ to the flesh, Christ to humanity. For Bonaventure, Christ's incarnation is the key that sets into motion multiple transformations symbolized by the miracle of water changed to wine. This broad theme informs Bonaventure's commentary, which he organizes to focus on the *occasion* of the wedding, Mary's *petition*, the miraculous *transformation*, the *recognition* of the miracle, and, finally, Christ's *manifestation* and *edification* of the disciples.[22]

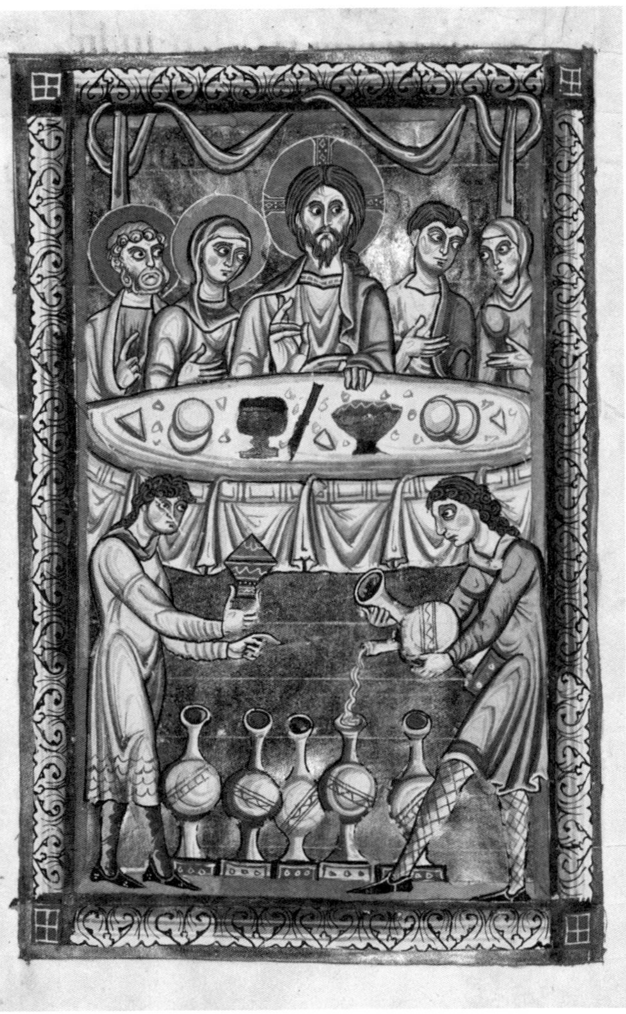

FIGURE 10. Pericopes of St. Ehrentraud, Salzburg, *c.* 1140; Munich, Bayerische Staatsbibliothek, clm. 15903, fol. 22ᵛ, the Miracle at Cana. (photo: Bayerische Staatsbibliothek).

The Occasion

The artists of the Assisi fresco and the *Supplicationes* drawing chose to depict Christ and Mary seated at the wedding-feast. This would have been an important point. Explaining how Christ came to be at the wedding, Bonaventure stresses that Christ has gone to Cana

20. Munich, Bayerische Staatsbibliothek, clm. 15903, fol. 22ᵛ; M. Pippal, *Das Perikopenbuch von St. Erentrud: Theologie und Tagespolitik* (Wiener Kunstgeschichtliche Forschungen 7, Vienna, 1997), on Cana, 42–3, 165, 183; E. Klemm, *Die romanischen Handschriften der Bayerischen Staatsbibliothek*, vol. 1, *Die Bistümer Regensburg, Passau und Salzburg* (Wiesbaden, 1980), cat. 272.

21. *Comm Jn* 2.1, 269; trans., Karris, 139.

22. *Comm Jn* 2.1, 269; trans. Karris, 139. Italics are used for these points in the Quaracchi edition and in Karris's translation. I have used *recognition* instead of Karris's *acknowledgment* to translate Bonaventure's term, *approbatio*, which means recognition, witness, or approval.

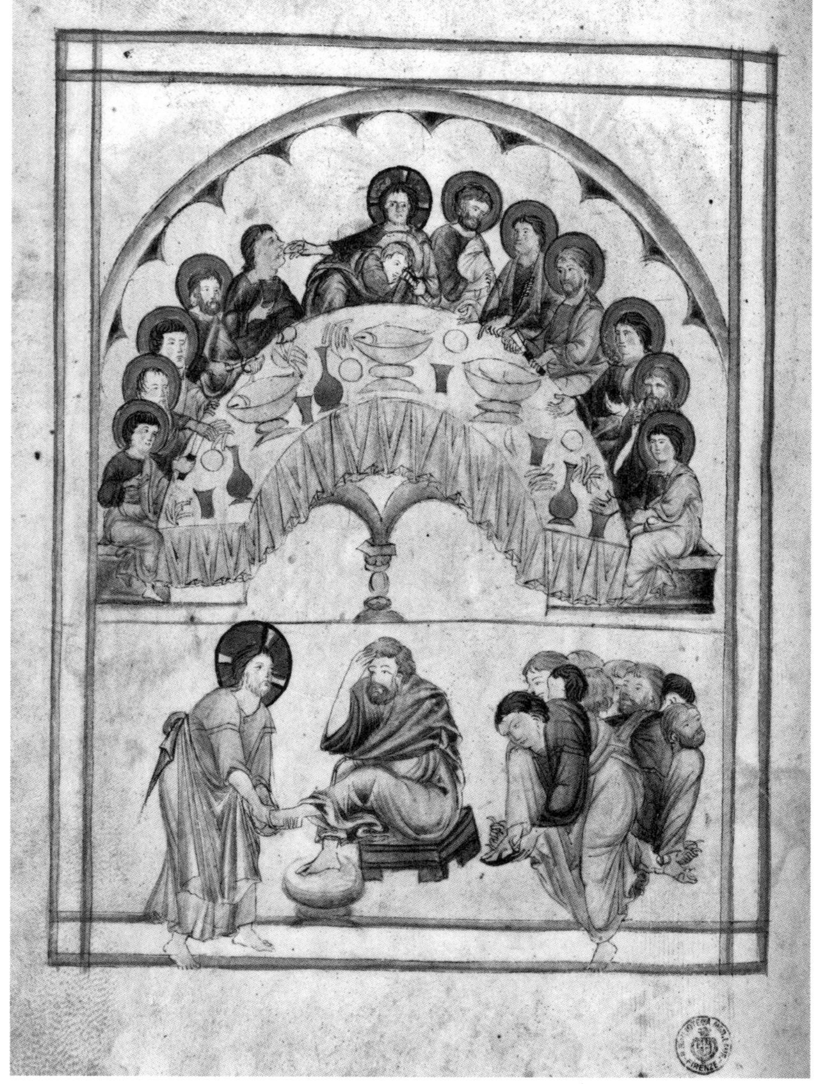

FIGURE 11. *Supplicationes variae*, Last Supper. Florence, Biblioteca Medicea Laurenziana, Plut. 25.3, fol. 372v (by permission of the Ministero per i Beni e le Attività culturali).

"not as someone great," but as a man, the son of Mary, who is kin to the groom. By accepting the invitation, Christ lowers himself to assume bonds of human relationship; "he, being humble, did not spurn the invitation, but went."[23] The miracle at Cana thus pertains to a central tenet of Franciscan theology: the descent of God that is effected through Christ's self-humbling. While the iconography of Ferentillo or Castel Appiano depicts the supernatural power of a miracle-worker, isolated from the marriage-feast, the late thirteenth-century Franciscan images show Christ with the guests as one of them, fully human. The lowly position that Christ assumes on this occasion is especially emphasized in the Byzantine composition adapted at Assisi, which seems inspired by a passage that Bonaventure quotes from Luke's parable on humility: "When you are invited to a wedding, go and recline in the last place" (Luke 14:10–11).[24]

23. *Comm Jn* 2.2, 269; trans. Karris, 140, who points out that Bonaventure here summarizes passages from his cited source, John Chrysostom.

24. *Ibid.* The Franciscan *Meditationes vitae christi* makes a similar point, that Christ sat among the other guests in the humblest place in order to exemplify Luke's parable; I. Ragusa and R. B. Green, ed., *Meditations on the Life of Christ: An Illustrated Manuscript of the Fourteenth Century. Paris, Bibliothèque nationale, Ms. ital. 115* (Princeton, 1961), 143.

The Petition

Bonaventure continues: "The stage is set for the second point, namely, the petition for a miracle."[25] Unlike most earlier commentaries in the Latin tradition, Bonaventure emphasizes the critical importance of Mary's *petition*, without which the miracle of Cana would not have taken place.[26] Although Mary was often included in medieval representations of *Cana*, her gestures vary. She may engage Christ in earnest conversation, telling him of the lack of wine, as in a ninth-century ivory panel now in the British Museum (Fig. 12), or she may react to the miracle that has already occurred, as in Pacino's miniature (Fig. 7). However, several Byzantine and a smaller number of western images depict Mary requesting the miracle, for example, in the Pericopes of St. Ehrentraud (Fig. 10). This action is emphasized at Assisi and in the *Supplicationes variae* with exceptional clarity. Because of damage to the painted surface, Mary's hand is now barely visible in the Assisi fresco, but originally it would have stood out, outstretched, silhouetted against a bright blue curtain.[27] In the *Supplicationes*, Mary's hands are more softly curved, but they are equally visible, isolated against the blank background of the page. The viewer should not miss Mary's gesture, the classic Byzantine pose of supplication and intercession, which was not consistently used in medieval images of *Cana*.

The intercessory posture, however, perfectly expresses Bonaventure's interpretation of Mary's petition, which is described as an act of charity.[28] According to Bonaventure, when Mary says, "They have no wine," her words are a prayer spoken out of commiseration with the bridegroom's poverty. Moreover, Mary's singular petition at Cana has universal application, demonstrating her relationship to all of mankind, who, in their human misery, imperfection, and sin are

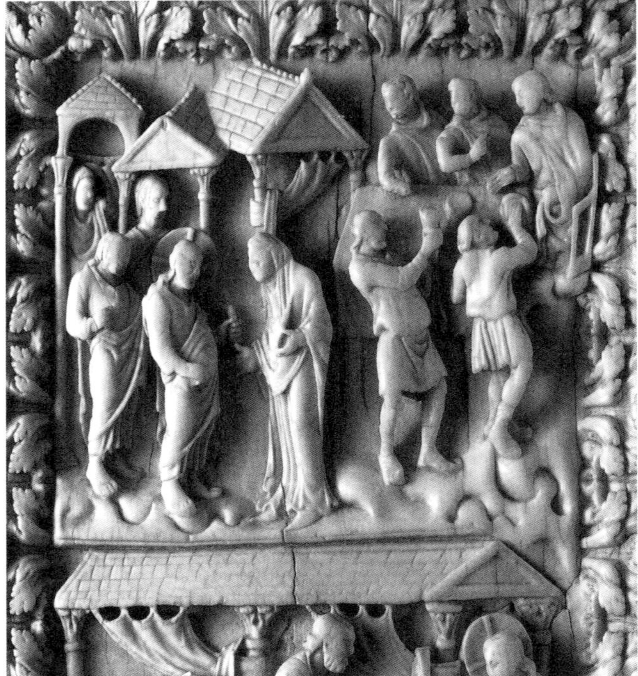

FIGURE 12. British Museum. Ivory panel, with the *Miracle at Cana*, ninth century (© Trustees of The British Museum).

"the poor." At Cana, Mary is the merciful advocate for the needy, intermediary between man and God. She is also an exemplary model who teaches mankind the path to salvation through obedience, faith, and prayer. Mary offers "to the poor at the banquet the solace of compassion, the counsel of instruction, and the suffrage of prayer."[29]

Cross-references to other images visually clarify the broad implications of Mary's prayer. In the *Supplicationes*, Mary takes the exact same pose in only one other scene, the *Last Judgment*, where she intercedes for the salvation of humanity (Fig. 13). At Assisi, Mary's gesture at Cana, with vertical forearm and outstretched hand, is repeated in the *Deësis* painted on the vault of

25. *Comm Jn* 2.3, 269; trans. Karris, 140.

26. Bonaventure develops a line of interpretation from Bernard of Clairvaux, who notes the compassion and mercy of Mary's words and their efficacy as intercession in sermons on Cana; *Dominica prima post Octavam Epiphaniae. Sermo* I and II, in Migne PL 183: 155, 159.

27. The current red color was underpaint to blue.

28. See Derbes and Sandona, *The Usurer's Heart* (as in note 1), 74, for other Franciscan writings that emphasize Mary's charity at the Cana wedding-feast.

29. *Comm Jn* 2.3, 269; trans. Karris, 140; also *Coll Jn* 2, coll. 9.1, 547. Both texts describe Mary's compassion for the poor in her petition; my quote is from the *Coll Jn*.

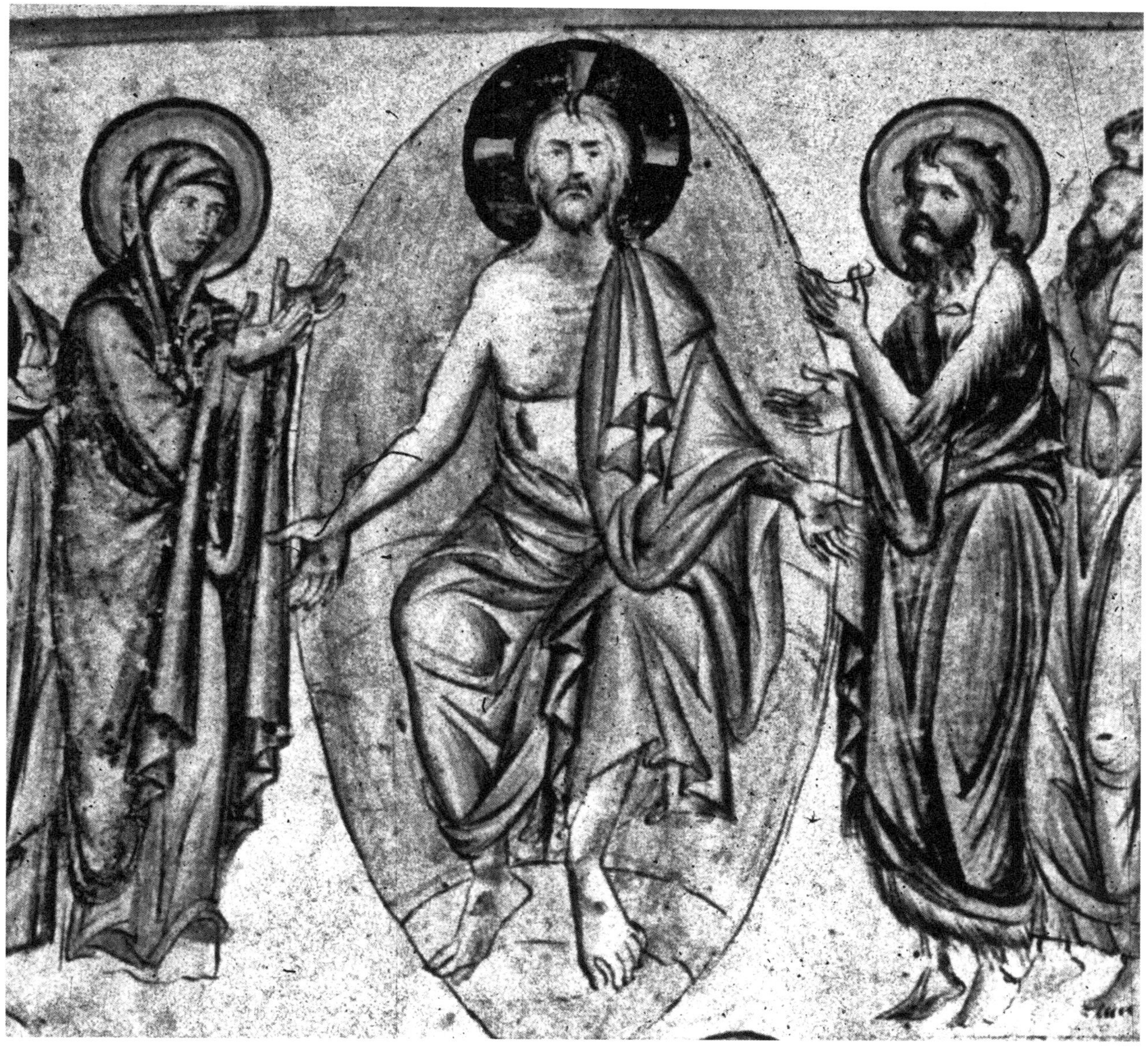

FIGURE 13. *Supplicationes variae*, Last Judgment. Florence, Biblioteca Medicea Laurenziana, Plut. 25.3, fol. 381v (by permission of the Ministero per i Beni e le Attività culturali).

the Upper Church nave, where Mary, John the Baptist, and St. Francis act as mankind's primary intercessors (Fig. 14).[30] Whether perusing the Franciscan manuscript or standing in the Upper Church nave, the viewer would receive a strong and reassuring message that what Mary did at Cana, she does for all humankind.

Mary's supplicatory gesture also teaches prayer, an important point for our monuments, since one is a manual of prayer, the other a site of prayer. According to Bonaventure, spiritual conversion begins with mankind's realization of its own defectiveness—its sinfulness and misery without God. Recognizing its existential

30. The pose is also repeated in the *Annunciation*, discussed below. On the *Deësis* at Assisi, see A. Neff, "Byzantine Icons and Franciscan Prayer: Images of Intercession and Ascent in the Upper Church of San Francesco, Assisi," in *Franciscan Prayer* (The Medieval Franciscans, 3), ed. T. J. Johnson (Leiden, 2007), 357–84.

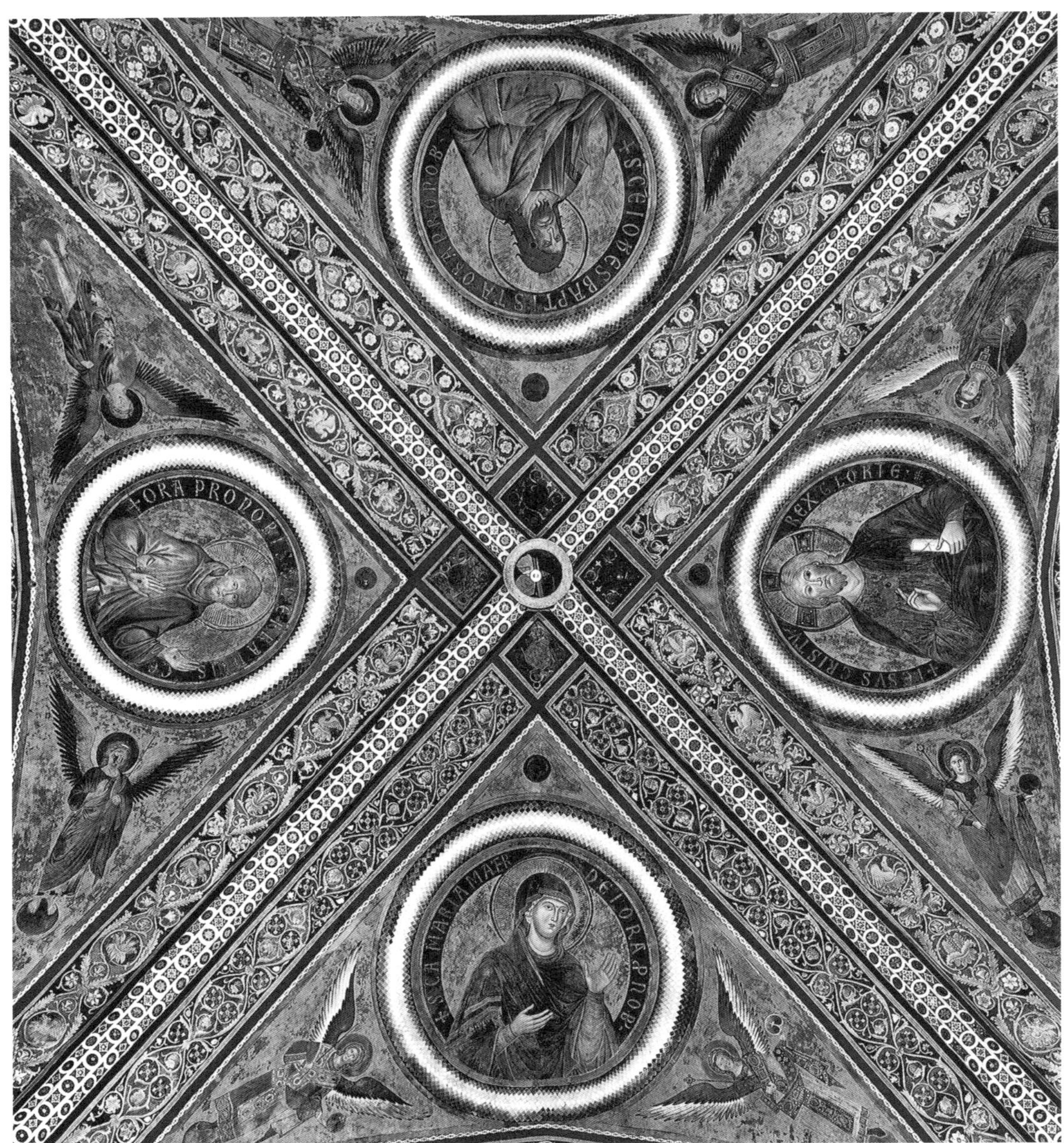

FIGURE 14. Assisi, San Francesco, vault of the Upper Church nave, *Deësis* (photo © Stefan Diller).

misery, mankind's first prayers are vocal and petitionary, cries for help.[31] This is precisely what Mary does at Cana. Her vocal supplication of Christ articulates the guests' neediness; her compassionate prayer enables them to receive the "best wine of devotion."[32] Bonaventure extends this allegory: the empty water-jars of Cana represent defects in the human soul, but when the soul repents, the jars are filled with tears of remorse. The water of penitence is what Christ transforms into wine of faith: "Because of the prayer of the Virgin, who had compassion for those in misery, God *filled the jugs* with the water of compunction, which was converted into the sweetness of devotion."[33] Miniatures in the *Supplicationes'* Office of the Virgin reinforce the idea that

31. On Bonaventure's theology of prayer, see T. J. Johnson, *The Soul in Ascent: Bonaventure on Poverty, Prayer, and Union with God* (Quincy, Ill., 2000).

32. *Comm Jn* 2.13, 271; trans. Karris, 149.

33. *Comm Jn* 2.13, 271; trans. Karris, 147.

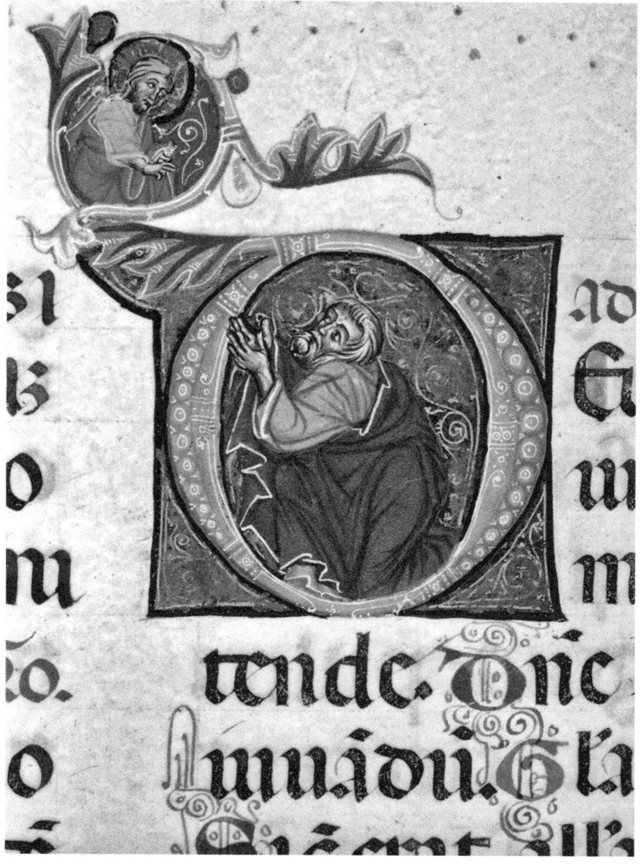

FIGURE 15. *Supplicationes variae*, supplicant in the Office of the Virgin. Florence, Biblioteca Medicea Laurenziana, Plut. 25.3, fol. 69v (by permission of the Ministero per i Beni e le Attività culturali).

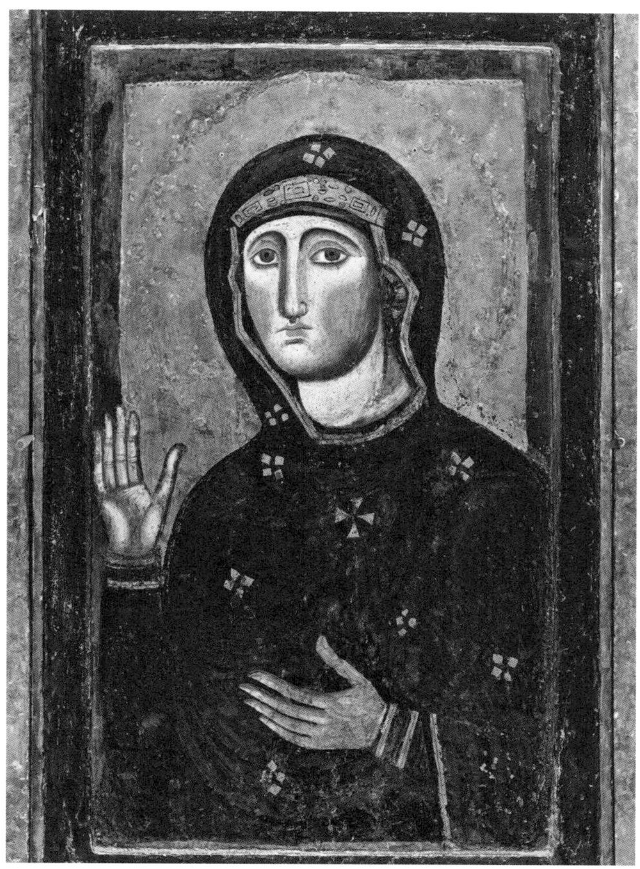

FIGURE 16. Rome, Sta. Maria in Aracoeli, replica of the *Madonna Advocata*, twelfth century (photo: Scala/Art Resource, N.Y.).

Mary's prayer at Cana teaches humans what they must do to escape their earthly misery. At the incipit of each hour, a supplicant prays with slightly parted, cupped hands—Mary's gesture at Cana. Like Mary, each supplicant calls aloud in prayer, seeking God's aid, as at the hour of Terce (Fig. 15): "O God, come to my assistance" (Ps. 69:2).

In the Assisi fresco of *Cana*, Mary's prayer has a different visual reference. Here, as Julian Gardner has pointed out, the figure of Mary is modeled after one of Rome's most venerated early Marian icons, the *Madonna Advocata*, which in the thirteenth century was kept in the Dominican convent of Rome.[34] But possibly, the Franciscan image at Assisi directly refers to a later medieval copy of this icon, an appealing thesis, since one of the many copies of the *Advocata* was "Franciscan," housed in the Order's Roman convent of Sta. Maria in Aracoeli (Fig. 16). By reproducing the icon within the Assisi fresco of *Cana*, the friars might have wanted to promote its status; the implication that the icon accurately replicates Mary's historic appearance at a Gospel event is a strong claim to its authenticity.

34. J. Gardner, "Pope Nicholas IV and the Decoration of Santa Maria Maggiore," *Zeitschrift für Kunstgeschichte* 36 (1973), 47, n. 119; see also Romano (as in note 10), 192. On the Roman *Madonna Advocata*, see H. Belting, *Likeness and Presence: A History of the Image before the Era of Art* (Chicago, 1994), 40, 314–23; Serena Romano, "Il ciclo di San Pietro in Valle: struttura e stile," in Tamanti (as in note 12), 65–70.

In the context of the *Miracle at Cana*, use of the iconic type emphasizes Mary's role as mankind's advocate and beautifully represents the duality of her prayer. While Mary enacts the New Testament narrative, noting the lack of wine, she also gazes outward toward viewers of the fresco—"the poor"—who stand in the church below her image. Taking the form of an icon, she invites their prayers and promises her mercy.

Transformation & Recognition

Mary's prayerful petition initiates the miracle at Cana, exemplifies compassionate charity, and obtains gifts of faith, penitence, and devotion for the poor. These gifts are attendant upon the occasion: Christ's union with humanity. Joined to Christ, who has humbled himself for this purpose, humankind is enabled to turn from a miserable earthly existence to faith. Thus, Christ's miraculous *transformation* turns water (remorse and repentance) to wine (faith and devotion). Bonaventure seems to emphasize the theme of individual penitence and conversion more so than most earlier commentators, but his interest in Cana as a site of transformation draws on long-standing exegetical tradition.[35] The Venerable Bede, one of Bonaventure's main sources, points out that the word *Cana* signifies zeal, while *Galilee* signifies transmigration.[36] The wedding miracle teaches that God's grace is especially for those "aflame with the zeal of pious devotion," who can "emigrate from vices to virtues by doing good works, and from earthly to eternal things by hoping and loving."[37] Each Franciscan image of Cana illustrates these transmigrations, but in different ways.

Transmigration in the *Supplicationes* drawing concerns transformation from vice to virtue and from indifference to faith. While the guests pictured at Assisi seem genteelly indifferent to the food before them, in the drawing, the bride firmly holds onto the roast meat. Granted, this is not a picture of base depravity, but it does place the *Supplicationes* drawing in a pictorial tradition that shows the marriage-feast as a site of indulgence. Castel Appiano is an especially unrestrained example: the bridal couple embraces with gusto, and a guest stuffs his dinner into his mouth (Fig. 6). The Cana feast pictured at Chartres Cathedral, *c.* 1220–1230, shows the bride holding a bowl, seemingly of red fruit, and the couple's gestures are like Adam and Eve's at the Fall (Fig. 17).[38] As in the *Supplicationes*, there are signs that the wedding-feast is Jewish; at Chartres, the Architriclinus wears a pointed hat, while in the *Supplicationes*, the bride wears a turban, a type of headgear worn in the manuscript only by Jews and marginal hybrid creatures.

In feast-scenes of this type, Christ generally does not sit at the table, and the guests are unaware of the miracle. The *Supplicationes*' imagery of Christ mingling with those who indulge is a strong statement of his voluntary self-humbling. And there are several signs that Cana's transmigrations have been set into action, leading to *recognition* and the *manifestation of divine glory*.[39]

35. Bernard, *Dominica prima* (as in note 26), 156, also links the Cana water-jars to individual conversion, but for him, the jars represent progressive stages that lead from purgation and compunction to obedience to the Church's teachings; the water is compared to the purifying waters of baptism and the fountain of life. Gottfried of Admont (*c.* 1100–1165) compares the water of the second jar, the jar of conversion, to the flood of cleansing tears in the time of Noah; Migne PL 174: 112. The direct source from which Bonaventure developed his allegory may have been the Dominican scholar and cardinal Hugh of St. Cher (d. 1263); Karris (as in note 8), 148 n. 35.

36. *Homily I.14 on the Gospels*, in *Bede the Venerable. Homilies on the Gospels. Book One. Advent to Lent*, trans. Lawrence T. Martin and David Hurst (Kalamazoo, Mich., 1991), 136. As the editors note, these widely used definitions were established in Jerome's *Book of Hebrew Names*.

37. Bede, *Homily I.14* (as in note 36), 136; *In S. Joannis Evangelium Expositio*, in Migne PL 92: 657.

38. The story of Cana is placed below the famous *Belle verrière* of Chartres, where it unfolds in six consecutive scenes. The placement of the feast-scene indicates that it depicts a moment before the miracle of transformation has occurred.

39. For the essential role of *recognition* as a prelude to salvation in Bonaventure's exegesis, exemplified in the story of Cana, see T. J. Herbst, *The Road to Union: Johannine Dimensions of Bonaventure's Christology* (Grottaferrata, 2005), 287–90. Another example in which Christ sits at the table with guests who indulge is carved on the side-portal of the Abbey Church of Charlieu, early twelfth century. Although this scene differs significantly from that in the *Supplicationes* in other respects, it has also been interpreted as depicting the transformation from vice to virtue; Jochen Zink, "Zur dritten Abteikirche von Charlieu (Loire), inbesondere zur Skulptur der

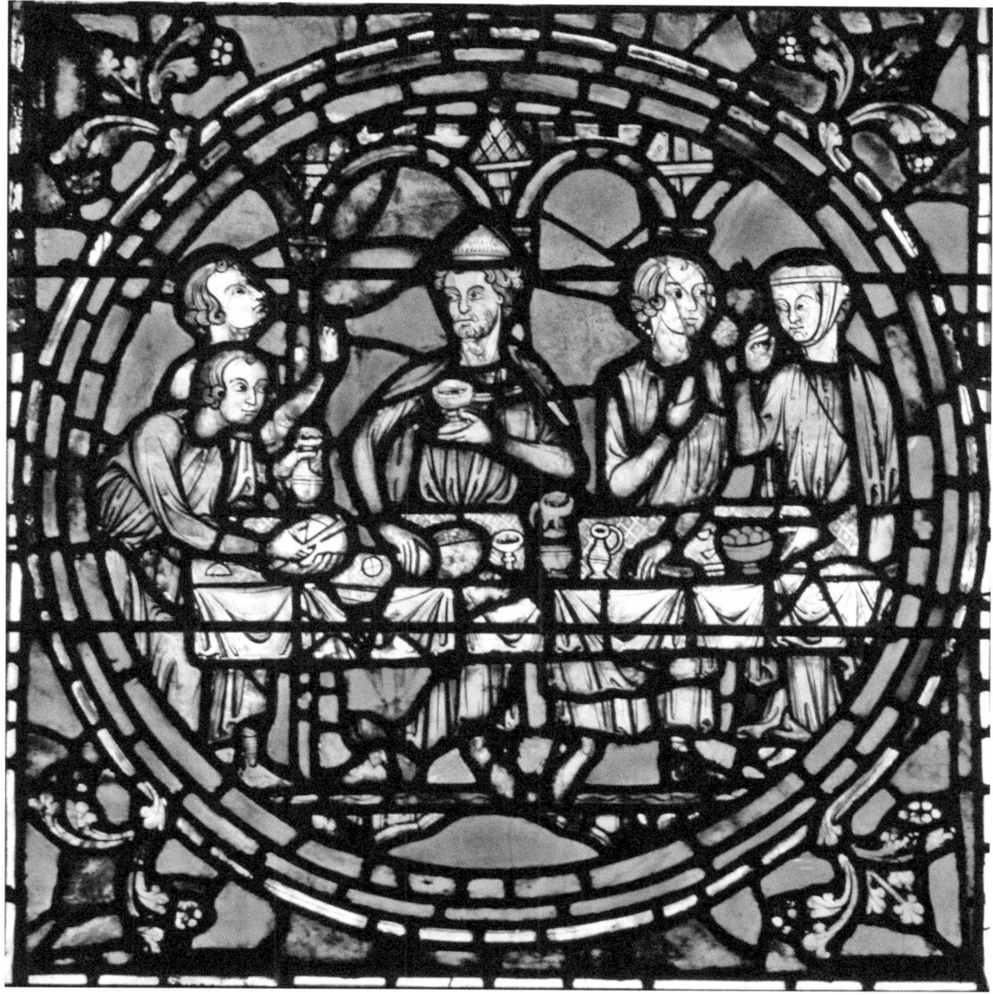

FIGURE 17. Chartres Cathedral, the *Belle verrière* window, detail: Miracle at Cana, *c.* 1220–1230 (photo: courtesy of Sacred Destinations Photography).

The casual stance of the youth who stands in the right foreground with crossed arms, one hand tucked under, is unusually naturalistic, truly exceptional not only for the *Supplicationes* artist but for most artists of the Duecento. In at least one example, however, the cross-armed pose characterizes courtly leisure. The partially preserved wall-painting of the Casa Finco, in Bassano del Grappa (Vicenza), shows a youth standing at ease, with his arms comfortably crossed, one hand tucked under, as he listens attentively to the music played by a troubadour.[40] This secular scene would surely have had no negative connotations, but in a Christian context, idleness often connotes inattention to God; in Christian art, the natural gestures of leisure often

Vorhalle und ihrer künstlerischen Nachfolge," *Wallraf-Richartz-Jahrbuch* 44 (1983), 99.

40. The date of this fresco is disputed, but probably falls in the third quarter of the thirteenth century; for a summary and bibliography, see G. Ericani, "Bassano," in *La pittura nel Veneto: Le origini*, ed. F. d'Arcais (Milan, 2004), 135–42. A cross-armed pose was also used by Nicola Pisano for a witness to the resurrection of Napoleone Orsini sculpted on the Arca di San Domenico, 1265–67; the pose moves to a heavenly realm in Simone Martini's *Maestà*, *c.* 1315, where two female saints stand with crossed arms and tucked hand. Their leisure might suggest not only elegant courtliness but also a paradise exempt from labor, mankind's punishment after the Fall.

indicate sloth, whether in physical laziness or lack of spiritual commitment.[41] The specific pose pictured in the drawing of *Cana* illustrates this vice well, finding scriptural reference in the slothful man who "hides his hand under his armpit" (Prov. 19 : 24, 26 : 15), and in the fool who will not labor but "folds his hands together" (Eccles. 4 : 5). That the pose could be widely associated with sloth is suggested by cross-armed figures depicting laziness, or *paresse*, in some manuscripts of the *Somme le roi*, the popular moral treatise written in 1279; the same idea is apparent in the folded hands of a figure representing *Acedia* in the Chapter House of Salisbury Cathedral, sculpted *c.* 1265.[42]

Yet despite his pose of leisure, the youthful attendant in the *Supplicationes* drawing responds to the miracle taking place. His companion at the left of the scene still has one arm folded but has been moved to obey Mary's command, "Do whatever he tells you" (John 2 : 5); he directs the servants to pour water. Bonaventure's *Commentary on John* interprets Mary's command as a warning precisely against spiritual indifference and lack of belief—sins of sloth. "Do not be diffident," writes Bonaventure, quoting John 11 : 10, "'if you believe, you will see the glory of God.'"[43] And in the drawing, the youth at the right turns to gaze at Christ—perhaps only now seeing and recognizing the "manifestation of the Word Incarnate." Giotto, working a little over a decade later than the *Supplicationes* artist, includes a similar cross-armed figure (Fig. 18).[44] The servant's stance is more erect and less casual, but recognition and conversion to belief are unmistakable in the intensity of the figure's gaze.

Those seated at the table also react to the miracle. In Bonaventure's *Commentary*, the Architriclinus discerns the superiority of the new wine, but, not recognizing its source, he questions the groom. The *Supplicationes* drawing differs from Bonaventure in this detail, showing the Architriclinus addressing the greedy bride with a raised hand and pointing finger. With the same gesture, two guests admonish or instruct their companions who hold bread, as if urging them to consider their action. It seems odd that the Apostle Peter, seated at the left, is among those receiving a lecture, but in this vignette, Peter may—like the attendants—represent recognition of Christ's miracle, conversion to faith, and "transmigration" from vice to virtue. In several gospel stories, Peter exemplifies human frailty, as when he lacks sufficient faith to walk on the water. Yet these moments of weakness are always followed by realization and renewed faith, and Peter's name was given the meaning *agnoscens*—recognizing or realizing.[45] Peter was also associated with sobriety or temperance, the antithesis to the bride's gluttony. When writing on the need to resist lust and indulgence in food or drink, Bonaventure often cites Peter's exhortations to sobriety (1 Peter 1 : 13 and 5 : 8), a virtue that may be suggested in the *Supplicationes* drawing by Peter's action.[46] Several manuscripts of the *Somme le roi* illustrate the virtue of

41. Excellent works on the classical, medieval, and Renaissance traditions include B. Vickers, "Leisure and Idleness in the Renaissance: The Ambivalence of *otium*," *Renaissance Studies* 4/1 (1990), 1–37; 4/2 (1990), 107–54; and S. Wenzel, *The Sin of Sloth: Acedia in Medieval Thought and Literature* (Chapel Hill, 1960).

42. British Library MS. Add. 28162, fol. 8ᵛ; for the visual representation of laziness with folded hands in the *Somme le roi*, see R. Tuve, "Notes on the Virtues and Vices. Part II," *JWarb* 27 (1964), 50; at Salisbury, R. B. Green, "Virtues and Vices in the Chapter House Vestibule in Salisbury," *JWarb* 31 (1968), 148–58. For other fourteenth-century and post-medieval examples, see S. Koslow, "Frans Hals's *Fisherboys*: Exemplars of Idleness," *Art Bulletin* 57 (1975), 418–32.

43. *Comm Jn* 2.5, trans. Karris, 142. Karris's translation of *non diffidatis* might also be read, "do not lack faith" or "do not despair." All these types of diffidence contrast to belief.

44. For R. Schumacher-Wolfgarten, the pose in the Arena Chapel fresco emphasizes the figure's thoughtful concentration on Christ; "Wein- und Speisewunder Jesu aus Oberitalien in Spätantike und Mittelalter," in *Vivarium: Festschrift Theodor Klauser zum 90. Geburtstag* (*Jahrbuch für Antike und Christentum Ergängungsband* 11, Munich, 1984), 298. For another Trecento example, see the Sta. Chiara Triptych in the Civico Museo Sartorio, Trieste. The gesture is modified in a drawing in the *Meditationes vitae christi* in Paris, so that the arms are raised and crossed over the chest in a pose of acceptance or reverence that sometimes appears in images of the *Annunciation*; Ragusa and Green, *Meditations* (as in note 25), 146, 148.

45. As in Jerome's *Book of Hebrew Names* and Walafrid Strabo's *Commentary on the Gospel of Matthew*; Migne PL 23: 843, 1153; 114: 87. The explanation given is that Peter recognizes the identity of Christ, saying, "Thou art Christ, the Son of the living God" (Matt. 16:16).

46. As far as I know, Bonaventure does not associate Peter with sobriety in his writings on Cana, but he often does so when writing about restraint from sins of excess; see, for example, *Opera Omnia* (as in note 8), vol. 9, 681.

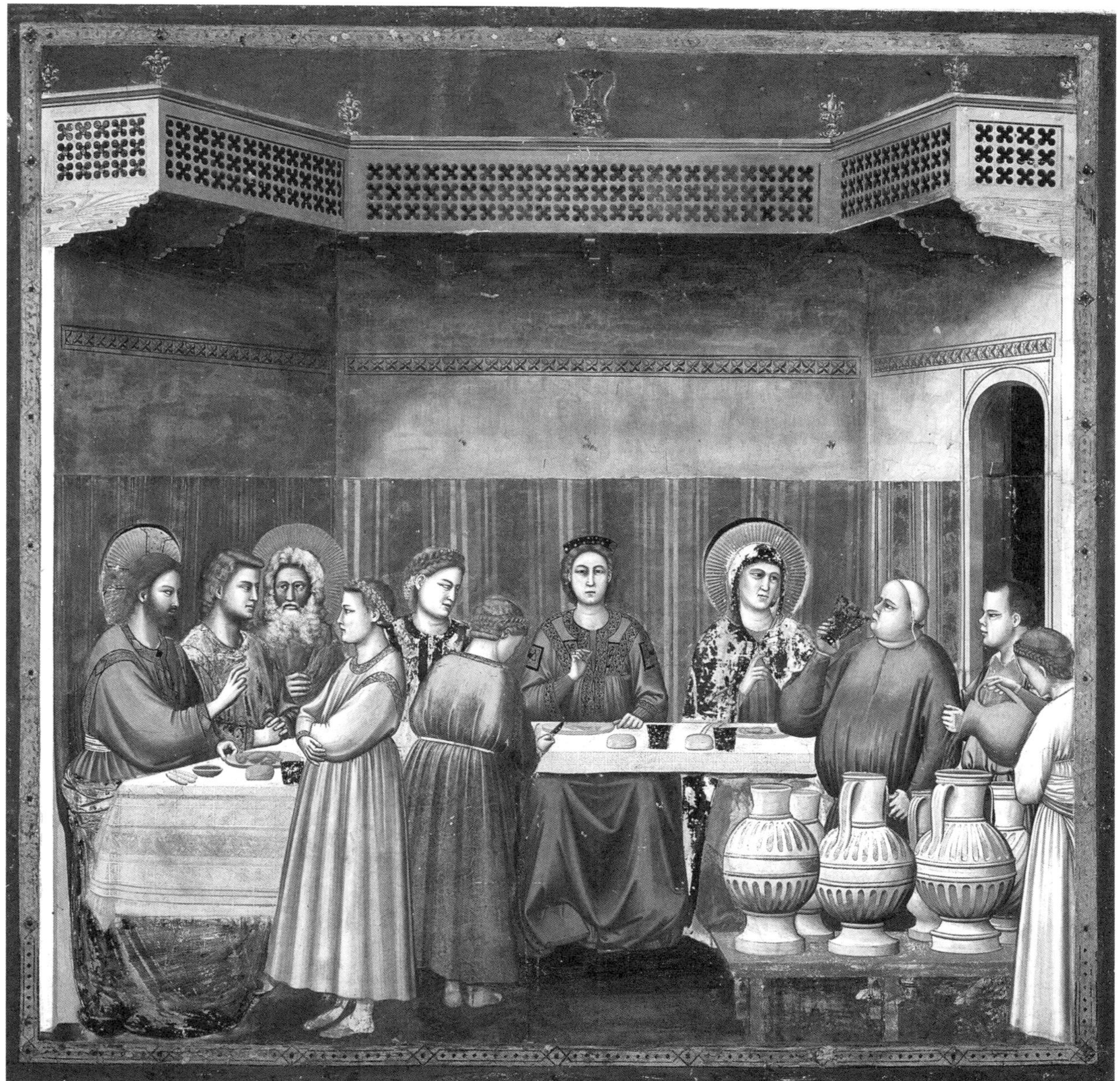

FIGURE 18. Giotto, the Miracle at Cana, Padua, Arena Chapel, *c.* 1305 (photo: Scala/Art Resource, N.Y.).

sobriety with a bearded man who sits at a meal, cutting a loaf of bread.[47] His is a measured consumption of food, which contrasts to the gluttony of the rich man's banquet. When sobriety appears at Cana, the new wine has been acknowledged, vice has been converted to virtue, and the disciples turn anew to faith.

Imagery of food and abstention links the *Miracle at Cana* to a theme that runs through the *Supplicationes variae*: the contrast between carnal eating and sacred eating. The manuscript's introductory poem addresses the guest at the banquet-table, "you who dine," advising abstinence, sobriety, and charity, for Christ's sake:

47. The meaning of this figure is clear from the inscription that accompanies it; see E. Kosmer, *A Study of the Style and Iconography of a Thirteenth-Century Somme le roi (British Museum Ms. Add. 54180)*, Ph.D. Diss., Yale Univ., 1973 (Ann Arbor, 1976), Pt. 1, 151, 327.

When [food] is held back from the mouth, you give
Christ what is better.
When you are at the table, think first of the poor man.
When you feed him, [my] friend, you feed God.[48]

Like Mary at Cana, the guest at the banquet-table should think of the poor and practice charity. And just as Cana's bread and wine prefigure the Eucharist, after a few lines the introductory poem shifts its focus from secular banquets to the sacred table of the Mass, affirming Christ's true presence and repeating the scriptural lesson that those who eat worthily will be saved, while unworthy eating merits damnation. These lessons were commonplace in a century preoccupied with the significance of the Eucharist, but they nonetheless help us appreciate the moral scope and sacramental implications of the *Supplicationes* drawing. When dinner-guests abstain, when they follow the counsel of the Virgin Mary, they do Christ's will (John 2:5), practicing charity—transmigrating "from vices to virtues by doing good works." The carnal wedding can then be transformed to a spiritual wedding whose guests will be worthy of the Eucharistic eating prefigured in the *Supplicationes* drawing by Christ's gesture.[49]

The ultimate transmigration is "from carnal things to heavenly things." Bonaventure's *Collation* on Cana notes four varieties of wedding: carnal, spiritual, sacramental, and eternal, which are explained as weddings of guilt, of grace, of the Eucharist, and of glory.[50] The first pertains to human concupiscence; the second to the marriage between God and the soul; the third and fourth to the marriage of Christ and the Church. The *Supplicationes* drawing alludes to all of these weddings. We have seen the carnal sin of self-indulgence, the individual's reception of grace in recognition, faith, and devotion, and the prefiguration of Eucharist. An unusual detail, the Architriclinus' crown, is a reminder of the fourth wedding, which Bonaventure identifies with the eternal banquet described in Matthew's parable: "The kingdom of heaven is like a king, who made a marriage for his son" (Matt. 22:2).[51] The guests admitted to this celestial banquet have obeyed Christ and spurned the goods of the world—like those in the *Supplicationes* drawing who abstain from the earthly, carnal feast.[52]

Bride & Church

In the *Supplicationes' Miracle at Cana*, reference to the wedding of Christ to the Church is muted, but at Assisi, the Church takes primary place, personified by *Cana*'s bride (Figs. 1, 4).[53] The bride is a striking figure; her dignified, formal stature and her crown separate her from the western medieval iconographic tradition, in which the bride wears either a head-cloth, as in the miniature from Salzburg (Fig. 10), or a contemporary fashion—for example, a low, round hat and barbette in the window at Chartres (Fig. 17). Nor is the crown like the wreath or simple metal circlet worn at medieval Italian

48. Plut. 25.3, fol. 1: "Ut retrahatur ori das christo de meliori. | Cum fueris in mensa primo de paupere pensa. | Dum pascis eum pascis amice deum."

49. *Comm Jn* II.13 (VI); trans., Karris, 147.

50. *Coll Jn* 2.coll. 8.2, 545. A ranked listing of three or four levels of marriage seems a common feature in thirteenth-century mendicant sermons on Cana; D. L. d'Avray, *The Preaching of the Friars: Sermons Diffused from Paris before 1300* (Oxford, 1985), 250, 257; D'Avray publishes several examples in his two books, *Medieval Marriage Sermons* (as in note 6) and *Medieval Marriage: Symbolism and Society* (Oxford, 2005). The details of these lists vary, but Bonaventure's system is not unique, appearing, for example, in a contemporary sermon by another Franciscan, Pierre de Saint-Benoît; see D'Avray, *Medieval Marriage Sermons*, 190–92, 211–25.

51. The crown is unusual but not unique. A crown is worn by the bearded Architriclinus in the *Cana* scene in a late eleventh-century ivory panel in Salerno; R. P. Bergman, *The Salerno Ivories: Ars Sacra from Medieval Amalfi* (Cambridge, 1980), fig. 25; a crowned young man—the Architriclinus or the groom—sits at the table in the Salzburg Lectionary, *c.* 1060 (New York, Pierpont Morgan Library, MS. M.780, fol. 17). Bonaventure's comparisons of the Cana wedding to Matthew's parable are in *Comm Jn* 2.12, 270; Karris, 145; and *Coll Jn* 2, coll. 8.12, 546.

52. *Coll Jn* 2, coll. 8. 10, 546.

53. For the iconography of the Cana scene at Assisi, see G. Ruf, *Die Fresken der Oberkirche San Francesco in Assisi. Ikonographie und Theologie* (Regensburg, 2004), 171–4; P. Burkhart, *Franziskus und die Vollendung der Kirche im siebten Zeitalter: Zum Programm der Langhausfresken in der Oberkirche von San Francesco in Assisi* (Frankfurt, 1992), 66–71, 87, 169; D. Rigaux, *A La Table du Seigneur: L'Eucharistie chez les Primitifs italiens (1250–1497)* (Paris, 1989), 79; A. Monciatti, in *La Basilica di San Francesco ad Assisi*, ed. G. Bonsanti (*Mirabilia d'Italia*, 11; Modena, 2002), II, 502. My analysis independently comes to some conclusions that are similar to Burkhart's.

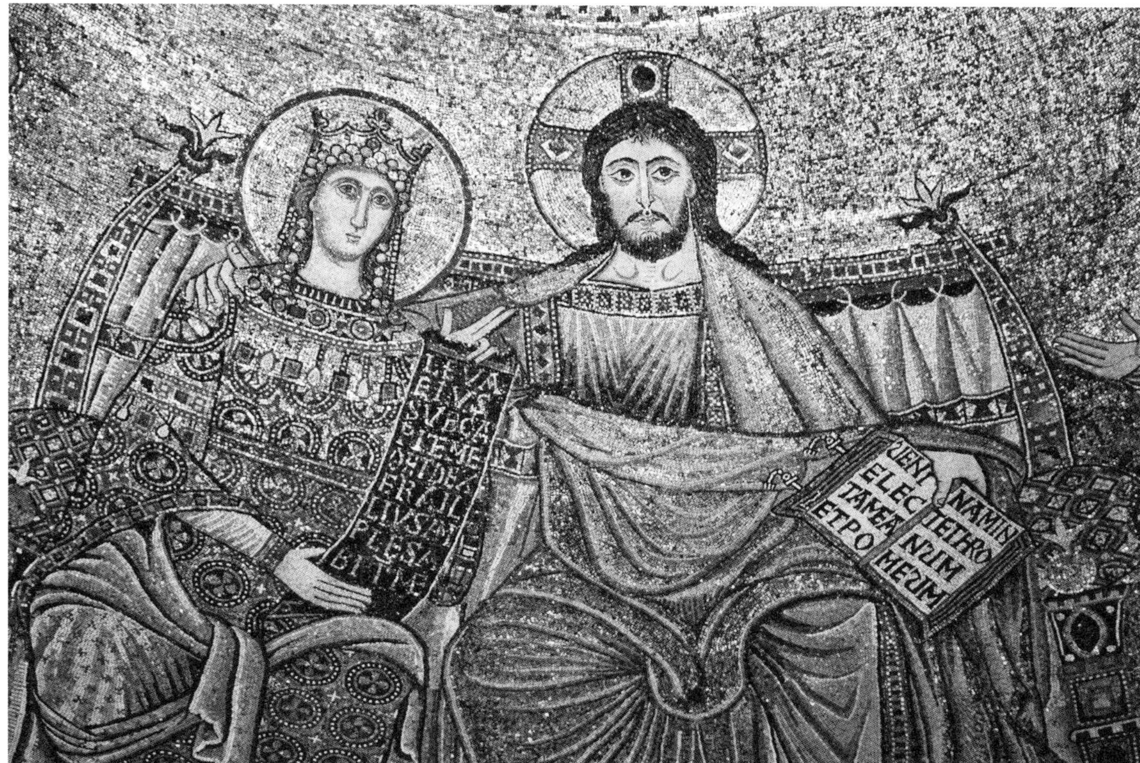

FIGURE 19. Rome, Sta. Maria in Trastevere, detail from the apse mosaic of Christ Enthroned with Mary, *c.* 1130–1140 (photo: courtesy of Stefan Gehring).

weddings, for example, in Giotto's fresco of Mary wed to Joseph in the Arena Chapel, Padua.[54] To medieval viewers at Assisi, the high, box-like crown with hanging gems would probably have looked foreign and exotic, in keeping with the event's distant locale, Cana in Galilee. However, considering the artist's Roman training and the Franciscan Order's close ties to the Roman papacy, *Cana*'s bride is surely related to Roman images of *Maria-Regina;* specifically, the bride resembles the crowned and jeweled bride of Christ as pictured in Rome.[55] For example, in the apse-mosaic of Sta. Maria in Trastevere, Mary sits enthroned as Christ's spouse (Fig. 19). Her crown is not boxy, but the rows of gems that frame her face are like those adorning Assisi's bride.

Two closely related iconographic types offer further comparisons. Across the façade of Sta. Maria in Trastevere, a mosaic frieze shows processions of wise and foolish virgins approaching Mary enthroned with the Christ child.[56] Each wise virgin wears a high crown that highlights her role as a prudent and virginal spouse of

54. For illustrations of late medieval bridal wreaths and crowns in Italy, see M. Seidel, "Hochzeitsikonographie im Trecento," *Mitteilungen des Kunsthistorischen Institutes in Florenz* 38 (1994), 1–47. At Assisi, on the crossing-vault of the Lower Church, the scene of St. Francis wed to Lady Poverty shows the Lady wearing a wreath made of a knotted cord.

55. While the artist of the *Miracle at Cana* is unknown, he is generally considered Roman; Belting, *Die Oberkirche* (as in n. 10), 226; A Monciatti, in *La Basilica* (as in note 53), II, 463; A. Tomei, *Iacobus Torriti Pictor. Una vicenda figurativa del tardo Duecento romano* (Rome, 1990), 67. The crown can also be compared to examples worn by brides or empresses in Byzantine art, and the artist probably modeled the figure after a Byzantine bride like that pictured in Iviron 5 (Fig. 9). Nevertheless, western medieval viewers at Assisi, unfamiliar with Byzantine bridal costume and prompted by sermons on the allegorical meanings of Cana, could readily have associated the bride's crown with the imagery of spouse, virgin, and Church.

56. For the mosaic and earlier bibliography, see C. Harding, "Images of Authority, Identity, Power: Facade Mosaic Decoration in Rome during the Late Middle Ages," *RACAR* 24/1 (1997), 19–21.

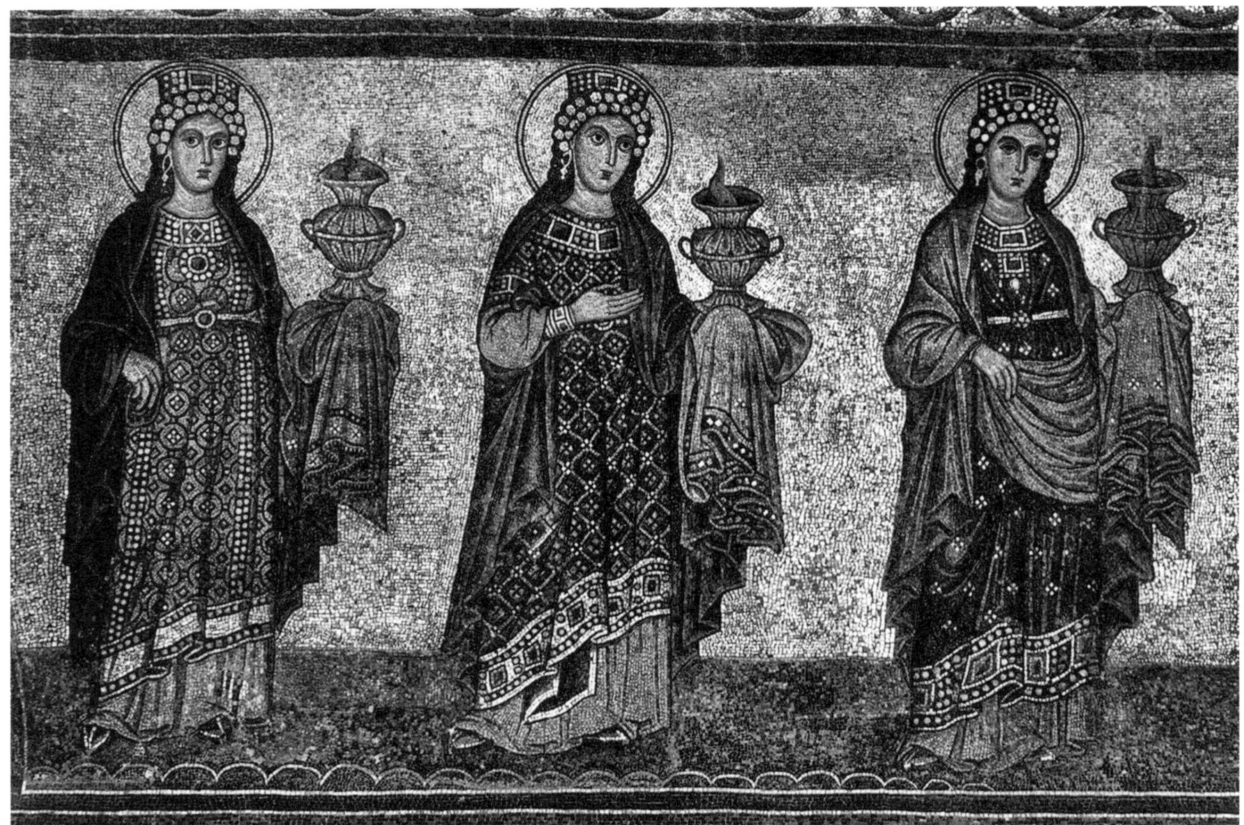

FIGURE 20. Rome, Sta. Maria in Trastevere, detail from the façade mosaic, the Wise Virgins, late thirteenth century (photo: Alinari/Art Resource, N.Y.).

Christ (Fig. 20); the foolish virgins, in contrast, wear head-scarves, like the Jewish bride in the *Supplicationes*. The wise virgins pictured at the Roman church wear costumes that vary in detail—not surprisingly, since the figures date to two or three distinct campaigns. But two of the thirteenth-century figures are especially close to the Assisi bride; curving rows of large gems frame the brow, and at the neckline, there is a wide jeweled band or necklace, to which a large brooch or pendant is attached, centered on the chest.[57] Another Roman comparison is more approximate, but still worthy of note. Only the head of *Ecclesia* survives from a full-length figure that was once part of the medieval apse mosaic of St. Peter's (Fig. 21).[58] Her crown is tall, angular, and boxy, like that in the fresco of *Cana*, with round knobs along the top edge.

If the bride's costume in the Assisi fresco suggests comparison with virgin-bride and *Ecclesia*, these allusions are perfectly suited to the interpretation of the Wedding at Cana as the union of Christ with the Church. When Bonaventure introduces his *Commentary* on Cana with the statement that the miracle was "about

57. A late thirteenth-century panel of Sta. Lucia in the Musée de Grenoble is also closely related in iconography to the wise virgins of Sta. Maria in Trastevere. Depicted as a bride holding a burning oil-lamp, Lucy wears a costume like those of the wise virgins, adding another similarity to Assisi's bride: the broad gold-colored bands around the upper arm. For the Grenoble panel, see Tomei, *Iacobus Torriti* (as in note 55), 44 n. 161, 67, 139–40, fig. 151.

58. The surviving mosaic of *Ecclesia* dates to the renovations made by Innocent III (1198–1216) to the apse of St. Peter's; see A. Iacobini, "Il mosaico absidale di San Pietro in Vaticano," in *Fragmenta picta* (as in note 11), 119–29; *idem*, "*Est Haec Sacra Principis Aedes*: The Vatican Basilica from Innocent III to Gregory IX (1198–1241)," in *St. Peter's in the Vatican*, ed. W. Tronzo (Cambridge, 2005), 49–52; M. Andaloro and S. Romano, *Arte e iconografia a Roma dal Tardoantico alla fine del Medioevo* (Milan, 2002), 94, 96–7.

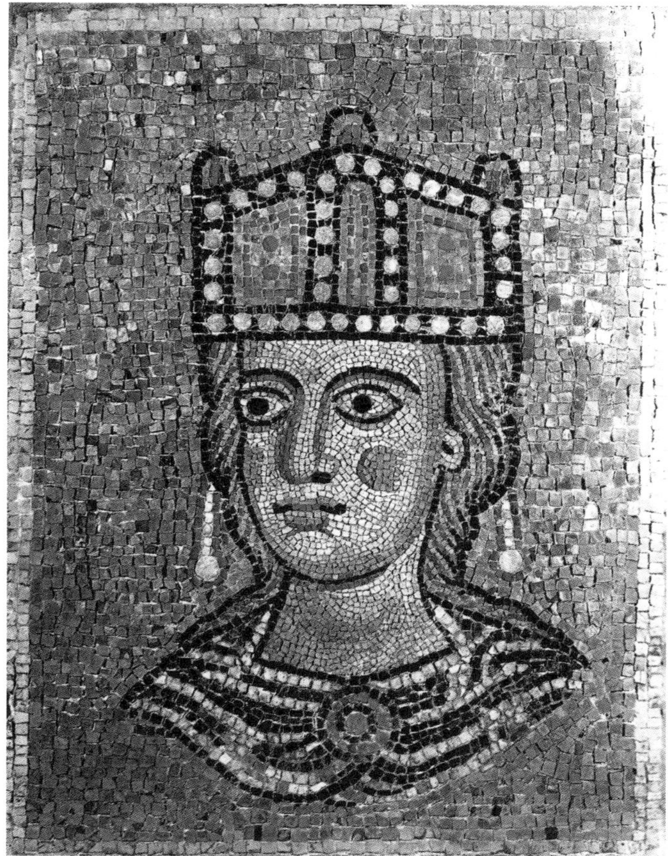

FIGURE 21. Rome, Museo di scultura antica Giovanni Barracco, *Ecclesia Romana*, from the apse mosaic formerly in the Basilica of St. Peter, Rome, *c.* 1205 (photo: Museo Barracco).

the Word Incarnate," God become man, he understands that Christ's joining of divinity to flesh is not only a matter of Christ's singular assumption of manhood; it also signifies Christ's marriage with all Christians, the community of the Church.[59] This common medieval reading links Cana to other fundamental Christian allegories of marriage, most importantly, to the Song of Songs, understood as a celebration of the nuptials of Christ and the Church, a notion applied to several Christological events, such as the Annunciation. While Christ's first marriage to the flesh takes place in the virgin's womb at the Annunciation, the wedding at Cana confirms and manifests this union. The connection between these incarnational weddings is explained by one of Bonaventure's main sources on Cana, the Venerable Bede: Christ "descended from heaven to earth in order to join the Church to himself in spiritual love," taking as his wedding chamber the womb of the Virgin.[60] At Cana, where he has gone to "a marriage celebrated on earth in the customary fleshly way," the "same joyful marriage vows" are proclaimed, when the gentiles are "called to faith."[61] At Assisi, the juxtaposition of the *Annunciation* with the *Miracle at Cana* seems to intentionally highlight the essential link between these two marriages (Fig. 2).[62] The fresco's placement also underscores the fact that *Cana*'s marriage specifically concerns the Church; it is placed directly opposite the scene of the *Building of the Ark* on the north wall of the nave—Noah's ark being a common typological figure for the Church.

The theme of the Church as bride supports allegorical interpretation of several objects in the Assisi fresco. In Bonaventure's listing of the four weddings represented by Cana, the sacramental and celestial weddings of Christ to the Church take place within the tabernacle of the Church, which is the house that Wisdom built out of seven pillars (Prov. 9:1).[63] In the Assisi fresco, two columns hold up the portico at the right; three more are hidden by the curtain behind the wedding guests, but capitals and impost blocks establish their presence. Adding the two columns that would have stood at the ruined left side of the fresco, there

59. In *Coll Jn* II, coll. 8.8, 546, Bonaventure explains that in a sacramental allegory, Cana is a wedding of the mystical body, i.e., the congregation of the Church united in Christ, quoting Rom 12:5, "We ... are one body in Christ." For the incarnational character of the Cana wedding, see also *Comm Jn* II.12, 270; trans. Karris, 145; and *De Assumtione B. Virginis Mariae. Sermo VI*, in *Opera Omnia* (as in note 8), vol. 9, 700.

60. Bede, *Homily 1.14* (as in note 36), 135.

61. *Idem*, 135, 136.

62. The conception in Mary's womb is likened to a wedding at least as early as Augustine, and frequently repeated by many, including Bonaventure; the metaphor seems to have originated in exegesis of the bridal chamber of Psalm 18.6, taken to signify the virginal womb, tabernacle of the union between the Word and flesh, Christ and the Church; see Migne PL 36: 495.

63. For the wedding of Cana in the tabernacle of the Church, see *Coll Jn* II, coll. 8.3, 545. For the Church as the house of wisdom, see *Dominica IX. post Pentecosten. Sermo I* in *Opera Omnia* (as in n. 8), vol. 9, 388; *Collationes de Septem Donis Spiritus Sancti* 9.8, in *idem*, vol. 5, 500.

are seven, the pillars of the house of Wisdom. In her house, Wisdom has prepared a meal and "set forth her table" (Prov. 9:2). This Bonaventure interprets as the altar of the cross; the table in the house of Wisdom is, like the table at Cana, prefigurative of the Eucharist.[64] And while Christ ceremonially displays sacramental bread in the *Supplicationes* drawing, at Assisi that role falls to the bride, the Church, who holds a piece of bread broken from a twisted pretzel on the table—an oddly shaped but significant reference. Broken bread is, for Bonaventure, a potent, multivalent symbol. Pertaining to the Eucharist, it signifies the suffering of the passion.[65] The broken bread of another supper, that at Emmaus, is a sign of the disciples' recognition of Christ, a theme that Bonaventure highlights in interpreting Cana as he does for Emmaus, citing Luke 24:35, "They knew him in the breaking of the bread."[66] Furthermore, Bonaventure explains that the bread is broken so that the individual soul may join in union with the Church: "*The bread is one. We, though many, are one body*" (1 Cor. 10:17).[67] In the *Miracle at Cana* at Assisi, recognition of Christ takes place in the house of Wisdom, at Christ's table, for those who become members of the Church, partaking of the Eucharistic sacrament of broken bread.

But perhaps the strangest object in the Assisi fresco is directly below the bride: a plate holding two fish, one whole and one boned. Although fish were commonly depicted at any meal attended by Christ, this configuration is odd, perhaps unique. Its placement seems to require an explanation related to the Church, and indeed, the scriptural language of marriage may provide an interpretation. When the Lord brings Eve, newly created, to Adam, Adam responds, "This now is bone of my bones, and flesh of my flesh" (Gen. 2:23)—words that are followed by the classic trope of marriage, "and they shall be two in one flesh" (Gen. 3:24). Several other passages in the Bible adapt Adam's phrase, "bones and flesh," to describe the union of separate parts into one. Most pertinent to the miracle at Cana is St. Paul's Letter to the Ephesians, which includes the well-known text counseling men to model their marriages on that of Christ and the Church. In this passage, "Church" signifies the corporate aggregate of church members, united to Christ in soul and body, Christ's own flesh. As Paul teaches, as each man loves his own flesh, Christ nourishes and loves the Church, "because we are members of his body, of his flesh and of his bones" (Eph. 5:30). In the same vein, Bonaventure parallels the union of Christ and the Church to the union of Adam and Eve, "bone of my bones and flesh of my flesh."[68] In the Assisi fresco, the traditional symbol of Christ, the fish, may be represented as bone and flesh to picture the mystery of each Christian's marriage to and membership in the Church, Christ's body.

The bride at Assisi is also vertically aligned with Cana's miraculous transformation, where a servant, obedient to Mary's command, pours the water. The artist of the fresco has clearly distinguished between the clear, poured water and the red wine filling the jug, underlining the moment of transformation taking place. Acknowledging the miracle, the servant turns to look at Christ—a conversion, literally a turning, to faith. The six water-jars correspond to the description in John's gospel, a number that prompted multiple interpretations by exegetes; particularly influential was Augustine's analogy to the six eras of history prophetically fulfilled in the last, the era of Christ's advent.[69]

64. *Dominica IX* (as in note 63), 388.

65. R. J. Karris, trans., *St. Bonaventure's Commentary on the Gospel of Luke, Chapters 17–24* (St. Bonaventure, N.Y., 2004), 2050. The odd, twisted, pretzel-like breads instead of loaves also appear in some Salzburg manuscripts. See, for example, the *Miracle at Cana* and *Last Supper* in the Pericopes of Custos Perhtolt (1060–1080); New York, Pierpont Morgan Library, MS. M.780, fols. 17, 27ᵛ.

66. See Karris, *Bonaventure's Commentary on the Gospel of Luke* (as in note 65), 2220–2223.

67. *Ibid.*, 2223.

68. *Collationes de Septem Donis Spiritus Sancti*, 6.20, in *Opera Omnia* (as in note 8), vol. 5, 487. Bonaventure also uses the image of bone and flesh to teach the significance of the incarnation, mankind's fraternal union in Christ, citing Adam's words from Genesis and 2 Kings 19:13, "Art not thou my bone, and my flesh?"; *Feria secunda post Pascha. Sermo*, in *Opera Omnia* (as in note 8), vol. 9, 282. Similar nuptial and fraternal imagery of union with Christ is used by many authors predating Bonaventure. Of particular interest in relation to Cana is the use of the "bone and flesh" metaphor in a sacramental context; the congregant is joined to Christ, bone and flesh, through the Eucharist; for example, Innocent III, *De Sacro Altaris Mysterio*, in Migne PL 217: 886.

69. The analogy to the six eras of history is found in Augustine and frequently repeated; see Augustine, *In Joannis Evangelium. Trac-*

The fresco seems to take this schema into account; it is in the sixth jar that the miracle occurs, filling all the jugs with new wine. And it is the sixth jar that has the most suggestive decoration. Each of the *hydriae* has three horizontal bands with geometric patterns or letters, which on the sixth jug form an alphabet. The *A* and *B* have flaked off the painted wall surface, but the rest, up to *L*, are clearly visible.[70]

Depictions of the *Miracle at Cana* often include contemporary utensils and vessels, and to a degree, the water-jug at Assisi with its alphabet is no exception. The alphabet-bowl known as the Studley bowl, from England, *c.* 1400, is a unique survivor of a type that might have been fairly common; alphabets arranged in horizontal registers circle the bowl and its cover, with a didactic decoration that could help whoever used the bowl—most likely a privileged child—to learn his or her letters.[71] The Studley bowl is a luxury object made of gilded silver, but plausibly similar objects were made in other materials. Nevertheless, the frescoed alphabet-jar at Assisi probably does not depict an actual object, since a large, heavy storage-vessel would be used by servants, and not held in the hand to be studied by an individual. The jar's spiritual meaning is more important than its realistic portrayal.

In the thirteenth century, learning the alphabet was considered valuable, even necessary, to spiritual growth; the presence of alphabets in psalters and books of hours demonstrates the value of literacy as an important step toward reading sacred texts.[72] By the mid-thirteenth century, even the order of St. Francis, himself a simple, unlearned man, discouraged admission of unlettered friars. However, in exegesis of Cana, letters represent not simple literacy but the most essential "transmigration," the historic and spiritual transformation from the Old Law to the New, effected by the incarnation. This is another trope that Bonaventure derives from Bede; in the sixth era, when the water is changed to wine, when Old Testament prophecy is fulfilled, a "better wine" replaces the teaching of the Pharisees, changing the "letter of the law to the gospel virtue of heavenly grace."[73] As Bonaventure puts it, the "water that is vapid and without nutritive value [becomes] flavorful and joyful wine" in a new era, when souls join to Christ in the sacraments and "the water of literal understanding [becomes] the wine of spiritual understanding."[74]

One last attribute of the bride deserves attention: the large moon-shaped pendant worn on her breast, a type of necklace often worn by young women in Roman Antiquity.[75] *Lunulas* are mentioned in the Vulgate among the female adornments condemned by Isaiah

tatus IX, in Migne PL 35: 1461–66. Other analogies for the jars include the six ages of man's life, six defects or vices, and six redeeming virtues or stages of penitence and conversion.

70. It is not clear whether the letter-shapes on the jug next to the sixth represent *S* and *F*—possibly for San Francesco? The only other image in which I have found letters on the jars at Cana is in Iviron 5 (Fig. 9): there is a Π (*pi*) on one jar and a Ρ (*rho*) on another. This peculiarity remains unexplained. My thanks to Annemarie Weil Carr and Kathleen Maxwell for answers to my questions on Iviron 5 and the iconography of Cana in Byzantine art.

71. R. Marks and P. Williamson, ed., *Gothic: Art for England 1400–1547* (London, 2003), cat. 183. For the alphabet associated with nourishment, whether physical or spiritual, see D. Alexandre-Bidon, "La lettre volée. Apprendre à lire à l'enfant au Moyen Age," in *Annales. Économies. Sociétés. Civilisations* 44/4 (1989), 971–5. The alphabet on antique and medieval vessels might also have apotropaic or magical significance; see F. Dornseiff, *Das Alphabet in Mystik und Magie* (Berlin, 1925), 76 ff.; Dornseiff lists twenty-four examples of vessels decorated with the Greek, Latin, or Etruscan alphabet, 158-61.

72. For example, in a window at Chartres, the saintly future of the shepherd Albinus is shown by his study of the alphabet, in contrast to his illiterate companions. See also J. H. Oliver, "A Primer of Thirteenth-Century German Convent Life: The Psalter as Office and Mass Book (London, BL, MS. Add. 60629)," in *The Illuminated Psalter: Studies in the Content, Purpose and Placement of its Images*, ed. F. O. Büttner (Turnhout, 2004), 268–69, for brief but valuable remarks on the alphabet and spiritual education.

73. Bede, *Homily I.14* (as in note 36), 136.

74. *Comm Jn* 2.12, 270; trans. Karris, 145, and *Dominica II. Post Epiphaniam. Sermo I*, in *Opera* (as in note 8), vol. 9, 180; trans. T. J. Johnson, *The Sunday Sermons of St. Bonaventure* (Saint Bonaventure, N.Y., 2008), 133. Burkhart, *Franziskus* (as in note 53), 70, also finds ecclesiastical symbolism in the letters. In the ritual dedication of a church, the bishop wrote Latin and Greek alphabets on the church floor. The jar nearest to the bride would thus represent the emergence of the Church in the sixth age. Although this symbolism is consistent with the overall meaning of the fresco, it seems less likely to have been intended, since the Greek alphabet is not depicted.

75. P. Réfice, *Pulchra ut Luna. La Madonna de Braye in S. Domenico a Orvieto* (Rome, 1996), 29–30. I am very grateful to Giovanni Freni

(3:18), and Isidore of Seville preserves the memory of Roman *lunulas* in his definition, "*Lunulae* are feminine ornaments in the likeness of the moon, hanging like small golden *bullae*."[76] In medieval Italian art, however, to my knowledge, similar jewelry is worn by only one other figure of a bride, the Virgin, or the Church. The pendant worn by Arnolfo di Cambio's figure of Mary on the tomb of Cardinal Guglielmo de Braye (d. 1282) is smaller than the Assisi bride's, but it hangs identically, with the crescent's tips symmetrically disposed and pointed downward.[77] The question of any relationship between the de Braye Madonna, made for the Dominican church of Orvieto, and the bride at Assisi leads beyond the scope of this essay, but Arnolfo's sculpture provides a striking contemporary example in which the moon-necklace adorns a figure who is allegorically Christ's bride and Church.[78]

Moon, Church, and bride were not uncommon companions in a variety of thirteenth-century religious contexts. For example, in its explanation of the creation of sun, moon, and stars, the Old French *Bible moralisée* states: "The sun signifies the whole divinity. The moon signifies the Holy Church...."[79] In the accompanying miniature, the moon-Church who transmits the divine light of the sun is illustrated as a crowned woman, holding aloft an unveiled, open book, the Word of God. The moon as Church is a key symbol for Bonaventure, discussed at length in his *Hexaemeron*, or *Collation on the Six Days of Creation*. The moon is the Church Militant, defined as the earthly church, its sacraments and members.[80] As the moon receives and reflects the brilliance of the sun, the Church is mediator of the divine Word. Just as the moon softens the sunlight, the Church veils the dazzling brilliance of the divine through sacraments and symbols; thus divinity is made accessible to human perception.[81] Citing Dionysius the pseudo-Areopagite, Bonaventure writes, "It is impossible for us to make the divine radiance shine forth, except surrounded mystically with a variety of sacred veils."[82] In the fresco of *Cana*, the viewer sees sacraments and symbols pictured within the veiled house of wisdom, tabernacle of the Church.

The moon also figures in nuptial imagery inspired by the Song of Songs, in which the bride "ascends like the rising dawn, beautiful as the moon, chosen as the sun...." (Cant. 6:9).[83] Bonaventure's contemporary, Hugh of St. Cher—whose works Bonaventure often used—describes the bride of the Song of Songs shining "like the moon with the advent of the sun of justice."[84] For Bonaventure, the soul distant from God is like the

---

for making this work available to me. On the *lunula* in ancient Roman costume, see K. Olson, "The Appearance of the Young Roman Girl," in *Roman Dress and the Fabrics of Roman Culture*, ed. J. C. Edmondson and A. Keith (Toronto, 2008), 144–5, 149.

76. "Lunulae sunt ornamenta mulierum in similitudinem lunae bullulae aureae dependentes," Migne PL 82: 701. *Bullae* are pendants, often containing amulets, worn by Roman children, male and female; examples can be seen on the *Ara Pacis Augustae*.

77. For a complex reading of the necklace, see Réfice, *Pulchra ut Luna* (as in note 75); her interpretation is rejected by V. Pace, "Arnolfo a Orvieto: una nota sull sepolcro de Braye e sulla ricezione dell'antico nella scultura del Duecento," in *Saggi in onore di Renato Bonelli*, ed. C. Bozzoni et al. (Rome, 1992), 190–91. On the Madonna de Braye, see A. M. Romanini, "La sconfitta della morte. Arnolfo e l'antico in una nuova lettura del monument de Braye," in *Bonifacio VIII e il suo tempo. Anno 1300 il primo Giubileo*, ed. M. Righetti Tosti-Croce, Exhib. Cat., Rome, Palazzo Venezia (Milan, 2000), 24–50; cat. 106. Réfice's interpretation of the necklace (*Pulchra ut Luna*, as in note 75) is overly complex but includes many valid points. I have not been able to consult F. Pomarici, "L'iconografia della Vergine nell'opera di Arnolfo di Cambio: il sepolcro De Bray e la facciata di Santa Maria del Fiore," in *Il monumento del Cardinale Guillaume de Bray di Arnolfo di Cambio dopo il restauro* (*Bollettino d'arte*, *Volume speciale*, 2009, in press).

78. For other scriptural, patristic, and medieval metaphors linking the moon to Mary and the Church, see Réfice, *Pulchra ut Luna* (as in note 75), 27–60.

79. See the facsimile, *Bible Moralisée. Codex Vindobonensis 2554. Vienna, Österreichische Nationalbibliothek*, ed. G. Guest (London, 1995), fol. 1 and p. 54.

80. *Collations on the Six Days*, trans. J. de Vinck, in *The Works of Bonaventure* 5 (Paterson, N.J., 1970), 307–16, 341–42, 344, 361–2. The Church Militant is the earthly exemplar of the heavenly Church Triumphant.

81. *Ibid.* 20.15, 308.

82. *Ibid.* 20.14, 308.

83. As translated by R. Fulton, in "'Quae est ista quae ascendit sicut aurora consurgens?': The Song of Songs as the *Historia* for the Office of the Assumption," *Mediaeval Studies* 60 (1998), 55–122.

84. Quoted in M. A. Lavin, "Cimabue's Life of Mary: Mother and Bride," in *idem* and I. Lavin, *The Liturgy of Love: Images from the Song of Songs in the Art of Cimabue, Michelangelo, and Rembrandt* (Lawrence, Kans., 2001), revised from *Liturgia d'Amore: Imagini dal Cantico dei Cantici nell'arte di Cimabue, Michelangelo, e Rembrandt*

moon at its wane, but, "as the bride is attracted to the groom," it desires union with the sun, becoming "completely filled with light." [85]

The lunar imagery of the Church and bride thus relates, on the one hand, to the Church's (or Mary's) role as mediator of the divine Word and, on the other, to ascent and mystical union with God.

Assumption

Perhaps the most frequent context for associating moon and bride is the Assumption of the Virgin.[86] Bonaventure's sermons of the Assumption make it clear that the Assumption pertains not only to the glorification of Mary as an individual, but also to the heavenly ascent and glorification of the Church and its members. As a figure of the Church, spouse of Christ, the bride of the *Miracle at Cana* thus prefigures this ascent. According to Bonaventure's fifth and sixth sermons on the *Assumption*, when Mary is exalted, the Church Militant rises to become the celestial Church Triumphant, which is crowned, "beautiful as the moon, chosen as the sun," and "like a bride adorned with her necklace" (Is. 61:10).[87] In Bonaventure's sermon, it is clear that he is aware of Isaiah's context for the bride's necklace, which is an adornment God gives to the soul clothed in the garments of salvation. Ascent and salvation are also suggested by the bride's crown, another gift from the bridegroom, which links the bride to the Apocalyptic Woman. In his sermons and in the *Collation on the Six Days*, Bonaventure identifies the Woman with Mary, the Church, and the individual soul risen to God.[88] It is worth noting that in the Assisi fresco, the bride's crown has four gems at the front and two at the side—with the gems of the unseen sides, a total of twelve, like the twelve stars of the Apocalyptic Woman's crown (Rev. 12:1).

Many of these themes come together in the *Coronation of the Virgin* in the apse of Sta. Maria Maggiore, Rome; the mosaic is contemporary with the Upper Church frescoes of Assisi and was commissioned by the same Franciscan pope, Nicholas IV (Fig. 22).[89] As Christ places a crown on the head of his mother and bride, the sun is at his feet, while the moon is at Mary's. The artist, Jacopo Torriti, also worked at Assisi; the *Wedding at Cana* is often attributed to a member of his Roman workshop. Indeed, in her heavenly appearance in the Roman mosaic, Mary holds her arm in the same pose as Mary's in the *Miracle at Cana*, the *Advocata*'s gesture of supplication.

No crown, moon, or necklace appears in the *Assumption of the Virgin* painted in the apse of San Francesco, Assisi; nevertheless, Cimabue's fresco of *c.* 1275–1280 is thematically linked to the *Miracle at Cana* (Fig. 23). Marilyn Aronberg Lavin's seminal study of the *Assumption* at Assisi highlights its significance as a marriage that is both physical and mystical.[90] In this

---

(Modena, 1999), 119, n. 148. Hugh's commentaries were an essential source for Bonaventure; see B. Smalley, *The Gospels in the Schools, c. 1100–c. 1280* (London, 1985), 206–11. Hugh was buried in 1263 at San Domenico, Orvieto, site of the de Braye Madonna (1282).

85. *Collations* (as in note 80), 20.19, 311. In a related metaphor, the moon is sister of the sun: of all created things the moon is closest to the sun and most susceptible to its rays. Those who are chaste and pure like the moon are joined to Christ as sister; *Opera Omnia* (as in note 8), vol. 9, 212.

86. Fulton, "'Quae est ista...,'" (as in note 83) discusses the Song of Song's association with the Assumption of Mary.

87. *De Assumtione B. Virginis Mariae. Sermo V* and *Sermo VI*, in *Opera Omnia* (as in note 8), vol. 9, 699–706, for the quoted passages, 700. Isaiah 61:10 reads, "et quasi sponsam ornatam monilibus suis." Although English versions of the bible translate *monilibus* generically as jewels, the Latin more specifically refers to a necklace or collar. In Song of Songs 1:9, *monilia* are at the bride's neck. For other thirteenth-century texts on the bride's necklace, a wedding gift from the Spouse, adorning the Church, see Réfice (as in note 75), 38–40.

88. *Collations* (as in note 80), 22.39, 361. For Bonaventure's interpretation of the Apocalyptic Woman, see R. S. Beal, "Bonaventure, Dante and the Apocalyptic Woman Clothed in the Sun," *Dante Studies* 114 (1996), 209–28.

89. For Nicholas IV and the Upper Church nave, see Cooper and Robson, "Pope Nicholas IV" (as in note 3). On the Sta. Maria Maggiore apse mosaic, see Gardner, "Pope Nicholas IV"(as in note 34); Andaloro and Romano (as in note 58), 100–102. Jacopo Torriti's placement of the moon and sun in the *Coronation of the Virgin* was frequently repeated by Paolo Veneziano and his followers, sometimes for Franciscan or Dominican patrons. A Franciscan example is the *Coronation of the Virgin* from the Sta. Chiara Polptych, in the Gallerie dell'Accademia, Venice.

90. Lavin, in *The Liturgy of Love* (as in note 80), 4–47. On Cimabue's *Assumption*, see also Ruf, *Die Fresken* (as in note 53), 46–7, 58–64, 68, 72–3.

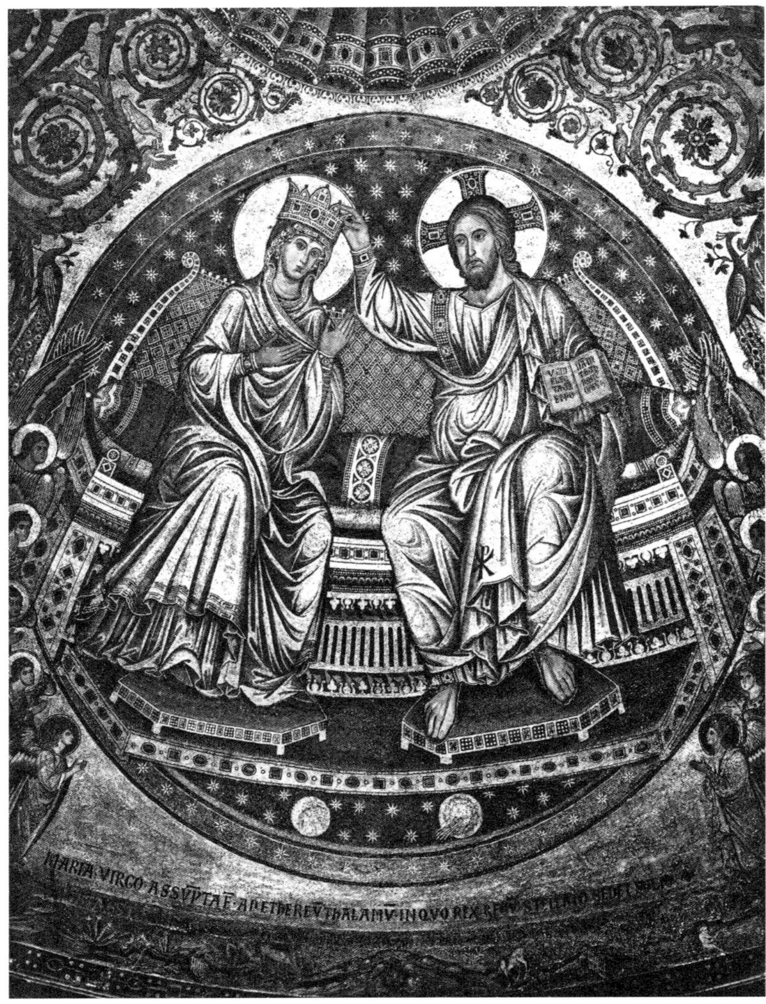

FIGURE 22. Jacopo Torriti, Coronation of the Virgin, *c.* 1292, detail from the apse mosaic, Rome, Sta. Maria Maggiore (photo: Alinari/Art Resource, N.Y.).

respect, the *Assumption of the Virgin* can also be seen as the fulfillment of Christ's earlier unions of spirit and flesh, the *Annunciation* and the *Wedding at Cana* (Fig. 2). Christ is wed to the body of the Church in his mother's womb, at the Wedding at Cana, and, finally, in glory, at the Assumption. This sequence of weddings moves from humility on earth—Christ's abasement in the womb of the Virgin, and Mary's humble consent—to supreme, heavenly exaltation. Because Mary is the Church, the *Assumption* pictures the glorification of the Church Militant, ascending into the eternal Church Triumphant, the heavenly Jerusalem.[91] As an exemplary model—a human lifted to heaven—and as the embodiment of the Church, Mary in her *Assumption* holds out the promise of bodily resurrection and glorification to all members of the Church, Christians admitted to the king's celestial banquet. In the fresco of *Cana*, the bride's moon-pendant and crown presage heavenly ascent, as do the broken bread and the plate of fish, for membership in the Church—mystically, union to Christ's body, bone, and flesh—is required for mankind's ascent. In order to see Christ in glory and in flesh, Bonaventure writes,

91. Belting, *Die Oberkirche* (as in note 10), 60–61, emphasizes this theme, contextualizing the *Assumption* within a programmatic glorification of the Church linked to Bonaventure's theology.

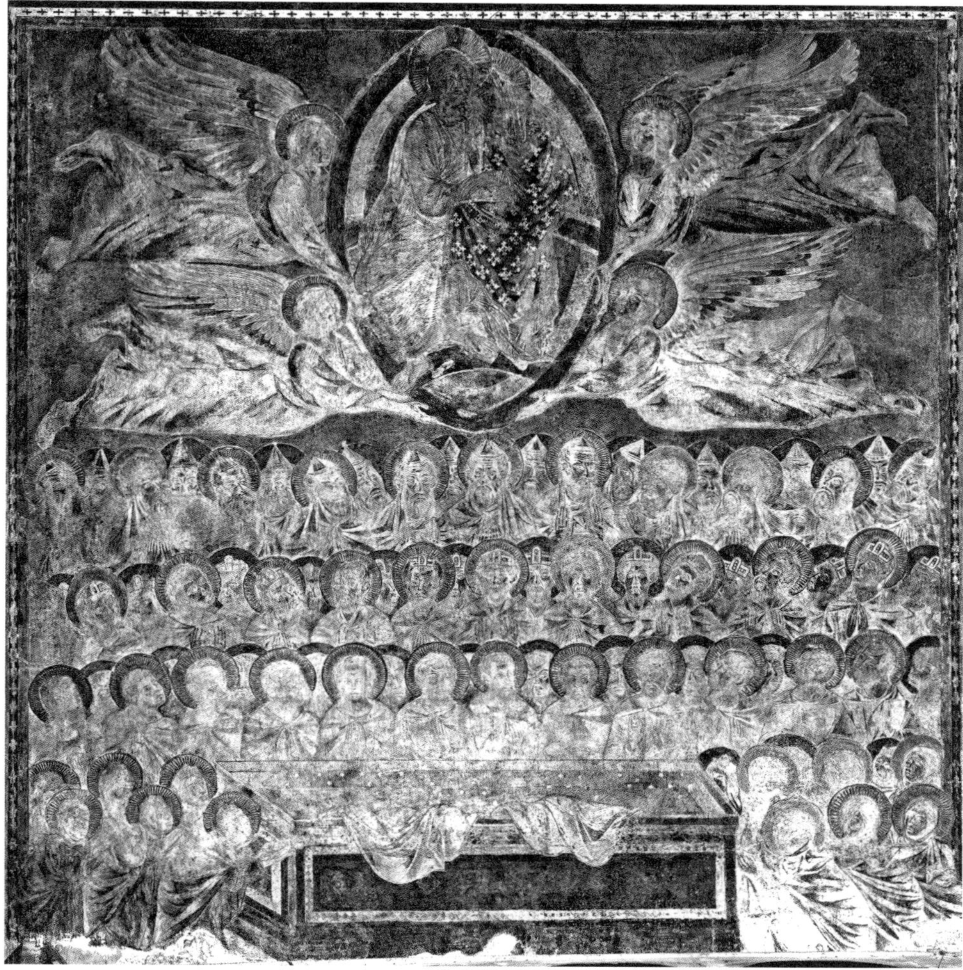

FIGURE 23. Assisi, Church of San Francesco, apse of the Upper Church, the Assumption of the Virgin, *c.* 1275 (photo: courtesy of G. Ruf).

mankind must be reborn through the sacraments, joined to Christ's body, "of his flesh and of his bones" (Eph. 5:30).[92]

It is fitting that the *Miracle at Cana*, Christ's bonding in marriage to the members of the Church, is situated within the congregational space of the church. A medieval visitor looking directly at the *Wedding at Cana* would stand near the choir-screen that once separated the nave from the apse of the Upper Church. Symbols of the "higher weddings" that Cana prefigures are nearby: the altar, site of the sacramental wedding, and the *Assumption of the Virgin*, the celestial wedding. If the viewer stood in the center of the nave, on axis with the altar, he or she might have been able to view *Cana*, the main altar of the church, and the fresco of the *Assumption* simultaneously, the latter two through the central opening of the choir-screen. From other positions, the altar and apse paintings would have been hidden by the choir-screen; the full range of wedding imagery would have been obscured. One may wonder how much the average visitor understood when viewing the fresco of the *Miracle at Cana*. The basic story and the effectiveness of Mary's intercession are clear, but beyond that, explanation from a friar, whether formally in a sermon, or informally, would be most helpful. Numerous thirteenth-century sermons on Cana survive, demonstrating the

92. *Dominica IV. Adventus. Sermo VI*, in *Opera Omnia* (as in note 8), vol. 9, 82.

popularity of the theme and the sophisticated symbolism preached to lay audiences.[93] Without explanation, however, the significance of the image would be only partly understood. But perhaps a measure of obscurity and complexity is part of the fresco's message. The full illumination of Christ's wisdom is veiled and hidden. One must seek the spiritual truth behind the letters. To understand Christ's wedding to the Church and mankind, one has need of the Church's mediation in teaching and sacraments.

Conclusion

Although significantly different, each of our two Franciscan images of the *Miracle at Cana* brings out essential themes from Bonaventure's interpretation of the miracle. While iconographic study of the Franciscan *Cana* brings no sweeping revisions to the broader study of Franciscan art, a few small points may add to the scholarship on this very large topic.

Just as Bonaventure's exegesis is greatly indebted to patristic and monastic sources, these two images of the *Miracle at Cana* are largely dependent on traditional iconography. For all their self-conscious emphasis on novelty, it is important to recognize the Franciscans' deep roots in monastic tradition. Moreover, the innovative features of the Franciscan scenes broadly reflect major concerns of the period. A dual focus on the incarnation and on Mary is hardly exclusive to the Franciscans. Yet it is undeniable that these themes are presented through the lens of Franciscan poverty. Even if some knowledge of Franciscan teaching is necessary to supplement the visual evidence, both illustrations of the wedding make strong statements about fundamental Franciscan teachings: that mankind's salvation is enabled by Christ's descent in the flesh to join to humans in poverty and is assisted by Mary's compassionate intercession for the poor.

The Franciscan *Miracle at Cana* also displays exceptional richness and specificity of imagery. The *Supplicationes* drawing not only shows guests touching the food, as in several earlier images, but also suggests several stages in the process of conversion: recognizing Christ, reproaching vice, and teaching virtue, all presented in a plausibly natural ensemble. In the Assisi fresco, the complexity of metaphor is like a virtuoso performance. Unusual objects—the plate of fish, the necklace, the letters on the water-jars—give unprecedented tangibility to religious metaphors. By their very oddness, these objects seem to ask the viewer to look at the scene allegorically—to not be diffident but to pay attention and recognize divine meaning.[94] At the same time, the physical presence of portico, necklace, plate, and jars creates a sense of concrete reality that is due to the detailed descriptive naturalism of individual objects. Christ, in his humility, seems indeed to have come down into the worshiper's human world.

The differences between our two images are also telling. Each addresses a specific audience. Created for a young man's private study and prayer, the *Supplicationes* drawing is more didactic in the pastoral sense of teaching concrete morals and behavior: obey the Virgin, turn away from indifference and vice, pray devoutly, and act with charity, in preparation for the heavenly banquet. The fresco in the Upper Church is more complex and erudite, a rich *mélange* of metaphor and pictorial reference that cannot be easily summarized. Although the *Miracle at Cana* is painted in the congregational space of the nave, plausibly it would have required explanation by a well-educated friar, as many Franciscans were by the end of the thirteenth century. Its dense pictorial and scriptural allegory might even be seen to display the Order's intellectual standards in the late thirteenth century, as appropriate for the church that was, on the one hand, the Franciscans' institutional and spiritual head, and, on the other, a special church, Rome's "*ecclesia specialis*," an honorific granted by the papacy exempting San Francesco from any ecclesiastical jurisdiction, save that of the papacy.[95] Within a "special church," the ecclesiastical emphasis of the *Miracle at*

93. D'Avray, *Medieval Marriage Sermons* (as in note 6) and *idem*, *Medieval Marriage: Symbolism* (as in note 52), esp. 72–3.

94. Ilene H. Forsyth suggests a similar role for puzzling letters sculpted on cloister capitals of Moissac; "Word-Play in the Cloister at Moissac," in *Romanesque Art and Thought in the Twelfth Century* (The Index of Christian Art Occasional Papers, x), ed. C. Hourihane (Princeton, 2008), 154–78.

95. On this dual nature of the church at Assisi, see Belting, *Die Oberkirche* (as in note 10), 17–29.

Cana is striking. The fresco's visual quotations—of the *Madonna Advocata* and Roman types of bride and *Ecclesia*—carry distinct institutional connotations, advertising the Franciscans' ties to papal Rome. Most importantly, in its elaboration of the bride and her attributes, Assisi's *Miracle at Cana* emphatically focuses on the Church, institutional and mystical, Militant and Triumphant, in its privileged status as glorified spouse of Christ and mediator of each Christian's ascent to salvation.

In their diversity of character and nuance in telling the same story, our two Franciscan images might suggest one last comparison: that of mendicant preaching. Along with other mendicant orders, the Franciscans were primary players in the great expansion of preaching that followed the Fourth Lateran Council of 1215.[96] For the Franciscans, teaching the word of God was a defining mission, an essential part of the apostolic life prescribed in the order's rule; the gospel commentaries that have shed so much light on the meaning of our images were written not as academic exercises but as sources for preaching.[97] Bonaventure was concerned that the preacher should be universal in proclaiming his message, in imitation of Christ, teacher of all. While this was an important concern for many preachers of the period, it may find visual expression in the Franciscan iconography of *Cana*, in the image of broken bread.[98] In Bonaventure's commentaries, broken bread signifies mankind's recognition of Christ and membership in his body, as discussed above. But Luke's statement that "they knew him in the breaking of bread" (Luke 24:35) has yet one more meaning for Bonaventure: the art of preaching. By "breaking down" the Lord's sacred bread for his audience, the preacher breaks down his words, adjusting them to the circumstances and capabilities of those who listen.[99] The images of *Cana* depicted at Assisi and in the *Supplicationes variae* give variants well suited for different audiences and circumstances. Perhaps this limited example is indicative of the mendicants' general desire to preach to *all people*, and the Franciscans' particular belief in the power of visual images to advance this agenda. In this, our images help clarify one of the many ways in which Franciscans contributed to the pastoral efforts of the thirteenth-century Church.

96. D. d'Avray, *The Preaching of the Friars: Sermons Diffused from Paris before 1300* (Oxford, 1985), 13–16, 43–48, and *passim*; M. Robson, "A Ministry of Preachers and Confessors: The Pastoral Impact of the Friars," in *A History of Pastoral Care*, ed. G. R. Evans (London, 2000), 126–47.

97. On the use of Bonaventure's gospel commentaries, see Karris, Introduction to *Commentary* (as in note 8), 1–3, 15, 20–21.

98. See d'Avray, *The Preaching of the Friars* (as in note 96), 127.

99. *Sermo. Feria secunda post Pascha*, in *S. Bonaventura Opera Omnia*, ed. PP. Collegii a S. Bonaventura (as in note 8), vol. 9, 281. Bonaventure compares the preacher to a nurse who "breaks down" her voice so that it is like the voice of the child she cares for who is in need of bread.

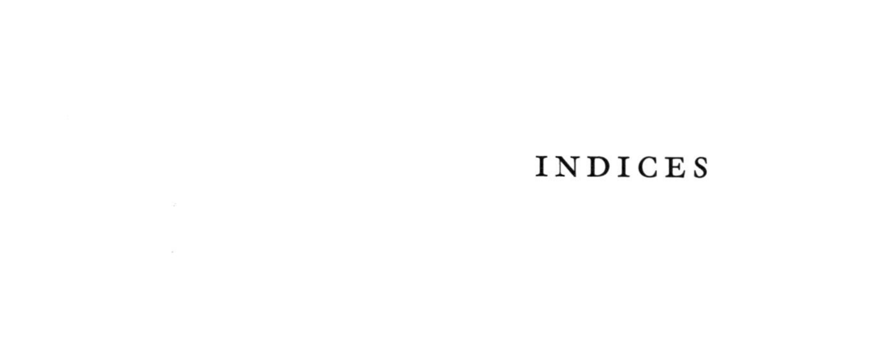

INDICES

GENERAL INDEX

(italic numbers indicate text illustrations)

H

I

J

K

INDEX OF MANUSCRIPTS

(italic numbers indicate text illustrations)

PRINTED BY
CAPITAL OFFSET COMPANY, INC.
CONCORD, NEW HAMPSHIRE

BOUND BY THE
NEW HAMPSHIRE BINDERY, CONCORD
NEW HAMPSHIRE

DESIGNED AND COMPOSED BY
MARK ARGETSINGER
ROCHESTER
NEW YORK

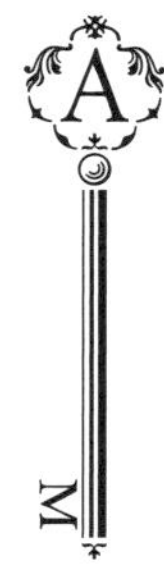

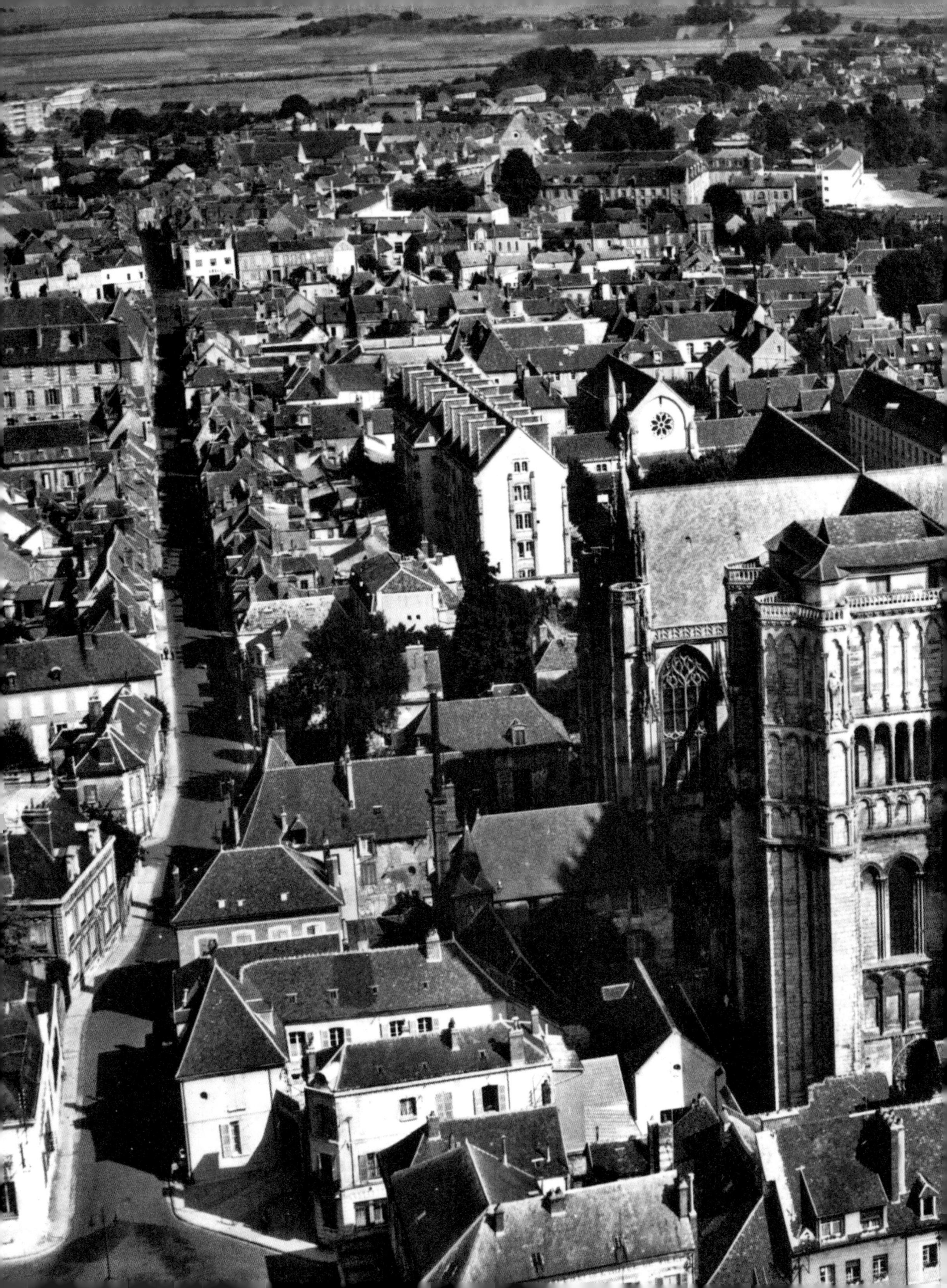